Lecture Notes in Information Systems and Organisation

Volume 83

Lecture Notes in Information Systems and Organization (LNISO) is a series of scientific books that explore the current state of information systems studies, in particular in the context of organizations, as well as behavioral and design aspects of information systems. The series offers an integrated publication platform for high-quality conferences, symposia and workshops proceedings. Books accepted for publication are selected based on a double-blind peer-review evaluation made by invited reviewers.

The series is indexed in Scopus.

Christoph M. Flath · Gunther Gust ·
Frédéric Thiesse · Axel Winkelmann
Editors

Digital Innovation and Organizational Transformation

Proceedings of the 19th International Conference on Wirtschaftsinformatik, Würzburg, Germany, 2024—Vol. 2

Springer

Editors
Christoph M. Flath
Julius-Maximilian University of Würzburg
Würzburg, Germany

Gunther Gust
Julius-Maximilian University of Würzburg
Würzburg, Germany

Frédéric Thiesse
Julius-Maximilian University of Würzburg
Würzburg, Germany

Axel Winkelmann
Julius-Maximilian University of Würzburg
Würzburg, Germany

ISSN 2195-4968 ISSN 2195-4976 (electronic)
Lecture Notes in Information Systems and Organisation
ISBN 978-3-032-08482-8 ISBN 978-3-032-08483-5 (eBook)
https://doi.org/10.1007/978-3-032-08483-5

This Springer imprint is published by the registered company Springer Nature Switzerland AG
The registered company address is: Gewerbestrasse 11, 6330 Cham, Switzerland

Contents

Enterprise Modeling

Addressing the Schema Representation Problem in Process Models Using Petri Nets—First Results Illustrated by the Dining Philosophers Problem 3
Sebastian Stephan, Josip Lovrekovic, and Peter Fettke

Internet of Things & Cyber-physical Systems

Smart Homes, Smart Strategies? An Empirical Study on Organizational Trust Repair After Breaches of Privacy 13
Björn Konopka, Kay Hönemann, Ning Yang, Jason Bennett Thatcher, and Manuel Wiesche

Tourism in the Era of Internet of Things: Design Principles for Smart Tourism 29
Leonardo Banh and Gero Strobel

Process Science

Experts versus Novices: Analyzing Behavioral Variability in Complex Process Environments 41
Nico Elbert and Christoph M. Flath

How Can Generative AI Empower Domain Experts in Creating Process Models? 57
Nataliia Klievtsova, Juergen Mangler, Timotheus Kampik, Janik-Vasily Benzin, and Stefanie Rinderle-Ma

Interactive Resolution of Inconsistencies in Declarative Process Models 73
Sabine Nagel and Patrick Delfmann

Orchestrating Enterprise Transformation and Business Processes Through Data-Driven Steering ... 87
Benedict Lösser and Robert Winter

Pre-Processing Inertial Measurement Unit-Based Data for Process Mining Using Convolutional Neural Networks ... 103
Daniel Polle, Milda Aleknonytė-Resch, Dominik Janssen, Clint Hansen, Elke Warmerdam, Walter Maetzler, and Agnes Koschmider

Service Innovation, Engineering & Management

"Was This Answer Helpful?"—A Taxonomy for Feedback Mechanisms in Customer Service Chatbots ... 119
Daniel Schloss, Saskia Haug, and Alexander Maedche

Characterizing the Roles of AI-Enabled Non-Human Agents in Service Systems ... 137
Matthäus Wilga, Layla Hajjam-Demir, Nina Lugmair, Martin Schymanietz, and Angela Roth

Business Models, Digital Transformation & Entrepreneurship

Data-Driven Business Models from an Internal Automotive OEM Perspective: Categories and Challenges ... 155
Norbert Michael Homner

Digital Platform Strategies and Profitability—The Role of Strategy Type and Chief Digital Officers ... 171
Yongli Huang, Maximilian Schreieck, Yiwen Gao, and Jason B. Thatcher

Dynamic Capabilities to Manage Generative Artificial Intelligence in Digital Transformation Efforts ... 189
Daria Höhener

Changing Nature of Work

Completing the Skills Puzzle: Developing a Skills Profile Data Model ... 207
Leonie Rebecca Freise and Ulrich Bretschneider

Conceptualizing the Agile Mindset in Agile Software Development Teams ... 223
Kristin Geffers, Ulrich Bretschneider, and Karen Eilers

Navigating the New Norm: Employees' Continuous Data Sharing in AI-Driven Workplaces ... 233
Mena Teebken, Thomas Hess, and Alexander Pretschner

Skills in Flux: Challenges in AI-Based Skills Management and Skills Profiles 247
Leonie Rebecca Freise, Ulrich Bretschneider, and Sarah Oeste-Reiss

Transparency of Algorithmic Control Systems and Worker Judgments 263
Maximilian Kempf, Filip Simić, Armin Alizadeh, and Alexander Benlian

Under the Neurodivergent Umbrella: A Qualitative Exploration of Neurodivergence and Remote Work 281
Lisa Kuhn and Florian J. Meier

Understanding Algorithmic Management in the Traditional Work Context: A Quantitative Analysis 299
Amelie Lena Schmid and Manuel Wiesche

Digital Finance

Deciphering Crypto Risks: Crypto Asset Risk Management Requirements for Financial Service Providers 329
Christian Zeiß, Konstanze Lang, and Axel Winkelmann

Evaluation of Outlier Detection Methods for Anomaly Detection in Journal Entries: A Use Case Analysis 345
Tobias Schreier, Nicolai Gnoss, Marina Tropmann-Frick, and Martin Schultz

When to Use Smart Contracts Instead of Traditional Contracts—A Conceptual Analysis 361
Anna Hupe

Digital Industry and Retailing

Development and Future Research Directions of AI-Based Anomaly Detection in Smart Manufacturing: A Bibliometric Analysis 379
Maximilian Nebel, Philip Stahmann, and Christian Janiesch

Monte Carlo Simulation to Analyse the Impact of Uncertain Telemetry Data on the Calculation of CO_2e Emissions for Trailer Traffic 387
Justus Leskow, Steffen Greiser, Laura Gregorc, and Stelios Damalas

Overcoming Lemon Markets with Business Reputation Ecosystem—A Multi-Agent Simulation on Monetary Ratings 403
Ulvi Ibrahimli, Simon Hemmrich, Simon Zauke, and Axel Winkelmann

Enterprise Modeling

Addressing the Schema Representation Problem in Process Models Using Petri Nets—First Results Illustrated by the Dining Philosophers Problem

Sebastian Stephan, Josip Lovrekovic, and Peter Fettke

Abstract In this paper, we introduce the schema representation problem using the example of dining philosophers: The difference between a system model of five eating philosophers and a schema model for a set of eating philosophers is of major importance. In a Petri net model, each philosopher and each fork would be considered as separate entities with their relating states and transitions. However, this approach lacks due to scalability and dynamic behavior, as adding more philosophers and forks significantly increases the model's size. To model any set of dining philosophers, a Petri net schema is useful. However, there is no modeling technique to model an infinite set of philosophers and forks, and to access its single elements. To address this problem, we provide the *elm*-notation, which allows us to dynamically unfold and aggregate any sets whereby behavior can be described for each philosopher and fork on schema level.

1 Introduction

In modeling, it is of major interest to distinguish between a *system model* and a *schema* for system models [1]. Typically, a modeler begins shaping system behavior based on concrete runs. Once detailed, the modeler adopts a universal interpretation, transforming runs into a complete system model, ensuring the system only behaves as described by its structure [2, 3].

S. Stephan · J. Lovrekovic (✉) · P. Fettke
German Research Center for Artificial Intelligence (DFKI), Kaiserslautern, Germany
e-mail: josip.jelicic-lovrekovic@dfki.de

Saarland University, Saarbrücken, Germany

S. Stephan
e-mail: sebastian.stephan@dfki.de

P. Fettke
e-mail: peter.fettke@dfki.de

C. M. Flath et al. (eds.), *Digital Innovation and Organizational Transformation*, Lecture Notes in Information Systems and Organisation 83,
https://doi.org/10.1007/978-3-032-08483-5_1

A system model is intended to represent just one concrete system with its finite sets of real or imagined world items and data objects. Using a so-called *term language* as presented in Genrich and Lautenbach [4] or Reisig [5], the structure can be abstracted from the system model. This makes it possible to describe a set of similar system models represented by a *schema*. Analogous to an algebra and its interpretation, by changing the interpretation, the net behavior can be changed without becoming externally visible [6]. Usually, a structure comes with a signature, providing a symbol for each of the structure's components like domains, functions, predicates, constants, and propositions [1, 7]. Based on system models that describe a concrete domain, the question now arises how the behavior of each element can be taken into account in a schema model. A symbolic representation of the set itself would be inaccurate and also incorrect, as this would represent the set itself as a token and system behavior is not described by its single elements. This does not allow a dynamic handling of sets where elements are produced, event-driven transformed, and then synchronized in a structured manner [8].

Thus, the problem we are focusing on is concerned with finding a suitable technique dealing with set symbols in a Petri net schema (schema representation) that accurately and efficiently depicts both structures and behavior of similar system models, but at the same time remains flexible, understandable and manageable for design and analysis. Before we present the solution more in detail, we motivate the schema representation problem using the example of the dining philosophers [9] in Sect. 2. In Sect. 3, we introduce the *elm*-notation provided by the modeling infrastructure HERAKLIT [8] and describe how it contributes to solve the motivated problem. Section 4 gives an overview of related work. Finally, Sect. 5 summarizes the key findings and provides an outlook on our further research work.

2 Motivating Example

The dining philosophers problem illustrates common pitfalls and challenges associated with designing concurrent systems [9]. It describes a situation in which five philosophers are thinking and eating. Sitting around a table with five forks, each philosopher needs his left and right fork to eat. This illustrates the challenges of synchronization and deadlocks in distributed systems. A run of the system would involve setting specific numbers of places and transitions for each philosopher and fork [10]. While the state and behavior of each element is modeled explicitly, a system model makes the problem more descriptive, but also complex and large for extensive systems, which may include hundreds of philosophers and forks. Another possibility how to describe the dining philosophers is to use a structure, which assembles real world items, data, constants, functions, predicates and propositions that can be updated, generated, deleted, computed and transformed by a system [1].

As depicted in Figure 1, a structure with five philosophers and forks is given. As shown, the system model is limited with regard to its expressiveness. First, only five philosophers and forks are considered. While this type of modeling works for

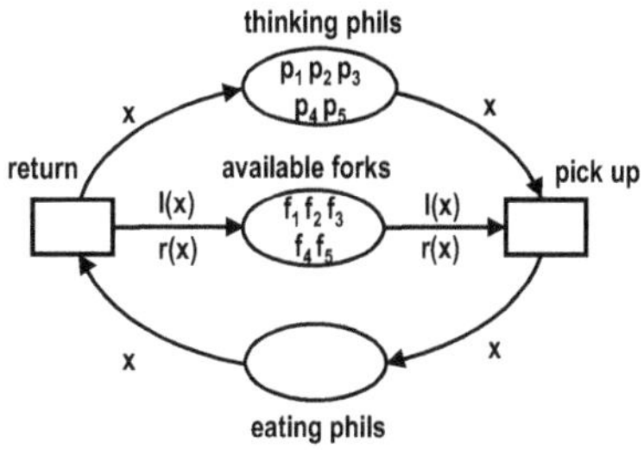

a structure:

domains	*functions*	*predicates*	*constants*	*variable*
phils = {p_1, p_2, p_3, p_4, p_5}	l,r: phils → forks	thinking phils, eating phils: phils	p_1, p_2, p_3, p_4, p_5: phils	x: phils
forks = {f_1, f_2, f_3, f_4, f_5}	$l(p_i) = f_i$	available forks: forks	f_1, f_2, f_3, f_4, f_5: forks	
	$r(p_i) = f_{i+1}$			
	$f_6 =_{def} f_1$			

Fig. 1 System model of the dining philosophers (based on Reisig [12])

domains with a finite set of elements, this approach fails for domains that are often not entirely known during modeling. Second, the concrete amount of elements has to be modeled in the places *thinking phils* and *available forks*. However, this makes Petri nets less readable and complex, especially when dealing with similar structures which might contain hundreds of different philosophers. Due to the close coupling of the structure to the system model, as many system models as there are structures would be needed. Third, given the two functions *l(x)* and *r(x)*, the case that only one philosopher (*x*) can eat with two forks, namely with his left and right fork, is reflected. This means that the dependency of which philosopher is allowed to eat with which fork is explicitly described in the model. Changes to the system behavior, for example to allow a philosopher to eat with any subset of forks (e.g. eating with only one or even three forks), need to be changed directly in each system model and structure respectively.

In order to represent similar structures by a model, the question now arises how any (in)finite set of philosophers and forks can be modeled in a Petri net model, for which any subset of philosophers can pick up any subset of forks. One possibility could be to further abstract the system behavior using a *schema*. Usually, a structure comes with a signature, which provides a symbol for each of the structure's components [1, 7]. For the dining philosophers, each domain gets its symbol (*phils* and *forks*) denoted as its type, analogous to the types of components of structures. As depicted in Figure 2, the schema model consists of two domain symbols, one function symbol, three predicate symbols, and two constant symbols. By the two domain symbols, an arbitrary set of philosophers and forks can be modeled and represented symbolically in the places. This kind of modeling means that the symbols *P* and *F* hold the complete set of philosophers and forks, respectively. However, representing a set of philosophers and forks in one token each does not correspond to the system behavior we want to describe. Behavior resulting from the single elements of a set is not

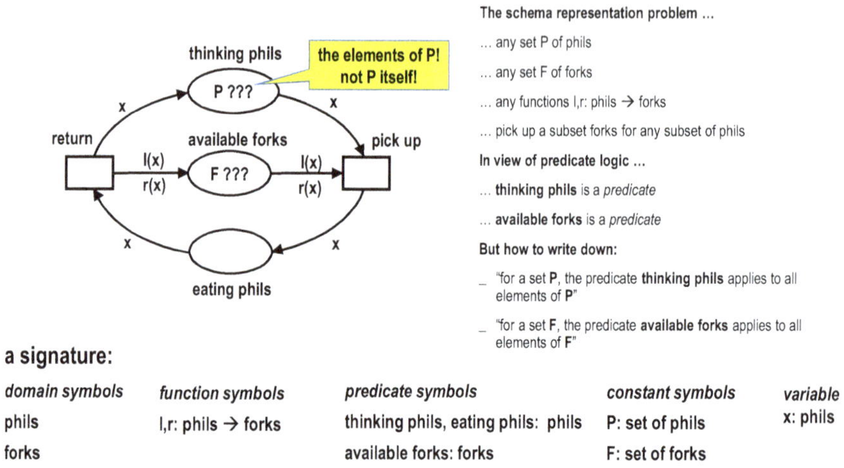

Fig. 2 Schema representation problem (based on Reisig [12])

reflected properly. This is also reflected in the functions *l(x)* and *r(x)*, which assign a left and right fork for a given philosopher. In the case that every philosopher can only eat with a left and right fork, this type of modeling might be sufficient and more descriptive. However, a more general representation that makes it possible to return the corresponding number of forks depending on the philosopher is not possible. For example, there might be a system model where philosophers can eat with only one fork, or even more. In other words, behavior like picking up or returning any subset of forks for any subset of philosophers is not described in such a schema model.

To the best of our knowledge, there is no suitable technique to address this modeling issue, which we refer to as the *schema representation problem*. In general, the universal quantifier of predicate logic is missing on modeling level not only to describe rules or conditions that apply to all elements of a given set symbol, but also to access them individually and describe their behavior, and thus consider additional concurrency.

3 The *elm*-Notation

Now, we want to sketch a solution for the schema representation problem. Given a signature as shown in Figure 3, we define different symbols, which describe aspects of our system. For example, there are *phils* and *forks* representing any set of philosophers and forks, respectively. The function *g* describes abstractly that a philosopher can have any sets of forks. Instead of having one token representing each set *P* and *F*, we now need a logical expression which allows us to generate five tokens in each place *thinking phils* and *available forks*. By this, we are able to describe each philosopher and fork by a local place for which the predicates *thinking phils* and

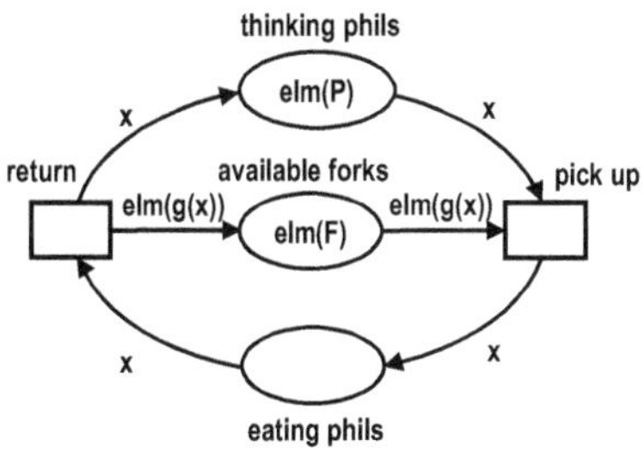

a signature:

domain symbols	*function symbols*	*predicate symbols*	*constant symbols*	*variable*
phils	g: phils → sets of forks	thinking phils, eating phils: phils	P: set of phils	x: phils
forks		available forks: forks	F: set of forks	

Fig. 3 Solution (based on [11])

available forks applies. At run level this means that each philosopher and fork is represented separately in one place. However, to consider this behavior not only in one run, but also for an arbitrary set of runs, which together describe a system model, a technique on schema level is required to deal with set symbols and to access its single elements.

Therefore, we introduce a predicate logic expression, called *elm*-notation, that allows us to generate a set of tokens from a fitting term. The *elm*-notation allows us to unfold any set symbol in a schema model and system model. In terms of the universal quantifier as provided in predicate logic, we can create as many tokens in one place as there are elements in the set for which the predicates apply. By this, we avoid an instantiation with just one token containing all philosophers (P) and forks (F). As shown in Figure 3, two domain symbols *phils* and *forks* are defined, which represent any set of philosophers and forks. For example, given a structure with five philosophers and forks (see Figure 1), the expressions *elm*(P) and *elm*(F) state that for each element of set P and set F the predicates *thinking phils* and *available forks* apply. Thus, for all philosophers (or forks), the *elm*-notation stands for the logical expression:

$$\forall p \in P : \quad \text{thinking phils}(p) \tag{1}$$

Using the *elm*-notation with the function $g(x)$ as arc description, we are able to model *pick up* and *return* for any subset of forks for any subset of philosophers, allowing a synchronization detached from a specific structure and its system model. Using $g(x)$, we use a function which maps a philosopher to a set of forks. Which forks are returned is not specified on schema level. This decoupling allows similar structures and any number of system models to be represented by one schema model. Furthermore, we can not only describe behavior as a sequence of occurrences of states for which typically a global timestamp is assumed. Rather a causal relationship can be described between philosophers and forks. Considering a strict partial-order instead of a strict total order, causal independence and dependency can be considered. Described by a run, for example two philosophers p_1 and p_2 could eat in parallel whereas p_1 eat with one fork and p_2 with two forks. In order to restrict the schema to the original dining philosophers problem, where philosophers can only eat with their left and right fork, constraints can be easily added for each structure.

4 Related Work

There is a plethora of other modeling techniques discussed in the literature to describe complex system behavior and dynamics. Techniques like state charts [13], process algebras [14, 15] or finite automaton [16] assume abstract events, abstracting away from concrete data to keep formalism better manageable. However, as the complexity of a system increases, the number of places and transitions using these techniques can grow exponentially, making the models difficult to manage, analyze, or simulate. In addition, they lack in direct support for detailed data manipulation and representation, but also representing partial-ordered runs. Petri nets are also a well-known formal approach. Various Petri net extensions like Colored Petri nets (CPN) [17], Predicate/transition-nets (PrT-nets) [4, 18], algebraic-specified nets [5] or other high-level Petri nets [19–21] are discussed in literature. For example, CPNs introduce the concept of "colors", which allows distinguishing between tokens based on their data attributes [17]. While the CPN language is based on Standard ML, it combines the strength of Petri nets and high-level programming languages to describe compactly system models in which communication, synchronization, and resource sharing play an important role [22]. Other approaches discussed are Oclets [3] and Proclets [23, 24]. While Oclets focus on a formal process model for describing scenarios with operational semantics using Petri nets, Proclets deal with the description of system behavior based on many-to-many interactions of its data objects. However, one limitation of these approaches is that they do not know the concept of a Petri net schema. For complex systems, this can lead to very large and incomprehensible process models. In contrast, PrT-nets use predicates to describe conditions under which transitions can fire and tokens are seen as bindings of variables that satisfy these predicates. A PrT-net describes a Petri net schema with an algebra as a free variable. This allows not to represent just one system, but many similar ones. However, PrT-nets lack in generating a set of tokens from set symbols for which the corresponding term fits. A similar approach is described by Glausch and Reisig ([25]. They present the concept of a Petri net schema to deal with set symbols. However, similar to a PrT-net, their approach lacks in accessing elements from set symbols itself to describe concurrent behavior, not only at run or system model level, but also on schema level.

5 Conclusion and Outlook

In this paper, we introduce the *elm*-notation to solve the schema representation problem. On the example of the dining philosophers, the idea of a universal quantifier was shown to model any set of philosophers and forks and to unfold it. By this, similar system models with their structures can be described by one schema model. We showed that the usage of the *elm*-notation is not only limited to places. Set unfolding and set aggregation can also be used as an arc label, which allows different behaviors to be taken into account depending on the underlying structure and properties. For the modeling of information systems, which deal with complex data structures, the *elm*-notation describes a promising approach. Especially, the nested hierarchical structure of business documents consisting of head and position data, like it is the case in enterprise resource planing systems (e.g. SAP), adds a layer of complexity for the description of system behavior resulting from position data. Formal approaches like HERAKLIT, which uses Petri nets, overcome the limitations of semi-formal modeling languages by representing system behavior more precisely and accurately. Semi-formal languages like BPMN or EPC often lead to ambiguities, scalability issues, and challenges in managing large systems due to lack of rigorous formalism [26]. In this context, we are convinced that using the *elm*-notation, we can not only consider an arbitrary set of data objects, but also describe their behavior resulting from its single elements. For example, the processing of a purchase order can depend on the properties of its order positions like availability. Moving forward, future research endeavors will encompass additional case studies to further demonstrate the advantages of the *elm*-notation along with the provision of best practices for its effective application in modeling computer-integrated systems.

References

1. Fettke, P., & Reisig, W. (2022). Breathing life into models: The next generation of enterprise modeling. In H.-G. Fill, M. van Sinderen, & L. Maciaszek (Eds.), *ICSOFT 2022. Proceedings of the 17th international conference on software technologies* (pp. 7–14). SCITEPRESS. https://doi.org/10.5220/0011376600003266
2. Desel, J. (2008). From human knowledge to process models. In R. Kaschek, C. Kop, C. Steinberger, & G. Fliedl (Eds.), *UNISCON 2008. LNBIP* (Vol. 5, pp. 84–95). Springer. https://doi.org/10.1007/978-3-540-78942-0_10
3. Fahland, D. (2009). Oclets---Scenario-based modeling with Petri Nets. In G. Franceschinis & K. Wolf (Eds.), *PETRI NETS 2009. LNTCS* (Vol. 5606, pp. 223–242). Springer. https://doi.org/10.1007/978-3-642-02424-5_14
4. Genrich, H. J., & Lautenbach, K. (1981). System modeling with high-level Petri-nets. *Theoretical Computer Science, 13*(1), 109–136. https://doi.org/10.1016/0304-3975(81)90113-4
5. Reisig, W. (1991). Petri nets and algebraic specifications. *Theoretical Computer Science, 80*(1), 1–34. https://doi.org/10.1016/0304-3975(91)90203-E
6. Starke, P. H. (1990). *Analyse von Petri-Netz-Modellen*. Springer. https://doi.org/10.1007/978-3-663-09262-9

7. Fettke, P., & Reisig, W. (2022). Discrete models of continuous dehavior of collective ddaptive systems. In T. Margaria, & B. Steffen (Eds.), *ISoLA 2022. LNCS* (Vol. 13703, pp. 65–81). Springer. https://doi.org/10.1007/978-3-031-19759-8_5
8. Fettke, P., & Reisig, W. HERAKLIT. https://heraklit.dfki.de/. Accessed 27.03.2024.
9. Dijkstra, E. W. (1971). Hierarchical ordering of sequential processes. *Acta Informatica, 1*(2), 115–138. https://doi.org/10.1007/BF00289519
10. Reisig, W. (2007). The decent philosophers: An exercise in concurrent behaviour. *Fundamenta Informaticae, 80*(1–3), 273–281.
11. Reisig, W. (2023). HERAKLIT—*A modeling infrastructure* [Presentation]. Sixth Advanced Course on Petri Nets 2023 (ACPN), Torun, Poland. https://heraklit.dfki.de/assets/documents/mittwoch_heraklit.pdf. Accessed 27.03.2024.
12. Reisig, W. (2023). *The essence of Petri Nets* [Presentation]. Sixth Advanced Course on Petri Nets 2023 (ACPN), Torun, Poland. https://heraklit.dfki.de/assets/documents/torun_sonntag_essence.pdf. Accessed 27.03.2024.
13. Harel, D. (1987). Statecharts: A visual formalism for complex systems. *Science of Computer Programming, 8*(3), 231–274. https://doi.org/10.1016/0167-6423(87)90035-9
14. Milner, R. (1996). Calculi for interaction. *Acta Informatica, 33*(8), 707–737. https://doi.org/10.1007/s002360050067
15. Milner, R. (1999). *Communicating and mobile systems: The Pi calculus* (176 pages). Cambridge University Press.
16. Hopcroft, J. E., Motwani, R., & Ullman, J. D. (2001). *Introduction to automata theory, languages, and computation*. Columbia, MO: Addison-Wesley.
17. Jensen, K. (1996). *Coloured Petri Nets. Basic concepts, Analysis methods and practical use* (Vol. 1). Springer.
18. Lindqvist, M. (1991). Parametrized reachability trees for predicate/Transition net. In K. Jensen, & G. Rozenberg (Eds.), *High-level Petri Nets: Theory and application* (pp. 301–324). Springer.https://doi.org/10.1007/978-3-642-84524-6_12
19. Chiola, G., & Dutheillet, C. (1993). Stochastic well-formed colored nets and symmetric modeling applications. *IEEE Transactions on Computers, 42*(11), 1343–1360.
20. Lakos, C. (2002). The challenge of object orientation for the analysis of concurrent systems. In J. Esparza & C. Lakos (Eds.), *ICATPN 2002. LNCS* (Vol. 2360, pp. 59–67). Springer. https://doi.org/10.1007/3-540-48068-4_4
21. Girault, C., & Valk, R. (2003). *Petri nets for systems engineering. A guide to modeling, verification, and applications*. Berlin, Heidelberg: Springer.
22. van der Aalst, W. M. P., & Stahl, C. (2011). *Modeling business processes. A Petri Net-oriented approach*. MIT Press.
23. van der Aalst, W. M. P., Barthelmess, P., Ellis, C. A., & Wainer, J. (2001). Proclets: A framework for lightweight interacting workflow processes. *International Journal of Cooperative Information Systems, 10*(4), 443–481. https://doi.org/10.1142/S0218843001000412
24. Fahland, D. (2019). Describing behavior of processes with many-to-many interactions. In S. Donatelli & S. Haar (Eds.), *PETRI NETS 2019. LNTCS* (Vol. 11522, pp. 3–24). Springer. https://doi.org/10.1007/978-3-030-21571-2_1
25. Glausch, A., & Reisig, W. (2006). How expressive are Petri Net Schemata? In S. Donatelli & P. S. Thiagarajan (Eds.), *ICATPN 2006. LNTCS* (Vol. 4024, pp. 201–220). Springer. https://doi.org/10.1007/11767589_12
26. Lana, C. A., Guessi, M., Antonino, P. O., Rombach, D., & Nakagawa, E. Y. (2019). A systematic identification of formal and semi-formal languages and techniques for software-intensive systems-of-systems requirements modeling. *IEEE Systems Journal, 13*(3), 2201–2212. https://doi.org/10.1109/JSYST.2018.2874061

Internet of Things & Cyber-physical Systems

Smart Homes, Smart Strategies? An Empirical Study on Organizational Trust Repair After Breaches of Privacy

Björn Konopka, Kay Hönemann, Ning Yang, Jason Bennett Thatcher, and Manuel Wiesche

Abstract Previous research has identified customer trust and privacy concerns as key factors for predicting the adoption and continued use of technology, especially for emerging technologies like the smart home. However, there is only limited empirical data on how trust can be restored after privacy violations, which are known to be common in smart home contexts. This study uses a scenario-based policy-capturing design to collect data from long-term smart home users. We examine the effectiveness of verbal (apology, reticence, denial) and substantive (compensation, regulation, third-party involvement) trust repair strategies for two types of privacy violations. Our results indicate that the effectiveness of verbal strategies varies depending on the type of violation, while regulation is the most effective substantive strategy across violation types. Combining verbal and substantive strategies is found to be more successful than isolated approaches. The study concludes with implications and recommendations for future research.

B. Konopka (✉) · K. Hönemann · M. Wiesche
Chair of Digital Transformation, TU Dortmund University, Dortmund, Germany
e-mail: bjoern.konopka@tu-dortmund.de

K. Hönemann
e-mail: kay.hoenemann@tu-dortmund.de

M. Wiesche
e-mail: manuel.wiesche@tu-dortmund.de

N. Yang
Quinlan School of Business, Loyola University Chicago, Chicago, IL, USA
e-mail: nyang1@luc.edu

J. B. Thatcher
Leeds School of Business, University of Colorado Boulder, Boulder, CO, USA
e-mail: jason.thatcher@colorado.edu

C. M. Flath et al. (eds.), *Digital Innovation and Organizational Transformation*, Lecture Notes in Information Systems and Organisation 83,
https://doi.org/10.1007/978-3-032-08483-5_2

1 Introduction

In the rapid evolution of smart home technology, privacy concerns have emerged as a significant issue for consumers. Convenience and efficiency offered by smart home devices are increasingly overshadowed by the potential of breaching privacy, which is unfortunately very common in this sector [1]. Smart home devices deployed in users' personal and most private home environments are uniquely vulnerable to privacy risks compared to other Internet-connected technologies [2, 3]. To provide their functionality, smart home devices such as home security cameras, smart speakers, and other sensors are designed to collect sensitive data continuously. Compared to other devices like laptops or smartphones, smart home devices cannot easily support comprehensive security systems, especially control systems for users with limited IT expertise, due to limitations in hardware design, computing power, or energy consumption [4]. A single breached smart home device can compromise the entire home network, exposing highly sensitive private information about users' daily routines and habits that would not be accessible through other technologies, thus having an immediate impact on smart home consumers [1, 5]. High-profile incidents like Amazon's Alexa smart speakers eavesdropping on customers and recording their conversations without authorization have heightened consumers' apprehension and eroded their trust in smart home as an emerging technology and the most consumer-facing side of the Internet of Things (IoT) [6, 7].

This erosion of trust is a crucial issue, contributing to limited technology adoption, with many smart home companies not being perceived as trustworthy but as excessive collectors of customer data [2]. A 2019 market survey found that a large proportion of respondents who don't own smart home devices do not plan to purchase any, with concerns about trust, privacy and security being considered as important as the price of the devices. Even among smart home device owners, 75% of consumers don't trust how companies will protect, use, and share data collected from smart home devices. The level of trust among customers is generally low due to numerous incidents and issues they have experienced or that have been reported [8]. Likewise, previous research has confirmed that trust is among the most important factors in predicting technology adoption and continued use ([9] or [10]). Findings like these show that smart home companies must prioritize rebuilding consumer trust if smart home technology is to reach its full market potential [7].

However, research on effectively repairing trust after privacy breaches, especially in domestic IoT contexts like the smart home, remains limited. Most existing trust repair research focuses on interpersonal or organizational contexts, with limited research on trust repair from an information systems perspective facing privacy violations [11]. Existing studies mainly focus on verbal strategies to repair trust, such as apologies or denials, rather than substantive strategies that include actual changes or consequences for the violator [12, 13]. In addition, most research on trust has focused on examining initial trust rather than more mature, longer-established trust [14]. This gap in research is significant because the dynamics of trust repair may differ substantially between initial and mature trust stages, as well as between verbal and substantive strategies when applied to different contexts [15]. This paper provides an empirical investigation into the effectiveness of various verbal and substantive trust repair strategies in a smart home context with the following research question (RQ): *What are the most effective strategies to repair existing customers' trust after a privacy-related violation of trust?*

Our study uses a scenario-based policy-capturing design to examine how long-term smart home users perceive different trust repair strategies in specific scenarios that mimic real-life privacy breaches. We contribute by providing insights for researchers and practitioners on the dynamics of trust repair in the smart home sector and for the broader discourse on how technology providers should navigate the challenges of privacy and trust violation challenges.

2 Theoretical Background

2.1 Trust and Trust Violations

Trust represents a far-reaching and complex construct studied across various research fields like Information Systems (IS) and Psychology. We define trust as the willingness of one party (the trustor, who gives the trust) to be vulnerable to the actions of another party based on the expectation that the other party (the trustee, who receives trust) will perform some action that is important to the trustor [16, 17]. This definition reflects that trust consists of beliefs and expectations derived from experiences and interactions in situations of risk and uncertainty [18, 19].

The level of trust is determined through trusting beliefs (TB). Mayer et al.'s [17] framework established three distinct dimensions of TB: Ability, Integrity, and Benevolence. Ability describes the belief that the trustee holds the skills, competencies, and traits that enable them to provide a desired outcome. Integrity is the belief that a trustee abides by an ethical set of principles. Benevolence describes the belief that the trustee is acting in good faith and is not motivated by self-interest. These three TBs combined are also denoted as the trustee's trustworthiness because they represent the trustor's assessment of whether the trustee exhibits desired characteristics that warrant trust [20].

The trust between two parties is not static but changes over time. The development of trust is often conceptualized as a progression from initial, calculative forms to deeper, sometimes emotional, stages. This progression occurs as the relationship develops over time, with higher and more complex levels of trust being attained [16]. The development of trust in smart home devices may follow similar stages, starting with a calculus-based assessment of the risks and benefits, potentially evolving into a more relational form as users become more familiar with and reliant on the technology [2, 15].

Trust violations are defined as a negative event or transgression attributable to the trustee. A reduction of trust may occur when the trustee's actions fail to meet the trustor's expectations or deviate from their beliefs. The trustor evaluates the transgression by considering the causality, controllability, and stability of the trustee's actions, potentially leading to a reassessment of the relationship [20]. Violations of trust can be classified into two major types: integrity-based violations of trust (IBV) and competency-based violations of trust (CBV) [13].

Dishonest or unethical behavior by the trustee violating the trustors' expectations of integrity is perceived as IBV, i.e. the trustees' intentional disregard of privacy laws leading to the excessive collection of data in customer's homes by smart home devices or the unauthorized sharing of customer data with third parties [11, 21]. CBV occur by actions showing a lack of ability or skill, and they indicate a failure in performance rather than improper conduct. A CBV in this context could be exemplified by a smart home organization's failure to implement robust cybersecurity measures [11, 13].

Both types of trust violations have significant implications for the trustor-trustee relationship, potentially leading to a loss of trust and damaging the trustee's reputation. [15, 22]. This reduced trust is defined as post-violation trust [13, 23]. The trustor evaluates the economic or psychological benefits of maintaining the relationship using a cost–benefit analysis, adjusting trust and behavior accordingly. In extreme cases, the user will terminate the relationship completely, i.e. no longer using a smart home device [9, 24].

2.2 Trust Repair

Trust repair is defined as the efforts taken by a trustee to restore the damaged trust after a violation from a state of post-violation trust back to repaired trust, where the trustor's willingness to rely on the trustee is reinstated [20, 25]. Previous research has distinguished between verbal and substantive trust repair strategies, which differ in their effectiveness depending on the type of violation [12, 13, 15].

Verbal trust repair strategies, also known as social accounts, involve verbal statements to address and mitigate the negative consequences of a violation of trust [20]. Previous research has shown that major verbal strategies include apologies, denial, and reticence. Apologies (APO) are statements that acknow-ledge responsibility and express regret for a trust violation towards the victim, potentially leading to positive trust repair effects. Denial (DEN) is a verbal statement rejecting the alleged violation, i.e. refusing to acknowledge that a violation has occurred, or refusing to accept responsibility, usually shifting the blame to external factors. Reticence (RET) does not imply that the trustee does not respond at all. Instead, a statement is given that neither confirms nor denies both the violation and the responsibility [13, 21].

Substantive strategies for trust repair are actions taken to address the breach of trust, usually including changes in behavior and processes of the trustee to mitigate the occurrence of future repeat transgression. Previous research has identified compensation, regulation, and third-party involvement as major forms of substantive trust repair strategies [13, 26]. Compensation (COMP) involves a transfer of tangible or intrinsic values to the victim, such as financial reimbursements or other forms of reparation to rectify the harm done [12, 27]. Regulation (REG) refers to the trustor implementing policies, changes in procedures and structures, or monitoring to prevent future violations [12, 13]. Third-party involvement (TPI) can include intervention by a third-party stakeholder to facilitate the repair process, whose involvement may help repair trust from the perspective of the trustor. An example could be the intermediary in a smart home ecosystem or a governmental institution that punishes the trustor for their transgressions and monitors their subsequent behavior [13, 28].

2.3 Hypotheses Development: Trust Repair After Violations of Privacy

In this section, the hypotheses regarding the effectiveness of verbal and substantive strategies in isolation as well as in combination are presented.

When a smart home technology company incurs a CBV, such as a database being hacked by criminal actors, it signals to customers that the company lacks the ability to adequately protect their private data, eroding customers' trust in the provider [2, 11]. Previous research proposes that for CBV, APO is more effective than RET or DEN [11, 29]. Using APO as a repair tactic may indicate to the customer that the trustee is taking responsibility, expresses remorse for the harm caused, and commits to improving its competence going forward [20, 30]. In contrast, RET and DEN may reinforce the perceived lack of competence by failing to address the issue [13, 15]. Previous empirical research in organizational literature has shown support for a higher effectiveness of APO for CBV compared to other strategies (e.g. [21]). Similarly, we hypothesize for the smart home context that: *H1: In competence-based trust violations, apologies will be more effective at repairing trust than Reticence or Denial.*

Behaviors like unauthorized excessive data collection by the trustee could be perceived as an IBV, as trustors may feel that the smart home company intentionally deceived them and violated their privacy for financial gain. For IBV, which are recognized as more difficult to repair than CBV, an APO that admits responsibility may backfire by confirming the company's lack of integrity [13, 21]. Instead, DEN may be the most effective response to IBV. For example, by denying intentionality or shifting responsibility to an unrelated party, the trustee can challenge the trustor's perception that a lack of integrity caused the breach. Previous research has found that following an IBV, an APO may actually decrease trust compared to not responding at all, while DEN or RET were able to restore trust to some degree (e.g. [29, 31]). Likewise, we want to gather data for the smart home context and hypothesize that: *H2: In integrity-based trust violations, denial will be more effective at repairing trust than apology or reticence.*

RET reflects an in-between response that combines elements of APO and DEN, i.e. not accepting responsibility or confirming intentionality [11, 13]. RET is generally considered a suboptimal response compared to the superior verbal response of APO or DEN, respectively, for CBV and IBV [21, 26]. For CBV, RET was found to be less effective than APO but more effective than DEN, as RET leaves the door open for potential future actions to address the transgression while also avoiding the issue of claiming innocence. For IBV, RET could repair trust better than a potentially damaging APO that admits responsibility and guilt. While RET avoids admitting this and distances the trustee from the transgression and the alleged lack of integrity, it also fails to provide a compelling counter-narrative, likely making it less effective than DEN [11, 21]. Thus, we propose, depending on the violation type, that: *H3a: In competence-based trust violations, reticence will be more effective at repairing trust than denial but less effective than apologies; H3b: In integrity-based trust violations, reticence will be more effective at repairing trust than apologies but less effective than denial.*

As key substantive strategies discussed in the theoretical literature, we chose to examine COMP, REG, and TPI for privacy-related violations of trust in the smart home context [13, 15]. As there is a lack of empirical data for these strategies in previous studies, the effectiveness of each strategy is tested for the smart home context.

The use of COMP involves the violating party providing monetary restitution or other valuable considerations to restore the relationship. This might help restore trust after a violation by balancing out the distribution of costs and benefits between trustor and trustee [12, 13]. However, one could also argue that by simply offering COMP after a privacy violation, smart home companies are attempting to "pay off" affected users without making meaningful changes. COMP alone, particularly minor COMP compared to the scale of the violation or the trustees' resources, could be insufficient to repair trust [15, 32]. Nevertheless, organizational research, e.g. [12] has found evidence that COMP is indeed an effective strategy to regain trust. To confirm these findings for the smart home context, we hypothesize: *H4: Compensation will repair trust after a) an integrity-based violation; b) a competency-based violation.*

REG involves implementing rules, policies, and control systems to directly address the root causes of the trust violation, i.e. by implementing new rules regarding customer data usage [13, 26]. By complying with REG, even voluntarily self-imposed, the trustor signals a commitment to restore trustworthiness and prevent future trust violations by restricting the ability to engage in future untrustworthy behavior. Considering REG provides substantive, observable changes in organizational practices that go beyond verbal responses like APO (e.g. [12, 33], we hypothesize that: *H5: Regulation will repair trust after a) an integrity-based violation; b) a competency-based violation.*

TPI, a strategy that may combine elements of both compensation and regulation, has been recognized for maintaining fairness and promoting proper behavior in various contexts. By accepting penalties determined and enforced by an external entity, the trustee endures a cost while also facing restrictions on future behavior [13, 28]. In previous research, there are mixed findings on the effectiveness of TPI. Some authors argue that when the trustee engages with a credible third party to address a trust violation, it signals a commitment to accountability and the willingness to establish corrective changes. In contrast, others hypothesize that if a third party has to get involved with the trustee after a violation, it may be perceived as less credible and effective in repairing trust. Customers may question the sincerity and sustainability of these changes, and the trustee may revert to their previous behavior once the TPI subsides [28, 31, 34]. To gain additional data for this less-researched trust repair strategy, we predict that for smart home contexts: *H6: Third-party involvement will repair trust after a) an integrity-based violation; b) a competency-based violation.*

Finally, previous research has primarily focused on examining the effectiveness of either verbal or substantive trust repair strategies in isolation [13]. Verbal strategies, such as APO aim to address the cognitive and affective aspects of short-term trust repair by providing information and expressing remorse. Substantive strategies, such as REG focus on implementing tangible actions to restore trust and prevent future breaches. However, as authors like Kahköhnen et al. (2021) or [13] have argued, there is a need for research that explores the potential synergistic effects of combining verbal and substantive trust repair strategies. The combination of these strategies may provide a more comprehensive approach to trust repair by addressing both the psychological and tangible factors related to the breach. For the context of smart home privacy violations, we hypothesize that: *H7: Combinations of verbal and substantive strategies are more effective at repairing trust than (a) only using verbal repair strategies and (b) only using substantive repair strategies.*

3 Method

We use a policy-capturing design to explore the relative effectiveness of the various trust repair strategies found in the literature in the context of privacy breaches involving smart home devices. Policy-capturing is a method used to investigate how the participants' decision-making processes depend on the information available to make their decisions [35]. Rather than simply providing survey questions, this method accurately represents real-world conditions, with participants grounding their decisions on information contained in a series of distinct text-based scenarios [36]. Considering that this method has seen frequent use in previous research to study trust repair (e.g. [28] or [22]), we believe this method is well suited to test our hypotheses. In our study, participants are tasked to evaluate different repair strategies applied by a fictional smart home brand attempting to recover customer trust following a privacy breach. Regression analyses are used to calculate the relative restorative power of each strategy and the combination of strategies on participants' post-violation trust [35].

3.1 Sample, Design, and Procedure

We used the specialized panel service Prolific to recruit participants for our policy-capturing survey. Our selection criteria required participants to be active users of smart home products and services, having used at least two different types of smart home devices in their households for at least one year. They also needed to be residents of Western European countries and be proficient in English. Seventy-seven participants were recruited (47 males, 30 females), with an average age of 30.36 (SD 9.73 ranging from 18–71 years). The survey took participants an average of 36 min to complete.

Before starting the policy-capturing online survey, participants were informed that the purpose of this study was to determine how they, as customers, would judge different combinations of strategies used to restore trust and that they would be asked to rate different combinations of strategies. Next, participants received background information, i.e., their use of smart home devices from a fictional smart home brand. The primary purpose of this information was to help participants form a cognitive relationship with the fictional smart home brand and provide details about the context in which the data breach occurred. This background was the same for all the participants.

Afterward, participants were randomly assigned to one of two treatments using a fictional newspaper report that either described an integrity-based (excessive data collection) or competency-based (hacking of customer database) data breach involving the fictional smart home brand. These reports for the smart home-specific data breach were modeled after Bansal and Zahedi [11], where an IS organization is either hacked or shares customer data with an unauthorized third party, as well as real-world breaches involving smart home technology like those reported by Baker [6] or Winder [37]. The nature of the breach described in the newspaper report, either an IVT or CBT, was investigated as a between-subjects factor, as previous research has found differences in effective trust repair between CBV and IBV [13]. The participants were then instructed to assume the role of a victim of this breach of trust between the smart home company and the customer.

Following the newspaper report, participants were exposed to 16 trust repair scenarios in which the fictional smart home brand attempted to regain their trust. In a full factorial design, verbal and substantive trust repair strategies were evaluated as a within-subjects factor: 4 verbal strategies (apology, reticence, denial, no response) * 4 substantive strategies (compensation, regulation, third-party involvement, no action), enabling us to examine both the isolated effectiveness of each strategy as well as the impact of strategy combinations. We asked participants to rate post-repair trust as the dependent variable for each scenario. Consistent with prior policy-capturing research, participants were asked to view and evaluate each of the 16 scenarios as an individual and isolated event [35].

For effective policy-capturing, it is necessary to balance between having enough scenarios to generate robust results and not having too many scenarios to prevent participants from becoming exhausted or bored [35]. Because our study provided much more detailed background information than other studies using this method (i.e. detailed descriptions of the trust repair strategies), we intentionally limited the number of scenarios well below the range of 40 to 80 scenarios recommended in the literature [38]. To help control for order effects and to increase the likelihood that participants would consider each scenario as distinct, the scenarios were presented in a randomized order [39].

3.2 Measures

Whenever possible, validated scales from previous research were adapted to measure the constructs using a scale from 1 (negative) to 7 (positive). As dependent variable, trusting beliefs (TB) were measured using nine items adapted from Bansal and Zahedi [11]. TB were measured at the beginning of the study (Pre-violation trust), after the newspaper report on the breach was provided (Post-violation trust), and for each of the 16 trust repair scenarios.

We controlled for two demographic variables (age, gender) as well as trust and context-specific variables. Disposition to trust (DTT) was adapted from using three items from Mayer and Davis [18] and Propensity to forgive (PTF) was measured with four items from Wang and Huff [40]. General privacy concerns (GPC) was adapted from Malhotra et al. [41], and user awareness of smart home technology (ASH) was measured with three items from the artificial intelligence awareness scale by Yang [42]

4 Analysis and Results

We followed established procedures from previous research for analyzing the data gathered through the policy-capturing survey (i.e. [22, 34] or [35]). Dummy coding was used to specify the presence or absence of the respective repair strategies within each scenario [43, 44]. Fixed regression analysis was used to test our hypotheses and determine the effects of isolated repair strategies as well as combinations of repair strategies on the trustee's post-repair trust. These effects were estimated for both the full sample and compared between the two treatments of IBV and CBV, as reported in Table 2.

Since the observed sample size for a policy-capturing design is equivalent to the number of scenarios assessed by the participants, the number of observations available for a pooled fixed regression analysis is 1232 (77 participants $\times$ 16 scenarios) [43]. The policy-capturing approach allows for the collection of multiple observations from the same participants. However, the validity of the observations is contingent upon the assumption that participants evaluate each scenario independently, as a separate data point [35, 45]. Potential autocorrelation was evaluated using the Durbin-Watson-Test. A resulting value of 1.79 for our regression analysis indicates slight autocorrelation in our data [46]. However, as Rynes et al. [44] and Tomlinson et al. [22] show, utilizing the aforementioned dummy variables in fixed effects regression analysis cancel out the idiosyncratic variance of each participant. This controls not only autocorrelation but also participant characteristics such as age, gender, DTT or PTF. Therefore, this approach automatically accounted for variance attributable to these variables [22, 47]. The participants' control variables accounted for 35% of the variance of the participants' post-repair trust as the dependent variable, which implies that the participant's individual characteristics cause 35% of the variance in post-repair trust. Adding the repair strategies explains an additional 18% of the variance, supporting our hypotheses (all values significant at $p < 0.01$) [22].

Descriptive statistics are reported in Table 1. Using a completely crossed scenario-based design with dummy coding to assess the effects of different strategy combinations on post-repair trust, the correlations among these strategies are zero and therefore excluded from the table due to space constraints [22]. The results of the fixed-effects regression analysis, which demonstrate the efficacy of the respective strategy or combination in restoring trust, are presented in Table 2 and illustrated in Fig. 1. All individual strategies besides TPI and all combinations have statistically significant regression coefficients in the expected positive direction.

For individual verbal repair strategies for the full sample, the coefficient for APO is highest, followed by DEN and RET. For IBV, DEN is followed by RET and then APO. For CBV, APO is highest, followed by RET and then DEN.

These results imply support for H1, H2, as well as H3a and H3b. For individual substantive strategies in the full sample, there are significant positive effects for REG and COM but not for TPI.

The same applies for IBV, whereas for CBV, there is a significant effect on TPI. Therefore H4a, H4b, H5a, H5b and H6b are supported, while H6a cannot be supported.

There are significant positive effects for all combinations of verbal and substantive strategies. However, H7 cannot be confirmed because combinations involving TPI feature comparatively lower coefficients than using only the respective verbal strategy.

5 Discussion

Our study provides empirical evidence for several verbal and substantive trust repair strategies found in the literature by investigating both competency and integrity-related privacy breaches with scenario data from long-term smart home users.

For verbal trust repair strategies, we provide additional data to confirm previous research. When considering the type of violation, we provide additional evidence for [11] showing that DEN, RET and APO are ordinal in effectiveness with the order depending on the type of violation. The order of effectiveness is DEN > RET > APO for IBV, while for CBV the order is APO > RET > DEN. We provide additional

Table 1 Means, standard deviations and correlations

Variable	Mean	SD	1	2	3	4	5	6	7	8
1. Age	30.36	9.73								
2. Gender	_a	_a	0							
3. DPT	4.38	1.2	−0.02	−0.01						
4. PTF	3.05	1.32	−.06*	−0.09**	0.31**					
5. GPC	4.77	1.62	0.05	−0.11**	0.09**	−0.03				
6. ASH	4.08	1.25	0.13**	−0.28**	0.04	−0.02	0.18**			
7. PRVT	5.14	0.75	0.15**	0.16**	0.03	0.16**	−0.14**	−0.04		
8. POVT	1.99	0.54	−0.10**	0.04	0.05*	0.11**	−0.16**	0.12**	0.06*	
9. PORT	2.92	1.47	−0.05	0.02	−0.13**	0.14**	−0.08**	−0.03	0.12**	0.12**

*$p < 0,05$; ** $p < 0,01$; $N = 1232$; PRVT = Pre-violation trust, POVT = Post-violation trust; PORT = Post-repair trust;
a: Gender was coded female 1 and male 0

Table 2 Results of the fixed-effects regression analysis

	Full sample	IBV only	CBV only
Strategy combinations	β	β	β
APO	1.194**	0.931**	1.450**
APO + COMP	1.58**	1.398**	1.757**
APO + REG	2.111**	1.961**	2.256**
APO + TPI	1.234**	1.062**	1.401**
RET	1.092**	1.090**	1.094**
RET + COMP	1.528**	1.472**	1.582**
RET + REG	2.106**	2.017**	2.193**
RET + TPI	0.916**	0.848**	0.982**
DEN	1.173**	1.369**	0.982**
DEN + COMP	1.711**	1.469**	1.953**
DEN + REG	2.041**	2.050**	2.031**
DEN + TPI	0.777**	0.556*	0.992**
COM	0.840**	0.690*	0.985**
REG	1.459**	1.269**	1.644**
TPI	0.501	0.308	0.689*

*p < .05; ** p < .01; APO = Apology, COMP = Compensation; REG = Regulation; TPI = Third-Party Involvement; RET = Reticence; DEN = Denial

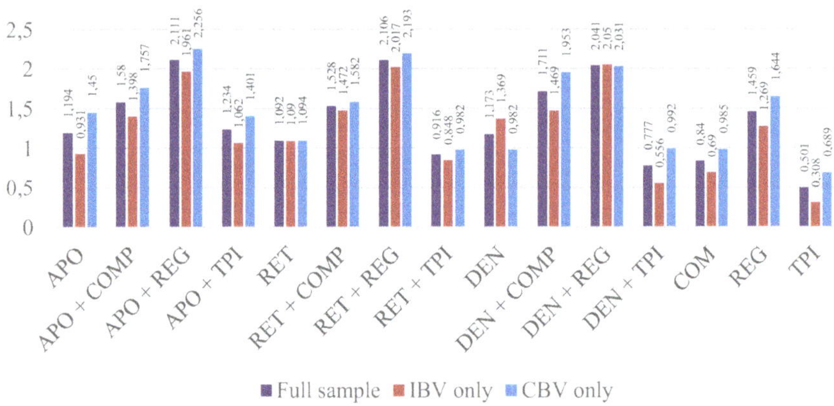

Fig. 1 Visualization of the results of the fixed-effects regression analysis

evidence for privacy-related violations for the argument that reticence is a second-best verbal trust repair strategy that should be utilized in situations when the most effective strategy can't be used [21].

We also provide insights on the effectiveness of substantive repair strategies, for which only limited empirical research is available [13]. For both CBV and IBV, REG was found to be most effective, followed by COMP. We find that REG, where the trustor makes efforts to address the transgression, is more beneficial to trust repair than the trustee just compensating the trustor [48]. Our data implies that TPI is unlikely to effectively restore trust compared to company-driven REG and COMP, though this could only be confirmed for CBV. The lower effectiveness of this repair strategy seems reasonable, considering that for this scenario, the transgressor is forced to take corrective actions by the platform intermediary as a third party under the threat of punishment. As these actions are not out of genuine remorse, our participants seem to doubt the authenticity of an organization that cannot be trusted to self-correct after transgressions [28, 34].

Furthermore, we follow calls for a holistic approach to research in trust repair (i.e. [12, 13, 15]) by examining combinations of verbal and substantive trust repair strategies rather than studying them in isolation. The findings show that combining certain strategies might have compounding effects on restoring trust after a privacy violation [48]. Strategy combinations involving COMP and REG are more effective than using only verbal strategies for both violation types. When faced with CBV like criminal actors hacking a customer database, the trustee should use APO + REG as a response,for IBV like excessive data collection through the trustee, they should use DEN + REG as the most effective response. The data also shows that adding REG to verbal strategies is relatively more effective at restoring trust compared to combinations including COMP. This seems to imply that money can buy back trust to a limited degree [12, 32]. Combining verbal strategies with TPI barely increases the effectiveness of verbal repair strategies, and in some cases, i.e. RET + TP in IBV, actually decreases effectiveness. This is probably due to an illogical combination of these two strategies from the customer's perspective.

5.1 Practical Implications, Limitations, and Future Research

This research also offers practical implications for smart home companies and other organizations aiming to recover trust after breaches of customer data, which are an unavoidable risk when conducting business using the internet [49]. As trust is recognized as vital prerequisite for gaining and retaining customers, our findings offer guidance on choosing suitable trust repair strategies when faced with CBV or IBV. Additionally, organizations should recognize that using only verbal responses or only substantive changes might not be enough and that a combination of well-matched strategies should restore trust better after a privacy breach.

This study has limitations that offer avenues for future research. First, while using a scenario-based policy-capturing design is an effective method for gathering decision-making data, it cannot fully capture the complexities of real-world trust violations and corresponding customer responses. Research with customers who have personally experienced privacy-related violations of trust could prove valuable, as well as research with users from different countries and cultural backgrounds. Second, to manage the complexity of the experimental design, we focused on a core set of trust repair strategies pulled from previous research. We also limited each strategy to a single level rather than examining different configurations of the same strategy, i.e. like [34] using different values for compensation. There might be other verbal and substantive strategies that could prove relevant for repairing trust. Future research should also try to develop new trust repair strategies for IoT and privacy-related contexts. Third, the data for this survey was measured at a single point in time, while trust repair is a continuous process [15]. Longitudinal studies are needed to provide more data on the effectiveness of trust-repair strategies and corresponding trustor reactions.

In conclusion, this research provides insights into the effective use of verbal and substantive trust repair strategies. We hope our findings will be useful to researchers and practitioners interested in understanding trust repair following breaches of privacy in the smart home context.

Acknowledgements This research was sponsored by the German Federal Ministry for Education and Research in the project Opt-In (Ref. num. 16KIS1935K) and by the Gambrinus Fund at TU Dortmund University.

References

1. Zheng, S., Apthorpe, N., Chetty, M., & Feamster, N. (2018). User perceptions of smart home IoT privacy. *Proceedings of the ACM on Human-Computer Interaction*, *2*(CSCW), 1–20.
2. Cannizzaro, S., Procter, R., Ma, S., & Maple, C. (2020). Trust in the smart home: Findings from a nationally representative survey in the UK. *PLoS ONE, 15*(5), Article e0231615.
3. Zeng, E., Mare, S., & Roesner, F. (2017). End user security and privacy concerns with smart homes. In *Thirteenth symposium on usable privacy and security (SOUPS 2017).*
4. Bugeja, J., Jacobsson, A., & Davidsson, P. (2016). On privacy and security challenges in smart connected homes. In *2016 European intelligence and security informatics conference (EISIC 2016): Uppsala, Sweden, 17–19 August 2016* (pp. 172–175). IEEE.
5. Abdi, N., Zhan, X., Ramokapane, K. M., & Such, J. (2021). Privacy norms for smart home personal assistants. In Y. Kitamura (Ed.), *ACM digital library, Proceedings of the 2021 CHI conference on human factors in computing systems* (pp. 1–14). Association for Computing Machinery.
6. Baker, P. (2023, June 15). Smart home security: your questions answered. *The Verge.* https://www.theverge.com/23753752/smart-home-privacy-security-questions-explained
7. Jaspers, E. D., & Pearson, E. (2022). Consumers' acceptance of domestic Internet-of-Things: The role of trust and privacy concerns. *Journal of Business Research, 142*, 255–265.
8. Consumers International and Internet Society. (2019). *The trust opportuinity: Exploring consumers' attitudes to the internet of things.* https://www.internetsociety.org/wp-content/uploads/2019/05/CI_IS_Joint_Report-EN.pdf
9. Lankton, N., McKnight, D. H., & Tripp, J. (2015). Technology, humanness, and trust: Rethinking trust in technology. *Journal of the Association for Information Systems, 16*(10), 880–918.
10. Pavlou, A. P. (2003). Consumer acceptance of electronic commerce: Integrating trust and risk with the technology acceptance model. *International Journal of Electronic Commerce, 7*(3), 101–134.
11. Bansal, G., & Zahedi, F. M. (2015). Trust violation and repair: The information privacy perspective. *Decision Support Systems, 71*, 62–77.

12. Dirks, K. T., Kim, P. H., Ferrin, D. L., & Cooper, C. D. (2011). Understanding the effects of substantive responses on trust following a transgression. *Organizational Behavior and Human Decision Processes, 114*(2), 87–103.
13. Sharma, K., Schoorman, F. D., & Ballinger, G. A. (2023). How can it be made right again? A review of trust repair research. *Journal of Management, 49*(1), 363–399.
14. McKnight, D. H., Carter, M., Thatcher, J. B., & Clay, P. F. (2011). Trust in a specific technology. *ACM Transactions on Management Information Systems, 2*(2), 1–25.
15. Lewicki, R. J., & Brinsfield, C. (2017). Trust repair. *Annual Review of Organizational Psychology and Organizational Behavior, 4*(1), 287–313.
16. Lewicki, R. J., & Bunker, B. B. (1996). Developing and maintaining trust in work relationships. In R. Kramer & T. Tyler (Eds.), *Trust in organizations: Frontiers of theory and research* (pp. 114–139). Sage.
17. Mayer, R. C., Davis, J. H., & Schoorman, F. D. (1995). An integrative model of organizational trust. *Academy of Management Review, 20*(3), 709.
18. Mayer, R. C., & Davis, J. H. (1999). The effect of the performance appraisal system on trust for management: A field quasi-experiment. *Journal of Applied Psychology, 84*(1), 123–136.
19. McKnight, D. H., Choudhury, V., & Kacmar, C. (2002). Developing and validating trust measures for e-commerce: An integrative typology. *Information Systems Research, 13*(3), 334–359.
20. Tomlinson, E. C., & Mayer, R. C. (2009). The role of causal attribution dimensions in trust repair. *Academy of Management Review, 34*(1), 85–104.
21. Ferrin, D. L., Kim, P. H., Cooper, C. D., & Dirks, K. T. (2007). Silence speaks volumes: The effectiveness of reticence in comparison to apology and denial for responding to integrity- and competence-based trust violations. *Journal of Applied Psychology, 92*(4), 893–908.
22. Tomlinson, E. C., Dineen, B. R., & Lewicki, R. J. (2004). The road to reconciliation: Antecedents of victim willingness to reconcile following a broken promise. *Journal of Management, 30*(2), 165–187.
23. Bies, R. J., & Tripp, T. M. (1996). Beyond distrust: "Getting even" and the need for revenge. In R. Kramer & T. Tyler (Eds.), *Trust in organizations: Frontiers of theory and research* (pp. 246–260). Sage.
24. Morgan, R. M., & Hunt, S. D. (1994). The commitment-trust theory of relationship marketing. *Journal of Marketing, 58*(3).
25. Xie, Y., & Peng, S. (2009). How to repair customer trust after negative publicity: The roles of competence, integrity, benevolence, and forgiveness. *Psychology & Marketing, 26*(7), 572–589.
26. Bozic, B. (2017). Consumer trust repair: A critical literature review. *European Management Journal, 35*(4), 538–547.
27. Tomlinson, E. C., Nelson, C. A., & Langlinais, L. A. (2021). A cognitive process model of trust repair. *International Journal of Conflict Management, 32*(2), 340–360.
28. Yu, Y., Yang, Y., & Jing, F. (2017). The role of the third party in trust repair process. *Journal of Business Research, 78*, 233–241.
29. Kim, P. H., Ferrin, D. L., Cooper, C. D., & Dirks, K. T. (2004). Removing the shadow of suspicion: The effects of apology versus denial for repairing competence- versus integrity-based trust violations. *Journal of Applied Psychology, 89*(1), 104–118.
30. Gao, S., & Yan, J. (2022). Verbal or written? The impact of apology on the repair of trust: Based on competence- vs. integrity-based trust violation. *Frontiers in Psychology, 13*.
31. Schweitzer, M. E., Hershey, J. C., & Bradlow, E. T. (2006). Promises and lies: Restoring violated trust. *Organizational Behavior and Human Decision Processes, 101*(1), 1–19.
32. Haesevoets, T., Reinders Folmer, C., & van Hiel, A. (2015). Is trust for sale? The effectiveness of financial compensation for repairing competence- versus integrity-based trust violations. *PloS One, 10*(12).
33. Gillespie, N., & Dietz, G. (2009). Trust repair after an organization-level failure. *Academy of Management Review, 34*(1), 127–145.
34. Cugueró-Escofet, N., Fortin, M., & Canela, M.-A. (2014). Righting the wrong for third parties: How monetary compensation, procedure changes and apologies can restore justice for observers of injustice. *Journal of Business Ethics, 122*(2), 253–268.

35. Aiman-Smith, L., Scullen, S. E., & Barr, S. H. (2002). Conducting studies of decision making in organizational contexts: A tutorial for policy-capturing and other regression-based techniques. *Organizational Research Methods, 5*(4), 388–414.
36. Graham, M. E., & Cable, D. M. (2001). Consideration of the incomplete block design for policy-capturing research. *Organizational Research Methods, 4*(1), 26–45.
37. Winder, D. (2019). *Confirmed: 2 billion records exposed in massive smart home device breach.* https://www.forbes.com/sites/daveywinder/2019/07/02/confirmed-2-billion-records-exposed-in-massive-smart-home-device-breach/
38. Cooksey, R. W. (1996). *Judgment analysis: Theory, methods, and applications.* Academic Press. http://www.loc.gov/catdir/description/els032/95044361.html
39. Spence, J. R., & Keeping, L. M. (2010). The impact of non-performance information on ratings of job performance: A policy-capturing approach. *Journal of Organizational Behavior, 31*(4), 587–608.
40. Wang, S., & Huff, L. C. (2007). Explaining buyers' responses to sellers' violation of trust. *European Journal of Marketing, 41*(9/10), 1033–1052.
41. Malhotra, N. K., Kim, S. S., & Agarwal, J. (2004). Internet users' information privacy concerns (IUIPC): The construct, the scale, and a causal model. *Information Systems Research, 15*(4), 336–355.
42. Yang, N. (2022). *Technology that rocks the cradle: Introducing artificial intelligence awareness* [Dissertation]. University of Alabama.
43. Judge, T. A., & Bretz, R. D. (1992). Effects of work values on job choice decisions. *Journal of Applied Psychology, 77*(3), 261–271.
44. Rynes, S. L., Weber, C. L., & Milkovich, G. T. (1989). Effects of market survey rates, job evaluation, and job gender on job pay. *Journal of Applied Psychology, 74*(1), 114–123.
45. Hays, W. L. (1994). *Statistics* (5th ed.). Harcourt Brace College Publishers.
46. Chatterjee, S., & Simonoff, J. S. (2013). *Handbook of regression analysis.* Wiley.
47. Huang, F. L. (2016). Alternatives to multilevel modeling for the analysis of clustered data. *The Journal of Experimental Education, 84*(1), 175–196.
48. Kähkönen, T., Blomqvist, K., Gillespie, N., & Vanhala, M. (2021). Employee trust repair: A systematic review of 20 years of empirical research and future research directions. *Journal of Business Research, 130*, 98–109.
49. Sen, R., & Borle, S. (2015). Estimating the contextual risk of data breach: An empirical approach. *Journal of Management Information Systems, 32*(2), 314–341.

Tourism in the Era of Internet of Things: Design Principles for Smart Tourism

Leonardo Banh and Gero Strobel

Abstract The tourism industry plays a crucial role in many countries and has suffered under the global events of the last years (e.g., COVID-19, economic recession) with a decline in visitors and economic contributions. Through digitalization efforts of cities and states, smart tourism destinations use emerging technologies like the Internet of Things and Smart Services to provide rich on-site experiences for visitors, hoping to increase their competitiveness and attract new tourists. By conducting a design science research project in collaboration with a German municipality, this paper aims to explore how digital assistants should be designed in the context of smart tourism. Based on expert interviews and a multi-case study of 37 tourism apps, we were able to develop twelve key design principles for smart tourism applications, evaluated through a prototypical instantiation, to create de-sign knowledge for the digitalization of tourism.

1 Introduction

Many cities have undergone extensive structural change for decades due to modernization and digitalization efforts in various industry sectors [1–3]. For instance, the Ruhr Area in Germany transformed from a former industry and mining region into a service-oriented region, providing services and producing economic information. Nevertheless, or particularly because of this change, these areas are becoming more attractive for touristic activities as much history gets intertwined with modern recreation sites, resulting in various cultural goods for locals and tourists [1].

As digitalization also affects more and more sectors, cities and states invest in modernization efforts through targeted digitalization strategies, aiming to develop smart cities in many areas of urban life. Smart cities incorporate information and

L. Banh (✉) · G. Strobel
University Duisburg-Essen, Essen, Germany
e-mail: leonardo.banh@uni-due.de

G. Strobel
e-mail: gero.strobel@uni-due.de

C. M. Flath et al. (eds.), *Digital Innovation and Organizational Transformation*, Lecture Notes in Information Systems and Organisation 83,
https://doi.org/10.1007/978-3-032-08483-5_3

communication technologies (ICT) with traditional infrastructures to improve life concerning social, environmental, and economic quality [4, 5]. By optimizing resources, monitoring security, and providing valuable services to the citizens in an intelligent and coordinated way, the goal is to create integrated, habitable, and sustainable urban centers [6, 7].

Following the closing of borders due to the COVID-19 pandemic, many regions and countries were affected negatively due to the absence of visitors and shrinking economic contributions. 66% of countries worldwide closed their borders entirely or partially to international tourists in 2021 [8]. The result was a decrease in travelers, from 1.5 billion people in 2019 before the pandemic to only 400 million in 2020 and 415 million in 2021 [9]. The decline also led to lower economic contribution (50.4% decline to 2019) and the demise of 62 million jobs in 2020 [10]. While the numbers have been recovering lately, with almost 97% of pre-pandemic levels observed in 2024-Q1 [11], destinations seek to attract tourists and deliver an exciting and unforgettable stay. Smart tourism can provide means to attract touristic travelers, enhance their stay, and provide meaningful and entertaining services. Smart tourism destinations use technologies such as Internet of Things (IoT) or Smart Services to enhance touristic experiences by providing rich on-site experiences for visitors [12, 13]. Especially the popularity of portable digital media devices like smartphones and tablets has led to opportunities for touristic providers to create mobile applications in combination with sensors enhancing tourists' experiences [14], leveraging technological concepts like augmented reality (AR) to provide interactive means [15]. Because of the ubiquity of smart devices and services, tourists can be supported throughout all stages of their travels [16, 17]. Cities such as Amsterdam or Brisbane have developed interactive applications to support tourists during their stay and integrate, for instance, radio-frequency identification (RFID) beacons to provide location-based information [12]. Features such as theme routes, audio and video content, multi-lingual guides, and suggestions for points of interest bring value to the tourists and can serve as smart assistants during their visits.

Although research activities have been focused on the smart tourism phenomenon as well as the development of smart services to enrich the touristic experience [e.g., 18–20], the results are primarily trimmed toward single case study solutions and isolated technologies [e.g., 21–23]. Against this backdrop, this paper investigates the smart tourism phenomenon from a design perspective to provide design knowledge supporting researchers and practitioners in leveraging the use of IoT and information systems for touristic destinations. Hence, we explore the following research question: *How to design smart tourism applications?*

To answer our question, we conduct a design science research (DSR) project in collaboration with a German municipality to develop design principles. This research-in-progress paper addresses the first iteration of the research process from the elicitation of requirements to the prototyping phase. The remainder of this paper is structured as follows: First, we analyze related literature on the topics of smart tourism and their potential to improve the touristic experience. Second, we elaborate on our research methodology, i.e., how we apply DSR with expert interviews and a multi-case study to gather our data. Third, we present our preliminary findings in form of design principles and the prototype of the smart tourism assistant. Last, we conclude our work and give an outlook on future steps of the research project.

2 Smart Tourism

The transition from tourism destinations to smart tourism destinations by integrating digital technologies has been a trending research topic in recent years. Cities see the use of ICT as a key factor in creating and enhancing smart tourism destinations. Besides improving tourists' stays with seamless and personalized experiences, e.g., via mobile applications or IoT technologies, destinations also aim to increase their competitiveness [13, 24–26]. ICT and IoT especially can be utilized in various ways to support smart tourism destinations. For example, the use of analytical approaches based on the data provided by various types of IoT devices facilitate real-time insights into tourist behavior, preferences, and needs, allowing for better targeting and personalization of tourist services and products [27, 28]. IoT devices such as smart sensors collect data on tourist traffic and behavior, enabling destination managers to optimize tourist flow as well as create better crowd management strategies [12, 29]. Thus, tourist attractions can be relieved, and visitors, as well as residents, benefit from less crowded spaces. Ubiquitous computing throughout the city in the form of RFID beacons, Wi-Fi connectivity, or near-field communication tags further elevate the tourists' experience by providing location-based services [13, 30, 31].

Smart Services play a vital role in the offerings to residents and visitors by enabling them to accomplish information seeking by means of interactive and intelligent technology [32]. Providing tourists with personalized and relevant information or services, smart services enhance the individual experience [33]. For instance in Amsterdam or Brisbane, smart services use real-time data from IoT devices to offer context-aware and location-based recommendations to tourists, making it easier for them to discover nearby attractions and activities [12]. Furthermore, they can provide personalized recommendations based on tourists' interests and preferences, creating a tailored and immersive experience [34]. The goal is to provide a holistic and unified experience for the user without too much active involvement. Overall, previous research shows that smart tourism destinations created by leveraging IoT technologies and smart services play a crucial role in enhancing tourists' trips. Combining these technologies provides tourists with novel experiences and personalized information to improve the overall satisfaction of tourists [35]. However, research is lacking in the design of holistic solutions that combine smart tourism with the value-creating benefits of IoT.

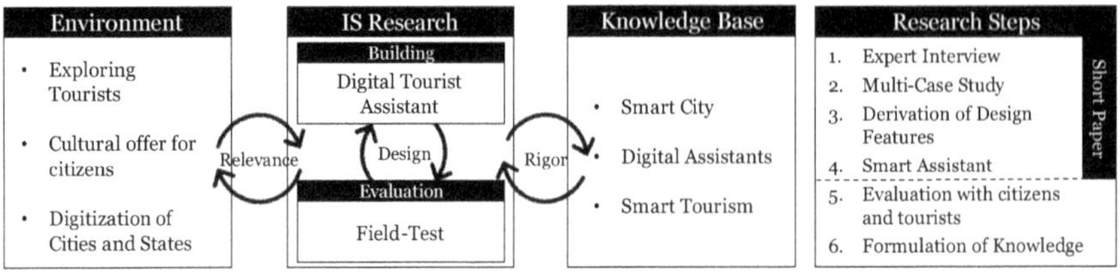

Fig. 1 Research design

3 Research Method

To achieve our overall goal of providing descriptive design knowledge for the design of smart tourism assistants, we conducted a DSR project [36] following the DSR approach of 37 [37]. This short paper addresses the first DSR cycle up to prototype development (see Fig. 1).

Problem awareness. The starting point for our research process was an examination of the smart tourism situation in the municipality. For this purpose, expert interviews[1] were conducted with three project managers from the IT, digitalization, and municipal utility resorts as part of a focus group [38] (1). To triangulate the findings and enrich them with empirical knowledge, a multi-case study of 37 smart tourism applications[1] (e.g., Munich) was conducted based on publicly available information [39] (2).

Suggestion of a solution. Based on the analysis of the expert interviews in an open coding process [40] and the conceptualization of smart tourism application capabilities from the case study, twelve design principles could be derived (3).

Development. We transferred the extracted design principles into a prototype (4) in the form of a mobile application to make the findings testable in the real world. The prototype was designed as a cross-platform application to include a large user base.

Demonstration and evaluation. As a first proof of concept [41], the prototype was tested by resort managers. User-centered artifact development is a central quality criterion in DSR. Therefore, as a subsequent step, additional stakeholders (i.e., citizens and tourists) will be included in the assessment (5) as the project progresses [42] to ensure the overall usefulness of the results.

4 Preliminary Results

Based on our data analysis, we identified 12 design principles for a smart tourism assistant to enhance user experience and provide personalized recommendations to tourists. Table 1 provides an overview of the first design principles we formulated.

[1] Further information about the expert interviews and case study: http://bit.ly/3Ta8Hbd.

Table 1 Design principles

#	Design principle	Description
DP1	Tailored Recommendations	Provide personalized recommendations to enhance the stay of different types of tourist groups.
DP2	Information Augmentation	Provide meaningful information that augments the tourists' stay (e.g., historical background knowledge).
DP3	Location-based Services	Provide context-aware and location-based offerings that are tailored toward the user's location.
DP4	Push Principle	Provide information automatically and context-aware, without the need of active user involvement.
DP5	Accessibility	Provide inclusive access for everyone, regardless their condition (e.g., enhanced auditive or visual options).
DP6	Multilingualism	Provide multiple language options to reach a large and diverse touristic user base.
DP7	Ease of Use	Provide a self-explanatory experience with low technical requirements to promote higher use.
DP8	Mobile Access	Provide mechanisms so that users have independent access (e.g., in offline situations).
DP9	Rich Interaction	Provide rich interactions with the environment and other users (e.g., augmented reality and social functions).
DP10	Gamification	Provide gamified incentives for users to actively continue the use throughout their stay.
DP11	Navigation	Provide navigation functions to the users for better orientation in an unknown city.
DP12	Ticket Provisioning	Provide virtual ticket counters to book tickets beforehand.

Providing **tailored recommendations** (DP1) is the first design principle we identified, and it pursues adaptive features and information for different types of tourist groups. This principle enables a personalized and inclusive experience for all tourists, as different groups have distinct expectations of their stay [43, 44]. For instance, the analysis of our case study municipality revealed tourist groups that could be classified into culture and history, nature, and sport. Depending on the personal interests of the tourists, the smart tourism application should present features and information to enhance their stay.

Information augmentation (DP2) and **location-based services** (DP3) address the type and delivery of information provided to tourists. To avoid overwhelming tourists with irrelevant data, it is important to provide only meaningful information that adapts to the personal context [45]. The **push principle** (DP4) enables the automatic provision of context-aware information, without the need for active user involvement. Hence, tourists can discover nearby attractions and activities and receive valuable information in relation to their location, fostering the engagement and discovery of new experiences and attractions.

Inclusive and accessible design principles enable every tourist to benefit from a smart tourism application [46, 47]. Thus, **accessibility** options (DP5), **multiple**

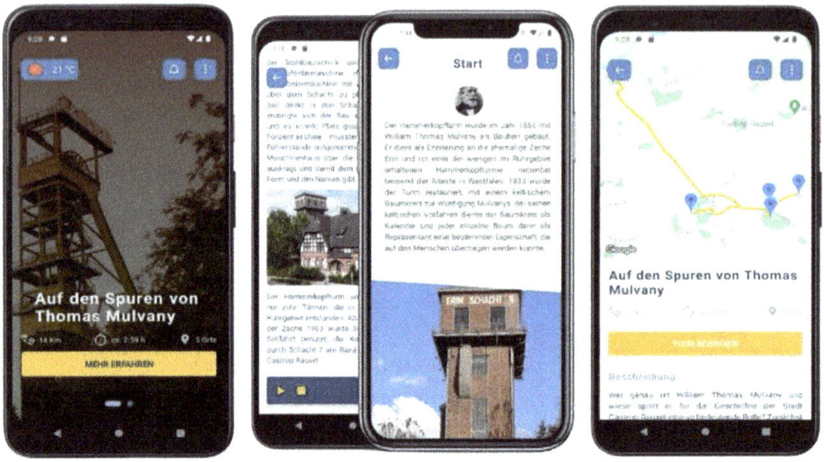

Fig. 2 Prototypical implementation of the smart tourism assistant

languages (DP6), and a focus on **ease of use** (DP7) are important design principles to be considered. **Mobile access** (DP8), e.g., via offline data, facilitates widespread use among users who may not have access to the Internet. And lastly, innovative design principles attract users to try out the smart tourism application and profit from functionalities that make the stay more comfortable and enjoyable, e.g., by providing **rich interaction** modes (DP9), **gamification** incentives (DP10), **navigation functions** (DP11), or **ticket provisioning** possibilities for attractions in the area (DP12).

By instantiating our design principles into a prototypical application, we developed a smart tourism assistant for a German municipality (Fig. 2) to provide a tangible evaluation basis and baseline for the formulation of design knowledge for the artifact class. We believe that the assistant can help improve the overall tourism experience and provide a personalized, inclusive, and engaging experience for all tourists.

5 Conclusion and Outlook

This paper has investigated the design of smart tourism applications by presenting the first results of a DSR project. Through eliciting and developing a prototypical smart tourism assistant for a German municipality, we have gathered preliminary design knowledge regarding design principles for smart tourism applications. Our work has shown the importance of personalization, context-awareness, and interactivity for assistants in the field of tourism. The proposed smart assistant can provide tailored recommendations, location-based information, and multimedia content to enrich the tourist's experience. In our next steps, we will derive further design knowledge for the artefact class based on succeeding evaluations of the smart assistant in the real-world. The design principles we have identified in this paper will be refined through a field experiment with citizens und visitors to prove their effectiveness in enhancing tourists' experiences. Future research will also explore the potential of emerging technologies, such as virtual and augmented reality, to further enhance the smart assistant's capabilities.

References

1. Copic, S., Djordjevica, J., Lukic, T., Stojanovic, V., Djukicin, S., Besermenji, S., Stamenkovic, I., & Tumaric, A. (2014). Transformation of industrial heritage: An example of tourism industry development in the Ruhr area (Germany). *Geogr Pannon, 18*, 43–50.
2. Kunzmann, K. R. (1998). *World city regions in Europe: Structural change and future challenges Globalization and the world of large cities.* (pp. 37–75). United Nations University Press.
3. Matthess, M., & Kunkel, S. (2020). Structural change and digitalization in developing countries: Conceptually linking the two transformations. *Technology in Society, 63*, Article 101428.
4. Batty, M., Axhausen, K. W., Giannotti, F., Pozdnoukhov, A., Bazzani, A., Wachowicz, M., Ouzounis, G., & Portugali, Y. (2012). Smart cities of the future. *European Physical Journal: Special Topics, 214*, 481–518.
5. Lombardi, P., Giordano, S., Farouh, H., & Yousef, W. (2012). Modelling the smart city performance. *Innovation: The European Journal of Social Science Research, 25*, 137–149.
6. Barrionuevo, J. M., Berrone, P., & Ricart Costa, J. E. (2012). Smart cities, sustainable progress: Opportunities for urban development. *IESE Insight*, 50–57.
7. Hall, R., Bowerman, B., Braverman, J., Taylor, J., Todosow, H., & Wimmersperg, U. (2000). *The vision of a smart city.* 2nd International Life Extension Technology Workshop.
8. UN Tourism. (2021). *Tightened travel restrictions underline current challenges for tourism.* https://www.unwto.org/news/tightened-travel-restrictions-underline-current-challenges-for-tourism
9. UN Tourism. (2022). *Tourism grows 4% in 2021 but remains far below pre-pandemic levels.* https://www.unwto.org/news/tourism-grows-4-in-2021-but-remains-far-below-pre-pandemic-levels
10. WTTC. (2022). *Economic impact reports.* https://wttc.org/research/economic-impact
11. UN Tourism. (2024). *International tourism reached 97% of pre-pandemic levels in the first quarter of 2024.* https://www.unwto.org/news/international-tourism-reached-97-of-pre-pandemic-levels-in-the-first-quarter-of-2024
12. Gretzel, U., Sigala, M., Xiang, Z., & Koo, C. (2015). Smart tourism: Foundations and developments. *Electron Markets, 25*, 179–188.
13. Jeong, M., & Shin, H. H. (2020). Tourists' experiences with smart tourism technology at smart destinations and their behavior intentions. *Journal of Travel Research, 59*, 1464–1477.
14. Brown, B., & Chalmers, M. (2003). Tourism and mobile technology. In K. Kuutti, E. H. Karsten, G. Fitzpatrick, P. Dourish, & K. Schmidt (Eds.), *ECSCW 2003* (pp. 335–354). Springer.
15. Chung, N., Han, H., & Joun, Y. (2015). Tourists' intention to visit a destination: The role of augmented reality (AR) application for a heritage site. *Computers in Human Behavior, 50*, 588–599. https://doi.org/10.1016/j.chb.2015.02.068
16. Höpken, W., Fuchs, M., Zanker, M., & Beer, T. (2010). Context-based adaptation of mobile applications in tourism. *Information Technology & Tourism, 12*, 175–195.
17. Kenteris, M., Gavalas, D., & Economou, D. (2011). Electronic mobile guides: A survey. *Personal and Ubiquitous Computing, 15*, 97–111.
18. Smirnov, A., Kashevnik, A., Shilov, N., Teslya, N., & Shabaev, A. (2014). Mobile application for guiding tourist activities: Tourist assistant—TAIS. In *Proceedings of 16th conference of open innovations association FRUCT* (pp. 95–100). IEEE.

19. Souto, V. T., Cristo, C., Araújo, M. G., & Santos, L. (2015). Designing apps for tourists: A case study. Lecture Notes in Computer ScienceIn A. Marcus (Ed.), *Design, user experience, and usability: Interactive experience design* (Vol. 9188, pp. 425–436). Springer International Publishing.
20. Tsaih, R.-H., & Hsu, C. (2018). Artificial intelligence in smart tourism: A conceptual framework. *ICEB 2018 Proceedings* (Guilin, China).
21. Boes, K., Borde, L., & Egger, R. (2015). The acceptance of NFC smart posters in tourism. In I. Tussyadiah & A. Inversini (Eds.), *Information and communication technologies in tourism 2015* (pp. 435–447). Springer International Publishing.
22. Lobao, F., Neto, M., & Aparicio, M. (2019). Smart tourism—City tourism radar: A tourism monitoring tool at the city of Lisbon. In *CAPSI 2019 Proceedings*.
23. Mutch, A. (1993). Successful use of information technology in a small tourism enterprise: The case of Country Holidays. *The Journal of Strategic Information Systems, 2*, 264–275.
24. Buhalis, D., & Amaranggana, A. (2015). Smart tourism destinations enhancing tourism experience through personalisation of services. In I. Tussyadiah & A. Inversini (Eds.), *Information and communication technologies in tourism 2015* (pp. 377–389). Springer International Publishing.
25. Gretzel, U., & Koo, C. (2021). Smart tourism cities: A duality of place where technology supports the convergence of touristic and residential experiences. *Asia Pacific Journal of Tourism Research, 26*, 352–364.
26. Li, Y., Hu, C., Huang, C., & Duan, L. (2017). The concept of smart tourism in the context of tourism information services. *Tourism Management, 58*, 293–300.
27. Kontogianni, A., Alepis, E., & Patsakis, C. (2022). Promoting smart tourism personalised services via a combination of deep learning techniques. *Expert Systems with Applications, 187*, Article 115964.
28. Xiang, Z., Du, Q., Ma, Y., & Fan, W. (2017). A comparative analysis of major online review platforms: Implications for social media analytics in hospitality and tourism. *Tourism Management, 58*, 51–65.
29. Xiang, Z., Stienmetz, J., & Fesenmaier, D. R. (2021). Smart tourism design: Launching the annals of tourism research curated collection on designing tourism places. *Annals of Tourism Research, 86*, Article 103154.
30. Meehan, K., Lunney, T., Curran, K., & McCaughey, A. (2013). Context-aware intelligent recommendation system for tourism. In *2013 IEEE international conference on pervasive computing and communications workshops (PERCOM workshops)* (pp. 328–331). IEEE.
31. Wise, N., & Heidari, H. (2019). Developing smart tourism destinations with the internet of things. In M. Sigala, R. Rahimi, & M. Thelwall (Eds.), *Big data and innovation in tourism, travel, and hospitality* (pp. 21–29). Springer Singapore.
32. Maedche, A., Legner, C., Benlian, A., Berger, B., Gimpel, H., Hess, T., Hinz, O., Morana, S., & Söllner, M. (2019). AI-based digital assistants. *Business & Information Systems Engineering, 61*, 535–544.
33. Paukstadt, U., Strobel, G., & Eicker, S. (2019). Understanding services in the era of the internet of things: A smart service taxonomy. In *Proceedings of the 27th European conference on information systems (ECIS)*.
34. Jiménez-Barreto, J., Rubio, N., Mura, P., Sthapit, E., & Campo, S. (2023). "Ask Google assistant where to travel" tourists' interactive experiences with smart speakers: An assemblage theory approach. *Journal of Travel Research, 62*, 734–752.
35. Goo, J., Huang, C. D., Yoo, C. W., & Koo, C. (2022). Smart tourism technologies' ambidexterity: Balancing tourist's worries and novelty seeking for travel satisfaction. *Information Systems Frontiers: A Journal of Research and Innovation, 24*, 2139–2158.
36. Hevner, A. R., March, S. T., Park, J., & Ram, S. (2004). Design science in information systems research. *MIS Quarterly, 28*, 75.
37. Kuechler, B., & Vaishnavi, V. (2008). On theory development in design science research: Anatomy of a research project. *European Journal of Information Systems, 17*, 489–504.
38. Tremblay, M. C., Hevner, A. R., & Berndt, D. J. (2010). The use of focus groups in design science research. In A. R. Hevner & S. Chatterjee (Eds.), *Design research in information*

systems. Integrated Series in Information Systems (vol. 22, pp. 121–143). Springer US. https://doi.org/10.1007/978-1-4419-5653-8_10
39. Yin, R. K. (2018). *Case study research: Design and methods*. Sage.
40. Bandara, W., Furtmueller, E., Gorbacheva, E., Miskon, S., & Beekhuyzen, J. (2015). Achieving Rigor in literature reviews: Insights from qualitative data analysis and tool-support. In *CAIS* (Vol. 37).
41. Nunamaker, J. F., Briggs, R. O., Derrick, D. C., & Schwabe, G. (2015). The last research mile: achieving both rigor and relevance in information systems research. *Journal of Management Information Systems, 32*, 10–47.
42. Rosemann, M., & Vessey, I. (2008). Toward improving the relevance of information systems research to practice: The role of applicability checks. *MIS Quarterly, 32*, 1.
43. Arnegger, J., Woltering, M., & Job, H. (2010). Toward a product-based typology for nature-based tourism: A conceptual framework. *Journal of Sustainable Tourism, 18*, 915–928.
44. McKercher, B. (2016). Towards a taxonomy of tourism products. *Tourism Management, 54*, 196–208.
45. Gorgoglione, M., Panniello, U., & Tuzhilin, A. (2019). Recommendation strategies in personalization applications. *Information & Management, 56*, Article 103143.
46. Huang, C. D., Goo, J., Nam, K., & Yoo, C. W. (2017). Smart tourism technologies in travel planning: The role of exploration and exploitation. *Information & Management, 54*, 757–770.
47. Tussyadiah, I., & Fesenmaier, D. R. (2007). Interpreting tourist experiences from first-person stories: A foundation for mobile guides. In *European conference on information systems (ECIS 2007)*.

Process Science

Experts versus Novices: Analyzing Behavioral Variability in Complex Process Environments

Nico Elbert and Christoph M. Flath

Abstract This paper introduces a novel approach to studying user behavior through the User Behavior Mining Framework, analyzing a unique log of 948,251 complex user interaction traces across 78,547 individuals featuring logs of low-level activities in a complex process environment. Employing methods such as directly-follows-graph analysis and trace clustering and next action prediction, the research uncovers the impact of varying experience levels on user interaction patterns and enhances predictive modeling for action forecasting in complex scenarios. This work not only addresses a significant gap in the field by leveraging an underutilized data source but also highlights the importance of rich, detailed datasets for a comprehensive understanding of user behavior and system interaction.

1 Introduction

Information systems (IS) are increasingly focused on enhancing user interactions through automation and optimization. To accomplish this goal understanding user behavior is key. It allows researchers to better comprehend, predict, or influence how users interact. By analyzing these interactions, researchers can map the underlying processes, reveal behavioral influences, and ultimately enhance these digital environments. As highlighted by Rehse et al. [18], the study of user behavior has been approached through qualitative methods [2], laboratory experiments [4], and the solicitation of direct user feedback [16]. While valuable, these methods have limitations as they tend to primarily capture the behaviors users actively perceive. This may give an incomplete picture as users tend to be unable to track their behavior over extended periods [12].

N. Elbert (✉) · C. M. Flath
Julius-Maximilians-Universität Würzburg, Würzburg, Germany
e-mail: nico.elbert@uni-wuerzburg.de

C. M. Flath
e-mail: christoph.flath@uni-wuerzburg.de

C. M. Flath et al. (eds.), *Digital Innovation and Organizational Transformation*, Lecture Notes in Information Systems and Organisation 83,
https://doi.org/10.1007/978-3-032-08483-5_4

With the User Behavior Mining (UBM) Framework, Rehse et al. [18] put forward a principled approach to studying user behavior in a data-driven way, through the analysis of user interaction (UI) logs. Such logs offer rich behavioral traces of user interactions, allowing for an in-depth examination of user behaviors at a scale and granularity not previously feasible [9]. Rehse et al. [18] note a significant challenge in this research area: the reluctance of individuals and organizations to share detailed data necessary for such studies, caused by concerns about privacy, regulatory restrictions, and considerations of competitive advantage [21, 23]. While some datasets capturing user interactions are publicly available [22], they tend to represent fairly simple processes. These datasets,[1] covering areas like customer interaction Dees and van Dongen [8], order management [25], and incident handling [24], provide valuable snapshots of user-system engagement and process management, but often fall short in complexity and lack the comprehensive user metadata needed for an in-depth analysis of user behavior. This limitation points to a significant gap in the field, underlining the need for a broader range of intricate and accessible data sources that not only highlight different aspects of complex user interaction but also include rich, detailed user metadata for a more complete understanding of user behavior and system interaction.

Our paper aims to contribute to the methodological advancement of UBM by showcasing how the UBM Framework can be employed to systematically examine behavioral variability between different user groups. We leverage a novel data set featuring a UI log of 948,251 complex traces across 78,547 unique users, demonstrating the framework's capability to uncover meaningful patterns from complex user interaction data. The log contains low level activities, consisting of *Case ID, Timestamp, Target Element, Action Type* and *Context Parameters*.

The log captures competitive interactions in the real-time strategy (RTS) game *Age of Empires II*. The environment features complex time-critical action sequences, so called build orders. These build orders are in principle comparable to chess openings, yet due to uncertainty, hidden information and a much larger game environment significantly richer. Driven by personal and intrinsic motivation, users exhibit highly rational decision-making, engage in long-term skill learning and collaborate within organizational structures for collective success [19]. As noted by Wagner [26] these interactions capture human behavior in a naturalistic environment over extended time periods, addressing the challenges highlighted by Ho mann et al. [12]. To the best of our knowledge this is the first study applying UBM to such data in a process mining context. However, other studies, such as the works of Clement [7] and Ching et al. [6] recently demonstrated, how such data can serve as a large-scale controlled experimental proxy.

We leverage the UBM framework to make several key contributions to the field. Notably, we explore the relationship between user experience and behavior variability. Through directly-follows-graph analysis and trace clustering, we uncover how various levels of experience affect interaction patterns within the environment. Furthermore, we enhance predictive modeling techniques for user actions in complex

[1] https://www.processmining.org/event-data.html.

scenarios. Our work investigates the predictability of actions across different experience levels, aiming to accurately forecast decisions in challenging contexts. Lastly, we address a notable research gap by introducing a novel data source. The use of RTS UI logs presents a unique, underexplored opportunity for UBM research.

2 UBM Methodology

Our approach is grounded in the UBM Framework as conceptualized by Rehse et al. [18]. This section recaps the framework's component and in turn sets the stage for its application in our study. The UBM Framework presents a systematic method for analyzing user interactions within software applications. This four-part framework encompasses UBM data, UBM technology, UBM objectives, and theoretical contributions, aiming to provide a holistic approach to understanding and improving user-system interactions.

2.1 Data

Central to the UBM Framework is the utilization of UI logs, which are detailed records of user activities during software interaction. These logs, capturing everything from basic clicks to complex task executions, serve as the atomic units for analysis. The framework emphasizes the challenge of categorizing these diverse interactions, acknowledging the need to discern between different user actions for a meaningful analysis of behavior.

2.2 Technology

UBM technology integrates a wide range of data analysis techniques tailored for UBM data, spanning from innovative to adapted existing methods designed to address the unique demands and objectives of UBM. Process mining is recognized as a critical tool, providing both a conceptual and technical framework suitable for exploring and confirming aspects of user behavior through UBM data. Despite its potential, the specific traits of UBM data, such as its variability and granularity, as well as the integration of behavioral theories, may limit the direct applicability of standard process mining methods.

Rehse et al. [18] categorize the landscape of available techniques into exploratory and confirmatory data analysis techniques. Exploratory techniques aim to reveal new knowledge about user behavior captured in the data, addressing questions related to user interactions, navigation efficiency, usability issues, and identifying abnormal or fraudulent behaviors through process mining. This includes process discovery to visualize user navigation paths, process enhancement for identifying usability bottlenecks, anomaly detection for spotting unusual behaviors, and process prediction to forecast future actions, interaction durations or the ultimate outcome of a process.

Confirmatory techniques focus on testing hypotheses about user behavior, seeking to validate or refute assumptions regarding deviations from intended design, reasons for user drop-offs, efficiency improvements through new features, or changes in behavior following software updates. These techniques often require adapting existing process mining methods, like stochastic conformance checking, to assess user behavior against expected models, and exploring concept drift detection and causal analysis to investigate changes in behavior or causal relationships within user interactions.

2.3 Objectives

The objectives of the UBM Framework are highly depended on the underlying software application and the tasks for which it is used. Rehse et al. [18] categorize resulting objectives in the areas analysis, assistance, and automation. In context of analysis, UBM aims to provide insights into user behavior, identifying usability problems, system design deviations, and user groups with similar patterns. For assistance, the focus shifts towards supporting users in navigating and utilizing complex or flexible software more efficiently. This involves leveraging UBM to offer real-time, context-specific guidance and recommendations, potentially steering users away from common pitfalls or optimizing their navigation through the system based on their current activities and past user behavior patterns. Lastly, automation through UBM targets the identification and execution of repetitive tasks that can be automated, typically employing Robotic Process Automation techniques. By analyzing user actions, UBM facilitates the discovery of high-potential automation opportunities and the generation of automation scripts, streamlining operations and reducing manual effort.

By delving into UI logs, the framework seeks to uncover usability issues, tailor user interfaces to distinct user groups, and identify opportunities for automating repetitive tasks. This tripartite goal underlines the framework's commitment to enhancing both user experience and system efficiency.

2.4 Theory

According to the UBM framework, data, technology, and objective are sufficient to instantiate a UBM application, especially in technical domains. By leveraging established theories regarding system usage or real-life behavior, UBM applications can enrich their analytical depth and prediction capabilities and gain access to general and causal explanations about the interactions between humans and IT artifacts. The integration of such theories from IS and Human-Computer Interaction provides a structured approach to analyzing user behavior, enriching both practical outcomes and theoretical advancements in the field.

3 Study Design

Using the UBM framework, our study seeks to systematically analyze user behavior, drawing on the rich data available from user interactions in a complex RTS environment. We appply the UBM framework to elucidate the influence of user experience on behavior and to demonstrate the practical application of such UI logs as a novel source for such analysis.

3.1 Data Sourcing

For our study, we collected a log of 948,251 publicly available UI traces, featuring complex competitive interactions in the RTS game *Age of Empires II*. This dataset was compiled by systematically scraping *AoE2 Insights*, a public analytics platform.[2] The log contains low level activities per user and interaction, consisting of *Case ID*, *Timestamp*, *Target Element*, *Action Type* and *Context Parameters*, as depicted in Table 1. The log is annotated with a range of meta data features, specifying the configuration of the environment. Our dataset features 78,547 different users, each with multiple appearances between April 2020 and September 2023. Every user is associated with an Elo rating, assessing a users experience and skill level at the time of the interaction. As we can identify users by their respective User ID, our dataset also features the development of this Elo rating alongside a record of all historic interactions as well as the user's nationality and preferences regarding the configuration of the environment. Further, a subset of 188,068 traces is annotated with an exogenous label, categorizing the featured trace-type.

3.2 Data Preprocessing

To analyze influential factors on user behavior, comparable subgroups in the dataset are crucial. Given the complexity of the underlying processes, especially for process mining related methodologies, we focus on similar processes, using the exogenous labels and narrow configurations for filtering.

The filtering is applied progressively over three stages of configuration adjustments (S1, S2, S3), each further constraining various settings within the environment.

[2] http://www.aoe2insights.com.

Table 1 Sample of the Dataset

CaseID	Timestamp	Target element	Action type	Parameters
138015780_1	00:00:01	TC-01	Queue 17	Amount:1
138015780_1	00:00:02	TC-01	Queue 17	Amount:1
138015780_1	00:00:03	TC-01	Queue 17	Amount:1
138015780_1	00:00:04	TC-01	Queue 17	Amount:1
138015780_1	00:00:04	S-01	Move	(x=14,y=17)
138015780_1	00:00:04	V-01	Build 70	(x=9,y=12)
138015780_1	00:00:05	V-02	Build 70	(x=12,y=8)
...	...	...	...	...

In S1 and S2 we apply filters on the general environmental settings, specified by the level type (S1) and the through the user selected set of available actions (S2). To standardize the processes further, we define a critical stop event, which represents a crucial part in the process of the interaction. In S3 we filter for this and other process related features. This step-by-step constriction results in a series of logs with user interaction traces, the quantities of which are depicted in Fig. 1 (left).

We partition the refined dataset into three Elo classes –low, medium, and high– to represent user groups of varying skill levels. Our goal is to generate substantial databases for each subgroup to ensure statistical robustness. These subgroups are determined not to be contiguous to one another to maximize intragroup homogeneity and intergroup heterogeneity. The intervals for these subgroups are selected based on the sample distribution of specific trace types within the overall population, as illustrated in Fig. 1 (right).

Given the different numbers of samples in each Elo class, we employ a subsampling strategy aimed at maintaining a target standard deviation (SD) of user Elo ratings within our dataset. To achieve this, we iteratively exchange samples of the larger populations, until we meet the SD of the smallest subgroup within a tolerance of 5%. This method ensures that the heterogeneity of users skill levels is consistent across our groups, allowing for more reliable comparisons. This strategic separation facilitates an examination of user behavior across varied levels of skill with a focus on retaining comparative integrity within each subgroup.

To maintain consistency among our approaches, we use the same set of configurations for all of our analysis, defined by the selected trace type 'A' and the level of granularity, achieved by including and excluding specific action types from the log. To analyze the behavioral variability and demonstrate the suitability of such UI logs, we conceptualize two UBM applications as proposed by Rehse et al. [18].

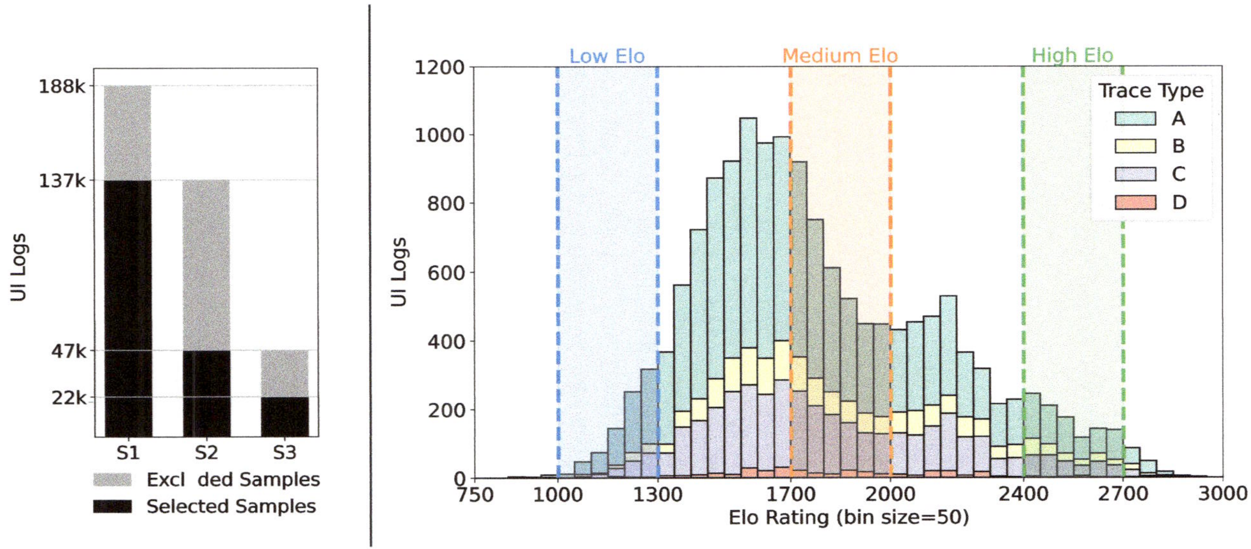

Fig. 1 Number of UI traces in logs of filter stages (S1,S2,S3) [left] and distribution of UI traces by trace type over Elo values annotated with defined Elo classes [right]

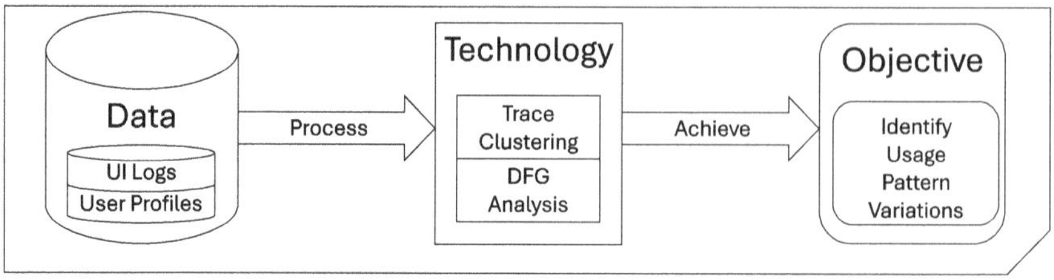

Fig. 2 Applying the UBM framework to identify usage patterns variations

3.3 Usage Pattern Variation

In our first application, summarized in Fig. 2, we aim to validate and understand the impact of user skill level on behavioral patterns in user interaction logs. Abb et al. [1] propose to address the challenge often posed by the complexity of the UI log data [15], by applying trace clustering. In line with Song et al. [20] and Elbert et al. [10], we utilize the Euclidean distance between aggregated traces to group similar behaviors, allowing us to verify the exogenous labels initially used for categorization.

Subsequent to the clustering process, we generate Directly-Follows Graphs (DFGs) by deploying timeline-based methods [13]. Given the nature of the captured interactions, we annotated the actions with a counter, enhancing the structure and interpretability of the timeline-based DFGs. Further we initially limit the horizon of possible number of actions or time passed in a process, and increase these limits iteratively. This allows us to compare the processes of getting to a certain state of an interaction, in addition to analyzing the full process. These DFGs serve as a tool to visualize and analyze the sequence and variance in user interactions, effectively capturing the flow of activities and user engagement over time.

To assess the influence of user skill on interaction patterns, we measure and compare several DFG metrics across various user skill levels. Key metrics include DFG variance, the count of unique traces, trace lengths and number of edges within these graphs. For conformance checking we calculate the Earth Mover's Distance (EMD), among the different comparable DFG populations [14]. These metrics provide insights into the complexity and diversity of user behavior, revealing the influence of skill level on interaction patterns within the environment.

3.4 Predictive Modeling

Our second application, summarized in Fig. 3, concentrates on process prediction, which aims to forecast the future behavior of a running process instance [11]. We aim to predict user's subsequent actions and overall process outcomes based on their interaction traces.

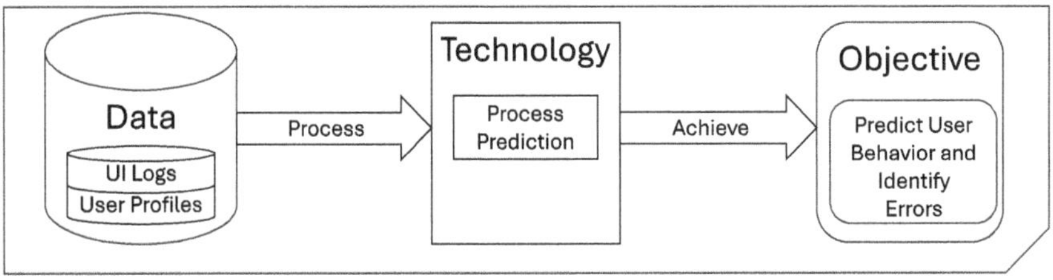

Fig. 3 Applying the UBM framework to predict user behavior and identify frrors

We utilize a transformer-based model, GPT-2 [17], to forecast the next action within a user's log sequence. This approach leverages the sequential nature of user actions, aiming to predict subsequent steps based on historical data and create recommendations for next process steps as demonstrated by Rehse et al. [18].

Further, we employ aggregate trace representations to predict the final outcome of a process (success or not) using gradient boosted trees [5]. This methods allows us to assess the overall performance of users and identify potential errors in their interaction sequences. By evaluating the quality of predictions across different skill levels, we can determine the extent to which user experience influences the predictability of their actions and the likelihood of successful outcomes.

4 Results

This section presents the tangible outcomes of our applications, illustrating the framework's broad applicability and effectiveness.

4.1 Usage Pattern Variation

In our analysis of usage pattern variations, as outlined by our first UBM application (see Fig. 2), we apply trace clustering to our dataset to segregate distinct trace types into multiple clusters. The aggregation of trace representations within the process allows us to verify the exogenous trace type labels with which the log is annotated.

We create timeline-based DFGs as suggested by Kaur et al. [13], illustrated in an excerpt in Fig. 4. The complexity of the interactions and resulting DFGs, even when narrowed down significantly, posed a challenge in comprehension. However, the simplification of the DFGs through adjustments in log horizon and granularity facilitated insights into the early steps and phases of the underlying processes.

To quantitatively compare the impact of user skill levels on user behavior, we computed the EMD as well as other key metrics like DFG variance, number of nodes, edges, and unique traces across different Elo classes. The comparative results

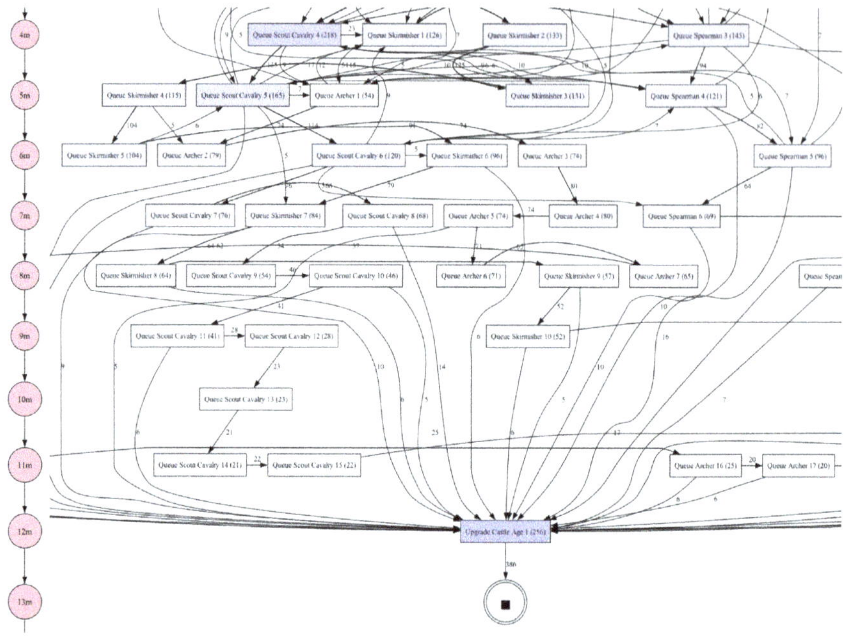

Fig. 4 Excerpt of the timeline-based DFG for high Elo users performing trace type A

for the EMD over all created DFGs are depicted in Fig. 5. The results highlight a significant difference between the different DFGs, increasing with the size of the skill gap.

Figure 6 illustrates the development of the number of unique traces per DFG over elapsing process time. After 5 minutes into the process, a difference in the number of unique traces becomes evident, underlying a higher uniformity in the behavior of higher skilled users. In a later stage of the game, around 20 minutes, the highest Elo class rapidly increase the number of unique traces, which can be an indicator for a higher adaptability in the later stages of the process.

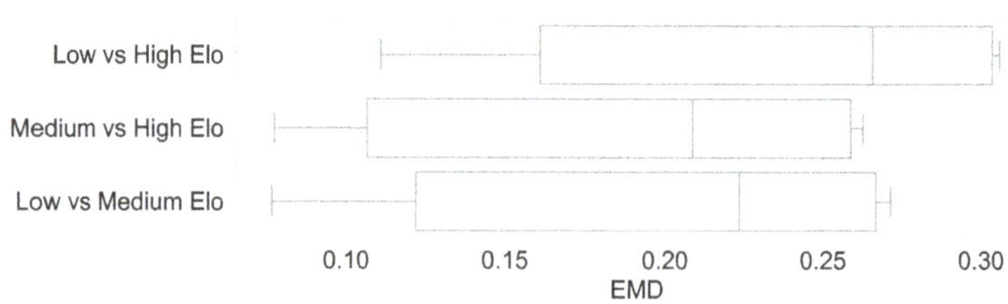

Fig. 5 EMD between DFGs of different Elo classes over all different configurations

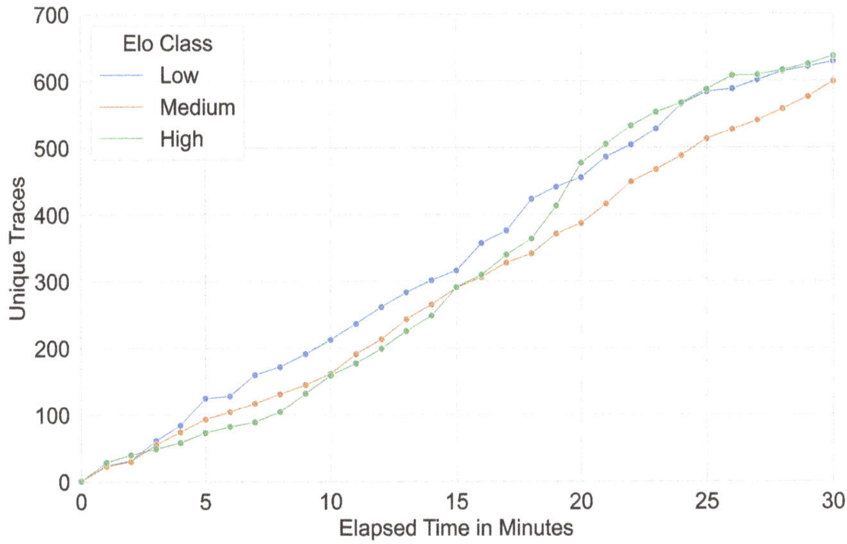

Fig. 6 Number of unique traces over the elapsed game time in minutes

4.2 Predictive Modeling

Our investigation into predictive modeling focused on the predictions of subsequent actions and process outcomes. Employing traces represented as sequences of actions, our transformer based model [17] was tasked with forecasting the subsequent action.

To systematically evaluate the model's predictive performance across different user expertise levels, we constructed action sequences for each Elo class. These sequences were formulated by restricting the number of actions from the beginning of the process, referred to as the action depth. Each sequence was then utilized to train and subsequently validate independent models specific to that action depth range. Figure 7 presents the aggregated results, illustrating the model's accuracy across incremental action depth intervals, each spanning five actions. This interval grouping was chosen to mitigate the variability in the data and to present a clearer picture of the model's predictive capabilities at varying stages of action sequences. As depicted in Fig. 7 the model demonstrated high accuracy, particularly for traces early in the process. This accuracy decreased with the depth of the action sequence, yet remained commendable across all Elo classes. These findings imply that the predictability of user actions at the onset of interaction is relatively consistent across skill levels, a notable point considering the distinct variations in the number of unique traces observed among different Elo classes.

To further our analysis, we applied gradient boosted trees [5] based on aggregated traces to predict the final outcome of a process, evaluating success probability as time progressed. Figure 8 depicts the growing accuracy of our outcome predictions as the elapsed time of interaction increases. The quality of these predictions did not exhibit a

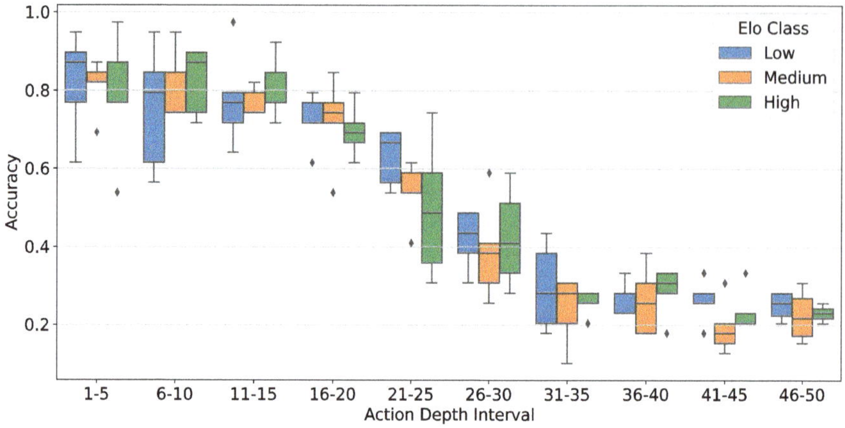

Fig. 7 Accuracy for next action prediction for full graces with restricted action depth

marked difference across Elo classes, demonstrating that our model could uniformly assess user performance over time, regardless of skill level.

The proficiency of the outcome prediction model offers a useful tool for identifying which actions may decrease the probability of success, thus pinpointing potential errors in process execution. The consistent quality of predictions across different user experiences suggests that the model is capturing fundamental aspects of user behavior that are common across skill levels, offering insights into process execution that are largely independent of individual user skill or experience.

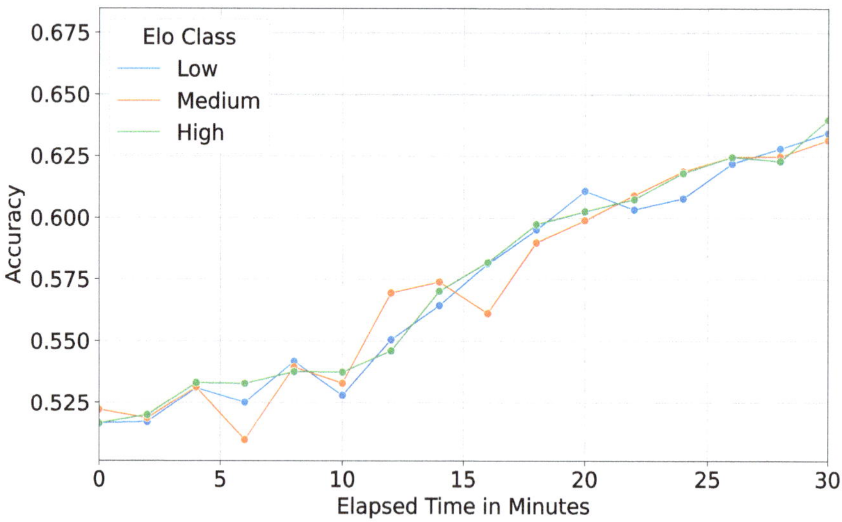

Fig. 8 Accuracy of outcome prediction for full traces with increasing elapsed time

5 Discussion

The analysis of usage patterns revealed through our UBM applications necessitates a discerning examination of the metrics employed. Particularly in complex environments, such as the one featured in our UI log, the interpretation of metrics like the number of unique traces demands contextualization. Contrary to typical process environments where high variance may signify inefficiency or deviation from the standard, in such complex environments, this variance can reflect a more nuanced scenario.

The usage of objective labels pertaining to the user's skill level offers a lens through which we can view higher Elo users' actions as more optimal [3]. For example, the initial proliferation of unique traces among lower Elo users may be indicative of randomness and a lack of strategic coherence, whereas higher Elo users exhibit more uniform behaviors early in the process. This trend inverts later in the interaction, where an uptick in unique traces among more skilled users signals their ability to adapt and navigate the process flexibly, thereby optimizing their behavior.

The application of the EMD in our study has quantitatively captured the qualitative differences in behaviors among users of varying skill levels. The increase in EMD with the skill gap suggests nuances in behavior that conventional metrics such as the number of edges, unique traces, or trace lengths do not capture.

Our next action prediction models shed light on the predictability of user actions, demonstrating high accuracy across all Elo classes early in the process. Yet, this finding prompts a closer inspection of whether alternative metrics, like top-n accuracy, could provide a more fitting evaluation. Given the frequency and partial interchangeability of actions in such complex environments, a broader accuracy measure could account for the marginal impact of different action orders on the resultant process state.

These findings underline the importance of careful metric selection and interpretation in complex process environments within the domain of UBM. It is clear, that while certain metrics can provide valuable insights, they must be chosen and analyzed with consideration of the unique dynamics present in the domain of study. This acknowledgment paves the way for more sophisticated and contextually aware approaches in future UBM research, particularly as we venture into environments with highly variable and intricate user behaviors.

6 Outlook and Conclusion

Our study demonstrates the ways in which user behavior varies according to user experience, particularly in the context of navigating complex processes within RTS environments. Our research has not only addressed the question posed by Rehse et al. [18] regarding the behavioral differences between experienced and inexperienced users but has also leveraged large-scale UI log datasets to perform comprehensive UBM.

The successful implementation of our UBM applications underscores the potential of environments such as RTS games for UBM research. The detailed and publicly available dataset used has proved to be an invaluable resource, circumventing common privacy and security concerns, as described by Rehse et al. [18], while providing the necessary features for a thorough UBM study, including user identification and the complexity of processes involved.

Looking forward, our research opens for several promising directions in the field of UBM, allowing researchers to address the challenges outlined by Rehse et al. [18]:

- **Conceptualization and Standardization:** The variety of log types and levels of granularity offered by this and comparable environments create a unique opportunity to develop sophisticated methods for log homogenization. This includes the creation of standardized exchange formats that could serve as benchmarks for other domains experiencing high log heterogeneity. The presence of publicly accessible logs, in combination with transparent underlying processes, provides an excellent foundation for efforts aimed at achieving a greater level of uniformity and interoperability in UBM datasets.
- **Theoretical Expansion and Grounding:** Our findings highlight the opportunity for theoretical development within UBM. Future studies have the potential to integrate complex user behaviors with existing theories or to devise new frameworks that more accurately reflect the intricate nature of user interactions in a variety of settings.
- **Confirmatory and Causal Analysis Techniques:** The dataset enables the development and benchmarking of techniques aimed at deriving insights from logs that are both highly variable and finely granular. There is ample scope for both developing and applying confirmatory and causal analysis techniques for complex UI data and advancing our general understanding of user behavior.

By delving into these domains, subsequent research can further enrich the discipline of UBM, enhancing our ability to analyze complex user behaviors and contributing to the evolution of more intuitive, secure, and efficacious models of user interaction. In reflecting upon our work, it's crucial to recognize the challenges in applying complex UI logs from RTS environments to UBM. The process of accurately mapping these logs for process-oriented analysis demands rigorous precision to maintain validity. Despite these challenges, when handled carefully, this approach unlocks significant insights, enriching the UBM field. Therefore, we advocate for the strategic use of such data, asserting that, with thoughtful analysis, it broadens our understanding of user behavior and opens new pathways for research.

References

1. Abb, L., Bormann, C., van der Aa, H. & Rehse, J.-R. (2022), Trace clustering for user behavior mining. In *ECIS*.
2. Amoako-Gyampah, K. (2007). Perceived usefulness, user involvement and behavioral intention: An empirical study of ERP implementation. *Computers in Human Behavior, 23*(3), 1232–1248.
3. Anderson, A., Kleinberg, J., & Mullainathan, S. (2017), 'Assessing human error against a benchmark of perfection', *ACM Transactions on Knowledge Discovery from Data (TKDD),* **11**(4), 1–25.
4. Burton-Jones, A., & Straub, D. W., Jr. (2006). Reconceptualizing system usage: An approach and empirical test. *Information Systems Research, 17*(3), 228–246.
5. Chen, T., & Guestrin, C. (2016). Xgboost: A scalable tree boosting system. In *Proceedings of the 22nd ACM SIGKDD international conference on knowledge discovery and data mining* (pp. 785–794). KDD '16, Association for Computing Machinery.
6. Ching, K., Forti, E., & Rawley, E. (2021). Extemporaneous coordination in specialist teams: The familiarity complementarity. *Organization Science, 32*(1), 1–17.
7. Clement, J. (2023). Missing the forest for the trees: Modular search and systemic inertia as a response to environmental change. *Administrative Science Quarterly, 68*(1), 186–227.
8. Dees, M., & van Dongen, B. (2016). *Bpi challenge 2016: Questions.* https://data.4tu.nl/articles/dataset/BPI_Challenge_2016_Questions/12687320/1
9. Dumais, S., Jeffries, R., Russell, D. M., Tang, D., & Teevan, J. (2014). Understanding user behavior through log data and analysis. In *Ways of Knowing in HCI* (pp. 349–372).
10. Elbert, N., Stein, N., & Flath, C. M. (2023). Process and strategy mining in real-time strategy games. In *Wirtschaftsinformatik 2023 Proceedings* (Article 98). https://aisel.aisnet.org/wi2023/98
11. Evermann, J., Rehse, J.-R., & Fettke, P. (2017). Predicting process behaviour using deep learning. *Decision Support Systems, 100*, 129–140.
12. Hoffmann, P., Mateja, D., Spohrer, K., & Heinzl, A. (2019). Bridging the vendor-user gap in enterprise cloud software development through data-driven requirements engineering. In *ICIS*.
13. Kaur, H., Mendling, J., Rubensson, C., & Kampik, T. (2023). *Timeline-based process discovery.* arXiv preprint arXiv:2401.04114.
14. Leemans, S. J., Syring, A. F., & van der Aalst, W. M. (2019, September 1–6). Earth movers' stochastic conformance checking. In *Business process management forum: BPM forum 2019, Vienna, Austria, Proceedings 17* (pp. 127–143). Springer.
15. Leno, V., Polyvyanyy, A., Dumas, M., La Rosa, M., & Maggi, F. M. (2021). Robotic process mining: Vision and challenges. *Business & Information Systems Engineering, 63*, 301–314.
16. Parks, N. E. (2012). Testing & quantifying ERP usability. In *Proceedings of the 1st annual conference on research in information technology* (pp. 31–36).
17. Radford, A., Wu, J., Child, R., Luan, D., Amodei, D., & Sutskever, I. (2019). *Language models are unsupervised multitask learners.*
18. Rehse, J.-R., Abb, L., Berg, G., Bormann, C., Kampik, T., & Warmuth, C. (2024). User behavior mining. *Business & Information Systems Engineering*, 1–18.
19. Reitman, J. G., Anderson-Coto, M. J., Wu, M., Lee, J. S., & Steinkuehler, C. (2020). Esports research: A literature review. *Games and Culture, 15*(1), 32–50.
20. Song, M., Günther, C. W., & van der Aalst, W. M. (2009). Trace clustering in process mining. In *Business process management workshops: BPM 2008 international workshops, Milano, Italy, September 1-4, 2008. Revised Papers 6* (pp. 109–120). Springer.
21. Tenopir, C., Allard, S., Douglass, K., Aydinoglu, A. U., Wu, L., Read, E., Manoff, M., & Frame, M. (2011). Data sharing by scientists: practices and perceptions. *PLoS One, 6*(6), Article e21101.
22. van der Aalst, W. M., Adriansyah, A., De Medeiros, A. K. A., Arcieri, F., Baier, T., Blickle, T., Bose, J. C., Van Den Brand, P., Brandtjen, R., Buijs, J. et al. (2012). Process mining

manifesto. In *Business process management workshops: BPM 2011 international workshops, Clermont-Ferrand, France, August 29, 2011, Revised Selected Papers, Part I 9* (pp. 169–194). Springer.
23. van der Aalst, W. M., Bichler, M., & Heinzl, A. (2017). *Responsible data science.*
24. van Dongen, B. (2014). *Bpi challenge 2014: Activity log for incidents.* https://data.4tu.nl/articles/dataset/BPI_Challenge_2014_Activity_log_for_incidents/12706424/1
25. van Dongen, B. (2019). *Bpi challenge 2019.* https://data.4tu.nl/articles_12715853/1
26. Wagner, M. (2006). On the scientific relevance of esports. In *International conference on internet computing* (pp. 437–442).

How Can Generative AI Empower Domain Experts in Creating Process Models?

Nataliia Klievtsova, Juergen Mangler, Timotheus Kampik, Janik-Vasily Benzin, and Stefanie Rinderle-Ma

Abstract Considering the human factor in information systems is a key to future digitalization efforts, as stated in the Industry5.0 research and innovation actions of the EU. Especially in the design phase of a process-oriented information system, the human factor includes the empowerment of domain experts in process model creation lowering the entry hurdle for process modeling, and increasing modeling speed. In this work, we investigate how generative AI methods can support domain experts in creating process models in interaction with a chatbot based on textual process descriptions. We explore the amount of necessary information required as input to create process models with immediate visual representation using markdown-inspired languages and extend existing evaluation methods for assessing generated models, focusing on their completeness and correctness. Overall, an evaluation method has to consider the complex relationships between model completeness, correctness, textual process description, textual representation, and prompt engineering to support the domain expert.

N. Klievtsova (✉) · J. Mangler · J.-V. Benzin · S. Rinderle-Ma
Technical University of Munich, TUM School of Computation, Information and Technology, Garching, Germany
e-mail: nataliia.klievtsova@tum.de

J. Mangler
e-mail: juergen.mangler@tum.de

J.-V. Benzin
e-mail: janik.benzin@tum.de

S. Rinderle-Ma
e-mail: stefanie.rinderle-ma@tum.de

T. Kampik
SAP Signavio, Berlin, Germany
e-mail: timotheus.kampik@sap.com

C. M. Flath et al. (eds.), *Digital Innovation and Organizational Transformation*, Lecture Notes in Information Systems and Organisation 83,
https://doi.org/10.1007/978-3-032-08483-5_5

1 Introduction

The design of process documentation and the creation of corresponding process models can be a complex and time-consuming task [6]. Yet, in conditions where an organization is an "open" system, constantly undergoing adaptations caused by internal or external changes, business processes are continuously redesigned based on their performance in day-to-day execution [14], requiring constant (re-) documentation and modeling.

One of the challenges during process modeling is the acquisition of knowledge from domain experts, considering that knowledge is often tacit and that even explicit knowledge is frequently distributed across a variety of sources and representation formats [41]. Domain experts might prefer process models in natural language (i.e., process descriptions), especially if they have not enough experience in and knowledge of (graphical) process modeling [5, 32]. Nevertheless, there are several reasons why utilizing process models can still be beneficial for domain experts and other stakeholders (e.g., documenting, analyzing, and improving business processes). Process models can help domain experts and other stakeholders facilitate a clearer understanding of the underlying process, particularly if its complexity is high. In addition, process models can bring more clarity: although on surface level, natural language in a *lingua franca* such as English may be almost universally understood in a given organization, the ambiguity of natural language can lead to misunderstandings.

The traditional approach to process modeling, where only the process modeler carries out the model design based on her interpretation of the domain experts' views, bears several disadvantages. First, the modeling expert can become a filter and bottleneck in capturing the process knowledge from the stakeholders [29], leading to wrong modeling decisions. Additionally, the absence of a direct involvement of the domain expert might have a negative impact on its quality. Moreover, the emergence of psychological ownership during the domain expert's participation in the modeling process could have a positive effect on affective commitment [26].

Consequentially, domain experts might be reluctant to input information into the first version of a model due to lack of modeling skills [17]. Hence, the ability to convert natural language text into business process models holds considerable appeal, offering added value to the organization, i.e., by overcoming the communication gap not only between process modelers and domain experts during the process model generation phase [33], but also among diverse stakeholders involved in the actual process. As first studies show [24], Large Language Models (LLM) may offer a simple and effective way to automatically generate process models from text. **The overarching question of this work is thus how and to which degree LLMs can generate process models from process descriptions with sufficient process model quality.**

This study focuses on the evaluation of the quality of process models resulting from an LLM-based generation based on provided process descriptions, and is a continuation of our first analysis provided in [30] which focused on task extraction. To this end, we provide a method to generate BPMN 2.0 (bpmn.org) process models from textual process descriptions based on different LLMs (cf. Sect. 2). Although, at first glance, it seems that GPT is capable of creating some process models in `.bpmn` format (XML-based), this output does not contain crucial layout information, and the output becomes too long even for simple process models with fewer tasks. In addition, to our knowledge, there are no evaluation studies exploring the quality of these generated models. Hence, we opt for a combination of LLM and graphical tools such as Mermaid.js and Graphviz, reflected in the prompts. The quality of the generated process models is assessed based on completeness (quantitative) and correctness (qualitative) (cf. Sect. 3), yielding, in turn, a way to assess different LLMs w.r.t. their ability to generate process models. The evaluation is based on two detailed data sets containing both textual process description and associated graphical process models created by humans. Related work is discussed in Sect. 5, before Sect. 6 concludes this work.

2 How to teach BPMN 2.0 to LLMs?

This section provides the building blocks for control flow extraction by LLMs from text, i.e., the selection of suitable graphical representations and prompt engineering.

Selection of Graphical Representations: Due to the context length limitation of LLMs, it is not possible to utilize standard XML serialization of BPMN models: a regular language model input/output limit is between 1,000–8,000 tokens. At the same time, even a simple BPMN model with 7 tasks in XML representation might exceed 10,000–15,000 tokens [3], depending on its complexity. Therefore, it is required to work with an abstract graphical representation of the BPMN model. Multiple comprehensible graphical representations (GR) of various types of event logs or process models (e.g., directly-follows graphs or Petri net) are suggested in [13] and pre-specified intermediary textual notations (TN) of BPMN are proposed in [24]. However, ordinary TNs require further conversion into diagrams (i.e., GNs) and do not allow us to see and analyze the output of a language model immediately in a user-friendly/understandable manner.

Nowadays, multiple TNs such as DOT[1], Mermaid.js[2], Penrose[3], D2[4], and PlantUML[5] exist [43]. Mermaid.js (MER) and Graphviz (GV) have been selected, because they are widely used, well-documented and thus it is reasonable to assume that LLMs might yield consistent results when generating them (see Sect. 3.1).

The TN contains the following elements: At first, we define the orientation of the graph and custom structure for all nodes and edges in it. Then, specific features

[1] https://graphviz.org/doc/info/lang.html.

[2] https://mermaid.js.org/.

[3] https://penrose.cs.cmu.edu/.

[4] https://d2lang.com/tour/intro.

[5] https://plantuml.com/.

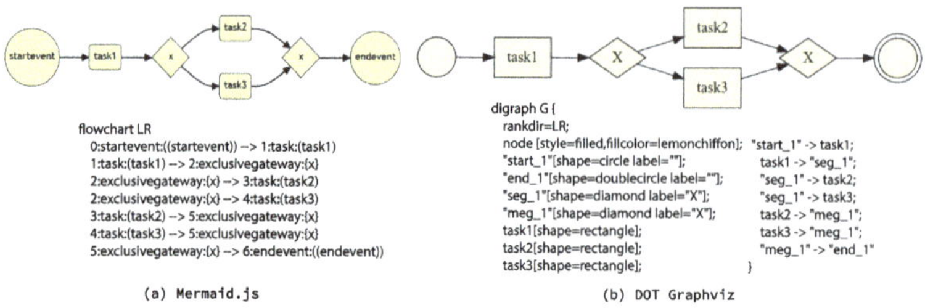

Fig. 1 TN & GN of text fragment given in TF1

are assigned for every node to represent particular BPMN element. For example, the simple process description

> "After task1, either task2 or task3 are conducted." (Text Fragment TF1)

can be converted by a LLM into the TN and finally into the GN shown in Fig. 1.

Prompt Engineering: LLMs like GPT are general-purpose models performing a wide range of tasks. Usually, fine-tuning is required to allow an LLM to generate output that corresponds to the preferences of a particular user/task, making it task-specific [7]. However, fine-tuning can be computationally and storage-intensive [28], and its performance is closely connected with the amount of available training data, which could be an issue in some domains [15].

Prompt engineering (i.e., the design of a prompt providing clear instructions such that LLM can perform the required task in the best and the most efficient way) can be employed to overcome these limitations [34].

Figure 2 shows how the prompts for the approach presented in this paper have been designed. Each prompt consists of three parts: [1] a process description, [2] some additional information, and [3] the actual task that should be solved by the LLM, i.e.,

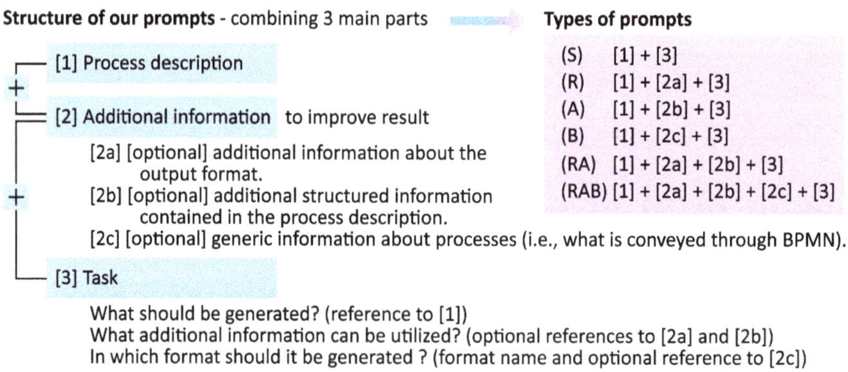

Fig. 2 Prompt structure and types of prompts

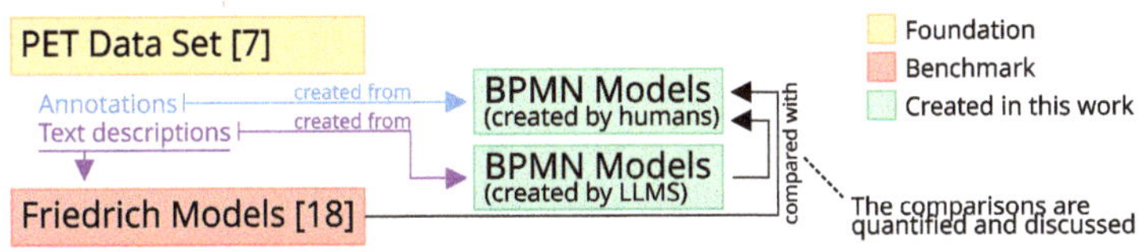

Fig. 3 Evaluation design

"generate a graph" (cmp.[6]). Each part of the prompt is designed separately with the help of iterative learning, where the prompt is tested and refined continually based on the output from the previous version of a prompt [37]. By combining various parts of the optional pieces of information, such as those in [2a], [2b], and [2c] in different ways, we create six different prompts (see Fig. 2, Types of prompts). The custom user input, e.g., the process description [1], and the actual task to be performed by the LLM [3] remain unchanged. Thus, the core task, passed to the LLM remains the same. Each prompt can be considered distinct, as the additional information can greatly impact the language model response. For the experiment, we employ a zero-shot prompting strategy, providing instructions to LLMs without the use of examples, enabling them to perform tasks for which they have not been explicitly trained [37].

3 Evaluation

We evaluate the LLMs by comparing the process models generated by them to process models created by humans in terms of completeness (cf. Sect. 3.1) and correctness (cf. Sect. 3.2). Overall we use two data sets: the PET data set[7] [8] for the evaluation and an independent (real-world) data set [35] (see Sect. 3.3) to validate the results.

The PET dataset is used for process extraction from natural language text. It contains 45 textual process descriptions together with human-annotated process elements in a corpus of these process descriptions. Out of 45 process descriptions only seven examples are taken over [9], as they are of different lengths and complexity. The variety in length and complexity is crucial, because the prompt length and content supplied to the LLM directly affect the quality of the generated response [25].

Based on the human annotations from the PET dataset, for seven selected examples, BPMN models are created. These models are to be considered as correct ground-truth process models and to be compared with the models generated by LLMs and models from the benchmark (see Fig. 3).

For benchmarking purposes, we employ the models outlined in [21]. These models fall into two categories: BPMN models designed by a human modeler **F.Human** and those generated by an automated system **F.System** described in [21].

[6] https://github.com/com-pot-93/convermod/tree/main/prompt_engineering.

[7] https://huggingface.co/datasets/patriziobellan/PET.

Despite the fact that **F.Human** models were created by human modelers, they cannot be considered as gold standard references and are used only for benchmarking for several reasons. First, many of these models were translated by the same authors from other process modeling languages without expert validation [12]. Second, human modelers tend to extend the models with the content that was not originally provided in the process description or reduce the information in the model based on their comprehension, modeling experience, domain knowledge, defined model purposes, and perspectives pursued by stakeholders [39].

For the evaluation, two basic categories of BPMN elements are considered: (a) flow objects (start and end events, tasks, exclusive and parallel gateways) and (b) connecting objects (sequence flows). The concept of merging gateways is addressed as follows: if the LLM does not generate a merging gateway, we do not consider it as an error, as a merging gateway concept is not a strict principle of the BPMN standard, and is often ignored by human modelers. If two tasks are merged into one, we consider it as a correct LLM response and split it manually into distinct tasks (e.g., "check and repair hardware" is equal to a sequence of two tasks "check hardware" and "repair hardware").

As LLMs, we choose GPT3 and GPT4, as they show promising performance [31]. Using the 6 prompts described in Sect. 2 and 7 PET examples, both GPT3 and GPT4 are instructed to create MER and GV graphs. All models (see Fig. 3) are transformed into a list of 3-tuples, where every tuple is an ordered sequence (source, connector, target). One tuple represents an edge of a model/graph (see Fig. 4).

3.1 Assessing Process Model Completeness

The following metrics are selected to quantitatively assess the generated models, i.e., the Jaccard index, precision, and recall.

In the NLP domain, precision and recall are used for classification problems or information retrieval evaluation [36]. We compute precision and recall metrics to assess the overall quality of the generated models.

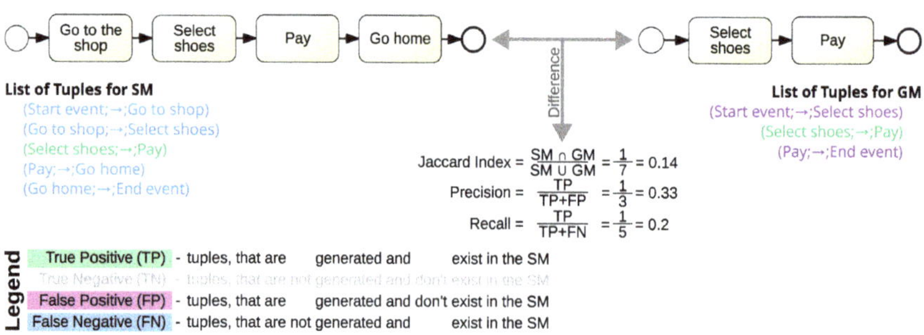

Fig. 4 Quantitative evaluation metrics for generated models

However, precision and recall are metrics that are mostly biased towards the positive class and are not useful when used in isolation [20]. Thus, Jaccard similarity is considered as a third metric. This method can efficiently determine the proximity of two data sets without data redundancy, providing a balanced similarity measure and a straightforward indicator of how similar two sets are [38]. Additionally, it is unaffected by the size of the dataset, making it a reliable option for determining similarity when the sets are of various sizes [19]. It also allows us to determine the similarity between two sets without considering the sequence order of the items in a sample set. We use the Jaccard index to measure the similarity between the model generated by the LLM and the standard model (see Fig. 4). All parameters and formulas for the metrics are shown in Fig. 4.

In Table 1, the results for the Jaccard Index (JI) are presented. As we can see, by using prompts with only the process description or with the process description and additional information that does not provide sufficient instructions about the textual representation format (i.e., (S), (A) or (B)), the JI value does not reach more than 27% in the best case (20% on average).

For the rest of the cases, using GPT3, a maximum of 52% similarity is achieved. However, there is a 13% decrease between models built with (R) and (RAB) prompts. This might suggest that the more content is supplied, the worse the LLM's understanding of the instructions is. By generating models with GPT4, we attain JI values of 59, 57% and 54% with (RAB), (RA) and (R) prompts, respectively. These results are similar to those reached by the automated system and 10% higher than the result obtained by a human modeler from the benchmark.

Similar to the JI results (see Tables 1, 2) shows that when providing less informative instructions to LLMs models, models with lower precision are created. Only between 32–45% of all generated tuples are correct. Nonetheless, models designed by a human modeler score 38% precision compared with the standard. With more content-substantial prompts, mostly 53–70% precision is reached. Hence, generated model precision is 5%-points better compared to the benchmark with the automated system and almost 2 times better compared to the human-designed models.

Table 3 presents recall values. In most cases, using (R),(RA) and (RAB) prompts, a recall of 51–71% is achieved. That is similar to the benchmark, where 58% and 69% recall was obtained by a human modeler and an automated system, respectively. Executing less descriptive prompts, only between 5% and 30% of target tuples were covered by generated models.

Table 1 Average Jaccard Index for PET standard models and textual notations (TNs) generated with GPT3 and GPT4; abbreviations see above

LLM	TN	S	A	R	RA	RAB	B	F. Human	F. System
GPT3	GV	0.03	0.11	0.44	0.47	0.15	0.03	0.47	0.58
	MER	0.18	0.22	0.52	0.47	0.39	0.19	0.47	0.58
GPT4	GV	0.13	0.17	0.50	0.56	0.46	0.40	0.47	0.58
	MER	0.14	0.22	0.54	0.57	0.59	0.27	0.47	0.58

Table 2 Average Precision for PET standard models and textual notations (TNs) generated with GPT3 and GPT4; abbreviations see above

LLM	TN	S	A	R	RA	RAB	B	F. Human	F. System
GPT3	GV	0.06	0.24	0.57	0.58	0.26	0.07	0.38	0.65
	MER	0.37	0.45	0.70	0.60	0.55	0.38	0.38	0.65
GPT4	GV	0.28	0.36	0.60	0.66	0.53	0.48	0.38	0.65
	MER	0.32	0.43	0.65	0.67	0.70	0.38	0.38	0.65

Table 3 Average Recall for PET standard models and textual notations (TNs) generated with GPT3 and GPT4; abbreviations see above

LLM	TN	S	A	R	RA	RAB	B	F. Human	F. System
GPT3	GV	0.04	0.14	0.53	0.58	0.26	0.05	0.58	0.69
	MER	0.23	0.28	0.57	0.57	0.51	0.25	0.58	0.69
GPT4	GV	0.20	0.25	0.62	0.70	0.61	0.51	0.58	0.69
	MER	0.19	0.30	0.65	0.70	0.71	0.30	0.58	0.69

Summary: In general, better results are achieved by applying prompts with more explanatory content, i.e., (R), (RA), and (RAB). Results of JI over 50% along with both recall and precision exceeding 70% can be considered satisfactory. However, there is a room for the further improvement.

We can see from Table 4 that utilizing MER, GPT3 is able to achieve 15–20%-points better scores compared to GV. On average, using MER, GPT3 achieves almost as good results as GPT4 showing only a 5%-points decrease in performance in contrast to GPT4. At the same time GPT4 reaches 20%points better results using GV. There is a slight difference (3%-points) between both text-based graph representations applying GPT4.

In addition, we considered the same metrics for the task extraction evaluation by taking out the set of tasks from the standard models and models created by LLMs. Despite relatively low JI values of models in general (between 21 and 39%), executing different prompts, LLMs are able to achieve 51–71% JI when comparing task sets. Recall and precision for the task extraction reach up to 85% on average, and are mostly similar or even better than by the human modeler and an automated system

Table 4 Average of average: Jaccard Index, Recall, Precision for Models and Tasks; abbreviations see above

Metric	JI		Precision		Recall		JI		Precision		Recall	
TN	GV	MER	GV	MER	GV	MER	GV	MER	GV	MER	GV	MER
	Models						Tasks					
GPT3	0.21	0.33	0.3	0.51	0.2	0.4	0.51	0.68	0.73	0.85	0.57	0.76
GPT4	0.37	0.39	0.48	0.53	0.48	0.47	0.71	0.69	0.78	0.84	0.85	0.78

from the benchmark (see Table 4 and https://github.com/com-pot-93/convermodGit repository).

3.2 Assessing Process Model Correctness

Process modeling typically results in model variability, i.e., the same process can be modeled in multiple variations from a different perspective, level of abstraction, and granularity [42]. Figure 5 depicts an example for different process models created for the same process description.

Model variability complicates model evaluation. For instance, if we consider the results presented in Tables 1, 2, 3, models designed by a human modeler have at least 10% -points lower metric values in comparison with the values gained by an automated system. The precision of a human modeler was two times worse than that of an automated system, reaching only 38%.

Low precision indicates that a human modeler tends to use another level of abstraction during process model design and tends to add further tasks, i.e., read between the lines. Thus, quantitative metrics cannot be considered objective and universal (see Fig. 5). Quantitative metrics could be used to evaluate the completeness of the model with respect to the original process description, but not its correctness.

In this work, we refer to semantic correctness, i.e., whether the generated model corresponds to its original process description. Due to model variability (see Fig. 5), we acknowledge the possibility of certain tasks being omitted or new tasks being introduced. However, this is acceptable only to the extent that it does not violate the

Process Description: You want to buy a new pair of shoes. To do so, at first you need to go to the shop. In the shop, select a pair of shoes that you like the most and pay the bill. After you finish, go home.

Models	Preci-sion	Recall	JI	T/F
	-	-	-	-
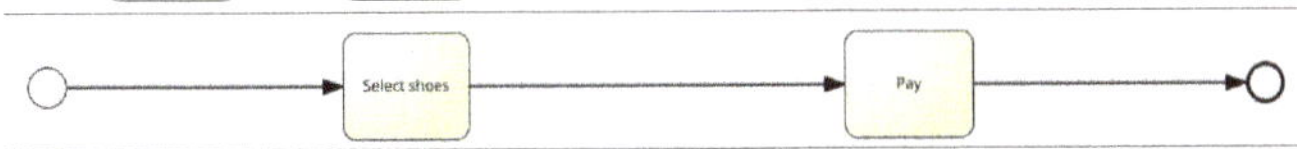	0.2	0.33	0.14	T
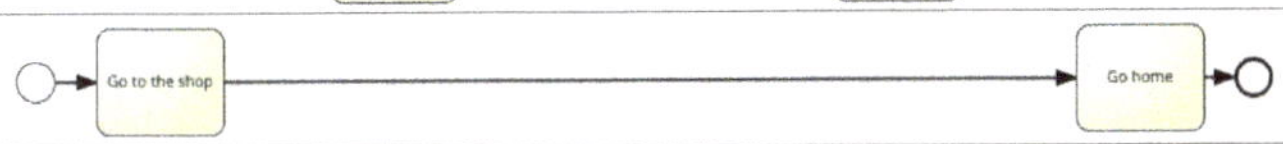	0.4	0.66	0.33	F
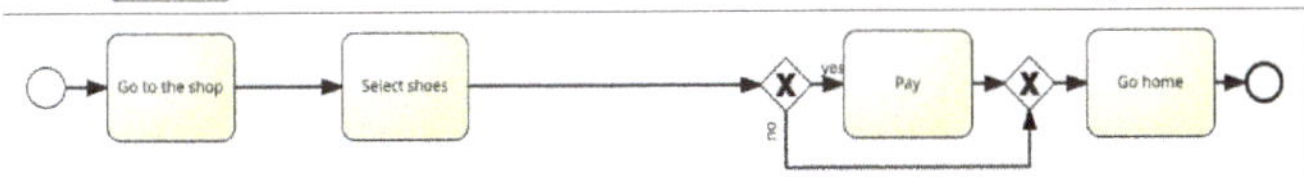	0.6	0.43	0.33	T
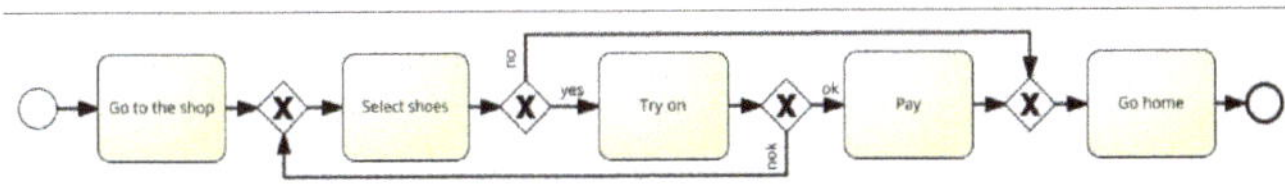	0.4	0.16	0.13	T

Fig. 5 Model variability example: different granularities and perspectives

semantic information or logical flow of the provided process description and must align with the introduced domain framework.

Hence, every model is evaluated by a modeling expert to determine whether the models generated by LLMs truly adhere to the original process descriptions. Both the process description and the process model are studied by an expert to assess whether the model covers all aspects mentioned in the text description and if semantic consistency between both representations is maintained. Based on this evaluation, a 'true' or 'false' value (1 or 0) is assigned to each model, respectively. A model is deemed correct if it captures all logical aspects of the process description.

Table 5 shows the average results of models generated by GPT3 and GPT4 by executing (R),(RA) and (RAB) prompts. Each row represents the number of correctly generated models out of seven selected PET process descriptions for a particular prompt.

None of the LLMs are able to achieve the same result as human modelers. GPT3 is able to generate only three correct models out of seven possible with both MER and GV representations, which is one model worse than automated systems. However, GPT4 generated six logically correct models (again, see Table 5). That is only one model less, when compared to a human modeler's result and 30%-points better as opposed to an automated system from the benchmark [21].

Regarding the correctness of models grouped by cases, the worst result occurred for case 1.3 in Table 6. In this case, none of the generated models are correct. The underlying textual description is the longest and has the highest number of tasks. The best results are achieved by both GPT3 and GPT4 for cases 10.1 and 10.6. These descriptions are the shortest. These observations suggest a correlation between the

Table 5 Correctness of models generated by GPT3 and GPT4

LLM	**TR**	**R**	**RA**	**RAB**	**F. Human**	**F. System**
GPT3	GV	2	3	2	7	4
	MER	3	2	1	7	4
GPT4	GV	6	4	2	7	4
	MER	6	6	5	7	4

Table 6 Average Ratio of Correctly Generated Models per Case

Case	# Words	# Tasks	GPT3	GPT4	AVG
10.13	39	3	0.33	0.67	0.50
10.6	30	4	0.67	1.00	0.83
10.1	29	4	0.67	1.00	0.83
5.2	83	7	0.50	0.67	0.58
3.3	71	7	0.00	0.83	0.42
1.3	162	11	0.00	0.00	0.00
1.2	100	10	0.00	0.67	0.33

Table 7 Number of Correctly Generated Models (NCM) for all Cases

LLM	GPT3		GPT4	
TR	GV	MER	GV	MER
NCM	7	6	12	17
Accuracy in %	33	29	50	81

complexity of the process and the quality of the generated model. However, not only the complexity of the process is critical. Case 10.13 is one of the shortest and most simple, containing three tasks. However, 50% of the models generated for this case are incorrect.

The possible explanation for this bad performance may be poor clarity, high complexity, and bad readability of the given process description for case 10.13.

This might imply that, above all, it is essential to convey the process using straightforward and unambiguous language to enhance the comprehensibility and readability of its description in order to achieve a high-quality model.

Summary: Considering the maximum number of correctly generated models, both types of textual representations got the same results. Nonetheless, taking into account the number of correct generated models, GPT4 produces 17 correct models out of 21 with MER, reaching a performance of 81%. GV achieved a 57% accuracy. Using GPT3, the average accuracy of 30% is reached (see Table 7).

3.3 *Validation*

Since all prompts and their corresponding artefacts are generated using the PET dataset and a trial-and-error approach, we decide to conduct a control evaluation with our initial dataset [35], introduced in [30]. The validation set contains 21 textual process descriptions from 6 topics or domains. This is done to check whether considered prompts and artefacts can yield the optimal results with other data, or they are affected by potential biases, overfitting, or lack of generalization. In addition, due to our limited knowledge about the training process of GPT models, it is impossible to determine whether the LLM has been trained with any particular dataset already [4].

For this purpose only the best results from quantitative and qualitative evaluations, as well as survey feedback, are considered, i.e., GPT4 with MER, (R), and (RA) prompts. Every generated model is labeled as correct if it adheres to the BPMN standard and does not include any elements or relations, that contradict the original process description. In addition to correctness, we take completeness into account (see Sect. 3.1).

Despite the fact that with both (R) and (RA) the average text similarity of 74% was reached, utilizing (R) prompt, 10 models out of 21 are generated correctly, and with (RA) only 8 (see Git). The average achieved accuracy is only 43%, which is half of what was attained using the PET dataset (see Table 7).

Surprisingly, only 52% of all models got the same labels for the same process description, i.e., they are either both considered as correct or incorrect. The 50% variation in labeling can be attributed to the ambiguity of language, the complexity of interpreting tasks, and the model's inherent variability in processing such tasks.

4 Discussion

Considering only the completeness of a model there is no substantial difference between the performance of GPT3 and GPT4. However, looking at completeness and correctness of a model (qualitative and quantitative metrics) GPT4 performs significantly better (50%) than GPT3. Prompt engineering and the quality of input information significantly influence model completeness and correctness. A good prompt provides sufficient information about the process and its desired output format and additional details about task specifics (such as BPMN descriptions) may not always be necessary (see Sect. 3.1, 3.2).

Not only factors such as selected textual representation, complexity of the provided process and instructions, the length of textual description have an influence on the quality of a generated model, but also the clarity and the structure of the process description itself are important. The existing dependency between the quality of a generated model and its textual description (see Sect. 3.2) emphasizes that LLM models generate human-like text based on predefined patterns but may not possess true comprehension (i.e., can LLM models really 'reason' or it is still just a stochastic parrot) and leads to a reasonable question, whether LLMs can be used for specific tasks, where human understanding and experience are required.

Completeness and correctness of a model are vital characteristics, but they alone do not provide sufficient information. Generated models cannot be correct without being complete up to a certain level, and vice versa. At the same time, both completeness and correctness can be insufficient. Completeness is influenced by selected metrics, model complexity, and the chosen level of abstraction. Correctness strongly relies on the expertise of the modeling expert. The expert's background and experience determine their judgments, potentially resulting in varying interpretations and subjective assessments of what constitutes correctness.

Finally, empirical results merely represent a snapshot in time of (largely) commercial LLM capabilities. In order to assess the frontier of what is currently possible, we opted to focus our assessment on proprietary, closed LLMs (or rather: on the commercial product capabilities containing these LLMs) instead of recent, yet currently arguably weaker, openly available LLMs[8].

[8] https://huggingface.co/spaces/lmsys/chatbot-arena-leaderboard.

5 Related Work

According to [27] business process models can be generated from different sources, such as business rules, standard operating procedures, spreadsheets and unstructured text. This paper focuses on unstructured text, as not everyone understands specific formats and notations, but essentially everyone understands at least one natural language [16]. The idea of transforming unstructured text into a structured, diagram-based representation such as UML, ER diagrams, BPMN, and DECLARE, is not novel. Most existing methods rely on text pattern search, rule-based approaches, or semantic analysis (e.g., [21, 23, 44]). [2, 40] propose techniques for automatic annotation of textual process descriptions utilizing supervised machine learning-based approaches. Nonetheless, due to the absence of suitable publicly available datasets containing real-life complex data, applying machine learning techniques becomes challenging [10]. Even with proprietary datasets, confidentiality requirements may not allow for the training of specialized models on much of the data that is potentially available within organizations. Hence, natural language processing (NLP) holds additional promise for research, particularly when applied in the context of utilizing Large Language Models (LLMs). [11] propose the extraction of process elements and relations using prompts with different levels of pre-knowledge and in [30] language models were utilized to extract tasks with different label length. In [24], the generation of an entire model using a specific level of abstraction is presented. [18] utilizes the JSON format to improve LLMs' capabilities to generate BPMN models, Entity-Relationship (ER), and UML Class Diagrams. There exists no methodology for creating process models that provide both LLM-compliant and graphical representation. Instead, only intermediate textual notations that must be further parsed and converted into graphical models are used. Additionally, so far, only syntactical correctness to a selected format and quantitative evaluation of the generated models have been performed, without considering their semantic correctness (how well they adhere to the provided process description). The evaluation of model correctness can offer new insights into the process of process model creation, since the ambiguity of natural language can lead to multiple interpretations of the described process, depending on the assumed contexts [1].

6 Conclusions and Research Directions

Overall, chatbots are in principle ready to be applied in practice. Yet the domain expert should always check the results, although this might still lead to variations in model quality. Additionally, the particular chatbot implementation should take into account the complex relationships between model completeness, correctness, textual process description, textual representation and prompt engineering such that the modeling capability of the chatbot can be tuned towards the respective needs of the domain expert. The results for these relationships, given the quantitative and qualitative evaluation, should be risen to the awareness of the domain expert via training before roll-out of the chatbot or added to the conversational user interface of the chatbot, e.g., by means of selecting the textual representation of the generated model. Considering that the acquisition of as-is models consumes up to 60% of the time spent on process management projects [22], chatbot-based partial automation as T2M transformation can be sufficiently impactful, even if substantial human refinement is required. Future research will focus on integrating the strong language capabilities of chatbots with the specialized capabilities of existing knowledge-based tools. The integrative research direction is more promising than chatbot training with specialized process modeling training sets featuring native process models, e.g., process models in BPMN format and a number of semantic targets, such as information on the existence of deadlocks in a process model. First, pure chatbot training ignores the vast modeling knowledge encoded in existing tools and is futile unless it serves as an intermediate step that unlocks further value.

References

1. van der Aa, H., Carmona, J., Leopold, H., Mendling, J., & Padró, L. (2018). Challenges and opportunities of applying natural language processing in business process management. In *Computational Linguistics* (pp. 2791–2801).
2. Ackermann, L., Neuberger, J., & Jablonski, S. (2021). Data-driven annotation of textual process descriptions based on formal meaning representations. In *Advanced Information Systems Engineering* (pp. 75–90).
3. Ali, M., Fromm, M., Thellmann, K., Rutmann, R., Lübbering, M., Leveling, J., Klug, K., Ebert, J., Doll, N., Buschhoff, J.S., et al. (2023). *Tokenizer choice for llm training: Negligible or crucial?*. arXiv preprint arXiv:2310.08754
4. Arkoudas, K. (2023). *GPT-4 can't reason.* CoRR **abs/2308.03762**. https://doi.org/10.48550/ARXIV.2308.03762
5. Azevedo, L. G., Rodrigues, R. D. A., & Revoredo, K. (2018). BPMN model and text instructions automatic synchronization. In *Enterprise Information Systems* (pp. 484–491). https://doi.org/10.5220/0006809604840491
6. Badakhshan, P. (2023). Process modeling lifecycle—A comprehensive view derived from multiple case studies. https://blogs.sap.com/2023/09/07/process-modeling-lifecycle-a-comprehensive-view-derived-from-multiple-case-studies/
7. Bakker, M., Chadwick, M., Sheahan, H., Tessler, M., Campbell-Gillingham, L., Balaguer, J., McAleese, N., Glaese, A., Aslanides, J., Botvinick, M., et al. (2022). Fine-tuning language models to find agreement among humans with diverse preferences. *Advances in Neural Information Processing Systems, 35*, 38176–38189.
8. Bellan, P., van der Aa, H., Dragoni, M., Ghidini, C., & Ponzetto, S. P. (2022). PET: An annotated dataset for process extraction from natural language text tasks. In *Business Process Management Workshops* (pp. 315–321).
9. Bellan, P., Dragoni, M., & Ghidini, C. (2020). A qualitative analysis of the state of the art in process extraction from text. In *Italian Association for Artificial Intelligence* (pp. 19–30). CEUR Workshop Proceedings.
10. Bellan, P., Dragoni, M., & Ghidini, C. (2021). Process extraction from text: Benchmarking the state of the art and paving the way for future challenges. https://api.semanticscholar.org/CorpusID:238531683

11. Bellan, P., Dragoni, M., & Ghidini, C.: Extracting business process entities and relations from text using pre-trained language models and in-context learning. In *Enterprise Design, Operations, and Computing* (pp. 182–199).
12. Bellan, P., Ghidini, C., Dragoni, M., Ponzetto, S. P., & van der Aa, H. (2022). Process extraction from natural language text: The pet dataset and annotation guidelines. In *Workshop on Natural Language for Artificial Intelligence.*
13. Berti, A., & Qafari, M.S. (2023). Leveraging large language models (llms) for process mining. *CoRR* **abs/2307.12701**. https://doi.org/10.48550/arXiv.2307.12701
14. Beverungen, D. (2014). Exploring the interplay of the design and emergence of business processes as organizational routines. *Business and Information Systems Engineering (BISE), 6*(4), 191–202.
15. Busch, K., Rochlitzer, A., Sola, D., Leopold, H.: Just tell me: Prompt engineering in business process management. In *Enterprise, Business-Process, and Information Systems Modeling* (pp. 3–11).
16. Dalianis, H. (1992). A method for validating a conceptual model by natural language discourse generation. In Advanced Information and System Engineering (pp. 425–444).
17. Doren, A., Markina-Khusid, A., Cotter, M., Dominguez, C. (2019). A practitioner's guide to optimizing the interactions between modelers and domain experts. In *Systems* (pp. 1–8)
18. Fill, H., Fettke, P., & Köpke, J. (2023). Conceptual modeling and large language models: Impressions from first experiments with chatgpt. *Enterprise Modelling and Information Systems Architectures An International Journal on Conceptual Modelling, 18*, 3.
19. Fletcher, S., Islam, M. Z. (2018). Comparing sets of patterns with the Jaccard index. *Australasian Journal on Information and System, 22.* https://journal.acs.org.au/index.php/ajis/article/view/1538
20. Foody, G. M. (2023). Challenges in the real world use of classification accuracy metrics: From recall and precision to the Matthews correlation coefficient. *PLoS One, 18*(10), Article e0291908.
21. Friedrich, F. (2010) Automated Generation of Business Process Models from Natural Language Input. Master's thesis, Humbold-University zu Berlin.
22. Friedrich, F., Mendling, J., Puhlmann, F. (2011). Process model generation from natural language text. In *Advanced Information Systems Engineering* (pp. 482–496)
23. Ghose, A., Koliadis, G., & Chueng, A. (2007). Process discovery from model and text artefacts. In *Services Computing Workshops* (pp. 167–174).
24. Grohs, M., Abb, L., Elsayed, N., & Rehse, J. (2023). *Large language models can accomplish business process management tasks* (pp. 453–465).https://doi.org/10.1007/978-3-031-50974-2_34
25. Gu, X., Yoo, K. M., & Lee, S. (2021). Response generation with context-aware prompt learning. *CoRR.* https://arxiv.org/abs/2111.02643
26. Gutschmidt, A., Lantow, B., Hellmanzik, B., Ramforth, B., Wiese, M., & Martins, E. (2022). Participatory modeling from a stakeholder perspective: On the influence of collaboration and revisions on psychological ownership and perceived model quality. *SoSyM, 22*, 1–17.
27. Honkisz, K., Kluza, K., Wisniewski, P. (2018). A concept for generating business process models from natural language description. In *Knowledge Science, Engineering and Management* (pp. 91–103).
28. Hu, Z., Wang, L., Lan, Y., Xu, W., Lim, E., Bing, L., Xu, X., Poria, S., & Lee, R. K. (2023). LLM-adapters: An adapter family for parameter-efficient fine-tuning of large language models. In *Empirical Methods in Natural Language Processing* (pp. 5254–5276).
29. Kannengiesser, U., & Oppl, S. (2015). *Business processes to touch: Engaging domain experts in process modelling* (Vol. 1418).
30. Klievtsova, N., Benzin, J., Kampik, T., Mangler, J., & Rinderle-Ma, S. (2023). Conversational process modelling: State of the art, applications, and implications in practice. In *Business Process Management Forum* (pp. 319–336)
31. Klievtsova, N., Benzin, J., Kampik, T., Mangler, J., & Rinderle-Ma, S. (2023). Conversational process modelling: State of the art, applications, and implications in practice. *CoRR.* https://doi.org/10.48550/ARXIV.2304.11065

32. Leopold, H., van der Aa, H., Pittke, F., Raffel, M., Mendling, J., & Reijers, H. (2019). Searching textual and model-based process descriptions based on a unified data format. *Software and Systems Modeling, 18*.https://doi.org/10.1007/s10270-017-0649-y
33. Leopold, H., Mendling, J., & Polyvyanyy, A. (2014). Supporting process model validation through natural language generation. *IEEE Transaction on Software Engineering, 40*(8), 818–840.
34. Liu, P., Yuan, W., Fu, J., Jiang, Z., Hayashi, H., & Neubig, G. (2023) Pre-train, prompt, and predict: A systematic survey of prompting methods in natural language processing. *ACM CSUR, 55*(9).
35. Mangler, J., & Klievtsova, N. (2023). *Dataset: Textual Process Descriptions and Corresponding BPMN Models*. https://doi.org/10.5281/zenodo.7783492
36. Manning, C.D., & Schütze, H. (1999) Foundations of Statistical Natural Language Processing. The MIT Press. http://nlp.stanford.edu/fsnlp/
37. Marvin, G., Hellen Raudha, N., Jjingo, D., & Nakatumba-Nabende, J. (2024). *Prompt Engineering in Large Language Models* (pp. 387–402).https://doi.org/10.1007/978-981-99-7962-2_30
38. Niwattanakul, S., Singthongchai, J., Naenudorn, E., & Wanapu, S. Using of Jaccard coefficient for keywords similarity. https://api.semanticscholar.org/CorpusID:14040055
39. Pinggera, J., Zugal, S., Furtner, M., Sachse, P., Martini, M., Weber, B. (2014). The modeling mind: Behavior patterns in process modeling. In Bider, I., Gaaloul, K., Krogstie, J., Nurcan, S., Proper, H.A., Schmidt, R., Soffer, P. (Eds.), *Enterprise, Business-Process and Information Systems Modeling - 15th International Conference, BPMDS 2014, 19th International Conference, EMMSAD 2014, Held at CAiSE 2014, Thessaloniki, Greece, June 16-17, 2014.* Proceedings. Lecture Notes in Business Information Processing (Vol. 175, pp. 1–16). Springer. https://doi.org/10.1007/978-3-662-43745-2_1
40. Qian, C., Wen, L., Kumar, A., Lin, L., Lin, L., Zong, Z., Li, S., & Wang, J. (2020) An approach for process model extraction by multi-grained text classification. In *Advanced Information Systems Engineering* (pp. 268–282)
41. Shaw, M. L., & Woodward, J. B. (1990). Modeling expert knowledge. *Knowledge Acquisition, 2*(3), 179–206.
42. Smirnov, S., Reijers, H. A., Weske, M., & Nugteren, T. (2012). Business process model abstraction: A definition, catalog, and survey. *Distributed Parallel Databases, 30*(1), 63–99.
43. Whatley, D., Goldman, M., & Miller, R. C. (2021). Snapdown: A text-based snapshot diagram language for programming education. In *Visual Languages and Human-Centric Computation* (pp. 1–9).
44. Yue, T., Briand, L. C., & Labiche, Y. (2010). An automated approach to transform use cases into activity diagrams. In *Modelling Foundations and Application* (pp. 337–353).

Interactive Resolution of Inconsistencies in Declarative Process Models

Sabine Nagel and Patrick Delfmann

Abstract When declarative process models (DPMs) contain contradictory constraints, they immediately become unsatisfiable. Recognizing the challenges of automated inconsistency resolution approaches in real-world scenarios, we present an interactive and comprehensive approach for resolving inconsistencies in DPMs. Our approach targets both design-time and run-time inconsistencies through incremental resolution of inconsistency cores. To guide users effectively and lower the mental effort required during the resolution process, we rank inconsistency cores based on customizable complexity measures. We also consider user preferences and familiarity with different inconsistency characteristics. Additionally, we dynamically integrate prior user decisions and resolution operations to ensure an efficient and user-centric approach. By presenting users with one inconsistency core at a time and providing decision support, our approach aims to minimize cognitive overload. Furthermore, it offers flexibility and adaptability by allowing users to apply their preferred resolution operations, reflecting the complexity of real-world scenarios.

1 Introduction

Handling inconsistencies in declarative process models (DPMs) has been of increased interest, as models containing even a single contradiction make the entire model unsatisfiable, meaning that no valid execution trace exists [1, 2]. Unlike procedural process models, which require explicit modeling of each valid execution path, DPMs implicitly define a process through a set of constraints [3]. Here, the general idea is that every process execution is allowed as long as it satisfies all constraints, allowing for more flexible process definitions. DPMs can be created manually or automatically extracted from sources like event logs [1, 4]. However, both approaches are

S. Nagel (✉) · P. Delfmann
University of Koblenz, Koblenz, Germany
e-mail: snagel@uni-koblenz.de

P. Delfmann
e-mail: delfmann@uni-koblenz.de

C. M. Flath et al. (eds.), *Digital Innovation and Organizational Transformation*, Lecture Notes in Information Systems and Organisation 83,
https://doi.org/10.1007/978-3-032-08483-5_6

error-prone, potentially leading to contradictory constraints being modeled. Manual modeling requires humans to be able to work with and understand declarative constraints and is particularly affected by comprehension issues, such as hidden dependencies between constraints, as highlighted by various studies [3, 5–7]. Meanwhile, automatic modeling approaches tend to extract constraints without considering (potentially inconsistent) interrelations between them [1]. Besides inconsistencies in the classic-logical sense that can be identified during design-time and that immediately make the entire model unsatisfiable, recent works have also explored potential inconsistencies, i.e., contradictory constraints that only make a model unsatisfiable if certain activities occur during run-time [8]. Consider, for example, the declarative constraint set {INIT(a), RESPONSE(a, b), NOTRESPONSE(a, b)}, which implies that each trace must start with activity a and that if a occurs in a trace, it is both required and prohibited that a is followed by b. This is an inconsistency in the classic-logical sense, as there is no valid trace that satisfies all three constraints. However, if only the two relation constraints are considered, any trace that does not contain a would be allowed, as the problem only occurs after activity a is executed. In this case, we refer to this subset as a *potential issue* that is activated by a.

As a result of this, the ability to resolve such inconsistencies before executing the process is crucial. Various works have introduced approaches for resolving inconsistencies in DPMs, including fully automated methods that iteratively remove constraints until consistency is reached [1, 2, 9, 10], as well as a first approach that incorporates interactive elements when semi-automatically resolving constraint sets [2]. However, these works merely aim to restore consistency in an efficient manner as opposed to supporting humans in understanding inconsistencies and helping them to identify erroneous rules.

Therefore, the aim of this work is to develop an interactive and stepwise approach for resolving inconsistencies in DPMs. In contrast to existing works, our approach prioritizes giving users full flexibility when performing resolution operations while attempting to lower the mental effort required to understand and resolve the problems at hand. The idea is to expose humans to one inconsistency at a time and ask them to resolve the problem by freely choosing from a list of possible resolution operations. Here, in addition to deleting entire constraints, we also introduce weakening as a less drastic resolution operation. By isolating problems in the form of inconsistency cores and only presenting a subset of the model at a time, the user's focus is limited to relevant parts of the model. This so-called fragmentation is expected to decrease the cognitive load when working with the model [5, 11].

To further lower the overall cognitive complexity, we introduce a customizable and dynamic complexity ranking that allows to present less complex inconsistencies first. That way, as constraints are commonly involved in multiple inconsistencies, more complex inconsistencies might be resolved automatically based on prior user decisions, without the modeler having to be exposed to the problem. To ensure maximum flexibility of our approach, the ranking is based on an arbitrary complexity measure and is recalculated after each iteration, so the effects of user experience on perceived complexity can be taken into account. This includes exposing the user to already known concepts (e.g., templates the modeler has worked with in a previous iteration) before moving on to foreign ones, as experience with certain templates has been found to have a notable effect on the required mental effort [12].

The remainder of this work is structured as follows. In Sect. 2 we provide preliminaries and related work by introducing all relevant concepts regarding DPMs and inconsistencies, including a discussion on related works on DPM and inconsistency understanding. Next, we present our interactive approach for inconsistency resolution in Sect. 3 by describing and demonstrating all steps using a running example. We conclude with a discussion in Sect. 4.

2 Preliminaries and Related Work

2.1 Declarative Process Models

Declarative process models (DPMs) implicitly model the allowed process behavior using a set of constraints. The following definition includes the different components of DPMs and is derived from the formalization provided by Di Ciccio and Montali [13].

Definition 1 (Declarative Process Model) A declarative process model is a tuple **DPM** = (**T**,**A**,**C**), where

- **T** is a finite, non-empty set of templates with each template being a unary $P(x_1)$ or binary predicate $P(x_1, x_2)$ representing existence and relation templates, respectively.[1]
- **A** is a finite, non-empty set of activities
- **C** is a finite set of constraints with a constraint $c \in \mathbf{C}$ being a pair (t, m) with t being a template $\in \mathbf{T}$ and m being a mapping that assigns each variable x an activity $a \in \mathbf{A}$. For simplicity, we will note existence and relation constraints in their textual form of representation, being $P(a_1)$ and $P(a_1, a_2)$, respectively.

In this paper, we consider the declarative process modeling language Declare, which is based on linear temporal logic (LTL) and provides a set of pre-defined templates that can be used to model constraints [13]. Generally, we distinguish between Existence and Relation templates. While the former category describes properties of single activities (e.g., how often and where they must occur in a trace) the latter defines relations between two activities (e.g., whether a target activity must eventually or immediately follow or precede a source activity). Furthermore, Relation templates represent "if"-statements, so the condition only applies when the source activity occurs in a trace. In this case, we say that the source activity is the *activation* of a constraint and any trace not containing the activation automatically satisfies that constraint.

[1] We acknowledge that there can be templates with a larger arity; however, we only consider templates with a maximum arity of two in this paper.

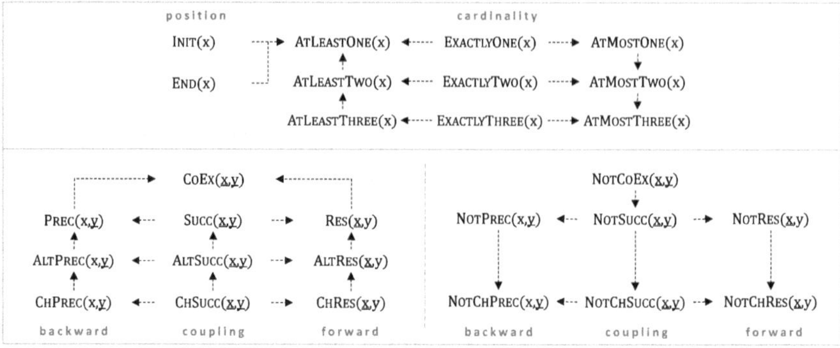

Fig. 1 Subsumption hierarchy of Declare templates

Figure 1 provides an overview of the templates considered in this paper. For a more detailed description and formalization of the individual templates, we refer to [13]. All templates can be displayed as a subsumption hierarchy. More specifically, the arrows point from a more restrictive template to a more general one, meaning that the language of the restrictive template is fully included in the more general one. For example, the language of CHAINRESpONSE (x,y), which comprises of all traces that either not contain x or where x is immediately followed by y, also satisfies ALTERNATERRESPONSE (x,y) ("if x occurs, it must eventually be followed by y before x reoccurs") and RESPONSE(x,y) ("if x occurs, it must eventually be followed by y"). Formally, we say that a constraint ϕ subsumes a constraint ψ if $\phi \vdash \psi$.

2.2 *Inconsistencies*

As we consider different types of inconsistencies in this paper, we first provide a generic definition.

Definition 2 (Inconsistency) An inconsistency is a tuple $I = (Act, C)$ with $Act \subseteq \mathbf{A}$ and $C \subseteq \mathbf{C}$ so that

$$C \cup \bigcup_{act \in Act} \text{ATLEASTONE}(act) \models \bot$$

We say that I is a minimal inconsistency if there is no $Act' \subset Act$ or $C' \subset C$ such that (Act', C') is an inconsistency.

To be able to differentiate between design-time and run-time inconsistencies, we now formalize different inconsistency types, extending the definition by Nagel and Delfmann [14]. This includes inconsistencies in the classic-logical sense (also referred to as *classic inconsistencies*) and potential inconsistencies, the latter comprising of so-called *actual issues* and *potential issues*.

Definition 3 (Classic Inconsistency) A minimal inconsistency $I = (Act, C)$ is considered a classic inconsistency iff $C \models \bot$ and $Act = \varnothing$.

Potential inconsistencies only lead to unsatisfiability if they are activated by the occurrence of one or more activities. This means that the constraint set itself is consistent and only becomes inconsistent when the activating activities occur in a trace.

Definition 4 (Potential Inconsistency) A minimal inconsistency $I = (Act, C)$ is called a potential inconsistency iff

1. $C \models \top$
2. $C \cup \bigcup_{act \in Act} \textsc{AtLeastOne}(act) \models \bot$

Furthermore, I is considered an actual issue if $|Act| = 1$ and a potential issue if $|Act| > 1$.

Example 1 Consider an exempl DPM M_1 with

$$\mathbf{T} = \text{the set of templates introduced in Figure 1}$$
$$\mathbf{A} = \{a, b, c, d\}$$
$$\mathbf{C} = \{\textsc{Init}(a), \textsc{Response}(a, b), \textsc{ChainResponse}(b, c), \textsc{ChainResponse}(c, d), \textsc{ChainResponse}(b, e), \textsc{NotResponse}(b, d), \textsc{Precedence}(b, d)\}$$

As multiple inconsistencies can have a shared core problem, we now formalize the concept of inconsistency cores following the initial definitions by [14] and provide examples of inconsistencies that extend these cores afterward.

Definition 1 (Inconsistency Core) An inconsistency core is a tuple $IC = (Act_C, C)$, where $Act_C \subseteq \mathbf{A}$ is a finite set of activities that serve as core activations and $C \subseteq \mathbf{C}$ is a set of constraints. Furthermore, IC must be a minimal classic or potential inconsistency and there is no $Act' \subseteq A$ or $C' \subseteq C$ such that (Act', C') is a minimal classic or potential inconsistency.

When recalling the DPM and contained inconsistencies shown in Example 1, we can identify three inconsistency cores defined via

$$IC_1 = (\{b\}, \{\textsc{ChainResponse}(b, c), \textsc{ChainResponse}(b, e)\})$$
$$IC_2 = (\{b\}, \{\textsc{ChainResponse}(b, c), \textsc{ChainResponse}(c, d), \textsc{NotResponse}(b, d)\})$$
$$IC_3 = (\{d\}, \{\textsc{Precedence}(b, d), \textsc{NotResponse}(b, d)\})$$

As previously implied, multiple (minimal) inconsistencies can have a shared core. For example, IC_1 can be extended to the minimal inconsistencies $I_1 - I_4$ by combinations of constraints that (externally) activate the respective core activations, with the resulting combination still meeting the previously defined minimality requirement. If a core has no core activation, it cannot be extended any further and represents a single classic inconsistency. If an inconsistency core has multiple core activations, it can be extended to any of the previously defined inconsistency types.

$I_1 = (a, \{\textsc{Response}(a, b), \textsc{ChainResponse}(b, c), \textsc{ChainResponse}(b, e)\})$
$I_2 = (\varnothing, \{\textsc{Init}(a), \textsc{Response}(a, b), \textsc{ChainResponse}(b, c), \textsc{ChainResponse}(b, e)\})$
$I_3 = (b, \{\textsc{ChainResponse}(b, c), \textsc{ChainResponse}(b, e)\})$
$I_4 = (d, \{\textsc{Precedence}(b, d), \textsc{ChainResponse}(b, c), \textsc{ChainResponse}(b, e)\})$

2.3 *Inconsistency and Culpability Measurement*

Related works have introduced a variety of measures for quantifying inconsistency. An inconsistency measure $\mathcal{I}$ is a function $\mathcal{I} : \mathcal{D} \rightarrow \mathbb{R}^{\infty}_{\geq 0}$ that assigns a numerical value to a set of rules (here: declarative constraints) with a higher value implying a higher degree of inconsistency [15, 16], the value 0 representing a consistent model. As there are many different ways of expressing this so-called "severity", a variety of inconsistency measures have been introduced [15, 17]. This includes, for example, the drastic inconsistency measure $\mathcal{I}_D$ that only differentiates between consistent and inconsistent constraint sets, and the MI-inconsistency measure $\mathcal{I}_{MI}$ that counts the number of minimally inconsistent subsets within a DPM.

In addition to measuring the overall inconsistency of a model, it is also possible to measure the severity of individual constraints, which is referred to as culpability measurement [9]. A culpability measure $\mathcal{C}$ is a function that assigns a numerical value to a constraint with a higher value implying a higher degree of culpability [8, 9]. A common example is the $C_{\#}$ culpability measure, which counts the number of minimally inconsistent subsets a constraints is involved in. For Example 1, we have the following $C_{\#}$ values, with the remaining constraints having a value of 0 as they are not involved in any inconsistency core.

$$\textsc{ChainResponse}(b, c) = 2 \qquad \textsc{ChainResponse}(b, e) = 1$$
$$\textsc{ChainResponse}(c, d) = 1 \qquad \textsc{NotResponse}(b, d) = 2$$
$$\textsc{Precedence}(b, d) = 1$$

2.4 *Inconsistency Resolution*

As already mentioned in Sect. 1, various works have introduced approaches for inconsistency resolution in DPMs. This mainly includes fully automated methods that iteratively remove constraints until consistency is reached [1, 9, 10]. The main problem with these approaches is their inability to guarantee minimal information loss w.r.t. the number of deleted elements, as they can run into local optima due to being designed as greedy algorithms [2]. As a result, Corea et al. [2] have proposed an approach making use of minimal hitting sets in the context of minimal repair in DPMs. More specifically, they use minimal hitting sets to identify minimal correction sets, i.e., sets of constraints that can be deleted to achieve consistency. When resolving inconsistencies based on these minimal correction sets, minimal information loss w.r.t. the number of deleted elements can be guaranteed. Following the definition of [2], the minimal correction sets for resolving the cores $IC_1 - IC_3$ include the following.

$$MCS_1 = \{\textsc{ChainResponse}(b, c), \textsc{NotResponse}(b, d)\}$$
$$MCS_2 = \{\textsc{ChainResponse}(b, c), \textsc{Precedence}(b, d)\}$$
$$MCS_3 = \{\textsc{ChainResponse}(b, e), \textsc{NotResponse}(b, d)\}$$
$$MCS_4 = \{\textsc{ChainResponse}(b, e), \textsc{ChainResponse}(c, d), \textsc{Precedence}(b, d)\}$$

However, these existing approaches may not always be applicable in real-life scenarios, as the elements deleted by the algorithm might not always be the ones that were incorrectly modeled, leading to potentially unwanted model behavior after the resolution process. As a result, the approach by Corea et al. [2] allows human intervention in the form of weights or whitelisting constraints. However, the user is confronted with entire pre-calculated correction sets instead of being able to look at individual inconsistencies to understand and resolve the problem, which is why the latter will form the basis of our approach.

2.5 *Declarative Process Model and Inconsistency Comprehension*

Related studies have identified several key factors influencing DPM comprehension, including the complexity of the model, the nature of individual constraints, combinations of constraints, their graphical or textual representation, the order in which models are read, and the background and experience of the model interpreters [3, 5, 7]. Here, complex models, high density of constraints, and hidden dependencies were found to particularly challenge users.

Works on DPM comprehension have direct implications for understanding inconsistencies in DPMs, as minimal inconsistencies are always subsets of DPMs. To be able to identify and resolve inconsistencies, comprehension of the involved constraints and their interplay is required. To investigate effects of inconsistency characteristics on understanding inconsistencies in DPMs, [12] have conducted an exploratory study to gain first insights into this matter. They were able to show that users found it challenging to comprehend inconsistencies, attributing this difficulty primarily to complex interrelations among sets of constraints. Moreover, the complexity, especially regarding the quantity of constraints and the variety of distinct templates within an inconsistency, notably influenced the time and mental effort required for understanding. Formally, so-called complexity metrics are similar to inconsistency measures in the sense that they assign a numerical value to a constraint set; however, with a different goal: measuring complexity. Most works apply complexity measurement to entire DPMs [18, 19]. However, all measures are also applicable to subsets of DPMs, which allows us to measure the complexity of minimally inconsistent subsets, as also suggested by Nagel and Delfmann [5, 12].

For example, considering that the primary metrics influencing the comprehension of inconsistencies appear to be the quantity of constraints and the variety of distinct templates present within an inconsistency, IC_1 comprises of two constraints based on one template, IC_2 contains three constraints based on two templates and IC_3 has a size of two based on two different templates.

Furthermore, backward constraints (e.g., PRECEDENCE) were identified as especially challenging [12]. Given that our approach aims to reduce cognitive load while preserving complete flexibility during the process of restoring consistency in a DPM, these findings serve as an important foundation.

3 Interactive Inconsistency Resolution

In this work, we present an approach for interactively resolving inconsistencies in a stepwise manner. Figure 2 provides an overview of the different steps in our approach, which can be divided into two main phases: The preparation phase includes the selection and calculation of measures, identifying the least complex core and determining valid resolution operations. This is followed by the actual resolution phase, where the user is presented with a core, viable resolution operations and additional decision support before having to decide which resolution operation should be performed. The operation is then executed and the resolution process can either be completed (if all cores have been resolved) or iteratively repeated until consistency is reached. For all steps, the resulting or altered artifacts are displayed in gray. Furthermore, any tasks direcly involving users are marked with a respective icon, while all other tasks can be executed automatically.

In the following, we will describe all steps in more detail and demonstrate them using the running example provided in Sect. 2.2. Furthermore, we implemented our approach as a proof-of-concept[2] in Java to demonstrate its potential to effectively support interactive inconsistency resolution in DPMs.

[2] https://uni-ko.de/declare-inconsistency-resolution.

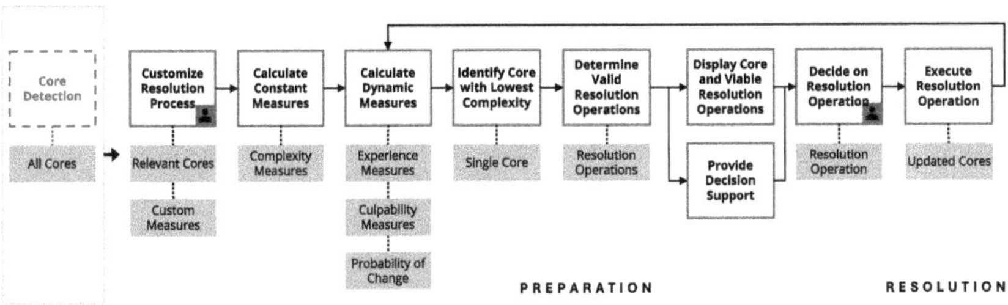

Fig. 2 Overview of interactive resolution approach

3.1 Preparation

Our approach takes a set of inconsistency cores as input. Next, the user can customize the resolution process. First, the cores that should be included in the approach can be narrowed down. Here, the priority should always be to resolve cores that are extended to one or more classic inconsistencies, as their resolution is crucial for restoring consistency. It is also recommended to resolve cores that occur in actual issues, as the core either leads to an inconsistency or is never activated, making one or more constraints irrelevant. Resolving cores that can only be extended to potential issues is optional, as all contained constraints can individually be activated and result in valid traces. One possibility to automatically determine combinations of co-occurring events that activate potential inconsistencies is to extract this information from existing event logs, as shown by Corea et al. [20]. In the running example, $IC_1 - IC_3$ can only be extended to classic inconsistencies and actual issues.

Before resolving inconsistencies, the user has the possibility to resolve redundancies based on the hierarchy presented in Fig. 1, i.e., removing all constraints that are subsumed by others and keeping the strictest constraints in the hierarchy. Generally, it might make sense to handle redundancy already before the detection of cores and inconsistencies to optimize the detection process and prevent the detection of inconsistencies that would already have been resolved otherwise. However, redundant constraints can also be leveraged to provide insights and allow for a partial and semi-automated resolution before starting the interactive approach, as explained in the following. Consider the following constraint set C_3 and its single inconsistency core IC_4.

$$C_3 = \{\textsc{Response}(a, b), \textsc{ChainResponse}(a, b), \textsc{NotChainResponse}(a, b)\}$$
$$IC_4 = (a, \{\textsc{ChainResponse}(a, b), \textsc{NotChainResponse}(a, b)\})$$

When resolving redundancy based on the hierarchy in Fig. 1, $\textsc{Response}$(a,b) would be deleted, as it is fully subsumed by $\textsc{ChainResponse}$ (a,b). To be able to utilize this information later, all removed constraints can be stored with the respective parent constraints, which not only allows to measure the likelihood of a constraint to be kept (as its condition occurs multiple times in the original model), but also provides possible weakening options that could be executed automatically. In this example, weakening CHAINREPONSE (a,b) to RESPONSE(a,b) would automatically resolve IC_4.

Next, the user can select measures to be used for calculating the complexity ranking. Generally, we distinguish between different types of metrics that can be included in a cumulative metric: complexity metrics, user-defined weights (e.g., to distinguish between easy-to-understand and more difficult templates) and experience metrics. In this example, we calculate a core's complexity as follows. We chose the number of constraints and the variability (i.e., the number of templates) as our base complexity measures. Furthermore, we assume that the user increased the weight (w_C) of backward constraints by multiplying them with a factor of 1.5, as they tend to be harder to comprehend for humans [12]. Lastly, experience with constraints and templates is included by multiplying all constraints and templates the user has been exposed to before with a factor of 0.5 (e_C and e_T, respectively). As a result, our custom measure is defined as

$$\gamma : IC \rightarrow \sum_{C \in IC} (1 \cdot w_C \cdot e_C) + \sum_{T \in IC} (1 \cdot e_T)$$

Please note that complexity can be calculated using arbitrary measures and that this is just an example for demonstration purposes. While the different components (complexity, user-defined weights, and experience) may provide a sensible basis for a cumulative measure, the final calculation can be fully customized according to the user's needs.

Now, the actual measures can be calculated. Here we distinguish between constant measures that are calculated once and remain the same (e.g., the size of a core) and dynamic measures, which can change after each iteration and therefore require recalculation (e.g., experience or culpability measures). This also includes an optional probability of change, which can be calculated based on a constraint's participation in minimal hitting sets (cf. Sect. 2.4) and insights gained from previously executed resolution operations. Based on all calculated metrics and the custom complexity measure defined by the user, we can now determine the least complex core. To this aim, we now define a general ranking of inconsistency cores based on an arbitrary (complexity) measure γ.

Definition 5 (Complexity Ranking) Consider a declarative process model **M** and the resulting set of inconsistency cores **IC**. Furthermore, consider any complexity measure $\gamma : \mathbf{IC} \rightarrow \mathbb{R}^{\infty}_{\geq 0}$ that assigns a non-negative numerical value to each inconsistency core. As a result, a complexity ranking over all $IC \in \mathbf{IC}$ is any ranking $\langle IC_1, \ldots, IC_n \rangle$ that satisfies $\gamma(IC_1) \leq \ldots \leq \gamma(IC_n)$.

Next, we can identify all valid resolution operations for this core. To this aim, we first introduce, formalize, and discuss all inconsistency resolution operations considered in our approach. As part of their stepwise resolution approach, [21] propose three functions for resolving inconsistencies in knowledge bases: deletion, weakening, and splitting. As we only consider a pre-defined set of declare templates with a maximum arity of two, the splitting operation is not applicable in our context. Therefore, we only focus on deleting and weakening constraints to restore consistency, which we define by adapting the functions proposed by [21].

Definition 6 (Change Operation) A change operation is a function that can be applied to constraint set C resulting in the updated constraint set C'. We consider the following change operations with $\{\phi, \psi\} \subseteq C$:

- **(Deletion)** $d(C, \phi) = C \setminus \{\phi\}$
- **(Weakening)** $w(C, \phi, \psi) = (C \setminus \{\phi\}) \cup \{\psi\}$ with $\phi \vdash \psi$

If C is minimally inconsistent, $d(C, \phi)$ automatically resolves the inconsistency, as minimality in terms of set inclusion implies that there must not exist a proper subset of C that is inconsistent. However, weakening one or more constraints in a minimally inconsistent constraint set does not automatically resolve inconsistency, which is why we only consider weakening operations that lower the overall number of cores in a DPM. To demonstrate viable change operations, consider constraint set C_4 and its resulting cores IC_5 and IC_6.

$$C_4 = \{\textsc{ChainResponse}(m, n), \textsc{ChainResponse}(m, o), \textsc{NotResponse}(m, n)\}$$
$$C_5 = (\{m\}, \{\textsc{ChainResponse}(m, n), \textsc{ChainResponse}(m, o)\})$$
$$C_6 = (\{m\}, \{\textsc{ChainResponse}(m, n), \textsc{NotResponse}(m, n)\})$$

For IC_5, weakening any constraint by one level (i.e., replacing either ChainResponse constraint with AlternateResponse) would resolve the core. However, for IC_6, weakening the constraints by one level (ChainResponse to AlternateResponse or NotResponse to NotChainResponse does not resolve the problem. Therefore, we now provide possible resolution operations for each constraint in that core. Please note that these are the minimal changes that have to be executed to achieve consistency, but any stronger operation (e.g., deleting instead of weakening or weakening a constraint by more levels than required) also successfully resolves the inconsistency.

(i) $w(C_3, \textsc{ChainResponse}(m, n), \textsc{CoExistence}(m, n))$
(ii) $d(C_3, \textsc{NotResponse}(m, n))$
(iii) $w(C_3, \textsc{ChainResponse}(m, n), \textsc{AlternateResponse}(m, n))$ and
$w(C_3, \textsc{NotResponse}(m, n), \textsc{NotChainResponse}(m, n)$

3.2 Resolution

The actual resolution starts by presenting the user with the lowest-ranked core. In the running example, this is IC_1 as it only contains two constraints and one distinct template without any additional weight. Next, the user is provided with possible resolution operations for each constraint in the core and is asked to resolve the problem. To provide decision support, additional metrics, such as the constraints' culpability and (if available) their probability of change can be provided. For C_1, the weakest possible resolution operations include weakening either constraint from CHAINRESPONSE to ALTERNATERESPONSE. After providing the user with the respective culpability measures (e.g., indicating that CHAINRESPONSE (b,c) has a higher culpability value), they now have the full flexibility to execute the resolution operation of their choice. For example, we will assume that the user decides to execute the weakening operation $w(C, \text{ChainResponse}(b, c), \text{AlternateResponse}(b, c))$, which fully resolves IC_1, which will then be executed. All cores containing a deleted constraint are no longer inconsistent and can be removed. If a constraint has been weakened, an additional consistency check is required as cores containing this constraint are not automatically resolved as well. In this iteration, no other core is affected, as the altered constraint had a $C_{\#}$ value of 1. If redundancy has not been resolved prior to the resolution process, all constraints subsuming the deleted one or being subsumed by the weaker constraint replacing the original one can be removed as well.

All remaining cores serve as input for the next iteration, where the dynamic measures are updated. Now, the complexity ranking can be recalculated and the process is repeated until consistency is reached. In the running example, the remaining two cores are now ranked again and IC_2 is determined to be the least complex one. Here we can see that even though it contains more constraints than IC_3, the complexity is considered lower due to containing both an already known constraint and template, as well as not containing any backward constraints, which are commonly considered hard to understand. If the user now decides to weaken or delete NOTRESPONSE (b,d), not only the current core but also the last one in the ranking is automatically resolved. As a result, the user did not have to look at all cores separately and was never exposed to backward constraints.

4 Conclusion

In this work, we introduced an interactive approach for resolving inconsistencies in DPMs, emphasizing the reduction of mental effort for users while maintaining maximum flexibility regarding the executed resolution operations. To this aim, we enable the prioritization of inconsistency cores by complexity and incorporate customizable user weights and insights acquired during the resolution process, such as familiarity with specific templates. Our approach is particularly advantageous for models with a high degree of inconsistency, as this increases the culpability of individual constraints, which – in turn – allows users to restore consistency without having to be exposed to every single inconsistency. As we provide the user with inconsistencies in order of their (cognitive) complexity, the user can likely be spared from being exposed and having to understand and resolve more complex problems. This strategy is designed to significantly reduce mental effort. Models containing fewer inconsistencies also benefit from our approach, as we provide many opportunities for user-centric customization and dynamically integrate user experience into the ranking calculation. That way, we leverage learning effects to gradually guide the user from simple to more complex inconsistencies.

Our concept is based on related works in the area of DPM comprehension and is supported by a proof-of-concept implementation, showcasing its potential to aid in the interactive resolution of DPM inconsistencies. However, this is only the first step towards a comprehensive resolution approach. When providing inconsistencies in order of their (user-defined) complexity compared to providing them in random order, the average complexity the user is exposed to can only be lower or remain the same. However, to identify optimal complexity measures that are tailored to the individual executing the resolution, further studies are needed. Future work includes enhancing the presented approach with a user interface that supports improved visualization and interactivity. This allows us to conduct user studies using eye-tracking to measure the mental effort involved in the resolution process and assess the effectiveness of our approach.

Furthermore, we plan to introduce additional impact measures to inform users about the implications of different resolution strategies on the resulting model. Here, Schützenmeier et al. [22] have introduced a first approach to detect behavioral changes when comparing DPMs based on finite state automata, which could be leveraged to compare the impact of different resolution operations. Here, the first challenge is to efficiently compute impact of a change operation locally, which already requires the comparison of the language of n subsets with $n = |IC|$. However, global impact measures are needed to assess the overall impact of an entire resolution strategy on the model's allowed language. Here, our goal is to alter the model minimally while ensuring consistency is restored, aiming for the least possible expansion of the model's language. This perspective will enrich our approach by combining automated methods with interactive human-in-the-loop features, presenting a comprehensive strategy for resolving and, ultimately, preventing inconsistencies in DPMs.

References

1. Di Ciccio, C., Maggi, F. M., Montali, M., & Mendling, J. (2017). Resolving inconsistencies and redundancies in declarative process models. *Information Systems, 64*, 425–446. https://doi.org/10.1016/j.is.2016.09.005
2. Corea, C., Nagel, S., Mendling, J., & Delfmann, P. (2021). Interactive and minimal repair of declarative process models. In *Business Process Management Forum. BPM 2021* (pp. 3–19). https://doi.org/10.1007/978-3-030-85440-9_1
3. Figl, K., Di Ciccio, C., & Reijers, H. A. (2020). Do declarative process models help to reduce cognitive biases related to business rules? In *International conference on conceptual modeling* (Vol. 12400, pp. 119–133). https://doi.org/10.1007/978-3-030-62522-1_9
4. Maggi, F. M., Bose, R. P. J. C., & van der Aalst, W. M. P. (2012). Efficient discovery of understandable declarative process models from event logs. In *Advanced Information Systems Engineering. CAiSE 2012*. https://doi.org/10.1007/978-3-642-31095-9_18

5. Nagel, S., & Delfmann, P. (2022). Investigating inconsistency understanding to support interactive inconsistency resolution in declarative process models. In *ECIS 2022 Research-in-Progress Papers*.
6. De Smedt, J., De Weerdt, J., Serral, E., & Vanthienen, J. (2016). Improving understandability of declarative process models by revealing hidden dependencies. In S. Nurcan, P. Soffer, M. Bajec, & J. Eder (Eds.), *Advanced Information Systems Engineering. LNCS* (pp. 83–98). Springer. https://doi.org/10.1007/978-3-319-39696-5_6
7. Haisjackl, C., Barba, I., Zugal, S., Soffer, P., Hadar, I., Reichert, M., Pinggera, J., & Weber, B. (2016). Understanding declare models: Strategies, pitfalls, empirical results. *Software & Systems Modeling, 15*(2), 325–352 (2016). https://doi.org/10.1007/s10270-014-0435-z
8. Corea, C., & Delfmann, P. (2019). Quasi-inconsistency in declarative process models. In *Business Process Management Forum. BPM 2019* (pp. 20–35). https://doi.org/10.1007/978-3-030-26643-1_2
9. Corea, C., Deisen, M., & Delfmann, P. (2019). Resolving inconsistencies in declarative process models based on culpability measurement. In *Proceedings der 14.* Internationalen Tagung der Wirtschaftsinformatik.
10. Maggi, F. M., Westergaard, M., Montali, M., & van der Aalst, W. M. P. (2012). Runtime verification of LTL-based declarative process models. In *International Conference on Runtime Verification* (Vol. 7186, pp. 131–146). Springer. https://doi.org/10.1007/978-3-642-29860-8_11
11. Andaloussi, A. A., Soffer, P., Slaats, T., Burattin, A., & Weber, B. (2020). The impact of modularization on the understandability of declarative process models: A research model. In *Information Systems and Neuroscience* (Vol. 43, pp. 133–144). Springer. https://doi.org/10.1007/978-3-030-60073-0_15
12. Nagel, S., & Delfmann, P. (2024). Exploring cognitive effects of inconsistency characteristics on understanding inconsistencies in declarative process models. In *Proceedings of the 57th Hawaii International Conference on System Sciences (HICSS)*.
13. Di Ciccio, C., & Montali, M. (2022). Declarative process specifications: Reasoning, discovery, monitoring. In *Process Mining Handbook* (Vol. 448, pp. 108–152). Springer. https://doi.org/10.1007/978-3-031-08848-3_4
14. Nagel, S., & Delfmann, P. (2023). Identification, abstraction and classification of inconsistency structures in declarative process models. In *ECIS 2023 Research Papers*.
15. Thimm, M. (2019). Inconsistency Measurement. In *Proceedings of the 13th International Conference on Scalable Uncertainty Management* (pp. 9–23). https://doi.org/10.1007/978-3-030-35514-2_2
16. Corea, C., & Thimm, M. (2020). Towards inconsistency measurement in business rule bases. In *Proceedings of the 24th European Conference on Artificial Intelligence (ECAI 2020)*.
17. Thimm, M. (2018). On the evaluation of inconsistency measures. In *Measuring Inconsistency in Information* (Vol. 73, p. 42). Studies in Logic, College Publications.
18. Andaloussi, A. A., Burattin, A., Slaats, T., Kindler, E., & Weber, B. (2023). Complexity in declarative process models: Metrics and multi-modal assessment of cognitive load. *Expert Systems with Applications, 233*, 120924. https://doi.org/10.1016/j.eswa.2023.120924
19. Andaloussi, A. A., Burattin, A., Slaats, T., Kindler, E., & Weber, B. (2021). Assessing the complexity of declarative process models using model-based metrics. In *A framework for enhancing the modeling and comprehension of declarative process models* (pp. 179–204).
20. Corea, C., Mansour, R., & Delfmann, P. (2022). Advanced auditing of run-time conflicts in declarative process models using time series clustering. In *Proceedings der 17.* Internationalen Tagung der Wirtschaftsinformatik (WI 2022).
21. Grant, J., & Hunter, A. (2011). Measuring the good and the bad in inconsistent information. In *IJCAI'11: Proceedings of the twenty-second international joint conference on Artificial Intelligence* (pp. 2632–2637).
22. Schützenmeier, N., Corea, C., Delfmann, P., & Jablonski, S. (2023). Efficient computation of behavioral changes in declarative process models. In *BPMDS 2023* (Vol. 479, pp. 136–151). Springer. https://doi.org/10.1007/978-3-031-34241-7_10

Orchestrating Enterprise Transformation and Business Processes Through Data-Driven Steering

Benedict Lösser and Robert Winter

Abstract Organizations are compelled by a variety of strategic and contextual shifts, as well as the pervasive nature of digital changes, to undertake enterprise transformation (ET). Such endeavors typically entail profound and emergent changes across multiple organizational levels and key constituencies, with business processes being a particularly sensitive aspect due to their ongoing dynamics. Despite the practical significance of business processes within enterprise-level change, there is only little research on the dynamic interplay between business processes and the ET. This study aims filling the gap by proposing an integrated, data-driven ET and business process steering. The designed method framework is based on the utilization of existing data sources of an enterprise. It is informed by a real-world case, dynamic capabilities as kernel theory and the existing literature on business process dynamics, ET, and digital twins in context of processual phenomena. We validated the proposal using a focus group of technology-related executives.

1 Introduction

In the fast-paced landscape of today's business, managing and sustaining enterprise transformation (ET) is a daunting challenge for incumbent organizations [1–4]. ET is an umbrella term for different transformation types (e.g., digital transformation, agile transformation, etc.) on an enterprise level, that are emergent by nature and comprise various concurrent initiatives on different levels while changing various business processes and architectural patterns ongoingly with high uncertainty and volatility [3, 5, 6]. Amidst this complexity, the ongoing dynamics and changes of operational business processes emerge as a particularly vulnerable facet. Having significant impact

B. Lösser (✉) · R. Winter
Institute of Information Systems and Digital Business, University of St. Gallen, St. Gallen, Switzerland
e-mail: benedict.loesser@unisg.ch

R. Winter
e-mail: robert.winter@unisg.ch

C. M. Flath et al. (eds.), *Digital Innovation and Organizational Transformation*, Lecture Notes in Information Systems and Organisation 83,
https://doi.org/10.1007/978-3-032-08483-5_7

both to ongoing operations and to the overarching ET, business process dynamics claim for particularly high management attention [7–10]. If steering committees or other ET-related governance bodies do not grasp the complex interrelationships between ET and business processes—and consider these dependencies in their analysis and decision making—, this may endanger the overall success of ETs for the organization. This is also reflected in the extremely high number of ET and business process change projects that fail to achieve the desired benefits [11, 12]. A common root cause for information gaps and analysis faults is if steering committees not have access to relevant and timely information on these dynamic interrelations [13].

Surprisingly, the dynamics of interconnected business processes and its structural impacts on ET have not been considered often in academic research, an exception being the rather siloed and fragmented portraits following the business process reengineering ideas in the 1990s [14]. These remain largely focused on the reengineering of individual processes—and not on the interplay between ET initiatives and multiple relevant business processes. Furthermore, there are no adequate metrics to measure the impact of business process reengineering on overall organizational performance. However, in the last years we have seen increasing capabilities for data-driven analysis and simulation of (complex) business processes in research and practice [15]. Recent research has even emphasized the application of the concept of digital twins to the management of business processes or entire organizations, with a particular focus on leveraging existing data sources, especially trace data [16–18]. Furthermore, ETs as strategic processual phenomena are increasingly often rigorously supported by digital tools from which a correspondingly large amount of data is collected and could be analyzed. Leveraging these extensive datasets, conceptual frameworks from research, and existing data-driven analytical tools, the ability to effectively analyze the complex interplay of organizational change encompassing ET emergence and business process dynamics, and consequently the ability to effectively steer these in an integrated manner could be significantly enhanced.

Thus, we pose our research question: How to systematically orchestrate the interaction between enterprise transformation and business process dynamics?

To address the research problem at hand, we propose a hypothesis-driven method framework that signifies a pivotal step towards unlocking the vast potential inherent in the automated utilization of different data sources. We build on a conception of steering as dynamic capability, recent literature on the digital twin of processual phenomena, and a real-world case of OTTO to inform the initial design for the "(Business) **P**rocess and **E**nterprise **T**ransformation **S**teering" (PETS) method framework. We validate our initial proposal with a focus group consisting of technology- and transformation-related executives. Our approach casts not only an abstract overview and synthesis of different data sources, but also enhances the structured gathering of management-relevant information for improved and integrated decision-making for ETs and business processes. Amidst this examination, we acknowledge not only the inherent complexity of ET, but also the dynamic interplay of changing business processes. As a conclusion, we outline a research agenda for future empirical studies based on our initial design contribution.

The study is structured as follows: In Sect. 2, we provide an overview of the conceptual underpinnings of ET and business process dynamics as well as on data-driven steering. Furthermore, we introduce the case of OTTO. In Sect. 3, we give an overview of our design and validation procedure. In Sect. 4, we introduce our method framework to address the research problem at hand. In Sect. 5, we discuss our results and provide an outlook for future research.

2 Background

2.1 *Enterprise Transformation and Business Process Dynamics*

ET as fundamental, non-routine change of one or several key constituencies serves as more than just a means for companies to better respond to evolving environmental conditions [6]. It also plays a pivotal role in ensuring long-term success for businesses, as successful operating models become obsolete and eventually fade when product innovations or novel combinations of production methods gain traction in the market [19]. Consequently, effectively utilizing appropriate transformation methods and tools becomes a fundamental component of a competitive strategy [19, 20]. ET encompasses profound shifts that extend beyond the singular impact on individual processes, organizational units, information technology (IT) systems, or products. Instead, they influence multiple components of enterprise architecture concurrently [21]. Achieving the overarching objectives of ET necessitates a holistic, enterprise-wide vantage point that spans across the entire organizational landscape [22]. We consider the research streams of organizational transformation [23], IT-enabled organizational transformation [24, 25], digital transformation [1, 26], and also agile transformation [27, 28] to be closely related to ET. ET is thus an umbrella term for different types of intentional organizational change, i.e., transformation, at an enterprise level [6, 29]. While there is a plethora of literature on all these different ETs from a variety of philosophical stances and different operational foci, the steering and management of business processes as aspect in ET steering is largely neglected.

This is remarkable as managing the dynamics of business processes is fundamentally central to achieving organizations objectives [8, 30]. According to Pentland, Vaast and Wolf [16] dynamics of business processes result from two different phenomena: (1) process change, meaning the change of the internal structure of a (single) business process and (2) process variety, meaning multiple execution paths of one given process structure. While in an ET we have both, high process variety and high structural process change, our main focus here is on the structural change of business processes and, importantly, their interdependence. In the case of an ET, this means not only the selective change of a single business process structure, but also the impact on many other business processes. This results in interdependencies and repercussions that are highly complex and difficult to grasp in practice [1, 10,

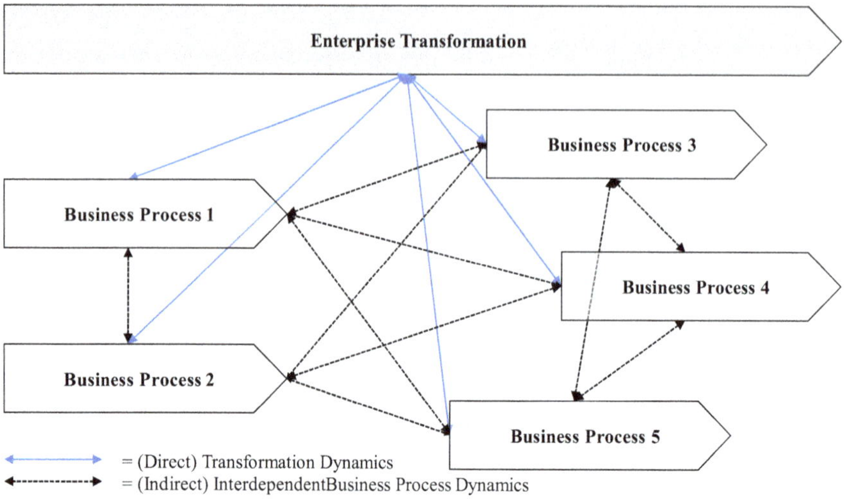

Fig. 1 Interdependencies of enterprise transformation and business processes

31]. In addition, this also might have strong implications on the ET as processual phenomenon itself which in turn has a strong impact on the structure of the business processes [10, 12, 32]. Thus, we face a wicked problem to steer the complexities and interdependencies of business processes among each other and to the overarching ET. A schematic representation of the interrelationships and the bi-directional interdependencies is depicted in Fig. 1.

Previous approaches to deal with these dynamics can be divided into business process-oriented and ET-oriented approaches. Business process-oriented approaches include the pursuit of agile business process management (BPM) concepts (Baiyere et al., 2020; Badakhshan et al., 2019) and data-driven, process mining-based techniques [33, 34]. While Baiyere, Salmela and Tapanainen [10] and Badakhshan, Conboy, Grisold and vom Brocke [8] shed light on the need to enable flexibility and leanness in BPM through altering fundamental logics, the data-driven, process mining-based techniques focus on dynamic modelling, monitoring and action-oriented concepts, usually for single business processes and thereby highly dependent on data quality [33, 35].

On the other hand, the ET-oriented approaches focus on balancing ET-inherent tensions through appropriate governance structures [5, 13]. For example, Jöhnk et al. (2022) highlight the challenging interplay and interdependencies between different ET initiatives and the "core" organization. Their solution to this challenge is a hybrid ambidexterity approach, applying structural and contextual ambidexterity in the ET to balance the tradeoffs.

However, while there is a call for an integrated perspective on business goals, processes, systems, participants, and data in the BPM domain [9], neither business process-oriented nor ET-oriented research have an explicit approach to managing the dynamics of business processes in the context of an ET. Nevertheless, the bi-directional interdependence of the ET and business processes holds immense strategic relevance. This is all the more evident as ETs still fail at an estimated rate of 70% despite a plethora of research on success factors and effective project and process management methods [36].

2.2 Data-Driven Steering

The traditional concept of ET deals with change that is generally initiated and steered in a top down manner [22]. As scaled agile methodologies gain relevance, a central steering committee still often remains pivotal in guiding the decentralized initiatives and securing the desired value generation [27, 29, 37, 38]. These steering committees, typically composed of senior managers, serve as the decision-making authority for strategic and disputed matters. They regularly oversee change activities, monitor progress, and make necessary decisions to initiate specific measures and facilitate organizational restructuring [39].

Following this notion, we regard the integrated steering of ETs and business processes as a dynamic capability according to the definition of a dynamic capability as the role of upper-level management in adapting, integrating, and reconfiguring skills and resources to renew competences and achieve congruence with the changing business environment [40]. As a consequence of this consideration, the integrated steering of ET and business processes consists fundamentally of the triad sensing, seizing and transforming.

Since ETs as well as end-to-end business processes affect the entire enterprise, the potential information and knowledge base is usually broad and spread across the organization. Furthermore, the specific information needs for such a steering are unclear, and the dependencies between ET and business processes are not thoroughly and empirically established [10]. Thus, typical steering committees lack information on the scope, relevance, and consequences of their decisions [41]. However, recent research towards the digital twin of organization sheds light on the usage of existing data sources for decision-support [42–44]. In line with these approaches for utilizing existing data sources to inform decision makers, we lie on the generic approach by Moser and Grossmann [42] for addressing decision-makers in complex projects as depicted in Fig. 2.

According to this scheme for a specified digital twin, the real-world provides data which are complemented by a model. Data and model then lead to analytics, which process the data and conveys the results to the user interface—and back to the model to improve its real-world fidelity. Insights are inferred from the user interface, leading to decisions in the reality which in turn lead to specific actions. These actions have impact in the real-world which also (directly) impacts the actions and provides (new) data for a new cycle. This way of thinking outlines a feedback loop where real-world outcomes are fed back into the system, indicating a continuous process of adaptation and refinement of the model and decisions based on real-world interactions and data analysis in the virtual representation.

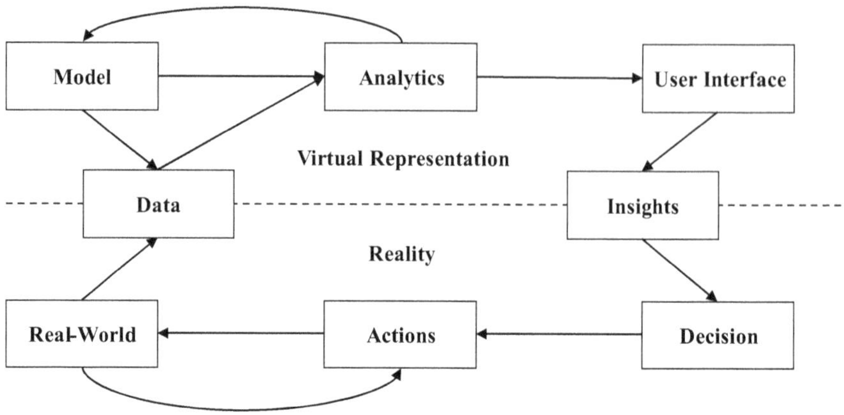

Fig. 2 Schematic digital twin of complex projects based on Moser and Grossmann (2023)

2.3 *OTTO Case*

We consider OTTO to be already advanced in the elaboration of an information system to support steering committees, showcasing specific results as well as potential design options, which can at least partially inform our solution design.

Established in the 1940s as a mail-order business, OTTO innovated its model by launching one of the first retailer websites in the mid-1990s, becoming the only surviving ex-mail-order business in Germany. E-commerce has become crucial to OTTO, transforming it into a highly digital organization. The shift from catalog to online retail has now evolved into a hybrid digital platform, offering OTTO products and those of other retailers, creating diverse revenue streams from trade, platform commissions, and monetizing platform data. To maintain customer relevance and scale network effects, OTTO's business processes have undergone significant transformation. All ET efforts follow a minimum viable product (MVP) approach, prioritized quarterly by the executive group. The transition from retailer to digital platform involved several phases, each requiring recalibration in the quarterly steering process. Strategic management issues and effective change patterns were continuously addressed. OTTO developed an overarching dashboard on an exploratory, hypothesis-based foundation, using integrated data from existing systems to capture strategic dynamics and relevant insights, such as those from the enterprise resource planning system.

The internal process of the tool development methodology at OTTO as a tangible manifestation of an ET information system is based on a 6-step process, that is oriented at hypothesis rather than requirements: *Listening and Relevance Filtering* aims at discovering which issues are affecting the steering of the organizations and where current control or bottleneck problems are. *Hypothesis formation* refers to the fundamental question on how to answer the issues (at least partially) with data—and what the relevant dimensions or metrics for the question are, *Discovery* means to identify where they might have the data that could help and how they could use existing data differently than before by linking and enriching it. *Provisioning* means how to make the data usable on the tool and interface side. *Integration* refers to the linking with overarching structural models (e.g., process or capability maps) to connect perspectives and *Interpretation* means the identification of patterns and how to learn from these for the future.

3 Research Design

To design a method framework for PETS, we opted for a research approach rooted in logics of the DSR paradigm. DSR is well established in the field of IS [45], aimed at enhancing organizational and human capabilities by creating innovative artifacts [46].

The DSR process builds on existing theory and practical knowledge to inform the design [45]. We therefore rely on Hevner's DSR methodology as it proposes a flexible process for designing artifacts [47]. The process consists of three combinable research cycles: the *relevance*, *rigor* and *design* cycle [47]. Below we first describe the design procedure along the three design cycles before outlining the validation procedure.

3.1 Design Procedure

The *relevance cycle* initiates DSR by providing research requirements and an application context. In this paper, the application context is motivated in the introduction and conceptually discussed in Sect. 2. As the implementation of an artifact is not a mandatory step for early designs [48] and due to the great effort in terms of time and costs to field test the artifact, this study does not yet include the evaluation in an application context but features a conceptual validation with practitioners based on a focus group, as further elaborated below in Sect. 3.2.

The *rigor cycle* functions as a feedback loop that supplies previous knowledge to the research project, ensuring its innovative contribution [47]. Grounding DSR can be achieved by including additional knowledge on the problems, existing artifacts, analogies as well as metaphors, and theories [47]. For this paper, the knowledge base is provided in Sect. 2 through the justificatory knowledge from literature, practice and dynamic capabilities as kernel theory. The knowledge base will be enhanced by extensions to existing knowledge on digital twins in the context of ET and business process change.

The *design cycle* represents the core of DSR and requires the most effort and particularly the decision for the artifact type to design. Due to the complexity, emergence and high variance of different ETs and business processes strong, normative reference models seem to be inaccessible. Based on the high degree of diversity of ET steering approaches, we propose a method framework as an artifact. Brinkkemper [49] defines a method as a systematic approach for executing a systems development project. This approach is rooted in a particular way of thinking, encompassing explicit guidelines and rules that organize the progression of development tasks and their associated deliverables. A method offers the advantages of being able to describe the path precisely without presenting a normative, direct solution that is at best unprepared for a large number of real-world scenarios. As a basis for a generic, abstract use concept, we develop an initial method framework that contains the essential method elements. In analogy to the architectural framework definition of ISO/IEC/IEEE [50], we understand a framework as a common practice for creating, interpreting, analyzing and using descriptions pertinent to a specific field of application or within a community of stakeholders.

3.2 Validation Procedure

To fundamentally validate the method framework, we must ensure that the proposal is effective, efficient, and user centered [51, 52]. As we could not validate the solution in the field yet, we summarize here a first concept validation through a focus group. Focus groups allow to tap into the collective wisdom of individuals who possess diverse experiences and perspectives [53]. Through moderator-led, but open discussions on the topic of interest, we can explore the ideas and opinions of knowledgeable and potentially interested individuals on the PETS method framework.

We conducted a focus group with 14 senior managers, mostly holding CIO or innovation officer positions in large companies. We divided the 90-min meeting into two halves. In the first round, the focus was particularly on the basic idea of data-driven steering in general, and participants were briefed by mostly conceptual materials and the OTTO case in general. In the second round, the focus was on specific tool support and (integrated) steering needs for ET and business processes.

The first round featured an in-depth discussion on data-driven steering and decision-making in general. Participants sorted contributions based on data utilization in decision-making, emphasizing the importance of specific data. However, one participant noted that data-drivenness is sometimes overemphasized, arguing that many steering decisions rely on common sense rather than extensive data analysis. Despite this, the potential for improved data-driven steering and information logistics for ET and business process dynamics was seen as highly beneficial.

The second round focused on OTTO's case and the proposed method framework. The solution and conceptual developments garnered interest and approval. The relevance of decision-making support was re-emphasized, and the PETS method framework was recognized as innovative and viable. Critical comments highlighted the complexity of implementing a comprehensive solution due to ET and business process dynamics. Over time, the method's application can help identify and represent emergent, dynamic factors effectively, despite the challenge of perfect mapping.

Overall, the approach was appreciated for capturing organizational change complexities effective and efficiently, though user-centric aspects could not be definitively assessed.

4 The PETS Method Framework

The PETS method framework as initial design solution to our research problem encompasses six activity clusters (Fig. 3). These are informed by the OTTO case and the scientific discourses on the digital twin of an organization, ET, in particular its emergent nature and complex decision-making [41, 54], general aspects of the business process dynamics and process mining discourse, i.e., the maintenance of high data quality standards [35, 55], and the dynamic capabilities perspective on the act of steering, i.e., sensing, seizing, and transforming [40]. The different activity clusters comprise specific activities along the joint steering of emergent ET and dynamic business processes. The representation is based on the interaction of the emergence in the real-world organization with the data derived from it, both for the ET itself and for the business processes. As the real-world organization is always emergent, the ET as well as the business processes change permanently and form dependencies, continuing to adapt to each other as a result of the respective changes [16]. In many cases, it is possible to capture changes comprehensively in business processes due to the ubiquity of trace data and analyses from process mining tools. The ET can also be traced, for example, by data stored in project management tools or in ET-related decision support systems. In order to successfully steer the complex and enterprise-specific interdependencies and dynamics, a structured approach, in the sense of a method, is needed to capture issues and utilize information to ultimately translate them into decisions and actions.

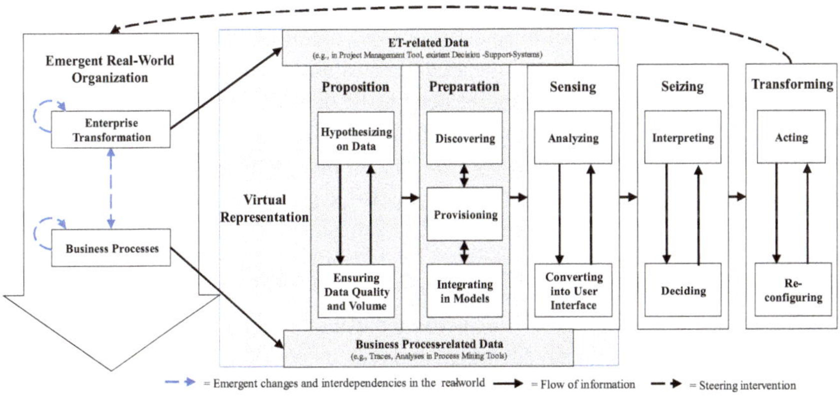

Fig. 3 PETS method framework

Typically, the process commences with a specific question or issue originating from the *Emergent Real-World Organization*. These questions could pertain to steering the *ET* or the management of a variety of *Business Processes*, or a combination of both. One of the most important questions is how well-orchestrated the ET actually is, i.e., how agile, widely autonomous teams could be steered to reach transformation targets, taking into account the concurrent change initiatives and the operational business processes as main objects of investigation.

From such real-world inquiries, the transition unfolds into the realm of virtual representation through PETS. This transition begins with the *Proposition* activity cluster, where managerial hypotheses about potential data sources for providing answers guide both technical and cognitive preparations. This ensures the use of relevant data of the appropriate quality. For example, *Hypothesizing on Data* could be based on the consideration that the ET is staggered as a sequence of quarterly initiatives and that these exist not only concurrent, but are also interdependent—both from each other and with existing business processes. They therefore need clear prioritization to avoid bottlenecks. The data that can potentially be utilized for this purpose, might be sourced from the project management tool as it reflects the progression of the ET. Furthermore, already given indicators from relevant business processes in process mining and analysis tools could be utilized. *Ensuring Data Quality and Volume* would also be of relevance in this case. The quality and the volume of relevant data might not be sufficient at first because, for example, tickets in the ET management tools are not tracked and managed for such an analysis case or relevant business processes are only insufficiently digitally represented and standardized.

The subsequent activity clusters delineate a systematic progression in the context of data utilization. The *Preparation* activity cluster encompasses the discovery and interconnection of available data, aligning them with existing structural models to serve the predefined use cases effectively. The activity *Discovering*, i.e., the open consideration of which, if any, enriched data could help, might lead to the selection of the initiative's tickets from the strategic change portfolio process, as these potentially indicate the ET's process structure and interdependencies of initiatives. In addition, the cycle time of business processes could be identified to be relevant. This may lead to demanding technical challenges as potential functional sequences and logical technical interfaces might need to be newly created. *Provisioning* then means specifically how this data can be utilized on the tool side. This could be done in a business intelligence tool. *Integrating in Models* then means merging created information with existing, overarching models—e.g., strategically specified milestones along the broad ET journey or existing business process maps. This allows examining and evaluating the progress of the ET and the business process dynamics in relation to strategic planning objectives.

When transitioning to the *Sensing* activity cluster, the focus shifts towards a technical analysis of the previously identified and linked data. The primary objective is to transmute this data into a user-friendly format, making it accessible and comprehensible for human stakeholders. During *Analyzing*, the data considered to be relevant, should be integrated and evaluated by an appropriate tool for dependency analysis and illustration for relevant stakeholders. *Converting into User Interface* means preparing clear figures and graphs for steering committee members. This might include two-dimensional graphs, depicting the effects of the development of the business process indicators over time and in relation to the ET milestones.

The *Seizing* activity cluster marks the convergence of virtual representation and real-world organizational impact. In this activity cluster, insights derived from earlier stages are interpreted to inform decision-making for the steering committee. For *Interpreting*, enterprise architects or well-trained portfolio managers could create a preliminary interpretation of the depicted relationships, which can then be discussed by the steering committee members. Thus, in *Deciding* the steering committee should be able to discuss specific thematic cuts to improve ET and business process orchestration. Typical decisions in this context could be, e.g., a reduction of parallel initiatives or new combinations in the business processes while changing business logics.

Decisions are then executed in *Transforming* with corresponding effects on the real-world organization, the ET and its business processes [16]. *Acting* means clear steering interventions to leverage current capabilities and resources effectively, while *Reconfiguring* refers to the change of the organizations structure and dynamics in the long-term. The consequences of such tactical or strategical interventions are automatically 'monitored' so that the success could be measured continuously. Any adjustments to the decisions can therefore be made, data-driven at any time. Accordingly, this method framework leads to more and more analyses and an increasing wealth of data and experience from past decisions. Over time, this will therefore enable better and more comprehensive steering and can therefore also be linked to the digital twin discourse, according to the paradigm: start where you are and then incrementally improve your systematic data assessments step by step [56].

5 Discussion and Conclusion

Our manuscript aims to shed light on the persistent challenges and the development path towards an increasingly integrated steering for ET and business processes. Thereby, we build upon the high availability of data for both worlds. Following a conceptual approach, informed by dynamic capabilities as kernel theory, a real-world case of OTTO, recent developments in the field of digital twins of organizations as well as discourses in the ET and BPM domain, we address a problem that has no apparent, systematic solution yet. That is providing timely, authentic decision support for steering committees, highlighting the interrelations of ET as strategic process and operational business processes. This manuscript is part of a larger research project towards improving steering in large enterprises, focusing on data-driven solutions to inform steering committees. Accordingly, we discuss our conceptual approach in three aspects, while highlighting future paths for research.

First, the novel perspective on BPM through ET glasses is particularly important in order to make the multitude of business processes in a superimposed ET understandable and manageable from a perspective of mutual dependencies and dynamics.

Here we outline a path to a solution—without sketching out an overfitted solution model yet. While we do not dissolve the logics of BPM [10], we enable a more data-driven, comprehensive and integrated steering of ET and business processes by applying the PETS method framework. In this way, we would like to broaden the discourse on BPM to focus more on the orchestration of diverse businesses processes and in interrelation to overarching strategic change processes as an object of investigation. In this sense, we present a valid proposal that paves the way towards a more data-driven, integrated steering of ET and business processes. However, our proposal is highly generic and universal at this stage and might be over-reliant on data, neglecting qualitative factors of human judgment in complex decision-making. Based on the in-depth analysis of additional real-world cases, a next step will be the empirical identification of contingencies and context factors and, as a consequence, the extension of our proposal into a situational method, following a design science or action design research approach. Such situational methods could relate to different situations or their foci (e.g., on ET or the orchestration of business processes).

Second, ETs as highly complex, emergent and interdependent, processual phenomena could benefit greatly from work on the more systematic use of data to improve information logistics and decision-making in steering committees [41]. While existing knowledge on the steering of ET is distributed and practical adaptation is limited due to the emergence and complexity of the system, the PETS method framework attempts to classify these parameters and make them applicable for future research and practice. As in the course of increased recognition and exploration of processual phenomena outside of traditional business processes, under the umbrella of process science [32], it is also becoming increasingly relevant to better understand strategic change and steering processes and to consider them in complex, holistic contexts. This study is intended to provide a conceptual foundation for an information system that could help to generate novel, practical insights into enterprise-level change in a hypothesis-oriented manner. In this line of thinking the proposal can also be interpreted in the direction of taking up the ideas of process mining and giving a first conceptual proposal on how to transfer these thoughts to more abstract, strategic processes. Additionally, there could be a wide range of research opportunities based on the insights of such an information system. For example, it seems to be a valuable endeavor to investigate data-driven decision-making by executive committees more specifically in the future. Based on an increasing number of investigated use cases and documented data-driven decisions, it may become possible to ultimately identify important context-input-mechanism-output patterns of steering decisions [57].

Third, while the concept of digital twins, that inform our proposed method framework among others, remains a vision, it appears to be increasingly worthwhile to start creating a digital infrastructure for real-time management support, especially for aspects of the organization that are subject to major changes. Accordingly, Moser and Grossmann [42] have described an interesting approach to make the metaphor of the digital twin more applicable to the context of processual phenomena in general. Our PETS method framework serves as an initial foundational step in understanding the dynamics of organizational change, particularly in the context of ET and dynamic business processes. This could serve as a foundational step towards a directed digital twin of the organization. In the context of ET and business processes, the exploration and exploitation of relevant data is particularly useful, as relevant data repositories can often be identified quickly and can already generate a high potential value lever. However, due to the diversity of organizational settings and design requirements, various issues still need to be addressed during active implementation of such a solution [44]. Thus, we expect future research to focus more on transferring conceptual approaches of the digital twin of the organization into practice, describing specific, empirical cases and working out what tangible impact such digital twins actually have on the way organizations steer their enterprise-level change.

References

1. Vial, G. (2019). Understanding digital transformation: A review and a research agenda. *The Journal of Strategic Information Systems, 28*, 118–144.
2. Volpentesta, T., Spahiu, E., & De Giovanni, P. (2023). A survey on incumbent digital transformation: A paradoxical perspective and research agenda. *European Journal of Innovation Management, 26*, 478–501.
3. Matt, C., Hess, T., & Benlian, A. (2015). Digital transformation strategies. *Business & Information Systems Engineering, 57*, 339–343.
4. Verhoef, P. C., Broekhuizen, T., Bart, Y., Bhattacharya, A., Dong, J. Q., Fabian, N., & Haenlein, M. (2021). Digital transformation: A multidisciplinary reflection and research agenda. *Journal of Business Research, 122*, 889–901.
5. Jöhnk, J., Ollig, P., Rövekamp, P., & Oesterle, S. (2022). Managing the complexity of digital transformation—How multiple concurrent initiatives foster hybrid ambidexterity. *Electronic Markets, 32*, 547–569.
6. Rouse, W. B. (2005). A theory of enterprise transformation. *Systems Engineering, 8*, 279–295.
7. Pentland, B. T., Liu, P., Kremser, W., & Hærem, T. (2020). The dynamics of drift in digitized processes. *MIS Quarterly, 44*, 19–14.
8. Badakhshan, P., Conboy, K., Grisold, T., & vom Brocke, J. (2019). Agile business process management. *Business Process Management Journal, 26*, 1505–1523.
9. Kerpedzhiev, G. D., König, U. M., Röglinger, M., & Rosemann, M. (2020). An exploration into future business process management capabilities in view of digitalization. *Business & Information Systems Engineering, 63*, 83–96.
10. Baiyere, A., Salmela, H., & Tapanainen, T. (2020). Digital transformation and the new logics of business process management. *European Journal of Information Systems, 29*, 238–259.
11. Mankins, M., & Litre, P. (2024). Transformations that work. *Harvard Business Review, 103*(5–6), 86.
12. Sarker, S., Sarker, S., & Sidorova, A. (2006). Understanding business process change failure: An actor-network perspective. *Journal of Management Information Systems, 23*, 51–86.
13. Kiselev, C., Winter, R., & Rohner, P. (2020). Project success requires context-aware governance. *MIS Quarterly Executive, 19*, 199–211.
14. Hammer, M., & Champy, J. (1993). *Reengineering the corporation - A manifesto for business revolution*. HarperCollins Publishers.
15. Martin, N., Fischer, D. A., Kerpedzhiev, G. D., Goel, K., Leemans, S. J. J., Röglinger, M., van der Aalst, W. M. P., Dumas, M., La Rosa, M., & Wynn, M. T. (2021). Opportunities and challenges for process mining in organizations: Results of a Delphi study. *Business & Information Systems Engineering, 63*, 511–527.
16. Pentland, B., Vaast, E., & Wolf, J. R. (2021). Theorizing process dynamics with directed graphs: A diachronic analysis of digital trace data. *MIS Quarterly, 45*, 967–984.

17. van der Aalst, W. M. P., Hinz, O., & Weinhardt, C. (2021). Resilient digital twins. *Business & Information Systems Engineering, 63*, 615–619.
18. Dumas, M. (2021). Constructing digital twins for accurate and reliable what-if business process analysis. *CEUR Workshop Proceedings*, 23–27.
19. Teece, D., Peteraf, M., & Leih, S. (2016). Dynamic capabilities and organizational agility: Risk, uncertainty, and strategy in the innovation economy. *California Management Review, 58*, 13–35.
20. Fiedler, M., Hutzschenreuter, T., Klarmann, M., & Weißenberger, B. E. (2023). Transformation: Challenges, impact, and consequences. *Schmalenbach Journal of Business Research, 75*, 271–279.
21. Winter, R., Bender, B., & Aier, S. (2024). Enterprise-level IS research – Need, conceptualization, exemplary knowledge contributions and future opportunities. In *Proceedings of the 57th Hawaii International Conference on System Sciences (HICSS 2024)*, Honolulu, HI, USA, 6402–6411.
22. Proper, H. A., Winter, R., Aier, S., & de Kinderen, S. (Eds.). (2017). *Architectural coordination of enterprise transformation.* Springer.
23. Greenwood, R., & Hinings, C. R. (1993). Understanding strategic change: The contribution of archetypes. *Academy of Management Journal, 36*, 1052–1081.
24. Henderson, J. C., & Venkatraman, N. (1999). Strategic alignment: Leveraging information technology for transforming organizations. *IBM Systems Journal, 38*, 472–484.
25. Lyytinen, K., & Newman, M. (2008). Explaining information systems change: A punctuated socio-technical change model. *European Journal of Information Systems, 17*, 589–613.
26. Sebastian, I. M., Ross, J. W., Beath, C., Mocker, M., Moloney, K. G., & Fonstad, N. O. (2017). How big old companies navigate digital transformation. *MIS Quarterly Executive, 16*, 133–150.
27. Carroll, N., Conboy, K., & Wang, X. (2023). From transformation to normalisation: An exploratory study of a large-scale agile transformation. *Journal of Information Technology, 38*(3), 267–303.
28. Horlach, B., Schirmer, I., & Drews, P. (2019). *Agile portfolio management: Design goals and principles.* Twenty-Seventh European Conference on Information Systems (ECIS2019), Stockholm.
29. Kiselev, C., & Winter, R. (2020). Governance of mixed agile/Traditional digital transformation programs. In *AMCIS 2020 Proceedings*. AIS, Salt Lake City.
30. Kohlbacher, M., & Reijers, H. A. (2013). The effects of process-oriented organizational design on firm performance. *Business Process Management Journal, 19*, 245–262.
31. Gust, G., Flath, C. M., Brandt, T., Strohle, P., & Neumann, D. (2017). How a traditional company seeded new analytics capabilities. *MIS Quarterly Executive, 16*(3), 215–230.
32. vom Brocke, J., van der Aalst, W., Grisold, T., Kremser, W., Mendling, J., Pentland, B., Recker, J., Roeglinger, M., Rosemann, M., & Weber, B. (2021). *Process science: The interdisciplinary study of continuous change.* Available at SSRN 3916817.
33. Park, G., & Van Der Aalst, W. M. P. (2021). Realizing a digital twin of an organization using action-oriented process mining. *2021 3rd International Conference on Process Mining (ICPM)*, 104–111.
34. van der Aalst, W. M. P. (2019). Object-centric process mining: Dealing with divergence and convergence in event data. In *Software engineering and formal methods* (pp. 3–25). Lecture Notes in Computer Science.
35. Fischer, D. A., Goel, K., Andrews, R., van Dun, C. G. J., Wynn, M. T., & Röglinger, M. (2020). Enhancing event log quality: Detecting and quantifying timestamp imperfections. In *Business process management* (pp. 309–326). Lecture Notes in Computer Science.
36. Wade, M., & Shan, J. (2020). Covid-19 has accelerated digital transformation, but may have made it harder not easier. *MIS Quarterly Executive, 19*(3), 213–220.
37. Dikert, K., Paasivaara, M., & Lassenius, C. (2016). Challenges and success factors for large-scale agile transformations: A systematic literature review. *Journal of Systems and Software, 119*, 87–108.

38. Fitzgerald, M., Kruschwitz, N., Bonnet, D., & Welch, M. (2013). Embracing digital technology: A new strategic imperative. *MIT Sloan Management Review, 55*, 3–12.
39. Lechler, T. G., & Cohen, M. (2009). Exploring the role of steering committees in realizing value from project management. *Project Management Journal, 40*, 42–54.
40. Teece, D. J., Pisano, G., & Shuen, A. (1997). Dynamic capabilities and strategic management. *Strategic Management Journal, 18*, 509–533.
41. Labusch, N., Aier, S., & Winter, R. (2014). A reference model for the information-based support of enterprise transformations. In *9th International Conference, DESRIST 2014* (pp. 194–208). Springer International Publishing.
42. Moser, B. R., & Grossmann, W. (2023). Digital twins of complex projects. In *The digital twin* (pp. 677–702). Springer.
43. Wurm, B., Becker, M. C., Pentland, B. T., Lyytinen, K., Weber, B., Grisold, T., Mendling, J., & Kremser, W. (2023). Digital twins of organizations: A socio-technical view on challenges and opportunities for future research. *Communications of the Association for Information Systems, 52*, 552–565.
44. Lyytinen, K., Weber, B., Becker, M. C., & Pentland, B. T. (2023). Digital twins of organization: Implications for organization design. *Journal of Organization Design.*
45. Gregor, S., & Hevner, A. R. (2013). Positioning and presenting design science research for maximum impact. *MIS Quarterly, 37*, 337–355.
46. Hevner, A. R., March, S. T., Park, J., & Ram, S. (2004). Design science in information systems research. *MIS Quarterly, 28*, 75–105.
47. Hevner, A. R. (2007). A three cycle view of design science research. *Scandinavian Journal of Information Systems, 19*, 87–92.
48. Dresch, A., Pacheco Lacerda, D., & Valle Antunes Jr, J. A. (2015). *Design science research.* Springer.
49. Brinkkemper, S. (1996). Method engineering - Engineering of information systems development methods and tools. *Information and Software Technology, 38*, 275–280.
50. ISO/IEC/IEEE. (2011). *Systems and Software Engineering - Architecture Description (ISO/IEC/IEEE Std 42010:2011).* ISO/IEC and IEEE Computer Society.
51. Straub, D. (1989). Validating instruments in MIS research. *MIS Quarterly, 13*, 147–169.
52. Gibson, M., & Arnott, D. (2007). The use of focus groups in design science research. In *18th Australasian Conference on Information Systems.* University of Southern Queensland, Toowoomba, Australia.
53. Tremblay, M. C., Hevner, A. R., & Berndt, D. J. (2010). the use of focus groups in design science research. In *Design research in information systems. Integrated series in information systems* (Vol. 22, pp. 121–143). Springer.
54. Carroll, N., Hassan, N. R., Junglas, I., Hess, T., & Morgan, L. (2023). Transform or be transformed: The importance of research on managing and sustaining digital transformations. *European Journal of Information Systems, 32*, 347–353.
55. Wynn, M. T., & Sadiq, S. (2019). Responsible process mining - A data quality perspective. In *Business Process Management. Lecture Notes in Computer Science* (pp. 10–15). Springer.
56. Caporuscio, M., Edrisi, F., Hallberg, M., Johannesson, A., Kopf, C., & Perez-Palacin, D.: Architectural concerns for digital twin of the organization. In *Software Architecture. Lecture Notes in Computer Science* (pp. 265–280). Springer.
57. Denyer, D., Tranfield, D., & van Aken, J. E. (2008). Developing design propositions through research synthesis. *Organization Studies, 29*, 393–413.

Pre-Processing Inertial Measurement Unit-Based Data for Process Mining Using Convolutional Neural Networks

Daniel Polle, Milda Aleknonytė-Resch, Dominik Janssen, Clint Hansen, Elke Warmerdam, Walter Maetzler, and Agnes Koschmider

Abstract The analysis of inertial measurement unit (IMU)-based data allows tracking human behavior, detecting anomalies, and predicting human activity changes. As IMU-based data is unstructured and continuous, the application of process mining could provide additional insights into the underlying human performance. Therefore, the data has to be efficiently pre-processed in order to be used by process mining algorithms. This paper presents an approach to convert IMU-based data into structured event data for process mining. Particularly, the approach relies on methods for time-series segmentation and convolutional neural networks. In this way, activities of daily living can be identified from the unstructured data. The evaluation results show that convolutional neural networks are suitable for discovering activities when window sizes are previously known and have low cutoff values. The combination with a fixed sliding window approach for unknown window sizes appears superior.

Daniel Polle and Milda Aleknonytė-Resch have contributed equally.

D. Polle · D. Janssen (✉) · A. Koschmider
Department of Business Informatics and Process Analytics, University of Bayreuth, Bayreuth, Germany
e-mail: dominik.janssen@uni-bayreuth.de

D. Polle
e-mail: daniel.polle@uni-bayreuth.de

A. Koschmider
e-mail: agnes.koschmider@uni-bayreuth.de

M. Aleknonytė-Resch
Department of Computer Science, Kiel University, Kiel, Germany
e-mail: mar@informatik.uni-kiel.de

C. Hansen · W. Maetzler
Department of Neurology, Kiel University, Kiel, Germany

E. Warmerdam
Werner Siemens Endowed Chair of Innovative Implant Development (Fracture Healing), Saarland University, Saarbrücken, Germany

C. M. Flath et al. (eds.), *Digital Innovation and Organizational Transformation*, Lecture Notes in Information Systems and Organisation 83,
https://doi.org/10.1007/978-3-032-08483-5_8

1 Introduction

Process mining is a data-driven approach to discover processes within a dataset, reveal deviations between as-is and to-be processes, and predict changes between ongoing and past process executions. While traditionally, process mining uses structured data as input (e.g., business processes), there is a high demand to process unstructured data for process mining [12]. Data from wearable sensors like inertial measurement units (IMUs) can be considered unstructured since the data is not necessarily provided in a format fitting for process discovery algorithms. Related works focus on specific algorithms (e.g., walking-bout detection [19]) to gain insights into specific human behavior and its changes.

IMUs usually include multiple sensors (i.e., accelerometer, gyroscope, and magnetometer) to capture the orientation of the sensor by integrating angular velocity, acceleration, and rotation of an object [3]. IMU-based sensors have been successfully used in many disciplines, such as medicine, sports, and consumer behavior. However, the application of process mining on IMU-based data has yet to receive more attention.

This paper presents a novel approach to translating IMU-based data into structured event data, which is crucial to be processed by process mining techniques. The approach includes data cleaning (e.g., noise reduction), time-series segmentation, and event-activity abstraction. We conducted a comparative study with two convolutional neural network (CNN) algorithms with various parameters to identify everyday activities of daily living and abstract them into events. Often, activities' start and end events are unknown for unlabeled data. We used fixed sliding windows and change point detection to overcome this challenge. We compared our evaluation results against a baseline (i.e., a random assignment of activity labels to windows based on time). Our approach outperformed the baseline, particularly for shorter window sizes.

2 Processing IMU-Based Data for Process Mining

2.1 *The Process from IMU-Based Data to Event Log*

Below, we summarize the process of event log extraction from IMU-based data. The pre-processing step is explained in detail in Sect. 2.2. Human body movements using IMUs are tracked with devices like smartwatches or smartphones, which refer to the **Recording** phase (see left-hand side of Fig. 1). Several sensors attached to various locations on the body are used to acquire time-series data. Usually, the time-series data has a lot of noise, which requires efficient data cleaning. The **pre-processing** step handles the data cleaning and preparation. To efficiently process the time series, ideally time-based windows are split in a way, that one window refer to an activity of daily living. So, we segment the time-series data into multiple windows of a particular

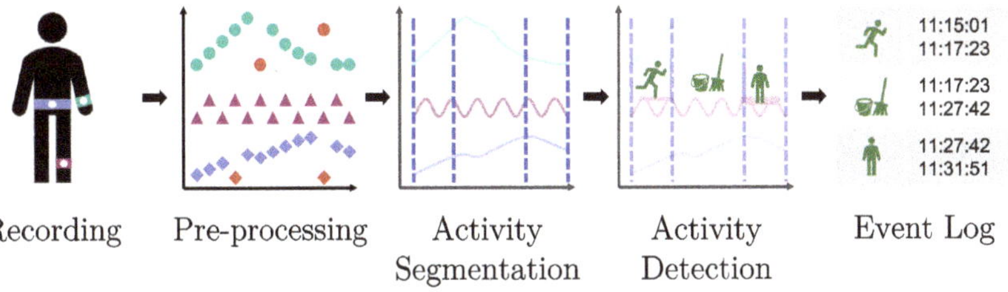

Fig. 1 The process from IMU-based data recording to an event log

window size. This is managed in **Activity Segmentation**. The divided data is fed directly to e.g., a deep learning technique for **Activity Recognition** where a window size is mapped to an activity. Finally, an event log is extracted for process mining.

The use cases appropriate for our pipeline must satisfy specific requirements. The source of IMU-based data shall be mapped to an entity (i.e., individual) supporting case identification (i.e., caseID). The data should be continuous without interruptions. Activities should be pre-defined and be on a similar abstraction level without mixed levels of details (i.e., not detailing every step in a recipe or categorizing every event of an activity).

2.2 *Processing Pipeline for IMU-Based Data*

The proposed approach to process IMU-based data for process mining consists of the following steps, as depicted in Fig. 1:

1. *Pre-processing: Data Cleaning and Preparation.* The data cleaning step includes checking if the raw data has the relevant sensor types/locations and if erroneous data entries in the ground truth (e.g., missing frame data) have been deleted. To reduce the computational time, we recommend starting with a minimal set of related sensor data like the accelerometer and gyroscope of the right forearm, pelvis, and right ankle as described in Tarantova et al. [21] and Huang et al. [5]. Activities and their granularity need to be carefully selected based on the purpose of the analysis. In case activities are too homogeneous (e.g., "picking up a box" and "picking up a book"), they should be subsumed. Scarce activities should be excluded to increase the accuracy of the results. In our approach, we consider rare events to have occurred less than 20 times. In future research, we plan to integrate advanced approaches for outlier detection [11]. The output of the data cleaning is time series data without erroneous data entries or rare activities.
2. *Activity Segmentation.* To ensure optimal performance of CNNs, the data needs to be segmented into inputs of the same length (i.e., every sample of an activity has to be provided with the same amount of frames as every other sample). We identified padding as a good compromise between computing power and the quality of the results (see for a reference Bier et al. [1]). Particularly, we applied

zero-padding, which adds zero values to each vector of the input until a specific frame length is achieved. In the following "cutoffs" refer to both the maximum frame length for model training and the standardized length for padding samples.
3. *Activity detection: Splitting Time Series into Windows.* We need to find the activities' start and end times for further processing. Start and end times are usually unknown in real-world applications. Therefore, we need to divide the time series into smaller parts that ideally contain exactly one activity. In our evaluation, we compared two methods of splitting time series into windows: fixed sliding window and change point detection. The output of this step is segmented and padding time series data, which is necessary for the subsequent step.
4. *Activity detection: CNN Training and Application.* To train the CNNs, the data of related activities needs to be labeled. First, the (usually multidimensional) input is transformed into a one-dimensional output through a CNN transformer with default settings [2]. After the transformation, a normalization around zero with a standard scaler follows before a ridge regression classifier is fitted on the normalized data as described in Dempster et al. [2]. The trained CNN models can be applied to unlabeled data to generate an event log with a caseID, corresponding activities and time stamps.

Given the multiple configurations for steps 2-4, we compared different approaches to each other (see Sect. 3). This included testing multiple cutoff values for activity segmentation, applying two distinct approaches for splitting time series into windows (fixed sliding window and change point detection), and applying two different CNN models (MiniRocket [2] and MultiRocket [20]). We chose the Rocket variants since they dominate the current CNN methods regarding computational efficiency [20].

3 Evaluation of the Process Mining Pipeline

3.1 IMU-Data

The data used for our evaluation is described in [22]. It refers to healthy adults and patients with neurological abnormalities (e.g., Parkinson's disease) who performed ten common activities of daily living, further referred to as activities (e.g., setting a table, ironing) while wearing 16 IMUs. The activities were performed in a laboratory setting. Typically, all activities were recorded at 200 Hz through IMUs (Noraxon USA Inc., myoMOTION, Scottsdale, AZ, USA) equipped with a triaxial accelerometer, triaxial gyroscope and triaxial magnetometer. Data used in our paper included 109 participants for whom IMU-based data and 3392 manually labeled activity tags were available. The data is available upon request.

The dataset is particularly suitable for the proposed approach, i.e., applying a pre-processing pipeline that employs CNNs to transform IMU-based data into a structured event log. The controlled environment under which the activities were performed allows for appropriate data labeling, which is essential as a baseline for evaluating our approach. Moreover, including data from individuals with neurological abnormalities introduces atypical movement patterns. This is beneficial for training our CNN model to generalize across both typical and atypical patterns of activities accurately.

3.2 Evaluation Setup

In our evaluation, we explored multiple approaches and configurations for steps 3 and 4 to assess how they affect the quality of activity recognition. In step 3, we considered three scenarios: predefined window sizes referring to an activity, random window size, which were then split using fixed-size sliding windows, and random window sizes, which were then split using change point detection. Furthermore, in step 4, we evaluated two CNN models, MiniRocket (**Mini**mally **R**and**o**m **c**onvolutional **ke**rnel **t**ransformation) and MultiRocket (extension of MiniRocket) in order to compare their performance and determine the most accurate output quality across these different scenarios.

The fixed sliding window approach generates a set of potential windows and selects those with the highest prediction confidence through an exhaustive search, as suggested by [15]. Concerning our dataset, this means that the sliding window creates many windows that can include an activity, and the windows that fit best are kept, i.e., show the highest confidence in the prediction of the window. Change point detection, specifically the Pruned Exact Linear Time (Pelt) method [10], identifies transitional movements between activities. The approach works well even for an unknown number of change points.

The classification of activities was done with MiniRocket and MultiRocket. MiniRocket transforms the input time series using a small, fixed set of convolutional kernels. The transformed features are the foundation for training a linear classifier. The computational load can be partially improved by dilation on the kernels. MiniRocket uses the proportion of positive values metric for the pooling layer and reduces randomness on the kernel parameters [2]. This reduction makes the method much faster while still being effective for classification.

We applied each configuration of time series segmentation (known windows, fixed sliding window and change point detection) and CNN algorithm (MiniRocket and MultiRocket) with four distinct cutoff values (1000, 2000, 3000, 10000) to evaluate our approach's performance. We evaluated the CNNs' performance across all activities collectively and then inspected each activity individually. For simplicity, when examining each activity individually, we present only the most promising results of the 1000 cutoff values.

To assess the validity of our evaluation results, we calculated a baseline for each scenario and cutoff value. Depending on the activity-based window search process, the random baseline process differed:

Known Windows:
Activity labels are randomly assigned to activities. The original probability distribution of activities was kept, i.e., activities that occur often in the original dataset will also be assigned more often.

Sliding Windows:
Window sizes were randomly selected and activities were assigned to them randomly.

Change Point Detection:
Relies on windows identified by the PELT algorithm [10]. Labeling was based on the distribution of labels learned during the final training phase, assigning weights to each label to mirror the model's exposure to the data distribution, ensuring fair comparison between model predictions and coincidence.

3.3 *Evaluation Criteria*

To evaluate the CNN models, we used a 5-fold cross-validation, splitting the data into 80% training and 20% test data. Three metrics were used to evaluate the results of the CNN models: Mean Jaccard Similarity (MJS), balanced accuracy (BAcc), and weighted average F1-Scores [19]. When comparing individual activities for each scenario and parameter combination, we considered the F1-Score. The Jaccard Similarity index measures the model's ability to predict the correct activity label at the proper position. It is defined as the ratio between the intersection and union of the predicted segmentation and the ground truth segmentation [6]. A standard accuracy value does not fit our purpose, as our dataset has a strong label imbalance [19]. The unbalanced distribution of labels is shown in Fig. 2: two activity labels describe around 60% of all occurring activities.Therefore, a balanced accuracy is calculated by considering the true positive rate and the true negative rate. Furthermore, we calculated the weighted average F1-Scores with the weights being the frequencies of the different activities.

3.4 *Results*

We removed rare activities and subsumed homogeneous activities such as "Sitting with reading out loud," "Sitting without a table (talking)," and "Sitting at a table" into one common activity labeled "Sitting." A complete list of activities, their frequencies, and median duration are shown in Figs. 2 and 3. As described in Sect. 2, we further pre-processed the data using CNNs by selecting three sensors and zero-padding. Furthermore, for step 3 of our approach we used the three scenarios as presented above: known windows, unknown windows with the application of fixed-size sliding widows, and unknown windows with change point detection. Then, MiniRocket and

MultiRocket were applied to the pre-processed data for each scenario. Both models underwent a standard training procedure, transforming multidimensional inputs into one-dimensional outputs, followed by normalization and fitting with a regression classifier.

The analysis results of the different cutoffs for MiniRocket and MultiRocket are shown in Fig. 4. The figure also includes benchmarks for random activity assignment, serving as a baseline. The baseline is depicted as a red line for each window/cutoff combination. The figure reveals a trend where smaller cutoff values correspond to

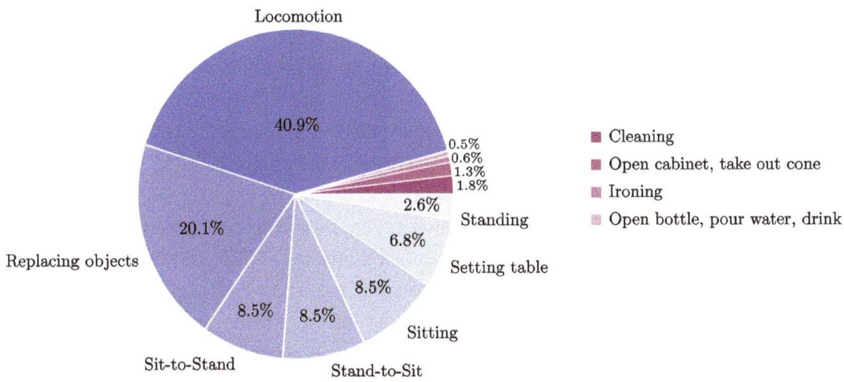

Fig. 2 Distribution of activities in the dataset. A total of 3392 activities were labeled. Red activities were excluded due to their infrequent occurrence

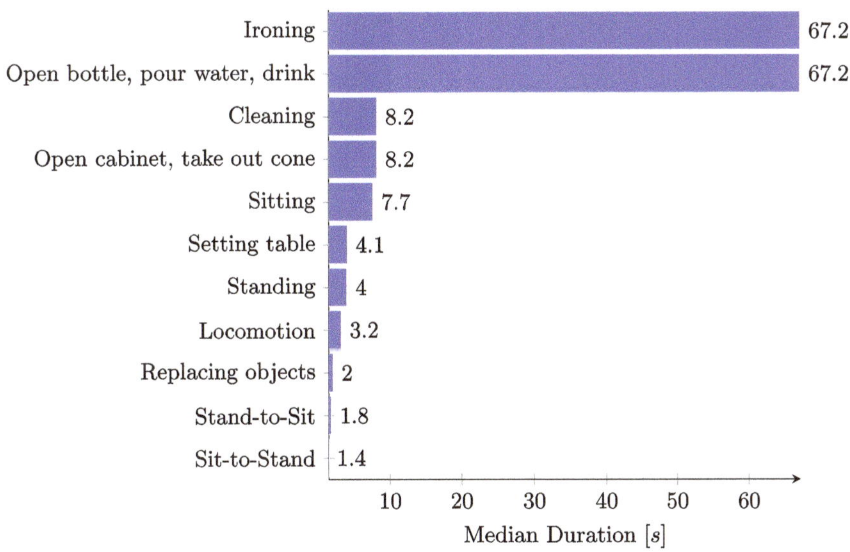

Fig. 3 Median duration of all observed activities

higher weighted F_1-Scores. Specifically, at the 1000 cutoff value, the weighted F_1-Score is much higher than the baseline, indicating accuracy of the CNN model or window detection method employed.To evaluate the CNN models, we used a 5-fold cross-validation, splitting the data into 80% training and 20% test data. Three metrics were used to evaluate the results of the CNN models: Mean Jaccard Similarity (MJS), balanced accuracy (BAcc), and weighted average F_1-Scores [18]. When comparing individual activities for each scenario and parameter combination, we considered the F_1-Score. The Jaccard Similarity index measures the model's ability to predict the correct activity label at the proper position. It is defined as the ratio between the intersection and union of the predicted segmentation and the ground truth segmentation [6]. A standard accuracy value does not fit our purpose, as our dataset has a strong label imbalance [18]. The unbalanced distribution of labels is shown in Fig. 2: two activity labels describe around 60% of all occurring activities. Therefore, a balanced accuracy is calculated by considering the true positive rate and the true negative rate. Furthermore, we calculated the weighted average F_1-Scores with the weights being the frequencies of the different activities.

The evaluation for the 1000 cutoff value reveals varying performance depending on the three-time series segmentation scenarios and two CNN models as shown in Table 1. Across all scenarios, model performance surpasses baseline. MiniRocket consistently outperformed MultiRocket across all scenarios and quality metrics. Notably, with known window size based on activities, both MiniRocket and MultiRocket exhibit high-quality scores, especially considering the BalAcc metric (0.88 and 0.82, respectively). The fixed sliding window approach outperforms change point detection when windows are unknown. However, for unknown windows, the ranges of MJS (0.60 to 0.41), BAcc (0.71 to 0.61), and weighted F_1-Scores (0.40 to 0.30) show lower effectiveness (see Table 1).

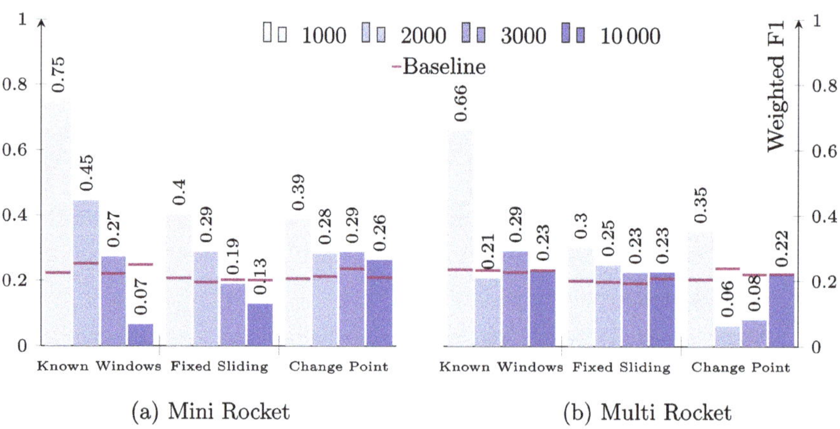

Fig. 4 Weighted F_1-Score for various cutoff values and activity-based window search processes for MiniRocket (**a**) and MultiRocket (**b**)

Table 1 Quality metric score comparison of MiniRocket and MultiRocket search process (Cutoff = 1000)

		MJS		BalAcc		W-F1	
	Rocket	Impl	Base	Impl	Base	Impl	Base
Known Windows	Mini	0.74	0.16	0.88	0.58	0.75	0.22
	Multi	0.59	0.16	0.82	0.58	0.66	0.23
Fixed Sliding Window	Mini	0.60	0.24	0.71	0.56	0.40	0.21
	Multi	0.58	0.23	0.61	0.55	0.30	0.20
Change Point Detection	Mini	0.49	0.25	0.64	0.56	0.39	0.21
	Multi	0.41	0.23	0.61	0.55	0.35	0.20

Source Authors

Next, we analyzed the performance of the MiniRocket algorithm, employing a 1000 cutoff and fixed-size sliding window for each activity (see Fig. 5). The results revealed a pattern where frequently performed activities, like locomotion, were identified with higher precision than less common ones, such as setting a table. The CNN's performance seems to be unaffected for activity duration. For instance, activities with longer durations, like sitting ($7.7s$), were not necessarily recognized more accurately than shorter ones, like Sit-to-Stand ($1.8s$). The F_1-Score, as depicted in Fig. 5, varied based on the activity and the knowledge window size. When the window size was pre-defined, MiniRocket excelled in classifying most activities, achieving an F_1-Score of over 0.92 for four activities. When the windows were unknown, the fixed sliding window outperformed change point detection for activities such as "Locomotion," "Stand-to-Sit," "Sit-to-Stand," and "Sitting." However, change point detection yielded higher F_1-Scores for "Replacing Objects," "Standing," and "Setting Table." This means that the fixed sliding window can be more effective for monotone activities, while change point detection can be superior for activities with varying executions (e.g., "Setting a Table").

After applying the CNNs, an event log is extracted, which serves as the input for process mining. Table 2 illustrates an exemplary event log. For multiple entities or individuals, the event log requires an additional column for case IDs to distinguish between entities. Process discovery algorithms can be applied to the event log, allowing in-depth analysis. For instance, it allows for identifying executed activity sequences and predicting changes between activities. Additionally, process mining can uncover potential bottlenecks, pinpointing areas where activities slow down or become inefficient, offering opportunities for improvement or intervention. It also enables conformance checking, comparing observed activities against predefined models or expectations to evaluate adherence or deviations. In the context of activity recognition, these insights could be beneficial in, e.g., the domains of rehabilitation, symptom management, and quality of life analysis. One specific example involves patients with neurodegenerative diseases. Their daily lives would be observed before and after an intervention, such as surgery. The quality of life could be measured based

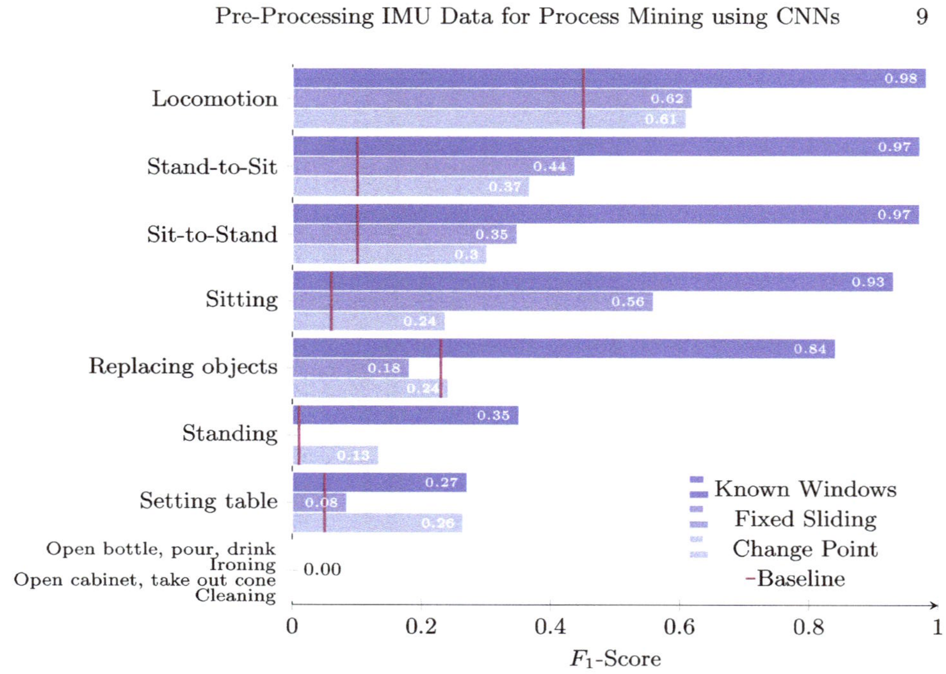

Fig. 5 F_1-Score by Activity and activity-based window search process (Cutoff = 1000, MiniRocket)

Table 2 Exemplary event log for the data set

Timestamp	Activity	Status
...	...	...
2024-03-01 15:35:23	Sitting	Start
2024-03-01 15:38:35	Sitting	End
2024-03-01 15:38:35	Sit-to-Stand	Start
2024-03-01 15:38:38	Sit-to-Stand	End
2024-03-01 15:38:38	Standing	Start
2024-03-01 15:40:02	Standing	End
...	...	...

Source Authors

on the process of their daily activities–specifically, the number of different activities executed in a day or the number of breaks a patient needs in their day-to-day life.

4 Related Work

Plenty of related works exist for human activity recognition. A comprehensive literature review on this topic has been published by Liu et al. [14]. The review studied wearable sensor data (e.g., [13]) and video data (e.g., [8]) for this purpose. The number and granularity of daily human activities varies. For instance, Zebin et al. [24] identified six activities related to movements. Pham and Oliver [17] recognized 11 activities related to food preparation.

Yuan et al. [23] present a comprehensive overview of the techniques involved in wearable sensor-centered human activity recognition, covering the spectrum from sensor types and activities recognized to data pre-processing, feature learning, and classification methods. Further interesting studies include Gholamiangonabadi's [4] paper, which critically examines the generalization capabilities of human activity recognition models across new subjects using Leave-One-Subject-Out Cross-Validation, demonstrating the effectiveness of a specific CNN architecture in providing accurate, subject-independent performance estimates. Meanwhile, Nweke's [16] review sheds light on the pivotal role of feature extraction in human activity recognition systems, advocating for a shift towards deep learning for automatic feature learning from multi modal sensor data.

Recent literature indicates that process mining can significantly benefit from sensor data analysis, as highlighted by Koschmider et al. [12], who explored the potential of process mining techniques in enhancing the understanding and utilization of sensor data. A recent paper by Khowaja et al. [9] addresses the challenges faced by smart healthcare services during the COVID-19 pandemic, particularly in tracking human behavior, complex patterns, and the subjective nature of physical activities. The paper introduces a novel approach called Process mining and Paravector Tensor for physical health monitoring. This approach aims to track subjective human behavior and manage the intensity variations associated with inertial measurement units, marking a significant step towards addressing variability and behavior dynamics in healthcare monitoring.

5 Conclusion and Future Work

This paper presented an approach for extracting event logs from IMU-based data for human activity recognition, employing scenarios with known and unknown window sizes using MiniRocket and MultiRocket with various configurations. Our evaluation relied on a dataset involving 109 participants performing daily living activities in a laboratory setting, with all activities labeled. We found that overall, CNNs identify human activities well when activity-based windows are known and a smaller (in our case, 1000) cutoff value is chosen. When the activity-based windows are unknown, a fixed sliding window approach combined with MiniRocket provided mostly the overall best results.

A missing unified classification of activities hampers the comparison of human activity recognition models. Our approach shows promise, but segmenting time series data requires additional investigation. Real-world applications include more noise as well as variability in IMU-driven data and lack predefined window sizes, posing challenges for CNN-based recognition systems. Scenarios in which this approach is beneficial are laboratory settings, where patients are explicitly asked to engage in daily living activities under observation, and staff can accurately identify activity-based windows. From these controlled observations, it becomes possible to evaluate the health status of patients by analyzing their ability to perform these activities.

Practical implications of our research include accurate identification of human activities through CNNs, which allows healthcare providers to monitor patient progress, tailor rehabilitation programs, and improve symptom management strategies. In scientific terms, our work contributes to the development of robust activity recognition models, facilitating more precise and reliable analysis of IMU-based data and incorporating the analysis of activities of daily living. This advancement supports the identification of more effective interventions, symptom monitoring and enhances our understanding of human behavior through quantitative observation of activities of daily living.

Future research directions shall address two main topics: further evaluation of the CNN models and the inclusion of additional sensor data, such as location information [7], to enrich context understanding since certain activities are specific to environments like kitchens or outdoor settings. The further evaluation of the CNN models could include a comparative study including multiple other machine learning approaches for activity recognition as well as a comparison of the performance of the CNN models depending on the status of the observed individual (patient vs. healthy control). The next steps in our research involve tuning the hyperparameters of the CNNs and applying our pipeline to IMU-based data collected in home settings. The derived event log from home settings could then be used for discovering process models and thus generating insights. These insights can include identifying the most common sequences of daily activities, detecting deviations from typical behavior patterns, and understanding the temporal distribution of activities throughout the day. This in turn could improve efficiency or support health-related outcomes.

Acknowledgements This project has received funding from the State of Schleswig-Holstein under the Datencampus project grant no. 220 21 016. We thank Noelle Kist, Arvid Lepsien and Frederik Fonger for their valuable discussions on this work.

References

1. Bier, A., Jastrzebska, A., & Olszewski, P. (2022). Variable-length multivariate time series classification using ROCKET: A case study of incident detection. *IEEE Access, 10*, 95701–95715. https://doi.org/10.1109/ACCESS.2022.3203523
2. Dempster, A., Schmidt, D. F., & Webb, G. I. (2021). MiniRocket: A very fast (almost) deterministic transform for time series classification. In *Proceedings of the 27th ACM SIGKDD Conference on Knowledge Discovery & DM. KDD 21. Virtual Event* (pp. 248–257). ISBN: 9781450383325. https://doi.org/10.1145/3447548.3467231
3. Demrozi, F., et al. (2020). Human activity recognition using inertial, physiological and environmental sensors: A comprehensive survey. *IEEE Access, 8*, 210816-210836.
4. Gholamiangonabadi, D., Kiselov, N., & Grolinger, K. (2020). Deep neural networks for human activity recognition with wearable sensors: Leave-one-subject-out cross-validation for model selection. *IEEE Access, 8*, 133982–133994. https://doi.org/10.1109/ACCESS.2020.3010715
5. Huang, E. J., Yan, K., & Onnela, J. P. (2022). Smartphone-based activity recognition using multistream movelets combining accelerometer and gyroscope data. *Sensors*. https://doi.org/10.3390/s22072618
6. Jaccard, P. (1912). The distribution of the flora in the alpine zone. 1. *New Phytologist, 11*(2), 37-50.
7. Janssen, D., et al. (2020). Process model discovery from sensor event data. In *ICPM* (pp. 69–81). Springer.
8. Ke, S. R., et al. (2013). A review on video-based human activity recognition. In *Computers. Pre-processing IMU data for process mining using CNNs* (Vol. 2, No. 2, pp. 88–131).
9. Khowaja, S. A., et al. (2023). PROMPT: Process mining and paravector tensor-based physical health monitoring framework. *IEEE Sensors Journal, 23*(2), 989–996. https://doi.org/10.1109/JSEN.2022.3195613
10. Killick, R., Fearnhead, P., & Eckley, I. A. (2012). Optimal detection of changepoints with a linear computational cost. *Journal of the American Statistical Association, 107*(500), 1590–1598. https://doi.org/10.1080/01621459.2012.737745
11. Koschmider, A., et al. (2021). Demystifying noise and outliers in event logs: Review and future directions. In *BPM 2021 int. Workshops*, Revised Selected Papers (Vol. 436, pp. 123–135). LNBIP. Springer. https://doi.org/10.1007/978-3-030-94343-1_10
12. Koschmider, A., et al. (2023). Process mining for unstructured data: Challenges and research directions. arXiv preprint arXiv:2401.13677.
13. Lara, O. D., & Labrador, M. A. (2012). A survey on human activity recognition using wearable sensors. *IEEE Communications Surveys & Tutorials, 15*(3), 1192-1209.

14. Liu, Y., et al. (2016). From action to activity: Sensor-based activity recognition. *Neurocomputing, 181*, 108–115. https://doi.org/10.1016/j.neucom.2015.08.096
15. Mathe, S., Pirinen, A., & Sminchisescu, C. (2016). Reinforcement learning for visual object detection. In *Proceedings of the IEEE Conference on CVPR.*
16. Nweke, H. F., et al. (2018). Deep learning algorithms for human activity recognition using mobile and wearable sensor networks: State of the art and research challenges. *Expert Systems with Applications, 105*, 233–261. https://doi.org/10.1016/j.eswa.2018.03.056
17. Pham, C., & Olivier, P. (2009). Slice & Dice: Recognizing food preparation activities using embedded accelerometers. In Tscheligi, M. et al. *Ambient Intelligence* (pp. 34–43). ISBN: 978-3-642-05408-2.
18. Rizwan, I., Haque, I., & Neubert, J. (2020). Deep learning approaches to biomedical image segmentation. *Informatics in Medicine Unlocked, 18*, 100297. https://doi.org/10.1016/j.imu.2020.100297
19. Romijnders, R., et al. (2023). Ecological validity of a deep learning algorithm to detect gait events from real-life walking bouts in mobility-limiting diseases. *Frontiers in Neurology, 14*, 1247532.
20. Tan, C. W., et al. (2022). MultiRocket: Multiple pooling operators and transformations for fast and effective time series classification. *Data Mining and Knowledge Discovery, 36*(5), 1623–1646.
21. Tarantova, Y. S., Makarov, K. V., & Orlov, A. A., et al. (2019). Features selection for human activity recognition in the telerehabilitation system. In *Problems of Information Technology.* https://doi.org/10.25045/jpit.v10.i2.08
22. Warmerdam, E., et al. (2022). Full-Body mobility data to validate inertial measurement unit algorithms in healthy and neurological cohorts. *Data, 7*(10), 136. https://doi.org/10.3390/data7100136
23. Yuan, G., et al. (2019). An overview of human activity recognition based on smartphone. *Sensor Review, 39*(2), 288–306.
24. Zebin, T., et al. (2018). Human activity recognition from inertial sensor time-series using batch normalized deep LSTM recurrent networks. In *2018 40th annual international conference of the IEEE engineering in medicine and biology society (EMBC)* (pp. 1-4). https://doi.org/10.1109/EMBC.2018.8513115

Service Innovation, Engineering & Management

"Was This Answer Helpful?"—A Taxonomy for Feedback Mechanisms in Customer Service Chatbots

Daniel Schloss, Saskia Haug, and Alexander Maedche

Abstract Chatbot technology has rapidly spread, especially in digital customer service. However, the automation potential of chatbots can only be realized if customers are satisfied with their service. Collecting explicit feedback is a promising technique for assessing customer satisfaction and identifying issues with the chatbot. It enables chatbot managers and developers to enhance performance and design of operational chatbots on an informed basis. The evident significance of explicit customer feedback comes with a multitude of design options available. However, there is a lack of research on chatbot feedback mechanisms and practical as well as theoretical clarity. In this paper, we address this gap by introducing a chatbot feedback taxonomy derived from existing research and a sample of N = 72 real world customer service chatbots. Furthermore, based on a cluster analysis, we identify four archetypes of feedback mechanisms and provide strategic guidelines for the informed use of each of those feedback design variants.

1 Introduction

Chatbots have become an integral part of the customer service repertoire of organizations and institutions [1], accelerated by the recent technological advancements and popularity of the GPT models. For practitioners, such as customer service managers, who strive for a satisfactory but efficient digital service offering, it is essential to continuously monitor chatbots in operation and identify opportunities for improvement [2, 3]. Beyond log data like conversational transcripts, leveraging

D. Schloss (✉) · S. Haug · A. Maedche
Human-Centered Systems Lab, Karlsruhe Institute of Technology, Karlsruhe, Germany
e-mail: daniel.schloss@kit.edu

S. Haug
e-mail: saskia.haug@kit.edu

A. Maedche
e-mail: alexander.maedche@kit.edu

C. M. Flath et al. (eds.), *Digital Innovation and Organizational Transformation*, Lecture Notes in Information Systems and Organisation 83,
https://doi.org/10.1007/978-3-032-08483-5_9

explicit customer feedback is of particular value [4, 5]. Requesting feedback allows customers to articulate perceptions and opinions that might have remained hidden in the basic log data. With explicit feedback, customers can provide ratings, highlight issues, and propose improvements. Consequently, it is advisable to solicit feedback explicitly from customers using feedback mechanisms within customer service chatbots [3, 5]. However, the design of feedback mechanisms in chatbots has hardly been researched compared to the non-conversational web (e.g., [6]). Furthermore, explicit feedback mechanisms have particular characteristics, as the feedback can be embedded variously in the conversation. For example, the feedback wording could be more response-oriented ("Is this answer helpful?") or service-oriented ("How satisfied were you with my service?"). Other factors such as timing, initiation or survey design also vary. Yet there are always advantages and disadvantages associated with each feedback mechanism. One design may have a greater impact on the customer's user experience, while another may only lead to a smaller amount of feedback [4]. For this reason, in addition to usability heuristics and findings from general feedback research, decision-makers benefit from an overview and conceptual clarity [7, 8]. However, yet, there is no framework for chatbot feedback mechanisms though feedback can be valuable to understand and improve the customer experience and service quality [4, 9, 10]. For this reason, in this paper, we aim to answer the following research questions (RQ):

RQ1 Which explicit feedback mechanisms exist for customer service chatbots?

RQ2 How and according to which criteria can they be classified in a taxonomy?

Answering the RQ, in this paper we provide a taxonomy on feedback mechanisms for the collection of explicit feedback in customer service that is not only theoretically derived but also practically validated. To do so, we began reviewing related research on chatbots and user feedback (chapter 2). We then outlined the methodology for our taxonomy development project (chapter 3) [11]. Since chatbot feedback already is practically established but theoretically unaddressed, we chose an inductive approach for taxonomy development, collecting a sample of N = 72 customer service chatbots, which served as empirical data basis (chapter 4.1) [11]. Then, we iteratively developed the taxonomy by gradually adding and coding samples (chapter 4.2). We applied a clustering method to our taxonomy to identify relevant clusters in our sample (chapter 4.3). Ultimately, we were able to identify 4 chatbot feedback archetypes which we named and discussed based on existing research with regard to their characteristics and suitable applications (chapter 4.4). This paper concludes this study with a discussion, limitations and a research outlook (chapter 5).

2 Related Work

2.1 *Customer Service Chatbots*

Digital customer service is increasingly supported by automation through web-based chatbots, which have a task-oriented design [1, 12]. They can be found at the websites of service providers as in telecommunication, energy, finance, banking, insurance and mobility industry [13]. When users seek assistance from those, they expect precise and reliable information or transactions and ultimately task fullfillment [14–16]. For this purpose, an established approach is user intent classification (of the user request) via Natural Language Understanding (NLU) followed by an answer which is either retrieved from a database or generated via Natural Language Generation (NLG). Experts predict that hybrid models consisting of controllable NLU and NLG elements will become the standard in highly specialised contexts like customer service applications (Greyling, 2023; Von Straußenburg & Wolters, 2023). In addition to the natural language processing (NLP), customer experience is also shaped by dialog or frontend design or backend performance [17–19]. If it is negative, it casts a negative light on chatbot technology as well as the associated company [20]. Therefore, researchers have pointed out the importance of quality testing and criteria for chatbots early on [21, 22]. However, the majority of existing evaluation concepts, involving both experts and test users, focuses on the pre-deployment phase and controlled environments [22]. Due to their widespread adoption from 2016 onward, however, chatbots are required to demonstrate their effectiveness in daily operation [23, 24]. This can be supported by collecting explicit chatbot feedback in the field. On the one hand, it indicates performance and satisfaction, on the other hand, it is a pointer for weaknesses in the chatbot [4, 9, 16]. Since continuous monitoring and updating of chatbots is a critical success factor, chatbot feedback becomes part of product development [3, 21], either asynchronously or directly feedbacking AI training in the case of NLG chatbots [25, 26].

2.2 *Customer Feedback for Customer Service Chatbots*

In user feedback research, feedback is categorized according to explicitness, structure, initiation and valence. First, users or customers can provide *explicit* feedback by participating in surveys or reviews. *Implicitly*, they provide feedback through their actions, for example clicks or view times [27, 28]. In the case of chatbots, implicit feedback is available in the form of conversation log data, while our study focuses on explicit feedback which is often *structured* with (numerical) scales, thumbs or stars combined with an option for *unstructured* text input. While unstructured feedback is more time-consuming to analyze, it can offer greater insights for companies [27, 29]. Regarding *initiation* chatbot feedback provision may be a *passive* option (like a menu item), or the user is *actively* asked for feedback (“Was this response helpful?”)

[30]. Generally, active requests for feedback are often linked to a specific event, for example after a process has been completed ("How was your call quality?") and is known to have higher response rates than passive feedback, but interrupts customers in their task [8, 31]. Lastly, regarding valence, feedback can be negative, neutral or positive [32]. Unsatisfied customers are often more inclined to give feedback, which leads to a bias, yet negative feedback holds particular value [4, 33]. In chatbot literature, customer feedback is mentioned in the context of chatbot evaluation, but dedicated research on chatbot feedback design is scarce. However, it is a well-known problem that feedback in chatbots is rarely provided, response rates of 5% (passive to 18% (active have been observed [4, 16]. In the case of customer service chatbots, the incentives to provide feedback are low, since there is no opportunity to help others and no long-term usage [10, 34]. Nevertheless, customer service chatbots are well-suited for collecting customer feedback. On the one hand, they can leverage "in-app feedback mechanisms" and obtain situational feedback [5]. On the other hand, studies with dedicated feedback or interview chatbots have shown that requesting feedback via conversational interfaces has an engaging effect on users [10, 35, 36].

3 Method

The objective of this study was to develop a taxonomy for mechanisms to collect explicit feedback in customer service chatbots. Taxonomies can help to structure and organize the body of knowledge in a field, enabling researchers to study relationships and concepts [11, 37]. As Fig. 1 shows, we first examined related research literature (0). We then collected an empirical market sample consisting of 72 customer service chatbots (with 84 feedback mechanismus) of seven german service-oriented industries (1). Following an established methodology for taxonomy building [11], we set meta-characteristics and end conditions and iteratively developed dimensions and characteristics for the feedback mechanisms by repeatedly drawing a subset of our sample (2) [38, 39]. After the taxonomy was finalized, we statistically identified 4 clusters (3). In the next step, we defined and named the 4 general chatbot feedback archetypes we found (4). Finally, we discussed these archetypes regarding their suitability and applicability, deriving guidelines for feedback collection in customer service chatbots.

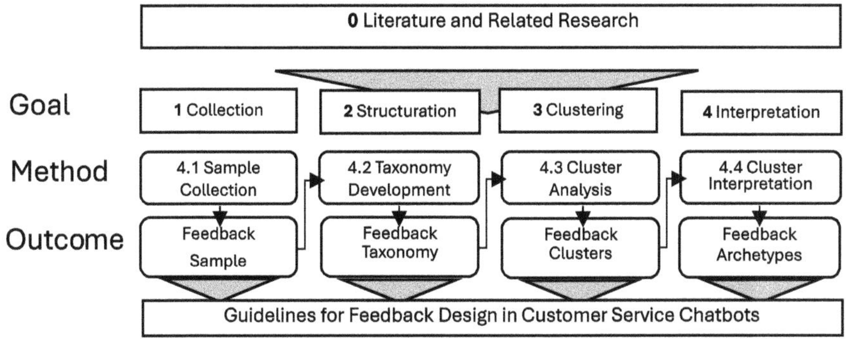

Fig. 1 Research method

4 A Taxonomy for Chatbot Feedback Mechanisms

4.1 Sample Collection

Having defined our research problem and goal, we collected chatbots with feedback mechanisms to form the sample of our targeted taxonomy. We focused on german service-oriented industries, namely energy and utilities, public administration, insurance, mobility, finance and banking, and telecommunications where the use of chatbots is typically worthwhile [16, 40]. We found a total of 79 chatbots across more than 200 website visits based on company registers. We excluded 7 chatbots which did not have any feedback mechanism. Of the remaining 72 chatbots, 34 were from energy and utilities, 11 from public administration, 11 from insurance companies, 7 from mobility and travel providers, 5 from financial institutions and 3 from the telecommunications sector. This distribution reflects the general presence of market participants, e.g. there are many more energy suppliers than telecommunications providers in germany and we do not expect any correlation between industry and feedback mechanisms. All companies are service providers that process typical customer service issues such as FAQ, bookings or cancellations [1]. Technologically, all of the chatbots in our sample used some kind of NLU-based intent classification and response retrieval, which was the market standard at the time of the sample collection (2023). All of them were supplemented with buttons for navigation and a partition included pre-defined multi step dialogs (23) or click paths (12, navigation without free text input). When collecting the sample, we noticed two interesting aspects: When we looked for the chatbot vendors, directly or via the embed code, we noticed that some companies had the same chatbot vendor or platform. This entails the risk of an imbalance in the sample and taxonomy [39, 41]. However, we found that, there were no major clusters, as the largest group were custom chatbots built in-house, see Fig. 2. Furthermore, we saw a broad spread of providers, a total of 24 plus 16 custom chatbots.

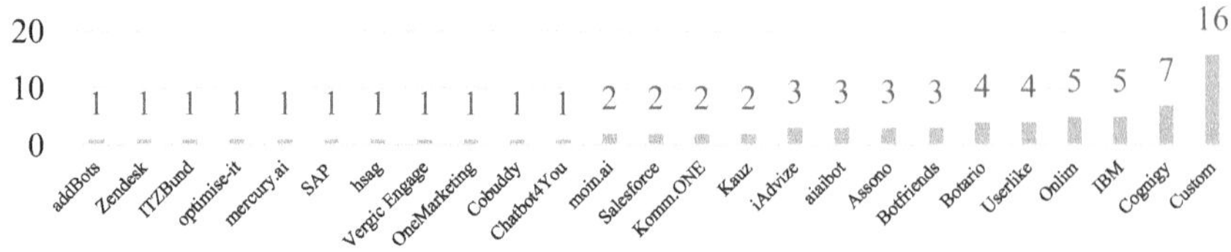

Fig. 2 Chatbot platforms and vendors in the chatbot sample

We could also detect that some chatbot platforms such as Cognigy offer several feedback mechanisms via in-house development, for example regarding feedback dialogs [42]. Additionally, some of the 72 chatbots had even more than one feedback mechanism within one interface. For example, one chatbot had a passive feedback item in the header of the chatbot interface but also actively asked customers whether their question had been answered. This led to a total of 84 samples to proceed.

4.2 Taxonomy Development

Building on [11], the first step in our taxonomy building was determining a meta-characteristic for the taxonomy, which is the basis for choosing *dimensions* and *characteristics* to include in the taxonomy. Our meta-characteristic to observe were the "feedback mechanisms in customer service chatbots." Next, we defined the following ending conditions under which the taxonomy development terminates:

- all chatbots in the sample have been examined
- at least one chatbot is classified under each characteristic of each dimension
- no dimensions or characteristics were added, merged or split in the last iteration
- every dimension is unique and not repeated
- every characteristic is unique and not repeated within its dimension

Having determined the ending conditions, there are two options to proceed. Researchers can decide to choose an empirical-to-conceptual, i.e., inductive, or an conceptual-to-empirical, i.e., deductive approach, depending on their data and domain knowledge [11]. Since we intended to use empirical samples to work inductively, we chose the empirical-to-conceptual approach in all our iterations. In this approach, a subset of samples that should be classified is chosen. This subset can be of random, convenient or systematic size [11]. We chose subsets of 2, 2, 1, 1, 1, 1, 11, 31 and 22 chatbots for the respective first to ninth iteration, which illustrates the gradual theoretical saturation [38]. In each iteration, we draw a subset of the feedback mechanisms and analyzed those individually among the three authors. The subsets were labeled and grouped independently and dimensions and characteristics in each dimension were individually defined. The assignment was then discussed: If a feedback mechanism was labeled differently or there were differences in the dimensions or characteristics, these were discussed in order to decide on a categorization for each mechanism and a final taxonomy variant. In order to avoid ambiguities regarding the preliminary taxonomy in any iteration, a coding guide was created and updated, detailing dimensions, characteristics and their differences with screenshots and examples. At the end of each iteration, the end conditions were checked. If they were not met, another iteration began, resulting in a new version of the taxonomy, possibly with dimensions or characteristics updated. After nine iterations, no dimensions or characteristics were added or altered, at least one object was classified under each characteristic of each dimension, and each of those characteristics and dimensions were unique and balanced [11].

The final taxonomy (see Table 1, next page) consists of the dimensions *Feedback Initiation, Feedback Access, Feedback Presentation, Feedback Structure, Pre-Labeling, Feedback Specificity* and *Feedback Scope.* The characteristics of all dimensions are exclusive, i.e. each chatbot feedback mechanism can only have one characteristic. The only exception is the *Feedback Structure*, as characteristics can be combined, e.g. when a scale and a free text field are used. Table 1 also shows at which iteration a dimension or characteristic was added (blue columns). Some characteristics were added while drawing further samples, others were formed on the basis of a differentiation of characteristics discussed by the authors. The first dimensions were created based on the user feedback literature (e.g. active vs. passive or feedback structure) and discussion of the authors guided by the overall sample data (e.g. [30]).

Our first defined dimension, *Feedback Initiation*, captures if feedback is actively or passively elicited (Sampson, 1996). Active initiation implies that the chatbot prompts the customer to provide feedback. This can be implemented within the chat or when closing the chatbot interface, for example. With passive initiation, the customer initiates the feedback e.g. by asking for a feedback option or clicking on UI elements. *Feedback Access* describes the situations in which a user can access the chatbot's feedback mechanism(s). At first we just divided between UI item access and system events but iteratively found more granular characteristics, the most common being the automatic display at the end of the conversation. This encompasses scenarios where the user him- or herself closes the chatbot as well as after predefined end events or timeouts. Another very common characteristic were feedback prompts after scripted multi-step dialogs. In this case, the feedback appears after completing a specific task, e.g. ordering a new credit card, allowing the user to provide feedback after ending the task dialog while the conversation can still continue [24]. The characteristic Top-level Item refers to a UI element located prominently at the top of the chatbot user interface, such as in the header bar, where feedback is accessed by clicking on the item. Similarly, the characteristic Menu Item describes a passive UI element, which can be accessed through a dropdown menu or similar UI elements. In-chat buttons after response are characteristic buttons (usually thumbs up/thumbs down) that are visible in the chat itself and usually located close to the text bubbles, i.e. responses, of the chatbot. Lastly, the characteristic Intent refers to feedback access via NLU-classification of messages like "i have a complaint" which was found distinct from second iteration.

Table 1 Final taxonomy

Dimension	Iteration	Characteristic	Iteration	N
Feedback Initiation	1	Active	1	44
		Passive	1	38
Feedback Access	1	End of conversation	3	23
		End of dialog	3	21
		Top-Level Item	8	15
		In-chat buttons after response	4	10
		Intent	2	10
		Menu Item	8	3
Feedback Presentation	2	Pop-Up Window	2	28
		In-chat buttons	6	26
		External Link	2	14
		Chat Widget	5	8
		Dialog	2	6
Feedback Structure	1	Scale	1	73
		Options	1	8
		Free Text	1	47
		Unstructured	2	8
Pre-Labeling	1	Pre-Labeling	1	61
		No Pre-Labeling	1	21
Feedback Specificity	4	Service Delivery	4	56
		Message Content	4	10
		Company	4	9
		Technology	8	1
		Unspecified	7	6
Feedback Scope	3	Conversation	3	44
		Dialog	3	20
		Single Response	4	10
		General	3	8

Feedback presentation characterizes the way the feedback items or surveys are presented to the customer. The characteristic Pop-Up Window refers to an overlay window within the chatbot covering the message interface. In-chat buttons are buttons directly below or on chat messages, while Chat widgets represent cards and forms located in between the chat messages. The characteristic Dialog implies the presentation of the feedback feature as a dialog, with the feedback survey having the same appearance as the normal chat. Lastly, the characteristic External Link denotes that the feedback feature is opened in a new browser tab or website. While the initial three dimensions primarily address the invocation and usability of feedback mechanisms in chatbots, the subsequent dimensions focus on the information captured and its context:

The *Feedback Structure* dimension refers to the form in which user feedback is captured, encompassing characteristics such as Scale (rating statements on a scale with two to n values), Options (choosing from non-numeric alternatives), Free text (providing textual input based on survey questions), and Unstructured (feedback without without specific survey questions). The *Pre-Labeling* dimension is binary and indicates whether the feedback query uses a form of pre-classification, e.g. complaint/suggestion or "I was not understood correctly" and "The information was insufficient". *Feedback Specificity* describes if the subject of the feedback is specified by the service provider. Given the formulation of feedback questions (e.g. "Do you like our service?") or feedback access, the feedback can relate more strongly to a single Message, overall Service Delivery, the chatbot Technology or the service Company. In instances where the relationship between feedback and these categories was undefined, the characteristic Unspecified was assigned. Conversely, the *Feedback Scope* dimension addresses the parts of the chatbot interaction that users refer to with their feedback. They may refer to the entire Conversation, specific Dialogs, Single Responses, or they may provide General Feedback, extending beyond the conversation. This broader feedback may prompt users to share their opinions on their overall service interaction with the company.

4.3 *Cluster Analysis*

The dimensions and characteristics found in our taxonomy can be used to describe the feedback collection in web-based customer service chatbots. However, each feedback mechanism is only described by the sum of its characteristics. Moreover, certain dimensions, for example feedback access and feedback scope, relate to each other. Therefore, the goal of this step was to find groups within the feedback sample that describe common combinations of the characteristics. If these can be determined, it is possible to abstract archetypes that can be used to structure the design knowledge on chatbot feedback [37]. In order to find those, a data-driven cluster analysis was conducted to form clusters in which the feedback mechanisms of one cluster are similar to each other while being dissimilar to others [43]. We used the K-mode clustering method, since it is particularly suitable for non-numeric, categorial data

[44]. In order to get a statistical indication for a reasonable K (number of clusters), we calculated the silhouette scores, a measure of cohesion and separation, for 2 to 10 clusters [45]. Given the results, we inspected the four-cluster and five-cluster solutions that showed the highest silhouette scores. Due to practical and statistical judgement we chose the four-cluster solution with a score of 0.37, showing the most interesting and plausible findings and correlations [46]. As Table 2 of the following chapter depicts given the distribution of our samples, a number of relationships become apparent with four chatbot feedback clusters. First, the different characteristics under the feedback access dimension can be clearly classified as to whether they occur along active or passive initiation. Additionally, the clusters are clearly split by feedback initiation and feedback access dimensions, as two clusters contain actively, the other two containing passively initiated feedback mechanisms.

Table 2 Frequency distribution of feedback dimensions and characteristics in 4 clusters

		Amount per cluster			
	Amount	Response-Prompted	Conversation-Prompted	Implicit Optional	Explicit Optional
Characteristics	**82**	**29**	**19**	**9**	**25**
Feedback initiation					
Active	44	25	19	0	0
Passive	38	4	0	9	25
Feedback access					
End of conversation	23	4	19	0	0
End of dialog	21	21	0	0	0
Intent	10	1	0	9	0
Top-level item	15	0	0	0	15
In-chat button after response	10	3	0	0	7
Menu item	3	0	0	0	3
Feedback presentation					
In-chat buttons	26	22	1	2	1
Chat widget	8	3	3	0	2
Dialog	6	3	2	1	0
Pop-Up Window	28	0	11	0	17
External Link	14	1	2	6	5
Feedback structure					
Scale	73	29	19	1	24
Options	8	2	3	1	2
Free text	47	5	17	1	24
Unstructured	8	0	0	8	0
Pre-labeling of feedback					
Pre-labeling	61	19	11	8	23
No pre-labeling	21	10	8	1	2
Feedback specificity					
Message content	10	3	0	0	7
Technology	1	0	0	0	1
Service delivery	56	26	18	1	11
Company	9	0	0	8	1
Unspecified	6	0	1	0	5
Feedback scope					
Single response	10	3	0	0	7
Sub-dialog	20	20	0	0	0
Conversation	44	6	19	1	18
General	8	0	0	8	0

4.4 Cluster Interpretation

The four clusters gained trough our taxonomy are shown in Table 2 in form of a sample distribution and are additionally visualized as chatbot interface examples in Fig. 3.

(1) The first cluster, the "Response-Prompted Feedback" archetype represents feedback mechanisms that are triggered when a dialog in the chatbot ends. This might be a response to a single question or the end of a multi-step dialog, but not the end of the entire conversation. The chatbot actively initiates the feedback process, e.g., by asking the user whether their goal was accomplished in a satisfactory manner. The user is provided with inputs in the form of buttons or scales that appear in the chat window among the other messages bubbles. The feedback is typically collected just in the chat interface. Due to the timing and the questions, the feedback is supposed to be provided with regards to the most recent dialog. The feedback questions of most samples in this cluster also focussed on the users' perceptions of the chatbot's performance.

(2) The second cluster, the "Conversation-Prompted Feedback" archetype is initiated by the chatbot as well. However, these feedback mechanisms are triggered once the entire conversation and the service delivery is finished, e.g. when the customer closes the chat or via a timeout. Instead of presenting the feedback

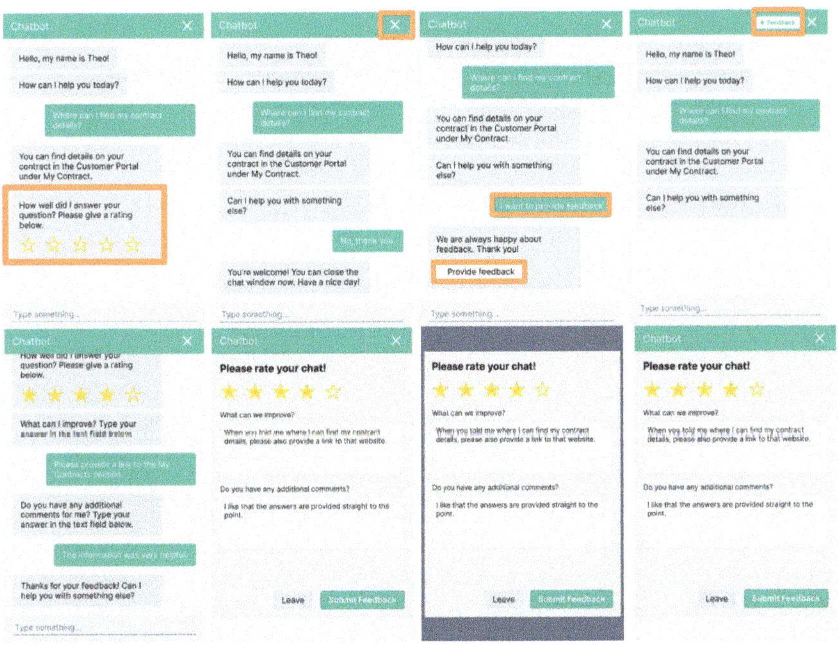

Fig. 3 Exemplary illustrations of the 4 feedback archetypes

between the chat messages, the feedback mechanisms in this cluster usually opt for a presentation in a new window that is laid over the chat window, having the user focus solely on the feedback form. These forms usually have both a rating scale and one or two questions that users have to answer by writing texts. The feedback is framed to address the service delivery of the chatbot. Instead of focusing on a specific dialog, this mechanisms prompts the user to think about the overall chat and service experience and the entire conversation.

(3) Unlike the previous two clusters, the feedback in the third cluster, the "Implicit Optional Feedback" is initiated by the user and not the chatbot [31]. These feedback designs are intent-based, meaning the chatbot uses NLU to detect intents or keywords like "feedback" or "complaint". Usually, when such an intent is detected, users receive a link to or can send an external contact form, e.g., the service company's general contact form. These forms often contain just a text input field for users to provide any feedback without being prompted to focus on the chatbot interaction. Accordingly, the feedback has a wider scope and is more related to the company.

(4) Lastly, the feedback mechanism of the fourth archetype, "Explicit Optional Feedback", is passive as well, meaning the user has to initiate the feedback process. This is done using a UI element, mostly located in the chatbot header, but also menu items or buttons belong to this cluster. While they often trigger the same feedback presentation, a feedback form overlaying the chat window or an external link, they are less visually prominent while the top-level item encourages or at least reminds the user to provide optional feedback. The feedback structure usually contains scales and free text fields, asking users to rate their experience and provide additional comments. The users therefore typically refer more to the chat experience then to specific events or the company.

5 Discussion

5.1 Guidelines for Chatbot Feedback Mechanisms

In this chapter, we discuss the special features and possible applications of chatbot feedback mechanisms, both in general and with reference to the results of our taxonomy and clustering. We then summarize our contributions and identify limitations and further research opportunities in the area of chatbot feedback.

As literature has shown, providing feedback is valuable for chatbot improvement, but often very scarce in the case of chatbots [4]. There is a general tendency for dissatisfied IS users to rather use (passive) feedback mechanisms to willingly provide feedback without being prompted [4, 33, 47]. This negative feedback is not reputationally damaging for service providers, as chatbot feedback is not publicly visible, but a bad chatbot is. On the other hand, non-public feedback means that the intrinsic motivation of feedback providers to help others is reduced [34]. However, the provision of feedback can be increased by actively prompting for feedback like more than 50% of our inspected chatbots did via Response- or Conversation-Prompted Feedback. Although this can annoy customers and impair the user experience, given that they only have very sporadic and short interactions with the chatbot anyway (3–4 turns), this does not weigh as heavily as being annoyed when using software on a daily basis (Schuetzler et al., 2019). The deterrence of feedback prompts in chatbots can also be reduced, as recommended by research, by introducing the feedback gradually and partially optionally, for example in a small click dialog without blocking the input field, instead of overwhelming the user immediately [19, 35, 36]. Nevertheless, when using active feedback mechanisms, chatbot managers should think about where feedback should be initiated. For example, the successful completion or the termination of pre-defined processes or dialogs is a good way to ask for feedback [19]. The end of a conversation, on the other hand, is always undefined within chatbots since users, aware of interacting with a machine, might simply close the browser tab instead of selecting a dedicated exit, as needed for the feedback mechanisms of cluster 2. Additionally, if, as 10 of the chatbots of our sample did, the feedback request is used undifferentiated, such as after every simple response ("Hello"—"Hi"), customers could be unnecessarily annoyed or the feedback could simply be completely unrelated to a real service task [48]. However, this is where the potential of chatbot feedback can be realized. With in-app feedback mechanisms, a connection to an IS, i.e. a chabot response, a conversation or a service process can be established, which is not possible with undifferentiated and general feedback forms [5]. Therefore, chatbot managers should be clear about the goal they are pursuing with the feedback: Do they want to identify dissatisfied customers? Do they want an evaluation of their services or company? Or do they explicitly want to improve the chatbot? The more the latter applies, the more the feedback initiation and structure must be visually and temporally linked to the actions of the chatbot. A typical example of this are the thumbs up/down buttons, which in some cases were completely undifferentiated clickable and did not trigger any further actions. For deploying NLG, like it can be seen in ChatGPT, however, the evaluation of AI generated responses can be a valuable feedback (in the future) to evaluate (or compare) the quality of responses with real users [25, 26]. However, such field test sets are more suited for chatbot developers than chatbot managers. If the latter are more interested in general feedback on the service and company, they can use the recognition of feedback intents (cluster 3 and the prominent placement of the passive feedback option (cluster 4. The specificity of the feedback received then depends above all on the feedback structure, scales and questions may narrow and guide the feedback, but also restrict the customer's expression [5, 49]. It is therefore advisable to combine easily analysable and relatable scales with free text. In general, we also found that some feedback mechanisms were mapped too little to the customer and too much to the chatbot developers, for example with regard to pre-labeling. Some chatbots suggested feedbacks such as "I was not understood" or "The answer did not help me", which are aimed at differentiating between NLU and knowledge base error, which the customer cannot necessarily follow.

5.2 *Limitations and Future Research*

In this paper we presented a taxonomy and a clustering that categorizes and explains feedback mechanisms of customer service chatbots based on literature and a real-world sample. We provide a theoretical structure for the knowledge on chatbot feedback and offer practical guidelines and orientation for feedback design, so chatbot managers can make informed decisions. Moreover, we equip researchers with a suitable framework for discussion and encourage for further research on chatbot feedback. Future research could broaden our context of task-oriented chatbots for customer service. Furthermore, we have focused on the specific channel of web- and text-based chatbots, while some of the findings of conversation-based feedback design apply to all media [10]. Finally, we have discussed the different feedback mechanisms only theoretically. Explicitly testing and comparing these feedback mechanisms in the field remains a precious and exciting possibility for future research. On top of that, our taxonomy is an intentional simplification that does not capture all real world manifestations. For example, even the choice of texts or emojis in the feedback initiation or survey structure alone could create differences in perceptions and feedback outcomes [50]. These or related aspects can be the subject of future research shedding light on the specifics of a chatbot feedback cluster or across different of our clusters.

References

1. De Keyser, A., Köcher, S., Alkire, L., Verbeeck, C., & Kandampully, J. (2019). Frontline Service Technology infusion: Conceptual archetypes and future research directions. *Journal of Service Management, 30*(1), 156–183.
2. Beaver, I., & Mueen, A. (2020). Automated conversation review to surface virtual assistant misunderstandings: Reducing cost and increasing privacy. *Proceedings of the AAAI Conference on Artificial Intelligence, 34*(8), 13140–13147.
3. Lewandowski, T., Heuer, M., Vogel, P., & Böhmann, T. (2022). Design knowledge for the lifecycle management of conversational agents, 17. Internationale Tagung Wirtschaftsinformatiok, Nürnberg. Proceedings.
4. Akhtar, M., Neidhardt, J., & Werthner, H. (2019). The potential of chatbots: Analysis of chatbot conversations. In *2019 IEEE 21st Conference on Business Informatics (CBI)* (pp. 397–404). IEEE.
5. Van Oordt, S., & Guzman, E. (2021). On the role of user feedback in software evolution: a practitioners' perspective. In *2021 IEEE 29th International Requirements Engineering Conference (RE)* (pp. 221–232). IEEE.
6. Fricker, R. D., & Schonlau, M. (2002). Advantages and disadvantages of internet research surveys: Evidence from the literature. *Field Methods, 14*(4), 347–367.
7. Nielsen, J. (1994). Enhancing the explanatory power of usability heuristics. In *CHI '94: Proceedings of the SIGCHI Conference on Human Factors in Computing Systems.*
8. Tizard, J., Rietz, T., & Blincoe, K. (2020). Voice of the users: A demographic study of software feedback behaviour. In *2020 IEEE 28th International Requirements Engineering Conference (RE)* (pp. 55–65). IEEE.

9. Pagano, D., & Bruegge, B. (2013). User involvement in software evolution practice: A case study. In *2013 35th International Conference on Software Engineering (ICSE)* (pp. 953–962). IEEE
10. Xiao, Z., Mennicken, S., Huber, B., Shonkoff, A., & Thom, J. (2021). Let me ask you this: How can a voice assistant elicit explicit user feedback? *Proceedings of the ACM on Human-Computer Interaction, 5*(CSCW2), 1–24.
11. Nickerson, R. C., Varshney, U., & Muntermann, J. (2013). A method for taxonomy development and its application in information systems. *European Journal of Information Systems, 22*(3), 336–359.
12. Schuetzler, R. M., Grimes, G. M., Giboney, J. S., & Rosser, H. K. (2021). Deciding whether and how to deploy chatbots. *MIS Quarterly Executive, 20*(1), 1–15.
13. Adamopoulou, E., & Moussiades, L. (2020). Chatbots: History, technology, and applications. *Machine Learning with Applications, 2*, Article 100006.
14. Brandtzaeg, P.B. and Følstad, A. (2017). Why people use chatbots. In I. Kompatsiaris, et al. (Eds.), *Internet Science*. Lecture Notes in Computer Science (pp. 377–392). Springer.
15. Grudin, J., & Jacques, R. (2019). Chatbots, humbots, and the quest for artificial general intelligence. In *Proceedings of the 2019 CHI Conference on Human Factors in Computing Systems* (pp. 1–11). ACM.
16. Kvale, K., Freddi, E., Hodnebrog, S., Sell, O. A., & Følstad, A. (2021). Understanding the user experience of customer service chatbots: What can we learn from customer satisfaction surveys? In A. Følstad, T. Araujo, S. Papadopoulos, E. L.-C. Law, E. Luger, M. Goodwin, & P. B. Brandtzaeg (Eds.), *Chatbot Research and Design*. Lecture Notes in Computer Science (pp. 205–218). Springer.
17. Gao, M., Liu, X., Xu, A., & Akkiraju, R. (2021). Chatbot or chat-blocker: Predicting chatbot popularity before deployment. In *Designing interactive systems conference 2021* (pp. 1458–1469). Virtual Event USA: ACM.
18. Li, T.J.-J., Chen, J., Xia, H., Mitchell, T. M., & Myers, B. A. (2020). Multi-modal repairs of conversational breakdowns in task-oriented dialogs. In *Proceedings of the 33rd Annual ACM Symposium on User Interface Software and Technology* (pp. 1094–1107). Virtual Event USA: ACM.
19. Zierau, N., Hausch, M., Bruhin, O., & Söllner, M. (2020). Towards developing trust-supporting design features for AI-based chatbots in customer service. In *ICIS Proceedings* (pp. 1–9).
20. Meyer-Waarden, L., Pavone, G., Poocharoentou, T., Prayatsup, P., Ratinaud, M., Tison, A., & Torné, S. (2020). How service quality influences customer acceptance and usage of chatbots? *Journal of Service Management Research, 4*(1), 35–51.
21. Janssen, A. H. A., Grützner, L., & Breitner, M. H. (2021). Why do chatbots fail? A critical success factors analysis. In *ICIS* (p. 18).
22. Maroengsit, W., Piyakulpinyo, T., Phonyiam, K., Pongnumkul, S., Chaovalit, P., & Theeramunkong, T. (2019). A survey on evaluation methods for chatbots. In *Proceedings of the 2019 7th International Conference on Information and Education Technology*. (pp. 111–119). ACM.
23. Dale, R. (2016). The return of the chatbots. *Natural Language Engineering, 22*(5), 811–817.
24. Følstad, A., & Taylor, C. (2021). Investigating the user experience of customer service chatbot interaction: A framework for qualitative analysis of chatbot dialogues. *Quality and User Experience, 6*(1), 6.
25. OpenAI. (2023). https://chat.openai.com/chat. Retrieved November 10, 2023.
26. Ricciardelli, E., & Biswas, D. (2019). *Self-improving chatbots based on reinforcement learning*.
27. Ordenes, F. V., Theodoulidis, B., Burton, J., Gruber, T., & Zaki, M. (2014). Analyzing customer experience feedback using text mining: A linguistics-based approach. *Journal of Service Research, 17*(3), 278–295.
28. Poblete, B., & Baeza-Yates, R. (2008). Query-sets: using implicit feedback and query patterns to organize web documents. In *Proceedings of the 17th international conference on World Wide Web* (pp. 41–50). ACM.
29. Witell, L., Kristensson, P., Gustafsson, A., & Löfgren, M. (2011). Idea generation: Customer co-creation versus traditional market research techniques. *Journal of Service Management, 22*(2), 140–159.

30. Wirtz, J., & Tomlin, M. (2000). Institutionalising customer-driven learning through fully integrated customer feedback systems. *Managing Service Quality: An International Journal, 10*(4), 205–215.
31. Sampson, S. E. (1998). Gathering customer feedback via the Internet: Instruments and prospects. *Industrial Management & Data Systems, 98*(2), 71–82.
32. Van Doorn, J., Lemon, K. N., Mittal, V., Nass, S., Pick, D., Pirner, P., & Verhoef, P. C. (2010). Customer engagement behavior: Theoretical foundations and research directions. *Journal of Service Research, 13*(3), 253–266.
33. Nasr, L., Burton, J., Gruber, T., & Kitshoff, J. (2014). Exploring the impact of customer feedback on the well-being of service entities: A TSR perspective. *Journal of Service Management, 25*(4), 531–555.
34. Hennig-Thurau, T., Gwinner, K. P., Walsh, G., & Gremler, D. D. (2004). Electronic word-of-mouth via consumer-opinion platforms: What motivates consumers to articulate themselves on the Internet? *Journal of Interactive Marketing, 18*(1), 38–52.
35. Han, X., Zhou, M., Turner, M., & Yeh, T. (2021). Designing effective interview chatbots: Automatic chatbot profiling and design suggestion generation for chatbot debugging. In *Proceedings of the 2021 CHI Conference on Human Factors in Computing Systems* (pp. 1–15).
36. Te Pas, M. E., Rutten, W. G. M. M., Bouwman, R. A., & Buise, M. P. (2020). User experience of a chatbot questionnaire versus a regular computer questionnaire: Prospective comparative study. *JMIR Medical Informatics, 8*(12), Article e21982.
37. Glass, R. L., & Vessey, I. (1995). Contemporary application-domain taxonomies. *IEEE Software, 12*(4), 63–76.
38. Glaser, B. G., & Strauss, A. L. (1999). *The discovery of grounded theory: Strategies for qualitative research.* Routledge.
39. Strauss, A. L., & Corbin, J. M. (1998). *Basics of qualitative research: Techniques and procedures for developing grounded theory* (2nd ed.). Sage Publications.
40. Fitzsimmons, J. A., & Fitzsimmons, M. J. (2011). *Service management: Operations, strategy, information technology* (7th ed.). McGraw-Hill.
41. Lin, W.-C., Tsai, C.-F., Hu, Y.-H., & Jhang, J.-S. (2017). Clustering-based undersampling in class-imbalanced data. *Information Sciences, 409–410*, 17–26.
42. Strohmann, T., Khosrawi-Rad, B., Schmidt, L., & Hiske, P. (2023). *AI-based technologies for conversational agent design– development tools and architectures for intelligent interactions.*
43. Kaufman, L., & Rousseeuw, P. J. (1990). *Finding groups in data: An introduction to cluster analysis* (1st ed.). Wiley.
44. Chaturvedi, A., Green, P. E., & Caroll, J. D. (2001). K-modes clustering. *Journal of Classification, 18*(1), 35–55.
45. Rousseeuw, P. J. (1987). Silhouettes: A graphical aid to the interpretation and validation of cluster analysis. *Journal of Computational and Applied Mathematics, 20*, 53–65.
46. Balijepally, V., Mangalaraj, G., Iyengar, K., & Prairie, V. (2011). Are we wielding this hammer correctly? A reflective review of the application of cluster analysis in information systems research. *Journal of the Association for Information Systems, 12*(5), 375–413.
47. Baumeister, R., Bratslavsky, E., Finkenauer, C., & De Vohs, K. (2001). Bad is stronger than good. *Review of General Psychology, 5*(4), 323–370.
48. Wang, R. Y., & Strong, D. M. (1996). Beyond accuracy: What data quality means to data consumers. *Journal of Management Information Systems, 12*(4), 5–33.
49. Haug, S., Benke, I., & Maedche, A. (2023). Aligning crowdworker perspectives and feedback outcomes in crowd-feedback system design. *Proceedings of the ACM on Human-Computer Interaction, 7*(CSCW1), 1–28.
50. Alismail, S., & Zhang, H. (2018). The use of emoji in electronic user experience questionnaire: An exploratory case study. In *Proceedings of the 51st Hawaii International Conference on System Sciences.*
51. Ashfaq, M., Yun, J., Yu, S., & Loureiro, S. M. C. (2020). I, Chatbot: Modeling the determinants of users' satisfaction and continuance intention of AI-powered service agents. *Telematics and Informatics, 54*, Article 101473.

52. Barki, H., & Hartwick, J. (1991). User participation and user involvement in information system development. In *Proceedings of the Twenty-Fourth Annual Hawaii International Conference on System Sciences* (pp. 487–492). IEEE Comput. Soc. Press.
53. Damodaran, L. (1996). User involvement in the systems design process-a practical guide for users. *Behaviour & Information Technology, 15*(6), 363–377.
54. Gopinath, K., & Kasilingam, D. (2023). Antecedents of intention to use chatbots in service encounters: A meta-analytic review. *International Journal of Consumer Studies., 47*(6), 2367–2395.
55. Gould, J. D., & Lewis, C. (1985). Designing for usability: Key principles and what designers think. *Communications of the ACM, 28*(3), 300–311.
56. Harris, M. A., & Weistroffer, H. R. (2009). A new look at the relationship between user involvement in systems development and system success. *Communications of the Association for Information Systems, 24*(1), 42.
57. Kujala, S. (2003). User involvement: A review of the benefits and challenges. *Behaviour & Information Technology, 22*(1), 1–16.
58. McKeen, J. D., & Guimaraes, T. (1997). Successful strategies for user participation in systems development. *Journal of Management Information Systems, 14*(2), 133–150.
59. Pagano, D., & Maalej, W. (2013). User feedback in the appstore: An empirical study. In: *2013 21st IEEE International Requirements Engineering Conference (RE)* (pp. 125–134). IEEE.
60. Sommerville, I. (2011). *Software engineering* (9th ed.). Pearson.

Characterizing the Roles of AI-Enabled Non-Human Agents in Service Systems

Matthäus Wilga, Layla Hajjam-Demir, Nina Lugmair, Martin Schymanietz, and Angela Roth

Abstract Machines are becoming more versed at adapting to environmental impulses and their operational contexts, changing their roles in service systems. These machines can autonomously fulfill goals within defined boundaries set by legal actors and thereby exhibit agency. As interactions are at the core of services, the integration of such non-human agents into value co-creation has the potential to heavily impact the innovation of services. Following a four-step type construction approach based on empirical open-source data on 130 services, we develop a multi-dimensional characterization of six roles that non-human agents fulfill in service systems. Taking a systemic perspective, we identify service system interactions involving non-human agents and how their contributions impact value propositions. Our findings forward the understanding of service processes involving non-human agents and their impact on value co-creation, benefiting both theory and practice through knowledge on the engineering of service systems and value-driven, user-centered human–machine interactions.

M. Wilga (✉) · L. Hajjam-Demir · N. Lugmair · M. Schymanietz · A. Roth
Chair of Information Systems, Innovation and Value Creation, Friedrich-Alexander-Universität Erlangen-Nürnberg, Nürnberg, Germany
e-mail: matthaeus.wilga@fau.de

L. Hajjam Demir
e-mail: layla.hajjam-demir@fau.de

N. Lugmair
e-mail: nina.lugmair@fau.de

M. Schymanietz
e-mail: martin.schymanietz@fau.de

A. Roth
e-mail: angela.roth@fau.de

C. M. Flath et al. (eds.), *Digital Innovation and Organizational Transformation*, Lecture Notes in Information Systems and Organisation 83,
https://doi.org/10.1007/978-3-032-08483-5_10

1 Introduction

Service systems, characterized as dynamic configurations of actors, technologies, and other resources interacting to realize value [1], undergo an evolution through the advent of AI-enabled machines as novel entities. AI-enabled technologies encompass both existing systems improved through the introduction of AI, commonly termed AI-enhanced, and entirely new systems developed with AI from the outset, commonly termed AI-based [2]. The integration of AI creates a pivotal change, as it endows machines with the capability to interact with their environment and autonomously adjust their actions based on external stimuli [3–6]. Growth in these AI interaction capabilities stems from progress in machine learning, which empowers machines to discern intricate patterns within data on social interactions [7] and facilitates the capturing of tacit knowledge, which is fundamental to human interactions but challenging to code explicitly [8]. Moreover, the integration of conversational interfaces based on Natural Language Processing and Generative AI has further transformed interactions with machines [9]. These collective advancements in the field of AI distinguish novel, AI-enabled interactive technologies from ordinary data-driven ones and catalyze the genesis of a new entity in service systems, referred to in this paper as AI-enabled non-human agents.

The capability to adaptively interact with their surroundings allows non-human agents to assume new roles in the co-creation of value and facilitates novel configurations of service systems [10]. When positioned within a system of actors, these capabilities enable technologies to exhibit agency, i.e. autonomous action in the pursuit of goals within a solution space defined by rules, norms and institutions through the concurrent interaction with and influencing of other actors in socio-technical systems [3, 4]. The advent of interactive AI-enabled technologies consequently demands novel abstractions and conceptual frameworks to characterize the contribution of non-human agents within the dynamics of value co-creation interactions in service contexts [4, 10–13].

The orchestration of the complex interplay between non-human agents and human actors is forwarded as the "key managerial issue of our time " [14], p. 1440, holding potential for profound impact on value co-creation [12] but also carrying the risk of harmful unintended consequences [15, 16]. Beck et al. [3] therefore encourage studies to gain a better understanding of the various forms of non-human agents and potential consequences of their introduction for individuals and firms. Seeber et al. [5] explicitly call for a typification of non-human agents to enhance the structured description of their facets, which can benefit their effective implementation in organizations. Although research has examined the roles of physical robots or digital assistants (e.g. [17, 18]), a comprehensive characterization of roles fulfilled by non-human agents in service system interactions and how they are integrated into such interactions is yet to be established. To address these research gaps, we pose the research question *"What roles do AI-enabled non-human agents fulfill in service systems?"*. We approach this research question by systematically analyzing empirical data on 130 services involving AI-enabled non-human agents obtained from the database Crunchbase.

2 Theoretical Background

2.1 *Service Systems*

The effective utilization of AI-enabled solutions goes beyond a fine-tuned algorithm or flooding data pipeline and has to consider the embedment and interplay of a solution with its social context [14]. A narrow focus on technical aspects critically underestimates the complexity and interdependencies involved in AI-enabled value co-creation, as value is increasingly co-created in dynamically changing actor configurations, commonly described with the terms service systems or service ecosystems [19]. A systemic perspective, like the one of service systems [1, 20], is therefore necessary to examine the role of adaptive, interactive technologies, i.e. non-human agents, in value co-creation. Service systems are socio-technical systems with a complex, dynamic interplay of human actors, technologies, and their environment to achieve specific outcomes [21]. These systems are conceptualized as sequenced ensembles of nine generic relations formed between humans, non-human agents and organizations in expectation of functional contributions [4]. To enhance comprehension, such systems can be further broken down into modular components [22]. In this realm, services can be decomposed into modularized service processes [23], with each module being specified by a clear functionality [24]. Traditionally, technologies have been rather seen as passive resources being used by actors to facilitate the co-creation of value [25]. Given recent technological advances, a wider array of service processes can be performed by AI-enabled non-human agents, giving rise to the concept of AI service modules [26]. Consequently, as the nature of activities non-human agents perform in AI service modules and how they are integrated into service system interactions remain open questions, in this study, we concentrate on elucidating the reciprocal relation between human actors and non-human agents. The delineation of non-human agent roles, which capture expected contributed activities [27], creates a framework for understanding complementary interactions between people, technologies and their environment and offers knowledge for the engineering, management, and innovation of service systems.

2.2 *Non-Human Agents*

Research on AI solutions as non-human agents in socio-technical systems is nascent and a common term for the phenomenon has yet to be established [28]. Research often refers to the underlying technological object, with labels such as *intelligent agents* (e.g., [37, 29]), *AI agents* [30], *technological agents* [31], or simply *algorithms* [32]. Other researchers delineate the overall phenomenon, *technological agency* [4] or *service AI* [15], or the researched activity, as with *algorithmic management* (e.g., [33, 34]). We use the term non-human agents, as it is technology-agnostic, omits misleading terms like autonomy and, through reference to agency, reflects a link to a responsible legal actor.

A clear delineation of attributes characterizing non-human agents is crucial to determine services in scope for analysis in this study. Although no consensus on the definition of non-human agents exists, an examination of recurring themes in literature on this topic can yield defining attributes. We will discuss commonalities along four fundamental characteristics of non-human agents forwarded by Dhiman et al. [35] and Russel and Norvig [36], which should not be considered as finite: Non-human agents (i) act upon their environment in an (ii) autonomous fashion (iii) without outside intervention for a certain time to (iv) pursue a goal. A prime unifying aspect is the described ability of non-human agents to adapt activities based on impulses from the environment [7, 11, 15, 35–39], Knote et al. [18]. A condition specifying this attribute is that the adaption of actions shall happen over a longer time or many interactions without the direct intervention of a designer or legal entity responsible for the non-human agent [3, 11, 35, 36]. We follow [37] that non-human agents can draw the inferences guiding their adaptive activities either from a static knowledge base or, as forwarded in stricter characterizations (e.g. [7, 35]), from an evolving knowledge base, modified by a backend learning from previous interactions. Other technologies have actuation capabilities as well, but rule-based, non-adaptive ones. Hence, the key distinction of non-human agents, and basis for discussions about their perceived autonomy, is that their activities are tailored to interactions with changing actors or changing contexts [3, 6, 39]. However, autonomy is a misleading term, as non-human agents only act autonomously within rules and contexts predefined by a legal actor responsible for it [3]. The condition that non-human agents require a liable legal actor, setting goals and boundaries for possible activities, is forwarded by a range of authors [4, 11, 35], hence can be interpreted as another defining aspect.

Taking into account the presented arguments, we establish a working definition for non-human agents by slightly adapting the attributes of Dhiman et al. [35] and Russel and Norvig [36]: Non-human agents interact with other service system entities and adapt their actions based on stimuli from humans, machines or the environment. Over longer periods of time or several interactions, they decide on activities to pursue a goal without the direct intervention of a responsible legal actor. Non-human agents perform actuations within a realm of boundaries preset by a designer or legal actor responsible for it, which represents an indirect intervention limiting the array of possible activities.

2.3 Roles of Non-Human Agents

Roles capture anticipated activities or contributions that an entity is expected to provide a system [27]. Research on non-human agent roles has been conducted in adjacent fields with different objectives. One academic discourse describes roles to aid the design and management of organizational settings involving non-human agents. Alter [28] offers frameworks to describe and evaluate functional non-human agent roles with regards to their suitability to perform various facets of work. Bittner et al. [40] and [41] outline roles for the subset of conversational agents to illustrate design options for non-human agents and modes of integration into the specific setting of collaborative teams. Another academic discourse probes how interactions with non-human agents and their functional contributions impact value co-creation. [18] do not provide roles, but identify five clusters of intelligent personal assistants, a subset of non-human agents, and link them to affordances they provide for value co-creation. However, the authors point out a limited data set and encourage research with a wider array of observations. For the context of elderly care, [17] use roles to categorize various forms of non-human agents based on their value co-creation and co-destruction potential. Concludingly, current research is conceptual [28] or literature-based and augmented with a sample of practical cases [18] or validated with experts [40]. Čaić et al. [17] base their findings on empirical data gathered in an artificial setting for hypothetical scenarios, which is common for studies on value co-creation involving non-human agents [42]. We aim to extend this research, which concentrates on specific settings and hardly covers real-world interactions with non-human agents, by providing a comprehensive analysis of non-human agent roles, grounded in empirical data, to reflect the status quo of commercially-available non-human agents and illustrate their integration into service system interactions as well as proposed value for interaction partners.

3 Research Approach

This study aims to uncover roles of non-human agents in interactions with other service system entities and how these interactions contribute to underlying value propositions. Typologies commonly serve to categorize individual observations by identifying shared characteristics [43] and roles represent a specific kind of types, which involve categorizing entities based on the expected activities or contributions they bring to a system [27]. Types provide valuable analytical advantages in service research, aiding the organization, comparison, and communication of research findings [44]. The roles in this study have been constructed in a desk-research approach, following four steps for the empirically grounded construction of types in qualitative research [45]: (1) developing relevant dimensions for analysis, (2) grouping cases, (3) constructing types, and (4) characterizing the constructed types.

In step (1), relevant dimensions for the analysis of empirical cases are established before data collection [45]. This study draws on the service systems perspective [1, 20], hence the initial analytical dimensions mainly revolve around the nature of different interactions non-human agents are involved in, coded based on the interaction dimensions for human-AI interaction [46], and their expected contribution to the co-creation of value.

In Step (2), cases are assigned to these dimensions and grouped along similar combinations of attributes [45]. The sample comprises services with non-human agents, i.e. AI-enabled technologies with the capability to adjust their conduct depending on the context of their interactions with humans, machines, or the environment. The sample is limited to digital non-human agents, falling into the category of virtual service robots [47], and focus on services for English-speaking users. While AI has historically been explored predominantly in academia, industry now plays a pivotal role in advancing and applying AI [11]. Consequently, this study uses data on commercially-available services instead of relying on literature sources. An initial sample was retrieved from Crunchbase, which constitutes a recognized practice in research on management and information systems (e.g., [48–50]), as it provides a comprehensive database on firms and their offerings. The search string combines common attributes describing non-human agents or its base technology (intelligent, autonomous, artificial intelligence and AI) with instantiations of digital technologies (agent, application and service), leading to twelve initial word pairs. Discussions of the search string at an international research seminar prompted advice to add the terms autonomous system and autonomous software as well as combinations of bot/bots and AI or machine learning, leading to the formation of a second search string. The first search string has contained these phrases: *"autonomous system"; "autonomous agent"; "autonomous software"; "autonomous application"; "autonomous service"; "intelligent agent"; "intelligent application"; "intelligent service"; "artificial intelligence agent"; "artificial intelligence application"; "artificial intelligence service"; "AI agent"; "AI application"; "AI service"*. The second search string was run with this syntax: *"bot" OR "bots" AND "artificial intelligence" or "machine learning"*. The search in August 2023 yielded 1004 unique companies. Crunchbase data was augmented with data from ancillary sources, including firm websites, journalistic reports, developer documentation, customer stories, social media posts and press releases. Data analysis was conducted in a rigorous multi-phase coding process to ensure accuracy, depth in the qualitative analysis and intercoder reliability. In the first phase, three researchers scrutinized these data sources to determine whether sampled companies offer a service involving an AI-enabled adaptive non-human agent fitting our working definition, which left 237 companies in scope. Common reasons for exclusion included firms not offering a solution involving an AI-enabled digital non-human agent, insufficient public information on coding dimensions defined in step (1), firms or websites no longer being operational, or information not being available in English. In another round of scrutiny, in-depth information on each service was collected until saturation was achieved [51] and three researchers examined in more detail whether the remaining services fit the sample criteria, reducing the final sample to 130 services from 99 companies. 48% of non-human agents are customer-facing, 42% for employees and 10% marketed as adaptable for both internal and external use. Most non-human agents are integrated into customer service and sales operations. However, analyzed non-human agents also contribute to IT development or human resource, legal, educational, and marketing activities. In the second coding process phase, data was coded in MAXQDA in two coding cycles. Initially, descriptive coding [52] was used to summarize the essence of passages with information on the coding dimensions defined in step (1: functional contributions, interaction partner value, integration type and links to other service system entities. An illustrative anchor example offers the passage "We empower your team to provide personalized and efficient support with generative AI, raising the bar for excellence in customer service [19AA5, Parloa]", which was described with 1st order code Interaction partner value and 2nd order code Efficiency (cf. coding scheme in Table 1).

Step (3) involves constructing types from groups with similar combinations of attributes. This step marks the final phase of the coding process and was performed

Table 1 Coding scheme with 1st and 2nd order codes and frequencies of roles in the sample

1st order code	2nd order code	IP	Con	Gen	Coa	Adv	AM
Functional contribution	Individual information	X					
	Task fulfillment		X				X
	Resource generation			X			
	Capability development				X		
	Behavior change advice					X	
Interaction partner value	Availability	X	X		X		
	Efficiency	X	X	X		X	X
	Effectiveness			X	X	X	
	Well-being				X		
Type of integration	Assistance	X	X	X			
	Augmentation				X	X	
	Automation						X
Interaction impulse	Human	X	X	X	X		X
	Non-human agent					X	
Action direction	Human	X	X	X	X	X	X
	Machine (Database/ Automation)	X	X				
Percentage of roles in the sample		40	24	10	6	5	15

using pattern coding, a method commonly applied after descriptive coding to identify commonalities and variations in data [52]. As roles capture expected contributions of an entity to a system [27], the construction of roles primarily focused on identifying patterns of services where non-human agents provide similar functional contributions. Initially, eight patterns of functional contributions to service system interactions were identified. Four functional contribution patterns were realized through distinctive interaction processes, hence were translated into the roles Information Provider, Generator, Coach and Algorithmic Manager. The functional contribution pattern pairs "Recommendation" and "Behavior change advice" as well as "Self-service enablement" and "Task fulfillment" were realized through similar interaction processes, hence the primary ones were integrated into the latter, more frequently observed ones, and eventually translated into the respective roles Advisor and Concierge. This condensed the sample to six roles, each characterized by a distinct combination of functional contribution and interaction process. The construction of roles was performed in discussions of three researchers, to ensure investigator triangulation [53] and internal homogeneity [45] of non-human agents grouped into respective roles.

Step (4) entails the communication of constructed types based on the identified combinations of attributes [45]. We present these findings in a multi-dimensional characterization of non-human agent roles in service interactions in the next section.

4 Results

We identified six roles non-human agents fulfill in service systems and characterize them by outlining their mode of integration into service systems, typical interactions with other service system entities and how these interactions are expected to contribute to the realization of proposed value. Three roles are expected to provide assistance to human actors: (A) Information Provider, (B) Concierge and (C) Generator. Two roles are expected to perform augmentation to human capabilities: (D) Coach and (E) Advisor. The sixth and final role is expected to automate processes in interactions between human actors: (F) Algorithmic Manager. Figure 1 and the ensuing paragraphs illustrate the integration of non-human agents in these six roles into service system interactions.

(A) Information Providers offer relevant or personalized information in an answer to a human query. In essence, non-human agents in this role assist human actors in accessing relevant information stored in external databases. Common use cases in our sample are, in the context of customer-facing interactions, the resolution of customer service inquiries or provision of personalized offerings, or, in internal organizational settings, responses to inquiries from employees regarding, for example, employment terms and conditions. The typical service system interaction described in connection to this role is (A1) a human actor giving the interaction impulse by inquiring for information with a textual or

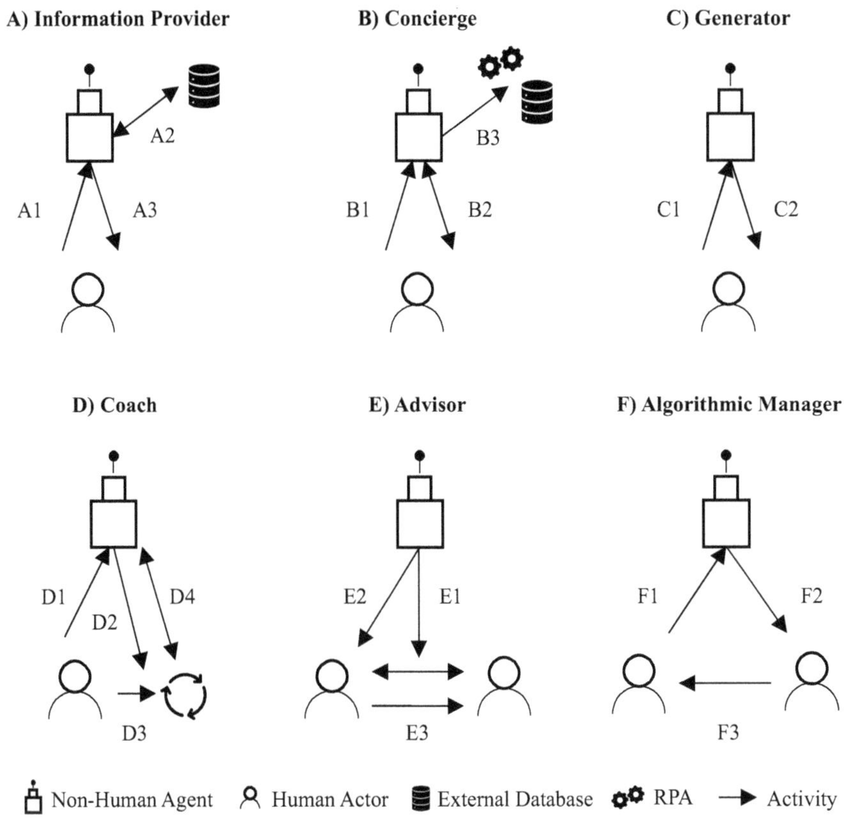

Fig. 1 Identified service system interactions of non-human agents

verbal directive and (A2) the non-human agent perceiving the intent of an inquiry and drawing on its knowledge-base or connected databases to (A3) provide relevant or personalized information adapted to the human inquiry. The objective of human actors to engage in this service system interaction is the reception of information. The primary proposed added value of the integration of a non-human agent in the Information Provider role for the human interaction partner is constant availability and efficiency, i.e. reduced contribution of own effort to receive desired information.

(B) The Concierge triggers automations to satisfy a perceived need of a human actor. In essence, non-human agents in this role assist human actors in triggering other machines for the fulfillment of tasks. Common use cases in our sample are the scheduling of appointments or processing of account operations, such as bank transactions. The typical service system interaction described in connection to this role is (B1) a human actor textually or verbally giving the interaction impulse by directing the non-human agent to solve a task, (B2) the non-human agent obtaining the necessary information for the fulfillment of this task and

(B3) subsequently performing a manipulation to a database or triggering a robotic process automation (RPA) to finalize the underlying task. The objective of human actors to engage in this service system interaction is to have a specific task fulfilled. The primary proposed added value of the integration of a non-human agent in the Concierge role for the human interaction partner is constant availability and efficiency, i.e. less own effort required to obtain a desired result.

(C) Generators produce content following a human directive. In essence, non-human agents in this role assist human actors in generating or adapting resources. Common use cases in our sample are the generation of text, visual media items and designs, or computer code. The typical service system interaction described in connection to this role is (C1) a human actor giving the interaction impulse by textually directing the non-human agent to generate content with specific attributes, in so called prompts, and (C2) the non-human agent generating the digital resource. The human actor can adapt the generated content or use it as it is for further actions. The objective of human actors to engage in this service system interaction is to receive a desired digital resource. The primary proposed added value of the integration of a non-human agent in the Generator role for the human interaction partner is efficiency, i.e. the creation of a digital resource with less contribution of own efforts, or effectiveness, i.e. at a higher quality than the human can produce with its own capabilities.

(D) Coaches suggest behavioral change and exercises or personalize learning units for personal development. In essence, non-human agents in this role augment human actors in the fulfillment of a desired activity. Common use cases in our sample are the support through adapted cognitive exercises or psychological approaches. The typical service system interaction described in connection to this role is (D1) a human actor giving the interaction impulse by textually or verbally setting a goal or articulating an issue to be solved, for example reaching a language proficiency level or well-being through stress relief. (D2) The non-human agent subsequently creates exercises or approaches adapted to this set directive, with (D3) the human counterpart executing the suggested exercise or approach while (D4) being accompanied by the non-human agent, which provides corrective guidance or solutions as needed. The objective of human actors to engage in this service system interaction is to improve their proficiency in performing specific actions and develop certain capabilities. The primary proposed added value of the integration of a non-human agent in the Coach role for the human interaction partner is constant availability, increased well-being and effectiveness, i.e. superior performance in certain actions compared to what the human actor can achieve solely with their existing skills or knowledge.

(E) Advisors suggest behavioral change to human actors in interactions with other human actors in the professional context. In essence, non-human agents in this role augment humans and their capabilities through advice for better task performance. Common use cases in our sample are the provision of responses or next best actions. The typical service system interaction described in connection to this role is (E1) the non-human agent following a social interaction between two human actors in the background and (E2) giving the interaction impulse by proactively suggesting one human actor responses or next best actions for an ongoing interaction, based on best practices learned from previous observed interactions or background information on the product or customer from internal systems. (E3) The human actor can take the content of the suggestion or follow the advice for behavioral change, adapt the generated advice or ignore it. The primary proposed added value of the integration of a non-human agent in the Advisor role for the human interaction partner is effectiveness, i.e. resolution of challenges at a higher quality than the human can produce with own capabilities, or efficiency, i.e. less contribution of own efforts to solve a problem.

(F) Algorithmic Managers assign tasks or hand over an interaction to a human actor. In essence, non-human agents in this role automate the matching between human actors. Common use cases in our sample are the adaptive routing of human actors to suitable human interaction partners for the resolution of customer inquiries or for the provision of personalized offerings, or, in internal organizational settings, connecting employees to human resource clerks. The typical service system interaction described in connection to this role is (F1) a human actor giving the interaction impulse by articulating a problem or need to a non-human agent, which perceives the intent of the inquiry and (F2) matches the human actor with a human counterpart at the service provider, who has sufficient skills and knowledge to (F3) solve the inquiry. The objective of human actors to engage in this service system interaction is to find the right human counterpart to solve a task. The primary proposed added value of the integration of a non-human agent in the Algorithmic Manager role for the human interaction partner is efficiency, i.e. less own effort required to find a suitable human counterpart for value co-creation.

A noteworthy observation in our data is the occurrence of certain roles being grouped within the same solution. For instance, the Information Provider is described to transition into an Algorithmic Manager and/or Concierge under specific circumstances. If the Information Provider cannot supply the requested information, fails to discern the customer intent or the customer explicitly prefers human interaction, solutions fulfilling this role often shift into the role of Algorithmic Managers, directing texts or calls to a human actor. Additionally, information inquiries may lead to the identification of an intent, which the AI-enabled solution can offer to fulfill by triggering automations, transforming into a Concierge. In turn, solutions assuming the roles of Coaches, Generators, or Advisors are commonly specialized and mostly only fulfill this specific role.

5 Discussion and Contributions

This empirical research illustrates six non-human agent roles in service system interactions and outlines the expected value of their contributions. We provide a first delineation of common service system interactions between non-human agents and humans and describe the sequence and direction of contributions and activities these technologies are involved in. The findings inform the scientific discourse about the changing role and nature of technology in value co-creation [10, 13]. This study addresses a gap on empirical research into the impact of non-human agents on value co-creation [42] and considers interactions with both service providers and beneficiaries, an aspect that has received limited attention in prior research [12, 42]. This paper augments existing research on types of AI-enabled solutions in adjacent fields (e.g. [17, 18, 28, 40, 41]) by drawing on findings from an approach using empirical open-source data on commercially-available services. Our study thereby provides a multi-dimensional conceptualization and abstraction of agentic AI-enabled information systems [54], which answers a call for structured descriptions of various facets of this phenomenon [5].

Our research contributes to the nascent literature on the engineering of service systems involving AI-enabled non-human agents. Each of the identified six roles is characterized by performing a specific function, thereby can be regarded as a service module [24]. More specifically, non-human agents fulfilling one of the six outlined roles constitute different AI service modules, which can be integrated into modular service structures [26]. By illustrating the systemic integration of non-human agents in different roles into service processes, we also uncover interfaces between service modules. The Concierge constitutes an AI service module, which commonly has an interface with another digital service module, as it is characterized by triggering automations. In turn, Algorithmic Managers constitute an AI service module, which hands over the interaction with a human actor to another human actor, thereby commonly has an interface with a traditional service module. Finally, in our sample, the Information Provider often transitions into the role of an Algorithmic Manager and/or Concierge, hence we infer it constitutes an AI service module, which commonly has an interface with another AI service module. Building on discussions on modular compositions of multiple machines involved in value creation on platforms [9], we explore connections between non-human agents and other machines within the roles of Information Provider and Concierge and thereby delineate existing compositions through which systems of multiple machines interact in service systems. Humans interact with service modules at different touchpoints during a customer journey [26] and we specify these interactions between a human actor and the AI service module, by describing whether a non-human agent in a specific role assists or augments the human actor. We furthermore contribute an empirical validation and extension for three of nine interaction dimensions for human-AI interaction [46] observable in our data. Human actors set the interaction impulse for interactions with Information Providers, Concierges, Generators, Coaches and Algorithmic Managers, while interactions with Advisors are triggered by non-human agents. Moreover, for each role, we describe the interaction result and depict action directions in Fig. 1. Finally, we draw on the actor relations conceptualized by [4] and illustrate empirically observable constellations of these different actor relations in practical settings. For instance, service system interactions involving Concierges encompass a constellation of human-to-machine, machine-to-human and machine-to-machine relations, while Advisors are embedded into interactions involving human-to-human and machine-to-human relations. The abstraction of ensembles of such relations from empirical data provides a basis for more in-depth examinations of the interplay and interdependencies in value co-creation with non-human agents.

AI-enabled non-human agents are projected to offer significant productivity gains in the service sector [47], but expectations need to be carefully managed for a successful introduction thereof [14]. The six roles with related integration types provide managers with an overview of embedding options, which demonstrably leads to a broader consideration of use cases and more innovative ideas for interactions between human and non-human agents [55]. Moreover, the roles can help to systematically uncover social attributes, which humans unconsciously ascribe to machines during interactions [56], and thereby enable managers to support employees in interactions with non-human agents.

6 Limitations and Future Research

The study is subject to limitations, which offer avenues for future research. Firstly, generalizability of results should be taken with a caveat. The sample is intentionally limited, given its exploratory nature. Future research can bolster robustness of findings with a representative sample from a specific industry and systematically explore roles applicable to that particular sector. Moreover, our open-source data does not cover service failure and value co-destruction, as it primarily stems from service provider sources. Hence, approaches observing interactions with deployed non-human agents can further increase the validity and breadth of findings. While we characterize roles based on value propositions by non-human agent providers, empirical studies show spikes in productivity triggered by AI-enabled solutions in the Advisor role [8, 57] and offer blueprints for research designs involving such real-world observations. Secondly, social and cultural aspects shape the roles non-human agents can assume in specific contexts [14]. Cultures differ across dimensions, such as uncertainty avoidance [58]. These cultural differences might lead to divergents attitudes towards contexts, in which AI is acceptable, across different regions. This study samples services targeted at English-speakers, hence replicating it with a focus on a particular societal context or cultural sphere, or conducting a comparative analysis among different types thereof, promises more nuanced insights into non-human agent roles. Thirdly, this study deliberately focuses on interactions with digital non-human agents, however, research indicates that anthropomorphism influences user well-being [59, 60] and sharing intensions [61]. Future research including physical robots might thus yield additional attributes to characterize non-human agent roles.

Acknowledgements The authors thank the German Federal Ministry for Economic Affairs and Energy (BMWE) for the funding of this research under the grant 01MK20006F (IIP-Ecosphere).

References

1. Maglio, P. P., Vargo, S. L., Caswell, N., & Spohrer, J. (2009). The service system is the basic abstraction of service science. *Information Science and e-Business Management, 7*, 395–406.
2. Rzepka, C., & Berger, B. (2018). User interaction with AI-enabled systems: A systematic review of IS research. In *Proceedings of the 39th International Conference on Information Systems* (pp. 1–21).
3. Beck, R., Dibbern, J., & Wiener, M. (2022). A multi-perspective framework for research on (sustainable) autonomous systems. *Business & Information Systems Engineering, 64*(3), 265–273.
4. Pakkala, D., & Spohrer, J. C. (2019). Digital service: Technological agency in service systems. In *Proceedings of the 52nd Hawaii International Conference on System Sciences* (pp. 1886–1895).
5. Seeber, I., Bittner, E., Briggs, R., de Vreede, T., de Vreede, G.-J., Elkins, A., Maier, R., Merz, A., Oeste-Reiß, S., Randrup, N., Schwabe, G., & Söllner, M. (2020). Machines as teammates: A research agenda on AI in team collaboration. *Information & Management, 57*, Article 103174.
6. Seeber, I., Waizenegger, L., Seidel, S., Morana, S., Benbasat, I., & Lowry, P. B. (2020). Collaborating with technology-based autonomous agents: Issues and research opportunities. *Internet Research, 30*(1), 1–18.
7. Andersen, J. V., Lindberg, A., Lindgren, R., & Selander, L. (2016). Algorithmic agency in information systems: Research opportunities for data analytics of digital traces. In *Proceedings of the 49th Hawaii International Conference on System Sciences* (pp. 4597–4605).
8. Brynjolfsson, E., Li, D., & Raymond, L. R. (2023). *Generative AI at Work, NBER Working Paper* 31161.
9. Schmidt, R., Alt, R., & Zimmermann, A. (2023). Assistant platforms. *Electronic Markets, 33*(1), 1–14.
10. Maglio, P. P. (2017). Editorial column—new directions in service science: Value cocreation in the age of autonomous service systems. *Service Science, 9*(1), 1–2.
11. Ågerfalk, P. J. (2020). Artificial intelligence as digital agency. *European Journal of Information Systems, 29*(1), 1–8.
12. Kaartemo, V., & Helkkula, A. (2018). A systematic review of artificial intelligence and robots in value co-creation: Current status and future research avenues. *Journal of Creating Value, 4*(2), 211–228.
13. Medina-Borja, A. (2015). Editorial column—Smart things as service providers: A call for convergence of disciplines to build a research agenda for the service systems of the future. *Service Science, 7*(1), ii–v.
14. Berente, N., Gu, B., Recker, J., & Santhanam, R. (2021). 'Managing artificial intelligence'. *MIS Quarterly, 45*(3), 1433–1450.
15. Bock, D. E., Wolter, J. S., & Ferrell, O. C. (2020). Artificial intelligence: Disrupting what we know about services. *Journal of Services Marketing, 34*(3), 317–334.
16. Enholm, I. M., Papagiannidis, E., Mikalef, P., & Krogstie, J. (2022). Artificial intelligence and business value: A literature review. *Information Systems Frontiers, 24*, 1709–1734.
17. Čaić, M., Odekerken-Schröder, G., & Mahr, D. (2018). Service robots: Value co-creation and co-destruction in elderly care networks. *Journal of Service Management, 29*(2), 178–205.
18. Knote, R., Janson, A., Söllner, M., & Leimeister, J. M. (2021). Value co-creation in smart services: A functional affordances perspective on smart personal assistants. *Journal of the Association for Information Systems, 22*(2), 418–458.
19. Barile, S., Lusch, R., Reynoso, J., Saviano, M., & Spohrer, J. (2016). Systems, networks, and ecosystems in service research. *Journal of Service Management, 27*(4), 652–674.
20. Spohrer, J. C., & Maglio, P. P. (2010). Toward a science of service systems. In *Handbook of service science* (pp. 157–194).
21. Böhmann, T., Leimeister, J. M., & Möslein, K. (2014). Service systems engineering. *Business & Information Systems Engineering, 6*(2), 73–79.

22. Parnas, D. L. (1972). On the criteria to be used in decomposing systems into modules. *Communications of the ACM, 15*(12), 1053–1058.
23. Peters, C. (2016). *Modularization of services—A modularization method for the field of telemedicine.* Kassel University Press.
24. Peters, C. (2014). Together they are strong—the quest for service modularization parameters. In *Proceedings of the 22nd European Conference on Information Systems.*
25. Vargo, S. L., & Lusch, R. F. (2016). *Service-dominant logic: Premises, perspectives.* Cambridge University Press.
26. Peters, C., & Zaki, M. (2018). *Modular service structures for the successful design of flexible customer journeys for AI services and business models—orchestration and interplay of services.* Working Paper Series of the Cambridge Service Alliance.
27. Biddle, B. J. (1979). *Role theory: Expectations, identities, and behaviors.* Academic Press.
28. Alter, S. (2023). How can you verify that i am using AI? Complementary frame-works for describing and evaluating AI-based digital agents in their usage contexts. In *Proceedings of the 57th Hawaii International Conference on System Sciences* (pp. 5856–5865).
29. Larivière, B., Bowen, D. E., Andreassen, T. W., Kunz, W. H., Sirianni, N. J., Voss, C. A., Wünderlich, N. V., & Keyser, A. D. (2017). "Service Encounter 2.0": An investigation into the roles of technology, employees and customers. *Journal of Business Research, 79*, 238–246.
30. Rai, A., Constantinides, P., & Sarker, S. (2018). Editor's comments: Next-generation digital platforms: Toward human–AI hybrids. *MIS Quarterly, 43*(1), iii–ix.
31. Yu, B., Vahidov, R., & Kersten, G. E. (2021). Acceptance of technological agency: Beyond the perception of utilitarian value. *Information and Management, 58*(7), Article 103503.
32. Tarafdar, M., Page, X., & Marabelli, M. (2022). Algorithms as co-workers: Human algorithm role interactions in algorithmic work. *Information Systems Journal, 33*(2), 232–267.
33. Benlian, A., Wiener, M., Cram, W. A., Krasnova, H., Maedche, A., Möhlmann, M., Recker, J., & Remus, U. (2022). 'Algorithmic management'. *Business & Information Systems Engineering, 64*(6), 825–839.
34. Möhlmann, M., Zalmanson, L., Henfridsson, O., & Gregory, R. W. (2021). Algorithmic management of work on online labor platforms: When matching meets control. *MIS Quarterly, 45*(4), 1999–2022.
35. Dhiman, H., Wächter, C., Fellmann, M., Trenz, M., & Fleisch, E. (2022). Intelligent assistants. *Business & Information Systems Engineering, 64*(5), 645–665.
36. Russell, S. J., & Norvig, P. (2020). *Artificial intelligence: A modern approach.* Pearson Education.
37. Kühl, N., Schemmer, M., Goutier, M., & Satzger, G. (2022). Artificial intelligence and machine learning. *Electronic Markets, 32*(4), 2235–2244.
38. Maedche, A., Morana, S., Schacht, S., Werth, D., & Krumeich, J. (2016). Advanced user assistance systems. *Business & Information Systems Engineering, 58*(5), 367–370.
39. Murray, A., Rhymer, J., & Sirmon, D. G. (2021). Humans and technology: Forms of conjoined agency in organizations. *Academy of Management Review, 46*(3), 552–571.
40. Bittner, E. A. C., Oeste-Reiß, S. & Leimeister, J. M. (2019). Where is the bot in our team? Toward a taxonomy of design option combinations for conversational agents in collaborative work. In *Proceedings of the 52nd Hawaii International Conference on System Sciences* (pp. 284–293).
41. Siemon, D. (2022). Elaborating team roles for artificial intelligence-based teammates in human-AI collaboration. *Group Decision and Negotiation, 31*(5), 871–912.
42. Lu, V. N., Wirtz, J., Kunz, W. H., Paluch, S., Gruber, T., Martins, A., & Patterson, P. G. (2020). Service robots, customers and service employees: What can we learn from the academic literature and where are the gaps? *Journal of Service Theory and Practice, 30*(3), 361–391.
43. Ragin, C. C. (1987). *The comparative method: Moving beyond qualitative and quantitative strategies.* University of California Press.
44. Vargo, S. L., & Lusch, R. F. (2004). Evolving service dominant logic: Perspectives on value creation and service ecosystems. *Marketing Theory, 4*(3), 381–400.

45. Kluge, S. (2000). Empirically grounded construction of types and typologies in qualitative social research. *Forum Qualitative Sozialforschung Forum: Qualitative Social Research, 1*(1).
46. Hinsen, S., Hofmann, P., Jöhnk, J., & Urbach, N. (2022). How can organizations design purposeful human-AI interactions: A practical perspective from existing use cases and interviews. In *Proceedings of the 55th Hawaii International Conference on System Sciences* (pp. 196–205).
47. Wirtz, J., Patterson, P. G., Kunz, W. H., Gruber, T., Lu, V. N., Paluch, S., & Martins, A. (2018). Brave new world: Service robots in the frontline. *Journal of Service Management, 29*(5), 907–931.
48. Engelbrecht, A., Gerlach, J., & Widjaja, T. (2016). Understanding the anatomy of data-driven business models—towards an empirical taxonomy. In *Proceedings of the 24th european conference on information systems*.
49. Hilbig, R., Hecht, S., Etsiwah, B., Mention, A.-L., & Torkkeli, M. (2020). The rise of data-driven business models in the berlin start-up scene. In *Managing digital open innovation* (pp. 353–377).
50. Riasanow, T., Galic, G., & Böhm, M. (2017). Digital transformation in the automotive industry: Towards a generic value network. In *Proceedings of the 25th European Conference on Information Systems* (pp. 3191–3201).
51. Creswell, J. W. (2007). *Qualitative inquiry and research design: Choosing among five approaches*. Sage Publications.
52. Saldaña, J. (2013). *The coding manual for qualitative researchers*. Sage Publications.
53. Yin, R. K. (2018). *Case study research and applications: Design and methods*. Sage Publications.
54. Baird, A., & Maruping, L. M. (2021). The next generation of research on is use: A theoretical framework of delegation to and from agentic is artifacts. *MIS Quarterly, 45*(1), 315–341.
55. Ringfort-Felner, R., Laschke, M., Neuhaus, R., Theofanou-Fülbier, D., & Hassenzahl, M. (2022). It can be more than just a subservient assistant. Distinct roles for the design of intelligent personal assistants. In *Proceedings of the nordic human-computer interaction conference* (pp. 1–17).
56. Nass, C., & Moon, Y. (2000). Machines and mindlessness: Social responses to computers. *Journal of Social Issues, 56*(1), 81–103.
57. Dell'Acqua, F., McFowland, E., Mollick, E. R., Lifshitz-Assaf, H., Kellogg, K., Rajendran, S., Krayer, L., Candelon, F., & Lakhani, K. R. (2023). *Navigating the jagged technological frontier: Field experimental evidence of the effects of AI on knowledge worker productivity and quality*. Harvard Business School Working Paper No. 24-013.
58. Hofstede, G. (2001). *Culture's consequences: Comparing values, behaviors, institutions, and organizations across nations*. Sage Publications.
59. Holthöwer, J., & van Doorn, J. (2023). Robots do not judge: Service robots can alleviate embarrassment in service encounters. *Journal of the Academy of Marketing Science, 51*(6), 767–784.
60. Pitardi, V., Wirtz, J., Paluch, S., & Kunz, W. H. (2022). Service robots, agency and embarrassing service encounters. *Journal of Service Management, 33*(2), 389–414.
61. Kim, T. W., Jiang, L., Duhachek, A., Lee, H., & Garvey, A. (2022). 'Do you mind if i ask you a personal question? How AI service agents alter consumer self-disclosure. *Journal of Service Research, 25*(4), 649–666.

Business Models, Digital Transformation & Entrepreneurship

Data-Driven Business Models from an Internal Automotive OEM Perspective: Categories and Challenges

Norbert Michael Homner

Abstract The automotive industry is undergoing a profound shift driven by digitalization, prompting the emergence of data-driven business models (DDBMs). As the original equipment manufacturers (OEMs) have already realised a number of DDBMs, their role in the traditional automotive industry is of great interest. This study investigates DDBMs within the European automotive sector, addressing two key objectives: a categorization of existing internal OEM DDBMs and internal OEM challenges. Interviews were made with sixteen automotive experts from four OEMs and two OEM suppliers, working in DDBM-related departments. Hence, five internal OEM DDBM categories were identified: Technical, Product Optimization, Marketing Analysis, Selling Raw Data, and Customer Services. The seven detected challenges that hinder DDBM development include legal constraints, technical complexities, organizational culture, and data knowledge gaps. These findings were guided by theoretical contributions to DDBMs in Information Systems (IS) and practical contributions such as DDBM advices for OEMs.

1 Introduction

The continuously growing importance of digital technologies such as cloud computing, mobile technology, or the Internet of Things lead towards a digitized world. This also affects primarily physical industries [1], including the automotive industry. Historically, the business models (BMs) in the automotive industry concentrate on producing and selling physical goods like the car itself and product-related services like the after-sales market, e.g. selling replacement parts. However, the transformation of the car into a "computing unit on wheels" [2] and its integration into an automotive ecosystem that includes other road users, vehicle manufacturers, service developers, and traffic infrastructure [3, 4] has opened up new possibilities

N. M. Homner (✉)
Digital Industrial Service Systems, Friedrich-Alexander Universität Erlangen-Nürnberg, Erlangen, Germany
e-mail: norbert.homner@fau.de

C. M. Flath et al. (eds.), *Digital Innovation and Organizational Transformation*, Lecture Notes in Information Systems and Organisation 83,
https://doi.org/10.1007/978-3-032-08483-5_11

for car manufacturers to develop new BMs [5]. These BMs seem to be necessary in the future, since car ownership is expected to decline, and car-sharing is predicted to increase in popularity [6]. Therefore, car manufacturers must find new ways to remain competitive. In this context, data-driven business models (DDBMs) based on the vast amount of data produced by connected cars represent a promising solution and can create new revenue streams [5].

Despite the digital potential in the automotive industry, the core industrial product, the car itself, cannot be digitized completely [7]. Hence, data-driven services will play an additional role [8]. Although there is a need to create DDBMs in the automotive industry, most incumbent car manufacturers struggle when it comes to building and creating DDBMs [9]. Furthermore, IS literature has not adequately explored the topic of connected cars and therefore car data and DDBMs [10, 11]. In addition, [10] call for a better understanding of DDBMs in the mobility domain, e.g., the automotive industry. This was the motivation to investigate an internal view from the automotive industry, as the field of DDBMs is developing very fast and internal development is years ahead of market maturity. For a better understanding of DDBMs in the automotive industry, this study focuses on a categorization of the DDBM market within the automotive industry. Since emerging areas such as DDBMs do not come without problems, there is a great interest in the challenges involved in creating DDBMs. Furthermore, the focus was set on an internal OEM perspective, since most authors in this field such as [3] or [11] focus on the ongoing ecosystematization of the car.

Thus, this paper addresses the following two research questions: *What are the distinct categories of DDBMs present within the European automotive OEMs?* and *Which challenges do the European automotive OEMs face regarding DDBMs?*

To answer these questions with an internal industry view, an exploratory interview study containing 16 semi-structured interviews with experts working in the domain of DDBMs development in the European automotive industry, which were subsequently coded following [12] and [13], was conducted.

2 Conceptual Background

2.1 Digitalization and Data in the Automotive Industry

Historically, the automotive industry has been a hardware-producing industry with the car at its center of product development. In recent years, digital transformation has also influenced incumbent industries like the automotive industry, e.g. with increasingly improved microprocessors or broadband communication [14]. Literature on digital transformation in the automotive industry discusses different aspects. Chanias and Hess [15] investigated strategies for digital transformation in the automotive industry and showed, that digital transformation begins with multiple organizational activities from a bottom-up perspective. Digital transformation in the automotive industry creates new roles for value creation [16].

In addition to the digital transformation in the automotive industry and hence also of the car, the technological advantages of big data and the interconnected DDBMs also influence the automotive industry. According to a study made by [17], all new cars will become connected in 2025. A connected car is equipped with hardware and software to connect the car to a cloud, which enables the OEMs to collect data from sensors [3]. Hence, the amount of car data will grow rapidly. One prominent example of the role of data in the automotive industry is autonomous driving, where data is the key to this technology. Data can also be used inside the OEM to improve organizational performance [18, 19]. In general, OEMs try to leverage their collected car data by improving their offers for customer needs [20]. Following a study made by McKinsey [5], car-generated data has the potential to be worth up to 750 billion USD by 2030. This indicates, that the role of data in the automotive industry will play a dominant role in the future. Having a look at European OEMs, data is already recognizable in either data-driven services like 'Mercedes me' [21] or 'First notification of loss' by Audi [22]. Hence, the potential of upcoming data brings also other companies on the track of car-data usage, leading to an additional value stream next to the traditional manufacturing of cars.

2.2 Data-Driven Business Models

Digitized cars lead to an extended amount of car data. To create value out of the car data, OEMs need a guiding architecture, i.e. a Business Model.

According to [23], there is no commonly accepted definition of BMs. However, one definition proposed by [24] describes a business model as the way how an organization creates and captures customer value by addressing customer relationships and channels, value proposition, resources, revenue and cost, and activities and partners. The creation of customer value is considered the core component of a business model [25], and the value proposition is a critical aspect of it [26]. In addition, BMs can be characterized as reflections of realized strategies [27] and representations of how organizations create value [28]. Now, with upcoming advantages of big data namely big data analytics and big data algorithms [29, 30], new DDBMs occur [31]. The value of DDBMs can be e.g. an improvement of business processes and decision-making [32] or the direct or indirect realization of value [33]. In terms of value proposition of DDBMs, several papers exist, e.g. [34] which provide a data insight generator, that links data to value proposition. Overall, the study of [31] pioneered the understanding and realization of DDBMs with a focus on start-ups. They defined DDBMs as a business model relying on data as a key resource [31, 35].

Furthermore, by analyzing literature on existing business model frameworks and data-related disciplines, [31] created a framework for DDBMs which contains six key dimensions: data sources, key activity, offering, target customer, revenue model, and specific cost advantage. Each dimension is subdivided, e.g. data sources unfold into ‘internal’ and ‘external data’, and characterizes a DDBM [31]. Other authors used this framework and the research on DDBMs to understand how companies innovate and develop DDBMs in consecutive phases, such as the ideation phase [36, 37] and the realization phase [38]. Both phases are interesting for incumbent firms since DDBMs are not core products of such firms.

Regarding the automotive industry, OEMs and new stakeholders in the market, (e.g. start-ups) try to gather valuable information out of the car generated data and built new business models upon that data [3, 39]. Due to the OEMs exclusive access to the car generated data, it is hard to get for third-party service providers such as start-ups [11]. Nevertheless, data marketplaces like Otonomo exist, acting as neutral intermediaries where multi-brand car data is sold to independent service providers [40] and research on DDBM archetypes of such data market-places is done. In the creation of DDBMs, different stakeholder types in data ecosystem [41] such as Data-Source, Data-Facilitator and Data-User exist [42, 43]. Bellin et al. [44] focus on the Data-Facilitator in an automotive industry-related case, showing the strong dependence of the Data-Facilitator on the Data-Source, i.e. the OEMs.

Hence, this research contributes to the body of knowledge by adding an internal OEM perspective on categories and challenges of DDBMs in the automotive industry, which is underrepresented in the current literature as the cited authors focus on an ecosystem perspective. Furthermore, “much of our current literature [on DDBMs] is conceptual, not empirical” [45], thus this study also contributes to this research stream.

3 Method

3.1 Case Description

The field of DDBMs is relatively new in the automotive industry and has not been studied extensively so far. Therefore, an exploratory interview study was conducted to create an understanding of this research field [46, 47]. The case selection followed a theoretical sampling approach by [12] and was planned, following the five components of case studies by [47]. The idea of investigating DDBMs and showing their status-quo in the automotive industry was inspired by the concept of DDBMs as proposed by [31] on a high level. This work theorizes in an inductive approach on a micro level [48]. To fullfil the research goal, the case must be the automotive industry. Due to feasibility, OEMs and digital companies working as suppliers as representatives for the automotive industry were chosen. To gain comparable results regarding data regulations, customer behavior, and legal situation the European market was investigated. Hence, four different European OEMs were chosen, and two digital companies that create data-driven solutions for the OEMs.

All OEMs, as well as digital companies want to stay anonymous, so key facts about them will be presented by cumulating all OEMs information. Therefore, a detailed description of each company cannot be provided. All OEMs have their headquarters in Europe and are commonly known since they have a long tradition in the car manufacturing business and have existed at least for more than 80 years. Together, they sell in total more than 15 Million vehicles worldwide and over 8 Million in Europe, with a total market share in Europe of more than 25% [49]. They all act globally, supply the volume or premium segment and have at least more than 100,000 employees worldwide. The digital companies have existed for at least 20 years and have at least more than 100 employees.

3.2 Data Collection and Analysis

Interview data was collected through a series of 16 semi-structured interviews in German or English conducted between April and September 2022 (see Table 1). The interview durations ranged from 32 min up to 67 min with a median of 43 min. Fifteen out of sixteen interviews were conducted online, e.g. via Microsoft Teams, and one in person. The requirements for the interviewees were, that they are working in a department (at an OEM or a related supplier company) that at least deals with data or ideally with DDBMs in the automotive industry, have at least 2 years of work experience in the field of DDBMs and have a company affiliation of at least 2 years. The interview guideline focused on the DDBMs in the automotive industry and the challenges in realizing them.

To prepare for the semi-structured interviews, a guideline was formulated in accordance with the recommendations provided by [50]. The guideline consisted of three main categories, that addressed questions about business models and DDBMs in the European automotive industry in general ("*What data driven business models do you have in Europe?*"), the design of DDBMs for the European market and their value proposition ("*What is the value proposition for the customer?*") and the development of DDBMs in the automotive industry ("*How was the data-driven business for the European market model developed?*").

The interview guidelines had to be approved by the labor union at some OEMs in advance. They prohibited recording the interviews, to guarantee privacy and anonymity of the interviewees. Therefore, notes were taken during the interviews. The aim was to transcribe the interviews manually as close to 'word by word' as possible (inspired by shorthand writing), with a focus on interesting statements, which serve as citations after translation from German to English. Subsequently, the interviews were sent back to the interviewees for further amendments or corrections. Following the approach by [12], three subsequent coding cycles were used: open coding, axial coding, and selective coding. Hereby, this research followed the active categorization framework for theory development proposed by [13] and analyzed the transcripts in three subsequent categorization cycles. This method was chosen, because it ensures a high rigor regarding coding. At the beginning of the first attempt, a large number of first-order open codes were identified in a line-by-line coding process. Subsequently, codes were dropped, merged, split, and revised [13]. By

Table 1 Details on interview Partners

Expert tag	Role description	Company	Duration
A	Engineer	OEM 1	40 Min
B	Big Data Developer	OEM 2	41 Min
C	Head of DDBM Development	OEM 1	37 Min
D	Big Data Developer	OEM 1	58 Min
E	Big Data Developer	SUP 1	32 Min
F	DDBM Strategy Developer	OEM 1	63 Min
G	DDBM Developer	OEM 1	56 Min
H	Head of DDBM Controling	OEM 1	43 Min
I	Head of DDBM Finance	OEM 2	60 Min
J	Technical DDBM Developer	OEM 2	33 Min
K	DDBM Purchaser	OEM 3	62 Min
L	DDBM Purchaser	OEM 1	55 Min
M	DDBM Developer	SUP 2	41 Min
N	DDBM Strategy Developer	OEM 4	33 Min
O	Technical DDBM Developer	OEM 1	67 Min
P	Technical DDBM Developer	OEM 1	43 Min

relating and contrasting the final codes, resulting in axial coding delivered a deeper understanding of the fundamental phenomenon [51]. These categories were linked to the research questions, to perform the final step: selective coding. Here, the axial codes were categorized into ‘core categories’ [51]. The coding led to two results: DDBM categories and DDBM challenges. Exemplary for the whole coding process, an example is shown in Fig. 1.

4 Results

4.1 DDBM Categories at Automotive OEMs

Based on the statements of the 16 interviewees, five categories were identified for DDBMs in Europe: Technical, Product Optimization, Marketing Analysis, Selling Raw Data, and Customer Services. In order to delimit from studies that deal with the ecosystematization like [3] or [11], the observed DDBMs in this study occur from an internal OEM perspective and only exist on the basis of vehicle data. While a permanent connection is not technically necessary for all DDBMs and hence not a basic requirement for all DDBMs, they must be able to establish a connection regularly (seconds to monthly).

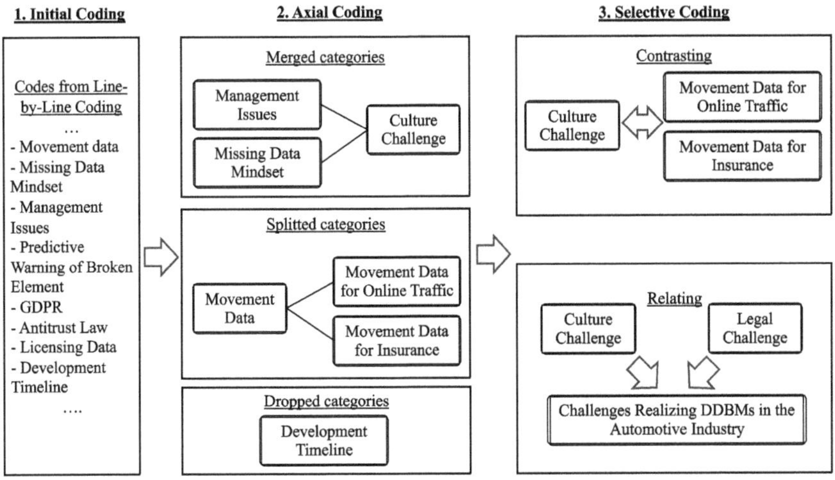

Fig. 1 Illustration of coding with the resulting challenge "Culture" as well as two codes ("Movement data for online traffic" and "Movement data for Insurance" resulting in the DDBM Category "Customer Service". Combination of [12] and [13]. Every step was followed by iterations

In Table 2, an overview of these DDBM categories is shown. The existing models vary by category, with some already available to customers and others still in the planning phase. Since the subcategory name would release too much detail about the DDBM itself, the substitute 'PLANNED' stands for subcategories which are not released yet and therefore cannot be mentioned.

Technical: These DDBMs focus on in-car features highly valued by customers and driven by technology. They primarily utilize data sourced from within the vehicle. Complementary data, like map information, relies on a mobile connection. If unavailable, an internal data source like a map version serves as backup. All data processing remains internal, ensuring the service operates independently. The value proposition centers on data-driven services that address customer needs, whether end-users or businesses. For example, in the sub-category predictive maintenance, customers are alerted to potential component failures (*'The plan is to report to the customer: 'Your component may break in the next 100 km'—A.'*), allowing proactive workshop visits to prevent breakdowns.

Product Optimization: The main objective of these DDBMs is to optimize the car as a product. Therefore, data is extracted from the car and processed outside the car in a backend system, where it is analyzed what kind of features or components such as control elements are used and how often they are used. Given the substantial size of OEMs, other company-departments can also be considered as customers, making this an internal OEM DDBM. Consequently, this study includes this DDBM, with the engineering departments acting as the customer, referred to as "B2E" (Business to Engineering) in this study. (*'Our [DDBM] is quite special since we have internal customers. We analyze usage behaviour*

Table 2 Details on the occurring DDBM categories. Design inspired by [52]. Elements taken from [31] and own ones

	Technical	Product Optimization	Marketing	Selling Raw Data	Customer Services
Sub-categories	Predictive Maintenance; Autonomous Driving; Replacing Constructional Elements	Usage Analysis of Features; PLANNED	Analyzing Subscriptions; PLANNED	Sensor Data; Anonymized Data; Personalized Data	Online Traffic; Insurance; Map Making; Seamless Integration; PLANNED
Data Sources	Anonymized Car-data	Anonymized Car-data	Anonymized and Personal Car-data	Anonymized and Personal Car-data	Anonymized and Personal Car-data
Key Activities	Data Aggregation and Predictive Analytics	Data Aggregation and Prescriptive Analytics	Data Aggregation and Prescriptive Data Analytics	Data Aggregation, Data Generation, Data Processing	Data Aggregation, Data Generation, Data Processing, Data Visualization
Value Proposition	Data-Based Services	Analytics Information	Analytics Information	Automotive-specific Raw Data	Data-based Services with Focus on Direct Customer Benefits
Target Customer	B2C and B2B	B2E (Business-to-Engineering, Internal Use)	B2R (Business-to-Retail, internal use)	B2B, B2C	B2B, B2C
Revenue Model	Single Payment per Car	Internal Costs	Internal costs, License Fee	Asset Sale, Lending/ Renting/Leasing, Licensing, Usage/ Subscription Fee	License Fee
Provider	OEM, Tier1, Start-Ups	OEM	OEM	OEM, Tier1	OEM, Tier1, Tier2, Start-Ups

regarding [control element] for them [Note: the engineering department]'—E). The value proposition is in the analytical insights provided, influencing future vehicle designs. Rarely used features may be omitted, while frequently used controls will receive special attention. The analytics service is sold internally, with the engineering-department paying a license fee to the analytics-department.

Marketing: Marketing DDBMs in the automotive industry have two primary objectives: to optimize campaigns and gather market feedback on car-specific topics. This DDBM relies solely on external data from customer feedback forms, online sources, and subscriptions. Similar to "Product Optimization" DDBMs, it is used by internal retail departments, termed "B2R" (Business to Retail) in this study.

The value proposition is analytical insights, such as assessing campaign effectiveness and developing recommendations based on subscription and crawled data. The analytics service is sold internally, with retail departments paying a license fee to use it.

Selling Raw Data: This DDBM is exclusively focused on selling automotive-specific raw data, either anonymized (e.g., anonymized movement data) or personalized (e.g., individual driving behavior), sourced from within the vehicle. The value proposition is providing third parties access to this data, enabling new services and DDBMs.

The financial model is multifaceted, with data sold via subscription fees, usage fees, licensing, renting, or asset sales. However, determining the final price and achieving effective monetization remains challenging.

Customer Services: Customer Services represent a highly diverse category within DDBMs, unified by their exclusive focus on direct customer benefits. Consequently, the data required for these DDBMs is equally varied. The primary data source is derived from within the vehicle, supplemented by complementary data, such as online crawled data. The value proposition of these services lies in their customer-oriented nature, offering data-based services that directly enhance customer experience, such as providing real-time traffic information. The DDBMs examined in this study were all financed through a license fee per vehicle.

4.2 Challenges for OEMs Regarding DDBM Development

The implementation of DDBMs inside the OEMs is not without challenges. The evolving market towards DDBMs endangers the automotive OEMs' market power. The main reason according to interviewees is that the OEMs face problems regarding the development of DDBMs. Having examined internal organizational resources, the findings from the interviews were analyzed and seven major challenge types were identified. Furthermore, the challenges are linked to the DDBM categories developed in 4.1 and are presented in Fig. 2.

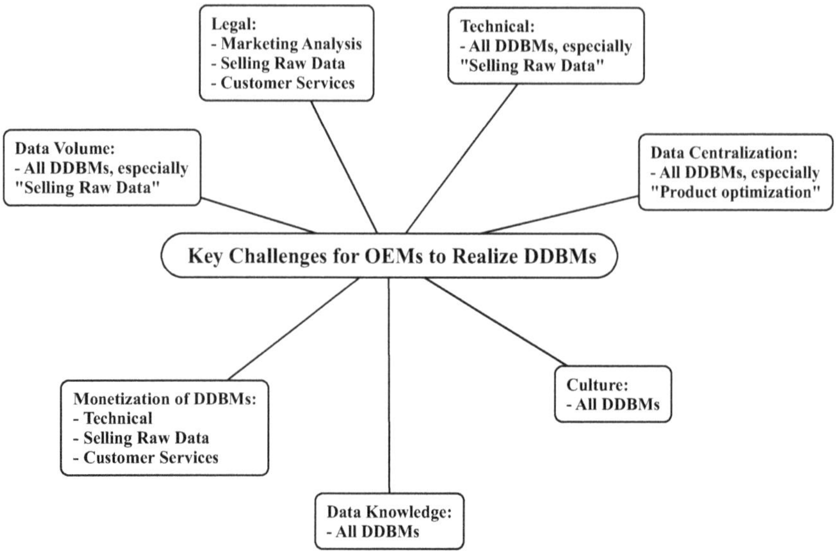

Fig. 2 Key challenges for OEM DDBM development and their linked categories

Legal: Creating a DDBM in the European automotive industry has legal boundaries that entail development efforts and hinder using the full potential. Interview partners stated, that the GDPR (General Data Protection Regulation) legislation entails development effort. According to the interviewees, this applies in particular to DDBMs where personalized data is required, i.e. Customer Services, Selling Raw Data and Marketing Analysis. Furthermore, the antitrust law and the law against unfair competition were mentioned as challenges regarding the use of the full potential of data. One interview partner stated: *'Something has to change in the legislation so that the automotive industry also makes progress here.'—C.*
Technical: The law situation leads to a technical challenge. Due to the anti-trust law, technical standardization of e.g., data formats in the automotive industry is hard to establish. This impedes data customers to create industry-wide DDBMs, according to interviewee F: *'For a potential customer it is difficult, he gets many different data formats/contents/frequencies from each OEM.'—F.* The challenge is valid for all DDBMs but interviewees mentioned that it is especially hard for the DDBM "Selling Raw Data", since a missing standard hinders a customer to integrate all the required raw data easily into their product. The DDBM category "Technical" is also affected, since the missing standard forces intermediate steps, before data analysis for "predictive maintenance" or "replacing constructional elements" can be done.
Data Centralization: Interviewees highlighted the issue of missing data centralization and an unfavorable company structure for DDBM development within OEMs. Data exists in various departments, from sales to R&D, and is not centralized, e.g., in a 'data lake'. One interviewee noted: *'At the beginning, there is*

the problem that data is in small silos.'—I. This lack of centralization leads to unstructured DDBM development and lost synergy effects. This issue affects all DDBMs, but especially those related to "product optimization," where incomplete data can lead to incorrect analysis results.

Culture: The main challenge identified in the interview data is the organizational culture at OEMs. Interviewees noted the unrecognized value of DDBMs and called for more proactive management: *'The leadership needs to do more in the direction [of DDBMs].'—C.* However, a manager from the same OEM stated: *'It [digitalization and DDBMs] has been anchored in the corporate strategy for several years.'—B.* This disparity suggests a lack of consensus on DDBMs within the company, echoed by interviewees from other OEMs. Consequently, a unified DDBM mindset in the automotive industry is absent, making DDBMs' importance unclear. This ambiguity can deter data experts, as one interviewee questioned: *'How can we as a company get into these mindsets that are attractive for experts?'—I.* The lack of data experts, resulting in missing knowledge about data in the automotive industry, was identified as a challenge affecting all DDBMs discussed in Sect. 4.1.

Data Knowledge: Interviewees mentioned that knowledge about, e.g., data analytics is missing. Frequently brought up by interviewees a reason for this mindset is surely the car industry itself, exemplary: *‚Because we come from engineering hardware and not from data topics and products. ‚—E.* In the classical engineering hardware world, constructional elements and Key Performance Indicators (KPIs) like several sold units are important and data plays a subsidiary role. This challenge is also a problem occurring in all DDBMs from 4.1 as the interviewees stated this challenge in the interviews.

Monetization of DDBMs: Another challenge identified in the interview data is the monetization of DDBMs and the resulting risk of disaffection of the management: *'You can't say that the risk [realizing a DDBM] is too high because I can't see it, I can't calculate it,* etc. ‚—*C.* Since monetization and therefore the economic value of DDBMs is hard to estimate, it is challenging for decision-makers to bring these DDBMs to market. In conclusion, OEMs become late penetrators for DDBMs since they only take the economic risk if someone else has already shown that the market demands it. This challenge is a problem for all externally sold DDBMs, i.e. interviewees mentioned this challenge for the categories "Technical", "Selling Raw Data" and "Customer Services".

Data Volume: The last identified challenge was the role of data volume. Here, the equation applies: more cars lead to more data: *'As a smaller brand that does not yet have so many cars in the market, it is very difficult to gain a foothold [in DDBMs].'—K.* A high amount of data yields to better DDBMs and therefore a higher economic value, especially for the DDBM "Selling Raw Data".

5 Discussion

5.1 Implications for Theory

Given the holistic approach of DDBMs in the automotive industry, the presented results carry three theoretical implications. First, the study contributes to the emphasized call to better understand DDBMs in the mobility domain by [10]. Categories were created for existing DDBMs in the automotive industry based on empirical data and showed their market characteristics. Additionally, taking into account [11] this study contributes to the topic of connected cars in IS with an internal OEM perspective. All presented DDBMs depend on automotive data, accessible solely through the connectivity of the vehicle, i.e. a connected car.

Second, our findings show that the framework from [31] needs to be extended or rearranged. For example, a physical product such as a car and its sensors can act as internal and external data sources. It depends on whether the data is personalized and therefore customer-provided or if it is anonymized and can therefore be tracked. This distinction holds paramount significance, particularly within the DDBM category of ‘Customer Services’. Within subcategories such as ‘insurance’ or ‘online traffic’, the initial consideration does not predominantly lie in discerning between internal and external data sources, rather, the primary differentiation centers on the classification of data as ‘personalized’ or ‘anonymized’. Hence, the ‘data sources’ dimension by [31] must be rearranged for the automotive industry towards a distinction between ‘personalized’ and ‘anonymized’ before it comes to ‘internal’ or ‘external’ data sources.

Third, referring to [45], this work adds an empirical study to the literature on DDBMs.

5.2 Implications for Practice

This study also offers implications for practitioners. First, this study shows that DDBMs are emerging in the automotive industry. Existing categories include Technical, Product Optimization, Marketing, Selling Raw Data, and Customer Services. B2B or B2C DDBMs like Technical, Selling Raw Data, and Customer Services generate additional revenue, while internal DDBMs like Product Optimization and Marketing optimize internal processes. Product Optimization is especially promising, as detailed usage analysis of features can lead to a more optimized car.

Second, this study identifies challenges for OEMs that they need to solve in order to maintain their market power in a market that is changing towards DDBMs, namely Legal, Technical, Company Structure, Cultural, Data Knowledge, Monetization of DDBMs, and Data Volume. These challenges are similar to the findings of [38] but are described in this study in the context of the automotive industry, while [38] investigated them in a broader context.

6 Conclusion, Limitations, and Future Work

In this study, an exploratory interview study was conducted to investigate the DDBMs in the mobility domain, e.g., the automotive industry. Therefore, 16 automotive experts spread over four OEMs and two OEM suppliers were interviewed, working in departments that deal with DDBMs. The interviews were guided by the question of how DDBMs within the market of the European automotive industry can be categorized as well as which challenges the European automotive industry face regarding DDBMs. Hence, five DDBM categories in the automotive domain were found: 'Technical', 'Product Optimization', 'Marketing Analysis', 'Selling Raw Data', and 'Customer Services' and seven challenges that the automotive domain deals with: legal, technical, company structure, cultural, data knowledge, monetization, and data volume. Furthermore, three This distinction holds paramount significance, particularly within the realm (DDBMs) of the category of 'Customer Services'. contributions to the theory occured. First, this study responded to a current call from [10] by emphasizing a better understanding of DDBMs in the mobility domain, e.g. the automotive industry. Second, this study shows that the framework from [31] needs to be reworked for the automotive industry. Third, by contributing an empirical study to the literature.

However, this study has limitations. For this study only four different European OEMs were interviewed. Hence, interviewing more OEMs inside Europe is beneficial to verify the results. This lowers subjectiveness in the results, even though it was tried to analyze the data as objectively as possible. Also interviewing experts outside Europe (e.g., Asian or American OEMs) would add new characteristics to the results of the study in the future. Furthermore, repeating the study as soon as data intensive technologies such as Large-Language-Models are established in the automotive industry, adds new characteristics.

Since this study deals with an internal OEM perspective, it is of great interest to investigate the whole ecosystem with other data suppliers and other competitors from outside the automotive industry. This extends the challenges from an internal OEM perspective to challenges that occur on a data ecosystem level.

References

1. Hanelt, A., Piccinini, E., Gregory, R. W., Hildebrandt, B., & Kolbe, L. M. (2015). Digital transformation of primarily physical industries—exploring the impact of digital trends on business models of automobile manufacturers. *Wirtschaftsinformatik Proceedings* 2015. 88. https://aisel.aisnet.org/wi2015/88
2. Bernhart, W., & Alexander, M. (2020, January). *Computer on wheels/Disruption in automotive electronics and semiconductors*. https://www.rolandberger.com/en/Insights/Publications/The-car-will-become-a-computer-on-wheels.html
3. Kaiser, C., Stocker, A., Viscusi, G., Fellmann, M., & Richter, A. (2021). Conceptualising value creation in data-driven services: The case of vehicle data. *International Journal of Information Management, 59*, Article 102335. https://doi.org/10.1016/j.ijinfomgt.2021.102335

4. Li, L., Wen, D., & Yao, D. (2014). A survey of traffic control with vehicular communications. *IEEE Transactions on Intelligent Transportation Systems, 15*(1), 425–432. https://doi.org/10.1109/TITS.2013.2277737
5. McKinsey. (2018). From buzz to bucks—automotive players on the highway to car data monetization. https://www.mckinsey.com/~/media/McKinsey/Industries/AutomotiveandAssembly/OurInsights/Acceleratingthecardatamonetizationjourney/From-buzz-to-bucks-automotive-players-on-the-highway-to-car-data-monetization-web-final.ashx
6. Bertoncello, M., Camplone, G., Gao, P., Kaas, H. W., Mohr, D., Möller, T., & Wee, D. (2016). *Monetizing car data: New service business opportunities to create new customer benefits*. McKinsey & Company.
7. Piccinini, E., Hanelt, A., Gregory, R. W., & Kolbe, L. M. (2015). Transforming industrial business: The impact of digital transformation on automotive organizations. *ICIS*.
8. Kaiser, C., Festl, A., Pucher, G., Fellmann, M., & Stocker, A. (2019). The vehicle data value chain as a lightweight model to describe digital vehicle services. In *WEBIST* (pp. 68–79).
9. Hodd, J., Hoda, O., & Robinson, R. (2019). *Monetizing data in the age of connected vehicles*. Deloitte Insights.
10. Ketter, W., Schroer, K., & Valogianni, K. (2023). Information systems research for smart sustainable mobility: A framework and call for action. *Information Systems Research, 34*(3), 1045–1065. https://doi.org/10.1287/isre.2022.1167
11. Sterk, F., Stocker, A., Heinz, D., & Weinhardt, C. (2024). Unlocking the value from car data: A taxonomy and archetypes of connected car business models. *Electronic Markets, 34*(1), 13. https://doi.org/10.1007/s12525-024-00692-5
12. Glaser, B. G., & Strauss, A. L. (1967). *The discovery of grounded theory*. Aldine Publishing Company.
13. Grodal, S., Anteby, M., & Holm, A. L. (2021). Achieving Rigor in qualitative analysis: The role of active categorization in theory building. *Academy of Management Review, 46*(3), 591–612. https://doi.org/10.5465/amr.2018.0482
14. Yoo, Y., Henfridsson, O., & Lyytinen, K. (2010). Research commentary: The new organizing logic of digital innovation: An agenda for information systems research. *Information Systems Research, 21*(4), 724–735.
15. Chanias, S., & Hess, T. (2016, June). Understanding digital transformation strategy formation: Insights from Europe's automotive industry.
16. Riasanow, T., Galic, G., & Böhm, M. (2017). Digital transformation in the automotive industry: Towards a generic value network. *Proceedings of the 25th European Conference on Information Systems (ECIS)*. http://aisel.aisnet.org/ecis2017_rip/
17. Gissler, A. (2015). Connected vehicle: Succeeding with a disruptive technology. Accenture. / abinteligencia/pdf/Accenture-digital- Connected-Vehicle.pdf.
18. Akter, S., Wamba, S. F., Gunasekaran, A., Dubey, R., & Childe, S. J. (2016). How to improve firm performance using big data analytics capability and business strategy alignment? *International Journal of Production Economics, 182*, 113–131. https://doi.org/10.1016/j.ijpe.2016.08.018
19. Dremel, C., Herterich, M., Wulf, J., Waizmann, J.-C., & Brenner, W. (2017). How AUDI AG established big data analytics in its digital transformation. *MIS Quarterly Executive, 16*(2), 81–100.
20. Stocker, A., Kaiser, C., & Fellmann, M. (2017). Quantified vehicles: Novel services for vehicle lifecycle data. *Business & Information Systems Engineering, 59*(2), 125–130. https://doi.org/10.1007/s12599-017-0465-5
21. Daimler. (2024). Mercedes ME. Retrieved March 29, 2024, from https://www.mercedes-benz.de/passengercars/services/mercedes-me.html
22. AUDI AG. (2024). *First Notification of Loss*. Retrieved March 29, 2024, from https://www.audi.de/de/brand/de/extended-vehicle-data/datenprodukte/first-notification-of-loss.html
23. Sorescu, A., Frambach, R. T., Singh, J., Rangaswamy, A., & Bridges, C. (2011). Innovations in retail business models. *Journal of Retailing, 87*, S3–S16. https://doi.org/10.1016/j.jretai.2011.04.005

24. Osterwalder, A., & Pigneur, Y. (2010). *Business model generation: A handbook for visionaries, game changers, and challengers*. Wiley.
25. Fielt, E. (2014). Conceptualising business models: Definitions, frameworks and classifications. *Journal of Business Models, 1*(1) (2013): Inaugural issue. https://doi.org/10.5278/OJS.JBM.V1I1.706
26. Demil, B., Lecocq, X., Ricart, J. E., & Zott, C. (2015). Introduction to the SEJ Special Issue on business models: Business models within the domain of strategic entrepreneurship: Introduction. *Strategic Entrepreneurship Journal, 9*(1), 1–11. https://doi.org/10.1002/sej.1194
27. Casadesus-Masanell, R., & Heilbron, J. (2015). Business models nature and benefits. *SSRN Electronic Journal*. https://doi.org/10.2139/ssrn.2606692
28. Teece, D. J. (2010). Business models, business strategy and innovation. *Long Range Planning, 43*(2–3), 172–194. https://doi.org/10.1016/j.lrp.2009.07.003
29. Chen, H., Chiang, R. H., & Storey, V. C. (2012). Business intelligence and analytics: From big data to big impact. *MIS Quarterly, 36*(4), 1165. https://doi.org/10.2307/41703503
30. Günther, W. A., Rezazade Mehrizi, M. H., Huysman, M., & Feldberg, F. (2017). Debating big data: A literature review on realizing value from big data. *The Journal of Strategic Information Systems, 26*(3), 191–209. https://doi.org/10.1016/j.jsis.2017.07.003
31. Hartmann, P. M., Zaki, M., Feldmann, N., & Neely, A. (2016). Capturing value from big data—a taxonomy of data-driven business models used by start-up firms. *International Journal of Operations & Production Management, 36*(10), 1382–1406. https://doi.org/10.1108/IJOPM-02-2014-0098
32. Woerner, S. L., & Wixom, B. H. (2015). Big data: Extending the business strategy toolbox. *Journal of Information Technology, 30*(1), 60–62. https://doi.org/10.1057/jit.2014.31
33. Akred, J., & Samani, A. (2018). *Your data is worth more than you think*. MIT Sloan Management Review. https://sloanreview.mit.edu/article/your-datais-worth-more-thanyou-think/.
34. Kühne, B., & Böhmann, T. (2019, June). Data-driven business models—building the bridge between data and value.
35. Homner, N. M., Bellin, P., Fielt, E., & Matzner, M. (2024). *Data-driven business models*. Elsevier.
36. Alfaro, E., Bressan, M., Satellogic, Girardin, F., Near Future Laboratory, Murillo, J., BBVA Group, Someh, I., University of Queensland, Wixom, B. H., & ' MIT Sloan Center for Information Systems Research'. (2019). BBVA's data monetization journey. *MIS Quarterly Executive*, 117–128. https://doi.org/10.17705/2msqe.00011
37. Chen, H.-M., Schütz, R., Kazman, R., & Matthes, F. (2017). How Lufthansa capitalized on big data for business model renovation. *MIS Quarterly Executive, 16*(2017), 19–34.
38. Lange, H. E., Drews, P., & Höft, M. (2021). Realization of data-driven business models in incumbent companies: An exploratory study based on the resource-based view. *ICIS 2021 Proceedings 2*. https://aisel.aisnet.org/icis2021/dig_innov/dig_innov/2
39. Nischak, F., & Hanelt, A. (2019). Ecosystem change in the Era of digital innovation—A longitudinal analysis and visualization of the automotive ecosystem. *ICIS 2019 Proceedings*.
40. Martens, B., & Mueller-Langer, F. (2020). Access to digital car data and competition in aftermarket maintenance services. *Journal of Competition Law & Economics, 16*(1), 116–141. https://doi.org/10.1093/joclec/nhaa005
41. S. Oliveira, M. I., Barros Lima, G. D. F., & Farias Lóscio, B. (2019). Investigations into data ecosystems: A systematic mapping study. *Knowledge and Information Systems, 61*(2), 589–630. https://doi.org/10.1007/s10115-018-1323-6
42. Schroeder, R. (2016). Big data business models: Challenges and opportunities. *Cogent Social Sciences, 2*(1), 1166924. https://doi.org/10.1080/23311886.2016.1166924
43. Wiener, M., Saunders, C., & Marabelli, M. (2020). Big-data business models: A critical literature review and multiperspective research framework. *Journal of Information Technology, 35*(1), 66–91. https://doi.org/10.1177/0268396219896811
44. Bellin, P., Homner, N., Mertes, D., Fielt, E., & Matzner, M. (2024). Data facilitator in a squeeze? Patterns of dependence in data-driven business models. In *Proceedings of the 32nd European Conference on Information Systems* (pp. 1–10).

45. Markus, M. L. (2017). Datification, organizational strategy, and IS research: What's the score? *The Journal of Strategic Information Systems, 26*(3), 233–241. https://doi.org/10.1016/j.jsis.2017.08.003
46. Klein, H. K., & Myers, M. D. (1999). A set of principles for conducting and evaluating interpretive field studies in information systems. *MIS Quarterly, 23*(1), 67. https://doi.org/10.2307/249410
47. Yin, R. K. (2018). *Case study research and applications: Design and methods* (6th ed.). Thousand Oaks.
48. Birks, D. F., Fernandez, W., Levina, N., & Nasirin, S. (2013). Grounded theory method in information systems research: Its nature, diversity and opportunities. *European Journal of Information Systems, 22*(1), 1–8. https://doi.org/10.1057/ejis.2012.48
49. Carsalesbase. (2022, November 10). *Carsalesbase*. https://carsalesbase.com/car-sales-europe-home-main/
50. King, N., Horrocks, C., & Brooks, J. M. (2019). *Interviews in qualitative research* (2nd ed.). SAGE.
51. Corbin, J. M., & Strauss, A. L. (2015). *Basics of qualitative research: Techniques and procedures for developing grounded theory* (4th ed.). SAGE.
52. Endres, H., Indulska, M., Ghosh, A., Baiyere, A., & Broser, S. (2019). Industrial Internet of Things (IIoT) Business Model Classification. *ICIS 2019 Proceedings*. https://aisel.aisnet.org/icis2019/practice_is_research/practice_is_research/2

Digital Platform Strategies and Profitability—The Role of Strategy Type and Chief Digital Officers

Yongli Huang, Maximilian Schreieck, Yiwen Gao, and Jason B. Thatcher

Abstract While companies in the IT industry—particularly the big tech companies—have profited from digital platform strategies, whether companies across industries al-so benefit from such strategies remains contested. Focusing on the S&P1500 companies, we show that digital platform strategies positively affect a company's profitability, albeit after a lag of several years. To further explore the relationship between digital platform strategies and profitability, we considered the impact of the type of digital platform strategy and the presence of a chief digital officer (CDO). First, the positive effect of a digital platform strategy is stronger for companies that implement the digital platform organically ("build strategy") rather than for companies that acquire a platform ("buy strategy"). Second, the presence of a CDO positively moderates the effect of digital platform strategy in the long but not in the short run. Overall, implementing digital platforms is not a quick-win strategy for companies, but it requires careful consideration.

Y. Huang (✉) · M. Schreieck
Department of Information Systems, Production and Logistics Management, Universität Innsbruck, Innsbruck, Austria
e-mail: yongli.huang21@gmail.com

M. Schreieck
e-mail: maximilian.schreieck@uibk.ac.at

Y. Gao
Wilbur O. and Ann Powers College of Business, Clemson University, Clemson, SC, USA
e-mail: yiweng@clemson.edu

J. B. Thatcher
University of Colorado Boulder, Leeds School of Business, Boulder, CO, USA
e-mail: jason.thatcher@colorado.edu

C. M. Flath et al. (eds.), *Digital Innovation and Organizational Transformation*, Lecture Notes in Information Systems and Organisation 83,
https://doi.org/10.1007/978-3-032-08483-5_12

1 Introduction

Many companies employ digital platforms to create value by unlocking third-party developers' innovative potential [1–3]. While some firms such as Alphabet/Google, Meta/Facebook, Apple, Tencent, and Alibaba have implemented successful digital platform strategies, there is mixed evidence of whether companies across a broader range of industries can realize the benefits of digital platform strategies. Previous work highlights the growth potential of digital platform strategies (e.g., [4, 5]) but also the challenges related to establishing a digital platform (e.g., [6, 7]). For example, opening internal systems to external third-party developers can lead to tensions within the companies. As a result, several leading companies abandoned their digital platforms, such as General Electric, which sold its digital platform Predix in 2018 [8].

Existing studies on digital platforms have predominantly focused on value generation mechanisms [9], platform governance strategies [10], multi-platform integration strategies [11], failed platforms [12], the strategic role of the Chief Digital Officer (CDO) [13], and the optimal digital platform strategy (build vs buy) [14]. Despite these contributions, the management and IS literature still lack a comprehensive analysis of whether companies profit from digital platforms and under which conditions. Therefore, this study aims to address this gap by empirically investigating the impact of digital platform strategies on firm profitability. Hence, we pose the following research questions: *How do digital platform strategies affect a firm's profitability? Additionally, will the implementation of a build strategy and the presence of a CDO strengthen a firm's profitability?*

To address these research questions, we first hypothesize that a digital platform contributes positively to the profitability of companies because it unlocks the generative power of third-party developers [15] and leverages network effects [9]. For a more nuanced understanding, we then consider whether companies implement the digital platform strategy organically ("build strategy") or through the acquisition of an existing digital platform ("buy strategy") [1]. We hypothesize that the effect of implementing a digital platform with a build strategy on a firm's profitability is stronger than that of a buy strategy because an internally developed digital platform will better align with the companies' overall digital infrastructure.

Finally, we consider the role of CDOs in implementing digital platform strategies because these strategies are often part of digital transformation agendas—which typically fall under the responsibility of the CDO [16]. We draw on the upper echelons theory [17, 18] and recent research on the CDO position [19–21] and the digital upper echelons [22, 23]. Given the importance of the CDO for digital transformation, we hypothesize that a CDO will positively moderate the relationship between digital platform strategies and companies' profitability.

We compiled a unique panel dataset from the S&P1500 companies (2000–2020), identifying those companies that reported launching a digital platform strategy in their SEC filings. We manually coded digital platform strategies as build or buy strategies and integrated BoardEx data on CDO Presence. Our findings reveal that digital platform strategies yield positive effects in the long run, particularly after five and six years, with build strategies showing more significant benefits. While the presence of a CDO also positively influences outcomes in the long term, there is no immediate benefit, and initial years might even show a slight negative impact.

Our findings contribute to the conversation about drivers of effective digital platform strategies by analyzing the overall impact of digital platform strategies on firms' profitability and probing the effect of strategy types and the CDO position on whether organizations create profitability from digital platforms. We suggest that when seeking to generate profitability from digital platform strategies, firms must plan with at least a five-year horizon and consider appointing a CDO, giving them sufficient time to implement the strategy.

2 Background and Hypotheses

This study investigates the impact of digital platform strategies on a firm's profitability. Specifically, we aim to determine whether a build or buy approach leads to greater profitability and whether the presence of a CDO further enhances these outcomes.

2.1 *Digital Platform Strategies and Profitability*

Digital platforms refer to the "extensible codebase of a software-based system that provides core functionality shared by the modules that interoperate with it" [24]. To support access to this functionality, digital platforms offer boundary resources—such as application programming interfaces (APIs), software development kits (SDKs), and developer portals [25]. Third-party developers then use these resources to create applications they make available to platform users. Examples of digital platforms include Google Android and Apple iOS, which support third-party developers of mobile applications [26, 27], the Sony PlayStation that enables developers of video games [28], and the Microsoft Azure Platform that enables developers of business applications [29].

Given that digital platforms create value in the IT industry, companies from non-IT industries have explored the applications of digital platforms. For instance, companies from the automotive manufacturing [7], machine and equipment manufacturing [6], insurance [30], and farming [31] industries have opened their core systems to establish digital platform ecosystems with third-party developers.

To unlock value from third-party developers, companies strive to build digital platform ecosystems populated by innovative third-party applications and services [1, 2, 32]. Thus, the platform owner and third-party developers co-created value in the digital platform ecosystem [33]. Digital platforms shift value creation from internal to external, thereby "inverting the firm" [5] and establishing value co-creation. For example, Apple has established a flourishing ecosystem of third-party developers that provide applications for Apple's mobile operating system, iOS. In Apple's App Store, sales generated by third-party applications are estimated to be between 70 and 85 billion US$ in 2021, with 60 billion US$ distributed to third-party developers and the rest captured by Apple [34]. Thus, revenue generated by external third-party companies represents a crucial part of Apple's overall revenue and profitability.

Digital platforms create indirect network effects because an increasing number of users attract more third-party developers [3, 9, 35]. These indirect network effects fuel value co-creation on the digital platform, allowing for more value capture by the platform owner. In sum, digital platforms enable companies to tap into the generative potential of third-party developers and capture a share of the co-created value. We hypothesize:

Hypothesis 1: *A digital platform strategy positively affects a firm's profitability.*

A digital platform strategy can be implemented by internally developing a digital platform, acquiring a company that has already implemented a digital platform, or forming a consortium with other companies to build a digital platform [1]. In this study, we exclude the strategy of platform consortia because they have been a rare phenomenon even though they have been promoted as a strategy to compete with dominant established digital platforms [36]. Instead, we focus on the first two strategies, which we label the build and buy strategies following [1].

With a build strategy, companies implement a digital platform themselves, with or without the support of an IT supplier. For example, the German enterprise software vendor SAP built a cloud platform for business applications [10], and Cisco implemented an Internet of Things platform for data analysis on routers and opened it to third-party developers [37]. Qualitative studies on digital platform strategies mainly focus on companies that built platforms organically. These studies, despite identifying challenges and internal tensions, show successful outcomes in the enterprise software [10, 38], automotive [7], network and telecommunications [37], and process automation industries [6].

While little evidence exists on the effect of buy strategies, anecdotal findings suggest that a high upfront investment and integration challenges might impede the benefits for the acquiring company [39, 40]. The company's legacy systems make integrating an acquired digital platform difficult and limit its generative potential [41].

By implementing digital platforms internally, companies control the platform architecture and can adapt it to the needs of the third-party developers in their industry. When third-party developers interact with the platform, they co-create value, part of which the platform owner captures. We hypothesize:

Hypothesis 2: *The effect of a digital platform strategy on a firm's profitability is stronger when the strategy is implemented internally (build strategy).*

2.2 *Moderating Role of the Chief Digital Officer Position*

The upper echelons theory postulates that it is insufficient to interpret organizations as functional structures [17]. Instead, individual top managers and the top management team significantly influence the organization. Various studies have empirically supported and refined the theory [42]. As firms face increasing demands to digitize, the role of the upper echelons in formulating digital strategies has drawn greater attention from management and information systems (IS) scholars. We refer to the executives with IT-related responsibilities as their primary role in the firm as digital upper echelons [22, 23].

In this study, we focus on the position of the CDO, which has become more widespread in recent years [16, 43]. The CDO is typically tasked with managing "initiatives that explore and harness new digital technologies," that is, digital transformation initiatives [44, 45]. As part of a broader digital transformation agenda, a CDO is expected to significantly impact the implementation of digital platform strategies.

Recent work has shown that firms who report transformation urgency and coordination needs tend to appoint CDOs [19] and that CDO presence may be linked to more innovation [46]. Furthermore, part of the job of CDOs is to navigate "tensions between the existing and emerging approaches to innovation with digital technologies" [21]. Digital platforms enable innovation, and a CDO's presence can help align the digital platform strategy with a firm's traditional business.

Due to their responsibilities, CDOs are crucial in implementing digital platform strategies. CDOs help create essential digital capabilities for successful digital transformation [21, 47]. Digital platform strategies, a specific type of digital transformation, may benefit from the expertise CDOs bring. Therefore, we hypothesize:

> **Hypothesis 3:** *The presence of a CDO positively moderates the effect of a digital platform strategy on a firm's profitability.*

3 Method

We conducted a quantitative analysis on the impact of digital platform strategies and the role of CDOs, using data from the S&P1500 companies. To determine if a firm implemented a digital platform strategy in a given year, we analyzed filings submitted to the United States Securities and Exchange Commission (SEC) from S&P1500 companies using the Wharton Research Data Services SEC Analytics Suite, searching for keywords indicative of platform strategies. This search encompassed annual reports (10-K forms), quarterly reports (10-Q forms), and significant event reports (8-K forms), including their full texts and exhibits. Our methodology involved crafting an initial list of keywords from known digital platform strategy implementations, refined through iterative searches of the filings. This process identified 231 firms with digital platform strategies and narrowed them down to 161 that actually implemented them.

Additionally, we corroborated our findings with the ProgrammableWeb dataset of public APIs, using public API availability as a proxy for identifying platform strategies [48]. This approach assumes that a strategy not mentioned in SEC filings is not strategically significant to the company. With the 161 firms, we generated an unbalanced panel dataset from 2000 to 2020, resulting in 26,906 firm-year observations, incorporating financial information from Compustat, manual coding for type of platform strategy (Build vs. Buy), and CDO presence from BoardEx. We chose this timeframe because digital platform strategies became significantly more prevalent in the 2000s [32], a trend supported by our review of SEC filings from the S&P1500, where 99% of mentions of digital platform strategies occurred from 2000 onwards.

3.1 Variables

Profitability. We measured profitability for the S&P1500 as return on assets (ROA), defined as the ratio of net income and total assets. ROA reflects the efficiency with which a company utilizes its assets to generate earnings. It offers a quantifiable metric of managerial efficacy and operational performance [49]. We apply a time lag to profitability, our dependent variable. In general, it has been shown that the effect of IT investments has a long-term impact on firm profitability rather than short-term [50, 51]. For example, lags of one to three years [51] and one to seven years [50] have been studied. In particular, implementing a digital platform strategy requires time. Its effect on profitability depends on third parties that enroll in the emerging digital platform ecosystem, a process that takes time [48]. We implemented a time lag of one to six years based on timelines for platform implementation reported in qualitative studies [6, 10, 37]. Because lagging reduces the number of available data points, shifting our data series back by one to six years caused our initial 26,906 observations for analysis to be reduced to 25,141, 23,487, 21,880, 20,300, 18,760, and 17,277, respectively.

Digital platform strategies. After identifying 161 firms from SEC filings that have implemented a digital platform strategy, we determined the year each firm implemented its digital platform. We then assigned a value of 1 to that year and to each subsequent year in the panel data for that firm; otherwise, the value is set to 0. For example, suppose a firm has panel data from 2000 to 2020 and implemented a digital platform strategy in 2018. That firm's digital platform strategy variable will be assigned a value of 1 from 2018 to 2020.

Buy and build strategy. In the next step, we distinguished build and buy platform strategies for the 161 firms. Drawing on [1] definition of the strategies, we manually searched firms' websites and online news for their platform launches. The build strategy is assigned a value of 1 if it is mentioned in the news that the firm developed their platform independently, otherwise, it is set to 0. We concluded that 126 firms had opted for a build strategy while 35 had applied a buy strategy.

The presence of a CDO. We extracted information on the presence of CDO of the S&P1500 companies from BoardEx and classified it as a binary variable. The presence of a CDO was indicated by either the job title containing the term "digit" or a role responsible for digital transformation as per the job description. Therefore, in our analysis, 'CDO presence' is assigned a value of 1 if a firm has a designated CDO position in a given year.

Control variables. We included control variables for top management team characteristics and firm-specific factors influencing decision-making and strategy. Digital Upper Echelons (DUE) Presence is a binary indicator for the presence of key digital officers (CDO, Chief Information Officer (CIO), Chief Technology Officer (CTO), Chief Information Security Officer (CISO). Similarly, CISO Presence and CIO/CTO Presence are binary variables indicating the presence of these specific roles. We also controlled for firm characteristics: firm size (log of total assets plus one), leverage (ratio of debt to equity), asset tangibility (ratio of net tangible assets to total assets), capital expenditure (capital expenditures to total assets ratio), R&D expenditure (R&D spending to total assets ratio), Tobin's Q (a valuation measure), and firm age (log of the difference between the current year and the year of the initial public offering plus one). Additionally, we considered industry factors like industry turbulence (entry and exit rates), market concentration (Herfindahl-Hirschman index), and industry growth (three-year total assets growth) that may affect digital platform strategies and profitability.

3.2 Panel Regression

To test the hypotheses, we used ordinary least squares (OLS) with clustered standard errors to estimate a linear fixed effect model. We included firm and year-fixed effects to control for time-invariant heterogeneity and time trends [52]. We estimate the model in Eq. (1) to test Hypothesis 1 on the main effect of digital platform strategy on profitability and the model in Eq. (2) to test Hypothesis 2 on the effect of a buy and a build strategy on profitability. Then, we estimate the model in Eq. (3) to test Hypothesis 3 on the moderating effect of CDO.

$$Y_{i(t+1)} = \alpha_i + \tau_t + \beta_0 \text{Digital Platform Strategy}_{it} + X_{it} + \varepsilon_{it} \tag{1}$$

$$Y_{i(t+1)} = \alpha_i + \tau_t + \beta_1 \text{Build Strategy}_{it} + \beta_2 \text{Buy Strategy}_{it} + X_{it} + \varepsilon_{it} \tag{2}$$

$$\begin{aligned} Y_{i(t+1)} = \alpha_i + \tau_t + \beta_3 \text{Digital Platform Strategy}_{it} + \beta_4 \text{CDO Presence}_{it} \\ * \text{Digital Platform Strategy}_{it} + \beta_5 \text{CDO Presence}_{it} + X_{it} + \varepsilon_{it} \end{aligned} \tag{3}$$

where $Y_{i(t+1)}$ indicates profitability. β_0, β_1, β_2 and β_4 are coefficients of interest. β_0 indicates the impact of a digital platform strategy. β_1 and β_2 indicates the impact of a build strategy and a buy strategy. β_4 indicates the moderating effect of a CDO. X_{it} indicates the time-variant control variables. α_i and τ_t indicate firm fixed effect and year fixed effect, which considers the time-invariant omitted variable bias and variables changing over time for all the individuals, respectively. ε_{it} indicates the error term.

To ensure our findings' robustness, we used the Generalized Method of Moments (GMM) for parameter estimation, effectively addressing endogeneity issues from unobserved variables or reverse causality—challenges not fully met by fixed effects models and a number of cross sections where N is large (e.g., 161 firms) while the number of periods T (e.g., 21 years) is small as in this case [53]. GMM's use of instrumental variables minimizes bias, particularly in dynamic panel data, making it ideal for robustness checks and managing dynamic endogeneity [54]. Followed by [55] and [56], we evaluate GMM's reliability by using serial correlation tests AR(1) and AR(2), which test for first-order and second-order serial correlation. The expected acceptance of the "no autocorrelation" null hypothesis for AR(2) confirms the validity of the model estimates. Moreover, we apply Sargan tests to validate the instrumental variables, aiming for higher p-values to verify their exogeneity.

We chose system GMM over differenced GMM for its enhanced ability to reduce biases from omitted variables, unobserved effects, measurement errors, and endogeneity, using instrumental variables to improve profitability estimates [55, 56]. To minimize bias and prevent overfitting, we employ the rule of thumb that the number of instruments should not be higher than the number of periods [57] and collapsed instruments to a maximum of two lags for both transformed and level equations, permitting longer lags for transformed equations. Therefore, 13 variables in our study, such as CISO Presence, DUE Presence, CIO/CTO Presence, Firm Size, Leverage, Asset Tangibility, Capital Expenditure, R&D Expenditure, Tobin's Q, Firm Age, Industry Turbulence, Market Concentration, and Industry Growth were treated as instrumental variables.

4 Results

4.1 The Effect of Digital Platform Strategies

First, we analyzed the impact of digital platform strategies on a firm's profitability. Digital Platform Strategy is the variable of interest. As shown in Table 1, our analysis of the lagged results reveals a complex pattern that unfolds over time.

In the initial year of implementing a digital platform strategy (year zero) and the subsequent four years, we observed positive effects on firm profitability, though these were not statistically significant. However, by the fifth ($\beta = 0.052$, $p < 0.05$) and sixth years ($\beta = 0.076$, $p < 0.01$), the positive impacts became statistically

Table 1 Effect of a digital platform strategy on firm profitability

DV	Profitability						
Lagged years	(0)	(1)	(2)	(3)	(4)	(5)	(6)
Digital Platform Strategy	0.070	0.0681	0.015	0.014	0.039	0.052**	0.076***
CDO Presence	−0.003	0.018	0.052	0.049	0.052	−0.039	0.026
CISO Presence	−0.011	0.003	−0.004	−0.025	−0.046**	−0.045**	−0.0419*
DUE Presence	−0.018	−0.014	−0.018	−0.009	−0.001	0.028	0.052
CIO/CTO Presence	0.011	−0.005	0.014	0.017	−0.011	−0.021	−0.052
Firm Size	0.058**	−0.046**	−0.06***	−0.056***	−0.074***	−0.054***	−0.051**
Leverage	−0.000	−0.001	−0.012	0.000	−0.001	−0.003	−0.003
Asset Tangibility	0.003	−0.044**	−0.024	−0.015	−0.000	−0.012	0.014
Capital Expenditure	−0.073	−0.025	−0.065	−0.041	0.057	−0.089	−0.161
R&D Expenditure	−0.19***	−0.10***	−0.081	−0.000	0.008	0.008	0.003
Tobin's Q	−0.001	0.02***	0.02***	0.012***	0.004	0.004	0.004*
Firm Age	0.05***	0.042**	0.037**	0.033*	0.014	−0.009	−0.009
Industry Turbulence	−0.222*	−0.103	0.172*	0.236**	−0.078	−0.319***	−0.031
Market Concentration	−0.046	−0.047	0.64***	0.584***	0.103	0.259	0.652***
Industry Growth	0.122	0.072	0.066	0.086**	−0.014	−0.019	−0.021
Firm Fixed Effects	Yes						
Year Fixed Effects	Yes						
Observations	26,906	25,141	23,487	21,880	20,300	18,760	17,277
Adj. *R*-squared	0.034	0.042	0.030	0.018	0.017	0.019	0.021

Notes Significance levels: $*p < 0.1$, $**p < 0.05$, $***p < 0.01$

significant, indicating an average increase in firm profitability of 5.2% and 7.6% in years five and six, respectively. This finding supports Hypothesis 1. In our robustness check, the relationship between digital platform strategy and firm profitability showed statistically significant positive impacts from the beginning, with notable increases in profitability in year zero ($\beta = 0.086, p < 0.10$), the first year ($\beta = 7.198, p < 0.10$), the third year ($\beta = 1.670$, $p < 0.01$), the fourth year ($\beta = 2.302$, $p < 0.01$), and the fifth year ($\beta = 12.237, p < 0.10$). In addition, low p-values below 5% for AR(1) from year zero to year six and high p-values above 5% for AR(2) affirm the validity of the estimated model. Moreover, the high p-values from the Sargan test, namely 0.780, 0.884, 0.257, 0.760, 0.276, 0.321, and 0.131, confirm the validity of the instrumental variables. These results further substantiate Hypothesis 1, confirming digital platform strategies' positive effect on firm profitability.

4.2 *The Effect of Build vs. Buy Strategies*

Next, we analyzed the effect of implementing a digital platform with a build strategy vs. a buy strategy. As shown in Table 2, both the build and buy strategies positively affect firm profitability from year zero to year six. However, the positive impact of a build strategy is statistically significant in years five and six ($\beta = 0.0492, p < 0.10$; $\beta = 0.075$, $p < 0.10$), suggesting that a build strategy could enhance firm profitability by 4.92% in the fifth year and 7.5% in the sixth year. These findings underscore the beneficial effect of digital platform strategies, mainly through implementing a build strategy, thus supporting Hypothesis 2.

In the robustness check, the stronger positive moderating effect of the build strategy is further confirmed for year zero ($\beta = 0.094$, $p < 0.05$) and the fourth year ($\beta = 0.067$, $p < 0.05$). The p-values below 5% for AR(1) and above 5% for AR(2) confirm the model's validity. Additionally, the p-values from the Sargan test, which were 0.775, 0.004, 0.057, 0.360, 0.412, 0.379, and 0.264, verified the validity of the instruments.

4.3 *The Moderating Effect of the CDO Position*

Finally, we examined Hypothesis 3, which posits that CDOs positively moderate the relationship between a digital platform strategy and a firm's profitability. As demonstrated in Table 3, significant positive effects were found in the fifth ($\beta = 0.132$, $p < 0.10$) and sixth ($\beta = 0.166$, $p < 0.10$) years, indicating CDO presence could enhance profitability by 13.2% and 16.6%, respectively. However, the year zero to year two showed a nonsignificant negative impact from CDOs.

Our robustness tests echoed these findings, showing a negative effect in year zero ($\beta = -0.101, p < 0.10$) but positive effects in the fifth ($\beta = 0.072, p < 0.10$) and sixth ($\beta = 0.196, p < 0.01$) years. The p-values below 5% for AR(1) and above 5% p-values

Table 2 Effect of build vs. buy strategy

DV	Profitability						
Lagged years	(0)	(1)	(2)	(3)	(4)	(5)	(6)
BuildStrategy	0.0868	0.0810	0.0071	0.0138	0.0357	0.0492*	0.075***
BuyStrategy	0.0096	0.0205	0.0445	0.0127	0.0530	0.0677	0.0805
CDO Presence	−0.0017	0.0192	0.0505	0.0489	0.0516	−0.0387	0.0261
CISO Presence	−0.0111	0.0031	−0.0047	−0.0258	−0.0459**	−0.0455**	−0.0419*
DUE Presence	−0.0177	−0.0135	−0.0182	−0.0094	−0.0011	0.0291	0.0521
CIO/CTO Presence	0.0107	−0.0054	0.0148	0.0171	−0.0112	−0.0206	−0.0519
Firm Size	0.0572**	−0.0464**	−0.061***	−0.057***	−0.075***	−0.0540***	−0.052**
Leverage	−0.0001	−0.0009	−0.0116	0.0000	−0.0009	−0.0032	−0.0036
Asset Tangibility	0.0031	−0.0437**	−0.0243	−0.0146	−0.0002	−0.0118	0.0140
Capital Expenditure	−0.0732	−0.0250	−0.0655	−0.0419	0.0571	−0.0897	−0.1612
R&D Expenditure	−0.192***	−0.095***	−0.0806	−0.0003	0.0083	0.0080	0.0028
Tobin's Q	−0.0014	0.01***	0.018***	0.012***	0.0041	0.0038	0.0040
Firm Age	0.053***	0.0420**	0.0368**	0.0329*	0.0142	−0.0094	−0.0094
Industry Turbulence	−0.2222*	−0.1026	0.1723*	0.2356**	−0.0783	−0.3190***	−0.0314
Market Concentration	−0.0430	−0.045***	0.640***	0.584***	0.1022	0.2587	0.652***
Industry Growth	0.1219	0.0718	0.0656	0.0857**	−0.0138	−0.0191	−0.0207
Firm Fixed Effects	Yes						
Year Fixed Effects	Yes						
Observations	26,906	25,141	23,487	21,880	20,300	18,760	17,277
Adj. *R*-squared	0.0342	0.0424	0.0293	0.0177	0.0172	0.0188	0.0206

Notes Significance levels: $*p < 0.1$, $**p < 0.05$, $***p < 0.01$

Table 3 The moderating effect of CDOs

DV	Profitability						
Lagged years	(0)	(1)	(2)	(3)	(4)	(5)	(6)
CDO Presence*Digital Platform Strategy	−0.125	−0.062	−0.024	0.026	0.005	0.132*	0.166*
CDO Presence	0.011	0.025	0.055	0.045	0.051	−0.045	0.016
Digital Platform Strategy	0.071	0.069	0.015	0.013	0.038	0.052**	0.075***
CISO Presence	−0.016	0.003	−0.005	−0.026	−0.046**	−0.046**	−0.042*
DUE Presence	−0.019	−0.014	−0.018	−0.009	−0.001	0.029	0.053
CIO/CTO Presence	0.011	−0.005	0.015	0.017	−0.011	−0.021	−0.053
Firm Size	0.058**	−0.046**	−0.061***	−0.057**	−0.08***	−0.054***	−0.051**
Leverage	−0.000	−0.001	−0.012	0.000	−0.001	−0.003	−0.004
Asset Tangibility	0.003	−0.044**	−0.024	−0.015	−0.000	−0.012	0.014
Capital Expenditure	−0.073	−0.025	−0.065	−0.042	0.057	−0.089	−0.161
R&D Expenditure	−0.19***	−0.09***	−0.081	−0.000	0.008	0.008	0.003
Tobin's Q	−0.001	0.016***	0.018***	0.012***	0.004	0.004	0.004*
Firm Age	0.053***	0.042**	0.0 37**	0.033*	0.014	−0.009	−0.009
Industry Turbulence	−0.221*	−0.102	0.172*	0.235**	−0.078	−0.319***	−0.032
Market Concentration	−0.046	−0.047	0.642***	0.584***	0.103	0.259	0.651***
Industry Growth	0.122	0.072	0.066	0.086**	−0.014	−0.019	−0.021
Firm Fixed Effects	Yes						
Year Fixed Effects	Yes						
Observations	26,906	25,141	23,487	21,880	20,300	18,760	17,277
Adj. R-squared	0.034	0.042	0.030	0.018	0.017	0.019	0.021

Notes Significance levels: $*p < 0.1$, $**p < 0.05$, $***p < 0.01$

for AR(2) further affirmed the model's validity. Moreover, the Sargan test p-values from year zero to year six were 0.780, 0.004, 0.109, 0.397, 0.644, 0.523, and 0.012, confirming the validity of all instrumental variables. These results indicate that CDOs significantly contribute to the long-term success of digital strategies, supporting our hypothesis.

5 Discussion

To understand the impact of digital platform strategies on firm profitability, we found that these strategies offer long-term benefits rather than immediate profits. This aligns with case studies showing that incumbents take several years for digital platforms to gain adoption by partners and customers [6, 37]. Our research suggests organically building digital platforms is more advantageous than acquisitions, as it avoids complexities in integrating information systems [39] and the difficulties associated with acquiring digital platforms [40].

The presence of CDOs enhances the positive long-term effects of digital platform strategies on profitability. This finding confirms work that shows that CDOs, who often spearhead digital innovation [21], can significantly influence profitability [58]. However, indications suggest that a CDO's presence might negatively impact in the short run. Misalignment between CDO initiatives and the firm's core needs or undue time pressure on CDOs could dampen the potential long-term positive impact. Confirming this will require qualitative studies on digital platform strategy implementation in companies with and without a CDO.

Implications for theory. Our findings add to the literature on digital platforms and digital upper echelons, offering insights into the debate on the value of digital platform strategies for companies. On the one hand, the management and IS literature provides theoretical foundations and anecdotal evidence of the success of digital platform strategies [5, 6, 37, 59]. On the other hand, many examples of failed platforms have been reported. In particular, for established companies from traditional industries, the struggle to develop digital platforms has become evident (e.g., [12, 60]).

Up to now, the management and IS literature lacks a comprehensive analysis of the potential of digital platform strategies for companies in general and not just for the big tech companies and digital startups. We contribute to this gap by confirming that the "inverting-the-firm" effect [5] of digital platforms contributes to a firm's profitability in the long term, particularly for firms that employ a build strategy rather than a buy strategy. We show that to establish a digital platform strategy successfully, it is not enough to acquire a digital platform; instead, the transformation has to be driven by internal actors.

We offer new insights into the role of CDOs in the success of digital platform strategies, complementing existing scholarship focused on platform characteristics—such as architecture [24], openness [61, 62], and boundary resources for developers

[25]—and platform owner attributes like organizational identity [63] and capabilities [64, 65]. We highlight the significance of CDOs in executing digital platform strategies. Future studies could explore how executive traits, technical systems, and reporting structures impact a firm's profitability, as well as CDOs' influence on firm innovativeness [46], where initial findings suggest a positive impact, could offer valuable perspectives for future research. Future research should examine the dynamics between CDOs and traditional digital leadership roles, such as CIOs and CTOs, during digital platform implementation [66]. Traditional roles may have goals differing from CDOs, while CISOs may have unique security concerns. A detailed study using both quantitative and qualitative methods could provide insights into how these roles impact the success of digital platform strategies.

Implications for practice. Our research provides insights for companies considering digital platform strategies. First, digital platforms often require time to yield benefits, necessitating patience. Second, firms adopting a build strategy should assess their leadership's digital expertise and consider appointing a CDO to address gaps while managing potential conflicts among multiple digital leadership roles. Third, acquiring digital platforms can accelerate ecosystem development but may present integration challenges. Additionally, joining an existing platform ecosystem, as an alternative strategy outlined by [1], allows companies to gain platform ecosystem experience and buy time for developing their own platforms, albeit at the risk of dependence on the ecosystem's orchestrator. These considerations highlight the nuanced decision-making process in effectively leveraging digital platform strategies.

Limitations. Our study has limitations, primarily in identifying digital platform strategies. We focus on those mentioned in SEC filings, assuming strategic importance leads to disclosure, but companies might not disclose all strategies. Additionally, we identify the first occurrence of a strategy without considering subsequent platforms. Future research could explore a detailed timeline of strategies, including success metrics and the impact of digital leadership roles beyond CDOs, such as digital middle management and roles like CISOs and Chief Data Officers. Broader sources like press releases or executive surveys could capture a wider range of strategies.

6 Conclusion

While digital platforms have made inroads into many industries, from banking to manufacturing to farming, it is still unclear to what extent these companies can benefit from these platforms. Drawing on the S&P 1500 companies, we show that digital platform strategies contribute to a firm's profitability in the long run, and the positive effect is higher for the build strategy, that is when the firm implements the platform internally. Next, we show that the emerging position of the CDO has a positive moderating effect on the firm's profitability. In sum, our study shows that companies seeking to realize profitability from a digital platform strategy must take at least a five-year perspective and consider appointing a CDO, giving them sufficient time to implement the strategy.

Acknowledgements This work was partly funded by the Deutsche Forschungsgemeinschaft (DFG, German Research Foundation) [project no. 444990299] and the Austrian Science Fund (FWF) [project no. I6567-G].

References

1. Cusumano, M. A., Gawer, A., & Yoffie, D. B. (2019). *The business of platforms: Strategy in the age of digital competition, innovation, and power*. Harper Business.
2. Kretschmer, T., Leiponen, A., Schilling, M., & Vasudeva, G. (2022). Platform ecosystems as metaorganizations: Implications for platform strategies. *Strategic Management Journal, 43*(3), 405–424.
3. Panico, C., & Cennamo, C. (2022). User preferences and strategic interactions in platform ecosystems. *Strategic Management Journal, 43*(3), 507–529.
4. Miller, C. D., & Toh, P. K. (2020). Complementary components and returns from coordination within ecosystems via standard setting. *Strategic Management Journal, 43*(3), 627–662.
5. Parker, G. G., Van Alstyne, M. W., & Jiang, X. (2017). Platform ecosystems: How developers invert the firm. *MIS Quarterly, 41*(1), 255–266.
6. Sandberg, J., Holmström, J., & Lyytinen, K. (2020). Digitization and phase transitions in platform organizing logics: Evidence from the process automation industry. *MIS Quarterly, 44*(1), 129–153.
7. Svahn, F., Mathiassen, L., & Lindgren, R. (2017). Embracing digital innovation in incumbent firms: How Volvo cars managed competing concerns. *MIS Quarterly, 41*(1), 239–253.
8. Edwards, D. (2018). General Electric puts Predix IIoT platform and its digital business up for sale. *Robotics & Automation.*
9. Parker, G. G., & Van Alstyne, M. W. (2005). Two-sided network effects: A theory of information product design. *Management Science, 51*(10), 1494–1504.
10. Schreieck, M., Wiesche, M., & Krcmar, H. (2022). From product platform ecosystem to innovation platform ecosystem: An institutional perspective on the governance of ecosystem transformations. *Journal of the Association for Information Systems, 23*(6), 1354–1385.
11. Schreieck, M., Ondrus, J., Wiesche, M., & Krcmar, H. (2023). A typology of multi-platform integration strategies. *Information Systems Journal, 43*(3), 828–853.
12. Yoffie, D. B., Gawer, A., & Cusumano, M. A. (2019, May). A study of more than 250 platforms reveals why most fail. *Harvard Business Review.*
13. Horlacher, A., & Hess, T. (2016). *What does a chief digital officer do? Managerial tasks and roles of a new C-level position in the context of digital transformation.* 49th Hawaii International Conference on System Sciences (HICSS), Hawaii, USA.
14. Bughin, J., Catlin, T., & Dietz, M. (2019). The right digital-platform strategy. *McKinsey Quarterly.*
15. Tiwana, A. (2014). *Platform ecosystems: Aligning architecture, governance, and strategy.* Morgan Kaufmann.
16. Singh, A., & Hess, T. (2017). How chief digital officers promote the digital transformation of their companies. *MIS Quarterly Executive, 16*(1), 1–17.
17. Hambrick, D. C. (2007). Upper echelons theory: An update. *Academy of Management Review, 32*(2), 334–343.
18. Hambrick, D. C., & Mason, P. A. (1984). Upper echelons: The organization as a reflection of its top managers. *The Academy of Management Review, 9*(2), 193–206.

19. Firk, S., Hanelt, A., Oehmichen, J., & Wolff, M. (2021). Chief digital officers: An analysis of the presence of a centralized digital transformation role. *Journal of Management Studies, 58*(7), 1800–1831.
20. Scuotto, V., Magni, D., Theofilos, T., & Giudice, M. D. (2022). Chief digital officer and organizational creativity toward digitalization. *IEEE Transactions on Engineering Management, 71*, 13775–13786.
21. Tumbas, S., Berente, N., & Brocke, J. (2018). Digital innovation and institutional entrepreneurship: Chief Digital Officer perspectives of their emerging role. *Journal of Information Technology, 33*(3), 188–202.
22. Gao, Y., & Thatcher, J. B. (2021). *IT governance, firm performance, and the rise of the digital upper echelon.* Forty-Second International Conference on Information Systems (ICIS), Austin, TX, USA.
23. Huang, Y. (2024). *The effect of AI integration into digital platforms—An event study in the banking industry.* Thirtieth Americas Conference on Information Systems, Salt Lake City, USA.
24. Tiwana, A., Konsynski, B., & Bush, A. A. (2010). Platform evolution: Coevolution of platform architecture, governance, and environmental dynamics. *Information Systems Research, 21*(4), 675–687.
25. Ghazawneh, A., & Henfridsson, O. (2013). Balancing platform control and external contribution in third-party development: The boundary resources model. *Information Systems Journal, 23*(2), 173–192.
26. Eaton, B. D., Elaluf-Calderwood, S., Sørensen, C., & Yoo, Y. (2015). Distributed tuning of boundary resources: The case of Apple's iOS Service System. *MIS Quarterly, 39*(1), 217–243.
27. Förderer, J., Kude, T., Mithas, S., & Heinzl, A. (2018). Does platform owner's entry crowd out innovation? Evidence from Google photos. *Information Systems Research, 29*(2), 444–460.
28. Cennamo, C., Ozalp, H., & Kretschmer, T. (2018). Platform architecture and quality tradeoffs of multihoming complements. *Information Systems Research, 29*(2), 461–478.
29. Pauli, T., Fielt, E., & Matzner, M. (2021). Digital industrial platforms. *Business & Information Systems Engineering, 63*, 181–190.
30. Riasanow, T., Jäntgen, L., Hermes, S., Böhm, M., & Krcmar, H. (2021). Core, intertwined, and ecosystem-specific clusters in platform ecosystems: Analyzing similarities in the digital transformation of the automotive, blockchain, financial, insurance and IIoT industry. *Electronic Markets, 31*(1), 89–104.
31. Perlman, C. (2017). From product to platform: John Deere revolutionizes farming. *HBS Digital Initiative.* https://digit.hbs.org/submission/from-product-to-platform-john-deere-revolutionizes-farming/
32. Parker, G. G., Van Alstyne, M. W., & Choudary, S. P. (2016). *Platform Revolution.* W. W. Norton & Company.
33. Hein, A., Schreieck, M., Riasanow, T., Setzke, D. S., Wiesche, M., Böhm, M., & Krcmar, H. (2019). Digital platform ecosystems. *Electronic Markets, 30*(1), 87–98.
34. Leswing, K. (2022). Apple implies it generated record revenue from the App Store during 2021. *CNBC.* https://www.cnbc.com/2022/01/10/apple-implies-it-generated-record-revenue-from-app-store-during-2021-.html
35. Armstrong, M. (2006). Competition in two-sided markets. *RAND Journal of Economics, 37*(3), 668–691.
36. Hermes, S., Töller, N., Hein, A., & Weking, J. (2020). *Gaining control over critical platforms: A comparative case study of European Consortia.* Twenty-Eigth European Conference on Information Systems (ECIS), Marrakech, Morocco.
37. Khanagha, S., Ansari, S. S., Paroutis, S., & Oviedo, L. (2022). Mutualism and the dynamics of new platform creation: A study of Cisco and Fog computing. *Strategic Management Journal, 43*(3), 476–506.
38. Sarker, S., Sarker, S., Sahaym, A., & Bjørn-Andersen, N. (2012). Exploring value cocreation in relationship between an ERP vendor and its partners: A revelatory case study. *MIS Quarterly, 36*(1), 317–338.

39. Baker, E. W., & Niederman, F. (2014). Integrating the IS functions after mergers and acquisitions: Analyzing business-IT alignment. *Journal of Strategic Information Systems, 23*(2), 112–127.
40. Toppenberg, G., Henningsson, S., & Eaton, B. (2016). *Reinventing the platform core through acquisition: A case study.* Hawaii International Conference on System Sciences (HICSS), Hawaii, USA.
41. Rolland, K. H., Mathiassen, L., & Rai, A. (2018). Managing digital platforms in user organizations: The interactions between digital options and digital debt. *Information Systems Research, 29*(2), 419–443.
42. Neely, B. H., Lovelace, J. B., Cowen, A. P., & Hiller, N. J. (2020). Metacritiques of upper echelons theory: Verdicts and recommendations for future research. *Journal of Management, 46*(6), 1029–1062.
43. Rickards, T., Smaje, K., & Sohoni, V. (2015). 'Transformer in chief': The new chief digital officer. *McKinsey Quarterly*, September 1.
44. Davison, R. M., Wong, L. H. M., & Peng, J. (2023). The art of digital transformation as crafted by a chief digital officer. *International Journal of Information Management, 69*, Article 102617.
45. Singh, A., Klarner, P., & Hess, T. (2020). How do chief digital officers pursue digital transformation activities? The role of organization design parameters. *Long Range Planning, 53*(3), Article 101890.
46. Salas, R. R., & Fernandez-Corrales, C. (2022). *Does a CDO enhance company inventiveness? An empirical study on new managerial positions and innovation.* Twenty-Eighth Americas Conference on Information Systems (AMCIS), Minneapolis, MN, USA.
47. Vial, G. (2019). Understanding digital transformation: A review and a research agenda. *Journal of Strategic Information Systems, 28*(2), 118–144.
48. Benzell, S. G., Hersh, J., & Alstyne, M. V. (2021). *How APIs create growth by inverting the firm.* SSRN. https://papers.ssrn.com/sol3/papers.cfm?abstract_id=3432591
49. Cho, S. Y., & Lee, C. (2019). Managerial efficiency, corporate social performance, and corporate financial performance. *Journal of Business Ethics, 158*, 467–486.
50. Brynjolfsson, E., & Hitt, L. M. (1998). Beyond the productivity paradox. *Communications of the ACM, 41*(8), 49–55.
51. Santhanam, R., & Hartono, E. (2003). Issues in linking information technology capability to firm performance. *MIS Quarterly, 27*(1), 125–153.
52. Tsionas, E. G., & Kumbhakar, S. C. (2014). Firm heterogeneity, persistent and transient technical inefficiency: A generalized true random-effects model. *Journal of Applied Econometrics, 29*(1), 110–132.
53. Hansen, L. P. (1982). Large sample properties of generalized method of moments estimators. *Econometrica: Journal of the Econometric Society*, 1029–1054.
54. Chan, K. C., Karolyi, G. A., Longstaff, F. A., & Sanders, A. B. (1992). An empirical comparison of alternative models of the short-term interest rate. *Journal of Finance, 47*(3), 1209–1227.
55. Arellano, M., & Bover, O. (1995). Another look at the instrumental variable estimation of error-components models. *Journal of Econometrics, 68*(1), 29–51.
56. Blundell, R., & Bond, S. (1998). Initial conditions and moment restrictions in dynamic panel data models. *Journal of Econometrics, 87*(1), 115–143.
57. Asongu, S. A., & Nwachukwu, J. C. (2018). Increasing foreign aid for inclusive human development in Africa. *Social Indicators Research, 138*(2), 443–466.
58. Kohli, R., & Melville, N. P. (2019). Digital innovation: A review and synthesis. *Information Systems Journal, 29*(1), 200–223.
59. Wang, P. (2021). Connecting the parts with the whole: Toward an information ecology theory of digital innovation ecosystems. *MIS Quarterly, 45*(1), 397–422.
60. Alstyne, M. W. V., Parker, G. G., & Choudary, S. P. (2016). 6 reasons platforms fail. *Harward Business Review.*
61. Benlian, A., Hilkert, D., & Hess, T. (2015). How open is this platform? The meaning and measurement of platform openness from the complementors' perspective. *Journal of Information Technology, 30*(3), 209–228.

62. Zhang, Y., Li, J., & Tong, T. W. (2022). Platform governance matters: How platform gatekeeping affects knowledge sharing among complementors. *Strategic Management Journal, 43*(3), 599–626.
63. Lindgren, R., Eriksson, O., & Lyytinen, K. (2015). Managing identity tensions during mobile ecosystem evolution. *Journal of Information Technology, 30*(3), 229–244.
64. Helfat, C. E., & Raubitschek, R. S. (2018). Dynamic and integrative capabilities for profiting from innovation in digital platform-based ecosystems. *Research Policy, 47*(8), 1391–1399.
65. Schreieck, M., Wiesche, M., & Krcmar, H. (2021). Capabilities for value co-creation and value capture in emergent platform ecosystems: A longitudinal case study of SAP's cloud platform. *Journal of Information Technology, 36*(4), 365–390.
66. Lorenz, F., & Buchwald, A. (2023). A perfect match or an arranged marriage? How chief digital officers and chief information officers perceive their relationship: A dyadic research design. *European Journal of Information Systems, 32*(3), 372–389.

Dynamic Capabilities to Manage Generative Artificial Intelligence in Digital Transformation Efforts

Daria Höhener

Abstract Incumbent firms face significant challenges due to rapid technological advancements, notably through generative artificial intelligence (genAI). By interviewing experienced digital leaders in a multiple-case study involving five organizations, this study elucidates eleven microfoundations, also referred to as low-level dynamic capabilities (DC). The specific focus centers on sensing, seizing, and transforming within the context of digital transformation (DT) efforts, offering insights into how organizations can navigate and leverage genAI to enhance their DT strategies. The identified microfoundations encompass 1) empowerment and knowledge utilization, 2) innovation ecosystem engagement, 3) organizational learning and openness, 4) interdisciplinary collaboration, 5) learning-driven innovation network, 6) organizational agility, 7) strategic leadership, 8) alignment and governance enhancement, 9) adaptive and informed culture, 10) organizational resilience, and 11) synergy creation. These foundations collectively provide a framework for leveraging genAI effectively from an organizational perspective.

1 Introduction

Generative artificial intelligence (genAI) marks a transformative era for organizations and industries, unlocking new paths for enhancing competitive advantage [1]. Yet, the primary challenge emerges as firms must evolve their capabilities to navigate this swiftly changing technological domain successfully [2]; 40% of the respondents of a large study [3] report that they are grappling to effectively implement artificial intelligence (AI) technologies, reflecting a gap in leveraging technologies' full potential to reshape business models, processes and products [4, 5].

Existing literature suggests that while genAI offers substantial opportunities for enhancing competitive advantage [6], the payoff from such technological investments often remains unclear [5], underscoring the significance of dynamic capabilities (DC)

D. Höhener (✉)
University of St.Gallen, St.Gallen, Switzerland
e-mail: daria.hoehener@unisg.ch

C. M. Flath et al. (eds.), *Digital Innovation and Organizational Transformation*, Lecture Notes in Information Systems and Organisation 83,
https://doi.org/10.1007/978-3-032-08483-5_13

as a means to elucidate the leveraging of technological resources for strategic advantage. Furthermore, the development of DC is highlighted as crucial for advancing successful digital transformation (DT) [7]. However, a key issue identified in the literature is the gap between the rapid advancement of genAI in industry practices and the pace of academic research [8], presenting a challenge in fully understanding and defining the capabilities required to harness genAI effectively. This paper responds to calls for more focused research on the organizational DC and conditions necessary for leveraging genAI by Banh & Strobel [9] and Feuerriegel et al. [10], emphasizing the need to closely examine and illuminate these capabilities to steer the technological possibilities of genAI in the direction for successful DT.

This qualitative multiple-case study enables the development of a nuanced understanding of how organizations utilize low-level DC, also referred to as microfoundations [11], to harness the transformative potential of genAI. The research question investigates: Which microfoundations, according to established organizations within the DC types of sensing, seizing, and transforming, are crucial for leveraging genAI in DT efforts? The study analyses five organizations, four from the private sector and one from public administration, drawing insights from thirteen experienced leaders through interviews and additional document reviews to provide a comprehensive perspective.

The research enriches the ongoing dialogue on DC within the information systems (IS) field (e.g., Steininger et al. [12]) by identifying eleven organizational microfoundations significantly impacting sensing, seizing, and transforming DT efforts. In doing so, the present study provides organizations with a guide on which aspects to concentrate on to leverage genAI.

2 Theoretical Foundation

2.1 DC to Achieve Competitive Advantage

DC theory evolved from Schumpeter's [13] early insights on the displacing of incumbent firms by entrants, Porter's [14] five forces model to understanding the positioning of the firm, and through the resource-based view (RBV) emphasizing valuable, rare, imperfectly imitable and non-substitutable (VRIN) resources as sources of competitive advantage [15]. Recognizing the static nature of RBV and the context-dependent attributes [11], the theory was extended to dynamic markets for which Teece et al. [16] introduced DC as the means by which firms integrate, build and reconfigure competencies to address volatile environments. This concept was refined by Eisenhardt & Martin [17], who argued that DC are specific, identifiable routines and that the competitive advantage comes from valuable, scarce, equifinal, interchangeable, and adaptable DC. Teece [18] clustered the DC into sensing, seizing, and transforming activities, marking a shift toward understanding how firms dynamically reconfigure resources in response to environmental shifts. Based on this classification, numerous contemporary publications have been published [19, 20].

Ordinary capabilities are the foundation for efficiency via key routines, also called best practices [21]. Dynamically built upon these are microfoundations, which are understood as processes to adjust, combine, and innovate upon a) existing capabilities and b) development of new ones, which both are guided by the higher-order capabilities [22]. The latter, categorized into sensing, seizing, and transforming, drive strategic adaptation and value creation [18, 22]. There are also other categorizations, such as that of Wang & Ahmed [23]; however, since the categorization according to Teece [18] is predominant in the DT literature, the approach of other authors, e.g., Warner & Wäger [19], is adopted. A balanced exploration-exploitation dichotomy is desired regarding the higher-order capabilities to address DT [11, 24]. Further, it can be noted that higher levels prioritize entrepreneurial management over organizational routines, emphasizing innovation and strategic agility [11].

DC are equivalent to the higher-order capabilities within the dynamic level and are defined as the strategic and organizational routines and processes that allow firms to adapt, integrate, build, upgrade, and reconfigure resources and competencies to address rapidly changing environments [16, 17, 23]. They are characterized by a forward-looking orientation and multidimensional nature, supporting particular activities, and typically require sustained commitments to specialized resources [11, 25, 26].

2.2 Leveraging on DC to Succeed in DT

DT is the further evolvment from digitization and digitalization, employing a shift in how digital technologies need to be viewed to innovate business models and enhance value creation [2, 27, 28]. DT, triggered by the disruption of digital technologies, necessitates a unified vision, aligning the technologies with firm objectives to improve performance and necessitating leadership that fosters a sense of urgency for transformation [5, 7, 28, 29].

DT relies on DC for successful implementation, highlighting the importance of systematically adapting to changes in today's market [7, 25]. DCs in DT are relatively unexplored [30], although they serve as a critical lens for understanding the DT process, especially in incumbent firms [19]. DC are intricately linked to digital maturity, with Marx et al. [31] and Vial [7] indicating that a firm's DC enhance its digital maturity.

DC, comprising discovering and creating opportunities, sensing and seizing capabilities, and executing ones, transforming capabilities, are essential for firms to effectively navigate the intricacies of DT [18, 19].

Sensing entails the vigilant identification, development, and interpretation of new opportunities and threats through a blend of scanning, learning, and creating [18], underpinned by sub-DC like scouting, scenario planning, and mindset crafting [19], to adapt to technological and environmental changes [32].

Seizing involves the strategic agility to capture value [30] from identified opportunities, necessitating changes across the organization to effectively utilize potential business prospects through rapid prototyping and balancing digital portfolios [32, 33].

Transforming entails the continuous renewal and reconfiguration of organizational routines [33] and structures essential for sustained growth as firms evolve and adapt to environmental changes [22]. This capability is underpinned by "redesigning internal structures", and "improving digital maturity" to ensure the firm remains competitive and agile in the digital age [19].

2.3 genAI Requiring Adapted DCs for DT

Digital technologies act as a pivotal driver in DT, enhancing firms' abilities to innovate, exploit external knowledge, and engage in novel business models, thereby fundamentally transforming business strategies, operations, and stakeholder relationships for competitive advantage [34, 35].

genAI is underpinned by deep generative models (DGM) as emergence from deep learning models, which are a subset of machine learning [9]. genAI is revolutionizing industries by enhancing knowledge management, products, services, and customer support through its ability to compress the information layer and generate knowledge from vast datasets [1, 36]. This technology, capable of producing diverse and realistic content across various input and output types [9], is positioned as a disruptive force in the digital realm [37], pushing the boundaries of innovation and redefining the management of AI in the new era of IT management, despite the ethical challenges it presents [8, 38].

Distinct from exploring the technical capabilities of the technology itself, such as those highlighted by Feuerriegel et al. [10] regarding generative pre-trained transformers (GPT) and their application in conversational agents, and examining the augmentation of human capabilities for enhanced speed and efficiency [37], the focus should center on DC of a firm. Leveraging incremental and radical innovation [39] through genAI for DT activities is crucial. With this, the approach outlined by McLaughlin [28] is adopted, concentrating on how organizations can develop sustainable DC to leverage a particular technology effectively to achieve competitive advantage. This emphasis lies in aligning with ever-evolving market conditions and operational challenges to ensure that the integration of genAI contributes substantial business value. As a consequence, DC and a deepened understanding of their underlying microfoundations are needed to excel in leveraging genAI.

3 Research Methodology

3.1 Study Design

Given the complex nature of DC and their critical role in navigating the technological shifts brought about by genAI, this study adopts an empirical case study method, aligning with the approach recommended by Helfat & Winter [26] and successfully employed in related research by Ellström et al. [30] and Jöhnk et al. [24]. This methodological choice is underscored by its effectiveness in deeply exploring contemporary phenomena within their real-world context [40]. This research is characterized by a multiple case study design, incorporating three units of analysis [40]: sensing, seizing, and transforming activities. Numerous case studies serve as a pivotal research strategy for developing theory, where cases are selected to illuminate and extend relationships among constructs, thereby creating a more robust study grounded in diverse empirical evidence [41].

The four case study tactics were meticulously applied to ensure the quality of the research design. These four principles encompass external validity, construct validity, reliability, and internal validity [40]. External validity involves replication logic, which is addressed through the diverse selection of cases examined (see Sect. 3. 2). Construct validity, addressed not only during data collection but also during data aggregation, includes triangulation with primary and secondary data in this study (see Chap. 3.3). Reliability is ensured through the case study database (see Sect. 3. 3). Finally, internal validity, addressed during data analysis, is maintained through systematic coding during the aggregation of insights (see Sect. 3.4).

3.2 Case Selection and Description

In the case selection process, adherence to theoretical sampling, as outlined by Eisenhardt [42], resulted in the identification of five cases at various stages of the AI-driven DT process (see Table 1), as described by Taherizadeh & Beaudry [43].

Table 1 High-level Comparison of the Cases

Case Dimension	A	B	C	D	E
Leading the transformation	◑	◕	◑	◑	◔
1. Evaluating transformation context	●	●	●	●	◕
2. Auditing organizational readiness	◑	◕	◕	◑	◔
3. Piloting the AI integration	◑	◕	◔	◔	◔
4. Scaling the implementation	◔	◑	◔	◔	◔

This diverse selection, indicative of the representativeness principle suggested by Dubé & Paré [44], encompasses the following organizations:

Case A, an insurance company, is integrating genAI use cases into its existing governance through a company-wide AI initiative, initially focusing on setting up an internal knowledge platform based on genAI to expedite information access for employees. Their (gen)AI approach is based on a maturity model of Gartner, contrasting complexity and use versus skills and maturity degree.

Case B, a retail and consumer goods firm that has merged its marketing and IT units, is proficient in data analytics and has defined seven pillars of digitalization, identifying meaningful genAI use cases for each. They have deployed genAI chatbots for customer interaction and leverage the technology for internal marketing enhancements.

Case C, operating in automotive, is enhancing its data-drivenness and digital maturity through a transformation tube map with AI as a core pillar. Currently, they are training employees to use integrated genAI solutions with *Promptathons*.

Case D, a global mobility group excelling in robotic process automation and conducting various genAI proof of concepts, sees significant advantages in managing organizational norms that vary significantly by country through the standardization capabilities of genAI.

Lastly, Case E, a large governmental entity, aims to boost attractiveness and gain insights through a sandbox approach to exploring regulatory and innovative (gen)AI questions, complemented by a DT unit evaluating (gen)AI options for public benefit.

3.3 Data Collection

Interviews were selected for their efficiency in collecting rich data [41], involving a diverse group of pioneers, investigators, and experimenters [3]. In total, twelve semi-structured interviews were conducted:

The interview questions targeted the sensing, seizing, and transforming efforts regarding genAI in DT.

Multiple sources of evidence were used for triangulation [44]. In addition to the interviews, supplementary secondary data consisting of 13 documents, both internal and publicly available, was considered to ensure the quality of the research findings. These secondary sources included annual reports, internal strategy presentations, project presentations, and company websites, which complemented the interview material. This approach helped close potential knowledge gaps and ensured a coherent representation of the cases studied. All documents were stored in a central case study database.

Table 2 Overview of Interview Participants

Case	Industry	Employees	ID	Interviewee(s)
A	Insurance	> 3′000	A1	Head of Advanced Analytics Solutions
			A2	Lead BI Solutions & Architecture
			A3	Head of BI & Analytics
B	Retail and Consumer Goods	> 95′000	B1	Head of Digital and Customer
			B2	Head of AI / ML Analytics
C	Automotive	> 7′000	C1	Head of Data and Advanced Analytics
			C2	Head of Customer Centricity; Ccustomer Retention Specialist
D	Mobility	> 70′000	D1	Chief Digital Officer
			D2	Head Digital Solutions & Data Management
			D3	Digital Solutions Manager
E	Public Administration	> 30′000	E1	Lead Digital Transformation
			E2	Project Lead New Technologies

3.4 *Data Analysis*

Interviews were digitally recorded and transcribed, except for one where notes served as the basis for analysis. The transcripts and secondary data underwent systematic coding [44] using qualitative data analysis software, adhering to the guidelines set by Yin [40] and employing an exploratory coding method of in vivo coding as per Strauss and Corbin [45]. Initially, 308 open codes were generated and subsequently clustered in each unit of analysis (sensing, seizing, transforming). Similarities and differences were consolidated to streamline data reduction [44], facilitating within-case analysis and cross-case analysis aiming for theoretical replication [42]. This approach enabled the meaningful extraction of microfoundations, respectively, low-level DCs discussed in the cases to address the overall research question. The methodology of Gioia et al. [46] was applied for data analysis, deriving a total of 118 first-order concepts. These concepts were then organized into 37 second-order themes and ultimately into 11 aggregate dimensions, enhancing the depth and comparability of the findings. For clarity, Chap. 4 visually represents the derivation of second-order themes to aggregated dimensions for each unit of analysis.

4 Results

4.1 Microfoundations of DC Category Sensing

Empowerment and Knowledge Utilization: Organizations like cases A and D utilize insights workshops to contextualize genAI use cases, enhancing their operational framework, as mentioned by interviewee D1: *"We know what is technically possible, but not necessarily what the business needs. Therefore, we must ensure the technology's tangibility in discovery workshops"*. Case B emphasizes leadership training for crowdsourcing genAI use cases alongside playgrounds that foster creative experimentation. Similarly, Case D's efforts to translate technology into actionable solutions, facilitated by internal advocates, highlight the critical role of equipping employees with the necessary knowledge and resources for effective genAI innovation and application.

Innovation Ecosystem Engagement: Engagement with the ecosystem is vital, as evidenced by case C's platforms for cross-disciplinary exchange and case E's sharing of expertise at the European Council. Moreover, case D highlights the critical need to define genAI's potential value from the start, using the ecosystem as a lever to validate user-centricity. Across all examined cases, strategic partnerships with major industry players and consultancy relationships facilitate a knowledge pull that empowers employees and enriches internal expertise. In addition, case B's market benchmarkings and case C's trend radar offer orientation towards market developments.

Organizational Learning and Openness: Cultivating a digital openness culture is crucial for adapting to genAI, promoting an environment that values curiosity, critical reflection, and outside-the-box thinking, observed in case B. Case D measures and promotes a digital mindset through annual assessments and targeted training, emphasizing the importance of scrutinizing as a core competency. Further, case E focuses on creativity enhancement within its innovation hub, recognizing the challenge of balancing resource constraints with the need for inspiring encounters that fuel iterative learning and innovation (Table 3).

4.2 Microfoundations of DC Category Seizing

Interdisciplinary Collaboration: Cases B and C showcase the critical role of sharing successes in multidisciplinary collaboration to make technology implications visible, enhancing decision-making and strategic flexibility. This approach emphasizes collecting internal learnings before external genAI application to strengthen decision capability, with case E directly applying learnings in services due to its unique mandate.

Learning-Driven Innovation Network: Starting small for complexity reduction and experimental mindset in case B highlights the importance of empirical testing

Table 3 Data Structure on Sensing Microfoundations to Leverage genAI

2nd order themes	Aggregarted dimensions
Contextualizing and Applying Insights	Empowerment and Knowledge Utilization
Creative Experimentation	
Employee Empowerment and Advocacy	
Cross-Disciplinary Collaboration	Innovation Ecosystem Engagement
User-Centric Innovation	
Strategic Partnerships	
Trend Assessment and Market Orientation	
Cultivating Digital Openness	Organizational Learning and Openness
Growth and Digital Mindset	
Iterative Learning and Creativity	

and real-world validation of genAI use cases. For case E, formalizing knowledge into guidelines fosters its usability, facilitating knowledge sharing and transfer. All organizations engage in experimenting with PoC for hypothesis testing, underlining the necessity of ongoing upskilling as integral, in alignment with Jackson et al. [47]'s insights on workforce training for effective genAI utilization.

Organizational Agility: Cases A and B focus on fostering adaptability through contextual understanding and sharing success stories, highlighting the need for continuous organization-specific adaptation and strategic alignment. Case D's resource optimization and exploring scaling effects in case B demonstrate a commitment to leveraging insights for multidimensional applications, ensuring governance flexibility.

Strategic Leadership: Case E's emphasis on operationalizing innovations for value creation and case A's balance of value, investment, and risk highlight the importance of leadership engagement in assessing the justification of risks and expenditures. This is strengthened by Fitzgerald et al. [5], who state that leading instead of doing technology-based transformations depends on leadership frameworks. Across all examined cases, strategic initiative planning involves prioritizing. As interviewee B1 explains: *"We prioritize our resources based on where we create the greatest customer value"* for maximum value addition and impact enhancement. This resonates with the broader strategic efforts to bundle decentralized initiatives, as mentioned in case E, and address psychological stakeholder reactions noted by Kanitz et al. [48] (Table 4).

4.3 Microfoundations of DC Category Transforming

Alignment and Governance Enhancement: Change leads serve as multipliers for transformation, as observed in case E. Further, cultivating organizational synergy

Table 4 Data Structure on Sensing Microfoundations to Leverage genAI

2nd order themes	Aggregarted dimensions
Enchanting Collaboratives	Interdisplinary Collaboratonn
Stategic Flexibitity and Decision Making	
Cultivating an Experimental and Reflective Mindset	Learning-Driven Innovation Network
Empirical Testing and Learning	
Knowledge Sharing and Documentation	
Promoting Organizatonal Learning	
Fostering Adaptability and Continuous Improvement	Organizational Agility
Organizational and Strategic Alignment	
Resoirce Optimization and Governance	
Scaling Innovations and Leveraging Synergies	
Maximaizing Valiue and Purposefuleness	Strategic Leadership
Prioritizing and Resoiuce Allocation	
Risk and Benefit Evaluation	
Stakeholders Engagementand Impact Evaluation	
Strategic Iinitiative Planning and Execution	

through shared experiences in case A and case E can be seen as an accelerator. This strategic alignment extends to formalizing scalability through structured methodologies in case A and harmonizing processes in case B, facilitating a coordinated approach to genAI adoption by connecting the dots of the insights gained.

Adaptive and Informed Culture: Continuous learning and knowledge sharing seem crucial for navigating the genAI landscape. Case B's emphasis on upskilling for comprehension, alongside case C's efforts to centralize knowledge, underscores the importance of an enabled workforce. Case A's approach to making insights actionable reflects a commitment to internal knowledge development that is relevant to fostering an innovative environment where genAI can thrive. Interviewee A1 points out: *"We provide them [the employees] with [genAI] dashboards they can operate themselves, allowing them to derive benefits via self-service."*

Organizational Resilience: Organizational resilience is strengthened by integrating critical reflection abilities, as demonstrated by cases A and B, and incorporating adaptive mechanisms like humans in the loop in case D. For scalable genAI solutions, visionary thinking, as encouraged by case C and case D, is closely linked to maintaining agility as a critical resilience factor as has been experienced in case E. Flexibility is enhanced by manifesting vision into tangible experiences for impactful reflections and adaptable actions in response to challenges, as practiced by case D.

Synergy Creation: Identifying and leveraging interdependencies, as case A shows, is critical to creating synergies and enhancing genAI utilization. Case B's establishment of a competence center for strategic coordination exemplifies how organizations can facilitate scaling, ensuring that genAI's transformative potential

Table 5 Data Structure on Transforming Microfoundations to Leverage genAI

2nd order themes	Aggregarted dimensions
Change Leads as Multiplier	Alignment and Governance Enhancement
Cultivation Organizational Synergy	
Formalizing Scalability	
Emncouraging a Culture of Continous Improvement	Adaptive and Informed Culture
Enhancing Knowledge Sharing	
Facilitating Innovation Through Comprehension	
Building Adaptive Capacity	Organizational Resilence
Fostering Visionary Thinking	
Promoting Flexibility	
Expanding Utilization and Creating Synergies	Synergy Creation
Leveraging on Competence Hubs for Scale-Up	
Stremlining Startegic Coordination and Insight	

is fully realized and integrated into organizational strategies for maximum impact (Table 5).

4.4 Putting it Together: Microfoundations of DCs for Leveraging genAI in DT

Drawing on the findings, this study elucidates how the delineated microfoundations can assist organizations in leveraging genAI within their DT endeavors. Advancing data foundations, enhancing quality and transparency, and fostering compliance and ethics awareness are pivotal information technology capabilities, as highlighted by Banh & Strobel [9]. However, the effective leverage of genAI transcends mere technological advances, necessitating a symbiotic integration of technology and human interaction [49], which is the latter this research aims to address. Swiftly responding to and managing new technologies [5] does not necessarily mandate a first-mover stance, a strategy exemplified by case B. In adopting a more measured approach, organizations can systematically apply these valuable microfoundations, building upon them progressively. Consistent with Eisenhardt & Martin [17], repeated practice is underscored as a critical learning mechanism within the DC framework, facilitating the integration of genAI into DT strategies (Table 6).

Drawing on the findings, this study elucidates how the delineated microfoundations can assist organizations in leveraging genAI within their DT endeavors. Advancing data foundations, enhancing quality and transparency, and fostering compliance and ethics awareness are pivotal information technology capabilities, as highlighted by Banh & Strobel [9]. However, the effective leverage of genAI transcends mere technological advances, necessitating a symbiotic integration of

Table 6 Microfoundations of DC to Leverage genAI for DT activities

Senzing	Seizing	Transformation
- Empowerment and Knowledge Utilization - Innovation Ecosystem Engagement - Organizatonal Learning nad Openness	- Interdisciplinary Collaboration - learning Driven Innovation Network - Organizational Agility - Strategic Leadership	- Alignment and Governance Enhancement - Adaptive and Informed Culture - Oganizational Resilience - Synergy and Creation

technology and human interaction [49], which is the latter this research aims to address. Swiftly responding to and managing new technologies [5] does not necessarily mandate a first-mover stance, a strategy exemplified by case B. In adopting a more measured approach, organizations can systematically apply these valuable microfoundations, building upon them progressively. Consistent with Eisenhardt & Martin [17], repeated practice is underscored as a critical learning mechanism within the DC framework, facilitating the integration of genAI into DT strategies.

5 Discussion of Results

5.1 Theoretical Contribution and Practical Implications

This multiple-case study expands the discourse on DC as extensively explored within IS research over recent decades [12]. It specifically explores the interplay between genAI and the essential microfoundations of DC in DT. By integrating insights from genAI studies and research on DT, including works by Ellström [30] and Warner and Wäger [19], this investigation bridges critical areas of inquiry, providing a comprehensive view on leveraging genAI in DT efforts.

This contribution aims to provide practitioners adopting genAI and seeking to establish functional DC at an organizational level with actionable and meaningful microfoundations. It seeks to empower them to effectively maximize the technological component to accelerate DT [19]. As observed across all cases dealing with genAI adoption, it is advisable to start small and then scale up to prevent overwhelming individuals and address complexity, in line with suggestions by Dwivedi, et al. [37]. The conceptualized non-technical microfoundations are intended to aid in the value generation of genAI in DT efforts.

5.2 *Limitations and Directions for Future Research*

This study, while providing valuable insights through qualitative exploratory research and leveraging the knowledge of experienced executives, acknowledges certain limitations. The multiple case study represents a snapshot in time without quantitative substantiation, relying exclusively on qualitative data. Additionally, although a diverse range of organizations in terms of sectors, sizes, and maturities (see Table 1) were selected to obtain a comprehensive view, the limited number of interviews suggests that expanding the sample and testing the findings with more case partners could enrich the research. Moreover, biases in the coding process cannot be completely eliminated, as the coding was performed by a single individual. Finally, while attempting to cover a broad spectrum of organizational contexts, it remains uncertain how the microfoundations of DC might evolve with more advanced stages of genAI adoption, a comparison that this study's scope cannot fully address.

In this research, we have concentrated on non-technical DC as defined by Dwivedi, et al. [37]. Exploring technological DC presents an exciting field for future research. While there has been significant attention to genAI as an entity within socio-technical systems across various applications such as text, image, video, speech, and code generation [9, 10, 37, 39], there remains a gap in understanding how genAI itself can create capabilities in regards of sensing, seizing, and transforming. This gap, noted as well by Dwivedi, et al. [37], represents an intriguing field for research, opening up discussions on the autonomous development of organizational capabilities through genAI.

6 Conclusion

In conclusion, technology represents merely one component of the broader picture [7]. This research identifies eleven pivotal microfoundations distributed across the DC framework, three for sensing, four for seizing, and four for transforming. This conceptual work enriches the ongoing discourse on genAI and its intersection with DC in the DT landscape.

The eleven concluding microfoundations are designed to be incrementally applied across the three categories of DC. It is crucial to recognize that the sub-DC of seizing builds upon the sub-DC of sense, and similarly, the sub-DC of transforming builds on the sub-DC of sensing and seizing [19], highlighting the interdependent and layered nature of scaling genAI.

Furthermore, DC's microfoundations contribute to the optimal allocation of organizational focus, enabling genAI's beneficial and scalable use. They offer organizations a source of inspiration on where to direct their efforts meaningfully to enhance the sustainable impact of genAI.

References

1. Alavi, M., Leidner, D. E., & Mousavi, R. (2024). A knowledge management perspective of generative artificial intelligence. *Journal of the Association for Information Systems, 25*(1), 1–12.
2. Van Veldhoven, Z., & Vanthienen, J. (2022). Digital transformation as an interaction-driven perspective between business, society, and technology. *Electronic Markets, 32*, 629–644.
3. Ransbotham, S., Khodabandeh, S., Fehling, R., LaFountain, B., & Kiron, D. (2019). Winning with AI: Pioneers combine strategy, organizational behavior, and technology. *MIT Sloan Management Review, 1–21.*
4. Matt, C., Hess, T., Benlian, A., & Wiesböck, F. (2016). Options for formulating a digital transformation strategy. *MIS Quarterly Executive, 15*(2), 123–139.
5. Fitzgerald, M., Kruschwitz, N., Bonnet, D., Welch, M.: Embracing digital technology: A new strategic imperative- MIT Sloan Management Review 55(2), 1–12 (2014).
6. Sætra, H. S. (2023). Generative AI: Here to stay, but for good? *Technology in Society, 75.*
7. Vial, G. (2019). Understanding digital transformation: A review and a research agenda. *The Journal of Strategic Information Systems, 28*(2), 118–144.
8. Stanford University: Artificial Intelligence Index Report 2023. Stanford University. https://hai.stanford.edu/ai-index/2023-ai-index-report, last accessed 2024/09/02.
9. Banh, L., & Strobel, G. (2023). Generative artificial intelligence. *Electronic Markets, 33*(1).
10. Feuerriegel, S., Hartmann, J., Janiesch, C., Zschech, P.: Generative AI. Business & Information Systems Engineering 66(1), 111–126 (2024).
11. Teece, D. J.: The Evolution of the Dynamic Capabilities Framework. In Adams, R., Grichnik, D., Pundziene, A., Volkmann, C. (ed.).: Artificiality and Sustainability in Entrepreneurship. Exploring the Unforeseen, and Paving the Way to a Sustainable Future, pp. 113–129. Springer, Cham (2023).
12. Steininger, D. M., Mikalef, P., Pateli, A., & Ortiz-de-Guinea, A. (2022). Dynamic capabilities in information systems research: A critical review, synthesis of current knowledge, and recommendations for future research. *Journal of the Association for Information Systems, 23*(2), 447–490.
13. Schumpeter, J. (1934). *The theory of economic development.* Harvard University Press.
14. Porter, M. E. (1980). *Competitive strategy: Techniques for Analyzing industries and competitors.* Free Press.
15. Barney, J. (1991). Firm resources and sustained competitive advantage. *Journal of Management, 17*(1), 99–120.
16. Teece, D. J., Pisano, G., & Shuen, A. (1997). Dynamic capabilities and strategic management. *Strategic Management Journal, 18*(7), 509–533.
17. Eisenhardt, K. M., & Martin, J. A. (2000). Dynamic capabilities: What are they? *Strategic Management Journal, 21*(10–11), 1105–1121.
18. Teece, D. J. (2007). Explicating dynamic capabilities: The nature and microfoundations of (sustainable) Enterprise performance. *Strategic Management Journal, 28*(13), 1319–1350.
19. Warner, K. S. R., & Wäger, M. (2019). Building dynamic capabilities for digital transformation: An ongoing process of strategic renewal. *Long Range Planning, 52*(3), 326–349.
20. Cannas, R. (2021). Exploring digital transformation and dynamic capabilities in agrifood SMEs. *Journal of Small Business Management, 61*(4), 1611–1637.
21. Teece, D. J. (2014). The foundations of enterprise performance: Dynamic and ordinary capabilities in an (economic) theory of firms. *Academy of Management Perspectives, 28*(4), 328–352.
22. Teece, D. J. (2018). Business models and dynamic capabilities. *Long Range Planning, 51*(1), 40–49.
23. Wang, C. L., & Ahmed, P. K. (2007). Dynamic capabilities: A review and research agenda. *International Journal of Management Reviews, 9*(1), 31–51.

24. Jöhnk, J., Ollig, P., Rövekamp, P., & Oesterle, S. (2022). Managing the complexity of digital transformation—How multiple concurrent initiatives foster hybrid ambidexterity. *Electronic Markets, 32*(2), 547–569.
25. Winter, S. G. (2003). Understanding dynamic capabilities. *Strategic Management Journal, 24*(10), 991–995.
26. Helfat, C. E., & Winter, S. G. (2011). Untangling dynamic and operational capabilities: Strategy for the (N)ever-changing world. *Strategic Management Journal, 32*, 1243–1250.
27. Verhoef, P. C., Broekhuizen, T., Bart, Y., Bhattacharya, A., Qi Dong, J., Fabian, N., & Haenlein, M. (2021). Digital transformation: A multidisciplinary reflection and research agenda. *Journal of Business Research, 122*, 889–901.
28. McLaughlin, S. (2017). Dynamic capabilities: Taking an emerging technology perspective. *International Journal of Manufacturing Technology and Management, 31*(1–3), 62–81.
29. Singh, A., & Hess, T. (2017). How chief digital officers promote the digital transformation of their companies. *MIS Quarterly Executive, 16*(1).
30. Ellström, D., Holtström, J., Berg, E., & Joseffson, C. (2022). Dynamic capabilities for digital transformation. *Journal of Strategy and Management, 15*(2), 272–286.
31. Marx, C., De Paula, D., & Uebernickel, F. (2021). Dynamic Capabilities & Digital Transformation: A quantitative study on how to gain a competitive advantage in the digital age. In *European conference on information systems (ECIS) 2021 proceedings*. Association for Information Systems AISeL.
32. Day, G. S., & Schoemaker, P. J. H. (2016). Adapting to fast-changing markets and technologies. *California Management Review, 58*(4), 59–77.
33. Yeow, A., Soh, C., & Hansen, R. (2018). Aligning with new digital strategy: A dynamic capabilities approach. *The Journal of Strategic Information Systems, 27*(1), 43–58.
34. Bharadwaj, A., El Sawy, O. A., Pavlou, P. A., & Venkat Venkatraman, N. (2013). Digital business strategy: Toward a next generation of insights. *MIS Quarterly, 37*(2), 471–482.
35. Kraus, S., Jones, P., Kailer, N., Weinmann, A., Chaparro-Banegas, N., & Roig-Tierno, N. (2021). Digital transformation: An overview of the current state of the art of research. *SAGE Open, 11*(3).
36. Mondal, S., Das, S., & Vrana, V. G. (2023). How to bell the cat? A theoretical review of generative artificial intelligence towards digital disruption in all walks of life. *Technologies, 11*(2), 44–60.
37. Dwivedi, Y. K., et al. (2023). Opinion paper: "So what if ChatGPT wrote it?" multidisciplinary perspectives on opportunities, challenges and implications of generative conversational AI for research, practice and policy. *International Journal of Information Management, 71*.
38. Berente, N., Gu, B., Recker, J., & Santhanam, R. (2021). Managing Artificial Intelligence. *MIS Quarterly, 45*(3), 1433–1450.
39. Mariani, M., & Dwivedi, Y. K. (2024). Generative artificial intelligence in innovation management: A preview of future research developments. *Journal of Business Research, 175*.
40. Yin, R. K. (2018). *Case study research and applications: Design and methods* (Sixth ed.). SAGE Publications.
41. Eisenhardt, K. M., & Graebner, M. E. (2007). Theory building from cases: Opportunities and challenges. *Academy of Management Journal, 50*(1), 25–32.
42. Eisenhardt, K. M. (1989). Building theories from case study research. *The Academy of Management Review, 14*(4), 532–550.
43. Taherizadeh, A., & Beaudry, C. (2023). An emergent grounded theory of AI-driven digital transformation: Canadian SMEs' perspectives. *Industry and Innovation, 30*(9), 1244–1273.
44. Dubé, L., & Paré, G. (2003). Rigor in information systems positivist case research: Current practices, trends, and recommendations. *MIS Quarterly, 27*(4), 597–635.
45. Strauss, A. L., & Corbin, J. M. (1990). *Basics of qualitative research: Grounded theory procedures and techniques*. SAGE Publications.
46. Gioia, D. A., Corley, K. G., & Hamilton, A. L. (2012). Seeking qualitative rigor in inductive research: Notes on the Gioia methodology. *Organizational Research Methods, 16*(1), 15–31.

47. Jackson, I., Ivanov, D., Dolgui, A., & Namdar, J. (2024). Generative artificial intelligence in supply chain and operations management: A capability-based framework for analysis and implementation. *International Journal of Production Research, 62*(17), 6120–6145.
48. Kanitz, R., Gonzalez, K., Briker, R., & Straatmann, T. (2023). Augmenting organizational change and strategy activities: Leveraging generative artificial intelligence. *Journal of Applied Behavioral Science, 59*(3), 345–363.
49. Agrawal, K. P. (2023). Towards adoption of generative AI in organizational settings. *Journal of Computer Information Systems, 1–16*.

Changing Nature of Work

Completing the Skills Puzzle: Developing a Skills Profile Data Model

Leonie Rebecca Freise and Ulrich Bretschneider

Abstract In today's working world, driven by technological progress, there is a growing need to adapt and update skills to remain competitive. Employers need qualified employees, and employees want to develop their job-related skills, so skills profiles are becoming more prevalent. These profiles comprise skills that individuals bring to their jobs and develop over employment. When used effectively, they offer benefits in attracting, retaining, and developing talent, as well as in staffing and performance management. This paper proposes a data model for such profiles. Drawing upon a systematic literature review and interviews with employees, we derived the critical aspects of a skill profile data model. We further demonstrate the complexity and the need for a structured approach to include a bottom-up perspective. This research contributes to the theoretical understanding of skills profile data models by including the employee perspectives. It further provides insights for organizations to develop a skilled workforce.

1 Introduction

The evolving labor markets, characterized by rapid technological advancements, such as artificial intelligence (AI), and digital processes, necessitate a paradigm shift in organizational practices toward skill-based approaches. The current dynamics within these environments underscore the inadequacy of traditional models in addressing the complexities of task allocation and the evolving nature of job requirements [17]. Accordingly, employees face two significant challenges. First, there is the challenge of remaining competitive in the job market, necessitating individuals to continuously update and acquire the latest and most relevant skills to fill emerging roles [30]. Secondly, employees must engage in ongoing development of their current skill sets

L. R. Freise (✉) · U. Bretschneider
Information Systems, University of Kassel, Kassel, Germany
e-mail: Leonie.freise@uni-kassel.de

U. Bretschneider
e-mail: Bretschneider@uni-kassel.de

C. M. Flath et al. (eds.), *Digital Innovation and Organizational Transformation*, Lecture Notes in Information Systems and Organisation 83,
https://doi.org/10.1007/978-3-032-08483-5_14

to align with the demands of twenty-first century skills, ensuring they can execute their tasks effectively [37]. Despite its importance, integrating complex skills like data literacy into skills profiles remains a challenge [23]. In response to these exigencies, data-driven skill profiles have emerged as a promising solution. Skills profiles involve recognizing and developing employees' diverse skills beyond their job roles [2]. Nonetheless, the efficacy of such profiles is contingent upon the availability of a robust datamodel, which serves as the foundational element for their successful implementation within organizational contexts. The growing emphasis on lifelong learning and the provision of personalized educational pathways underscores the need for a dynamic, adaptable data model. This model should be capable of mapping out the evolving skill sets required by more complex processes such as AI-integrated work, thereby ensuring that individuals remain competitive in their respective fields [56, 64]. In an increasingly digitized workplace, employees are required to rapidly adapt to technological advancements and embrace lifelong learning. As these learning requirements are often directed at employees at different levels, the inclusion of their perspectives is of particular relevance to ensure their commitment. Organizations and researchers further support the importance of humans' positions as vital contributors to the overall functioning of the digitized system [36]. Therefore, we aim to enhance an employee-focused perspective on the working system. Including an employee's perspective has far-reaching benefits. As [34] emphasize, perspective-taking helps to navigate social interactions. Also, [39] state that it can facilitate knowledge integration, which is considered crucial for organizational learning and innovation. However, the employee perspective on skills is kept out of focus [62]. Therefore, we aim to enhance an employee-focused perspective on the working system. A data model focused on skill profiles, informed by employee-driven insights, would cater to the necessity for nuanced skill profile strategies. Leveraging data analytics, such a model empowers organizations to precisely identify, assess, and enhance the varied competencies within their workforce [32]. Hence, a detailed examination and outline of a data model for skills management offers the potential for a deeper understanding of prerequisites from a bottom-up perspective. We thereby address the following research question (RQ): *What does a data model look like that integrates employees' perspectives?*

This research introduces a skills profile data model that uniquely derives individual skill data points and their intricate relationships from a literature review [68] and qualitative interviews. Unlike existing models that often focus solely on isolated skills, our approach offers a comprehensive framework capturing the complex interconnections of different involved instances within skill sets. This advancement significantly enhances the theoretical foundations of information systems research by providing a more holistic understanding of skills profiles. By elucidating these relationships, the model deepens our theoretical comprehension and facilitates more effective problem-solving methodologies. This offers a new approach for future research and practical applications, thereby providing valuable insights into skills development and deployment dynamics. Our research contributes to the field by incorporating the employee perspective through a bottom-up approach, thereby enriching the existing literature with practical, grounded insights for developing effective skill management strategies. Thereby, our research enriches various management disciplines, including Information Systems (IS), Data Science, Human Resources (HR), Business Research, Learning, and Education.

2 Background

2.1 Characteristics of Skills Profiles

A skills profile, whether in paper or electronic form, is a record that describes a person's skills and experience. It includes information on their experience, education, and training [23]. A skills profile provides a holistic overview of a person's skills and qualifications as an overview for themselves or for third parties, such as potential employers or clients [18, 65]. Thereby, it serves many beneficial purposes. For instance, a compiled account of skills enables the individual to prioritize development and improvement. With the data encapsulated in a skills profile, skill gaps can be detected to give a reference point for progress and performance evaluation [61] or long-term career path planning [57]. Further, the data can be used to optimize and facilitate project staffing [25]. These applications can be significantly enlarged by AI developments. For instance, AI can aid in identifying suitable candidates for specific projects and ultimately achieve strategic organizational goals based on data [15]. A skills profile can be developed by the individual or a third party, such as a manager or recruiter and should be updated regularly to reflect changes in a person's skills and expertise. Thereby, assessment is clearly tied to skills profiles.

However, assessment is not limited to this stage of the employee life cycle. It is also vital to document the status quo of employees' skills in order to provide employees with lifelong learning [51]. Some organizations are already investing in managing employee skills more professionally and with the help of AI. In that vein, Microsoft announced the introduction of Viva, an AI-driven qualification service and a multichannel communication center for employees. With this, Microsoft also recognizes the added value that skill-based approaches provide organizations to increase the engagement and productivity of their employees, which are crucial factors on their path to success [52]. Another example of a skills profile is LinkedIn. The usage of these personal profiles has been a significant breakthrough in personnel selection and recruitment [1]. Organizations regularly look at applicants' social media presence before making initial hiring selections [67]. In this context, it is assumed that profiles enable organizations to learn about an individual's personality, skills, experiences, and values, as well as to assess how well qualifications match job requirements or suit the organization's culture [3].

In conclusion, skill profiles offer significant benefits to both organizations and employees. However, the ambiguity in data requirements on skills profiles often leads to mismatches between employee expectations and organizational offerings regarding employee requirements.

2.2 Enhancing HR Systems with Data-Based Skills Profiles

Existing research is already looking at how to integrate skills or knowledge information in organization-wide HR management systems [9, 42]. It is argued that skills data often needs to be shared across different HR platforms like SAP [24, 28]. Therefore, detailed information is not easily used for personnel development. Additionally, the individual proficiency level in skills is difficult to be displayed in HR management systems as it requires constant revision and status updates [2], especially for employees with a long employment history in an organization. For instance, a software developer might quickly advance from basic to intermediate proficiency in a new programming language after completing an intensive course, requiring immediate updates in HR systems to reflect this growth accurately. This dynamic nature necessitates sophisticated tracking and frequent updates to maintain accuracy. These aspects should be solved by or supported by information technology. HR systems need to navigate the complexities of skills, which are polysemous, multi-dimensional, and multi-operational. This means that skills like 'communication' can have varying labels, posing evaluation challenges [43]. Skills are also multi-dimensional, composed of related sub-skills, e.g., project management involves time management and team coordination [33]. Furthermore, skills are multi-operational, adaptable across different contexts and may shift focus with job functions [45].

Skills-based HR management, including skills profiles, is not a novel concept but rather an underexplored approach [38]. The development of the skills-based models has been gradual, evolving from the experiences of organizations recognizing it as a source of competitive advantage [31]. While several organizations have incorporated practices aligned with this approach, many still maintain the prevailing job-based approach [12]. Our objective is to elucidate the underlying assumptions and principles of this model and the data structures necessary to establish and fully understand a skills profile. Within skills profiles with consistent data structures, the establishment of a coherent and comprehensive model is essential to effectively capture, assess, and utilize skills and subskills [22]. Structuring skills profiles is equally crucial for HR management and talent development [50]. In this regard, the interplay between skills, subskills, evaluation methods, and proficiency levels can be visualized as a data model, where each component contributes to the accuracy and utility of skills profiles. This model would serve as the basis for constructing and navigating the landscape of skills assessment and development, offering a clear reference point for evidence-based decision-making in workforce development. A good starting point for this is given by [28], who outlined a skill-competency management architecture to improve HR information systems. However, we aim to further build upon existing literature and interview data, tailoring it to the specific case of skills profiles. The model should symbolize the interdependent organization of skills, subskills, evaluation methods, proficiency levels, usage contexts, and their connections, resembling a structured data model to emphasize the importance of skills profiles.

3 Research Approach

3.1 Data Collection

We used a two-folded qualitative research approach to examine our RQ. The aim is to shed light on the requirements for skills profiles from an employee perspective. Based on a comprehensive understanding of the role of skills in everyday working life, we aim to evaluate the most important dimensions for conceptualizing skills profiles. Finally, these aspects will be translated into requirements that employees place on mapping their skills. We conducted a systematic literature review following the methodology of [68], targeting articles within IS, management studies, and education across four digital libraries: AISeL, ScienceDirect, ProQuest, and Web of Science. Our search strategy utilized key terms related to skills management, skills profiles and data models or data structures, adapted semantically for each database. We included English-language articles published between 2010 and January 2023, initially identifying 93 articles from titles, abstracts, and keywords. After screening for relevance and excluding duplicates or texts without full-paper access, we narrowed the selection to 50 publications. Further refinement excluded papers which did not directly refer to a specific skill or data, resulting in 21 papers. Final inclusion criteria led to 17 studies focused on developing data models on skills profiles of professional skills in adult education or workplace settings, evaluating more than one skill or competency. Additional searches on Google Scholar added two more studies, totaling 19 publications for detailed analysis. The detailed process is displayed in Fig. 1.

The second part of our research consists of interviews based on a semi-structured questionnaire [46]. The semi-structured questionnaire allows for a deeper and more nuanced analysis of the reported data [5]. The interview guide was created in eight steps: (1) defining the research area, (2) developing specific research questions, (3) determining the interview topics, (4) formulating the interview guide, (5) revising the questions, (6) conducting a mock interview, (7) identifying further guiding questions and (8) finalizing the guide [5]. The first section of the questionnaire collects demographic details, such as educational background and current job, to understand the professional context. The second section explores the application of skills in participants' jobs, identifying crucial skills and their usage in different contexts. The third section assesses perceptions of individual skills, including the importance of according to proficiency levels. Additionally, it explores the systematic resources and organizational support participants utilize or require to enhance or broaden their skill set. The final section of the questionnaire explores participants' experiences with skill development over their careers and their perspectives on the future evolution of skills in their work, focusing on anticipated changes in requirements.

A total of 20 participants from different work backgrounds, age groups, and hierarchical levels in organizations were interviewed to generate a meaningful sample. The interviews were conducted according to theoretical saturation, i.e., further data collection does not provide new insights into the research issues [26]. They took

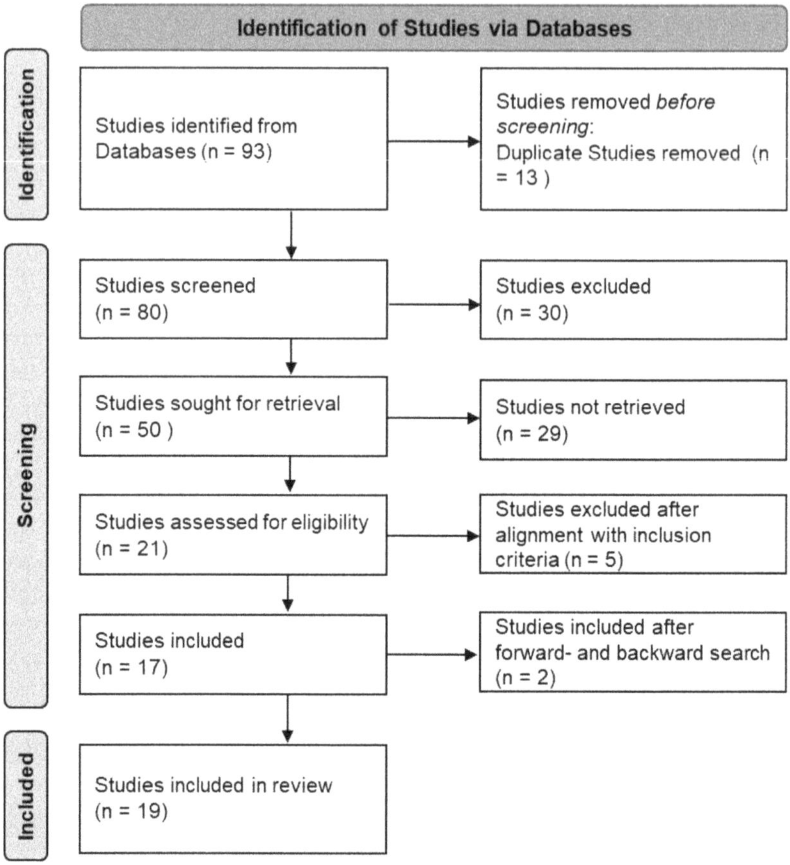

Fig. 1 Literature review process according to the PRISMA framework

approximately 30 min and were recorded and transcribed with prior consent. The average age was 35 years (34.8 years). 65% of the participants classified themselves as male and 35% as female. 15% of the participants had a secondary school certificate, 35% a high school diploma, 35% a bachelor's degree, and 15% a master's degree. The interviews revealed that 25% of participants are working students, 55% are regular employees and 20% are managers with leadership responsibilities. The participants worked in the Customer Quality Department, Test Planning, Engineering, Sales, Administration, Compliance, Customs, IT Project Management, and HR.

3.2 Data Analysis

Subsequently, the transcripts were examined, and a qualitative content analysis was carried out using MAXQDA. This process aimed to identify similarities, differences, and key themes in the data set. Our analytical method was guided by [46], starting with the generalization of interview content, followed by two reduction stages to distill the material into final observations and conclusions. In line with grounded theory's established methods, we employed open, axial, and selective coding as outlined by [14] and [63], further supported by [58] techniques in these coding processes. Within the 20 interviews, we coded four main categories and 15 subcodes and assigned 597 code segments.

4 Results & Discussion

4.1 Literature-Based Skills Profile Data Model

Based on our literature review, we developed a conceptual data model that involves an abstract representation of data in accordance with [4]. To achieve this, we started by conducting a comprehensive literature review to identify core papers and extract relevant data elements. Then, we systematically categorized these elements as higher-level constructs and noted their connections. Thereafter, we developed a conceptual model using visualizations, ensuring all necessary data elements and relationships are accurately represented.

When considering the data structure of skills profiles, it becomes apparent that evidence about skills, such as certificates, CVs, references, or micro-credentials, is required to validate the evaluation process, which in turn tracks this information [27]. In this stage, natural language processing techniques are already established. For instance, [20] and [41] used a text-mining method to identify semantic components from job descriptions. Methods like these produce a rich repository of recorded content demonstrating the individual's skills in different use contexts or areas of expertise. This is emphasized by [60], who distinguish between role-related and general skills. The use context provides essential skill-specific details necessary for correct evaluation. For instance, data literacy in business analytics might be assessed via KPI analysis [55].

In contrast, in scientific contexts, it could focus on experimental analysis, statistical testing, and preparing publications. The models' proficiency levels indicate varying degrees of mastery [53]. These levels differentiate the person's skills and subskills and inform their progress in a certain domain. One framework that particularly refers to proficiency levels is the Digcomp model [13]. Therein, the complexity of tasks, as well as the employee's autonomy in applying the skill, is considered. Next, the different skills are not isolated but interconnected with other skills, forming a network that can be represented in ontologies or taxonomies (e.g., [19, 21]). For example, a person with high ability in networking is likely to also show high ability in teamwork and negotiation, as shown by [54]. This outlines the need to consider related skill aspects in addition to the core skill set. Moreover, the skill relations together shape a semantic skill model. Within our literature review, [6] developed a competency model for IS and cybersecurity and argue for a better understanding of the relation between skill categories like social and methodological skills. A structured semantic skill model can assess an individual's proficiency across contexts like marketing, healthcare, or finance. It aligns evidence like certifications and project outcomes with skill proficiency standards, offering a solid basis for evaluating skills across professional fields.

Nevertheless, it needs to be considered that the data model described here mainly relies on research that includes the organizational perspective but not the employee perspective. In other words, it does not take into account what employees actually consider important for their skill assessment and development.

4.2 Employee Requirements for a Skills Profile Data Model

This section delves into the requirements that emerged from the qualitative interviews. We describe the employee perspectives in detail and provide exemplary quotes from the participants. Moreover, we position them in relation to our previously proposed data model. Each of these requirements contributes to a bottom-up understanding of skills' pivotal role in education, career development, and organizational success. By examining employee perspectives, we provide additions to our data model on skills profiles and enlarge the concrete use context applications for technology.

Identification of Skill Requirements: This involves systematically gathering and defining the skills needed in a particular job role or industry. This could be done through a rigorous analysis of job descriptions, industry standards, and skill models. One key element of this requirement on a skills profile is the semantic skill model that guides further development. This is outlined by a statement that highlights the multidimensional nature of skills like data literacy. As participant 7 (P7) states: *"I am not sure, I would say using the right data, the right way at the right time."*. To be as in this example, data literate, individuals must possess a blend of technical skills, critical thinking, and domain-specific knowledge to maximize the value of data in their respective roles and industries. This requirement was already described by [8], who discuss a framework for calculating employees' soft and hard skills, enhancing task assignment based on worker's skills. They describe that existing skill management is often based on job descriptions as the data basis that organizations can easily build upon to identify the skills needed for a position or a task. A longitudinal approach is described by [40]. They used curricula to identify changes in skills and the required subskills for IS over a fifty-year period. Referring to our profile model, this confirms the need for a semantic skill model that offers a general common understanding of the construct that is referred to in the evidence information.

Modeling and Structuring Skills Data: Following the principles of requirements data modeling, the gathered skills can then be organized into a structured format. This could involve categorizing skills into different areas such as technical, interpersonal, cognitive, and others. Each skill can be further defined with attributes like proficiency level required, relevance to specific job roles and use context, and interdependencies with other skills. As outlined in the interviews, many employees face difficulties in the evaluation of their own skills, especially because they do not have a systemized understanding of the different sub-skills and the concept behind. *"That depends, of course, on which skills we are talking about. Are we talking about technical skills or about the job?"* (P12). Databases like O*NET (The Occupational Information Network) from the U.S. Department of Labor/Employment and Training Administration [66] and ESCO (European Skills, Competences, Qualifications, and Occupations) by the European Commission [19] provide extensive collections of skill-related information, comprising numerous entries. However, the existence of these databases highlights the need to construct a data model that focuses on individual skills. This model is essential for accurately representing and establishing a robust conceptual basis for subsequent actions. In reference to our model, this requirement is related to the domain of skills and their contribution to the design of a semantic skills model.

Dynamic Update and Management: A skills profile model must allow easy updates and modifications. This aspect is crucial given the rapidly changing nature of job requirements and skill sets in the modern workplace. As P14 describes, it is challenging to keep up with changing requirements and regulations about data, so a skills profile and the underlying model need to be adaptable and flexible enough to stay up pace *"the challenge lies in being able to cope with the ever-increasing volume of data. (...) In addition, there are always system updates, and it feels like there are always new systems being added and I think the most difficult thing is to keep learning and always be up to date."*. Global organizations are facing increasing challenges in efficiently managing the skills of their employees [48]. In order to keep comprehensive records of employees' skills, experience, and knowledge, effective software support with detailed profiles of all employees is essential [8]. This enables tracking employees' changing skill sets and managing them efficiently for different purposes. Within our data model, this becomes particularly important in updating the definitions of skills and related skills based on changes or refinements in the semantic skills model. If those are constantly feedbacked and kept up-to-date, the subsequent steps can be accordingly adapted.

Integration with HR and Organizational Systems: The model could be integrated into human resource management systems, aiding in tasks like recruitment, employee development, and career planning. By aligning skills profiles with organizational needs and individual career paths, the model can support both strategic HR planning and personal development. This part is something that organizations struggle with, as emphasized by this statement: *"Our processes are still relatively unstructured, and you have to have a hands-on mentality to keep track of things."* (P16). The need for a holistic system is further illuminated by P6, who argues for as few independent solutions as possible but rather one HR system so that people do not have to be accustomed to many stand-alone programs. Similarly, many organizations are already transforming their HR management systems to more strategic HR Information Systems that include functions like HR planning, meaning to analyze learning. [49] showed that those systems increase the efficiency and effectiveness of HR through the integration of skills inventories and the combination with an analysis of unfilled job positions. They also stress the need for an integrated personnel system to benefit organizations. At this point, the requirements named in our interviews extend beyond the profile model and are referring to an even broader context that is important to consider in skills management. Similarly, [29] argue for integrating skill graphs into HR management systems and [24] emphasize the same for knowledge management.

Analytical Insights and Gap Analysis: By using the data provided by, for instance, assessments and evidence like CVs in the skills profile model, organizations can perform detailed analyses to identify skills gaps, predict future skill requirements, and plan necessary training and development interventions. *"It would also be interesting to find out about other analysis tools or the possibilities of simply obtaining more and more useful evaluations using current tools."* (P16). P18 describes a positive example. In this case, if the person had skill gaps, they wouldn't have to worry about keeping up to date themselves but would receive the necessary support from the company. To develop this aspect further, it would ideally be data-based, possibly automated, and therefore independent of individuals. This could be realized by online learning platforms that gather extensive data on the learning process. This includes how learners engage with course materials via system access patterns and video consumption habits [59]. In addition, analysis of this data provides practical insights into potential individual or organization-wide skills gaps [35] and can inform long-term decision-making processes such as strategic workforce planning [16]. The availability of data from online settings is essential for this step and confirms the domains of the data model. Insights into actual and target states at the skill level offer the possibility of concluding necessary further training in the context of use at the proficiency level.

Personalization and Individual Development Plans: Employees can use the model to understand their current skill levels, identify areas for improvement, and align their personal development goals with organizational needs. This is outlined by P8 *"In any case, targeted and planned and also implemented training measures which, depending on the data relationship concerned, are also implemented or generally made available for the time being, i.e. training measures in general."*. Further, P6 emphasizes the challenge of *"(...) learning the right things (...)"*, as a lot of information is often offered that is not relevant to individual needs. These statements emphasize the need for well-designed, customized, and relevant skill training programs. Such training should consider individuals' unique challenges and provide them with the skills and knowledge necessary to make informed decisions and contribute effectively to their roles within an organization. Additionally, training should be agile and adaptable to evolving needs and technology advancements, ensuring that individuals are well-prepared to navigate the complexities of the data-driven world. This finding aligns with [11], who call for a shift from on-site to online training as they

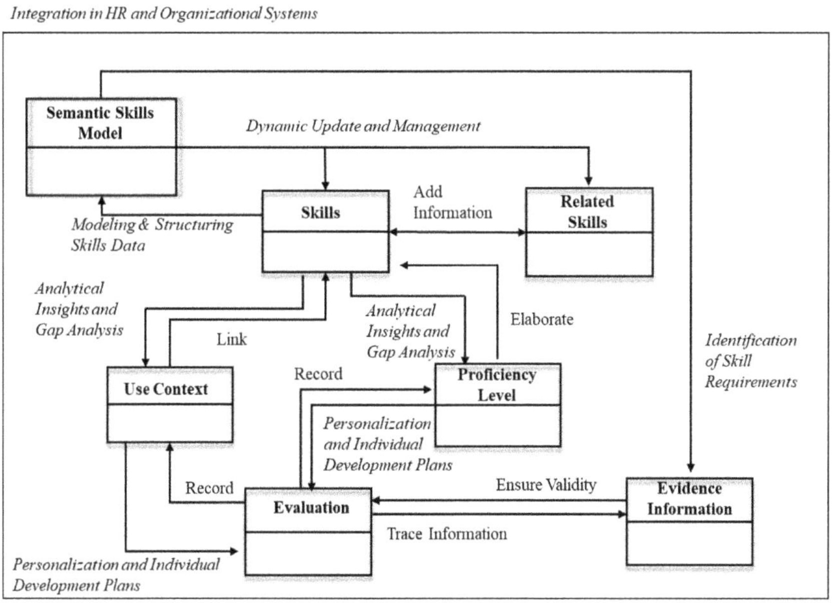

Fig. 2 Skills Profile Data Model including to the Employee Perspective

promise a high potential for personalized and interactive learning journeys. Further, employees should be able to develop more self-directed. Self-regulated learners can independently control their learning by setting goals and choosing effective strategies [69]. Prior research emphasized that adult education catalyzes empowerment [10]. Consequently, courses to improve and enhance skills should enable learners to take charge of their skill development [10]. Personalized learning journeys can be designed in various ways and are known as effective strategies to support learners [57]. Based on the previously based skill gaps in use context and proficiency level, these personalizations can be enabled and can be incorporated into a re-evaluation of skills.

Overall, our findings confirm and extend many domains of the data model outlined based on the literature. The data model shown in Fig. 2 represents the addition of the employee perspective. Such a model could help align employee skills with evolving industry requirements and individual career aspirations.

5 Limitations & Future Research Avenues

Our findings, while insightful, have limitations, highlighting areas for further research. Methodologically, the reliance on a small sample of 20 participants limits the generalizability and depth of the insights gained [44]. The size limits the representation of diverse opinions and experiences, potentially introducing bias. Despite efforts to ensure diversity among the participants regarding job positions, age, and gender, the limited demographic range may not fully capture diversity [47]. Additionally, the potential for socially desirable responses could skew the results [7]. Future research with larger and more diverse samples is needed for broader validation. Second, the absence of direct application in organizational settings limits the practical verification of our data model. This gap points to the need for empirical research that tests these models in practice, enhancing the relevance and applicability of our conclusions in organizational contexts.

For future research, the integration of AI in candidate selection raises questions about the necessity of structured data. While AI can process unstructured data, structured data ensures accuracy, transparency, and fairness, addressing ethical concerns and employee requirements. Future research can examine the optimal data structures for AI-based skills profiles in more detail. Moreover, research could examine what drives the acceptance and engagement with skill assessments. Longitudinal research is crucial for tracking how skill profiles adapt to changes in technology, the market, and demographics and assessing the sustainability of current models. Ethical issues, such as data privacy, assessment bias, and responsible data use, are critical areas to ensure fairness and transparency in skill management. Addressing these topics will improve our knowledge of skill management, enhance skill profile models, and help organizations optimize their workforce's skills. By pursuing these future research directions, scholars can contribute to optimizing skill sets and completing the skills puzzle.

6 Conclusion

Accurately measuring and developing employee skills is of paramount importance, especially in the context of the changing world of work. Therefore, it is essential to understand the underlying concepts, possible methods, and requirements of employees for a system that should support them in skills development. This research paper provides an understanding of the needs of employees for skills profiles. Furthermore, the insights from our interviews are broadened and used to develop and evaluate the data model for a skills profile model based on existing literature. We thereby present six different requirements that are emphasized for a holistic skills profile. Our work contributes to a better understanding of employees' perspectives on skills management and their needs in such a system. Overall, the results provide a deeper insight into how skills profiles can be designed and which underlying dimensions of skills are vital. In doing so, we enrich the literature on skills profiles from a bottom-up perspective. In addition, this overview provides actionable guidance for practitioners on what approaches can create a reliable and objective recording of employee skills. Based on this, it can empower employees to develop their skills independently, equip organizations with the necessary knowledge to use their employees' skills best, and identify suitable development paths. It should facilitate continuous learning, skill gap analysis, and the development of complementary skill sets.

References

1. Adams, S. (2013). New survey: Linkedin more dominant than ever among job seekers and recruiters, but facebook poised to gain. *Forbes, 2013*, 28–29.
2. Anwar, Z., Bibi, N., & Ahsan, A. (2013). Expertise based skill management model for effective project resource allocation under stress in software industry of Pakistan. In *6th International Conference On Information Management, Innovation Management And Industrial Engineering:* Xi'an, China, 23.11.2013–24.11.2013 IEEE Service Center (pp. 509–513).
3. Bangerter, A., Roulin, N., & König, C. J. (2012). Personnel selection as a signaling game. *The Journal of Applied Psychology, 97*(4), 719–738.
4. Batra, D., & Marakas, G. M. (1995). Conceptual data modelling in theory and practice. *European Journal of Information Systems, 4*(3), 185–193.
5. Bell, E., Bryman, A., & Harley, B. (2022). *Business research methods.* Oxford University Press.
6. Bendler, D., & Felderer, M. (2023). Competency models for information security and cybersecurity professionals: Analysis of existing work and a new model. *ACM Transactions on Computing Education, 23*(2), 1–33.
7. Bergen, N., & Labonté, R. (2020). "Everything is perfect, and we have no problems": Detecting and limiting social desirability bias in qualitative research. *Qualitative Health Research, 30*(5), 783–792.
8. Bibi, N., Anwar, Z., & Rana, T. (2021). Expertise based skills management system to support resource allocation. *Plos One, 16*(8), E0255928.
9. Biesalski, E., & Abecker, A. (2005). Integrated processes and tools for personnel development. *2005 IEEE International Technology Management Conference (ICE)* (pp. 1–8).
10. Boyadjieva, P., & Ilieva-Trichkova, P. (2023). Adult education as a pathway to empowerment: Challenges and possibilities. In J. Holford, P. Boyadjieva, S. Clancy, G. Hefler & I. Studená (Eds.), *Lifelong learning, young adults and the challenges of disadvantage in Europe* (pp. 169–191). Palgrave Macmillan.
11. Brinton, C. G., Rill, R., Ha, S., Chiang, M., Smith, R., & Ju, W. (2015). Individualization for education at scale: Miic design and preliminary evaluation. *IEEE Transactions On Learning Technologies, 8*(1), 136–148.
12. Cantrell S, Griffiths M, Jones R, Et Al. (2022, September 8) The Skills-Based Organization: A New Operating Model For Work And The Workforce. *Deloitte.*
13. Carretero, S., Vuorikari, R., & Punie, Y. (2017). *Digcomp 2.1: The digital competence framework for citizens.*
14. Charmaz, K., & Belgrave, L. (2012). Qualitative interviewing and grounded theory analysis. In J. F. Gubrium (Ed.), *The Sage Handbook of interview research: The complexity of the craft* (pp. 347–365). Sage.
15. Chowdhury, S., Dey, P., Joel-Edgar, S., Bhattacharya, S., Rodriguez-Espindola, O., Abadie, A., & Truong, L. (2023). Unlocking the value of artificial intelligence in human resource management through AI capability framework. *Human Resource Management Review, 33*(1), 100899.
16. Cotton, A. (2007). *Seven steps of effective workforce planning.* IBM center for The Business of Government.
17. Djumalieva, J., & Sleeman, C. (2018). An open and data-driven taxonomy of skills extracted from online job adverts. In C. Larsen, S. Rand, A. Schmid & A. Dean (Eds.), *Developing skills in a changing world of work* (pp. 425–454). Rainer Hampp Verlag.
18. Doherty-Restrepo, J. l., Perez, K., Creeden, M., Cram, B., & Charite, M. (2023). Closing the gap between students' career readiness and employers' expectations. *International Journal of Innovative Teaching and Learning in Higher Education, 4*(1), 1–14.
19. European Commission. (2022). Esco. Retrieved September 28, 2022, from https://Esco.Ec.Europa.Eu/De
20. Fareri, S., Fantoni, G., Chiarello F, Coli, E., & Binda, A. (2020). Estimating industry 4.0 impact on job profiles and skills using text mining. *Computers in Industry, 118*, 103222.

21. Fazel-Zarandi, M., & Fox, M. S. (2013). Inferring and validating skills and competencies over time. *Applied Ontology, 8*(3), 131–177.
22. Fernández-Sanz, L., Gómez-Pérez, J., & Castillo-Martínez, A. (2017). E-Skills match: A framework for mapping and integrating the main skills, knowledge and competence standards and models for ICT occupations. *Computer Standards & Interfaces, 51*, 30–42.
23. Freise, L. R., & Hupe, A. (2023). Transferring digital twin technology on employee skills: A framework to support human resources. In *83rd academy of management annual meeting.*
24. Fteimi, N., & Hopf, K. (2021). Knowledge management in the Era of artificial intelligence: Developing an integrative framework.
25. Gerogiannis, V. C., Rapti, E., Karageorgos, A., & Fitsilis, P. (2015). A fuzzy linguistic approach for human resource evaluation and selection in software projects. In *Proceedings of the 2015 International Conference on Industrial Engineering and Operations Management (IEOM)* Dubai, 3–5 March 2015. IEEE.
26. Glaser, B., & Strauss, A. l. (1967). *Discovery of grounded theory: Strategies for qualitative research.* Taylor and Francis.
27. Gottipati, S., & Shankararaman, V. (2018). Competency analytics tool: Analyzing curriculum using course competencies. *Education and Information Technologies, 23*(1), 41–60.
28. Hirata, K., & Brown, M. (2008). Skill-Competency management architecture. In *Proceedings of the 16th International Conference on Computers in Education* (pp. 179–185). Citeseer.
29. Holland, A.,& Fathi, M. (2005). Creating graphical models as representation of personalized skill profiles. *2005 IEEE International Conference on Systems, Man and Cybernetics, 1*, 560–565.
30. Jain, H., Padmanabhan, B., Pavlou, P. A., & Raghu, T. S. (2021). Editorial for the special section on humans, algorithms, and augmented intelligence: The future of work, organizations, and society. *Information Systems Research, 32*(3), 675–687.
31. Judrups J, Zandbergs U And Kazakovs M (2015) Competence Based Human Resource Development Solution. *Engineering for Rural Development, 14*, 669–674.
32. Kimble, C., de Vasconcelos, J. B., & Rocha, Á. (2016). Competence management in knowledge intensive organizations using consensual knowledge and ontologies. *Information Systems Frontiers A Journal Of Research and Innovation, 18*, 1119–1130.
33. Konstantinidis, I., Maragoudakis, M., Magnisalis I, Berberidis, C., & Peristeras, V. (2022). Knowledge-Driven unsupervised skills extraction for graph-based talent matching. In *Proceedings of The 12th Hellenic Conference on Artificial Intelligence:* Corfu Greece, 07 09 2022 09 09 2022. ACM.
34. Ku, G., Wang, C. S., & Galinsky, A. D. (2015). The promise and perversity of perspective-taking in organizations. *Research in Organizational Behavior, 35*, 79–102.
35. Laboissiere, M., & Mourshed, M. (2017). Closing the skills gap: Creating workforce-development programs that work for everyone. *Mckinsey & Company, 2.*
36. Lähteenoja, V., Flanagan, A. J., & Warren, S. (2021). *On the importance of human-centricity and data.* World Economic Forum.
37. Lanzl, J., Schnaak, F., Schöttl, F., & Gimpel, H. (2024). Der Einfluss Von Digitalen Technologien Auf Wissensarbeit: Kompetenzen Im Wandel. *Hmd Praxis Der Wirtschaftsinformatik, 61*(1), 141–158.
38. Lawler, E., & Ledford, G. (1992). A skill-based approach to human resource management. *European Management Journal, 10*(4), 383–391.
39. Litchfield, R. C., & Gentry, R. J. (2010). Perspective-Taking as an organizational capability. *Strategic Organization, 8*(3), 187–205.
40. Longenecker, H, Feinstein, D. l., & Clark, J. (2013). Information systems curricula: A fifty year journey. *Information Systems Education Journal, 11*, 71–95.
41. Lula, P., Oczkowska, R., Wiśniewska, S., & Wójcik, K. (2018). Ontology-Based system for automatic analysis of job offers. In *The 12th Professor Aleksander Zelias International Conference on Modelling and Forecasting of Socio-Economic Phenomena* (pp. 256–265).
42. Malik, A., Froese, F. J., & Sharma, P. (2020). Role of Hrm in knowledge integration: Towards a conceptual framework. *Journal Of Business Research, 109*, 524–535.

43. Markus, L., Thomas, H. C., & Allpress, K. (2005). Confounded by competencies? An evaluation of the evolution and use of competency models. *New Zealand Journal of Psychology, 34*(2), 117.
44. Marshall, B., Cardon, P., Poddar, A., & Fontenot, R. (2013). Does sample size matter in qualitative research? A review of qualitative interviews in is research. *Journal of Computer Information Systems, 54*(1), 11–22.
45. Maurya, A., & Telang, R. (2017). Bayesian multi-view models for member-job matching and personalized skill recommendations. In *2017 IEEE International Conference on Big Data (Big Data):* Boston, Ma, 11–14 December 2017 (pp. 1193–1202). IEEE.
46. Mayring, P. (2004). Qualitative content analysis. In B. Jenner, U. Flick, E. vonKardoff & I. Steinke (Eds.), *A companion to qualitative research.* Sage.
47. Mcintosh, M. J., & Morse, J. M. (2015). Situating and constructing diversity in semi-structured interviews. *Global Qualitative Nursing Research, 2*, 2333393615597674.
48. Minku, L. l., Sudholt, D., & Yao, X. (2013). Improved evolutionary algorithm design for the project scheduling problem based on runtime analysis. *IEEE Transactions on Software Engineering, 40*(1), 83–102.
49. Nagendra, A., & Deshpande, M. (2014). Human Resource Information Systems (HRIS) in HR planning and development in mid to large sized organizations. *Procedia—Social and Behavioral Sciences, 133*, 61–67.
50. Nikitinsky, N. (2016). Improving talent management with automated competence assessment: Research summary. In *Scientific-Practical Conference "Research and Development"*, 73–82.
51. Paiva, J. C., Leal, J. P., & Figueira, Á. (2022). Automated assessment in computer science education: A state-of-the-art review. *Acm Transactions on Computing Education, 22*(3), 1–40.
52. Patton, S. (2023). Introducing skills in microsoft viva, a new ai-powered service to grow and manage talent. Retrieved January 5, 2024, from https://Www.Microsoft.Com/En-Us/Microsoft-365/Blog/2023/10/10/Introducing-Skills-In-Microsoft-Viva-A-New-Ai-Powered-Service-To-Grow-And-Manage-Talent/.
53. Pellegrino, J. W. (2013). Proficiency in science: Assessment challenges and opportunities. *Science, 340*(6130), 320–323.
54. Pospelova, V., Baldominos, I. L., Sanz, L. F., Castillo-Martinez, A. (2021). Big data and skills frameworks to determine recommended profiled of soft skills for is development. *Proceedings of The International Conference on Information Systems Development (ISD).*
55. Ridsdale, C., Rothwell, J., Smit, M., Ali-Hassan, H., Bliemel, M., Irvine, D., Kelley, D., Matwin, S., Wuetherick, B. (2015). Strategies and best practices for data literacy education. *Knowledge Synthesis Report.*
56. Ritz, E., Donisi, F., Elshan, E., & Rietsche, R. (2023). Artificial socialization? How artificial intelligence applications can shape a new era of employee onboarding practices. In *56th Hawaii International Conference on System Sciences (HICSS).*
57. Ritz, E., Freise, L., Elshan, E., Rietsche, R., & Bretschneider, U. (2024). What to learn next? designing personalized learning paths for re-&upskilling in organizations. In *Hawaii International Conference on System Sciences (HICSS).*
58. Saldana, J. (2021). *The coding manual for qualitative researchers.* Sage Publications Ltd.
59. Santandreu Calonge, D., & Aman Shah, M. (2016). Moocs, graduate skills gaps, and employability: A qualitative systematic review of the literature. *International Review of Research in Open and Distributed Learning, 17*(5), 67–90.
60. Sciuk, C., & Hess, T. (2022). Governing digital transformation—The profiles of top managers. In *Pacific Asia Conference on Information Systems.*
61. Sebastião, L., Tirapicos, F., Payan-Carreira, R., & Rebelo, H. (2023). Skill profiles for employability: (Mis)understandings between higher education institutions and employers. *Education Sciences, 13*(9), 905.
62. Slayter, E., & Higgins, L. M. (2018). Hands-on learning: A problem-based approach to teaching microsoft excel. *College Teaching, 66*(1), 31–33.
63. Strauss, A., & Corbin, J. (1990). *Basics of qualitative research: Grounded theory procedures and techniques.* Sage.

64. Tarafdar, M., Beath, C. M., & Ross, J. W. (2019). Using AI to enhance business operations. *Mit Sloan Management Review, 60*(4).
65. Traynor, S., Wellens, M. A., & Krishnamoorthy, V. (2021). Job profile builder. In S. Traynor, M. A. Wellens & V. Krishnamoorthy (Eds.), *Sap successfactors talent: Volume 1* (pp. 65–111). Apress.
66. U.S. Department Of Labor/Employment And Training Administration. (2022). Occupational Information Network (O*Net). Retrieved September 28, 2022, from https://Www.Onetcenter.Org/
67. Van Iddekinge, C. H., Lanivich, S. E., Roth, P. L., & Junco, E. (2016). Social media for selection? Validity and adverse impact potential of a facebook-based assessment. *Journal of Management, 42*(7), 1811–1835.
68. Vom Brocke, J., Simons, A., Niehaves, B., Niehaves, B., Riemer, K., Plattfaut, R., & Cleven, A. (2009). Reconstructing the giant: On the importance of rigour in documenting the literature search process. In *17th European Conference on information systems*.
69. Zimmerman, B. J. (2002). Becoming a self-regulated learner: An overview. *Theory into practice*, 41(2), 64-70.

Conceptualizing the Agile Mindset in Agile Software Development Teams

Kristin Geffers, Ulrich Bretschneider, and Karen Eilers

Abstract Agile Software Development Teams (ASDTs) employ agile methodologies to navigate the dynamic landscape of the software industry, responding effectively to constant change and innovation. The success of ASDTs relies significantly on the individuals' mindset, referred to as the agile mindset (AM). Yet, a clear conceptualization of the AM remains elusive, as existing approaches do not meet scientific standards and fail to produce consistent results. This paper addresses this gap by systematically conceptualizing the AM within the context of ASDTs. Through a systematic review and evaluation of existing definitions and initial conceptualizations, we identified dimensions and consolidated insights, resulting in a comprehensive conceptualization of the AM. Our work represents a crucial step towards understanding the AM's role in ASDTs and lays the foundation for our planned future work: the empirical validation and development of a standardized measurement instrument for the AM.

1 Introduction

In today's rapidly evolving technological landscape, the software industry stands out as particularly susceptible to constant change and disruption. With innovation driving the industry forward at an unprecedented pace, companies within this sector face continuous challenges to remain adaptable and competitive [1, 2]. To address these challenges head-on, software development teams adopt agile methodologies and work according to the values captured in the Agile Manifesto [3]. These teams,

K. Geffers (✉) · U. Bretschneider
University of Kassel, Kassel, Germany
e-mail: kristin.geffers@wi-kassel.de

U. Bretschneider
e-mail: bretschneider@uni-kassel.de

K. Eilers
Institute for Transformation, Hamburg, Germany
e-mail: karen.eilers@in-transformation.com

C. M. Flath et al. (eds.), *Digital Innovation and Organizational Transformation*, Lecture Notes in Information Systems and Organisation 83,
https://doi.org/10.1007/978-3-032-08483-5_15

known as agile software development teams (ASDTs), employ iterative processes marked by frequent testing, feedback, and adaptation, all aimed at continuously delivering valuable outcomes to their customers [4]. The Agile Manifesto follows a people-focused approach, emphasizing individuals in the process of building software [5]. Consequently, the success of agile software projects is critically linked to people factors [6], referring to the human aspects, such as individual behavior, influencing the agile development process and overall project success. Many researchers have already explored various people factors in the field of ASDTs, such as agreeableness, morals, and motivation [7, 8, 9]. Although the significance of the mindset of individuals working in ASDTs, in the following referred to as the agile mindset (AM), has long been emphasized in both research and practice, the scientific knowledge surrounding this phenomenon remains limited. In particular, there is a pressing need for deeper and clearer conceptualizations of the AM [10]. Current concepts predominantly rely on a limited number of practice-driven insights and employ inconsistent dimensions in defining the AM [10, 11]. Moreover, these concepts are excessively broad and fail to address the specific context and requirements of ASDTs. Consequently, attempts to conceptualize the AM have fallen short of meeting scientific standards and delivering coherent results. Our paper works on the identified gap by answering the research question (RQ): How can the agile mindset among individuals working in agile software development teams be conceptualized?

Our research aims to conceptualize the AM in the context of ASDTs. By systematically reviewing and evaluating existing AM definitions and initial conceptualizations, we were able to a) identify all known dimensions, b) consolidate redundant insights, and c) eliminate irrelevant aspects. Further, we expand the existing knowledge base by adding additional insights that we derived from relevant theory. This process leads to a comprehensive conceptualization of the AM, which effectively addresses the gaps in understanding the construct. These outcomes represent a partial result of our ongoing research endeavors. Moving forward, our objectives include empirically evaluating and validating our findings, as well as developing a standardized measurement instrument for assessing the AM among individuals in ASDTs.

1.1 Agile Software Development Teams

Agile software development (ASD), using methodologies like Scrum and Extreme Programming, aligns with the values outlined in the Agile Manifesto [12]. These values prioritize individuals, working software, customer collaboration, and responsiveness to change [3]. Unlike traditional methods, agile approaches emphasize experimenting, shared ownership, and continuous stakeholder involvement [9], enabling frequent delivery and real-time adaptation [13]. ASD allows teams to respond rapidly and flexibly to changes, fostering learning and improvement [14]. Additionally, it enhances stakeholder satisfaction, productivity, and business alignment [15]. ASDTs operate in line with agile values and principles, consisting of small, cross-functional groups that make collective decisions [16, 17]. Close collaboration is essential in ASDTs [18], with roles typically including Agile Manager, Scrum Master, Product Owner, and Developer [9].

Research on ASDTs covers various aspects such as organizational, technical, technological, procedural, project, customer, team, and performance dimensions [6, 7, 19, 20]. However, ASD maintains a people-centric approach, with team members driving the development process, adapting to changing requirements, and ensuring the software's success [12, 13]. This human-centered focus has led to growing research on people factors. The outlined factors found in the literature can be categorized into several dimensions:

1) Scholars have investigated personal traits such as agreeableness, conscientiousness, team orientation, emotionality, extraversion, and honesty-humility in the context of ASDTs [8, 9].

2) Individual characteristics of the ASDT members significantly impact their performance. Autonomy, learnability, openness to experience, and self-organization are crucial for navigating agile project complexities [7, 21, 22, 23, 9].

3) The psychological well-being of members also plays a vital role in the success of ASDTs. Individual perceptions of participative safety, psychological safety, and mutual trust contribute to creating an environment where individuals feel supported and secure in expressing their ideas and concerns [7, 4, 8].

4) Further psychological factors such as motivation, morale, and value congruence were investigated in ASDTs [7, 19, 8, 24, 25, 22].

1.2 The Agile Mindset

Understanding the AM entails delving into the concept of "mindset", which originates from cognitive psychology. Mindset can be viewed as the inherent sense-making assumption of an individual, serving as a general framework of epistemology [26]. Scholars often describe mindset as a predisposition to perceive the world in a certain way, acting as a lens through which individuals interpret experiences. This implies that mindset shapes an individual's worldview and dictates how individuals view and interact with the world, portraying it as a fundamental aspect of their beliefs and identity [26]. This view corresponds to the psychological concept of attitude, which reflects an individual's predisposition towards a value and their reactions to various objects or behaviors, termed the attitude object [27]. Unlike mindsets, attitudes are more specific, focusing on particular objects or behaviors and indicating an individual's degree of favor or disfavor towards them [28]. Thus, attitudes can be positive or negative evaluations of the attitude object [27]. Applied to the context of the AM, it can be regarded as an attitude with a thematic focus on agility as its object, with agility understood as the company's ability to rapidly and effectively respond to external changes [29]. Similar to attitudes, the AM can be a positive or negative evaluation of agility by an individual [30]. Attitudes are generally resistant to change but can evolve through environmental experiences and learning processes [31].

2 Research Design

Clear, concise conceptualization is crucial for accurately defining constructs [32]. To conceptualize the AM, we followed a three-step process recommended by [33]: 1) review existing literature, 2) specify the construct, and 3) define it. We started by examining past research on the AM. This review aimed to identify previous definitions as well as initial conceptualizations and to assess their strengths and weaknesses. In December 2023, we conducted a systematic literature search using Google Scholar and Business Source Premier for works published until 2023 under the search criteria "Agile Mindset", "Mindset", "Attitude", and "Agile Attitude". This yielded 21 relevant studies from journals and conferences. Forward and backward citation searches from these studies identified nine additional sources. Following that, we reviewed these 30 articles, carefully assessing their abstracts for relevance. Of these, 23 articles used the keywords in contexts different from our focus, prompting their exclusion. Ultimately, we selected seven relevant studies (Table 1) for our analysis.

Our next step in conceptualizing the AM is to formally specify it by building on the strengths of prior definitions and conceptualizations identified in our literature analysis. This process entails leveraging the insights in a stepwise manner according to the criteria that we used for the literature analysis, namely the general type of property, entity to which the property applies, dimensions, and stability. The specification of the AM construct, including its dimensions, enabled us to provide a clear and concise conceptual definition of the AM in the final step. In the future, we aim to validate our findings through empirical testing and develop a standardized measurement tool for evaluating the AM among members of ASDTs.

Table 1 Overview of literature

Extant literature	Methodologies
Senapathi and Srinivasan (2013) [34]	Literature review
Van Manen and van Vliet (2014) [35]	Case study
Gannod et al. (2018) [1]	Interviews
Miler and Gaida (2019) [36]	Interviews and quantitative survey
Mordi and Schoop (2020) [37]	Literature review and interviews
Ozkan et al. (2020) [2]	Literature review and expert interviews
Eilers et al. (2022) [10]	Quantitative survey

3 Preliminary Findings: Conceptualization of the Agile Mindset

3.1 *Review and Analysis of the Literature*

As described in the previous section, we identified seven relevant studies (Table 1). All examined studies perceive the AM as an attitude towards a company's or a team's agility efforts, or at least as a closely related concept of mindset. Moreover, all studies consistently identify the individual employee as the entity to which this property applies. In contrast, scholars lack clarity on which dimensions of agility should form the attitude object. There is no consensus on the specific dimensions or their quantity and some crucial dimensions remain undiscovered. Additionally, we found significant overlaps between dimensions within the initial conceptualization. All these discrepancies in the dimensionality lead to the fact that, until today, there are inconsistent, varying, and unspecific definitions of the AM. Furthermore, only one paper by [10] addresses the stability of the AM. The authors suggest that, like psychological attitudes, the AM tends to be somewhat resistant to change but can evolve through experiences and resulting learning processes. This previously overlooked aspect should be a crucial component of a comprehensive conceptualization of the AM.

3.2 *Specification of the Construct*

(1) General type of property: All identified studies (Table 1) commonly interpret the AM as a psychological attitude or at least as a mindset closely related to the concept of attitude towards a company's or team's agility efforts. Derived from our research aim, we will take the team perspective, more precisely, that of the ASDTs for our conceptualization.

(2) Entity to which the property applies: All identified studies consistently apply the AM to individual employees. In our research, we refine this perspective to focus specifically on individuals within ASDTs.

(3) Dimensions: Our literature analysis revealed significant discrepancies in the identified works regarding the dimensionality of the AM. To ensure precision in defining the focal construct, we identify and clarify each relevant dimension and its interrelationships, following [33]. This involves meticulously analyzing each study and dimension to assess its relevance and distinctiveness. We examine the unique characteristics of each dimension and consider key questions: How distinct are these characteristics from each other, beyond their common theme? Would excluding any dimension significantly limit the construct's scope, particularly in the context of ASDTs? Dimensions that did not meet these criteria were excluded. In the final step, the remaining dimensions (Table 2) were grouped by categorizing those with similar thematic focuses into distinct and unique groups.

Table 2 Categorization of dimensions

Dimensions from extant literature (Table 1)	Newly-emerged dimensions
Opportunities for learning; continuous improvement; continuous learning; open mindedness; willingness to learn; seeking new insights for change response	Learning spirit: Positive attitude of an individual working in an ASDT towards the search for and the learning of new things and insights to respond to change
Collaboration; transparently share and discuss methods and work results	Collaborative exchange: Positive attitude of an individual working in an ASDT towards sharing knowledge, giving feedback, and collaborating with others for problem-solving
Proactivity; responsibility; proactive mind; decide for themselves how to proceed	Empowered self-guidance: Positive attitude of an individual working in an ASDT towards self-reflection, organizing themselves, decision-making, and taking ownership
Customer orientation in a co-creation process	Customer co-creation: Positive attitude of an individual working in an ASDT towards customer-centricity within a customer co-creation process

(4) Stability: Only the studies by [10] and [34] address the stability of the AM. Following their findings, we agree that the AM, defined as a psychological attitude, tends to exhibit stability over time but can evolve through experiences and learning processes influenced by the environment.

3.3 *Definition of the Construct*

Based on the specifications provided, we define the AM as the attitude of an individual working in an ASDT towards the ASDT's agility efforts. This, in turn, is expressed through the following dimensions: Positive attitude of an individual working in an ASDT 1) towards the search for and the learning of new things and insights to respond to change (learning spirit); 2) towards sharing knowledge, giving feedback, and collaborating with colleagues for problem-solving (collaborative exchange); 3) towards reflecting upon their working process, organizing themselves, making their own decisions, and taking responsibility for their work (empowered self-guidance); and 4) with a direct touch point with customers towards a proactive record of customer needs and a proactive transfer into appropriate actions in response to these needs (proactive interaction with customers). The AM tends to be more or less change-resistant in an individual employee. However, it can be changed over time through experiences in contact with the environment and the resulting learning processes.

4 Contributions and Outlook

Our study addresses the current gap in the scientific literature concerning the inconsistent understanding of the AM by providing a clear and concise conceptualization along with its dimensions. Thus, we reduce misunderstandings and interpretation errors regarding the AM and foster consistent communication across research and practice about this phenomenon. Furthermore, we lay the groundwork for further theoretical exploration of the AM's impacts and relationships, its theoretical differentiation from other constructs, and the development of precise measurement and validation of the AM construct. Moreover, a reliable conceptualization of the AM addresses the inconsistent and misleading applications observed in practice by providing practitioners, managers leading ASDTs, and human resources departments with a basis to comprehend AM's role and relevance in ASDTs and to identify strategies and measures to promote attitudes, competencies, skills, and values required for fostering an AM among employees. Looking ahead, we aim to empirically evaluate and validate our findings and develop a standardized tool to measure the AM among individuals in ASDTs.

References

1. Gannod, G. C. et al.: Establishing an agile mindset and culture for workforce preparedness: A baseline study. In: Sluss, J. et al. (eds.) Frontiers in education conference 2018, fie, vol. 48, pp. 1–9. Curran Associates, Inc., (2018).
2. Ozkan, N., Gök, M. Ş., & Köse, B. (2020). Ö.: Towards a better understanding of agile mindset by using principles of agile methods. In *Federated conference on COMPUTER SCIENCE and INFORMATION SYSTEMS 2020* (Vol. 15, pp. 721–730).
3. Fowler, M., & Highsmith, J. (2001). *The agile manifesto. Software Development, 9*(8), 28–35.
4. Buvik, M., & Tkalich, A. (2022). Psychological safety in agile software development teams: Work design antecedents and performance consequences. In: Bui, T. (ed.) HAWAII INTERNATIONAL CONFERENCE ON SYSTEM SCIENCES 2022. *HICSS, 55*, 7330–7339.
5. Beck, K. et al.: http://agilemanifesto.org/, last accessed 2024/03/03, (2001).
6. Aldahmash, A., Gravell, A. M., & Howard, Y. (2017). A review on the critical success factors of agile software development. In J. Stolfa, S. Stolfa, R. V. O'Connor, & R. Messnarz (Eds.), *SYSTEMS, SOFTWARE AND SERVICES PROCESS IMPROVEMENT: 24TH EUROPEAN CONFERENCE, EuroSPI 2017* (Vol. 24, pp. 504–512). Springer International.
7. Arcos-Medina, G., & Mauricio, D. (2020). Identifying factors influencing on agile practices for software development. *Journal of Information and Organizational Sciences, 44*, 1–31.
8. Fatema, I., Sakib, K.: Factors influencing productivity of agile software development teamwork: A qualitative system dynamics approach. In: Lv, J. (ed.) ASIA-PACIFIC SOFTWARE ENGINEERING CONFERENCE 2017, APSEC, vol. 24, pp. 737–742 (2017).
9. Zainal, D., Razali, R., & Mansor, Z. (2020). Team formation for agile software development: A review. *International Journal on Advanced Science, Engineering, and Information Technology, 10*, 555–561.
10. Eilers, K., Peters, C., & Leimeister, J. M. (2022). Why the agile mindset matters. *Technological Forecasting and Social Change, 179*, 121650.
11. Fuchs, C., & Hess, T. (2018). Becoming agile in the digital transformation: The process of a large-scale agile transformation. In: Baskerville, R., Nickerson, R. (eds.) INTERNATIONAL CONFERENCE OF INFORMATION SYSTEMS 2018. *ICIS, 39*, 1–17.

12. Alqudah, M. K., & Rozilawati, R. (2017). Key factors for selecting an agile method: A systematic literature review. *International Journal on Advanced Science, Engineering and Information Technology, 7*(2), 526–537.
13. Tam, C., Moura, E., Oliveira, T., & Varajão, J. (2020). The factors influencing the success of on-going agile software development projects. *International Journal of Project Management, 38*, 165–176.
14. Hameed, T. A., El, L., Abd El, M., & Kholief, S. (2016). Identify and classify critical success factor of agile software development methodology using mind map. *International Journal of Advanced Computer Science and Applications, 7*(5), 83–92.
15. Henderson-Sellers, B., & Ralyté, J. (2010). Situational method engineering: State-of-the-art review. *Journal of Universal Computer Science, 16*(3), 424–478.
16. Schwaber, K., Sutherland, J.: https://www.scrum.org/resources/what-is-scrum, last accessed 2024/02/15, (n.d.).
17. Moe, N. B., Aurum, A., & Dyba, T. (2012). Challenges of shared decision-making: A multiple case study of agile software development. *Information and Software Technology, 54*(8), 853–865.
18. Dingsøyr, T., & Lindsjørn, Y. (2013). Team performance in agile development teams: Findings from 18 focus groups. In H. Baumeister & B. Weber (Eds.), *AGILE PROCESSES IN SOFTWARE ENGINEERING AND EXTREME PROGRAMMING 2013, XP* (Vol. 14, pp. 46–60). Springer.
19. Chiyangwa, T. B., & Mnkandla, E. (2017). Modelling the critical success factors of agile software development projects in South Africa. *South African Journal of Information Management, 19*(1), a838.
20. Darwish, N. R., & Rizk, N. M. (2015). Multi-dimensional success factors of agile software development projects. *International Journal of Computer Applications, 118*(15), 23–30.
21. Chow, T., & Cao, D. B. (2008). A survey study on critical success factors in agile software projects. *Journal of Systems and Software, 81*, 961–971.
22. Stankovic, D., Nikolic, V., Djordjevic, M., & Cao, D. B. (2013). A survey study of critical success factors in agile software projects in former Yugoslavia IT companies. *Journal of Systems and Software, 86*(6), 1663–1678.
23. Subramanyam, V., & Prasad, C. G. (2013). Organizational practices that affects software quality in software engineering process. *International Journal of Engineering Trends and Technology, 2*(3), 25–30.
24. Fernández-Sanz, L., & Misra, S. (2011). Influence of human factors in software quality and productivity. In B. Murgante, O. Gervasi, & A. Iglesias (Eds.), *Computational SCIENCE and its applications 2011, ICCSA* (Vol. 11, pp. 257–269). Springer.
25. Kelle, E. V., Visser, J., Plaat, A., Wijst, P.: An empirical study into social success factors for agile software development. In: Begel, A. et al. (eds.) International workshop cooperative and human aspects of software engineering 2015, IEEE/ACM, vol. 8, pp. 77–80. Curran Associates, Inc., (2015).
26. French, R. P. (2016). The fuzziness of mindsets: Divergent conceptualizations and characterizations of mindset theory and praxis. *International Journal of Organizational Analysis, 24*(4), 673–691.
27. Perloff, R. M. (2017). *The dynamics of persuasion: Communication and attitudes in the twenty-first century*. Taylor & Francis.
28. Dweck, C. S. (2016). What having a "growth mindset" actually means. *Harvard Business Review, 13*, 213–226.
29. Youssef, A. B., Boubaker, S., Dedaj, B., & Carabregu-Vokshi, M. (2021). Digitalization of the economy and entrepreneurship intention. *Technological Forecasting and Social Change, 64*, 120043.
30. Eagly, A. H., & Chaiken, S. (1993). *The psychology of attitudes*. Harcourt Brace Jovanovich College Publishers.
31. Petrocelli, J. V., Tormala, Z. L., & Rucker, D. D. (2007). Unpacking attitude certainty: Attitude clarity and attitude correctness. *Journal of Personality and Social Psychology, 92*(1), 30–41.

32. Churchill, G. A. A. (1979). Paradigm for developing better measures of marketing constructs. *Journal of Marketing Research, 16*(1), 64–73.
33. MacKenzie, S. B., Podsakoff, P. M., & Podsakoff, N. P. (2011). Construct measurement and validation procedures in MIS and behavioral research: Integrating new and existing techniques. *Management Information Systems Quarterly, 35*(2), 293–334.
34. Senapathi, M., Srinivasan, A.: Sustained agile usage: a systematic literature review. In: INTERNATIONAL CONFERENCE ON EVALUATION AND ASSESSMENT IN SOFTWARE ENGINEERING, ABK., vol. 17, pp. 119–124 (2013).
35. Manen, H. van, Vliet, H. van: Organization-wide agile expansion requires an organization-wide agile mindset. In: A. Jedlitschka et al. (eds.) Product focused software process improvement 2014, PROFES, vol. 15, pp. 48–62. Springer, (2014).
36. Miler, J., & Gaida, P. (2019). On the agile mindset of an effective team: An industrial opinion survey. In *Federated conference on COMPUTER SCIENCE and INFORMATION SYSTEMS 2019* (Vol. 14, pp. 841–849).
37. Mordi, A., & Schoop, M. (2020). Making it tangible: Creating a definition of the agile mindset. In: EUROPEAN 2020 CONFERENCE ON INFORMATION SYSTEMS 2020. *ECIS, 28*, 1–17.

Navigating the New Norm: Employees' Continuous Data Sharing in AI-Driven Workplaces

Mena Teebken, Thomas Hess, and Alexander Pretschner

Abstract This study examines the changing nature of employee data sharing in AI-driven workplaces. AI tools, such as intelligent assistants embedded in daily routines, necessitate a reevaluation of data sharing paradigms due to their continuous data generation and processing. Despite the vast body of literature on data sharing, the constant nature of data sharing in AI-driven environments is rarely investigated. This gap between the practical relevance of such tools and our limited understanding of the changes they entail highlights the need for an extended understanding of the evolving nature of data sharing and its implications. We emphasize the concept of Continuous Data Sharing, transitioning from static decision-making to recognizing data sharing as an ongoing process characterized by changes in data dynamics, employee participation, and unpredictability. In summary, this work underscores the importance of redefining employee data sharing in the context of digital workplace transformation and increasing AI integration.

1 Introduction

The essence of digital work is continuously evolving through digital workplace solutions based on Artificial Intelligence (AI) [4]. This development reflects a change in job roles, the essence of digital work, and, crucially, the role of employee data [30]. The profound integration of AI-based solutions into the workplace is evidenced by its far-reaching adoption across various sectors, signaling a broad reevaluation of

M. Teebken (✉)
Bavarian Research Institute for Digital Transformation, Munich, Germany
e-mail: mena.teebken@bidt.digital

T. Hess
LMU Munich School of Management, Munich, Germany
e-mail: thess@lmu.de

A. Pretschner
Technical University of Munich, Munich, Germany
e-mail: alexander.pretschner@tum.de

C. M. Flath et al. (eds.), *Digital Innovation and Organizational Transformation*, Lecture Notes in Information Systems and Organisation 83,
https://doi.org/10.1007/978-3-032-08483-5_16

how work is conceived and executed [13]. With 61% of workers reporting increased productivity due to AI and 93% of managers endorsing its use for enhancing performance, the impact of AI on the workforce is definite [29, 34]. Furthermore, organizations' adoption rate of AI technology—now at 37%, marking a 270% increase over the span of four years [12]—underscores the growing reliance on AI as a critical driver of workplace transformation.

In today's digital workplaces, various AI tools are increasingly utilized, such as wearables, robotics or AI-based[1] assistants [6]. Given their substantial impact and growing prevalence, our study focuses on AI assistants as an exemplary application area of AI in workplaces. We chose Microsoft Copilot as an example of an AI assistant for several compelling reasons. First, Microsoft's Windows operating system dominates the global market with a share of around 72% [28]. Second, Microsoft Copilot is particularly popular because it seamlessly integrates into the Microsoft workflow and is widely used in professional settings [16]. Such AI assistants are designed to easily work with existing business processes, making them an attractive option for companies looking to enhance efficiency without extensive overhauls of their current systems.

As AI technologies transition from mere tools to integral partners and digital assistants, the challenge now lies in navigating this new terrain, where the distinction between humans and machines becomes increasingly intertwined [2, 4]. In particular, AI assistants require unrestricted access to employee data for full functionality, involving collecting, storing, analyzing, and acting upon a continuous stream of employee data. For instance, this includes user-generated content, interaction data, or data from integrated applications [22]. The constant, voluminous, and essential nature of data sharing for AI functionality, coupled with the blurred boundaries between professional and private life [30], demands reevaluating our understanding of employee data sharing in this context.

This study delves into the evolving dynamics of employee data sharing brought about by adopting AI technologies. Therefore, our research is guided by the pivotal question: *How does the nature of employee data sharing change in the context of AI-driven workplaces*? Following methodological guidelines for theory adaptation [17], our conceptualization process is divided into two interconnected steps. First, we begin with a critical examination of the existing literature on data sharing, highlighting the context of digital workplaces. Second, we outline the peculiarities of continuous data sharing and propose an adapted conceptualization that acknowledges the continuous and pervasive nature of data sharing facilitated by AI technologies. Through this theoretical lens, we develop propositions that articulate areas for future exploration.

The implications of this research are both timely and significant. For organizations, understanding the changing dynamics of data sharing in digital workplaces is crucial for developing effective data management policies, addressing potential employee concerns, and ensuring compliance with data protection regulations. Moreover, this

[1] In this study, the term "AI-based assistants" is interchangeably used with "AI assistants" for brevity and ease of reading. Both terms refer to the same concept of digital assistants powered by artificial intelligence technologies.

understanding is vital for societal implications, reflecting on the broader impacts of digital transformation on privacy, employment, and organizational culture. Furthermore, the implications of our research extend to the realm of policy-making and governance. As AI technologies become increasingly integral to workplace operations, there is a pressing need for policies that foster innovation and protect individual rights.

2 Theoretical Foundations

The growing integration of AI in the workplace represents a paradigm shift, transitioning AI from a mere operational tool to a pivotal component in enhancing productivity and redefining job roles [4, 6]. An AI system is a machine-based system that can make predictions, recommendations, or decisions for a set of human-defined objectives. AI in the workplace is defined as the technology enabling smart computer programs and machines to perform tasks that usually necessitate human intelligence [6, 20]. Cranefield [9] emphasizes the transformative potential of AI in the future of work, suggesting that AI-based systems increasingly become partners rather than mere tools.

AI assistants, also known as Intelligent Assistants or Intelligent Personal Assistants, refer to a sophisticated system of intelligent software agents designed to handle complex tasks without direct user intervention [4]. These assistants utilize advanced AI technologies, including machine learning and natural language processing, to provide personalized and contextual support, automate repetitive tasks, and offer actionable insights [19]. An example is Microsoft Copilot, which integrates deeply with Microsoft 365 to offer various functionalities, including document drafting, data analysis, email management, and presentation assistance [23]. Overall, AI assistants have the potential to represent a significant advancement in workplace technology, enhancing productivity and facilitating a higher level of human-AI collaboration [9].

Generally speaking, AI tools rely on a vast array of data, highlighting the critical role of employee data sharing for the effectiveness of AI [6]. The continuous nature of data generation in AI-based tools underscores the importance of data sharing as an integral part of everyday usage [8]. For example, Microsoft Copilot utilizes various types of employee data [22]: Amongst others, this can include user-generated data from Microsoft Office applications, user interaction data to tailor suggestions, email and calendar data for efficient communication management, data from integrated applications for context-relevant assistance, publicly available data and knowledge bases for informational support, organizational data for internal operations insight, and user feedback and interaction logs for continuous improvement of the AI model.

This data is profoundly sensitive, capturing not just the flow of information. The insights derived from this comprehensive data collection offer a deep dive into individuals' preferences and behavior, such as professional relationships, network structures, collaboration patterns, and communication styles [10]. This increasing generation of employee data feeds into AI tools and makes employees increasingly transparent [15]. As a result of the rising generation and processing of vast amounts of employee data, diverse concerns arise, particularly regarding the proper handling of employee data and privacy [30].

In conclusion, integrating AI in digital workplaces relies heavily on the continuous sharing of employee data, as opposed to one-time data sharing. AI assistants like Microsoft Copilot depend on a constant flow of diverse and sensitive data to function effectively and provide support. As AI technologies continue to evolve and integrate deeper into workplace processes, understanding the implications of continuous data generation becomes imperative.

3 Revising Our Current Understanding of Data Sharing

3.1 Conceptual Methodology

To ensure a structured methodology, we followed the conceptual paper guidelines outlined by [17]. The author describes various methods for conceptual papers, with theory adaptation being the most relevant to our goal of introducing a new lens of continuous data sharing. Thus, we chose this methodology to maintain a rigorous approach. Our methodology, as illustrated in Fig. 1, comprises a two-step approach: a systematic literature review followed by revising our understanding of the concept of data sharing.

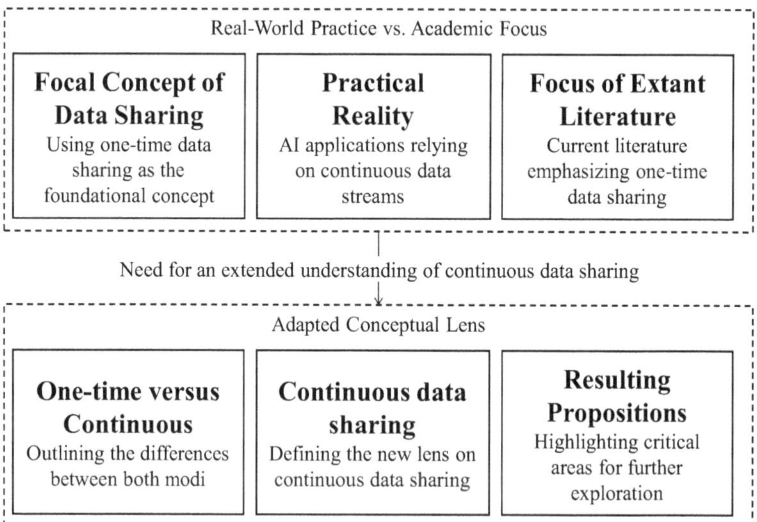

Fig. 1 Overview of the conceptual methodology

The first step involved conducting a systematic literature review on the focal concept of data sharing. Our review focused on the extent to which current literature addresses the context of continuous data sharing. As described in the conceptual foundations, we note that AI applications in digital workplaces increasingly rely on employees' continuous data streams. We found that while there is a substantial body of work on data sharing, it rarely investigates the constant nature of data sharing in AI-driven environments. This gap between practice and literature highlighted the need for an extended understanding of data sharing that includes continuous data generation and its implications.

Building on the findings from our literature review, we refined and expanded the concept of data sharing. We began with the established concept of data sharing and identified its limitations. We analyzed extant literature and concluded that it often deals with one-time data sharing, while in practice, the trend is towards continuous data sharing. The literature that deals with data generation in light of AI applications often does not investigate the continuous nature of data sharing. Therefore, our main goal was to revise the current understanding of data sharing by introducing a new lens focused on continuous data sharing. Our adapted conceptualization incorporates the constant aspect of data sharing, emphasizing its differences from one-time data sharing events. On this basis, we built propositions for future research.

In conclusion, our two-step methodology—systematic literature review followed by concept adaptation—allowed us to extend the understanding of data sharing by highlighting the unique characteristics of continuous data sharing in AI-driven workplaces. This approach aligns with the need for a revised theoretical understanding that better aligns with the realities of modern data sharing practices.

3.2 *Extant Data Sharing Literature*

For our study, we conducted a systematic literature review following the guidelines of [36]. These guidelines allowed us to scour available literature systematically, ensuring we did not miss potential information. The process of our systematic literature review is depicted in the PRISMA flow diagram in Fig. 2 [24].

Our search was structured around diverse keywords related to the act of sharing data, including various synonyms. We employed a Boolean keyword search system to obtain an overview of the available literature. The terms used were 'Data disclosure' or 'Information disclosure' or 'Data sharing' or 'Information sharing' or 'Willingness to disclose' or 'Self-disclosure' or 'Disclosure intention' or 'Disclosure behavior' appearing in titles or abstracts. This approach enabled us to cast a wide net and grasp the general landscape of data sharing research.

We searched multiple databases to retrieve relevant literature, including the Association for Information Systems (AIS) eLibrary and Web of Science. Additionally, we conducted forward and backward searches using Google Scholar to identify more relevant literature. Our exploration of journals focused on the Senior Scholars' List of Premier Journals, and to consider more recent publications, we also searched

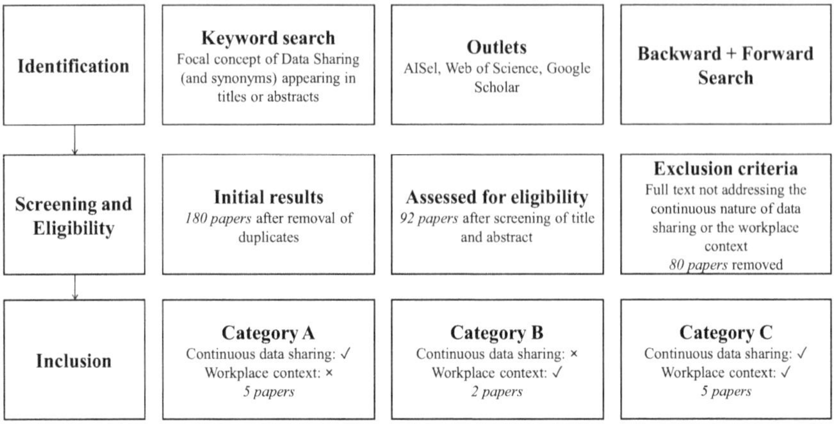

Fig. 2 Process of systematic literature review

for contributions to major IS conferences such as ICIS, ECIS, PACIS, AMCIS, and HICSS. The literature search was concluded towards the end of 2023.

The search, after the removal of duplicates, yielded 180 papers. We carefully assessed their relevance to our research question by screening their titles and abstracts. Out of the 92 papers that resulted in this, we excluded those that did not address the topics of interest suitably in the full text or were not topic-related. We filtered the papers according to two criteria: we included papers that referred to (a) continuous generation/sharing of data and/or (b) data sharing in workplaces. Specifically, in the workplace literature, we excluded studies on knowledge sharing that did not directly involve employee data, such as [33]. We excluded knowledge sharing literature because it primarily focuses on disseminating work-related information and expertise, which differs fundamentally from sharing personal data.

This rigorous approach ensured that our literature review was comprehensive and focused, providing a solid foundation for understanding the unique characteristics and implications of continuous data sharing in AI-driven workplaces. Ultimately, the literature search yielded 12 relevant papers, which we categorized into three groups based on their focus and context.

In Table 1, we present literature that concentrates on three main areas: (1) Continuous data sharing, (2) employee data sharing, and (3) continuous employee data sharing. Five papers focused on data continuously shared or data sharing in the context of AI applications without explicitly addressing the workplace environment. We noticed that literature assessing the continuous nature of data generation or sharing always assessed this concept in light of AI tools. Research in this category traditionally centers on understanding the drivers behind individuals' decisions to share data, often highlighting privacy concerns or risk-benefit trade-offs in various contexts such as connected vehicles, smart homes, wearables, or voice assistants [3, 5, 7, 8, 26]. For instance, studies emphasize the unique privacy concerns and risk considerations associated with the large volumes of user data generated by connected cars

Table 1 Overview of data sharing research

Context	Authors	Construct	Focus
Continuous data sharing	[3]	Data sharing	Wearables
	[5]	Information disclosure decisions	Smart home speakers
	[7]	Information disclosure	Voice assistant
	[8]	Data sharing	Connected cars
	[26]	Personal information disclosure	Voice assistants
Employee data sharing	[11]	Willingness to disclose	Enterprise social networks
	[32]	Willingness to disclose	Digital work, in general
Continuous data sharing + Employee data sharing	[18]	Self-disclosure	IoT Conversational Agents
	[21]	Data sharing mode	Wearables
	[27]	Intention to disclose	Smartwatches
	[35]	Willingness to share	Smart Factory Robots and Chatbots
	[37]	Willingness to share	People analytics

[8]. However, these studies tend to focus on the determinants affecting users' willingness to disclose data rather than on how the disclosure process itself is evolving. Two papers concentrated on the workplace context without focusing on continuous data sharing or AI applications. Here, the literature examines employees' one-time act of data sharing within general digital work processes or through platforms like enterprise social networks [11, 32].

Finally, five papers intersect both previous categories, addressing the continuous generation of employee data in the context of intelligent applications within digital workplaces. These studies recognize the shift towards a constant stream of data generated by employees using intelligent applications such as wearables, smartwatches or people analytics [21, 27, 37]. While these papers consider determinants like benefits, trust, and risks, the changing nature of employee data sharing is often only a side note. Some research acknowledges that the type of information shared in intelligent workplaces is increasingly personal, investigating how this influences employee sharing behaviors [18, 35]. However, they largely leave out the specific ways this shift affects the act of data sharing itself.

3.3 A New Lens on Employee Data Sharing

Comparing the practical use of AI-based tools like Microsoft Copilot to the state of extant literature reveals a gap concerning the investigation of the constant nature of data generation. Despite continuous data sharing being a by-product of digital interactions, existing studies do not capture how this phenomenon alters the dynamics of employee data sharing in AI-driven workplaces. This oversight underscores the need for a reevaluation of existing conceptualizations of data sharing. Following [17] conceptual methodology guidelines, we start from the premise that the current understanding of data sharing is incomplete, particularly in the context of continuous data generation. We propose that the practical developments in AI technologies and their pervasive integration into workplace processes have rendered existing understandings of data disclosure insufficient, necessitating a reconfiguration and a shift of perspective. Our analysis critically examines the evolving concept of data sharing driven by AI technology advancements based on the core functionalities of AI-based tools as outlined in the conceptual foundations.

We define one-time data sharing as a process where employees share their data during work without data being continuously generated as a by-product. Enterprise Social Networks are an example of a data-sharing context not associated with continuous data sharing but with active participation, where employees decide what information to share and when to share it [11]. For our research, we propose that the continuous disclosure of information in intelligent workplace tools introduces a new paradigm in the concept of data sharing. Unlike one-time data disclosure associated with non-intelligent tools, continuous data sharing in AI applications has unique characteristics that fundamentally change data sharing. As discussed in the following and displayed in Table 2, these characteristics can be categorized into three interrelated aspects: data dynamics, employee participation, and predictability.

First, *data dynamics* between both contexts are different. In the context of one-time data disclosure with non-intelligent tools, data is collected transactionally during specific events or through particular requests, where the scope and type of data are determined in advance and remain fixed. In contrast, continuous data sharing with AI applications involves ongoing and integrated data collection through constant interactions with digital tools and platforms. This continuous data sharing is facilitated by automated collection methods, which operate through persistent interaction with these tools, sharply contrasting with the episodic nature of one-time data collection. Furthermore, continuous data generation inherently lacks clear boundaries and

Table 2 Outlining the peculiarities of employee data sharing in AI-based contexts

Aspect	One-time data disclosure with non-intelligent tools	Continuous data sharing with AI applications
Data dynamics	Data is collected during specific events with predefined and static parameters	Data is continuously collected, lacking clear boundaries, and evolves over time through ongoing interactions with digital tools
Employee participation	One-time and explicit sharing, based on active participation	Employees passively participate, often unaware of ongoing data collection integrated into their routine activities
Predictability	More predefined and visible parameters, making it easier for employees to foresee the spectrum and use of the data	Persistent uncertainty over data use, heightened by the complex nature of AI systems, making it difficult to predict future uses of collected data

endpoints. Unlike one-time data sharing, continuous data generation can adapt and expand, capturing new types of information as interactions with AI systems evolve over time. This distinction is rarely addressed in the literature, but it is notably discussed by [8] in the context of the Internet of Things. They highlight that, like connected cars and many other IoT devices, data sharing is typically not a single, one-time transmission. Instead, individuals usually agree to continuous or repeated transmissions of data. This underscores a fundamental difference between one-time and continuous data sharing contexts, emphasizing the need for new approaches to data management and privacy considerations in AI-driven environments.

Second, *employee participation* differs significantly between the two contexts. Employees engage in explicit data sharing for one-time data disclosure with non-intelligent tools, which requires active participation. On the other hand, in continuous data sharing with AI applications, employee involvement shifts from an active role to a more passive one, where data is generated and shared often without their immediate awareness as part of their routine work activities. Employees may not be continuously aware of the data being collected as the process becomes an integrated part of the digital tools they use. This passive participation means that data is collected more seamlessly. This aspect of passive employee participation in continuous data sharing has not been addressed by extant literature so far but has been derived from the core functionalities of AI assistants.

Third, the *predictability* of data usage between one-time and continuous data sharing is markedly different. With one-time data disclosure, the parameters for data collection are more predefined and visible, making it easier for employees to foresee the spectrum and future use of their data. In contrast, continuous data sharing with AI applications often involves less transparent purposes and scopes, making it difficult for employees to predict how the data being collected will be used in the future. The persistent uncertainty over data use, heightened by the complex nature of AI systems, leads to difficulties in making informed decisions about data sharing. This unclarity affects how employees perceive and react to data-related issues, impacting their ability to anticipate and control their information's future trajectory. This aspect is supported by existing literature, which highlights the opacity and corresponding uncertainty of AI systems, leading to an inability of users to assess the consequences [1, 25].

Referring back to our practical example of AI assistants, such as Microsoft Copilot, continuous data generation with these tools fundamentally differs from one-time data sharing. Here, data is collected continuously, lacking clear boundaries and evolving over time through constant interactions with these digital tools. Continuous data generation with AI assistants involves passive participation while the ongoing data collection is integrated into routine activities. Moreover, the purposes of data collection by AI assistants are largely intransparent, making it difficult for employees to predict how their data will be used in the future. Generally speaking, the evolving, passive, and opaque nature of continuous data generation underscores the need for a reevaluation of data sharing practices with regard to intelligent workplace tools.

In summary, the transition to AI-based data sharing represents a fundamental change in how data is collected, and utilized in the workplace. The continuous and integrated nature of data sharing necessitates a fresh perspective accommodating the nuanced complexities introduced by AI technologies. The aspects of data dynamics, employee participation, and unpredictability collectively make continuous data sharing fundamentally different from one-time data disclosure, underscoring the need for a new understanding of employee interactions with AI-driven systems. Table 3 represents our definition of the new lens of continuous data sharing.

Stressing the continuous nature of data sharing, we derived a set of propositions to guide future research, as shown in Table 4. Together, these propositions advocate for a comprehensive reevaluation and adaptation of current understandings to effectively navigate the complexities of ongoing technological advancements.

Table 3 The emphasis on continuous data sharing

Continuous + **Data Sharing**
Continuous data sharing refers to the ongoing, integrated data collection and utilization through constant interactions with digital tools and platforms. It is characterized by automated, boundary-less data generation that evolves over time, involving passive employee participation. Data is seamlessly collected as part of routine activities and is associated with a certain degree of unpredictability

Table 4 Propositions on critical areas for exploration

Topics	Propositions
Data Management	AI-driven workplaces alter data sharing dynamics, necessitating a reevaluation of existing data management strategies to address emerging concerns related to privacy, security, and employee monitoring practices
Consent	The continuous nature of data sharing in AI-based workplaces requires a reevaluation of consent as a dynamic engagement rather than a one-time agreement
Motivations and Outcomes	Evolving functionalities of AI tools require a reassessment of the interplay of risk-benefit trade-offs that shape employees' willingness to share data
Methodological Considerations	The evolution of AI-driven data sharing requires developing and validating new measurement scales or adapting existing ones to accurately capture the nuances of continuous data sharing
Future of Data Sharing	Continuous advancements in AI technologies will fundamentally alter the landscape of employee data sharing, necessitating new governance frameworks and ethical considerations that are adaptive to the changing technological and social contexts

4 Conclusion, Implications, and Limitations

Our study illuminates the intricate relationship between AI technologies and employee data sharing, underscoring the need for understanding this interaction. AI assistants exemplify the continuous data exchange between employees and AI systems, illustrating how AI integration reshapes workplace data sharing dynamics and were chosen as an example in our study for their popularity and ease of integration. However, the findings are also relevant to other technologies involving continuous data generation and processing. Generally speaking, the emphasis on the constant nature of data sharing, developed through our study, serves as a foundation that offers a nuanced understanding of employee data sharing in the age of AI.

The exploration undertaken in this research underscores a notable gap in the existing literature: a comprehensive understanding of how the proliferation of AI technologies impacts employee data sharing. Despite the recognized importance of AI in digital workplaces as an emerging topic [6], there is a lack of insights into how these technologies change the concept of data sharing. We base our suggestions for future research on the propositions developed through our revised understanding of continuous data sharing. First, future research should explore how AI technologies and the corresponding generation of unprecedented amounts and types of employee data raise concerns about data generation and analysis, and develop data management strategies that address novel privacy and security issues, especially with regards to increasing transparency over employees [15].

Second, it is crucial to investigate informed, flexible, and user-friendly consent mechanisms, understand how employee attitudes differ between one-time and continuous consent models, and design mechanisms to avoid consent fatigue. Third, investigations into the motivations and outcomes of employees' data sharing within AI-driven workplaces are essential, particularly in exploring how employees balance the benefits and risks of data sharing. Fourth, methodological evaluations are needed to capture AI-driven data-sharing intentions accurately, requiring the development or refinement of measurement scales. Finally, research should address the ethical, legal, and social challenges of continuous data sharing, preparing adaptive strategies for future technological evolutions. Together, these research domains offer a comprehensive roadmap for addressing AI and data sharing dynamics in the workplace.

For practice, this research underlines the critical need to recognize and adapt to the continuous nature of data sharing inherent in AI systems. For organizations integrating AI technologies into their operations, the shifting landscape of data sharing presents challenges. For instance, it is questionable whether the one-time model of transactional consent is adequate in capturing the full spectrum of employee engagement with AI technologies and the ongoing data exchange this entails. To maintain the trust and confidence of their workforce, organizations must develop and implement data management strategies that are fundamental to fostering a culture of trust and transparency. Organizations can leverage AI technologies' full potential by implementing policies reflecting the continuous and dynamic nature of consent and designing AI systems prioritizing openness and user control [14]. This approach ensures ethical and responsible use of employee data and paves the way for the development of AI solutions that employees feel comfortable using.

On a broader scale, the nuanced understanding provided by this study is vital for informing policymaking and governance. The changing nature of employee data sharing underscores the urgency of updating legal frameworks to reflect the continuous nature of data sharing inherent in AI-based workplaces. Looking at specific national contexts, such as Germany, it becomes evident that existing regulatory frameworks may fall short of capturing the nuances of digital technology advancements, particularly in workplace settings [31]. In particular, regulation needs to reconsider foundational principles, such as data minimization, in the context of AI technologies. While fundamental to traditional data privacy legislation, these principles starkly contrast the requirements and realities of AI-driven environments where continuous data collection and analysis are pivotal [10]. Thereby, this study signals a call to adapt and evolve regulation, ensuring that legislation keeps pace with the changing dynamics of employee data in digital workplaces.

On another note, we acknowledge the limitations of our study. First, foundational to our conceptual methodology, the literature review spans relevant journals and conferences, supplemented by backward and forward searches. Despite this systematic approach, we cannot assert the exhaustive inclusion of all pertinent studies and acknowledge a potential limitation in the breadth of our literature base. Second, our conceptual methodology presents another limitation. The adapted conceptualization proposed is not verified by empirical data and may include biases or overlook certain aspects. We aimed to mitigate these limitations by grounding our argument in a structured literature review and illustrating our points with the practical example of the AI assistant Microsoft Copilot.

Finally, although our study originates from the workplace, it is also relevant to consumer environments like using personal voice assistants at home. However, the workplace is unique because of the blurred lines between professional and private life due to ongoing employee data collection and power imbalances between employees and employers that could lead to more monitoring—issues that are less common in personal settings [30]. Given these considerations, we invite scholars to engage with our adapted conceptualization of continuous data sharing, addressing the outlined propositions to be explored by future research.

References

1. Al-Natour, S., Cavusoglu, H., Benbasat, I., & Aleem, U. (2020). An empirical investigation of the antecedents and consequences of privacy uncertainty in the context of mobile apps. *Information Systems Research, 31*(4), 1037–1063.
2. Attaran, M., Attaran, S., & Kirkland, D. (2020). Technology and organizational change: harnessing the power of digital workplace. In *Handbook of research on social and organizational dynamics in the digital era* (pp. 383–408). IGI Global.

3. Banerjee, S., Hemphill, T., & Longstreet, P. (2018). Wearable devices and healthcare: Data sharing and privacy. *The Information Society, 34*(1), 1–9.
4. Baptista, J., Stein, M.-K., Klein, S., Watson-Manheim, M. B., & Lee, J. (2020). Digital work and organisational transformation: Emergent digital/human work configurations in modern organisations. *Journal of Strategic Information Systems, 29*(1), 1–10.
5. Bélanger, F., Resor, J., Crossler, R. E., Finch, T. A., & Allen, K. R. (2021). *Smart home speakers and family information disclosure decisions*. 'Proceedings of the 27th Americas Conference on Information Systems (AMCIS)', A Virtual AIS Conference.
6. Bhave, D. P., Theo, L. H., & Dalal, R. S. (2020). Privacy at work: A review and a research agenda for a contested terrain. *Journal of Management, 46*(1), 127–164.
7. Cao, G., & Wang, P. (2022). Revealing or concealing: Privacy information disclosure in intelligent voice assistant usage-a configurational approach. *Industrial Management & Data Systems, 122*(5), 1215–1245.
8. Cichy, P., Salge, O., & Kohli, R. (2021). Privacy concerns and data sharing in the internet of things: Mixed methods evidence from connected cars. *MIS Quarterly, 45*(4), 1863–1892.
9. Cranefield, J., Winikoff, M., Chiu, Y.-T., Li, Y., Doyle, C., & Richter, A. (2023). Partnering with AI: The case of digital productivity assistants. *Journal of the Royal Society of New Zealand, 53*(1), 95–118.
10. Ebert, I., Wildhaber, I., & Adams-Prassl, J. (2021). Big data in the workplace: Privacy due diligence as a human rights-based approach to employee privacy protection. *Big Data & Society, 8*(1), 1–14.
11. Engelbrecht, A., Gerlach, J., Benlian, A., & Buxmann, P. (2017). 'Analysing employees' willingness to disclose information in enterprise social networks: The role of organisational culture. In *Proceedings of the 25th European Conference on Information Systems (ECIS).*
12. Eser, A. (2023). Essential AI in the workplace statistics in 2024. Retrieved March 08, 2024, from https://zipdo.co/statistics/ai-in-the-workplace/
13. Gartner. (2020). 6 Trends on the gartner hype cycle for the digital workplace. Retrieved November 20 2020, from https://www.gartner.com/smarterwithgartner/6-trends-on-the-gartner-hype-cycle-for-the-digital-workplace-2020/
14. Gierlich-Joas, M., Baiyere, A., & Hess, T. (2024). Inverse transparency and the quest for empowerment through the design of digital workplace technologies. *Journal of the Association for Information Systems, 21*(1), 1–30.
15. Gierlich-Joas, M., Teebken, M. A., & Hess, T. (2022). *A synthesized perspective on privacy and transparency in the digital workplace*. Proceedings of the 54th Hawaii International Conference on System Sciences (HICSS), A Virtual AIS Conference.
16. Hamer, M. (2024). Chatgpt Vs Microsoft copilot: Which AI assistant comes out on top? Retrieved June 24, 2024, from https://www.netitude.co.uk/blog/chatgpt-vs-microsoft-copilot-ai-showdown
17. Jaakkola, E. (2020). Designing conceptual articles: Four approaches. *AMS Review, 10*(1), 18–26.
18. Li, Z., Rau, P.-L. P., & Huang, D. (2019), 'Self-Disclosure to an IOT conversational agent: Effects of space and user context on users' willingness to self-disclose personal information. *Applied Sciences, 9*(9), 1887.
19. Maedche, A., Legner, C., Benlian, A., Berger, B., Gimpel, H., Hess, T., Hinz, O., Morana, S., & Söllner, M. (2019). AI-Based digital assistants: Opportunities, threats, and research perspectives. *Business & Information Systems Engineering, 61*, 535–544.
20. Lane, M., & Williams, M. (2023). *'Defining and Classifying AI in the Workplace'* (Report, Social, Employment and Migration Working Papers). OECD.
21. Messer, U., & Lukas, N. (2023). *Wearables in organizations—The role of data sharing mode.* Proceedings of the 31st European Conference on Information Systems (ECIS), Kristiansand, Norway.
22. Microsoft. (2024a). Data, privacy, and security for Microsoft copilot for Microsoft 365' Retrieved March 08, 2024, from https://learn.microsoft.com/en-us/microsoft-365-copilot/microsoft-365-copilot-privacy

23. Microsoft. (2024b). Introduction to Copilot for Microsoft 365', Retrieved March 08, 2024, from https://learn.microsoft.com/en-us/training/modules/introduction-microsoft-365-copilot/
24. Moher, D., Liberati, A., Tetzlaff, J., Altman, D. G., & Group, P. (2009). Preferred reporting items for systematic reviews and meta-analyses: The prisma statement. *Annals of Internal Medicine, 151*(4), 264–269.
25. Moore, P. (2020). 'Data subjects, digital surveillance, AI and the future of work', report, panel for the future of science and technology. European Parliament.
26. Pal, D., Arpnikanondt, C., & Razzaque, M. A. (2020). Personal information disclosure via voice assistants: The personalization-privacy paradox. *SN Computer Science, 1*, 1–17.
27. Richter, A., Kühtreiber, P., & Reinhardt, D. (2022). *On the impact of information provided to employees on their intention to disclose data collected by smart watches to their employers.* Proceedings of the 30th European Conference on Information Systems (ECIS), Timisoara, Romania.
28. Statista. (2024). Global market share held by operating systems for desktop Pcs, from January 2013 to February 2024. Retrieved June 24, 2024, from https://www.statista.com/statistics/218089/global-market-share-of-windows-7/
29. SnapLogic. (2021). Employees want more AI in the workplace. Retrieved March 08, 2024, from https://www.snaplogic.com/resources/infographics/employees-want-more-ai-in-the-workplace
30. Teebken, M. (2021). *What makes workplace privacy special? An investigation of determinants of privacy concerns in the digital workplace.* Proceedings of the 27th Americas Conference on Information Systems (AMCIS), A Virtual AIS Conference.
31. Teebken, M., & Hess, T. (2024). Mehr ist Mehr: Besserer Beschäftigtendatenschutz für Umfassende Nutzung von Arbeitsplatzdaten, Impulse Paper, Bavarian Research Institute for Digital Transformation (bidt), Munich.
32. Tolsdorf, J., Reinhardt, D., & Lo Iacono, L. (2022). Employees' privacy perceptions: Exploring the dimensionality and antecedents of personal data sensitivity and willingness to disclose. In *Proceedings on Privacy Enhancing Technologies* (pp. 68–94).
33. Trier, M., Fung, M., & Hansen, A. (2017), 'Uncertainties as Barriers for Knowledge Sharing with Enterprise Social Media', *in* 'European Conference on Information Systems (ECIS)', Guimarães, Portugal.
34. Turner, J. (2023), The future of AI in the workplace: A survey of American managers. Retrieved March 08, 2024, from https://www.beautiful.ai/blog/2023-generative-ai-workplace-report
35. Vervier, L., Brauner, P., & Ziefle, M. (2023). Perception of privacy and willingness to share personal data in the smart factory. In *International Conference on Human-Computer Interaction* (pp. 213–231) Springer.
36. Webster, J., & Watson, R. T. (2002). Analyzing the past to prepare for the future: Writing a literature review. *MIS Quarterly, 26*(2), xiii–xxiii.
37. Zieglmeier, V., Gierlich-Joas, M., & Pretschner, A. (2022). Increasing employees' willingness to share: Introducing appeal strategies for people analytics. In *Proceedings of the 13th International Conference of Software Business (ICSOB)* (pp. 213–226). Springer.

Skills in Flux: Challenges in AI-Based Skills Management and Skills Profiles

Leonie Rebecca Freise, Ulrich Bretschneider, and Sarah Oeste-Reiss

Abstract The changing world of work, driven by automation and digital technologies, requires a workforce that continuously adapts its skills in order to be competitive and employable. This dynamic environment has fueled the demand for advanced skills management, with artificial intelligence (AI) playing a critical role in measuring and supporting individual skills development. This paper looks at AI-based competency profiles as a strategic tool for talent acquisition, retention, and development and highlights their potential challenges. Using semi-structured interviews with experts from HR, education, and industry, we explore the multiple challenges of AI-based skills management from a theoretical, conceptual, and practical perspective. Our findings reveal complex problems at the individual, team, organizational, and systemic levels that form a basis for the development of effective AI-based skills management strategies. This research highlights the importance of using AI to foster an adaptable and skilled workforce that meets both current needs and future challenges.

1 Introduction

The contemporary labor markets are in a constant state of flux due to a multitude of factors such as automation, artificial intelligence (AI), and the ongoing digital revolution that have sped up a reallocation of tasks in labor markets. These transformations necessitate continually adapting skills among the workforce to remain competitive and employable [51]. According to Bakhshi et al. [4], there will be a shift in focus toward interpersonal, higher-order cognitive, and systems skills. With jobs

L. R. Freise (✉) · U. Bretschneider
Information Systems, University of Kassel, Kassel, Germany
e-mail: Leonie.freise@uni-kassel.de

U. Bretschneider
e-mail: Bretschneider@uni-kassel.de

S. Oeste-Reiss
Information Systems, University of Kiel, Kiel, Germany
e-mail: sarah.oeste-reiss@informatik.uni-kiel.de

C. M. Flath et al. (eds.), *Digital Innovation and Organizational Transformation*, Lecture Notes in Information Systems and Organisation 83,
https://doi.org/10.1007/978-3-032-08483-5_17

being displaced or transformed by technology, a growing demand for re-&upskilling arises. According to a World Economic Forum report, 50% of employees will need a reskilling by 2025 [54]. As these numbers demonstrate, employers are confronted with the challenge of staffing positions with qualified individuals with the latest and most relevant job-related skills. Accordingly, there is a growing need for lifelong learning, where individuals receive personalized suggestions for continuing education [43]. Nevertheless, AI may not only be one relevant driver of skills changes, but it could also contribute to being the solution, As it can address the demand for personalized skills management, which is a comprehensive approach to identifying, assessing, and cultivating the skills of the workforce.

The foundational premise of our inquiry is predicated upon conceptualizing a virtual representation of an individual's skill set and proficiency [56]. In general, a skills profile, either physical or digital, encapsulates a comprehensive overview of a person's abilities, experiences, educational background, and training achievements [19]. The adoption of digital platforms for skills management, when executed proficiently, enhances capabilities in talent acquisition, retention, and the facilitation of skill advancement. Employing skill assessment tools serves to refine this process, rendering it more streamlined, efficient, and predicated on empirical data [18]. Within Human Resources (HR) technology, there is a notable trend toward integrating AI-based skills management systems. AI-based skills management involves the use of AI technologies to optimize the selection, training, and deployment of personnel based on their skills (e.g., [48]). These systems are designed to deliver bespoke strategic skill evaluations, personalized learning trajectories, and targeted training suggestions [5]. Despite the promise these AI-based skills management frameworks hold, their potential is not fully realized, with the challenges associated with their deployment and utilization uncharted due to barriers [13]. Academia currently lacks sufficient understanding of how to effectively harness these emerging technologies [1]. Nonetheless, the imperative to maintain competitiveness within the skills management sector and to address the emergent needs for re-& upskilling within organizations remains paramount. Accordingly, this paper endeavors to elucidate upon the research question (RQ): *What are challenges in establishing AI-based skill development?*

We apply a qualitative approach to identify these challenges, including interviews with professionals among skills management providers, human resources professionals working in the digital management of skills, and researchers on the topic. Subsequently, we categorize the described challenges into theoretical, conceptual, and practical dimensions and assign a multi-level perspective including systemic, organizational, team, and individual challenges. This paper sets the foundation for understanding the complexities of AI-based skills management and profiling, focusing on essential factors for research and practice for establishing reliable skills profiles and management. The resulting classification scheme relates the dimensions of challenges (theoretical, conceptual, and practical) to levels of consideration at the system, organization, team, and individual levels. This approach outlines the interrelations between dimensions and sheds light on the necessity to include multiple perspectives. We thereby enrich the discussions on the evolving nature of skills profiles in the rapidly changing labor market. Employing a 'proof-of-concept' approach, we highlight unresolved issues in skills management and profiling, crucial to concern for both research and practice [33]. Our findings and proposed frameworks aim to influence the future direction of skills management amidst ongoing skill transformations.

2 Theoretical Background

2.1 The Influence of AI on Skills in the Working World

Changing job skills due to advances in technology are driving a shift in organizational requirements. AI is one crucial development. AI can be thereby defined as systems that use data and algorithms to mimic human-like cognitive functions, such as decision-making, learning, perception, and reasoning [3]. Compared to the past, AI is now able to perform many routine tasks independently, such as calculations [24]. As a result, the adoption of AI has led to re-evaluating human skills, emphasizing the increasing importance of cognitive skills like creativity, critical thinking, communication, and collaboration that complement and enhance AI skills [53]. For instance, the demand for AI skills in software development was highlighted by Păvăloaia and Necula [37], who notes the importance of both technical and social skills, such as problem-solving and interpersonal communication, for the future of work. Furthermore, Morandini et al. [31] discuss the critical role of transversal skills in adapting to AI in organizations and highlight strategies to support workers in developing these skills. Accordingly, changing skills requires to re-&upskill employees. This highlights the challenge and opportunity for education and training to foster human-centered skills. For example, while AI can take over tasks such as for instance data analysis and decision-making, it still relies on human skills for skills such as critical thinking to interpret the data and to consider the context for decision-making [47]. However, while AI may be one of the most prominent drivers of changing skill requirements, it brings along opportunities to meet those demands. As people are known to have different abilities [46], it is necessary to take into account the different skills of employees during the learning process. However, traditional face-to-face evaluations are often limited by the availability of resources and the expertise of staff in the work context. Consequently, the use of AI for personalized recommendations can be beneficial [9]. This is confirmed by several studies examining AI's role in e-learning and education. For instance, AI can provide personalized learning experiences and support for learners with different needs improving the educational process by tailoring educational content and interactions to meet individual learners' unique needs, preferences, and pace [32, 45].

In addition, the impact of AI on employability and the workforce has been systematically explored, with findings showing that workers need to adapt to new technologies to maintain their employability and professional relevance [12]. The shift towards skills-based procedures like hiring suggests employers increasingly favor individual skills over formal qualifications, particularly in AI [23]. Accordingly, managing employee skills presents a challenging task, especially as organizations are faced with considerable pressure to attract and manage professionals [8]. This highlights the importance of strategic choices in skills management that can shape organizational competitive advantage [6, 7]. Integrating AI into skills management within IT-based Human Resources (HR) Management presents significant opportunities to enhance the identification and development of employee skills. This approach is foundational for informed staffing decisions and skill-centric strategies [17]. AI-based analytics can revolutionize skill acquisition and gap analysis, offering organizations insights to efficiently align skills with current and future needs [8]. Additionally, AI in skills assessment provides a more objective analysis of employee capabilities, facilitating tailored development plans [2]. The adaptability of AI to different environmental and organizational contexts indicates its potential to keep skills management strategies relevant over time [21]. However, the effectiveness of AI in skills management hinges on establishing a standardized framework and common language for skills, enabling uniform data interpretation and enhancing system interoperability [21, 39]. In essence, integrating AI into skills management could revolutionize how organizations approach the development and deployment of employee skills, provided challenges around standardization are addressed. This promises more dynamic, efficient, and personalized HR practices. As Pan and Froese [36] argue using AI has great potential for HR. Especially on the topic of integrating and establishing AI, more research is needed as this is an aspect often neglected in HR research. This can include challenges in regard to data usage, ethical considerations and technological integration.

2.2 *Digitally Mapped Skills Profiles*

Exploring the integration of AI in skills management unveils substantial opportunities for enhancing the creation and utilization of digitally mapped skills profiles. A digitally mapped skills profile includes an electronic record individual's skills and experience [19]. This record typically includes a list of the person's unique skills and abilities, along with information about their experience, education, and training. A profile can also refer to an individual's skillset deemed essential for performing effective job-related tasks, as noted by Sebastião et al. [49]. Employers underline the importance of skills profiles by consenting that when recruiting, they seek candidates who obtain a specific skills profile. The advantages of a skills profile are manifold, including providing a comprehensive view of an individual's skills and qualifications to potential employers or clients, identifying skill gaps, and facilitating the development of training programs [52]. The usage of AI in this domain promises to revolutionize how skills profiles are generated, analyzed, and updated. For instance, by automating the aggregation and analysis of skill data, AI can provide dynamic, real-time insights into skill gaps and emerging competencies [15]. This extends to the customization of career paths [44], optimizing project staffing [22], and facilitating efficient work allocation [30]. For example, M. Zhao et al. [57] described an automated skills recognition and normalization system that revealed gaps in skills profiles crucial for matching applicants to the right jobs, and that could be missed by human assessors due to inconsistencies and discrepancies in skills descriptions. Another example is Konstantinidis et al. [26], who illustrate an approach utilizing deep information retrieval and semantic similarity search for skill identification without the need for human-annotated databases. They introduce an end-to-end method combining text embeddings for skill extraction with a skills graph matching algorithm to compare similar resumes efficiently. Additionally, presenting a consolidated account of one's skills allows for the prioritization of personal development and improvement, serving as a reference point for progress and performance evaluation [35]. The creation of a skills profile can be undertaken by the individual or a third party, such as a manager or recruiter, and be in the form of text or graphics, such as lists or graphs. Regular updates are recommended to ensure the alignment of the skills profile with changes in the individual's skills and expertise.

In academia and research, the focus is often on profiles for a specific group of skills like AI literacy [38], occupations like engineering [34], or positions like CIO profiles [40]. Accordingly, many of these works have primarily concentrated on the theoretical development in one focus area of skills profiles rather than the establishment of exhaustive descriptions of profiles. Similarly, Pospelova et al. [39] call for reliable and generally applicable skill data. To answer this need, our work addresses the challenges associated with current skills management and skills profiles.

3 Research Approach

Due to the exploratory character of our RQ, we decided on a qualitative research approach. We included ten expert interviews to deepen the understanding of skills management and profiles and to analyze their profound knowledge. The experts were recruited from science and practice in the field of skills management, including researchers, providers, and HR professionals as we consider these groups as promising for expertise and diverse perspectives. The experts are characterized by their intensive engagement with the topic at a scientific level or practitioners who provide extensive experience in interacting with companies and in the implementation of skills management. We applied a semi-structured interview process and conducted online interviews. They took approximately 30 min and were recorded and transcribed with prior consent. Based on the literature, we outlined our problem space and defined the relevant concepts to answer the RQ. Afterward, we constructed a semi-structured interview guideline relying on Mayring's [29] problem-centric approach. The content and questions focused on the experts' perceptions and evaluation of existing skills management and profile approaches. The first interview questions focused on the relevance of skills management and profiles and the development in the last years, followed by a question on the specific work of the expert with skills.

Secondly, we asked for the challenges, limits, and non-functional aspects of current skill solutions (e.g., What challenges and opportunities arise from the identification and assessment of skills?). Next, the interview guideline considers the requirements for designing and establishing skills profiles. We concluded with an outlook on use cases and the potential of skills management and profiles. Demographic data was collected, including the experts' position.

Afterward, all transcripts were analyzed along qualitative content analysis using MAXQDA to identify similarities, differences, and overarching themes [25]. Our analysis followed Mayring [28] approach, starting with generalizing interview material before consolidating it in two reduction steps into resulting statements and insights. Due to the exploratory nature, an open coding approach based on Strauss and Corbin's [50] grounded theory was used to identify and segment pertinent data. Subsequently, axial coding was applied to discern and organize relationships among these codes. Within the interviews, we coded five main categories and seven subcodes and assigned 457 code segments. To conclude the analysis, selective coding was employed to interconnect the previously identified categories that encompass the research findings.

4 Findings

Drawing upon our interviews, we identified three dimensions of challenges. The challenges faced in establishing and utilizing AI in HR extend beyond the practical dimension, encompassing significant theoretical and conceptual issues as well. We refer to a multi-level approach to categorize the challenges of AI in skills profile and management due to the complexity and multifaceted nature of these challenges. Addressing these issues from multiple perspectives provides a comprehensive understanding. We thereby refer to the individual, team, organization, and system level. This categorization is depicted in Table 1. These challenges necessitate not only practical solutions but also research-driven requirements to fully address them.

4.1 Theoretical Challenges in Skills Profiles

Theoretical challenges pertain to foundational principles and assumptions, addressing theoretical gaps, and proposing new theoretical frameworks, which require rigorous academic research and critical analysis to advance knowledge.

On the dimension of the theoretical challenges, organizations necessitate the unambiguous articulation of the semantic concept within the organizational framework to delineate the specific evidence information required for establishing a robust and dependable database for subsequent AI-based projects.

The expert interviews shed light on critical aspects of developing and maintaining the data basis on a **system level**. One recurring theme was the challenge of creating a

Table 1 Synthesis of AI-based skills management challenges based on dimensions and levels

Dimensions	Level of challenges			
	Individual	Team	Organizational	System
Theoretical challenge	Preselection of evidence information influencing the data quantity and quality		Consistent semantic skill model within the organization	Solid and reliable data basis for skill categorization
Conceptual challenge	Transparency of the profile within the organization	Anonymity of skills within the team	Coordinated objectives for skills management	Data protection (rights for access, use, change)
			Data use rights (ownership of data)	
Practical challenge	Motivation for active use of skills management	Lack of objective rubrics/measures for skills evaluation of peers/ supervisors	Non-skill-ready corporate culture	Integration into existing systems (e.g., personnel management)
	Acceptance of the inherent change process and skills management	Unpredictable group dynamics influencing peer assessments	Adjusting needs to company size	Continuous maintenance of technical functions
	Cognitive distortions biasing self-assessment			

taxonomy or ontology as a data basis for skills, with experts expressing the difficulty of skills as unstructured data. They highlighted the inherent complexity in dealing with language data, particularly in the context of skills. Unlike other data types, language lacking a simple structure poses a significant challenge. The interviewees emphasized the multifaceted nature of skill formulation, citing examples where a skill could be articulated in numerous ways, and its interpretation could vary depending on the context. As expert 1 (E1) stated: "*This is because language in particular is not as simply structured as other data, which means that I can formulate a skill in 50 different ways and some things have a different meaning depending on the context.*" The interviews revealed problems in the development and maintenance of skills management on a system level. These insights, summarized by E3, highlight the crucial role of standardized language in the skill selection process and maintain its relevance: "*I think what you have to ensure is the definition and perception of what a skill means in the company.*" Similarly, E9 described the black-box character of skills management providers: "*With the data models behind it with the algorithms, the provider is like a black box. Especially in the sense that it remains unclear whether we can continue to work with this skill data*" (E8). The complexity of language as a data structure for taxonomies is further emphasized by researchers like Donini et al. [16]

and Das et al. [14]. The latter use Latent Dirichlet Allocation (LDA) and the BERT framework for automatic complexity identification, achieving accuracy rates of over 80% in text identification. Further, the risk of the AI being trained on insufficient or flawed data cannot be excluded. Based on the data, the AI could develop biasing decisions, like Amazon's recruiting tool, that showed a bias against women [42]. Therefore, requirement one (R1) states that on a system level a solid and reliable database for skill categorization should be ensured.

At the **organizational level**, the interviews underscored the foundational role of defining skills within a semantic framework. Many organizations struggle with the fundamental question of the concrete skills that are important for them and how to define them in an overarching model like a taxonomy or ontology. In more detail, E2 described the goal that their system should contribute to as crucial because it sets the stage for subsequent processes. "*(...) and I think that is the most important question that many companies still have – 'what exactly do I want?'*". The decision-making process on the organizational level is pivotal, necessitating appropriate expertise and time commitment. This is further highlighted by E10 "*The ever more specific requirements are due to the fact that we are developing so many new technologies and require specialist knowledge that is also becoming ever more specific. That's why we always need new experts.*" This highlights the challenge of necessitating increasingly specialized knowledge and the constant need for new expertise. This situation is closely related to change management theory, particularly the concepts of continuous learning and adaptability in organizational development [27]. Therefore, R2 includes that on an organizational level, consistent semantic skill models need to developed and integrated into organizational structures.

The critical issue of the pre-selection of evidence on the **individual level** and its influence on the quantity and quality of data is also emphasized: "*That is why we try to collect as much data as possible, which is not always easy. The differences in data quality are enormous*" (E7). We herein suppose this pre-selection occurs at the individual level, which our experts emphasize is usually true. In that case, the sovereignty over this selection lies with the individuals and is potentially susceptible to falsification. The strategy of collecting the most detailed data possible from various sources (e.g., managers and colleagues) is a challenge. However, it contributes significantly to reducing the risks associated with the pre-selection of documents [18]. A broader data set can potentially increase the representativeness and reliability of the results and minimize individual influences. Therefore, we propose R3 as: On an individual level, a preselection of evidence information in terms of quantity and quality should be ensured. Yet, it has to be considered that this aim to include as much data as possible also raises concerns about data privacy and ethical considerations, as sensitive data needs to be stored accordingly.

4.2 Conceptual Challenges in Skills Profiles

Conceptual challenges involve understanding and framing ideas, models, or frameworks, necessitating innovative thinking and clear, coherent concept development.

Organizations are required to contemplate the conceptual framework for the digital management of skills, which encompasses integrating it within existing operational processes and addressing concerns related to data protection. This consideration is oriented towards determining the strategic objectives the organization aims to achieve.

Further, they mentioned data security aspects to take into account on the **system level:** "*(…) of course, data protection issues, i.e., that the data is located in Germany or the EU*" (E4). The citation emphasizes the importance of data security and protection, explicitly highlighting the requirement for data storage localization. R4 underscores the need for skills management systems to integrate robust data security measures, ensuring the confidentiality, integrity, and availability of sensitive information. This adherence to high data protection standards can enhance trust among stakeholders and facilitate compliance with regulatory requirements, thereby supporting sustainable development and maintenance at a system level [10].

The experts shed light on the pivotal shift in the **organizational challenge** of providing a strategy toward a more proactive and coordinated approach to skills management. As E7 exemplifies, the focus was initially on identifying deficits in activities, but it evolved to emphasize the importance of future-oriented planning in learning and development. This strategic pivot underscores the complexity of aligning organizational objectives for effective skills management. The "*incredibly long process*" and "*endless discussions at the management level*" (E6) highlight a significant challenge: achieving a uniform understanding and commitment across leadership to implement this strategic shift. This illustrates the requirement five (R5) of clear communication, shared vision, and consensus-building on skills management objectives within an organization. Further, this contributes to a strategic approach towards the possible use cases of skills management: "*With the roll-out plan, we also have to learn about the other use cases in order to drive forward other skill-based topics, such as performance management. If things go well in the first stages if it's not effort without benefit, then you can argue this with our board members*" (E7). Another important challenge that we identified were questions regarding the management, ownership, and ethical considerations of data within organizational platforms. Data quality control and privacy need to be considered. This underscores need (R6) of data use rights, emphasizing the need for governance structures and policies around data ownership, quality control, and protection.

At the **team level**, one challenge mentioned in the interviews pertains to the reliable assessment of team skills when evaluations are conducted anonymously. E1 refers to this as follows: "*One of the problems with assessing teams and employees when everyone evaluates themselves anonymously could be that they don't know how the others evaluate themselves and there is a certain amount of uncertainty. 'Am I evaluating myself correctly or incorrectly?'*". This emphasizes the need for a uniform approach that either includes team comparisons, so that there is a corrective in the assessments (E8) or to ensure anonymity within the evaluation of teams. This translates into the requirement (R7) that the skills of team members and the associated group dynamics should be taken into account.

At the **individual level**, transparency was identified as critical in mitigating concerns. Individuals are more likely to create skills profiles when they perceive transparency in the evaluation process, reducing fears of potential negative consequences based on skill assessments. The statement from E2 underscores the need to balance individual benefit, psychological well-being, and transparent processes to foster engagement at the individual level: "*Acceptance is super relevant. The fact that people think 'This can only be to my disadvantage', especially for low-skilled workers, makes it much more difficult to gain trust. Transparency is also important. If people see that 'I can be checked and then I'm the first to be kicked out because I'm the least qualified, then I don't want to take advantage of that'*". The traceability of embedding in existing systems goes hand in hand with this transparency. Similarly, this was examined for knowledge management systems by Ramesh [41]. According to experts, if contextual factors such as time or monetary resources are clearly formulated, it is easier for employees to assess. This is aimed at the selectivity of the individual skills profiles: "*If it is unclear what the individual should be categorized as, motivation drops*" (E7). Therefore, transparency regarding the use of the skills profile needs to be ensured to ensure trust among individuals (R8).

4.3 Practical Challenges in Skills Profiles

Practical challenges are real-world issues encountered during the implementation or application of a solution, such as technical difficulties or resource limitations, requiring tangible solutions.

At the **system level,** the experts refer to skills analysis as one challenge for the skills management provider. The need for a robust maintenance strategy was also emphasized (R9) but described as not being the main point of problems: "*As few regulations as possible, but also as many as necessary*" (E7). Moreover, they directly mention the requirement (R10) of establishing a balance between the lean design of a model and its specificity to accommodate rapid implementation for future use cases within an organization. While meeting the desire for a flexible and adaptable platform to meet immediate and evolving organizational needs, it also needs to be specific enough in its functionalities to support skills management in the stage needed. Accordingly, "*It is necessary to compare the results precisely with those of competitors*" (E8).

One practical challenge at the **organizational level** is having sufficient human resources to propel the initiative forward comprehensively. E5 connects resource investment on the organizational level with the organization's mindset for skills as a holistic topic. This is also reflected in the need to consider differing opinions regarding implementing skills management within organizations. Some individuals may perceive the endeavor as unnecessary, impeding the establishment process. Interestingly, this is more pronounced in larger companies, where the scale of communication and explanation required is substantial: "*Backing from the company that the topic is important and is given the appropriate expertise and time (…). And having enough manpower to drive the topic forward is another practical challenge at a high organizational level*" (E5). As a result, organizations need a skill-ready corporate culture to succesfullly build up skills management (R11). Implementing skills management could be straightforward in smaller companies due to fewer stakeholders involved. However, the perceived impact of such systems may be less significant in smaller organizational settings compared to their larger counterparts, as outlined by E2: "*It's much easier in smaller companies. Because you simply have to talk to fewer people and explain less, but I don't think the effects that you can generate are quite as relevant in small companies as they are in large ones*". This translates into R12, which emphasizes that skills management approaches need to be adjusted to the company size.

Within the **team level**, group dynamics can lead to incorrect evaluations from other team members. This may also be due to insufficient assessment skills by other team members. Accordingly, with the introduction of skills management, teams need to be educated about different assessment methods and need comprehensive evaluation guidelines (R13). Further, the assessment methods within teams can range from evaluations by managers to those conducted by teammates or colleagues from project work. The choice of assessment method introduces additional complexity, with different approaches influencing the evaluation process. This variability underscores the requirement (R13) for clarity and standardization in the assessment procedures to ensure fairness and reliability in team and employee evaluations [11]. E7 outlines this: "*But managers in particular are not, in my opinion, in a position to evaluate on the basis or at the level of sub-skills*".

At the **individual level,** experts emphasized the importance of outlining the added benefit for the individual as a motivating factor for engagement (R14): "*That's perhaps the most important reason. So I should somehow benefit from it and if it only helps my company in some way and not me at all, then I have less motivation to do it*" (E2). They argued that employees experience a reluctance to participate if the benefits were perceived as solely favoring the company rather than contributing to individual growth or well-being. The need to ensure low-threshold access to learning content via mobile devices is also emphasized (R14): "*There are a lot of people who want to access learning content* via *smartphone, for example, which means you have to make sure that it is used on different devices*" (E9). Moreover, the interviews delved into the psychological dynamics at play, highlighting challenges related to cognitive dissonance phenomena like the Dunning-Kruger effect (i.e., incompetent people overestimate themselves while underestimating the performance of competent people) and impostor syndrome (i.e., people feel inadequate despite their professional success). "*Then you have the problem of narcissists and the impostor syndrome, i.e., people who rate themselves too poorly and people who rate themselves so highly. That can be demotivating*" (E1). The spectrum of self-assessment, ranging from overly critical to overly optimistic evaluations, can lead to demotivation that impacts individuals' engagement and confidence in their skills. Moreover, acceptance emerged as a potential challenge, especially among low-skilled workers. The perception that participation might be detrimental creates challenges in building trust. This can be translated into R15 that organizations need to control for cognitive distortions or group dynamics within self-assessments of skills, for instance by involving peer-assessments as further source.

4.4 Interdependence of Challenge Dimensions

The interdependence of challenge dimensions in skills management highlights the need for a dynamic, iterative approach that connects theoretical, conceptual, and practical aspects. Initially, defining skills clearly is crucial to avoid misunderstandings and establish a solid foundation for organization-wide understanding. Without a clear definition, subsequent phases, especially creating a database for AI initiatives, may face ambiguity. The next step involves tailoring the theoretical framework to the organization's context and needs and integrating it into existing processes. Finally, implementing skills management requires evaluating its effectiveness and acceptance, allowing for the reevaluation of initial theories based on practical insights. Skills management is cyclical, requiring ongoing refinement of strategies based on new insights. E9 highlights this by the requirement for taking an overview and adapting learning based on new insights:"*If we now take a 360-degree view of what someone needs, it is of course important to consider where I come from and where I want to go*". Like many processes that call for continuous adaption, feedback loops are emphasized in our interview. In more detail, feedback mechanisms enable the reassessment and modification of strategies, ensuring they stay aligned with organizational realities: "*That is why this healthy degree of self-reflection is necessary*" (E9). Maintaining open communication with stakeholders, especially employees and managers allows for adjusting in response to diverse perspectives and unforeseen challenges. This also refers back to the need to outline the inherent value of skills management for all involved parties: "*There are simply many more opportunities for employees themselves, and the more an organization uses its ecosystem for this and opens itself up to the opportunities of skill-based approaches, the more these opportunities multiply*" (E8). The rapid pace of AI advancements necessitates the flexible integration of technologies, necessitating regular updates to both theory and practice: "*So starting with the collection, from the assessments to the training, everything is actually digital. The whole process, there were of course corresponding software tools that were also data protection-compliant and suitable for the collection and for giving feedback and were precisely geared towards this*" (E4). Similar proceeses like change management further support this argumentation (e.g., [20]).

The levels of analysis, i.e., individual, team, organization and system, although not explicitly mentioned in our interviews, are related as well, influencing each other [55].

5 Conclusion

The systematic documentation of an individual's skills, experience, and qualifications offers a comprehensive overview that can significantly enhance various facets of AI-based skills management. We identified challenges at different levels for the successful establishment of skills management. At the system level, creating and maintaining a taxonomy for skills was highlighted. Experts expressed optimism about AI's potential but acknowledged technical issues, emphasizing the intricate nature of language data. On the organizational front, defining skills proves critical, with a focus on the specific goal of the organization. The commitment of expertise, time, and human resources emerged as pivotal. At the team level, the anonymity of self-assessments introduces uncertainty, and the diversity of assessment methods adds complexity, emphasizing the need for standardized procedures. On an individual level, the study highlights the crucial role of personal benefit as a motivator for engagement. Psychological dynamics were noted to impact self-assessments, influencing individuals' confidence and engagement. In summary, effective skills management necessitates addressing challenges at different levels—system, organizational, team-based, and individual. Striking a balance between technological optimism, organizational commitment, fair assessment practices, and individual well-being is integral to successfully developing and utilizing skills.

Our research faces some limitations. Qualitative expert interviews can be prone to subjectivity and bias, where personal views can skew interpretations. This can affect this research in two ways. First, during the expert selection, a bias could have influenced the results, and second, the expert's opinions can be influenced. The small sample size of ten limits the generalizability of findings.

Overall, our paper contributes to scholarly knowledge about skills management frameworks and challenges posed by skills management systems. In the future, our research will not only enhance our understanding of contemporary workforce and skill dynamics but also serve as a basis for developing practical implications for organizations striving to adapt and thrive as skill-based organizations. Future research should also focus on the negative implications of using AI for skills profiles and management to enrich our perspective.

References

1. Allal-Chérif, O., Yela Aránega, A., & Castaño Sánchez, R. (2021). Intelligent recruitment: How to identify, select, and retain talents from around the world using artificial intelligence. *Technological Forecasting and Social Change, 169*, Article 120822.
2. Anwar, Z., Bibi, N., & Ahsan, A. (2013). Expertise based skill management model for effective project resource allocation under stress in software industry of Pakistan. In *6th International Conference on Information Management, Innovation Management and Industrial Engineering* (pp. 509–513). IEEE Service Center.

3. Baird, A., & Maruping, L. M. (2021). The next generation of research on IS use: A theoretical framework of delegation to and from agentic IS artifacts. *Management Information Systems Quarterly, 45*(1).
4. Bakhshi, H., Downing, J. M., Osbrone, M. A., & Schneider, P. (2017). *The future of skills: Employment in 2030.* Pearson.
5. Bersin, J. (2023, October 10). Why Microsoft viva skills could disrupt the HR tech market. *The Josh Bersin Company.* https://joshbersin.com/2023/10/why-microsoft-viva-skills-could-disrupt-the-hr-tech-market/
6. Broadbent, M., & Weill, P. (1997). Management by maxim: How business and IT managers can create IT infrastructures. *MIT Sloan Management Review.*
7. Byrd, T. A., & Turner, D. E. (2000). Measuring the flexibility of information technology infrastructure: Exploratory analysis of a construct. *Journal of Management Information Systems, 17*(1), 167–208.
8. Cantrell, S., Griffiths, M., Jones, R., & Hiipakka, J. (2022, September 8). The skills-based organization: A new operating model for work and the workforce. *Deloitte.* https://www2.deloitte.com/us/en/insights/topics/talent/organizational-skill-based-hiring.html
9. CEDEFOP. (2017). *European inventory on validation of non-formal and informal learning—2016 update: Synthesis report.* https://www.cedefop.europa.eu/files/4153_en.pdf
10. Chang, S. E., Liu, A. Y., & Lin, S. (2015). Exploring privacy and trust for employee monitoring. *Industrial Management & Data Systems, 115*(1), 88–106.
11. Cicchetti, D. V. (1994). Guidelines, criteria, and rules of thumb for evaluating normed and standardized assessment instruments in psychology. *Psychological Assessment, 6*(4), 284–290.
12. Cramarenco, R. E., Burcă-Voicu, M. I., & Dabija, D. C. (2023). The impact of artificial intelligence (AI) on employees' skills and well-being in global labor markets: A systematic review. *Oeconomia Copernicana, 14*(3), 731–767.
13. Cubric, M. (2020). Drivers, barriers and social considerations for AI adoption in business and management: A tertiary study. *Technology in Society, 62*, Article 101257.
14. Das, S., Mandal, S. K. D., & Basu, A. (2020). Identification of cognitive learning complexity of assessment questions using multi-class text classification. *Contemporary Educational Technology, 12*(2), ep275.
15. Doherty-Restrepo, J. L., Perez, K., Creeden, M., Cram, B., & Charite, M. (2023). Closing the gap between students' career readiness and employers' expectations. *International Journal of Innovative Teaching and Learning in Higher Education, 4*(1), 1–14.
16. Donini, F. M., Lenzerini, M., Nardi, D., & Nutt, W. (1997). The complexity of concept languages. *Information and Computation, 134*(1), 1–58.
17. Dörsam, M., & Körfer, A. (2021). *Skill-management in Unternehmen der Industrie 4.0: Gute Beispiele aus der Praxis.* BIBB Discussion Paper. https://res.bibb.de/vet-repository_779563
18. Freise, L. R., & Bretschneider, U [U.] (2023). Automized assessment for professional skills—A systematic literature review and future research avenues. In *18. Internationale Tagung Wirtschaftsinformatik,* Paderborn, Germany.
19. Freise, L. R., & Hupe, A. (2023). Transferring digital twin technology on employee skills: A framework to support human resources. In *Academy of Management Annual Meeting,* Boston, MA, USA.
20. Galli, B. J. (2018). Change management models: A comparative analysis and concerns. *IEEE Engineering Management Review, 46*(3), 124–132.
21. Garcia-Arroyo, J., & Osca, A. (2021). Big data contributions to human resource management: A systematic review. *The International Journal of Human Resource Management, 32*(20), 4337–4362.
22. Gerogiannis, V. C., Rapti, E., Karageorgos, A., & Fitsilis, P. (2015). A fuzzy linguistic approach for human resource evaluation and selection in software projects. In *Proceedings of the 2015 International Conference on Industrial Engineering and Operations Management (IEOM).* IEEE.
23. Gonzalez Ehlinger, E., & Stephany, F. (2023). Finding talent for the twin transition: Are UK firms shifting towards skill-based hiring for AI and green jobs? *Available at SSRN 4603764.*

24. Kirkpatrick, K. (2017). AI in contact centers. *Communications of the ACM, 60*(8), 18–19.
25. Kohlbacher, F. (2013). The use of qualitative content analysis in case study research. *Forum: Qualitative Social Research, 7*(1), 1–30.
26. Konstantinidis, I., Maragoudakis, M., Magnisalis, I., Berberidis, C., & Peristeras, V. (2022). Knowledge-driven unsupervised skills extraction for graph-based talent matching. In *Proceedings of the 12th Hellenic Conference on Artificial Intelligence.* ACM.
27. Kontoghiorghes, C., Awbre, S. M., & Feurig, P. L. (2005). Examining the relationship between learning organization characteristics and change adaptation, innovation, and organizational performance. *Human Resource Development Quarterly, 16*(2), 185–212.
28. Mayring, P. (2004). Qualitative content analysis. In B. Jenner, U. Flick, E. von Kardoff, & I. Steinke (Eds.), *A companion to qualitative research.* Sage.
29. Mayring, P. (2015). *Qualitative Inhaltsanalyse: Grundlagen und Techniken, 12* (überarbeitete). Beltz Verlag.
30. Möhlmann, M., Zalmanson, L., Henfridsson, O., & Gregory, R. W. (2021). Algorithmic management of work on online labor platforms: When matching meets control. *MIS Quarterly, 45*(4), 1999–2022.
31. Morandini, S., Fraboni, F., de Angelis, M., Puzzo, G., Giusino, D., & Pietrantoni, L. (2023). The impact of artificial intelligence on workers' skills: Upskilling and reskilling in organisations. *Informing Science: The International Journal of an Emerging Transdiscipline, 26*, 39–68.
32. Murtaza, M., Ahmed, Y., Shamsi, J. A., Sherwani, F., & Usman, M. (2022). AI-based personalized e-learning systems: Issues, challenges, and solutions. *IEEE Access.*
33. Nunamaker, J. F., Briggs, R. O., Derrick, D. C., & Schwabe, G. (2015). The last research mile: Achieving both rigor and relevance in information systems research. *Journal of Management Information Systems, 32*(3), 10–47.
34. Pacher, C., Woschank, M., Rauch, E., & Zunk, B. M. (2022). Systematic development of a competence profile for industrial logistics engineering education. *Procedia Computer Science, 200*, 758–767.
35. Paiva, J. C., Leal, J. P., & Figueira, Á. (2022). Automated assessment in computer science education: A state-of-the-art review. *ACM Transactions on Computing Education, 22*(3), 1–40.
36. Pan, Y., & Froese, F. J. (2023). An interdisciplinary review of AI and HRM: Challenges and future directions. *Human Resource Management Review, 33*(1), Article 100924.
37. Păvăloaia, V.-D., & Necula, S.-C. (2023). Artificial intelligence as a disruptive technology—A systematic literature review. *Electronics, 12*(5), 1102.
38. Pinski, M., & Benlian, A. (2023). AI literacy-towards measuring human competency in artificial intelligence. In *56th Hawaii International Conference on System Sciences (HICSS)*, Waikiki, Hawaii, USA.
39. Pospelova, V., Baldominos, I. L., Sanz, L. F., & Castillo-Martinez, A. (2021). Big data and skills frameworks to determine recommended profiled of soft Skills for IS development. *Proceedings of the International Conference on Information Systems Development (ISD).*
40. Preston, D. S., Leidner, D. E., & Chen, D. (2020). CIO leadership profiles: Implications of matching CIO authority and leadership capability on IT impact. In *Strategic Information Management* (pp. 277–291). Routledge.
41. Ramesh, B. (2002). Process knowledge management with traceability. *IEEE Software, 19*(3), 50–52.
42. Reuters (2018, October 11). Insight—Amazon scraps secret AI recruiting tool that showed bias against women. *Reuters Media.* https://www.reuters.com/article/us-amazon-com-jobs-automation-insight/amazon-scraps-secret-ai-recruiting-tool-that-showed-bias-against-women-idUSKCN1MK08G/
43. Ritz, E., Donisi, F., Elshan, E., & Rietsche, R. (2023). Artificial socialization? How artificial intelligence applications can shape a new era of employee onboarding practices. In *56th Hawaii International Conference on System Sciences (HICSS).*
44. Ritz, E., Freise, L., Elshan, E., Rietsche, R., & Bretschneider, U. (2024). What to learn next? Designing personalized learning paths for re-&upskilling in organizations. In *Hawaii International Conference on System Sciences (HICSS).*

45. Ritz, E., Rietsche, R., & Leimeister, J. M. (2023). How to support students' self-regulated learning in times of crisis: An embedded technology-based intervention in blended learning pedagogies. *Academy of Management Learning & Education, 22*(3), 357–382.
46. Rychen, D. (2016, 9–10 November). *E2030 conceptual framework: Key competencies for 2030 (DeSeCo 2.0)*. Working Paper Edu/Edpc (2016) 23/Ann1, Beijing, China.
47. Samuel, Y., Brennan-Tonetta, M., Samuel, J., Kashyap, R., Kumar, V., Krishna Kaashyap, S., Chidipothu, N., Anand, I., & Jain, P. (2023). Cultivation of human centered artificial intelligence: Culturally adaptive thinking in education (CATE) for AI. *Frontiers in Artificial Intelligence, 6*, 1198180.
48. Schlippe, T., & Bothmer, K. (2023). Skill scanner. *International Journal of Advanced Corporate Learning, 16*(1), 55–64.
49. Sebastião, L., Tirapicos, F., Payan-Carreira, R., & Rebelo, H. (2023). Skill profiles for employability: (Mis)Understandings between higher education institutions and employers. *Education Sciences, 13*(9), 905.
50. Strauss, A., & Corbin, J. (1990). *Basics of qualitative research: Grounded theory procedures and techniques*. Sage.
51. Traumer, F., Oeste-Reiß, S., & Leimeister, J. M. (2017). Towards a future reallocation of work between humans and machines–Taxonomy of tasks and interaction types in the context of machine learning. In *38th International Conference on Information Systems*, Seoul, South Korea.
52. Traynor, S., Wellens, M. A., & Krishnamoorthy, V. (2021). Job Profile Builder. In S. Traynor, M. A. Wellens, & V. Krishnamoorthy (Eds.), *SAP SuccessFactors talent* (Vol. 1, pp. 65–111). Apress.
53. Whiting, K. (2020). *These are the top 10 job skills of tomorrow—And how long it takes to learn them*. https://www.weforum.org/agenda/2020/10/top-10-work-skills-of-tomorrow-how-long-it-takes-to-learn-them/
54. World Economic Forum (Ed.). (2023). *Future of jobs: Insight report.*
55. Wright, P. M., & Nishii, L. H. (2007). Strategic HRM and organizational behavior: Integrating multiple levels of analysis. *Cornell Working Paper Series*
56. Zhao, G., Cao, X., Xiao, W., Zhu, Y., & Cheng, K. (2019). Digital twin for NC machining using complete process information expressed by STEP-NC standard. In *Proceedings of the 4th International Conference on Automation, Control and Robotics Engineering.*
57. Zhao, M., Javed, F., Jacob, F., & McNair, M. (2019). SKILL: A system for skill identification and normalization. In *Proceedings of the Twenty-Seventh Conference on Innovative Applications of Artificial Intelligence.*

Transparency of Algorithmic Control Systems and Worker Judgments

Research Paper

Maximilian Kempf, Filip Simić, Armin Alizadeh, and Alexander Benlian

Abstract The use of algorithms to guide worker behavior, referred to as algorithmic control (AC), is increasingly prevalent in organizations. Despite its potential operational benefits, prior research indicates that workers often struggle with the opaque nature of such systems. Our research aims to explore how workers perceive, judge, and react to AC systems when exposed to two distinct facets of algorithmic transparency (AT): input and transformation AT. Through an experimental study with 121 participants, we provide empirical evidence that increased transparency about the algorithm's transformation process significantly enhances workers' perceived AT, which in turn positively impacts workers' judgments and, ultimately, their continuance intention and acceptance of an AC system. In doing so, we provide practical recommendations for organizations to mitigate the adverse effects associated with algorithmic control.

M. Kempf (✉) · F. Simić
Technical University of Darmstadt, Darmstadt, Germany
e-mail: maximilian.kempf@stud.tu-darmstadt.de

F. Simić
e-mail: filip.simic@stud.tu-darmstadt.de

A. Alizadeh · A. Benlian
Information Systems and Electronic Services, Technical University of Darmstadt, Darmstadt, Germany
e-mail: alizadeh@ise.tu-darmstadt.de

A. Benlian
e-mail: benlian@ise.tu-darmstadt.de

C. M. Flath et al. (eds.), *Digital Innovation and Organizational Transformation*, Lecture Notes in Information Systems and Organisation 83,
https://doi.org/10.1007/978-3-032-08483-5_18

1 Introduction

The modern workplace is being transformed by the continuous collection of data through ubiquitous digital devices and the integration of artificial intelligence for decision making [11]. This transformation has given rise to the concept of algorithmic control (AC), which refers to the use of these advanced technologies to guide worker activities in alignment with organizational goals [66]. While AC has been studied mainly within platform-based organizations (e.g., ride-hailing or food-delivery platforms), it has recently also spread into more conventional work settings [5, 14]. One particularly noteworthy example for AC in conventional work settings are employee management systems, such as Microsoft Viva. These systems utilize algorithms to monitor worker activity, such as calendar schedules, set productivity goals, and deliver feedback [37]. As a result, these systems are automating managerial tasks that were traditionally performed by human managers [39, 47].

Although the use of AC promises significant benefits to organizations, including enhanced efficiency and scalability of control mechanisms [39], it comes with significant drawbacks. One core issue associated with AC is the opaque nature of these systems [39]. Workers frequently report increased job-related uncertainties when subjected to AC systems due to a lack of transparency regarding the underlying algorithms and their decision-making processes [46]. This obscurity can lead to feelings of alienation and decreased job satisfaction, as workers struggle to understand the rationale behind task assignments and performance evaluations [43]. To mitigate these negative outcomes, scholars suggest that AC systems should be designed to provide more information about their inner workings to mitigate these negative aspects of AC [2, 5, 47]. However, despite these frequent recommendations, there is a notable lack of empirical research exploring the effects of increased transparency concerning AC systems on worker judgments of AC. Against this background, our study aims to answer the following research question:

How do varying levels of transparency in AC systems affect worker perceptions, judgments, and reactions toward AC?

To address our research question, we leveraged existing literature on algorithmic transparency [8] to describe two distinct forms of AT in AC systems: input and transformation AT. In an online experiment with 121 participants using a fictional employee management system, we found that transformation AT significantly increased perceived AT, unlike input AT, which had no significant effect. Perceived AT positively influenced workers' judgments of AC, which in turn positively correlated with their acceptance and continuance intention.

Our study makes two key contributions to AC research. First, while existing research often treats transparency in AC as an abstract requirement, we leverage AT literature to define two specific forms of transparency within AC systems: input and transformation AT as action. Second, we provide rare empirical evidence linking perceived AT to worker judgments in conventional work settings, demonstrating that not all forms of transparency positively affect workers' perceptions. Consequently, we recommend that future AC research adopts a more granular approach to transparency, in order to provide organizations with concrete recommendations for action.

2 Conceptual Background

Our study builds on recent advancements in research on AC and AT. Initially, we introduce the concept of AC and how it unfolds in different work settings. Subsequently, we review recent approaches to studying worker judgments of AC systems. Finally, we draw on an existing conceptualization of AT, detailing its relevance and application within the AC context, thereby laying the groundwork for our empirical investigation.

2.1 Opaqueness of Algorithmic Control and Worker Judgments

The notion of AC represents a new form of organizational control that leverages intelligent algorithms and advanced digital technologies to align worker activities with organizational goals [66]. Compared to previous forms of (human-based) control, AC is considered to be a more comprehensive, interactive, instantaneous, and opaque form of control [39]. AC is considered the backbone of platform-based organizations, such as Uber and Deliveroo, which guide millions of workers through their smartphone app [14, 66]. In more conventional work settings, AC becomes embedded within established power dynamics between managers and workers, redefining their roles, relationships, and information exchange, thereby resulting in a shift in power dynamics [35]. Therefore, in more conventional work settings, AC typically has a complementary character, replacing only some managerial functions and delivering control together with the human manager [35, 66]. A prominent example in this regard, which also builds the backdrop for our study, is employee management systems, such as Microsoft Viva, which provide individual-level recommendations to workers, such as "Stay connected with you collaborators - You don't have 1:1 meetings over next 2 weeks. Here are suggested times that work everyone" [37].

Research in the context of AC has identified both advantages and disadvantages for workers. On the positive side, AC can provide precise, real-time feedback, a capability beyond the scope of conventional human supervision [49, 5, 39]. AC systems can analyze vast amounts of data from different data sources in real time to assess individual working behaviors and recommend specific actions tailored to each worker [18, 33]. However, the widespread adoption of AC also introduces significant challenges, including concerns over job autonomy, constant surveillance, and the potential erosion of trust within the workplace [28, 39, 40, 46, 59].

Recently, a growing body of research has been investigating how specific design features of AC affect workers, aiming to amplify benefits and mitigate drawbacks of AC use [18, 49, 66]. A principal design recommendation emerging from these studies is the need for greater transparency, as "algorithmic opaqueness can be very frustrating to the workers exposed to algorithmic instructions, causing them to experience uncertainties about [...] the accuracy and fairness of algorithmic instructions" [5, p. 830). Surprisingly, empirical research on the relationship between increased transparency and worker perceptions is scant and yields mixed results. [28] identified a positive correlation between the disclosure of information and workers' retention intentions within a ride-hailing platform context. Conversely, Cram et al. observed that perceived AT did not significantly affect workers' perceptions of technostress under AC and therefore suggest to examine how different elements of transparency impact worker perceptions of AC [18].

To examine how different AC designs affect workers, recent studies have employed a three-step model of AC perception, judgment, and reaction [66]. With this study, we apply this approach to assess how different levels of transparency impact workers' perceptions (i.e., perceived AT of an AC system), judgments, and reactions. We specifically focus on two reactions that are frequently discussed in the literature and have significant practical implications: acceptance of an algorithmic recommendation and the continuance intention to use the system [43, 66]. Regarding judgments, our study concentrates on three key dimensions frequently highlighted in AC research: autonomy, privacy, trust. Additionally, considering the specific context of this research, we have also included credibility as a critical judgment dimension. It is common research practice to focus on the most relevant dimensions, though it is acknowledged that the list of possible judgments can never be exhaustive [66]. Table 1 provides detailed definitions and illustrative examples for these dimensions.

2.2 Algorithmic Transparency

The notion of algorithmic transparency was first articulated by Diakopoulos and Koliska [23]. They conceptualized algorithmic transparency as "the disclosure of information about algorithms to enable monitoring, checking, criticism, or intervention by interested parties" (p. 811). This perspective assumes that there are at least two distinct roles within the transparency dynamic: the disclosing party (i.e., the AC system within the scope of our study), which shares information about the algorithms, and the receiving party (i.e., workers in our study), which interacts with this information [6, 9].

Building on this definition, a recent literature review [9] conceptualized AT in terms of *AT as action* and *AT as perception.* AT as action involves the disclosing party providing information about an algorithm to its users. AT as perception focuses on how users observe and interpret this information. Although these concepts are related, not every facet and amount of information shared leads to a correspondent

Table 1 Dimensions of worker judgments

Dimension	Short description	Illustrative example in the traditional context	Reference
Privacy	Workers judge AC practices as appropriate, respecting their personal information during data collection, storage, and use.	A Microsoft viva user feels that the app-usage data collected by the company are relevant to her/his work and will contribute to better work outcomes.	Wiener et al. [66]
Autonomy	Workers judge AC practices as empowering, while allowing them to act independently.	A Microsoft viva user values the flexibility of working when and where he or she chooses.	Wiener et al. [66]
Trust	Workers judge AC practices as trustworthy.	A Microsoft viva user believes the application and recommendations are well-meaning and honest.	Bitzer et al. [10]
Credibility	Workers judge AC practices as believable.	A Microsoft viva user views the information presented by the application as authentic and unbiased.	Shin et al. [56]

perception. Instead, this relationship is dependent on the specific context and recipient of the information [9]. Additionally, Bitzer et al. [9] conceptualize AT along the algorithmic process itself. The definition of an algorithm, "encoded procedures for transforming input data into a desired output based on specified calculations" [26, p. 167), stresses that algorithms can be seen as a process. Thus, algorithmic information can be provided for every step of an algorithm's input, transformation, or output [9].

Recent research highlights that workers are also seeking insights into the inner workings of an AC system, particularly regarding what data is fed into the system (i.e., input transparency) and how the system processes this data to derive instructions (i.e., transformation transparency). For example, AC workers demand more transparency regarding the data collection and the processing of how tasks are assigned [2, 46]. Therefore, these two forms are in the focus of this study. Table 2 provides an overview of the concepts, including illustrative examples of the two transparency forms.

Table 2 Two forms of algorithmic transparency

Construct	Definition	Illustrative example
IATA	Input algorithmic transparency as action	Information on why and how data is collected (e.g., calendar for schedule optimization)
TATA	Transformation algorithmic transparency as action	Information on the algorithm's logic (e.g., schedule is generated based on analyzed work patterns)

3 Hypothesis Development

3.1 AT as Action and Perceived AT

Looking at the impact of AC on workers, stakeholders frequently demand greater transparency with respect to their usage [5]. However, the degree of perceived AT of workers differs remarkably when they are provided with different types of information. Some details about algorithms may not even influence individuals' perceptions of AT [9]. Nevertheless, despite the lack of direct investigation, the majority of studies implicitly suggest that greater AT as action is truly associated with increased AT as perception [9, 19, 44, 55, 64, 65]. In the context of this study, we scrutinize the disclosure of two different types of information. The first one is IATA. Workers demand a higher level of transparency regarding the data collection [2], since often they are not even aware of the existence or purpose of such data collections [39]. Providing workers with desired information about the input of algorithms may contribute to a higher perception of AT. Therefore, we propose the following hypothesis:

Hypothesis 1a: *IATA is positively related to workers' perceived AT.*

The second form is TATA. Scholars point out one main concern in human-algorithm interaction, which is the lack of perceived AT in regards to how the algorithms' output is generated [6, 61]. Hence, individuals who receive information about the inner logic of algorithms may perceive greater AT when provided in a way that humans can understand (no machine code). We propose the following hypothesis:

Hypothesis 1b: *TATA is positively related to workers' perceived AT.*

3.2 Perceived AT and Worker Judgments

Numerous of the impeding beliefs and perceptions, lowering worker judgments, come from the aspect of uncertainty [10]. One possible way to mitigate individuals' uncertainty is to disclose information, or, in other words, to increase their perceived AT [6, 10] and thereby positively influence their worker judgments. By increasing workers' perceived AT, they gain insights into the inner processes of AC systems and potentially drop their concerns about data misuse and incorrect calculations. In this study, we conceptualized worker judgments in terms of four dimensions (autonomy, privacy, trust, credibility), all of which appear to be affected by perceived AT. Regarding autonomy, Vaassen [63] argues that more transparent algorithms enable individuals to gain insights into the explanations behind algorithmic recommendations. This increased understanding allows them to make well-informed decisions about whether to accept or decline such recommendations, leading to higher levels of autonomy. Transparency and privacy are closely related [6] and research has been called to examine the effect of perceived AT on privacy [9]. Sharing information about why and how algorithms collect data might reduce users' privacy concerns and, thus, enhance their judgment about the privacy aspects of the underlying AC system. The relationship between AT and trust has shown contrasting findings when considering different contexts [44]. Regarding the context of our study, we draw upon the following assumptions: Through higher perceived AT, workers understand that organizations have nothing to conceal concerning their algorithms and provide relevant information with positive intentions [10]. Hence, we argue that enhanced perceived AT increases workers' trust judgments towards AC systems. When examining credibility, workers who view AC systems as transparent interpret the presented information as more authentic and recognize their output as unbiased [56]. Therefore, we conclude that increased perceived AT is related to higher judgments of credibility. Thus, we propose the following hypothesis:

Hypothesis 2: *Perceived AT is positively related to worker judgments.*

3.3 Worker Judgments and Behavioral Reactions

In this study, we focus on two common behavioral reactions of workers resulting from their judgments about AC systems. First, we examine the extent to which workers accept algorithmic recommendations. This is of great importance, as it is the most common approach to direct workers to specific decisions or behaviors intended by their employers [39]. The second reaction is the degree to which workers plan to continue working with a given AC system. Implementing AC systems in organizations requires substantial effort and investments [15]. Therefore, it is crucial for organizations to achieve high adoption rates to make the investment worthwhile. In the following paragraphs, we investigate each behavioral reaction. Algorithmic recommending is widely spread for the purpose of affecting workers by suggesting they behave in a certain way or perform desired actions [33, 39]. However, the effectiveness of such an instrument heavily depends on workers' acceptance of these recommendations.

From an organizational perspective, the concept can be compared to an advice-taking and decision-making scenario. Existing research in this context suggests that autonomy is positively associated with following the recommendations of credible advisors [41]. Conversely, workers who judge the advisor as questionable are unlikely to accept recommendations. Apart from this, Koestner et al. [41] further indicates that individuals would decline recommendations to a greater extent if they suspected the advisors' goals not to be aligned with their own, which may result in a positive relationship between trust and advice-taking. We assume these considerations are transferable to the context of workers and AC systems. Following the line of arguments, workers who experience no restriction on their autonomy and judge the underlying AC system as trustworthy and credible are more likely to accept recommendations from AC systems. Formally, we state this hypothesis as follows:

Hypothesis 3: *Worker judgments are positively related to workers' acceptance of algorithmic recommendations.*

The integration of AC systems in conventional organizations is associated with high costs and the effort of aligning AC systems and human employees, leading to an uncertain return on investment [13, 15]. In addition, organizations that implement AC systems are also characterized by high turnover rates [4, 12, 22]. As a consequence, organizations benefit from increasing workers' commitment to the organization and their AC system. Prior studies found that autonomy leads to less tension and higher job satisfaction [21, 40], indicating that workers may stay longer in the organization's ecosystem, including their AC system. In terms of privacy, individuals are aware of the surveillance practices and utilization of personal data by organizations, yet their perceptions vary [66]. Perceived invasions of workers' privacy are likely to result in reduced organizational commitment and a higher turnover rate [34, 57, 60]. Another aspect to consider concerning continuance intention is trust, since it contributes to loyalty towards a specific system. Prior research analyzed this relationship in the context of the sharing economy [36] as well as voice-controlled artificial intelligence [32] and revealed significant positive effects. The effects of credibility have not yet been investigated in the AC literature. However, the credibility of online platforms has been found to positively impact the continuance intention of their users [24]. We suppose this relationship is also transferable to the context of AC systems. Following the above lines of arguments, we assume that AC workers with enhanced judgments intend to continue working with AC systems more often and hypothesize the following:

Hypothesis 4: *Worker judgments are positively related to workers' continuance intention.*

4 Experimental Study

4.1 Design and Procedure

In the particular case of this study, we implemented a 2 × 2 between-subjects design experiment consisting of four randomly assigned scenarios, followed by a survey. Past Information Systems research conducted similar approaches for their experiments [28, 42].

The subject of our experiment was a fictional application called "WorkFlowZen", which simulated an employee management system, a prominent example of AC in conventional work settings. Such systems analyze employee data to provide managers with detailed insights into worker behaviors, activities, and performance, thereby offering recommendations to boost productivity [35]. WorkFlowZen offered the functionality of presenting personalized recommendations for weekly schedule optimizations.

The experiment started by asking the participants to imagine being in the following scenario: The attendees are employed in an office setting with flexible working hours. Their boss introduces them to an application called "WorkFlowZen". The participants are informed about the functions of the app, which include providing work and well-being improving analytics as well as recommendations tailored to their unique needs. They were instructed to carefully examine the application and decide whether they wanted to accept or decline the recommendation provided by WorkFlowZen.

The participants were then randomly assigned to one of four different experimental scenarios and directed to the initial page, imitating a first visit to the application. They were asked to provide access to their office suite usage data, screen time, and calendar. We varied the quantity of information considering IATA (low or high). Participants in the high information group received the following two pieces of information: "**This access enables us to personalize your tasks, track your activities, and enhance productivity while prioritizing your data privacy**"; "**The application discreetly captures your work hours at different times of the day, allowing it to evaluate data and offer personalized scheduling recommendations**." Participants in the low-information group received no additional information.

Next, participants were redirected to the second page of the experiment, where they were presented with analytical metrics and a personalized recommendation. Similarly, we manipulated the quantity of information associated with TATA (low or high). Participants in the high-information group received the following piece of information: "**This recommendation is based on our analysis of your work patterns using office suite usage data. We've observed that your peak productivity hours typically occur in the afternoon. Applying this recommendation, you can optimize your work schedule to align with your peak productivity, promoting overall well-being and efficiency**." Participants in the low-information group received no additional information.

After inspecting the page, participants decided whether they wanted to accept or decline the recommendation. Consequently, this resulted in a change in their fictional regular weekly schedule. After finalizing their decision, they were redirected to the survey.

4.2 Survey Instrument and Data Collection

In the first part of the questionnaire, all dependent and independent latent variables were measured reflectively on a 7-point Likert scale (1 = "strongly disagree" and 7 = "strongly agree"). We measured perceived AT by adapting existing scales to our specific context [65, 67]. The construct served as the dependent variable for hypotheses H1a and H1b as well as the independent variable for hypothesis H2. The four dimensions of worker judgments were assessed by implementing customized items from previous studies: privacy [3], autonomy [27], trust [20], credibility [62]. We combine these four variables into a reflective-formative second-order construct, following the notion of previous studies that view them as building parts of worker judgments [66]. Furthermore, this aggregation reduces the overall complexity of the measurement model [31, 51]. To capture workers' acceptance of recommendations and continuance intention, we applied constructs developed by Abraham et al. [1] and Goldbach et al. [27].

To check for potential confounded effects, we collected several control variables at the end of the questionnaire: general privacy concern [45], algorithmic literacy [25], technology use index at work and personally [1], positive and negative attitude towards technology [54]. To ensure external validity, we implemented a reality check [38, 28], asking participants to assess the presented scenario regarding its authenticity on a 7-point scale from "not realistic" to "very realistic". The results demonstrate participants perceived the experiment as realistic ($M = 4.73$, $SD = 1.62$). In addition, the survey included two attention checks to reject straight-liners and inattentive participants.

Our study recruited participants through the crowd-sourcing platform Prolific, providing high-quality data [50, 48]. The total sample size reached 121 after excluding incomplete responses and failed attention checks. The participants had a mean age of 28.5 (SD=8) years, and regarding gender, the sample was balanced, with 53.3% being male and 46.7% female.

4.3 Data Analysis

To test hypotheses H1a and H1b of our research model, we employed a two-way ANOVA. We evaluated the hypotheses H2, H3, and H4 of the research model through a structural equation model using SmartPLS 4 [52]. The partial least squares structural equation modeling (PLS-SEM) algorithm was the most suitable choice since it handles our reflective-formative second-order construct worker judgments [30, 53]. Following the set standards, we then performed a bootstrapping algorithm with 5000 subsamples to evaluate the significance of the relationships [30]. Due to the higher-order construct, the model was implemented using a two-step approach [31]. First, we calculated latent variable scores for the lower-order constructs, including privacy, autonomy, trust, and credibility. Afterward, these scores were combined to measure the higher-order construct worker judgments. During the first step, we evaluated several metrics of our measurement model to ensure valid results. Starting with indicator reliability, we analyzed the outer loadings of each item and removed one autonomy, one privacy, and one perceived AT item. The remaining items all passed the benchmark of 0.708 proposed by Hair et al. [29]. Subsequently, we looked at the internal consistency reliability and chose the reliability coefficient rho_{α}, whereby all values are in the acceptable range (0.6–0.95). For measuring convergent validity, we selected the average variance extracted. All constructs passed the threshold of 0.5. To assess discriminant validity, this study applied the Fornell-Larcker criterion, which all constructs passed. Concerning the second step, we recalculated our model with the assembled formative second-order construct and ensured the reliability and validity of the new model. However, the outer weight of the privacy item was above the significance level ($\beta = 0.137, p = 0.071$). Yet, all items' outer loadings are highly significant (autonomy: $\beta = 0.613, p < 0.001$; privacy: $\beta = 0.651, p < 0.001$; trust: $\beta = 0.941$, $p < 0.001$; credibility: $\beta = 0.887$, $p < 0.001$). Considering that formative indicators do not have to be excluded solely based on the statistical outcomes [29], we decided to keep privacy in the measurement model because of its conceptual importance for the research model [7, 66].

5 Results

5.1 Results of H1a & H1b

The results of the two-way ANOVA indicate no significance for hypothesis H1a ($F(1, 117) = 0.615, p > 0.05$). Participants who received information about why they should give access to their applications and how data is utilized did not show higher levels of perceived AT than participants who received no information about this criterion. However, hypothesis H1b is statistically significant ($F(1, 117) = 12.868$, $p < 0.01$). Participants who received information about why they got their personalized recommendation reported higher perceived AT compared to participants who received no information about this criterion. Regarding the descriptive statistics, the scenarios revealed the following characteristics: with IATA and TATA both low, the mean perceived AT is 4.208 (SD = 1.188, $N = 39$). With low IATA and high TATA, the mean is 4.946 (SD = 1.066, $N = 21$). High IATA and low TATA result in a mean of 4.423 (SD = 1.107, $N = 26$). Both high yield a mean of 5.029 (SD = 1.019, $N = 35$). The model explains 7.6% of the variance in perceived AT ($R^2 = 0.099$, adjusted $R^2 = 0.076$).

5.2 Results of H2 & H3 & H4

The results of the structural equation model suggest the following: The hypothesis H2 is statistically supported by the results ($\beta = 0.535$, $p < 0.001$). This indicates that workers who perceived the AC system as more transparent also showed greater judgments. Moreover, the results support hypothesis H3 ($\beta = 0.712$, $p < 0.001$), showing that workers with higher judgments tend to accept algorithmic recommendations more often. Likewise, hypothesis H4 is supported ($\beta = 0.729$, $p < 0.001$). Therefore, workers who express higher-level judgments are more likely to work with the AC system in the future. The control variables were not found to be significant. Figure 1 summarizes the results.

Lastly, the model was analyzed for any mediation effects of worker judgments. Therefore, we examined the effects of perceived AT on acceptance and continuance intention, respectively. To do so, we added direct connections to the existing research

Table 3 Analysis of mediation effects

	Direct effect		Indirect effects		
Path	Path coefficient	*p*-value	Path coefficient	*p*-value	Analysis results
PT → AC	**−0.217**	0.006	**0.441**	0.000	*Partial mediation*
PT → CI	0.025	0.753	**0.393**	0.000	Full mediation

Significant effects in bold
PT = Perceived AT, AC = Acceptance of recommendations, CI = Continuance intention

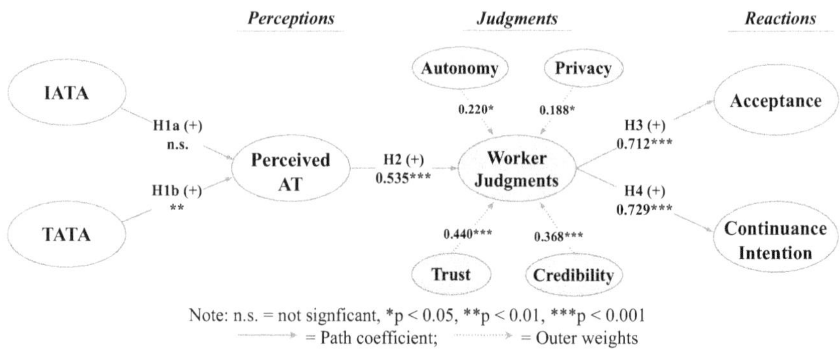

Fig. 1 Visualization of the research model and results

model, following the guidelines proposed by Hair et al. [29]. The outcomes reveal that both indirect effects (with worker judgments as mediators) are significant, while only perceived AT appears to influence acceptance through an immediate effect. As a consequence, the relationship between perceived AT and recommendation acceptance is *partially* mediated by worker judgments, whereas the connection between perceived AT and continuance intention is *fully* mediated (see Table 3). Given the opposite signs of the direct and indirect effects between perceived AT and acceptance (negative direct effect), the relationship is characterized by a competitive mediation effect [31].

6 Discussion and Conclusion

The purpose of this research was to examine whether more and different information about the inner workings of AC systems affects how workers perceive, judge, and react to AC systems. Thereby, workers' perceived AT, worker judgments, and behavioral reactions, namely acceptance of recommendation and continuance intention, were analyzed. The empirical results of our experimental study show that providing information about the transformation process of algorithms increases workers' perceived AT, whereas information about the input of algorithms seems to have no significant effect. One possible explanation is that the provided information about the algorithm's input was not sufficient. Participants were asked an additional optional question: *In which area of the application do they want to see enhanced transparency?* Multiple high IATA group responses requested more detailed information about when exactly the application captures data, where and how long the data is stored (regarding third parties), and reasons for collecting each type of data. Another reason may be that worker information needs vary greatly by context. We further observed the importance of worker judgments serving as a mediator in linking workers' perceived AT with their consequential reactions. Additionally, as an observation of our mediation analysis, we find a direct effect of perceived AT on acceptance of recommendations to be positively related, confirming prior studies [19]. This indicates that AC workers with enhanced perceived AT are more likely to accept AC recommendations.

6.1 Research Contributions

This research contributes to the existing research on AC in two ways: Conceptually, our study bridges the gap between recent AC and AT research. While calls for greater transparency within AC are a recurrent theme in the AC literature [5, 14, 46], these calls remained somewhat broad and often lacked specificity. This is why recent studies emphasized the need to examine different elements of transparency in more detail [17]. By leveraging the concepts of IATA and TATA, and distinguishing between AT as action and AT as perception [9], this research paves the way for future, more nuanced investigations into transparency in AC settings. Empirically, our study provides a rare insight into how workers' perceive, judge, and react to different levels of provided transparency in AC systems. Through experimental investigation, we observed a significant correlation between TATA and workers' perceived AT, while IATA showed no such relationship. These results may suggest that employees assign different importance to different types of information if they want to better understand the inner workings of the AC system. Additionally, we found a strong positive relationship between perceived AC, worker judgments, and reactions, aligning with prior assumptions in previous research [49]. However, it had not been demonstrated through an experimental setup.

6.2 Limitations and Future Research

Our paper acknowledges several limitations. First, our cross-sectional experimental design hinders the ability to establish cause-and-effect relationships [58]. Therefore, the causal interpretations we provide are based on recent literature and logical reasoning. Additionally, the distribution of the participants across the four scenarios was not perfectly balanced. Future research should address these limitations by implementing a longitudinal study to confirm the results suggested by our experimental study [16]. Second, as our research context, we focused on a prominent application of AC in conventional settings, namely employee management systems. While these systems represent a subtler form of AC, there exist more coercive applications of AC in traditional work environments, such as AC in warehouses [22]. This variation in AC manifestations raises questions about the generalizability of our findings. Hence, we recommend investigating the relationships in other conventional work contexts like warehouses [22].

References

1. Abraham, M., Niessen, C., Schnabel, C., Lorek, K., Grimm, V., Möslein, K., & Wrede, M. (2019). Electronic monitoring at work: The role of attitudes, functions, and perceived control for the acceptance of tracking technologies. *Human Resource Management Journal, 29*(4), 657–675.
2. Ajunwa, I. (2020). The "black box" at work. *Big Data & Society, 7*(2), 205395172096618.
3. Alge, B. J., Ballinger, G. A., Tangirala, S., & Oakley, J. L. (2006). Information privacy in organizations: Empowering creative and extrarole performance. *The Journal of Applied Psychology, 91*(1), 221–232.
4. Anderson, D. N. (2016). Wheels in the head: Ridesharing as monitored performance. *Surveillance & Society, 14*(2), 240–258.
5. Benlian, A., Wiener, M., Cram, W. A., Krasnova, H., Maedche, A., Möhlmann, M., Recker, J., & Remus, U. (2022). Algorithmic management. *Business & Information Systems Engineering, 64*(6), 825–839.
6. Bernstein, E. S. (2017). Making transparency transparent: The evolution of observation in management theory. *Academy of Management Annals, 11*(1), 217–266.
7. Bijlsma-Frankema, K. M., & Costa, A. C. (2010). Consequences and antecedents of managerial and employee legitimacy interpretations of control: A natural open system approach. In S. B. Sitkin, L. B. Cardinal, K. M. Bijlsma-Frankema, & K. Bijlsma-Frankema (Eds.), *Organizational control* (pp. 396–433). Cambridge companions to management, Cambridge University Press.
8. Bitzer, T. (2022). Algorithmic transparency in action: How and why do companies disclose information on algorithms? *AMCIS 2022 Proceedings*.
9. Bitzer, T., Wiener, M., & Cram, W. A. (2023). Algorithmic transparency: Concepts, antecedents, and consequences—A review and research framework. *Communications of the Association for Information Systems, 52*.
10. Bitzer, T., Wiener, M., & Morana, S. (2021). The role of algorithmic transparency in contact-tracing app adoption. *ICIS 2021 Proceedings*.
11. Brynjolfsson, E., & McAfee, A. (2014). *The second machine age: Work, progress, and prosperity in a time of brilliant technologies* (1st ed.). W.W. Norton.
12. Bujold, A., Parent-Rocheleau, X., & Gaudet, M.-C. (2022). Opacity behind the wheel: The relationship between transparency of algorithmic management, justice perception, and intention to quit among truck drivers. *Computers in Human Behavior Reports, 8*, 100245.
13. Burton, J. W., Stein, M., & Jensen, T. B. (2020). A systematic review of algorithm aversion in augmented decision making. *Journal of Behavioral Decision Making, 33*(2), 220–239.
14. Cameron, L., Lamers, L., Leicht-Deobald, U., Lutz, C., Meijerink, J., & Möhlmann, M. (2023). Algorithmic management: Its implications for information systems research. *Communications of the Association for Information Systems, 52*(1), 518–537.

15. Christin, A. (2017). Algorithms in practice: Comparing web journalism and criminal justice. *Big Data & Society, 4*(2), 205395171771885.
16. Cram, W. A., D'Arcy, J., & Benlian, A. (2024). Time will tell: The case for an idiographic approach to behavioral cybersecurity research. *MIS Quarterly, 48*(1), 95–136.
17. Cram, W. A., & Wiener, M. (2020). Technology-mediated control: Case examples and research directions for the future of organizational control. *Communications of the Association for Information Systems, 46*(1), 70–91.
18. Cram, W. A., Wiener, M., Tarafdar, M., & Benlian, A. (2022). Examining the impact of algorithmic control on uber drivers' technostress. *Journal of Management Information Systems, 39*(2), 426–453.
19. Cramer, H., Evers, V., Ramlal, S., van Someren, M., Rutledge, L., Stash, N., Aroyo, L., & Wielinga, B. (2008). The effects of transparency on trust in and acceptance of a content-based art recommender. *User Modeling and User-Adapted Interaction, 18*(5), 455–496.
20. Cyr, D., Head, M. M., Larios, H., & Pan, B. (2009). Exploring human images in website design: A multimethod approach. *MIS Quarterly, 33*(3), 539.
21. Deci, E. L., & Ryan, R. M. (1987). The support of autonomy and the control of behavior. *Journal of Personality and Social Psychology, 53*(6), 1024–1037.
22. Delfanti, A. (2021). *The warehouse: Workers and robots at Amazon* (1st ed.). Pluto Press.
23. Diakopoulos, N., & Koliska, M. (2017). Algorithmic transparency in the news media. *Digital Journalism, 5*(7), 809–828.
24. Filieri, R., Acikgoz, F., Ndou, V., & Dwivedi, Y. (2021). Is tripadvisor still relevant? The influence of review credibility, review usefulness, and ease of use on consumers' continuance intention. *International Journal of Contemporary Hospitality Management, 33*(1), 199–223.
25. Flynn, L. R., & Goldsmith, R. E. (1999). A short, reliable measure of subjective knowledge. *Journal of Business Research, 46*(1), 57–66.
26. Gillespie, T., Boczkowski, P. J., & Foot, K. A. (2014). *The relevance of algorithms, media technologies: Essays on communication, materiality, and society*. The MIT Press.
27. Goldbach, T., Benlian, A., & Buxmann, P. (2018). Differential effects of formal and self-control in mobile platform ecosystems: Multi-method findings on third-party developers' continuance intentions and application quality. *Information & Management, 55*(3), 271–284.
28. Göttel, V. (2021). Sharing algorithmic management information in the sharing economy—Effects on workers' intention to stay with the organization. *ICIS 2021 Proceedings*.
29. Hair, J. F., Hult, G. T. M., Ringle, C. M., & Sarstedt, M. (2017). *A primer on partial least squares structural equation modeling (PLS-SEM)* (2nd ed.). Sage.
30. Hair, J. F., Ringle, C. M., & Sarstedt, M. (2011). Pls-sem: Indeed a silver bullet. *Journal of Marketing Theory and Practice, 19*(2), 139–152.
31. Hair, J. F., Sarstedt, M., Ringle, C. M., & Gudergan, S. (2018). *Advanced issues in partial least squares structural equation modeling*. Sage.
32. Hasan, R., Shams, R., & Rahman, M. (2021). Consumer trust and perceived risk for voice-controlled artificial intelligence: The case of siri. *Journal of Business Research, 131*, 591–597.
33. Hirsch, F., Alizadeh, A., Wiener, M., & Cram, A. (2023). Algorithmic control in platform and traditional work settings: An updated conceptual framework. *ECIS 2023 Research Papers*.
34. Hodson, T. J., Englander, F., & Englander, V. (1999). Ethical, legal and economic aspects of employer monitoring of employee electronic mail. *Journal of Business Ethics, 19*(1), 99–108.
35. Jarrahi, M. H., Newlands, G., Lee, M. K., Wolf, C. T., Kinder, E., & Sutherland, W. (2021). Algorithmic management in a work context. *Big Data & Society, 8*(2), 205395172110203.
36. Jiang, Y., & Lau, A. K. (2021). Roles of consumer trust and risks on continuance intention in the sharing economy: An empirical investigation. *Electronic Commerce Research and Applications, 47*, 101050.
37. John, B., Alsamarra'i, Z., & Panteli, N. (2023). Enhancing employee experience in the era of hybrid work: The case of microsoft viva. *IEEE Software, 40*(2), 70–79.
38. Jones, D. A., Shultz, J. W., & Chapman, D. S. (2006). Recruiting through job advertisements: The effects of cognitive elaboration on decision making. *International Journal of Selection and Assessment, 14*(2), 167–179.

39. Kellogg, K. C., Valentine, M. A., & Christin, A. (2020). Algorithms at work: The new contested terrain of control. *Academy of Management Annals, 14*(1), 366–410.
40. Kinowska, H., & Sienkiewicz, Ł. J. (2022). Influence of algorithmic management practices on workplace well-being—Evidence from european organisations. *Information Technology & People, 36*(8), 21–42.
41. Koestner, R., Gingras, I., Abutaa, R., Losier, G. F., DiDio, L., & Gagné, M. (1999). To follow expert advice when making a decision: An examination of reactive versus reflective autonomy. *Journal of Personality, 67*(5), 851–872.
42. Lee, M. K. (2018). Understanding perception of algorithmic decisions: Fairness, trust, and emotion in response to algorithmic management. *Big Data & Society, 5*(1), 205395171875668.
43. Lee, M. K., Kusbit, D., Metsky, E., & Dabbish, L. (2015). Working with machines. In B. Begole, J. Kim, K. Inkpen, & W. Woo (Eds.), *Proceedings of the 33rd Annual ACM Conference on Human Factors in Computing Systems* (pp. 1603–1612). ACM.
44. Lehmann, C., Haubitz, C., Fuegener, A., & Thonemann, U. (2020). Keep it mystic? The effects of algorithm transparency on the use of advice. *ICIS 2020 Proceedings*.
45. Martin, K. D., Borah, A., & Palmatier, R. W. (2017). Data privacy: Effects on customer and firm performance. *Journal of Marketing, 81*(1), 36–58.
46. Möhlmann, M., & Henfridsson, O. (2019). What people hate about being managed by algorithms, according to a study of uber drivers.
47. Möhlmann, M., Zalmanson, L., Henfridsson, O., & Gregory, R. W. (2021). Algorithmic management of work on online labor platforms: When matching meets control. *MIS Quarterly, 45*(4), 1999–2022.
48. Palan, S., & Schitter, C. (2018). Prolific.ac–a subject pool for online experiments. *Journal of Behavioral and Experimental Finance, 17*, 22–27.
49. Parent-Rocheleau, X., & Parker, S. K. (2022). Algorithms as work designers: How algorithmic management influences the design of jobs. *Human Resource Management Review, 32*(3), 100838.
50. Peer, E., Brandimarte, L., Samat, S., & Acquisti, A. (2017). Beyond the turk: Alternative platforms for crowdsourcing behavioral research. *Journal of Experimental Social Psychology, 70*, 153–163.
51. Polites, G. L., Roberts, N., & Thatcher, J. (2012). Conceptualizing models using multidimensional constructs: A review and guidelines for their use. *European Journal of Information Systems, 21*(1), 22–48.
52. Ringle, C. M., Wende, S., & Becker, J.-M. (2022). *Smartpls 4*. http://www.smartpls.com
53. Ringle, C. M., Sarstedt, M., & Straub, D. W. (2012). Editor's comments: A critical look at the use of pls-sem in "mis quarterly". *MIS Quarterly, 36*(1), iii.
54. Rosen, L. D., Whaling, K., Carrier, L. M., Cheever, N. A., & Rokkum, J. (2013). The media and technology usage and attitudes scale: An empirical investigation. *Computers in human behavior, 29*(6), 2501–2511.
55. Salminen, J., Santos, J. M., Jung, S.-G., Eslami, M., & Jansen, B. J. (2020). Persona transparency: Analyzing the impact of explanations on perceptions of data-driven personas. *International Journal of Human-Computer Interaction, 36*(8), 788–800.
56. Shin, D., Lim, J. S., Ahmad, N., & Ibahrine, M. (2022). Understanding user sensemaking in fairness and transparency in algorithms: Algorithmic sensemaking in over-the-top platform. *AI & SOCIETY*.
57. Smith, W. P., & Tabak, F. (2009). Monitoring employee e-mails: Is there any room for privacy? *Academy of Management Perspectives, 23*(4), 33–48.
58. Spector, P. E. (2019). Do not cross me: Optimizing the use of cross-sectional designs. *Journal of Business and Psychology, 34*(2), 125–137.
59. Spiekermann, S., Krasnova, H., Hinz, O., Baumann, A., Benlian, A., Gimpel, H., Heimbach, I., Köster, A., Maedche, A., Niehaves, B., Risius, M., & Trenz, M. (2022). Values and ethics in information systems. *Business & Information Systems Engineering, 64*(2), 247–264.
60. Tabak, F., & Smith, W. P. (2005). Privacy and electronic monitoring in the workplace: A model of managerial cognition and relational trust development. *Employee Responsibilities and Rights Journal, 17*(3), 173–189.

61. Tarafdar, M., Page, X., & Marabelli, M. (2023). Algorithms as co–workers: Human algorithm role interactions in algorithmic work. *Information Systems Journal, 33*(2), 232–267.
62. Thielsch, M. T., & Hirschfeld, G. (2019). Facets of website content. *Human–Computer Interaction, 34*(4), 279–327.
63. Vaassen, B. (2022). Ai, opacity, and personal autonomy. *Philosophy & Technology, 35*(4).
64. Wang, W., & Benbasat, I. (2007). Recommendation agents for electronic commerce: Effects of explanation facilities on trusting beliefs. *Journal of Management Information Systems, 23*(4), 217–246.
65. Wang, W., & Benbasat, I. (2016). Empirical assessment of alternative designs for enhancing different types of trusting beliefs in online recommendation agents. *Journal of Management Information Systems, 33*(3), 744–775.
66. Wiener, M., Cram, W. A., & Benlian, A. (2023). Algorithmic control and gig workers: A legitimacy perspective of uber drivers. *European Journal of Information Systems, 32*(3), 485–507.
67. Zhou, L., Wang, W., Xu, J., Liu, T., & Gu, J. (2018). Perceived information transparency in b2c e-commerce: An empirical investigation. *Information & Management, 55*(7), 912–927.

Under the Neurodivergent Umbrella: A Qualitative Exploration of Neurodivergence and Remote Work

Lisa Kuhn and Florian J. Meier

Abstract It is estimated that one-fifth of the global population is neurodivergent. As remote work becomes more prevalent, there is a lack of knowledge about how neurodivergent individuals are affected by it. This paper explores how masking, a prevalent coping strategy affected by neuroableism, can be reduced through remote work. Masking is related to severe health consequences, even linked to suicide. We use a qualitative research approach and regular engagement with interviewees to deliver insights into neuromixed communication and collaboration. We show how *chronic technocomfort* and *episodic technorelief* reduce the need for masking. Emphasizing individual acknowledgment over diagnoses, this paper underscores the importance of alleviating workplace stressors induced by ableism. This paper contributes to the IS research stream of remote work by focusing on neurodivergent work experiences and interactions with video conferencing tools, employing collaboration and an intersectional perspective.

1 Introduction

It is not raining jobs when you're standing under the neurodivergent umbrella. Despite holding college degrees, a staggering 85% of autistic individuals in the US are unemployed [44]. Similarly, ADHD:ers [5] face a disproportionately high unemployment rate of around 8%, far exceeding the national average [43]. Further, ableist stereotypes contribute to a reduced *ability* to submerge in neuroconventional relational contexts [5, 64]. As such, ADHD:ers are subject to discrimination in employment, with cross-neurotype remote work being no exception. In general, cross-neurotype

L. Kuhn (✉) · F. J. Meier
Faculty of Business, Economics, and Law, University of Erlangen-Nuremberg, Erlangen, Germany
e-mail: lisa.kuhn@fau.de

F. J. Meier
e-mail: florian.j.meier@fau.de

C. M. Flath et al. (eds.), *Digital Innovation and Organizational Transformation*, Lecture Notes in Information Systems and Organisation 83,
https://doi.org/10.1007/978-3-032-08483-5_19

communication leads to the "Double Empathy Problem" [38], encompassing difficulties in reciprocal understanding between individuals with different cognitive clusters or dispositions. Particularly, the problem arises from differing perceptions of *the social world*, for instance between autistic and non-autistic spectrum individuals, leading to a breach in what is considered "social reality" for non-autistic spectrum individuals but is an everyday and often traumatic experience for autistic individuals [5, 38]. Bertilsdotter Rosqvist et al. [5] have introduced the term neuromixed conversations to relate to cross-neurotype communication. In neuromixed conversations, neurodivergent individuals might resort to masking, also referred to as camouflaging, as a coping strategy [2, 21, 31, 33, 70], to conceal one's true self [27] and to conform with neuroconventional norms [37]. Motivations for masking include concerns for safety and well-being due to the potential risks of verbal, emotional, and even physical assaults when not camouflaging [27]. Ableism forces affected persons to hide in plain sight. Masking drains mental health and is associated with threats to self-image and suicidality, as it brings about rejecting one's true self, inducing elevated levels of psychological stress [27, 48, 56].

Remote work, where individuals use information and communication technologies (ICTs) for virtual communication and collaboration [68], is prevalent among so-called knowledge workers and has become integral to everyday life [41].

With approximately one-fifth of the global population being neurodivergent [13], and masking—with its serious health implications—being a prevalent coping mechanism impacted by neuroableism, it becomes imperative to delve into neurodivergent experiences within the neuronormative remote workplace. Understanding the intricate relationship between ICT-induced aspects of remote work environments and neuromixed conversations is vital for unraveling how these factors contribute to masking.

This contribution explores perspectives and experiences pertaining to ICTs, including video conferencing (VC) tools, which often serve as sources of *technostress* in remote work settings [51, 68] and their connection to masking behaviors. *Technostress*, hereby, refers generally to adverse reactions individuals experience when interacting with information and communication technologies (ICTs) [51], which is linked to an overall decrease in well-being and performance [34, 35, 58, 63]. While this accounts for a broad spectrum of individuals, the concept of *technostress* may specifically affect cross-neurotype communication [56].

Instead of being named from external perspectives, participants are named by "someone who moves like [us]" [42, p. 147], aiming to contribute to a reframing of neuromixed communication within the critical discourse of neurodivergence [5, 37].In feminist tradition of *joint action* [15], with a "collective I", stressing "neurodivergent togetherness" [5, p. 5], neurodivergent individuals will be referred to as *one of us*. The research question collectively explored in the following is: How do neurodivergent individuals experience the remote workplace, and what factors contribute to un/masking behavior?

To answer the proposed research question, a qualitative approach was chosen. We conducted nine interviews with neurodivergent participants to highlight aspects of remote work adding to *technostress*, *technorelief*, and introducing *technocomfort* according to neurodivergent experiences. The findings of this paper contribute to the IS remote work research stream (e.g. [41]), emphasizing organizations' responsibility to acknowledge individuals rather than diagnoses. The neurodivergent gaze within the IS research stream on remote work, akin to other underrepresented groups, is notably underrepresented [36], signaling a substantial gap in the literature that warrants attention.

2 Background

2.1 Neurodivergence & Intersectionality

A recent study found evidence that approximately 10% of individuals who died by suicide in the UK were likely autistic but undiagnosed [8]. In general, autistic individuals are significantly more susceptible to experiencing suicidal thoughts and behaviors than non-autism spectrum people [7–9, 22, 49]. These prevalence rates are highest among adults who receive a diagnosis *later in life* [9]. In the context of ADHD, for instance, women or individuals assigned female at birth (AFAB) are more likely to be diagnosed *later in life* [11, 26, 39]. Both internalizing behaviors [30, 50, 71] and internalized ableism [39] as well as being socialized into normative gender roles with an emphasis on pleasing others [40, 67], *girls* are more likely to be misdiagnosed due to gender bias in ADHD assessments [6, 39, 46].

Not only gender but also racialized stereotypes lead to ADHD misdiagnoses [39]. This is *likely* due to biases from professionals, structural racism, imbalanced resources, stigma, and policies influencing service seeking in communities [72]. Neurodivergence, comprising about one-fifth of the global population, is prevalent, making up a significant part of the remote workforce. The next section explores emotional experiences in remote work, especially from a neurodivergent standpoint.

2.2 Technostress, Technorelief—But Make it Techno

When masking, neurodivergent people experience profound dissonance between their core identity and the ideal identity they feel pressured to pursue [27, 37, 56]. Despite recognizing masking as unhealthy, *one of us* might feel unsafe unmasking. According to a qualitative study by Saigot with autistic people, ICTs seems to simulate a "digital stage" filtering out "aspects of ambiguity", which supposedly reduces the strain of masking [56, p. 6925]. While ICTs cannot tackle the core problem of ableism, they nonetheless provide some relief in that moment and a digital space. One property of ICTs in that context is an input filter, which Saigot refers to as *technorelief*, and which is further described as facilitating "time outs" for autistic employees in which one can "tune into their perceptions and regain control of their collaborative experiences" [56, p. 6921]. Also, being able to use symbols such as emojis, allows for an outwardly display of emotions [56]. These findings are in line with other research indicating that ICTs are a preferred means for social connection in autistic people [24, 56]. However, where there is *technorelief*, there is *technostress*. Framed as the anti-pattern to *technorelief*, *technostress* can be defined as the adverse reaction to interacting with ICTs [51]. *Technostress* is associated with a decrease in well-being and a decline in so-called "user performance" [34, 35, 58, 63]. Evidence suggests that the level of perceived *technostress* is influenced by individual responses to ICT stimuli, this spectrum of perception is argued to be linked to personality traits [3, 35]. Research with individuals on the autism spectrum suggests that while ICTs present various advantages, they also entail significant drawbacks. For instance, social media's unpredictable interruptions can disrupt individual's workflow and potentially trigger emotional distress [3, 56]. The following Sect. 2.3 provides a more detailed overview of prior research on human interaction with VC tools.

2.3 Zoomed Out: Fatigue and Video Conferencing

Masking frequently involves concealing stimming behaviors, which serve as essential self-soothing mechanisms for navigating overstimulation [27, 56]. Suppression stimming behaviors can lead to significant distress, although individuals may feel safer hiding them, as mentioned earlier [56]. Videoconferencing fatigue, commonly known as "Zoom Fatigue" (ZF), refers to cognitive and emotional exhaustion resulting from the use of video conferencing (VC) tools, irrespective of the specific type of VC tool being utilized [14]. Bailenson [4] proposes four psychological causal mechanisms for Zoom Fatigue (ZF): visual distress, increased cognitive effort, mirror anxiety, and physical constraint. Visual distress arises from prolonged close-up eye gaze in virtual interactions, while increased cognitive effort is needed to interpret flattened visual impressions in virtual environments [4, 14, 45]. Mirror anxiety stems from constant self-evaluation prompted by seeing one's mirror image [14], and physical constraint arises from limited camera frames restricting mobility [4, 14]. According to Bailenson [4], these factors collectively contribute to the unique challenges of virtual communication, leading to fatigue not typically encountered in face-to-face interactions in non-neurodivergent people. There is some evidence that suggests that neurodivergent people navigate several stressors when interacting with VC tools, aggravated by a lack of technological accessibility and inadequate home environments [12, 66, 73]. These studies imply that VC environments are associated with higher levels of stress in people on the autism spectrum than in non-autism spectrum groups. For example, some studies imply that autistic people prefer looking at facial regions instead of looking for eye-contact [53]. As a result, staring eye-to-eye, close-up, into a VC tool, sometimes even at a "gallery" of faces is considered highly stressful [47]. By contrast, Saigot's findings highlight how the laptop's camera can act as an anchor point or proxy for eye-contact. Therefore, remote meetings are purportedly considered less stressful when it comes to eye-contact, than in-person meetings by autistic people [56]. Regardless, it is recommended that organizations take responsibility for mitigating stressors associated with VC tool interactions by optimizing the duration, frequency, and timing of VC meetings [66]. While some studies suggest that ICTs can alleviate barriers and enhance well-being for neurodivergent individuals in remote work settings [56], technostress may persist. The example of VC meetings with cameras on inducing Zoom Fatigue and potentially leading to masking behaviors contrasts with Saigot's [56] findings where participants viewed the camera as a convenient proxy for eye-contact, presenting conflicting perspectives. These discrepancies, especially regarding masking behavior, highlight the need for additional research or may reiterate the importance of prioritizing individual experiences over diagnostic labels.

3 Research Approach

3.1 Recruitment and Planning

In this qualitative study, flexible data collection techniques are employed to accommodate individualized collaboration and allow for adjustments and iterations as needed. To create a collaborative and communal experience from the get-go, relevant literature on collaborative qualitative research with neurodivergent groups [61] was consulted before recruitment and planning. The focus on a neurodivergent re-storying of neuromixed conversations is led by literature on neurodiversity studies [5, 55] and intersectionality [1, 18–20, 25, 29, 39, 52, 54]. Szulc [61] argues that in recruitment and planning, it is vital to include key information about the research project, provide sample questions, and share information on the research team through, for instance, a short bio [61]. Hence, the first author, who conducted and analyzed the interviews, furnished a comprehensive interview guide supplemented with a brief biography approximately two weeks prior to the interview scheduling. In that bio, the author stated that they are neurodivergent and shared their special interests. The interview guide includes a thorough explanation of key themes and why questions surrounding gender could be relevant. To emphasize the collaborative aspect, different ways of getting in touch before responding to the questions were offered. Further, it was emphasized that the interview guide was open for debate and adjustments. Participants engaged in improving the clarity and readability of the guide.

3.2 Data Collection

The interview guide, along with a brief biography of the first author, was disseminated to a private forum within the creative department of an international corporation with approximately four thousand employees headquartered in Asia, and to a semi-private network of neurodivergent professionals. A total of nine semi-structured interviews were conducted in English. The low response rate can be attributed to various factors, including the collaborative nature of the interviews, potentially inducing feelings of overwhelm. Additionally, some individuals hesitated due to (a) imposter syndrome, (b) fear of sounding "incompetent", and (c) uncertainty about their neurodivergence without clinical diagnoses. Again, obtaining clinical diagnoses is challenging due to biases, privilege, and time constraints [39, 72]. Moreover, research indicates a significant correlation between ADHD, stigma, low self-esteem, and imposter syndrome symptoms, potentially contributing to individuals' reluctance to share personal experiences [23].

All interviews were carried out by an AFAB neurodivergent researcher. The interviews, averaging twenty-five minutes each, prioritized participant agency and a low-sensory time and environment. Time, place, format, and means of the dialogue were chosen by interviewees [61] to allow for a comfortable setting. Three participants engaged via chat and two via email with the first author to improve the interview guide before the actual interviews took place. The interview questions primarily addressed experiences with neuromixed remote meetings and factors that enhance well-being during digital communication in the neuronormative work context. For example: (a) Do you or did you prepare yourself differently for online meetings compared to in-person meetings at the workplace? (b) Are there any aspects about remote meetings or work that you prefer as compared to in-person meetings or work situations? If so, why? The favored interview formats included conducting interviews either via Teams with cameras off, following a written interview guide, or through email correspondence. Interviewees received direct debriefing, including information on project milestones and deadlines for orientation. The median age of participants is 35, with three *of us* residing in East Asia and six in Europe. All participants hold a college degree. Two interviewees work in the wider field of information technology, and seven are engaged in creative fields, primarily involving translation, writing, and editing tasks. Participants were asked whether they would like to share their gender identity and/or the sex assigned at birth. Hereafter, 'assigned a female label at birth' and 'assigned a male label at birth' will be abbreviated as AFAB and AMAB, respectively. Additionally, the comorbidity of Autism Spectrum Disorder and ADHD will be referred to as AuDHD. One individual preferred not to disclose their diagnosis publicly and thus chose the label neurodivergent. Please refer to Table 1 for further details on the distribution of gender and neuro-identities among the interviewees.

3.3 Data Analysis

The methodological approach adopted in this study, incorporating regular engagement with interviewees, aims to mitigate potential bias and align with established literature [39, 69]. This approach cultivates reflective practices concerning researcher positionality, methodological choices, and interpersonal dynamics. Audio interviews

Table 1 Collaborators

One of Us	Gender Identity/Assigned Sex	Neurotype
A	Female/AFAB	ADHD
B	Female/AFAB	ADHD
C	Female/AFAB	ADHD
D	Female/AFAB	Neurodivergent
E	Non-Binary/AFAB	ADHD
F	Non-Binary/AFAB	AuDHD
G	Non-Binary/AMAB	AuDHD
H	Male/AMAB	ADHD & Dysthymia
I	Male/AMAB	AuDHD

were transcribed using the software ‘f4transcript’. As discussed in Sect. 3.1, to enable an intersectional exploration of the data and promote collaboration, prior works by Morgan [39] and Szulc [61] were consulted to guide the methodological approach. Using the Gioia method [17], the written interview texts underwent multiple readings to develop a comprehensive understanding of the narratives. Initial codes were generated through iterative line-by-line open-coding [10]. Subsequently, focused coding was conducted to consolidate initial codes and establish analytical coherence. The texts were then revisited considering these new focused codes [10]. Finally, the codes were aggregated into second-order themes and subsequently into three third-order dimensions: *episodic technorelief*, *chronic technocomfort*, and *technostress*, to subsume our data [17]. This approach facilitated an intersectional exploration of the data. Prioritizing intersectionality is crucial, particularly in areas with limited research, to amplify a broad spectrum of voices and experiences [39, 65]. Consequently, an interpretivist intersectional paradigm, which emphasizes multiple interpretations, was employed.

4 Findings

The findings of this paper comprise three major dimensions: individuals’ *chronic technocomfort* and *episodic technorelief* within neuromixed remote work. Additionally, themes related to *technostress* were identified. Overall, participants reached a consensus that remote work considerably reduces stress compared to the confines of a corporate office environment. As one interviewee succinctly put it, “I do not think that I can ever go back working in an office” (one of us C, ADHD). Due to the parsimony of the paper, we could not include the entire data structure table [17]. Figure 1 summarizes our findings, depicting the aggregated dimensions and reflecting both first and second order concepts. For example, the first order concept “I greatly benefit

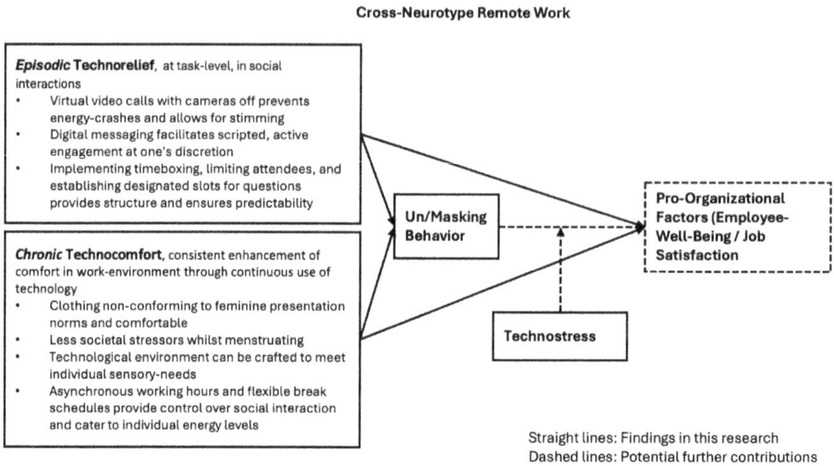

Fig. 1 Cross-neurotype remote work

from the focus on text communication' is aggregated into the second order theme 'use of ICTs alleviate stressors', referring to *episodic technorelief*.

4.1 Technocomfort

All AFAB participants noted that office environments often exert pressure to conform to feminine presentation norms, which can include expectations to wear uncomfortable clothes and makeup. Consequently, as emphasized by one interviewee, leveraging technology for remote work significantly enhances job-related well-being:

"Having no societal pressure to dress 'properly' is wonderful. I get to feel comfortable in sweatpants or pajamas, and I don't have to worry about dealing with menstrual issues in a public space" (one of us D, neurodivergent). Another interviewee further underscores the additional stress of menstruating while being at the office, explaining the challenge of managing conflicting situations while maintaining a composed demeanor: "I find it perplexing how I am supposed to maintain a smile while bleeding in public and enduring uncomfortable clothing, yet simultaneously fulfill my work obligations and remain prepared for trivial small talk at any moment" (one of us F, AuDHD). Remote work, within a more controlled and less hostile environment (e.g. at home), is considered less burdensome by the interviewees and hints toward feelings of *technocomfort*. Emphasized through *technocomfort*, individuals experience a reduced need for masking in the work environment, facilitated by the IT-enabled option for remote work. Furthermore, one person described the challenges of office dynamics, noting, "It is very hard to focus on my task when colleagues' emotional states seem to be constantly reflected in my body (…) It's exhausting" (one of us G, AuDHD). Another participant shared extreme measures taken to cope with frequent interruptions, including arriving at the office early to focus before distractions arose and staying late into the evening to work in peace, ultimately resulting in burnout (one of us F, AuDHD). This sets the stage for exploring how technology empowers individuals to control their work environment, fostering *technocomfort* and thereby enhancing productivity.

All of us unanimously agreed on the significant reduction of sensory stressors associated with office environments, particularly open-space offices, when working remotely.

Hereby, highlighting the adaptability of the home environment to individual needs, contrasting it with the often conflicting demands of colleagues in office settings, such as temperature preferences, lighting levels, and the need for social interaction. One interviewee noted that they "get much more work done at home, because nobody distracts me simply by passing by my office door" (one of us I, AuDHD). Additionally, having more control over environmental stimuli and social interactions was noted to limit the occurrence of meltdowns and energy crashes (one of us B, ADHD). Three interviewees pointed out that aforementioned stimuli present in office environments, can trigger migraines (F, AuDHD & I, AuDHD & D, neurodivergent). Furthermore, the ability to "follow routines independently" and experience "less supervisor control" were identified as key advantages of remote work in terms of autonomy, leading to *technocomfort* (E, ADHD & H, ADHD & Dysthymia & F, AuDHD & G, AuDHD & I, AuDHD). This decreased need to adapt to the environment results in reduced masking behavior: "When I work from home, I feel less pressured to conform to norms like sitting 'normally' or not wearing sunglasses, even though my eyes are sensitive", highlighting how remote environments allow "me to move and behave" without the need for masking (one of us F, AuDHD). Participants also emphasized the flexibility of remote work, allowing to work during most productive hours, even if it's later in the day. This theme emerged consistently throughout the conversations, indicating the importance of accommodating individual productivity peaks to enhance performance.

4.2 *Technorelief*

With the COVID-19 pandemic, remote work and digital written communication were embraced, being perceived as conducive to reducing stress. Participants appreciate the control over communication and interruptions afforded by digital platforms, contrasting with the disruptions experienced in office settings. The combination of setting boundaries and relying on text-based communication emerged as a recurring theme, facilitating active engagement at one's discretion: "I greatly benefit from the focus on text communication (…) With text messages, which is how most of our communication is handled with remote work, I get to actively decide when to engage and when to be left alone" (one of us D, neurodivergent). This alleviates the need for masking prompted by the stress of immediate responses and communication demands. Additionally, participants noted that using digital messages allowed them more time to *prepare* for conversations, crafting questions and potential responses. Again, this enhances sense of control during interactions, feeling reassured by having structured and scripted discourse to follow rather than needing to engage in spontaneous conversation. Some participants mentioned using tools like ChatGPT to reflect on their messages before sending them to colleagues (F, AuDHD & G, AuDHD). These findings underline feelings of *technorelief* as they portray how the use of technology alleviates stressors inherent to analog communication.

4.3 Technostress

Audiovisual online meetings generally require less preparation from participants but can be significantly more draining compared to in-person sessions when cameras are required to be switched on. One participant expressed, "It feels like I need to stare and perform the entire time (…) Camera meetings exhaust me immensely (…) I usually plan some time away from the PC or at least schedule 'solo work', aka tasks that require no further social interaction (…) Please let's make cameras always optional. Please." (one of us D, neurodivergent). Another participant likened online meetings with cameras to "having to stare into colleagues' soul" (one of us F, AuDHD). In contrast, when cameras are not mandatory during remote sessions, they are perceived as far less stressful than in-person meetings, because interviewees feel less compelled to mask. The absence of 'obnoxious face galleries' alleviates pressure, allowing individuals to engage in stimming. Examples provided by interviewees include simultaneously watching a show or pacing in circles. All agreed that keeping their hands busy, whether by doing chores like laundry or fidgeting, provides essential relief. As one interviewee stated, "I found that it is harder for me to focus if my hands 'rest', it helps my focus to have something to do while talking and thinking" (one of us D, neurodivergent).

Online meetings also introduce new sources of insecurity related to technology and meeting-culture. For instance, one participant expressed anxiety about differences in equipment usage, such as using a full-on headset versus a clip-on Bluetooth piece, and concerns about the quality of colleagues' microphones, having "them sounding like they're using a tin can and a piece of string" (one of us H, ADHD & Dysthymia). Also, navigating interruptions caused by lagging internet connections during conversations poses a challenge. Most participants noted a lack of structure in remote meetings, leading to unnecessary length and chaos. This included meetings scheduled abruptly without clear objectives, which could have been addressed more efficiently via "a three sentence E-Mail" (one of us A, ADHD). To address these issues, one participant suggested implementing timeboxing, limiting attendees to essential personnel, and establishing designated times for questions (one of us I, AuDHD). These recommendations are directed towards organizations to improve meeting efficiency.

5 Discussion

This study aims to gain a deeper understanding of underrepresented groups, in this case ADHD:ers, within information systems research [36]. We explore how neurodivergent individuals experience the remote workplace. Despite affecting approximately one-fifth of the population [13], neurodivergence has been largely overlooked in information systems research. From our findings, we conclude that for neurodivergent individuals, remote work can be advantageous in decreasing masking behaviors on two different levels: *chronic technocomfort* and *episodic technorelief*. However, evidence of *technostress* emerged when individuals lacked the freedom to control their technological setup and environment.

All participants in this research preferred remote work over in-situ work. The reported experiences around gender performance and menstruation align with recent studies suggesting that individuals on the autism spectrum may experience heightened sensory overstimulation and difficulties in regulating emotions and behavior during menstruation [59]. As such, Steward et al. (2020) note, menstruation intersects with social norms and stereotypes of femininity, shaping interactions in key realms, such as gender/sex identity and public bathroom access. These are influenced by the biologically and socially constructed gender/sex binary, imposing preexisting constraints on trans and genderqueer menstruators' experiences in social and physical environments [16, 59]. Hence, it makes sense that individuals find *technocomfort* in remote work, within a more controlled and less hostile environment. Additionally, according to participants, the *technocomfort* of exerting control over the work environment fosters feelings of contentment and, consequently, enhances productivity. Research indicates that digital communication tools alleviate cognitive burden and social anxiety, supporting participants' experiences with remote work dynamics [56]. *Technocomfort*, being chronic, arises from the continuous use of technologies in remote work, which consistently enhance individuals' comfort in their work environment.

Given the prevalence of sleep disorders among ADHD:ers and people on the autism spectrum [57], the *technocomfort* of asynchronous working hours can be particularly beneficial for individuals who struggle with insomnia or find themselves more productive during nighttime hours [28]. Providing employees with greater control and agency over their work schedules translates to fostering increased flexibility from an organizational standpoint.

Furthermore, digital communication fosters *technorelief*, promoting active engagement and boundary-setting, which reinforces findings from previous studies [56]. The *episodic technorelief* contrasts with *technocomfort*, emerging during virtual interactions and alleviating stress in social work-related situations. *Technorelief* is also experienced at the task-level, aiding individuals in communication and responding to colleagues' requests. Participants noted that digital messaging provided them with extra time to prepare for conversations, enhancing their sense of control during interactions. Some participants mentioned using tools like ChatGPT to reflect on their messages before sending. These findings align with previous research suggesting that individuals on the autism spectrum prefer the combination of flexible response time, preparedness, and written communication [27, 56]. However, remote work can also induce *technostress*, when the technological setup is forced upon individuals. Participants emphasized experiencing stress when required to turn on their cameras during remote meetings.

These experiences align with research suggesting that VC meetings feel draining, akin to staring closely and eye-to-eye at a "gallery" of faces, as mentioned in Sect. 2.3 [47]. However, this contrasts with some prior research with employees on the autism spectrum, which found the camera to be a less stressful proxy for eye contact [56]. Participants experience *technorelief* during meetings with VC tools when they can switch off their cameras, reducing the need to mask. Similarly, Saigot [56] suggests that engaging in stimming feels safer when it can be hidden from interlocutors. Furthermore, turning off cameras helps prevent sharing motor tics associated with Tourette's syndrome and reduces self-presentation-related concerns for individuals on the autism spectrum [60, 62, 73]. Discrepancies may be attributed to the comorbidity of ADHD among participants on the autism spectrum or individual variations in needs and comfort zones. Thus, organizations may benefit from focusing on individual characteristics and needs rather than diagnoses [28]. As indicated by previous research and this study, there is a tension in remote collaborations, where effectiveness often relies on a standardized setup, such as having cameras turned on [68]. However, previous research has largely overlooked the perspective of neurodivergent individuals, particularly in neuromixed remote work collaborations, where a nuanced understanding of the necessary technological setup and boundaries is crucial. This study initiates a novel discussion bridging previous findings on remote work with a heightened focus on individual differences, particularly for ADHD:ers. Interestingly, the proposed adaptions in this research might also benefit non-neurodivergent groups and those unaware of their neurodivergence. Organizations are invited to contemplate why it falls upon neurominorities, who have been *named* antisocial and worse, to facilitate both decent neuromixed conversations and work environments for all.

6 Limitations and Future Work

The collection of experiences in this article comes from individuals with different identities and positionalities regarding, for instance, class, gender, and a/sexuality. Some grew up with internalized ableism and/or were diagnosed *later in life*, therefore coping with and dismantling neuroconventional relational contexts and "dis/ability and the promises of neurodiversity" in different ways [5, 64]. In neuromixed conversations, neurominority positions are forced into hiding, or masking, which has dramatic consequences for health in neurominority populations. These structural aspects could contribute to a lower response rate, as well as potentially inducing feelings of overwhelm due to the collaborative nature of the research. Future studies from a neurodivergent perspective could further develop our findings to gain a more nuanced understanding of how *technocomfort* and *technorelief* affect un/masking behavior. While one technology might provide *technorelief* in some situations, another might cause *technostress.* Future research should explore how different technologies affect *technorelief*, *technostress*, and masking behavior in neuromixed communication and collaboration.

Future research could employ a longitudinal approach to investigate how un/masking behaviors are affected by *technorelief* and *technocomfort*, and how these influence job-related constructs such as job satisfaction and well-being. We recognize the partial explanatory power of person-environment fit [32] for a subset of our data concerning *technocomfort*, *technorelief*, and *technostress.* As outlined in prior sections, there exists a discernible correlation between privileges and the probability of diagnoses with ADHD [20]. Since all *collaborators* in this contribution have access to health care, it clearly lacks experiences of those who don't and/or are still struggling to be diagnosed. As this paper delves into issues concerning narratives about dis/ability and employment, it is imperative to underscore that an individual's value should never be contingent upon their professional pursuits or quantifiable work hours. This discussion is not aimed at, nor can it construct a programmatic tool for organizations to increase *participation* of neurodivergent individuals in the labor force solely to accrue more quantifiable work hours. Rather, it serves as an endeavor to reconceptualize communication dynamics, particularly within the workplace that can inform other kinds of conjunctural work with a primary emphasis on fostering greater empathy and compassion among individuals.

This collaborative research aims to provide insights from within the neurodivergent community rather than being viewed through an external, neurotypical gaze [5, 37]. The shared insights and recommendations are intended to improve neuromixed communication [25], challenging external perceptions, fostering longitudinal change beyond the neurodivergent community. In essence, by alleviating the burden of masking, it is evident that ICTs alone cannot address the fundamental issue of ableism. However, they may contribute to mitigating some of its consequences, albeit temporarily and within specific digital contexts.

References

1. Attoe, D. E., & Climie, E. A. (2023). Miss. diagnosis: A systematic review of ADHD in adult women. *Journal of Attention Disorders, 27*(7), 645–657. https://doi.org/10.1177/10870547231161533
2. Attwood, A. (2006). *The complete guide to Asperger's syndrome.* Jessica Kingsley Publishers.
3. Ayyagari, R., Grover, V., & Purvis, R. (2011). Technostress: Technological antecedents and implications. *MIS Quarterly, 35*(4), 831–858. https://doi.org/10.2307/41409963
4. Bailenson, J. N. (2021). Nonverbal overload: A theoretical argument for the causes of Zoom fatigue. *Technology, Mind, and Behavior, 2*(1). https://doi.org/10.1037/tmb000003
5. Bertilsdotter Rosqvist, H., Hultman, L., Österborg Wiklund, S., Nygren, A., Storm, P., & Sandberg, G. (2023). Naming ourselves, becoming neurodivergent scholars. *Disability & Society, 40*(1), 128–147. https://doi.org/10.1080/09687599.2023.2271155

6. Bruchmüller, K., Margraf, J., & Schneider, S. (2012). Is ADHD diagnosed in accord with diagnostic criteria? Overdiagnosis and influence of client gender on diagnosis. *Journal of Consulting and Clinical Psychology, 80*(1), 128. https://doi.org/10.1037/a0026582
7. Cassidy, S. (2020). Suicidality and self-harm in autism spectrum conditions. In *The Oxford handbook of autism and co-occurring psychiatric conditions*. Oxford University Press. https://doi.org/10.1093/oxfordhb/9780190910761.013.18
8. Cassidy, S., Au-Yeung, S., Robertson, A., Cogger-Ward, H., Richards, G., Allison, C., Bradley, L., Kenny, R., O'Connor, R., Mosse, D. et al. (2022). Autism and autistic traits in those who died by suicide in England. *The British Journal of Psychiatry, 221*(5), 683–691. https://doi.org/10.1192/bjp.2022.21
9. Cassidy, S., Bradley, P., Robinson, J., Allison, C., McHugh, M., & Baron-Cohen, S. (2014). Suicidal ideation and suicide plans or attempts in adults with asperger's syndrome attending a specialist diagnostic clinic: A clinical cohort study. *The Lancet Psychiatry, 1*(2), 142–147. https://doi.org/10.1016/s2215-0366(14)70248-2
10. Charmaz, K. (2014). *Constructing grounded theory*. Sage.
11. da Silva, A. G., Malloy-Diniz, L. F., Garcia, M. S., & Rocha, R. (2020). Attention-deficit/hyperactivity disorder and women. In J. Rennó Jr., G. Valadares, A. Cantilino, J. Mendes-Ribeiro, R. Rocha, & A. G. da Silva (Eds.), *Women's mental health: A clinical and evidence-based guide* (pp. 215–219). Springer. https://doi.org/10.1007/978-3-030-29081-8_15
12. Das, M., Tang, J., Ringland, K. E., & Piper, A. M. (2021). Towards accessible remote work: Understanding work-from-home practices of neurodivergent professionals. In *Proceedings of the ACM on Human-Computer Interaction 5*(CSCW1) (pp. 1–30). https://doi.org/10.1145/3449282
13. Doyle, N. (2020). Neurodiversity at work: A biopsychosocial model and the impact on working adults. *British Medical Bulletin, 135*(1), 108. https://doi.org/10.1093/bmb/ldaa021
14. Fauville, G., Luo, M., Queiroz, A. C., Bailenson, J. N., & Hancock, J. (2021). Zoom exhaustion & fatigue scale. *Computers in Human Behavior Reports, 4*, 100119. https://doi.org/10.1016/j.chbr.2021.100119
15. Francis, B., & Hey, V. (2009). Talking back to power: Snowballs in hell and the imperative of insisting on structural explanations. *Gender and Education, 21*(2), 225–232. https://doi.org/10.1080/09540250802680081
16. Frank, S. E., & Dellaria, J. (2020). Navigating the binary: A visual narrative of trans and genderqueer menstruation. In *The Palgrave handbook of critical menstruation studies* (pp. 69–76). Springer. https://doi.org/10.1007/978-981-15-0614-7_7
17. Gioia, D. A., Corley, K. G., & Hamilton, A. L. (2013). Seeking qualitative rigor in inductive research: Notes on the Gioia methodology. *Organizational Research Methods, 16*(1), 15–31. https://doi.org/10.1177/1094428112452151
18. Glasofer, A., & Dingley, C. (2022). Diagnostic and medication treatment disparities in African American children with ADHD: A literature review. *Journal of Racial and Ethnic Health Disparities, 9(5)*, 2027–2048. https://doi.org/10.1007/s40615-021-01142-0
19. Glenn, D. (2022). Neuroqueer Heresies: Notes on the neurodiversity paradigm, autistic empowerment, and postnormal possibilities. *World Futures, 78*(5), 339–341. https://doi.org/10.1080/02604027.2022.2094194
20. Goetz, T. G., & Adams, N. (2022). The transgender and gender diverse and attention deficit hyperactivity disorder nexus: A systematic review. *Journal of Gay & Lesbian Mental Health, 28*(1), 2–19. https://doi.org/10.1080/19359705.2022.2109119
21. Gould, J., & Ashton-Smith, J. (2011). Missed diagnosis or misdiagnosis? Girls and women on the autism spectrum. *Good Autism Practice (GAP), 12*(1), 34–41.
22. Griffiths, S., Allison, C., Kenny, R., Holt, R., Smith, P., & Baron-Cohen, S . (2019). The vulnerability experiences quotient (VEQ): A study of vulnerability, mental health and life satisfaction in autistic adults. *Autism Research ,12*(10), 1516–1528. https://doi.org/10.1002/aur.2162
23. Hailey, K. (2023). Diversity in diagnosis: A comparative relationship between the social behavioral effects and timing of ADHD diagnosis in African American adults. In *Senior Projects Spring*.

24. Hassrick, E. M., Holmes, L. G., Sosnowy, C., Walton, J., & Carley, K. (2021). Benefits and risks: A systematic review of information and communication technology use by autistic people. In *Autism in Adulthood, 3*(1), 72–84. https://doi.org/10.1089/aut.2020.0048
25. Hillary, A. (2020). Neurodiversity and cross-cultural communication. In *Neurodiversity studies: A new critical paradigm* (pp. 91–107). https://doi.org/10.4324/9780429322297-10
26. Hinshaw, S. P., Nguyen, P. T., O'Grady, S. M., & Rosenthal, E. A. (2022). Annual research review: Attention-deficit/hyperactivity disorder in girls and women: Underrepresentation, longitudinal processes, and key directions. *Journal of Child Psychology and Psychiatry, 63*(4), 484–496. https://doi.org/10.1111/jcpp.13480
27. Hull, L., Petrides, K., Allison, C., Smith, P., Baron-Cohen, S., Lai, M.-C., & Mandy, W. (2017). "Putting on my best normal": Social camouflaging in adults with autism spectrum conditions. *Journal of Autism and Developmental Disorders, 47*, 2519–2534. https://doi.org/10.1007/s10803-017-3166-5
28. Kalmanovich-Cohen, H., & Stanton, S. J. (2023). How can work from home support neurodiversity and inclusion? *Industrial and Organizational Psychology, 16*(1), 20–24. https://doi.org/10.1017/iop.2022.93
29. Kelly, C., Sharma, S., Jieman, A.-T., & Ramon, S. (2022). Sense-making narratives of autistic women diagnosed in adulthood: A systematic review of the qualitative research. In *Disability & Society* (pp. 1–33). https://doi.org/10.1080/09687599.2022.2076582
30. Klefsjö, U., Kantzer, A. K., Gillberg, C., & Billstedt, E. (2021). The road to diagnosis and treatment in girls and boys with ADHD–gender differences in the diagnostic process. *Nordic Journal of Psychiatry, 75*(4), 301–305. https://doi.org/10.1080/08039488.2020.1850859
31. Kopp, S., & Gillberg, C. (2011). The Autism Spectrum Screening Questionnaire (ASSQ)-revised extended version (ASSQ-Rev): An instrument for better capturing the autism phenotype in girls? A preliminary study involving 191 clinical cases and community controls. *Research in Developmental Disabilities, 32*(6), 28752888. https://doi.org/10.1016/j.ridd.2011.05.017
32. Kristof-Brown, A., & Guay, R. P. (2011). Person–environment fit. *APA handbooks in psychology*. https://doi.org/10.1037/12171-001
33. Lai, M.-C., Lombardo, M. V., Pasco, G., Ruigrok, A. N., Wheelwright, S. J., Sadek, S. A., Chakrabarti, B., Consortium, M. A., & Baron-Cohen, S. (2011). A behavioral comparison of male and female adults with high functioning autism spectrum conditions. *PLOS One, 6*(6), e20835. https://doi.org/10.1371/journal.pone.0020835
34. Maier, C., Laumer, S., & Eckhardt, A. (2015). Information technology as daily stressor: Pinning down the causes of burnout. *Journal of Business Economics, 85*, 349–387. https://doi.org/10.1007/s11573-014-0759-8
35. Maier, C., Laumer, S., Wirth, J., & Weitzel, T. (2019). Technostress and the hierarchical levels of personality: A two-wave study with multiple data samples. *European Journal of Information Systems, 28*(5), 496–522. https://doi.org/10.1080/0960085X.2019.1614739
36. Marabelli, M., Zaza, S., Masiero, S., Li, J., & Chudoba, K. (2023). Diversity, equity and inclusion in the AIS: Challenges and opportunities of remote conferences. *Information Systems Journal, 33*(6), 1370–1395. https://doi.org/10.1111/isj.12458
37. McDermott, C. (2021). Theorising the neurotypical gaze: Autistic love and relationships in the bridge (bron/broen 2011–2018). *Medical Humanities*. https://doi.org/10.1136/medhum-2020-011906
38. Milton, D. E. (2012). On the ontological status of autism: The 'double empathy problem'. *Disability & Society, 27*(6), 883–887. https://doi.org/10.1080/09687599.2012.710008
39. Morgan, J. (2023). Exploring women's experiences of diagnosis of ADHD in adulthood: Aqualitative study. *Advances in Mental Health* (pp. 1–15). https://doi.org/10.1080/18387357.2023.2268756
40. Mowlem, F., Agnew-Blais, J., Taylor, E., & Asherson, P. (2019). Do different factors influence whether girls versus boys meet ADHD diagnostic criteria? Sex differences among children with high ADHD symptoms. *Psychiatry Research 272*, 765–773. https://doi.org/10.1016/j.psychres.2018.12.128

41. Mueller, C., Maedche, A., Schwabe, G., Ackerman, M., & Wulf, V. (2023). Home office: Working from a private place. *Business & Information Systems Engineering, 65*(3), 233–234. https://doi.org/10.1007/s12599-023-00797-9
42. Mullis, C. (2019). Reflection: Autistic-coded characters and fans in fandom. *Canadian Journal of Disability Studies, 8*(2), 147–156. https://doi.org/10.15353/cjds.v8i2.495
43. MyDisabilityJob: ADHD Employment statistics—Update 2024. https://mydisabilityjobs.com/statistics/adhd-employment/
44. MyDisabilityJob: Autism and Employment Statistics—Update 2024. https://mydisabilityjobs.com/statistics/autism-employment/
45. Nadler, R. (2020). Understanding "zoom fatigue": Theorizing spatial dynamics as third skins in computer-mediated communication. *Computers and Composition, 58*, 102613. https://doi.org/10.1016/j.compcom.2020.102613
46. Nussbaum, N. L. (2012). ADHD and female specific concerns: A review of the literature and clinical implications. *Journal of Attention Disorders, 16*(2), 87–100. https://doi.org/10.1177/1087054711416909
47. Parmar, K. R., Porter, C. S., Dickinson, C. M., Pelham, J., Baimbridge, P., & Gowen, E. (2021). Visual sensory experiences from the viewpoint of autistic adults. *Frontiers in Psychology, 12*, 633037. https://doi.org/10.3389/fpsyg.2021.633037
48. Pearson, A., & Rose, K. (2021). A conceptual analysis of autistic masking: Understanding the narrative of stigma and the illusion of choice. *Autism in Adulthood, 3*(1), 52–60. https://doi.org/10.1089/aut.2020.0043
49. Pelton, M. K., Crawford, H., Robertson, A. E., Rodgers, J., Baron-Cohen, S., & Cassidy, S. (2020). Understanding suicide risk in autistic adults: Comparing the interpersonal theory of suicide in autistic and non-autistic samples. *Journal of Autism and Developmental Disorders, 50*, 3620–3637. https://doi.org/10.1007/s10803-020-04393-8
50. Quinn, P. O., & Madhoo, M. (2014). A review of attention-deficit/hyperactivity disorder in women and girls: Uncovering this hidden diagnosis. *The Primary Care Companion for CNS Disorders, 16*(3), 27250. https://doi.org/10.4088/PCC.13r01596
51. Ragu-Nathan, T., Tarafdar, M., Ragu-Nathan, B. S., & Tu, Q. (2008). The consequences of technostress for end users in organizations: Conceptual development and empirical validation. *Information Systems Research, 19*(4), 417–433. https://doi.org/10.1287/isre.1070.0165
52. Rainer, T., Lim, J. K., He, Y., Perdomo, J., Nash, K. A., Kistin, C. J., Tolliver, D. G., McIntyre, E., & Hsu, H. E. (2023). Structural racism in behavioral health presentation and management. *Hospital Pediatrics, 13*(5), 461–470. https://doi.org/10.1542/hpeds.2023-007133
53. Robertson, C. E., & Baron-Cohen, S. (2017). Sensory perception in autism. *Nature Reviews Neuroscience, 18*(11), 671–684. https://doi.org/10.1038/nrn.2017.112
54. Rosentel, K., López-Martínez, I., Crosby, R. A., Salazar, L. F., & Hill, B. J. (2021). Black transgender women and the school-to-prison pipeline: Exploring the relationship between anti-trans experiences in school and adverse criminal-legal system outcomes. *Sexuality Research and Social Policy, 18*, 481–494. https://doi.org/10.1007/s13178-020-00473-7
55. Rosqvist, H. B., Chown, N., & Stenning, A. (2020). *Neurodiversity studies: A new critical paradigm*. Routledge. https://doi.org/10.4324/9780429322297
56. Saigot, M. (2024). Unveiling technorelief: Enhancing neurodiverse collaboration with digital capabilities. In *Proceedings of the Annual Hawaii International Conference on System Sciences* (pp. 6921–6931). United States. https://doi.org/10.24251/hicss.2023.829
57. Singh, K., & Zimmerman, A. W. (2015). Sleep in autism spectrum disorder and attention deficit hyperactivity disorder. *Seminars in pediatric neurology* (Vol. 22, pp. 113–125). Elsevier. https://doi.org/10.1016/j.spen.2015.03.006
58. Srivastava, S. C., Chandra, S., & Shirish, A. (2015). Technostress creators and job outcomes: theorising the moderating influence of personality traits. *Information Systems Journal, 25*(4), 355–401. https://doi.org/10.1111/isj.12067
59. Steward, R., Crane, L., Roy, E. M., Remington, A., & Pellicano, E. (2020). "Life is much more difficult to manage during periods": Autistic experiences of menstruation. In *The Palgrave handbook of critical menstruation studies* (pp. 751–761). https://doi.org/10.1007/s10803-018-3664-0

60. Szulc, J. M. (2022). Amo model for neuro-inclusive remote workplace. *Personnel Review, 51*(8), 1867–1882. https://doi.org/10.1108/PR-02-2022-0085
61. Szulc, J. M. (2023). Towards more inclusive qualitative research: the practice of interviewing neurominorities. *Labour and Industry, 33*(2), 179–187. https://doi.org/10.1080/10301763.2022.2148853
62. Tang, J. (2021). Understanding the telework experience of people with disabilities. In *Proceedings of the ACM on Human-Computer Interaction 5*(CSCW1), 1–27. https://doi.org/10.1145/3449104
63. Tarafdar, M., Pullins, E. B., & Ragu-Nathan, T. (2015). Technostress: Negative effect on performance and possible mitigations. *Information Systems Journal, 25*(2), 103–132. https://doi.org/10.1111/isj.12042
64. Thomas, C. (2004). Rescuing a social relational understanding of disability. *Scandinavian Journal of Disability Research, 6*(1), 22–36. https://doi.org/10.1080/15017410409512637
65. Thomson, S. B. (2010). Sample size and grounded theory. *Journal of Administration and Governance, 5*(1), 45–52.
66. Tomczak, M. T., Mpofu, E., & Hutson, N. (2022). Remote work support needs of employees with autism spectrum disorder in Poland: Perspectives of individuals with autism and their coworkers. *International Journal of Environmental Research and Public Health, 19*(17), 10982. https://doi.org/10.3390/ijerph191710982
67. Waite, R. (2010). Women with ADHD: It is an explanation, not the excuse du jour. *Perspectives in Psychiatric Care, 46*(3), 182–196. https://doi.org/10.1111/j.1744-6163.2010.00254.x
68. Waizenegger, L., McKenna, B., Cai, W., & Bendz, T. (2020). An affordance perspective of team collaboration and enforced working from home during Covid-19. *European Journal of Information Systems, 29*(4), 429–442. https://doi.org/10.1080/0960085X.2020.1800417
69. Walsh, R. (2003). The methods of reflexivity. *The Humanistic Psychologist, 31*(4), 51–66. https://doi.org/10.1080/08873267.2003.9986934
70. Wing, L. (1981). Sex ratios in early childhood autism and related conditions. *Psychiatry Research, 5*(2), 129–137. https://doi.org/10.1016/0165-1781(81)90043-3
71. Young, S., Adamo, N., Ásgeirsdóttir, B. B., Branney, P., Beckett, M., Colley, W., Cubbin, S., Deeley, Q., Farrag, E., Gudjonsson, G. et al.: Females with ADHD: An expert consensus statement taking a lifespan approach providing guidance for the identification and treatment of attention-deficit/hyperactivity disorder in girls and women. *BMC Psychiatry, 20*(1), 1–27. https://doi.org/10.1186/s12888-020-02707-9
72. Zhao, X., Hayes, T., Timmons, A. C., Wu, W., & Frazier, S. L. (2023). Unpacking inequities in ADHD diagnosis: Examining individual-level race/ethnicity and state-level online information-seeking patterns. *Administration and Policy in Mental Health and Mental Health Services Research,50*(4), 576–590. https://doi.org/10.1007/s10488-023-01259-w
73. Zolyomi, A., Begel, A., Waldern, J. F., Tang, J., Barnett, M., Cutrell, E., McDuff, D., Andrist, S., & Morris, M. R. (2019). Managing stress: The needs of autistic adults in video calling. *Proceedings of the ACM on Human-Computer Interaction 3*(CSCW) (pp. 1–29). https://doi.org/10.1145/3359236

Understanding Algorithmic Management in the Traditional Work Context: A Quantitative Analysis

Amelie Lena Schmid and Manuel Wiesche

Abstract Algorithmic management (AM) is increasingly transferred to the traditional work context (TWC) and is applied to support the management of permanent workers. AM only partially replaces human managers here, but the core elements of AM remain similar. Hence, AM is implemented into pre-existing organizational structures to enhance processes and performance. While AM in the platform-based context is already well-researched, its implications for the TWC from a managerial perspective remain unclear. To enhance our understanding, we conduct a quantitative study analyzing the utilization of AM at an international automotive supplier. Using linear mixed modeling, we examine a data set of 12,743 error records and reveal that AM has performance advantages in the TWC as it reduces the error resolving time of workers. Furthermore, the impact of influencing factors such as workforce involvement, task complexity, time of work, and experience with AM are considered, evaluated, and discussed.

1 Introduction

The introduction of intelligent algorithms at the workplace heavily influences various aspects of work, such as the interaction among workers and managers. If algorithms are utilized to assume workforce management practices and increasingly take on managerial roles, it is also described as algorithmic management (AM) [150]. Its characteristics are mainly rooted in the gig economy, where well-known platforms such as Uber or Upwork are the key players [38]. AM can scale such platform-based businesses, enabling them to react to fluctuating demands. Since the workforce is

A. L. Schmid (✉)
TU Dortmund University, Dortmund, Germany
e-mail: amelie.schmid@tu-dortmund.de

A. L. Schmid · M. Wiesche
Robert Bosch GmbH, Reutlingen, Germany
e-mail: manuel.wiesche@tu-dortmund.de

C. M. Flath et al. (eds.), *Digital Innovation and Organizational Transformation*, Lecture Notes in Information Systems and Organisation 83,
https://doi.org/10.1007/978-3-032-08483-5_20

structured and managed by AM, it can be considered a critical success factor for their business models, significantly increasing their value contribution [22, 188].

Even outside the platform-based work context, AM gains more and more importance in the traditional work context (TWC) [22]. Well-established firms (e.g., in manufacturing, hospitality, or warehouses) envision how the AM approach can be integrated into their existing organizational structures and improve their processes and performance [38]. In this context, AM is perceived as a "sociotechnical process emerging from the continuous interaction of organizational members and the algorithms that mediate their work" [120]. Hence, managers of established organizations must consider minor adaptations before transferring AM from the platform-based work context to the TWC. For example, AM in the traditional work setting coexists with human managers. It results in a complementary character of the algorithm, as the human-to-human interaction is supported by AM [22, 274]. Moreover, the organizational logic in traditional work should still follow an organizational hierarchy and not a platform logic [12, 39, 156]. Despite these adaptations, the core elements of AM remain the same as AM in the TWC still includes the analysis of the massive amounts of data in real-time to improve learning algorithms that coordinate workers and inform automated managerial decision-making [164, 188]. Besides, AM in the TWC also increases managerial power by mediating the pre-existing relationship between managers and workers [120]. Finally, for managers in established organizations, using AM to manage their available workforce efficiently is highly relevant [38, 261].

While these performance advantages of platform companies are well noted [22], a validation of the impact of AM in the TWC is needed [206]. From this managerial perspective, further research on relevant moderators that influence the outcome of AM in the TWC is of high interest. Hence, we raise the following research question: *What performance impact does AM have in the TWC, and what are the relevant influencing factors?*

We anticipate the recent call of [38] for more quantitative approaches in this research area. Thus, we conducted a quantitative analysis within an international automotive supplier. We collected data on 15,297 manufacturing errors at a German manufacturing plant between January and September 2023. Analyzing the data with linear mixed modeling, we find that AM significantly reduces error resolving time. Further moderating aspects such as workforce involvement, task complexity, time of work, and experience with AM are investigated and discussed.

2 Theoretical Background

AM can take over coordination and control activities traditionally performed by human managers [188]. As a result, an ongoing interaction occurs between workers and the algorithms that facilitate their work [120]. In the platform-based context, these interactions are facilitated via digital interfaces such as mobile apps managed by hidden data processes. Thus, a real co-working environment between employees and managers does not exist, and the algorithm is considered as a co-worker asking to conduct a specific task [250]. In the platform-based work context, algorithmic matching and algorithmic control represent the two key dimensions. Algorithmic matching refers to the coordination of demand (customers) and supply (workers) and, e.g., serves as a marketplace. The platform aims to achieve the highest possible level of economic efficiency by, e.g., dynamic pricing strategies [188]. Algorithmic control makes use of algorithms capable of reviewing and controlling the actions of workers to ensure that their behavior aligns with the overall goals of the organization [54, 135]. This alignment can be realized, e.g., by implicit or explicit recommendations via the algorithm, restricting workers' access to complete information or targeting to reward high-performing workers with non-monetary or monetary incentives [135]. Based on this logic, algorithms create power asymmetries and constrain the actions of workers in the platform-based context [136, 277].

Whereas the utilization of algorithms for supervising freelance workers is well-established within the platform economy, there is an increase in AM usage in the TWC [22]. This increase holds for companies with traditional business models, such as Amazon or Deutsche Post [22, 156]. For managers in such organizations, using AM to manage workers is relevant for enhancing processes and performance [38]. It must be noted that traditional organizations must consider some adaptations for transferring the AM approach from the platform-based work context toward the TWC (Table 1). A vital adaptation is that AM only partially substitutes managers in the TWC, and the organizational logic still follows the organizational hierarchy as compared to the platform-based work context [156]. Besides, AM complements existing organizational structures, strengthens established operations, or is attached to existent processes [38, 274]. In addition, traditional companies organize work with AM around the established team structures of separate work units, while platform-based businesses are predominately task-centric [133]. Hence, the individual output within work units of traditional companies is more complex to optimize due to organizational intersections since work unit relevant outcomes might be preferred over organizationally preferred results [200]. Nevertheless, the fundamental elements of AM also apply to the TWC. For example, the existing hierarchical power dynamics between managers and workers are strengthened by AM [120]. Besides, the collected data enhances the algorithms that manage workers and improves automated decision-making of management [164, 188].

However, studies analyzing AM in the TWC are rare or predominantly focus on the workers' perspective. For example, Kellogg et al. [135] investigate literature-based the role of AM in reshaping established manager-worker relationships, especially when workers resist to its implementation. In the field of human resource management, [172] show the effects of AM on workers' autonomy and value creation. In sales organizations, the salespeople are instructed to follow algorithmic recommendations made by AM, which often leads to a defensive attitude. Finally, Lee [149] analysis the perceived fairness and trustworthiness of algorithmic decisions in the TWC. Especially with tasks that are attributed to humans, algorithms were recognized as less fair and trustworthy.

Table 1 From platform-based to the traditional work context

Elements to consider	Platform-based work context	Traditional work context	Sources
Role of management	Substituted by AM	Co-exists with AM	[156]
Role of AM	Foundation of any processes	Attached to pre-existing processes	[38, 136]
Communication	Via AM	Via AM & people	[22]
Form of organization	Task-centric	Team and work unit centric	[133, 200]
Optimization of output	Individual observation and tracking	Overall observation, tracking	[190]
Employment	Self-employed, no permanent contract	Direct employment, permanent contract	[12, 156]
Work environment	Isolated, AM as co-worker	Colleagues & AM as co-workers	[156, 250]

Overall, studies on AM in the TWC need to consider the managerial perspective for utilizing AM. For managers of established organizations, the validation of the performance effects of AM in the TWC, as well as possible influencing factors, are of high relevance [206].

3 Model and Hypotheses

It is well known that AM has an enormous efficiency potential and performance advantage in platform-based businesses [121]. Uber uses AM, e.g., to monitor the productivity and performance of its workers [188]. Besides, AM on platforms provides employees performance metrics. These metrics allow a comparison among employees and an overall performance evaluation of each individual to increase the productivity [60, 101]. Within the context of platforms, workers, therefore, aim to receive above-average ratings to avoid automatically sanctioning by the platforms' AM. Hence, sanctioning AM increases platform performance [140, 278]. Outside of the platform-based work context, it is generally acknowledged that algorithmic technologies benefit to employers, e.g., through improved efficiency in decision-making or coordination activities [135]. First researchers already show in a simulation study that AM can reduce the average duration of tasks in the TWC [131]. Hence, we suppose:

Hypothesis 1: AM decreases the error resolving time. In the TWC, AM is implemented in a pre-existing work environment with an established manager-worker relationship [156]. Thus, managers must actively involve workers in the implementation process to ensure successful outcomes [120, 283]. Enhanced algorithmic transparency, understandability, or explanations, e.g., regarding the general process and outcomes, can lead to better reactions and improve usability [139, 142]. Hence, managers need to empower workers to provide feedback on the algorithmic work and raise questions when encountering confusion in the new setting [250]. Based on these reasons, the following hypothesis is proposed:

Hypothesis 2: Workforce involvement positively moderates the relationship between AM and the error resolving time.

For successful AM utilization, managers within the TWC need to understand the role of task characteristics that directly influence the application of the algorithm and its outcomes. Kordzadeh and Ghasemaghaei [139] argue that for tasks with a high impact workers are more sensitive to algorithmic biases and might react unfairly to algorithmic processes. This reaction contrasts low-impact tasks, which are less prone to workers' concerns. In the field for automation, Vimalkumar et al. [266] show that variances in task complexity lead to distinctions in their potential for automation. Whereas simple tasks with a low complexity have a higher automation potential, complex tasks are much more challenging to automate. Based on these arguments, we propose to analyze the effects regarding differing complexity levels of tasks, which describe how demanding a specific task is for the worker [67]. Thus, we hypothesize the following:

Hypothesis 3: Task complexity negativly moderats the relationship between AM and the error resolving time.

Employees' well-being at the workplace is of high relevance for managers in the TWC, as workers are directly employed with a permanent contract [12]. However, working at nighttime is associated with increased health risks like sleep disturbances or disruption of the circadian rhythms [25]. Besides, the severe issues regarding workers' well-being and excessive sleepiness during night shifts can also harm performance [51]. First researchers show that AM can positively impact the overall work environment, e.g., by avoiding overwork or enhancing decision-making [131, 135, 206]. To analyze whether managers can use AM in the TWC to enhance the working conditions during the nighttime we posit:

Hypothesis 4: Time of work (nighttime) positivly moderates the relationship between AM and the error resolving time compared to daytime.

Previous studies show that more experience within a particular role or with a specific task enhances workers' knowledge or job performance [210]. According to the law of practice, performance within a job increases as workers practice a task more frequently [194]. The reasons lay in the fact that workers undergo a learning curve and enhance their performance based on task repetitions and training [89]. In the gig economy, recent results show that same-day experience increases workers' productivity [93]. Based on these assertions, the following hypothesis is proposed (Fig. 1):

Hypothesis 5: Experience with AM positively moderates the relationship between AM and the error resolving time.

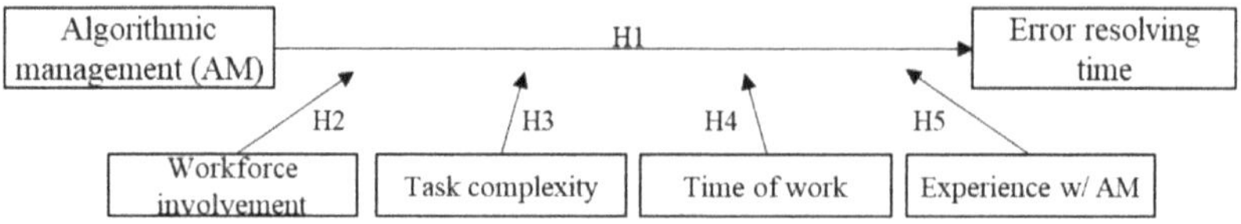

Fig. 1 Research model

4 Methodology

4.1 Research Setting, Data and Sample

We analyse the production data of an international automotive supplier to answer our research question. Our research object is using smart watches as an AM approach at a German manufacturing plant. The workers in our setting are responsible for ensuring the continuous operation of nine production lines, e.g., by maintaining equipment, promptly resolving any occurring errors, proactively preventing interruptions, and reducing downtime. They are split into four teams with similar backgrounds and demographics, working in a three-shift model. On average, two workers are responsible for three manufacturing lines representing a confusing working atmosphere. Moreover, the work environment is characterized by a high task fluctuation, which requires different skills and equipment. Hence, managers have the responsibility of overseeing and coordinating their employees' work efforts. Starting from April 1st 2023, AM is installed to optimize the communication on the shop floor and to deliver the right information at the right time to the right worker. AM informs the responsible worker in real time about machine alarms or events, also described as algorithmic recommending [135]. In addition, AM provides detailed information related to the error type, the position of the error, and how to fix it. Besides, it collects data on error resolving to predict patterns and to proactively identify upcoming errors. Finally AM learns from workers' responses, enabling managers to adjust the work processes accordingly. An illustrative example of the error report is shown in Fig. 2.

We collect production data between January 2023 and September 2023. The uncorrected dataset contains 15,297 data points, and each data point represents one occurring error at a production line. The following information is linked for each error: error duration in seconds [s], date, timestamp [CET], line number, and error number. We match additional descriptive data to each record, e.g., the shift, processing team, error complexity, and whether the error is processed with or without AM (smart watch). Based on process expert review, we removed all errors with an error duration below 5 s and above 300 s to enhance data quality. In addition, we clear out all errors with missing or wrong information. This results in the final data set of 12,743 errors.

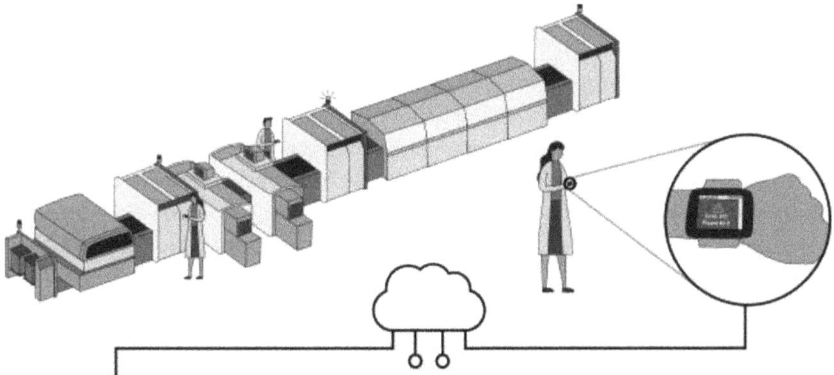

#	Error duration [s]	Date	Timestamp [CET]	Shift	Team	Line number	Error number	Error complexity	Smart watch
15	5.23	2023-01-02	22:59:53	night	4	9	100	1	0
16	119.25	2023-01-03	23:04:23	night	4	5	144	3	0
17	66.84	2023-01-03	23:06:02	night	4	7	145	1	0
…	…	…	…	…	…	…	…	…	…
8255	57.05	2023-04-03	13:59:48	early	2	2	101	2	1
8256	31.14	2023-04-03	14:00:54	late	3	7	118	1	1
8257	26.23	2023-04-03	14:02:18	late	3	6	122	1	1

Fig. 2 Research setting with table illustrating sample data

4.2 *Measures*

Dependent variable. We want to quantify the error resolving time as our dependent variable. Generally, minimizing error resolving time is essential for cycle time, which is fundamental for overall production performance [13, 16]. For that purpose, we use the specific indicator variable *error duration* in order to measure error resolving time. The definition of error duration is as follows: it refers to the time interval between the occurrence of an error and its resolution by an operator or expert. The primary goal is to reduce the error duration since therewith, production downtime can be decreased and thus overall plant performance can be increased. Accordingly, we are able to collect the error duration of 22 different error types, resulting in an overall 12,743 errors.

Independent variables. Starting from the 1st of April 2023, 8902 errors were processed by the operators using AM, resulting in a binary measure for AM (1 = w/ AM; 0 = w/o AM), which can be identified based on the error type. Besides, we included four independent variables in our model (H2-H5), namely workforce involvement, task complexity, time of work, and experience w/ AM. These independent variables will be defined in the following. The variable *workforce involvement* (H2) refers to the fact that the affected workers of a team were involved in the use case development of the AM approach at their workplace or not. In our case, the employees of team 4 were actively involved by providing feedback and bringing in their own ideas, whereas the employees of teams 1–3 were not involved. Thus, we measure workforce involvement by comparing team 4 with teams 1–3. In order to measure *task complexity* (H3), we use the variable error complexity. Error complexity is ordinally scaled and takes on values between 1 (low error complexity, can be easily solved by the worker) and 4 (high error complexity, workers cannot solve the error on their own). Process experts have categorized the complexity of the different error types according to a pre-defined scheme. Moreover, we considered the respective shift during which the errors were observed in order to measure the *time of work* (H4). The shift model includes the early shift (6:00 am–2:00 pm), late shift (2:00 pm–10:00 pm), and night shift (10:00 pm–6:00 am). As nighttime refers to the period between sunset and sunrise, we consider the night shift as nighttime and the early and late shifts as daytime. As the last dependent variable, we measure the experience effect of the workers with the AM by the variable *experience w/ AM* (H5). To measure it, we counted the number of days AM is in place and used by the workers, starting from the 1st of April 2023 onwards.

4.3 Data Analysis

We use linear mixed modeling for our data analysis. Longitudinal data from repeated observations of 22 different error numbers at nine manufacturing lines provides evidence for the verification of this kind of modeling [71]. It must be noted that linear mixed models (LMMs) are generally robust to violations of the model assumptions, such as data not following a normal distribution [229]. The LMM is an extension of the general linear regression, allowing to model and estimate fixed and random effects. Thus, the LMM is also called the random effects model [71]. In contrast to the fixed effects (unknown population parameters), random effects refer to subject-specific effects and can be described as grouping factors [168, 229]. The overall goal of including subject-specific effects is to enhance the estimation of the fixed effects [71]. We modeled two random effects: (i) manufacturing line and (ii) error number. The variable manufacturing line indicates which of the nine lines the error occurred. This is included as a random effect to avoid overlooking any bias coming from any line. Moreover, the error number was modeled as a random effect to consider modifications based on specific error types.

5 Results

5.1 Descriptive Statistics

Between January 2023 and September 2023, around 2/3 of the errors (8902) are processed w/ AM and around 1/3 (3841) errors w/o AM. In our sample—as a baseline—the average error duration without AM is 77.55 s. With AM, the error duration significantly decreases by 11.14 s (14.36%) to 66.41 s. The error processing is distributed across the four teams almost equally. While team 1 processed 2856 errors (22.4%), team 2 processed most errors (3381; 26.5%). Team 3 & 4 processed 3249 errors (25.5%) and 3257 errors (25.6%). The errors occur in three different shifts in which all teams rotate. 3864 errors occurred during the early shift, representing 30.3%, the smallest amount. 4057 errors (31.8%) occurred in the late shift and 4822 (37.8%) in the night shift. A total of 22 different error numbers are included in our sample, appearing on one of the nine production lines. Each error type occurs with varying frequency, between 3 and 4666 times within the nine months. Most occurring errors (11,257) are attributed to complexity level 1. Besides, 1096 errors are categorized as complexity level 2, 194 as complexity level 3, and 196 as complexity level 4.

5.2 Linear Mixed Model

Table 2 summarizes the descriptive statistical values such as estimate, standard deviation (SD), p-value of the dependent variable *error duration w/ AM,* and all independent variables. *Manufacturing line* and *error number* are modeled as random effects.

The coefficient of determination R^2 represents an essential indicator for the amount of variance explained by any linear model [71]. For LMMs, reporting R^2 has become increasingly relevant. In this specific case, R^2 can be categorized into two types: *marginal* R^2 (= variance explained by the fixed factors) and *conditional* R^2 (= variance explained by both fixed and random factors) [192]. Whereas the marginal R^2 can be reported with 0.015, the conditional R^2 reveals that 0.329 of variance can be explained by the entire model. It is acceptable, as most of our explanatory variables are statistically significant [203]. We start our analysis by examining the effect of AM on workers' performance. In particular, we consider the error resolving time (= error duration) to be a relevant performance outcome. Our results show that AM has a significant negative effect on the *error duration* (exp($b = 0.310$; $p < 0.001$. Thus, it can be confirmed that AM significantly reduces the error resolving time (H1 and thus enhances work performance. For *workforce involvement* (H2), we found mixed effects. We can support that team 4 is significantly faster than team 1 (exp(b) = 0.013; p = 0.025) if both teams apply AM. However, we do not find this effect in team 4 compared to team 2 (exp(b) = −0.069; p = 0.606) and team 3 (exp(b) = −0.024; p = 0.002). Analyzing the level of *error complexity* (H3) reveals that AM does not work for all error levels the same way. The error duration of errors with complexity level 3 (medium level) is significantly higher with AM compared to errors with complexity level 1 (exp(b) = 0.263; p = 0.021). In contrast, we cannot identify significant effects for errors with a complexity of 4 (exp(b) = 0.631; p = 0,250) and complexity of 2 (exp(b) = − 0.138; p = 0.285). Thus, we can only partially confirm *error complexity* as the assumed negative moderator (H3). The results concerning the *time of work* (H4) show that the early shift is significantly slower with AM compared to the night shift (exp(b) = 0.010; p = 0.008), whereas the late shift is

Table 2 Results of the linear mixed model

Parameter	Estimate	Standard deviation	*p*-value	95% conf. interval	
				Lower	Upper
Intercept	3.787	0.105	<0.001	3.578	3.905
Algorithmic management	−0.310	0.048	<0.001	−0.404	−0.217
Team (team 4)					
Team 1	−0.102	0.046	0.025	−0.192	−0.013
Team 2	−0.082	0.050	0.102	−0.180	−0.016
Team 3	−0.168	0.044	<0.001	−0.254	−0.081
Complexity (complexity = 1)					
Complexity = 2	−0.224	0.193	0.247	−0.605	0.157
Complexity = 3	−0.107	0.212	0.613	−0.523	0.309
Complexity = 4	0.142	0.255	0.578	−0.361	0.654
Shift (night)					
Shift (early)	−0.123	0.042	0.004	−0.205	−0.040
Shift (late)	0.019	0.042	0.650	−0.063	0.102
Workforce involvement (team 4)					
Workforce involve. (team 1)	0.123	0.055	0.025	0.015	0.231
Workforce involve. (team 2)	−0.028	0.054	0.606	−0.134	0.078
Workforce involve. (team 3)	0.163	0.053	0.002	0.059	0.267
Error complexity (compl. = 1)					
Error complexity (compl. = 2)	0.082	0.076	0.285	−0.068	0.232
Error complexity (compl. = 3)	0.438	0.189	0.021	0.067	0.808
Error complexity (compl. = 4)	0.224	0.195	0.250	−0.158	0.606
Nighttime (shift = night)					
Daytime (shift = early)	0.133	0.050	0.008	0.034	0.231
Daytime (shift = late)	−0.203	0.051	<0.001	−0.304	−0.103
Experience w/ AM (days)	0.002	0.000	<0.001	0.001	0.002

Dependent variable: Error duration [ln]
$N = 12{,}743$; R^2 (marginal) = 0.015; R^2 (conditional) = 0.329; SD of random effects: 0.070

significantly faster ($\exp(b) = -0.184$; $p < 0.001$) compared to the night shift. Hence, the hypothesized positive moderation effect of *nighttime* (H3) can only be confirmed for the early shift. Finally, we cannot support H5, as the error duration with AM is slightly increased with increasing *experience w/AM* ($\exp(b) = 0.002$; $p<0.001$).

We check the robustness of our results by analyzing the error duration of two error types that are not processed with AM starting April 1st, 2023. The robustness check reveals that the error duration without AM does not significantly decrease.

6 Discussion

As the first distinct contribution, we demonstrate with our study utilizing a quantitative analysis that the performance enhancements of workers observed in the platform business can also be recognized in the TWC. Interestingly, the performance increase is not based on individual tracking or related to penalties and sanctions in case of bad performance [189, 278]. Instead, it is based on the enhanced coordination of workers within the complex work environment and an increased decision-making efficiency related to the error resolving [135]. It is an important finding, as it can serve as a confirmation for traditional companies to implement AM to improve performance while respecting legal obligations and further encourage platform-based businesses to use AM ethically [189].

In addition, four relevant moderators are examined that influence the outcome of AM in the TWC. From a managerial perspective, the impact of (i) workforce involvement, (ii) task complexity, (iii) time of work, and (iv) experience w/ AM is considered. Strikingly, we find out that missing workforce involvement does not negatively affect performance outcomes. This clearly contradicts general studies on technology implementation, which promote a participatory approach as a relevant success factor [80, 120, 283]. Most probably, the reason is that we are dealing with highly standardized work, which generally eases automation [90]. Hence, AM is not considered disruptive in the TWC and represents a rather competence-enhancing than a competence-destroying technology [82, 257]. This can be explained by the fact that AM is attached to the pre-exisitng organizational environment. Hence, it augments a few managerial activities [120]. In the platform context, work is broken down into small parts (gigs), which disrupts the work identity, as the purpose of the work is more challenging to recognize due to this transience of work [12]. Besides, employees can hardly control the AM in the platform context, which means that autonomy is reduced [136]. The lack of autonomy leads to a classification of AM as a disruptive system since the algorithm replaces human roles step-by-step [118, 122].

On a generic level, it is recommended to structure tasks at varying degrees of complexity on a labor platform to attract the most suitable worker [251]. We advance the discussion by showing a U-shape relationship for the moderation effect of task complexity in the TWC. Whereas AM has limited functionality for easy and complex tasks, AM significantly impacts tasks with medium complexity. Consequently, managers need to look at the type of task before implementing AM in the TWC. Tasks with high complexity are more difficult to automate since there are multiple possibilities to achieve a desired outcome, and further expert knowledge is needed [67, 266]. This finding proves that AM does not enhance workers' performance for highly complex tasks. In contrast, work performance for relatively simple tasks is also not improved by AM. One reason might be that such tasks are too simple [206]. Hence, the support of AM is not relevant to the workers. Instead, AM is highly meaningful for tasks with medium complexity. Generally, medium complex tasks indicate that not all complexity contribution elements, such as the goal, input factors, or process components apply [157]. Here, AM reduces perceived task complexity and enables workers to enhance their work performance [45, 141].

Furthermore, we can show that AM eases the working environment, e.g. during night shifts. In warehouses, AM is considered to enhance working conditions by simplifying workers' jobs or by solving problems [206]. We contribute to these findings and display that AM can level out performance fluctuation during nighttime. Studies in the medical domain indicate that shifts at nighttime are linked to disturbed circadian rhythms and inadequate sleep [25]. Such conditions frequently result in psychosomatic stress, manifesting as depression, burnout, cognitive impairment, and an elevated risk of work-related errors [51, 160]. This compensating effect of AM during nighttime emphasizes that AM can be introduced by managers as a supportive IS in the TWC. Such supportive systems have already been proven to reduce perceived stress [68].

Finally, our results do not show an influence of experience w/ AM on performance in the TWC. The reasons might be that the workers are familiar with the existing processes and can thus immediately exploit the full potential of AM [122]. The role of increasing knowledge and experience with the algorithm is also highly debated within the platform-based work business. On the one hand, gig workers use their increasing algorithmic competency to work around or manipulate the algorithm. This effect is also called "algoactivism" and refers to the individual or collective resistance towards AM [122, 135]. On the other hand, Guha and Corsten [93] show that same-day experience can also benefit gig workers' productivity up to a certain threshold.

Overall, our study contributes to research on AM as it validates the positive performance impact of AM in the TWC. Besides, we highlight the managerial perspective and show relevant moderating aspects that influence the success of transferring the AM approach to the TWC.

6.1 Pracitcal Implications

AM has great potential for established companies. However, selecting the right application areas with distinct carefulness is essential. While AM has a considerable impact related to tasks with medium complexity, it is not reasonable to implement AM for every single task. Nonetheless, we can recommend further integrating relevant aspects from the platform-based work context within the TWC, e.g., adding competency profiles and considering task complexity. With this approach, the tasks could be deployed even more precisely to a specific worker, which leads to performance enhancement. Additional contributions, such as recommendations or instructions, could further increase the value contribution of AM in practice.

6.2 Limitations and Further Research

The present study is subject to some limitations. First, we acknowledge that work performance is a multidimensional concept that includes various additional dimensions besides error resolving time. Thus, further research could also consider soft aspects such as the leadership style [155]. Second, the analyzed sample is limited to a time period of 9 months. It might lead to the fact that the effect of experience w/ AM (H5) could not be confirmed. However, while experience w/ AM might cause enhanced performance, it can also stimulate workarounds and a manipulation of AM [122]. As a future work, it would be reasonable to collect further data to analyze such consequences. Third, the data set was limited to error types that were subjected to the usage of AM. Nevertheless, most of the collected error types have not been processed using AM since the 1st of April. Hence, these error types were excluded from the analysis, which might bias our results. Effort was taken to consider these errors in the robustness check. Nevertheless, further analysis might be needed as soon as AM is implemented for a more extensive range of errors.

References

1. Abbasi, A., Sarker, S., & Chiang, R. (2016). Big data research in information systems: toward an inclusive research agenda. *Journal of the Association for Information Systems*. https://doi.org/10.17705/1jais.00423
2. Adadi, A., & Berrada, M. (2018). Peeking inside the black-box: A survey on explainable Artificial Intelligence (XAI). *IEEE Access*. https://doi.org/10.1109/ACCESS.2018.2870052
3. Agarwal, R., & Dhar, V. (2014). Editorial—Big data, data science, and analytics: The opportunity and challenge for IS research. *Information Systems Research*. https://doi.org/10.1287/isre.2014.0546
4. Agrawal, A., Gans, J. S., & Goldfarb, A. (2019). Artificial intelligence: The ambiguous labor market impact of automating prediction. *Journal of Economic Perspectives*. https://doi.org/10.1257/jep.33.2.31
5. Alavi, M., Leidner, D. E., & Mousavi, R. (2024). Knowledge management perspective of generative artificial intelligence. *Journal of the Association for Information Systems*. https://doi.org/10.17705/1jais.00859
6. Allen, C., Wallach, W., & Smit, I. (2006). Why machine ethics? *IEEE Intelligent Systems*. https://doi.org/10.1109/MIS.2006.83
7. Alsheibani, S. A., Cheung, Y., Messom, C., et al. (2022). Winning AI strategy: Six-steps to create value from artificial intelligence. *AMCIS 2020 Proceedings*.
8. Alter, S. (2013). Work system theory: Overview of core concepts, extensions, and challenges for the future. *Journal of the Association for Information Systems*. https://doi.org/10.17705/1jais.00323
9. Anderson, K. J. B., Courter, S. S., McGlamery, T., et al. (2010). Understanding engineering work and identity: A cross-case analysis of engineers within six firms. *Engineering Studies*. https://doi.org/10.1080/19378629.2010.519772.
10. Anthony, C. (2018). To question or accept? How status differences influence responses to new epistemic technologies in knowledge work. *Academy of Management Review*. https://doi.org/10.5465/amr.2016.0334.

11. Arshad, Y., Ahlan, A. R., & Syed Ibrahim, S. N. (2013). Combining grounded theory and case study methods in IT outsourcing study. *Journal of Information Systems Research and Innovation*: 84–93.
12. Ashford, S. J., Caza, B. B., & Reid, E. M. (2018). From surviving to thriving in the gig economy: A research agenda for individuals in the new world of work. *Research in Organizational Behavior*. https://doi.org/10.1016/j.riob.2018.11.001
13. Ayabakan, S., Bardhan, I. R., & Zheng, Z. (2017). A data envelopment analysis approach to estimate it-enabled production capability. *MIS Quarterly, 41*(1), 189–205. https://doi.org/10.25300/MISQ/2017/41.1.09
14. Azmi, A., Kamin, Y., Noordin, M., et al. (2018). Towards industrial revolution 4.0: Employers' expectations on fresh engineering graduates. *International Journal of Engineering and Technology, 7*(28), 267–272.
15. Bala, H., & Venkatesh, V. (2013). Changes in employees' job characteristics during an enterprise system implementation: A latent growth modeling perspective. *MIS Quarterly*. https://doi.org/10.25300/MISQ/2013/37.4.06
16. Banker, R. D., Bardhan, I. R., Chang, H., & Lin, S. (2006). Plant information systems, manufacturing capabilities, and plant performance. *MIS Quarterly, 30*(2), 315. https://doi.org/10.2307/25148733
17. Barley, S. R., Bechky, B. A., & Milliken, F. J. (2017). The changing nature of work: Careers, identities, and work lives in the 21st century. *Academy of Management Discoveries*. https://doi.org/10.5465/amd.2017.0034
18. Barley, W. C., Leonardi, P. M., & Bailey, D. E. (2012). Engineering objects for collaboration: Strategies of ambiguity and clarity at knowledge boundaries. *Human Communication Research*. https://doi.org/10.1111/j.1468-2958.2012.01430.x
19. Bechky, B. A. (2003). Sharing meaning across occupational communities: The transformation of understanding on a production floor. *Organization Science*. https://doi.org/10.1287/ORSC.14.3.312.15162
20. Benbasat, I., Goldenstein, D., & Mead, M. (1987). The case research strategy in studies of information systems. *MIS Quarterly, 11*(3).
21. Benbya, H., Strich, F., & Tamm, T. (2024). Navigating generative artificial intelligence promises and perils for knowledge and creative work. *Journal of the Association for Information Systems*. https://doi.org/10.17705/1jais.00861
22. Benlian, A., Wiener, M., Cram, W. A., et al. (2022). Algorithmic management. *Business & Information Systems Engineering*. https://doi.org/10.1007/s12599-022-00764-w
23. Birkinshaw, J., & Gibson, C. (2004). Building ambidexterity into an organization. *MIT Sloan Management Review*.
24. Boer, E. de, Friligos, Y., Giraud, Y., et al. (2022). *Transforming advanced manufacturing through Industry 4.0*.
25. Boivin, D. B., & Boudreau, P. (2014). Impacts of shift work on sleep and circadian rhythms. *Pathologie-biologie*. Epub ahead of print 20 September 2014. https://doi.org/10.1016/j.patbio.2014.08.001
26. Boudreau, M.-C., & Robey, D. (2005). Enacting integrated information technology: A human agency perspective. *Organization Science*. https://doi.org/10.1287/orsc.1040.0103
27. Boudreau, P., Dumont, G. A., & Boivin, D. B. (2013). Circadian adaptation to night shift work influences sleep, performance, mood and the autonomic modulation of the heart. *PloS one*. Epub ahead of print 26 July 2013. https://doi.org/10.1371/journal.pone.0070813
28. van den Broek, E., Sergeeva, A., & Huysman Vrije, M. (2021). When the machine meets the expert: An ethnography of developing AI for hiring. *MIS Quarterly*. https://doi.org/10.25300/MISQ/2021/16559
29. Bryant, A., & Charmaz, K. (2007). *The SAGE handbook of grounded theory*. 1 Oliver's Yard, 55 City Road, London England EC1Y 1SP. Sage Publications Ltd, UK
30. Brynjolfsson, E., & McAfee, A. (2016). *The second machine age: Work, progress, and prosperity in a time of brilliant technologies*. W.W. Norton & Company.

31. Brynjolfsson, E., Hitt, L. M., & Kim, H. H. (2011, December 4–7). Strength in numbers: How does data-driven decisionmaking affect firm performance? In D. F. Galletta & T.-P. Liang (Eds.),*Proceedings of the 32nd International Conference on Information Systems.*
32. Brynjolfsson, E., & Mitchell, T. (2017). What can machine learning do? Workforce implications. *Science (New York, N.Y.).* https://doi.org/10.1126/science.aap8062
33. Buber, R., & Holzmüller, H. H. (Eds.). (2009). *Qualitative marktforschung*. Gabler.
34. Bughin, J. (2018). Why AI isn't the death of jobs. *MIT Sloan Management Review.*
35. Buttazzo, G. (2022). *Can we trust ai-powered real-time embedded systems?*
36. Calisto, F. M., Nunes, N., & Nascimento, J. C. (2022). Modeling adoption of intelligent agents in medical imaging. *International Journal of Human-Computer Studies.* https://doi.org/10.1016/j.ijhcs.2022.102922
37. Calisto, F. M., Santiago, C., Nunes, N., et al. (2021). Introduction of human-centric AI assistant to aid radiologists for multimodal breast image classification. *International Journal of Human-Computer Studies.* https://doi.org/10.1016/j.ijhcs.2021.102607
38. Cameron, L., Lamers, L., Leicht-Deobald, U., et al. (2023). Algorithmic management: Its implications for information systems research. *Communications of the Association for Information Systems.*
39. Cappelli, P., & Keller, J. R. (2013). Classifying work in the new economy. *Academy of Management Review.* https://doi.org/10.5465/amr.2011.0302
40. Carroll, N., Conboy, K., Hassan, N. R., et al. (2023). Problematizing assumptions on digital transformation research in the information systems field. *Communications of the Association for Information Systems.* https://doi.org/10.17705/1CAIS.05322
41. Carroll, N., Hassan, N. R., Junglas, I., et al. (2023). Transform or be transformed: The importance of research on managing and sustaining digital transformations. *European Journal of Information Systems.* https://doi.org/10.1080/0960085X.2023.2187033
42. Carroll, N., & Maher, M. (2023). How shell fueled digital transformation by establishing DIY software development. *MIS Quarterly Executive, 22*(2), 99–127.
43. Carter, M., & Grover, V. (2015). Me, my self, and I(T): Conceptualizing information technology identity and its implications. *MIS Quarterly.* https://doi.org/10.25300/MISQ/2015/39.4.9
44. Cascio, W. F. (2000). Managing a virtual workplace. *Academy of Management Perspectives.* https://doi.org/10.5465/AME.2000.4468068
45. Chan, S. H., Song, Q., & Yao, L. J. (2015). The moderating roles of subjective (perceived) and objective task complexity in system use and performance. *Computers in Human Behavior.* https://doi.org/10.1016/j.chb.2015.04.059
46. Charmaz, K. (2014). Grounded theory in global perspective. *Qualitative Inquiry.* https://doi.org/10.1177/1077800414545235
47. Chen, L. Y.-H. (2020, 21–25 September). A conceptual framework for AI system development and sustainable social equality. In *2020 IEEE/ITU International Conference on Artificial Intelligence for Good (AI4G)* (pp. 101–106). IEEE.
48. Christin, A. (2017). Algorithms in practice: Comparing web journalism and criminal justice. *Big Data & Society.* https://doi.org/10.1177/2053951717718855
49. Christmann, D. (2023). Bosch bringt generative KI in die Produktion. https://www.bosch-presse.de/pressportal/de/de/bosch-bringt-generative-ki-in-die-produktion-260806.html. Accessed 8 April 2024.
50. Corbin, J. M., & Strauss, A. L. (2015). *Basics of qualitative research: Techniques and procedures for developing grounded theory.* Sage.
51. de Cordova, P. B., Bradford, M. A., & Stone, P. W. (2016). Increased errors and decreased performance at night: A systematic review of the evidence concerning shift work and quality. *Work.* https://doi.org/10.3233/WOR-162250
52. Cortellazzo, L., Bruni, E., & Zampieri, R. (2019). The role of leadership in a digitalized world: A review. *Frontiers in psychology.* Epub ahead of print 27 August 2019. https://doi.org/10.3389/fpsyg.2019.01938

53. Cram, W. A., & Wiener, M. (2020). Technology-mediated control: Case examples and research directions for the future of organizational control. *Communications of the Association for Information Systems*. https://doi.org/10.17705/1CAIS.04604
54. Cram, W. A., Wiener, M., Tarafdar, M., et al. (2022). Examining the impact of algorithmic control on uber drivers' technostress. *Journal of Management Information Systems*. https://doi.org/10.1080/07421222.2022.2063556
55. Crisan A., Fiore-Gartland, B., & Tory, M. (2021). Passing the data baton: A retrospective analysis on data science work and workers. *IEEE transactions on visualization and computer graphics*. Epub ahead of print 28 January 2021. https://doi.org/10.1109/TVCG.2020.3030340
56. Danks D., & London, A. J. (2017, 19–26 August). Algorithmic bias in autonomous systems. In F. Bacchus & C. Sierra (Eds.), *Proceedings of the twenty-sixth international joint conference on artificial intelligence* (pp. 4691–4697). International Joint Conferences on Artificial Intelligence Organization.
57. Davenport, T. H. (2018). *The AI advantage*. The MIT Press.
58. Davenport, T. H., & Dasgupta, S. (2019). How to set up an AI center of excellence. https://hbr.org/2019/01/how-to-set-up-an-ai-center-of-excellence. Accessed 20 March 2023.
59. Davis, G. F. (2016). Can an economy survive without corporations? Technology and robust organizational alternatives. *Academy of Management Perspectives*. https://doi.org/10.5465/amp.2015.0067
60. van Doorn, N. (2017). Platform labor: On the gendered and racialized exploitation of low-income service work in the 'on-demand' economy. *Information, Communication & Society*. https://doi.org/10.1080/1369118X.2017.1294194
61. Dremel, C., Herterich, M. M., Wulf, J., et al. (2017) How AUDI AG Established Big Data Analytics in Its Digital Transformation. *MIS Quarterly Executive, 16*(3).
62. Duan, Y., Edwards, J. S., & Dwivedi, Y. K. (2019). Artificial intelligence for decision making in the era of Big Data—Evolution, challenges and research agenda. *International Journal of Information Management*. https://doi.org/10.1016/j.ijinfomgt.2019.01.021
63. Döring, N., & Bortz, J. (2016). *Forschungsmethoden und Evaluation in den Sozial- und Humanwissenschaften*. Springer Berlin Heidelberg.
64. EY (Ed). (2021). *EY Jobstudie 2021—Digitalisierung im Arbeitsleben: Ergebnisse einer Befragung von 1.550 Beschäftigten in Deutschland*.
65. Ebert, C., & Weyrich, M. (2019). Validation of autonomous systems. *IEEE Software*. https://doi.org/10.1109/MS.2019.2921037
66. Eckhardt, A., Endter, F., Giordano, A., et al. (2019). Three stages to a virtual workforce. *MIS Quarterly Executive*. https://doi.org/10.17705/2MSQE.00006
67. Efatmaneshnik, M., & Handley, H. A. H. (2021). Task complexity measurement framework for human systems integration. *IEEE Systems Journal*. https://doi.org/10.1109/JSYST.2020.3000499
68. Eisel, M., Schmidt, H., et al. (2014). Can information systems reduce stress? The impact of information systems on perceived stress and attitude. *ICIS 2014 Proceedings*(14).
69. Eisenhardt, K. M. (1989). Building theories from case study research. *Academy of Management Review*. https://doi.org/10.5465/AMR.1989.4308385
70. Fabri, L., Häckel, B., Oberländer, A. M., et al. (2023). Disentangling human-AI hybrids. *Business & Information Systems Engineering*. https://doi.org/10.1007/s12599-023-00810-1
71. Fahrmeir, L., Kneib T., Lang, S., et al. (2013). *Regression*. Springer Berlin Heidelberg.
72. Faltaous, S., Baumann, M., Schneegass, S., et al. (2018). Design guidelines for reliability communication in autonomous vehicles. In *Proceedings of the 10th International 2018 ACM Conference on Automotive User Interfaces and Interactive Vehicular* (pp. 258–267).
73. Fernandez-Vidal, J., Gonzalez, R., Gasco, J., et al. (2022). Digitalization and corporate transformation: The case of European Oil & Gas Firms. *Technological Forecasting and Social Change*. https://doi.org/10.1016/j.techfore.2021.121293
74. Ferràs-Hernández, X. (2018). The future of management in a world of electronic brains. *Journal of Management Inquiry*. https://doi.org/10.1177/1056492617724973

75. Fischer, T., & Riedl, R. (2017). Technostress research: A nurturing ground for measurement pluralism? *Communications of the Association for Information Systems*. https://doi.org/10.17705/1CAIS.04017
76. Fjeld, J., Achten, N., Hilligoss, H., et al. (2020). *Pincipled artificial intelligence: Mapping consensus in ethical and rights-based approaches to principles for AI*.
77. Flexera Software. (2023). *Priorities for IT technology initiatives in companies worldwide from 2020 to 2023*. https://www.statista.com/statistics/1106032/top-priorities-it-technology-initiatives/
78. Flyvbjerg, B. (2006). Five misunderstandings about case-study research. *Qualitative Inquiry*. https://doi.org/10.1177/1077800405284363
79. Forster, Y., Kraus, J., Feinauer, S., et al. (2018, 23, 25 September). Calibration of trust expectancies in conditionally automated driving by brand, reliability information and introductionary videos. In *Proceedings of the 10th International Conference on Automotive User Interfaces and Interactive Vehicular Applications* (pp. 118–128). ACM.
80. Gagné, M., Parent-Rocheleau, X., Bujold, A., et al. (2022). How algorithmic management influences worker motivation: A self-determination theory perspective. *Canadian Psychology*. https://doi.org/10.1037/cap0000324
81. Galton, F. (1886). Regression towards mediocrity in hereditary stature. *The Journal of the Anthropological Institute of Great Britain and Ireland*. https://doi.org/10.2307/2841583
82. Ghawe, A. S., & Chan, Y. (2022). Implementing disruptive technologies: What have we learned? *Communications of the Association for Information Systems*. https://doi.org/10.17705/1CAIS.05030
83. Giermindl, L. M., Strich, F., Christ, O., et al. (2022). The dark sides of people analytics: Reviewing the perils for organisations and employees. *European Journal of Information Systems*. https://doi.org/10.1080/0960085X.2021.1927213
84. Gillath, O., Ai, T., Branicky, M. S., et al. (2021). Attachment and trust in artificial intelligence. *Computers in Human Behavior*. https://doi.org/10.1016/j.chb.2020.106607
85. Gioia, D. A., Corley, K. G., & Hamilton, A. L. (2013). Seeking qualitative rigor in inductive research. *Organizational Research Methods*. https://doi.org/10.1177/1094428112452151
86. Glaser, B. G., & Strauss, A. L. (1967). *The discovery of grounded theory: Strategies for qualitative research*. Aldine.
87. Glaser, B. G. (1978). *Theoretical sensitivity*. Soc. Pr.
88. Glikson, E., & Woolley, A. W. (2020). Human trust in artificial intelligence: Review of empirical research. *Academy of Management Annals*. https://doi.org/10.5465/annals.2018.0057
89. Glock, C. H., Grosse, E. H., Jaber, M. Y., et al. (2019). Applications of learning curves in production and operations management: A systematic literature review. *Computers & Industrial Engineering*. https://doi.org/10.1016/j.cie.2018.10.030
90. Goel, K., Bandara, W., & Gable, G. (2021). A typology of business process standardization strategies. *Business & Information Systems Engineering*. https://doi.org/10.1007/s12599-021-00693-0
91. Gregory, R. W., Keil, M., Muntermann, J., et al. (2015). Paradoxes and the nature of ambidexterity in IT transformation programs. *Information Systems Research*. https://doi.org/10.1287/isre.2014.0554
92. Guevara, K., & Ord, J. (1996). The search for meaning in a changing work context. *Futures*. https://doi.org/10.1016/0016-3287(96)00030-4
93. Guha, R., & Corsten, D. (2023). The role of within-day learning on gig workers' performance and task allocation: Evidence from an on-demand platform. *SSRN Electronic Journal*. https://doi.org/10.2139/ssrn.4546690
94. Gulati, R., Puranam, P., & Tushman, M. (2012). Meta-organization design: Rethinking design in interorganizational and community contexts. *Strategic Management Journal*. https://doi.org/10.1002/smj.1975
95. Gupta, A. K., Smith, K. G., & Shalley, C. E. (2006). The interplay between exploration and exploitation. *Academy of Management Journal*. https://doi.org/10.5465/AMJ.2006.22083026

96. Günther, W. A., Rezazade Mehrizi, M. H., Huysman, M., et al. (2017). Debating big data: A literature review on realizing value from big data. *The Journal of Strategic Information Systems*. https://doi.org/10.1016/j.jsis.2017.07.003
97. Haenlein, M., & Kaplan, A. (2019). A brief history of artificial intelligence: On the past, present, and future of artificial intelligence. *California Management Review*. https://doi.org/10.1177/0008125619864925
98. Halaweh, M., Fidler, C., & McRobb, S. (2008). Integrating the grounded theory method and case study research methodology within IS research: A possible 'road map'. *ICIS 2008 Proceedings*(165).
99. Hanelt, A., Bohnsack, R., Marz, D., et al. (2021). A systematic review of the literature on digital transformation: Insights and implications for strategy and organizational change. *Journal of Management Studies*. https://doi.org/10.1111/joms.12639
100. Hauptman, A. I., Duan, W., & Mcneese, N. J. (2022, October 8, 22). The components of trust for collaborating with AI colleagues. In G. Hsieh, A. Tang, M. G. Ames, S. Ding, S. Fussell, V. Liao, et al. (Eds.), *Companion computer supported cooperative work and social computing* (pp. 72–75). Virtual Event Taiwan. ACM.
101. Healy, J., Nicholson, D., & Pekarek, A. (2017). Should we take the gig economy seriously? *Labour & Industry: A journal of the social and economic relations of work*. https://doi.org/10.1080/10301763.2017.1377048
102. Heinke, A. (2024). *Thinking ahead: Bosch Megatrend Report 12.*
103. Hengstler, M., Enkel, E., & Duelli, S. (2016). Applied artificial intelligence and trust—The case of autonomous vehicles and medical assistance devices. *Technological Forecasting and Social Change*. https://doi.org/10.1016/j.techfore.2015.12.014
104. Hernandez, C. A. (2009). Theoretical coding in grounded theory methodology. *Grounded Theory Review: An International Journal* 8.
105. Hess, T. (2022). *Managing the digital transformation*. Springer Fachmedien Wiesbaden.
106. Hess, T., Benlian, A., Matt, C., et al. (2016). Options for formulating a digital transformation strategy. *MIS Quarterly Executive, 15*(2), 123–139.
107. Hoda, R. (2022). Socio-technical grounded theory for software engineering. *IEEE Transactions on Software Engineering*. https://doi.org/10.1109/TSE.2021.3106280
108. Hodapp, D., Hawlitschek, F., Wortmann, F., et al. (2022). Key lessons from Bosch for incumbent firms entering the platform economy. *MIS Quarterly Executive*. https://doi.org/10.17705/2msqe.00061
109. Hoff, K. A., & Bashir, M. (2015). Trust in automation: Integrating empirical evidence on factors that influence trust. *Human factors*. Epub ahead of print 2 September 2014. https://doi.org/10.1177/0018720814547570
110. Hofmann, M., Neukart, F., & Bäck, T. (2017). Artificial intelligence and data science in the automotive industry. *arXiv*. https://doi.org/10.48550/arXiv.1709.01989
111. Holotiuk, F., Beimborn, D., & Hund, A. (2024). Mechanisms for achieving ambidexterity in the context of digital transformation: Insights from digital innovation labs. *JAIS Preprints*. https://doi.org/10.17705/1jais.00885
112. Holton, J. A. (2007). The coding process and its challenges. In A. Bryant & K. Charmaz (Eds.), *The SAGE handbook of grounded theory* (pp. 265–289). Sage.
113. Holzinger, A., & Muller, H. (2021). Toward human–AI interfaces to support explainability and causability in medical AI. *Computer*. https://doi.org/10.1109/MC.2021.3092610
114. Holzinger, A. (2021). The next frontier: AI we can really trust. In M. Kamp, I. Koprinska, A. Bibal, T. Bouadi, B. Frénay, L. Galárraga, et al. (Eds.), *Machine learning and principles and practice of knowledge discovery in databases* (pp. 427–440). Springer International Publishing.
115. Huy, L., Nguyen, H., Vo-Thanh, T., et al. (2024). Generative AI, why, how, and outcomes: A user adoption study. *AIS Transactions on Human-Computer Interaction, 16*(1), 1–27.
116. Huysman, M. (2020). Information systems research on artificial intelligence and work: A commentary on "robo-apocalypse cancelled? Reframing the automation and future of work debate." *Journal of Information Technology*. https://doi.org/10.1177/0268396220926511

117. Im, H., Jeon, S., Cho, H., et al. (2023). AI story relay: A collaborative writing of design fiction to investigate artificial intelligence design considerations. In C. Fiesler & F. Pinatti (Eds.), *The 2023 ACM International Conference on Supporting Group Work (GROUP '23) Companion* (pp. 6–8). ACM.
118. Jabagi, N., Croteau, A.-M., Audebrand, L. K., et al. (2019). Gig-workers' motivation: Thinking beyond carrots and sticks. *Journal of Managerial Psychology*. https://doi.org/10.1108/JMP-06-2018-0255
119. Jago, A. S. (2019). Algorithms and authenticity. *Academy of Management Discoveries*. https://doi.org/10.5465/amd.2017.0002
120. Jarrahi, M. H., Newlands, G., Lee, M. K., et al. (2021). Algorithmic management in a work context. *Big Data & Society*. https://doi.org/10.1177/20539517211020332
121. Jarrahi, M. H., Möhlmann, M. & Lee, M. K. (2023). Algorithmic management: The role of AI in managing workforces. *MIT Sloan Management Review*.
122. Jarrahi, M. H., & Sutherland, W. (2019). Algorithmic management and algorithmic competencies: Understanding and appropriating algorithms in gig work. In N. G. Taylor, C. Christian-Lamb, M. H. Martin, & B. Nardi (Eds.), *Information in contemporary society* (pp. 578–589). Springer International Publishing.
123. Javaid, M., Haleem, A., Singh, R. P., et al. (2022). Artificial intelligence applications for industry 4.0: A literature-based study. *Journal of Industrial Integration and Management*. https://doi.org/10.1142/S2424862221300040.
124. Jiang, H., Cheng, Y., Yang, J., et al. (2022). AI-powered chatbot communication with customers: Dialogic interactions, satisfaction, engagement, and customer behavior. *Computers in Human Behavior*. https://doi.org/10.1016/j.chb.2022.107329
125. Jobin, A., Ienca, M., & Vayena, E. (2019). The global landscape of AI ethics guidelines. *Nature Machine Intelligence*. https://doi.org/10.1038/s42256-019-0088-2
126. Johns, G. (2006). The essential impact of context on organizational behavior. *Academy of Management Review*. https://doi.org/10.5465/AMR.2006.20208687
127. Jones, M. (2019). What we talk about when we talk about (big) data. *The Journal of Strategic Information Systems*. https://doi.org/10.1016/j.jsis.2018.10.005
128. Joshi, M., Su, N., Austin, R., et al. (2021). Why so many data science projects fail to deliver. https://sloanreview.mit.edu/article/why-so-many-data-science-projects-fail-to-deliver/
129. Jung, J. Y., Steinberger, T., King, J. L., et al. (2022). How domain experts work with data: Situating data science in the practices and settings of craftwork. *Proceedings of the ACM on Human-Computer Interaction*. https://doi.org/10.1145/3512905
130. Kaganer, E., Gregory, R. W., & Sarker, S. (2023). A process for managing digital transformation: An organizational inertia perspective. *Journal of the Association for Information Systems*. https://doi.org/10.17705/1jais.00819
131. Kandemir, C., & Handley, H. A. H. (2019). Work process improvement through simulation optimization of task assignment and mental workload. *Computational and Mathematical Organization Theory*. https://doi.org/10.1007/s10588-018-9275-7
132. Kane, G. (2019). The technology fallacy. *Research-Technology Management*. https://doi.org/10.1080/08956308.2019.1661079
133. Karanović, J., Berends, H., & Engel, Y. (2021). Regulated dependence: Platform workers' responses to new forms of organizing. *Journal of Management Studies*. https://doi.org/10.1111/joms.12577
134. Kayabay, K., Gökalp, M. O., Gökalp, E., et al. (2022). Data science roadmapping: An architectural framework for facilitating transformation towards a data-driven organization. *Technological Forecasting and Social Change*. https://doi.org/10.1016/j.techfore.2021.121264
135. Kellogg, K. C., Valentine, M. A., & Christin, A. (2020). Algorithms at work: The new contested terrain of control. *The Academy of Management Annals*. https://doi.org/10.5465/annals.2018.0174
136. Kinder, E., Jarrahi, M. H., & Sutherland, W. (2019). Gig platforms, tensions, alliances and ecosystems. *Proceedings of the ACM on Human-Computer Interaction*. https://doi.org/10.1145/3359314

137. Kirsch, L. S. (1997). Portfolios of control modes and IS project management. *Information Systems Research*. https://doi.org/10.1287/isre.8.3.215
138. Koch, H., Chipidza, W., & Kayworth, T. R. (2021). Realizing value from shadow analytics: A case study. *The Journal of Strategic Information Systems*. https://doi.org/10.1016/J.JSIS.2021.101668
139. Kordzadeh, N., & Ghasemaghaei, M. (2022). Algorithmic bias: Review, synthesis, and future research directions. *European Journal of Information Systems*. https://doi.org/10.1080/0960085X.2021.1927212
140. Kuhn, K. M., & Maleki, A. (2017). Micro-entrepreneurs, Dependent contractors, and instaserfs: Understanding online labor platform workforces. *Academy of Management Perspectives*. https://doi.org/10.5465/amp.2015.0111
141. Kyndt, E., Dochy, F., Struyven, K., et al. (2011). The perception of workload and task complexity and its influence on students' approaches to learning: A study in higher education. *European Journal of Psychology of Education*. https://doi.org/10.1007/s10212-010-0053-2
142. Langer, M., & Landers, R. N. (2021). The future of artificial intelligence at work: A review on effects of decision automation and augmentation on workers targeted by algorithms and third-party observers. *Computers in Human Behavior*. https://doi.org/10.1016/j.chb.2021.106878
143. Langley, A. (1999). Strategies for theorizing from process data. *Academy of Management Review*. https://doi.org/10.2307/259349
144. Lankton, N., McKnight, D. H., & Tripp, J. (2015). Technology, humanness, and trust: Rethinking trust in technology. *Journal of the Association for Information Systems*. https://doi.org/10.17705/1jais.00411
145. Lebovitz, S., Levina, N., & Lifshitz-Assa, H. (2021). Is AI ground truth really true? The dangers of training and evaluating AI tools based on experts' know-what. *MIS Quarterly*. https://doi.org/10.25300/MISQ/2021/16564
146. Lebovitz, S., Lifshitz-Assaf, H., & Levina, N. (2022). To engage or not to engage with AI for critical judgments: How professionals deal with opacity when using AI for medical diagnosis. *Organization Science*. https://doi.org/10.1287/orsc.2021.1549
147. Lebovitz, S. (2019). Diagnostic doubt and artificial intelligence: An inductive field study of radiology work. In H. Krcmar & J. Fedorowicz (Eds.), *Proceedings of the 40th International Conference on Information Systems*.
148. Leclercq-Vandelannoitte, A. (2017). An ethical perspective on emerging forms of ubiquitous IT-based control. *Journal of Business Ethics*. https://doi.org/10.1007/s10551-015-2708-z
149. Lee, M. K. (2018). Understanding perception of algorithmic decisions: Fairness, trust, and emotion in response to algorithmic management. *Big Data & Society*. https://doi.org/10.1177/2053951718756684
150. Lee, M. K., Kusbit, D., Metsky, E., et al. (2015, April 18, 23). Working with machines. In B. Begole, J. Kim, K. Inkpen, & W. Woo (Eds.),*Proceedings of the 33rd Annual ACM Conference on Human Factors in Computing Systems* (pp. 1603–1612). ACM.
151. Leitner-Hanetseder, S., Lehner, O. M., Eisl, C., et al. (2021). A profession in transition: Actors, tasks and roles in AI-based accounting. *Journal of Applied Accounting Research*. https://doi.org/10.1108/JAAR-10-2020-0201.
152. Lewicki, R. J., & Bunker, B. B. (1996). Developing and maintaining trust in work relationships. In R. Kramer & T Tyler (Eds.), *Trust in organizations: Frontiers of theory and research* (pp. 114–139). Sage.
153. Li, X., Ye, P., Li, J., et al. (2022). From features engineering to scenarios engineering for trustworthy AI: I&I, C&C, and V&V. *IEEE Intelligent Systems*. https://doi.org/10.1109/MIS.2022.3197950
154. Li, Y., & Hahn, J. (2022). Review of research on human trust in artificial intelligence. *ICIS 2022 Proceedings*.
155. Li, C.-K., & Hung, C.-H. (2009). The influence of transformational leadership on workplace relationships and job performance. *Social Behavior and Personality: An International Journal, 37*(8), 1129–1142. https://doi.org/10.2224/sbp.2009.37.8.1129

156. Lippert, I., Kirchner, K., et al. (2023). Context matters: The use of algorithmic management mechanisms in platform, hybrid, and traditional work contexts. *56th Hawaii International Conference on System Sciences (HICSS).*
157. Liu, P., & Li, Z. (2012). Task complexity: A review and conceptualization framework. *International Journal of Industrial Ergonomics.* https://doi.org/10.1016/j.ergon.2012.09.001
158. Lu, X., & White, H. (2014). Robustness checks and robustness tests in applied economics. *Journal of Econometrics.* https://doi.org/10.1016/j.jeconom.2013.08.016
159. Lu, Q., Zhu, L., Xu, X., et al. (2022, May 16, 24). Towards a roadmap on software engineering for responsible AI. In I. Crnkovic (Ed.), *Proceedings of the 1st International Conference on AI Engineering: Software Engineering for AI* (pp. 101–112). ACM.
160. Maltese, F., Adda, M., Bablon, A., Hraeich, S., Guervilly, C., Lehingue, S., Wiramus, S., Leone, M., Martin, C., Vialet, R., Thirion, X., Roch, A., Forel, J.-M., & Papazian, L. (2016). Night shift decreases cognitive performance of ICU physicians. *Intensive Care Medicine, 42*(3), 393–400. https://doi.org/10.1007/s00134-015-4115-4
161. Mao, Y., Wang, D., Muller, M., et al. (2019). How data scientists work together with domain experts in scientific collaborations. *Proceedings of the ACM on Human-Computer Interaction.* https://doi.org/10.1145/3361118
162. Marabelli, M., Newell, S., & Handunge, V. (2021). The lifecycle of algorithmic decision-making aystems: Organizational choices and ethical challenges. *The Journal of Strategic Information Systems.* https://doi.org/10.1016/j.jsis.2021.101683
163. Matavire, R., & Brown, I. (2013). Profiling grounded theory approaches in information systems research. *European Journal of Information Systems.* https://doi.org/10.1057/ejis.2011.35
164. Mateescu, A., & Nguyen, A. (2019). *Explainer: Algorithmic management in the workplace.*
165. Mayer, R. C., Davis, J. H., & Schoorman, F. D. (1995). An integrative model of organizational trust. *Academy of Management Review.* https://doi.org/10.2307/258792
166. Mayer-Schönberger, V., & Cukier, K. (2013). *Big data: A revolution that will transform how we live, work, and think.* Houghton Mifflin Harcourt.
167. McAfee, A. (2006). Mastering the three worlds of information technology. *Harvard Business Review.*
168. McCulloch, C. E., & Searle, S. R. (2000). *Generalized, linear, and mixed models.* Wiley.
169. McKnight, D. H., Carter, M., Thatcher, J. B., et al. (2011). Trust in a specific technology. *ACM Transactions on Management Information Systems.* https://doi.org/10.1145/1985347.1985353
170. McKnight, D. H., Cummings, L. L., & Chervany, N. L. (1998). Initial trust formation in new organizational relationships. *Academy of Management Review.* https://doi.org/10.2307/259290
171. Meijerink, J., Boons, M., Keegan, A., et al. (2021). Algorithmic human resource management: Synthesizing developments and cross-disciplinary insights on digital HRM. *The International Journal of Human Resource Management.* https://doi.org/10.1080/09585192.2021.1925326
172. Meijerink, J., & Bondarouk, T. (2023). The duality of algorithmic management: Toward a research agenda on HRM algorithms, autonomy and value creation. *Human Resource Management Review.* https://doi.org/10.1016/j.hrmr.2021.100876
173. Menzel, H. C., Aaltio, I., & Ulijn, J. M. (2007). On the way to creativity: Engineers as intrapreneurs in organizations. *Technovation.* https://doi.org/10.1016/j.technovation.2007.05.004
174. Merchel, R., Iqbal, T., Süße, T., et al. (2021, December 12–15). Digital competencies and IT skills as employees' resources to cope with digitalization demands. In J. Valacich (Ed.), *Proceedings of the 42nd International Conference on Information Systems (ICIS 2021).*
175. Meyer, G., Adomavicius, G., Johnson, P. E., et al. (2014). A machine learning approach to improving dynamic decision making. *Information Systems Research.* https://doi.org/10.1287/isre.2014.0513
176. Mikalef, P., Boura, M., Lekakos, G., et al. (2019). Big data analytics and firm performance: Findings from a mixed-method approach. *Journal of Business Research.* https://doi.org/10.1016/j.jbusres.2019.01.044

177. Miles, M. B., Huberman, A. M., & Saldaña, J. (2020). *Qualitative data analysis: A methods sourcebook*. Sage.
178. Mingers, J. (2001). Combining IS research methods: Towards a pluralist methodology. *Information Systems Research*. https://doi.org/10.1287/isre.12.3.240.9709
179. Mingers, J., & Brocklesby, J. (1997). Multimethodology: Towards a framework for mixing methodologies. *Omega*. https://doi.org/10.1016/S0305-0483(97)00018-2
180. Morse, J. M. (1999). Qualitative generalizability. *Qualitative health research*. https://doi.org/10.1177/104973299129121622
181. Morse, J. M. (2009). Mixing qualitative methods. *Qualitative Health Research*. https://doi.org/10.1177/1049732309349360
182. Morse, J. (2022). *Amazon announces new employee tracking tech, and customers are lining up*. https://in.mashable.com/tech/18635/amazon-announces-new-employee-tracking-tech-and-customers-are-lining-up
183. Morse, J. M. (2015). Critical analysis of strategies for determining rigor in qualitative inquiry. *Qualitative health research*. Epub ahead of print 16 July 2015. https://doi.org/10.1177/1049732315588501
184. Mruck, K., & Mey, G. (2009). Der Beitrag qualitativer Methodologie und Methodik zur Marktforschung. In R. Buber & H. H. Holzmüller (Eds.), *Qualitative Marktforschung* (pp. 21–45). Gabler.
185. Muhuri, P. K., Shukla, A. K., & Abraham, A. (2019). Industry 4.0: A bibliometric analysis and detailed overview. *Engineering Applications of Artificial Intelligence*. https://doi.org/10.1016/j.engappai.2018.11.007
186. Muller, M., Lange, I., Wang, D., et al. (2019, May 9). How data science workers work with data. In S. Brewster, G. Fitzpatrick, A. Cox & V. Kostakos (Eds.), *Proceedings of the 2019 CHI Conference on Human Factors in Computing Systems* (pp. 1–15). ACM.
187. Myers, M. (2000). Qualitative research and the generalizability question: Standing firm with proteus. *The Qualitative Report*. https://doi.org/10.46743/2160-3715/2000.2925
188. Möhlmann, M., Zalmanson, L., Henfridsson, O., et al. (2021). Algorithmic management of work on online labor platforms: When matching meets control. *MIS Quarterly*. https://doi.org/10.25300/MISQ/2021/15333
189. Möhlmann, M. (2021). Algorithmic nudges don't have to be unethical. *Harvard Business Review*.
190. Möhlmann, M., & Henfridsson, O. (2019). What people hate about being managed by algorithms. According to a study of uber drivers.
191. Nah, F., Cai, J., Zheng, R., et al. (2023). An activity system-based perspective of generative AI: Challenges and research directions. *AIS Transactions on Human-Computer Interaction, 15*(3), 247–267.
192. Nakagawa, S., & Schielzeth, H. (2013). A general and simple method for obtaining R2 from generalized linear mixed-effects models. *Methods in Ecology and Evolution*. https://doi.org/10.1111/j.2041-210x.2012.00261.x
193. Nelson, A. J., & Irwin, J. (2014). "Defining what we do—All over again": Occupational identity, technological change, and the librarian/internet-search relationship. *Academy of Management Journal*. https://doi.org/10.5465/amj.2012.0201
194. Newell, A., & Rosenbloom, P. (1982). Mechanisms of skill acquisition and the law of practice. *Cognitive Skills and Their Acquisition* Vol. 1.
195. Ngereja, B. J., Hussein, B., & Wolff, C. (2024). A comparison of soft factors in the implementation and adoption of digitalization projects: A systematic literature review. *International Journal of Information Systems and Project Management* 12(2).
196. Niehaus, F., & Wiesche, M. (2021). A socio-technical perspective on organizational interaction with AI: A literature review. *ECIS 2021 Research Papers*.
197. Noesgaard, M. S., Nielsen, J. A., Jensen, T. B., et al. (2023). Same but different: Variations in reactions to digital transformation within an organizational field. *Journal of the Association for Information Systems*. https://doi.org/10.17705/1jais.00770

198. Oberländer, M., Beinicke, A., & Bipp, T. (2020). Digital competencies: A review of the literature and applications in the workplace. *Computers & Education*. https://doi.org/10.1016/j.compedu.2019.103752
199. Okamura, K., & Yamada, S. (2020). Empirical evaluations of framework for adaptive trust calibration in human-AI cooperation. *IEEE Access*. https://doi.org/10.1109/ACCESS.2020.3042556
200. Olkkonen, M.-E., & Lipponen, J. (2006). Relationships between organizational justice, identification with organization and work unit, and group-related outcomes. *Organizational Behavior and Human Decision Processes*. https://doi.org/10.1016/j.obhdp.2005.08.007
201. Oludapo, S., Carroll, N., & Helfert, M. (2024). Why do so many digital transformations fail? A bibliometric analysis and future research agenda. *Journal of Business Research*. https://doi.org/10.1016/j.jbusres.2024.114528
202. Orlikowski, W. J. (1993). CASE tools as organizational change: Investigating incremental and radical changes in systems development. *MIS Quarterly*. https://doi.org/10.2307/249774
203. Ozili, P. K. (2022). The acceptable R-Square in empirical modelling for social science research. *SSRN Electronic Journal*. https://doi.org/10.2139/ssrn.4128165
204. Pachidi, S., Berends, H., Faraj, S., et al. (2021). Make way for the algorithms: Symbolic actions and change in a regime of knowing. *Organization Science*. https://doi.org/10.1287/orsc.2020.1377
205. Parasuraman, R., & Riley, V. (1997). Humans and automation: Use, misuse, disuse, abuse. *Human factors*. https://doi.org/10.1518/001872097778543886
206. Parent-Rocheleau, X., & Parker, S. K. (2022). Algorithms as work designers: How algorithmic management influences the design of jobs. *Human Resource Management Review*. https://doi.org/10.1016/j.hrmr.2021.100838
207. Park, S., Wang, A. Y., Kawas, B., et al. (2021, April 14, 17). Facilitating knowledge sharing from domain experts to data scientists for building NLP models. In T. Hammond, K. Verbert, D. Parra, B. Knijnenburg, J. O'Donovan, & P. Teale (Eds.), *26th International Conference on Intelligent User Interfaces* (pp. 585–596). ACM.
208. Parmiggiani, E., Østerlie, T., & Almklov, P. G. (2022). In the backrooms of data science. *Journal of the Association for Information Systems*. https://doi.org/10.17705/1jais.00718
209. Paré, G. (2004). Investigating information systems with positivist case research. *Communications of the Association for Information Systems*. https://doi.org/10.17705/1CAIS.01318
210. Di Pasquale, V., Miranda, S., & Neumann, W. P. (2020). Ageing and human-system errors in manufacturing: A scoping review. *International Journal of Production Research*. https://doi.org/10.1080/00207543.2020.1773561
211. Passi, S., & Sengers, P. (2020). Making data science systems work. *Big Data & Society*. https://doi.org/10.1177/2053951720939605
212. Patton, M. Q. (2009). *Qualitative research & evaluation methods*. Sage.
213. Petriglieri, G., Ashford, S. J., & Wrzesniewski, A. (2019). Agony and ecstasy in the gig economy: Cultivating holding environments for precarious and personalized work identities. *Administrative Science Quarterly*. https://doi.org/10.1177/0001839218759646
214. Pinsonneault, A., & Kraemer, K. L. (1993). The impact of information technology on middle managers. *MIS Quarterly*: 271–292.
215. Power, D. J., Cyphert, D., & Roth, R. M. (2019). Analytics, bias, and evidence: The quest for rational decision making. *Journal of Decision Systems*. https://doi.org/10.1080/12460125.2019.1623534
216. Provost, F., & Fawcett, T. (2013). Data science and its relationship to big data and data-driven decision making. *Big data*. https://doi.org/10.1089/big.2013.1508
217. Puranam, P., Alexy, O., & Reitzig, M. (2014). What's "new" about new forms of organizing? *Academy of Management Review*. https://doi.org/10.5465/amr.2011.0436
218. PwC. (2023). *Internal technological and labor challenges in enterprises in the United States in 2023*. https://www.statista.com/statistics/1413045/internal-business-challenges-us/
219. Rahmati, P., Tafti, A., Westland, J. C., et al. (2021). When all products are digital: Complexity and intangible value in the ecosystem of digitizing firms. *MIS Quarterly*. https://doi.org/10.25300/MISQ/2021/15384

220. Reagans, R., Argote, L., & Brooks, D. (2005). Individual experience and experience working together: Predicting learning rates from knowing who knows what and knowing how to work together. *Management Science*. https://doi.org/10.1287/mnsc.1050.0366
221. Reay, T., Golden-Biddle, K., & Germann, K. (2006). Legitimizing a new role: Small wins and microprocesses of change. *The Academy of Management Journal, 49*(5).
222. Reis, L., Maier, C., & Weitzel, T. (2022). Mixed-methods in information systems research: Status quo, core concepts, and future research implications. *Communications of the Association for Information Systems*. https://doi.org/10.17705/1CAIS.05106
223. Robert Bosch GmbH. (2022). *Bosch digital strategy*. Internal document.
224. Russell, S. J., & Norvig, P. (2010). *Artificial intelligence: A modern approach*. Prentice-Hall.
225. Salam, A. F., Pervez, S., & Nahar, S. (2021). Trust in AI and intelligent systems: Central core of the design of intelligent systems. *AMCIS 2021 Proceedings*.
226. Sambasivan, N., & Veeraraghavan, R. (2022, April 29, May 5). The deskilling of domain expertise in AI development. In S. Barbosa, C. Lampe, C. Appert, D. A. Shamma, S. Drucker, J. Williamson, et al. (Eds.), *CHI Conference on Human Factors in Computing Systems* (pp. 1–14). ACM.
227. Sarker, S., & Lee, A. (2001). Using a positivist case research methodology to test three competing theories-in-use of business process redesign. *Journal of the Association for Information Systems*. https://doi.org/10.17705/1jais.00019
228. Sarker, S., Xiao, X., Beaulieu, T., et al. (2018). Learning from first-generation qualitative approaches in the IS discipline: An evolutionary view and some implications for authors and evaluators (PART 1/2). *Journal of the Association for Information Systems*. https://doi.org/10.17705/1jais.00508
229. Schielzeth, H., Dingemanse, N. J., Nakagawa, S., et al. (2020). Robustness of linear mixed-effects models to violations of distributional assumptions. *Methods in Ecology and Evolution*. https://doi.org/10.1111/2041-210X.13434
230. Schnellbächer, B., Heidenreich, S., & Wald, A. (2019). Antecedents and effects of individual ambidexterity—A cross-level investigation of exploration and exploitation activities at the employee level. *European Management Journal*. https://doi.org/10.1016/j.emj.2019.02.002
231. Seidel, S., & Urquhart, C. (2013). On emergence and forcing in information systems grounded theory studies: The case of strauss and corbin. *Journal of Information Technology*. https://doi.org/10.1057/jit.2013.17
232. Sharma, R., Mithas, S., & Kankanhalli, A. (2014). Transforming decision-making processes: A research agenda for understanding the impact of business analytics on organisations. *European Journal of Information Systems*. https://doi.org/10.1057/ejis.2014.17
233. Sheppard, S., Colby, A., Macatangay, K., et al. (2006). What is engineering practice? *International Journal of Engineering Education* 22(3).
234. Skog, D. A., Wimelius, H., & Sandberg, J. (2018). Digital disruption. *Business & Information Systems Engineering*. https://doi.org/10.1007/s12599-018-0550-4
235. Slota, S. C., Fleischmann, K. R., Greenberg, S., et al. (2020). Good systems, bad data? Interpretations of AI hype and failures. *Proceedings of the Association for Information Science and Technology*. https://doi.org/10.1002/pra2.275
236. Soh, C., Kien Sia, S., Fong Boh, W., et al. (2003). Misalignments in ERP Implementation: A dialectic perspective. *International Journal of Human-Computer Interaction*. https://doi.org/10.1207/S15327590IJHC1601_6
237. Staats, B. R., & Gino, F. (2012). Specialization and variety in repetitive tasks: Evidence from a Japanese bank. *Management Science*. https://doi.org/10.1287/mnsc.1110.1482
238. Stanton, J. M. (2001). Galton, Pearson, and the Peas: A brief history of linear regression for statistics instructors. *Journal of Statistics Education*. https://doi.org/10.1080/10691898.2001.11910537
239. Strauss, A. L. (1978). *Qualitative analysis for social scientists*. Cambridge University Press.
240. Strauss, A. L., & Corbin, J. (1998). *Basics of qualitative research: Techniques and procedures for developing grounded theory*. Sage.

241. Strich, F., Mayer, A.-S., & Fiedler, M. (2021). What do I do in a world of artificial intelligence? Investigating the impact of substitutive decision-making AI systems on employees' professional role identity. *Journal of the Association for Information Systems*. https://doi.org/10.17705/1jais.00663
242. Suddaby, R. (2006). From the editors: What grounded theory is not. *Academy of Management Journal*. https://doi.org/10.5465/amj.2006.22083020
243. Sunde, E., Pedersen, T., Mrdalj, J., et al. (2020). Blue-enriched white light improves performance but not subjective alertness and circadian adaptation during three consecutive simulated night shifts. *Frontiers in psychology*. Epub ahead of print 18 August 2020. https://doi.org/10.3389/fpsyg.2020.02172.
244. Svahn, F., Mathiassen, L., & Lindgren, R. (2017). Embracing digital innovation in incumbent firms: How Volvo cars managed competing concerns. *MIS Quarterly*. https://doi.org/10.25300/MISQ/2017/41.1.12
245. Sykes, T. A., Venkatesh, V., & Johnson, J. L. (2014). Enterprise system implementation and employee job performance: Understanding the role of advice networks. *MIS Quarterly*. https://doi.org/10.25300/MISQ/2014/38.1.03
246. Söllner, M., Hoffmann, A., & Leimeister, J. M. (2016). Why different trust relationships matter for information systems users. *European Journal of Information Systems*. https://doi.org/10.1057/ejis.2015.17
247. Söllner, M., Benbasat, I., Gefen, D., et al. (2016a). MIS quarterly research curation on trust. *MIS Quarterly*.
248. Tabrizi, B., Lam, E., Girad, K., et al. (2019). Digital transformation is not about technology. *Harvard Business Review*.
249. Tams, S. (2022). Helping older workers realize their full organizational potential: A moderated mediation model of age and IT-enabled task performance. *MIS Quarterly, 46*(1).
250. Tarafdar, M., Page, X., & Marabelli, M. (2022). Algorithms as co-workers: Human algorithm role interactions in algorithmic work. *Information Systems Journal*. https://doi.org/10.1111/isj.12389
251. Taylor, J., & Joshi, K. D. (2018). How IT leaders can benefit from the digital crowdsourcing workforce. *MIS Quarterly Executive, 17*(4).
252. Tesch, R. (2013). *Qualitative research: Analysis types and software*. Routledge.
253. Thiebes, S., Lins, S., & Sunyaev, A. (2021). Trustworthy artificial intelligence. *Electronic Markets*. https://doi.org/10.1007/s12525-020-00441-4
254. Tomitza, C., Schaschek, M., Straub, L., et al. (2023). What is the minimum to trust AI?—A requirement analysis for (generative) AI-based Texts. *Wirtschaftsinformatik 2023 Proceedings*.
255. Trenerry, B., Chng, S., Wang, Y., et al. (2021). Preparing workplaces for digital transformation: An integrative review and framework of multi-level factors. *Frontiers in psychology*. Epub ahead of print 23 March 2021. https://doi.org/10.3389/fpsyg.2021.620766
256. Trittin-Ulbrich, H., Scherer, A. G., Munro, I., et al. (2021). Exploring the dark and unexpected sides of digitalization: Toward a critical agenda. *Organization*. https://doi.org/10.1177/1350508420968184
257. Tushman, M. L., & Anderson, P. (1986). Technological discontinuities and organizational environments. *Administrative Science Quarterly*. https://doi.org/10.2307/2392832
258. Urquhart, C., & Fernández, W. (2013). Using grounded theory method in information systems: The researcher as blank slate and other myths. *Journal of Information Technology*. https://doi.org/10.1057/jit.2012.34
259. Urquhart, C. (2013). *Grounded theory for qualitative research: A practical guide*. Sage.
260. Vaast, E., & Walsham, G. (2005). Representations and actions: The transformation of work practices with IT use. *Information and Organization*. https://doi.org/10.1016/j.infoandorg.2004.10.001
261. Veen, A., Barratt, T., & Goods, C. (2020). Platform-capital's 'app-etite' for control: A labour process analysis of food-delivery work in Australia. *Work, Employment and Society*. https://doi.org/10.1177/0950017019836911

262. van de Ven, A. H., & Huber, G. P. (1990). Longitudinal field research methods for studying processes of organizational change. *Organization Science*. https://doi.org/10.1287/orsc.1.3.213
263. Venkatesh, V., Brown, S. A., & Bala, H. (2013). Bridging the qualitative-quantitative divide: Guidelines for conducting mixed methods research in information systems. *MIS Quarterly*. https://doi.org/10.25300/MISQ/2013/37.1.02
264. Venkatesh, V., Brown, S., & Sullivan, Y. (2016). Guidelines for conducting mixed-methods research: An extension and illustration. *Journal of the Association for Information Systems*. https://doi.org/10.17705/1jais.00433
265. Vial, G. (2019). Understanding digital transformation: A review and a research agenda. *The Journal of Strategic Information Systems*. https://doi.org/10.1016/j.jsis.2019.01.003
266. Vimalkumar, M., Gupta, A., Sharma, D., et al. (2021). Understanding the effect that task complexity has on automation potential and opacity: Implications for algorithmic fairness. *AIS Transactions on Human-Computer Interaction*. https://doi.org/10.17705/1thci.00144
267. de Vries, G. J., Gentile, E., Miroudot, S., et al. (2020). The rise of robots and the fall of routine jobs. *Labour Economics*. https://doi.org/10.1016/j.labeco.2020.101885
268. Waardenburg, L., Huysman, M., & Sergeeva, A. V. (2022). In the land of the blind, the one-eyed man is king: Knowledge brokerage in the age of learning algorithms. *Organization Science*. https://doi.org/10.1287/orsc.2021.1544
269. Wade, M., & Shan, J. (2020). Covid-19 has accelerated digital transformation, but may have made it harder not easier. *MIS Quarterly Executive*.
270. Walsham, G. (1995). Interpretive case studies in IS research: Nature and method. *European Journal of Information Systems*. https://doi.org/10.1057/ejis.1995.9
271. Wessel, L., Baiyere, A., Ologeanu-Taddei, R., et al. (2021). Unpacking the difference between digital transformation and it-enabled organizational transformation. *Journal of the Association for Information Systems*. https://doi.org/10.17705/1jais.00655
272. West, R. M. (2022). Best practice in statistics: The use of log transformation. *Annals of clinical biochemistry*. Epub ahead of print 19 October 2021. https://doi.org/10.1177/00045632211050531
273. Wibowo, S., Deng, H., & Duan, S. (2022). Understanding digital work and its use in organizations from a literature review. *Pacific Asia Journal of the Association for Information Systems*. https://doi.org/10.17705/1pais.14302
274. Wiener, M., Cram, W., & Benlian, A. (2021). Algorithmic control and gig workers: A legitimacy perspective of uber drivers. *European Journal of Information Systems*. https://doi.org/10.1080/0960085X.2021.1977729
275. Wiesche, M., Jurisch, M. C., Yetton, P. W., et al. (2017). Grounded theory methodology in information systems research. *MIS Quarterly*. https://doi.org/10.25300/MISQ/2017/41.3.02
276. Willcocks, L. (2020). Robo-apocalypse cancelled? Reframing the automation and future of work debate. *Journal of Information Technology*. https://doi.org/10.1177/0268396220925830
277. Wood, A. J. (2021). Algorithmic management consequences for work organisation and working conditions. *JRC Working Papers Series on Labour, Education and Technology*(7).
278. Wood, A. J., Graham, M., Lehdonvirta, V., et al. (2019). Good gig, bad gig: Autonomy and algorithmic control in the global gig economy. *Work, Employment & Society a Journal of the British Sociological Association*. Epub ahead of print 8 August 2018. https://doi.org/10.1177/0950017018785616
279. Yeow, A., Soh, C., & Hansen, R. (2018). Aligning with new digital strategy: A dynamic capabilities approach. *The Journal of Strategic Information Systems*. https://doi.org/10.1016/j.jsis.2017.09.001
280. Yin, R. K. (2010). *Case study research: Design and methods*. Sage.
281. Zhang, Z., Nandhakumar, J., Hummel, J. T., et al. (2020). Addressing the key challenges of developing machine learning AI systems for knowledge-intensive work. *MIS Quarterly Executive*. https://doi.org/10.17705/2msqe.00035
282. Zhou, J., Chen, F., Berry, A., et al. (2020, 1–4 December). A survey on ethical principles of AI and implementations. In *2020 IEEE Symposium Series on Computational Intelligence (SSCI)* (pp. 3010–3017). IEEE.

283. Zink, K. J., Steimle, U., & Schröder, D. (2008). Comprehensive change management concepts. Development of a participatory approach. *Applied ergonomics*. Epub ahead of print 18 April 2008. https://doi.org/10.1016/j.apergo.2008.02.015
284. van Giffen, B., & Ludwig, H. (2023). How siemens democratized artificial intelligence. *MIS Quarterly Executive, 22*(1).

Digital Finance

Deciphering Crypto Risks: Crypto Asset Risk Management Requirements for Financial Service Providers

Research Paper

Christian Zeiß, Konstanze Lang, and Axel Winkelmann

Abstract The emergence of decentralized finance and crypto assets has fundamentally changed the financial world and offers new potential to private investors and financial service providers. Despite the benefits, it is essential to face the risks. While initial regulation is already in place for risk management, financial service providers are often left to implement these measures on their own. This paper aims to identify the requirements for crypto assets risk management for financial service providers that go beyond implementing individual regulations. Guided by our research approach, we derive requirements from an academic and practical knowledge base. Accordingly, we evaluate the final requirements with a mixed-methods approach to receive feedback from portfolio managers, financial advisors, and blockchain experts. Finally, we will provide a comprehensive framework for financial service providers to effectively manage and mitigate crypto asset risks.

1 Introduction

A financial system that offers services and products with low transaction costs, high returns, and transparency [20, 48]—at first glance, it sounds like an ideal situation. But is it? Crypto assets have recently experienced enormous demand and are developing into financial products for the masses [34, 41]. Initially, crypto assets were a niche product held only in the portfolios by a small target group despite their high-profit potential [60]. As the number of financial products available and the number

C. Zeiß (✉) · K. Lang · A. Winkelmann
University of Würzburg, Würzburg, Germany
e-mail: christian.zeiss@uni-wuerzburg.de

K. Lang
e-mail: konstanze.lang@uni-wuerzburg.de

A. Winkelmann
e-mail: axel.winkelmann@uni-wuerzburg.de

C. M. Flath et al. (eds.), *Digital Innovation and Organizational Transformation*, Lecture Notes in Information Systems and Organisation 83,
https://doi.org/10.1007/978-3-032-08483-5_21

of websites providing them has increased rapidly, decentralized finance (DeFi) and cryptocurrencies are becoming widely available to the general public [46, 64].

Despite this, fraud and a lack of regulation are plaguing crypto assets [9, 13], leading to cases such as Cryptoqueen[1] and FTX[2] attracting media attention. Accordingly, it is crucial for all players in the crypto market to be aware of these risks and to understand them fully [57]. This heightened level of threat that requires appropriate risk management accompanies the novelty of crypto assets [17]. By this, financial service providers (FSP) need to identify, measure, and minimize threats to ensure private as well as institutional investors can safely participate in the crypto market [5, 46]. Currently, FSP encounter significant challenges in fulfilling this role partly due to a dearth of specific knowledge among organizational and individual level [63]. Additionally, FSP operating in the crypto market must adhere to new fundamental standards [17]. However, there are various regulation standards for FSP for crypto assets, but their consolidation and embedding in the organization still need to be clarified [36]. The multifaceted landscape of occurring challenges and regulatory demands highlights the critical need for robust research into efficient and effective risk management strategies for FSP in the crypto ecosystem.

The problems briefly described lead us to our research question:

RQ: *What are the requirements for establishing and improving risk management for crypto assets for financial service provider?*

To answer this question, we apply a design science research approach to develop requirements by conducting a structured literature review and supplementing this with interviews with practitioners to derive provider expectations. With our results, we contribute to blockchain governance, security management in FinTech, and DeFi risk management.

The paper is structured as follows: We briefly examine the role of FSP in DeFi and risk management (Chap. 2). Next, we describe our research design (Chap. 3) and present the requirements (Chap. 4). Further, we evaluate the requirements mixed-methods (Chap. 5). In Chap. 6, we discuss our research, concluding with limitations, further research, and implications (Chap. 7).

2 Research Background

Financial Service Provider in Decentralized Finance. Crypto assets are tokenized assets comprising objects traded as digital representations of physical or virtual assets [49]. Tokenization describes the digital securitization of virtual and physical rights and goods. Supply chain traceability [e.g., 43] have primarily used this tokenization. Nevertheless, many applications have emerged in developing the DeFi and crypto

---

[1] https://edition.cnn.com/2023/01/22/business/ruja-ignatova-cryptoqueen-fbi-most-wanted-cec/index.html.

[2] https://edition.cnn.com/2023/11/02/business/ftx-sbf-fraud-trial-verdict/index.html.

ecosystems [61]. Payment, utility, and asset tokens separate those crypto tokens [49]. These assets include cryptocurrencies, non-fungible tokens, and tokenized assets such as fractionalized real estate or art [22, 41]. With the upcoming blockchain technology and as a reaction to the economic crisis, a decentralized financial system emerged [48, 65]. This DeFi ecosystem emphasizes the role of transparency and trust and develops new innovative business models [10]. Contrary to DeFi, centralized finance relates to the traditional financial system, and investment opportunities typically comprise stocks, funds, or commodities [62]. Transactions require an intermediary, usually in the form of a central authority such as an FSP [52].

Technical innovations, new regulations, or increasing customer demands are changing the financial ecosystem and driving to a competitive environment [44, 52]. With the advent of DeFi, the formerly very powerful intermediaries, e.g., FSP, typical of the underlying blockchain technology and its pure peer-to-peer communication, have no longer been part of the system [47]. Banks were becoming considerably less influential, losing their customers and money [20]. However, due to re-intermediation, DeFi is now softening, and new FSP are gathering in the DeFi ecosystem where technology eliminated the old players [10]. For example, numerous crypto exchanges, trading platforms for tokenized assets, and service providers for custody exist [61, 64]. Consequently, the new FSP have gained power. Finally, traditional FSP need to strengthen their resilience to guard their position in the ecosystem and better resist future changes [39]. As DeFi and crypto market participants, FSP requires appropriate risk management to avoid total exposure to potential dangers and risks [13, 17].

Risk Management in the Financial Sector. Risk management plays a fundamental role in identifying, analyzing, and categorizing threats within an organization [23]. It aims to minimize risk by appropriately allocating economic resources [50]. In the financial sector, risk management aims to maintain profitability, security, and liquidity ratios while managing assets and liabilities [12]. Investing in crypto assets will likely involve higher financial and non-financial risks, so rigorous management is essential [27].

Managing non-financial risk is challenging for companies as historical data from other industries or even from the early stages of the crypto market often does not accurately reflect current risks. The crypto industry faces unique risks such as regulatory uncertainty, technological vulnerabilities (e.g., hacks, smart contract bugs), and market manipulation [27]. However, increasingly sophisticated measurement techniques are being used to assess these uncertainties accurately [30]. Quantifying non-financial risks is often challenging, so the appropriateness of different threat assessment frameworks may differ depending on the type and size of the organization, its regulatory environment, as well as best practices [35]. Scenario analysis has recently emerged as an essential method of risk assessment, particularly for FSP using advanced measurement approaches for operational risk [30].

The financial risks associated with crypto assets are higher than those associated with traditional assets [11]. Financial risks can be divided into credit, liquidity, and market risks. Value at Risk (VaR), Expected Shortfall, and stress testing are methods and strategies to assess these risks [27]. VaR measures the expected loss on investment at a given probability and over a given time [28]. Expected shortfall measures the severity of losses in an adverse scenario and is used to accurately estimate scenarios beyond a certain probability [27, 29].

3 Methodology

Examining and validating requirements is a common research objective [54, 58]. In order to derive our requirements for the risk management of crypto assets for FSP, we proceeded in four steps (Fig. 1). Since the risk management of crypto assets is a dynamic topic, we placed great importance on findings from practice. Therefore, we considered theoretical and practical perspectives when elaborating our requirements. We evaluated these requirements employing a mixed-methods approach [8].

Step 1: We conducted a structured literature review following [59] focusing on crypto asset risk management for including the scientific knowledge bases. For this review of scientific literature dealing with the risk management of crypto assets in the financial sector, we searched for relevant literature using the databases *ACM Digital Library, Web of Science, and Science Direct*. Including criteria was on peer-reviewed relevant articles. For exclusion, we removed paper without digital access and duplicates (Fig. 2). The literature search operated at the full-text level with the broadest possible scope using the following query string, which we adapted for each database: *("crypto asset" OR "digital asset" OR "cryptocurrency" OR "cryptocurrencies") AND "risk"*

Step 2: We performed in-depth interviews with practitioners to gain insights and expand our knowledge base for deriving our crypto asset risk management requirements. As the interviews were semi-structured, we prepared open-ended guiding

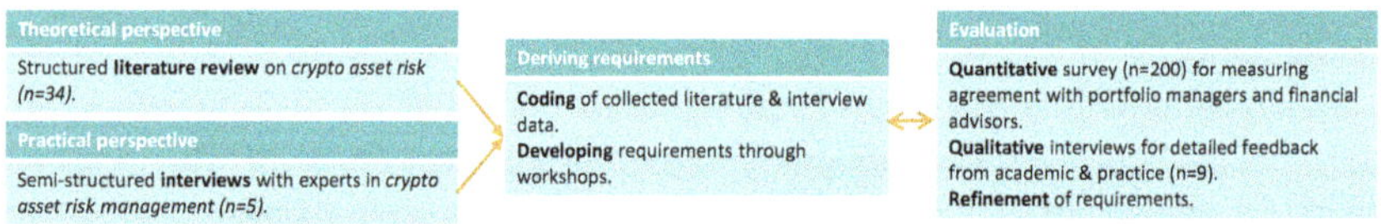

Fig. 1 Research approach for deriving requirements for crypto asset risk management

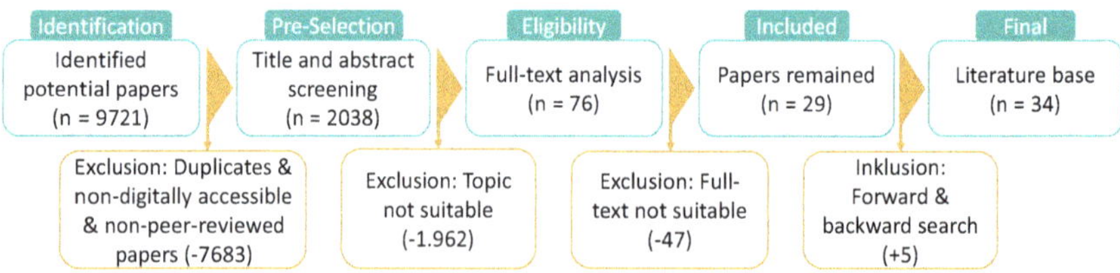

Fig. 2 Reduction of literature review with inclusion and exclusion

ID	Industry Sector	Focus of Knowledge
I1	FinTech	Senior Analyst for Crypto Risk
I2	FinTech	Investment advisor focused on crypto
I3	Consultant Banking	Certified Blockchain expert at FSFM and researcher
I4	Banking	Senior Risk Manager
I5	Financial Institution	Director in Blockchain solutions

Fig. 3 Overview of experts for interviews (I1–I5)

questions, discussed to steer the participant toward a specific topic [45]. As we emphasized the role of practical insights in our research approach, we selected experts with risk management experience and deep knowledge of the current trends in crypto assets, digital currencies, and the financial sector. Representatives from five FSP took part in the interviews, all of whom are experts with extensive experience in leadership positions within the company or ecosystem. The FSP surveyed all operate business models and provide risk management services within the crypto asset ecosystem. In addition, certain experts also serve as instructors at renowned academic institutions. The following figure provides a brief introduction to each interviewee (I1–I5) (Fig. 3).

Step 3: For elaborating our requirements, we summarized the data collected from the literature review and the expert interviews. First, the research team read the identified relevant papers and coded them. Second, we evaluated the interview data with the qualitative content analysis by [37]. In three workshops, our research team designed and formulated requirements for managing risks associated with crypto assets.

Step 4: The evaluation consists of a quantitative survey and qualitative interviews [8]. Using the platform Prolific, the survey is aimed at 200 portfolio managers and financial advisors, as these professional groups can provide valuable insights based on their work experience in risk management. The participants' age range was 19 to 60 (30,1 on average), and the gender-balanced audience mainly consisted of individuals from the UK, Germany, and the US. We start our study with a topical introduction. The next section of our survey presents the elaborated requirements with their titles and descriptions, each with a seven-point Likert-scale of agreement for the participants [54]. Participants can also contribute ideas if anything needs to be added. After conducting the survey, we analyze the responses and qualitative feedback to refine the requirements. Further, we evaluate our requirements for crypto asset risk management through nine semi-structured interviews with experts from academia and practice in crypto assets as well as risk management, which we obtain through our social environment. In these interviews, we explain our research objective, approach, and final requirements and gather their qualitative feedback on the requirements for refinement. During the evaluation process, we hold several workshop sessions with the research team to refine the requirements and continuously supplement them with feedback.

4 Requirements for Crypto Asset Risk Management

Categorizing risk management requirements for FSP of crypto assets into *Assessment, Strategy, and Control* dimensions offers a clear and structured approach to effectively managing crypto asset risks. Each dimension addresses specific meta-aspects within the risk management process, while the identified requirements examine each dimension in detail. In Fig. 4, we show the dimensions and requirements (REQ1–10) elaborated from literature and interviews (I1–I5) for crypto asset risk management from an FSP perspective:

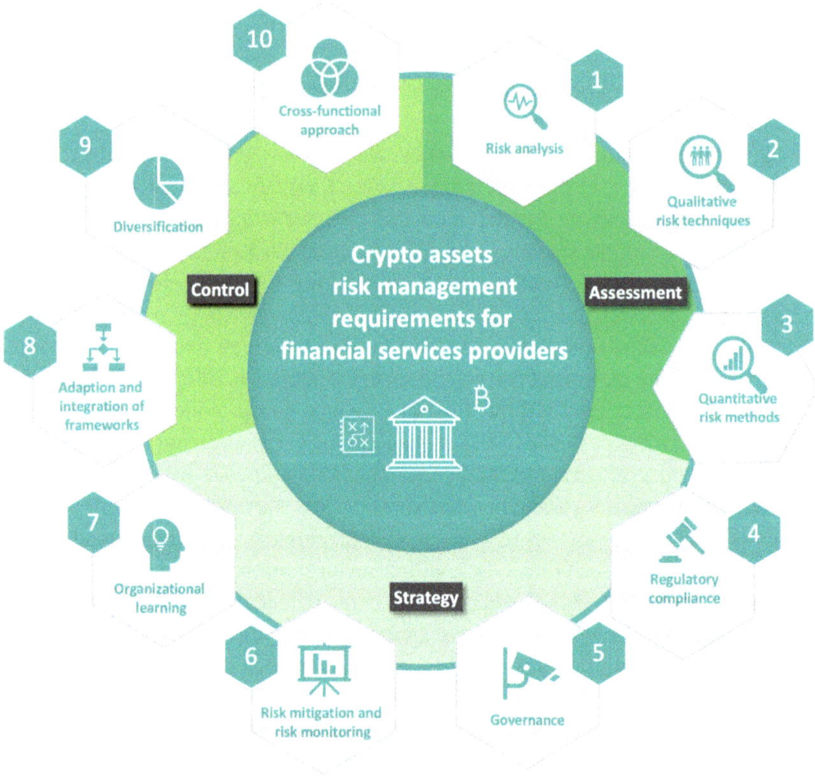

Fig. 4 Dimensions and requirements for crypto assets risk management

Assessment: The systematic identification and evaluation of risks is necessary to understand the nature, extent, and impact of various factors on the FSP. Use qualitative and quantitative techniques to estimate risk events' likelihood and potential impact.

REQ1: **Risk analysis** of crypto assets is crucial in their risk management due to the unique threats arising from volatility and the ever-changing regulatory environment (I1–5). "*Looking at the history, crypto assets or crypto instruments have a significantly higher volatility than traditional*" (I2). FSP should consider specific hazards regarding crypto activities, e.g., market, counterparty default, or operational risks [24]. When dealing with tokenized assets, organizations should be aware of issuer risk (I1, I3). The token is introduced with a promise, such as interest payments, dividends, or service delivery. That claim's credibility determines the token's corresponding value [47]. Furthermore, cyber and technical troubles [21] align with awareness (I1–5) of the risks of decentralized protocols, cyber criminals, and technological progress [1]. Additionally, the lack of an appropriate corporate strategy is indicative of the entire organization (I2, I4). Risk management for crypto assets must recognize the interdependence of multiple threats (I1–5).

REQ2: **Qualitative risk techniques** are a vital aspect of managing crypto assets. It involves evaluating subjective risks that depend on market conditions, regulations, or technical limitations (I1–5). Qualitative risk techniques are crucial for estimating risks through self-executing smart contracts [6]. The Financial Action Task Force (FATF) recommends using qualitative risk techniques to manage crypto assets threats [18]. This approach helps organizations identify and assess risks associated with crypto assets (I2). It should identify and evaluate the money laundering and terrorist financing risks (I1–5). In the United States, FSP are required by the Securities and Exchange Commission (SEC) to conduct a risk assessment before investing in or managing crypto assets [56]. Recently, major banks have adopted scenario analysis, which has become a crucial tool to employ advanced measurement approaches for operational risks, as mandated by supervisory authorities (I3, I4). It helps estimate and account for model risks that have not yet occurred or have only ensued to a limited extent (Kaiser, 2023). Scenario analysis is a technique for analyzing qualitative risks in traditional finance and applies to crypto assets (I4). "*To assess the risks, I would develop a list of criteria. Above all, I would have a look at the scenario calculation. In other words, I ask myself the question: what could actually go wrong*" (I4)?

REQ3: **Quantitative risk methods** employ mathematical and statistical tools (I2, I3, I4) to support FSP in making informed decisions to manage risks for crypto assets and estimate those threats [35]. This approach enables organizations to consider the level of risk they are willing to accept when investing in crypto assets. The Basel Committee on Banking Supervision (BCBS) suggests that quantitative risk methods should be employed to establish the capital level financial institutions should maintain to cover the risks associated with crypto assets [6]. According to the International Organization of Securities Commissions, assessing risks quantitatively can help FSP identify, evaluate, and prioritize crypto asset hazards and develop suitable strategies to manage them [26]. In addition, quantitative risk methods can assist organizations in complying with regulatory requirements related to crypto assets (I1, I3). The Fifth

Anti-Money Laundering Directive (5AMLD) in the European Union mandates financial institutions to evaluate the risks linked with crypto assets and establish suitable measures to alleviate those threats [16]. As crypto assets are a novel asset class with new and different risks [17, 20], the application of quantitative methods used in traditional finance should be explored when measuring crypto asset risks (I2, I3, I4, I5). We consider VaR, Monte Carlo simulations, and Economic Capital Models to be appropriate methods (I1–I5). All statistical methods can be used for crypto assets without limitations (I2, I3, I5). However, not all of them are currently used in practice (I5). "*VaR comes with certain weaknesses that do not work well in practice [...] VaR requires calibration for each asset class. This is very tedious*" (I2). "*It is relatively difficult to carry out something like a conventional VaR calculation with a 99.9 percent confidence level, simply because of the lack of data*" (I3). "*In traditional finance, we have credit scoring models, behavioral and application scoring. None of this exists yet and has therefore not been adapted to current and future market conditions*" (I5). A further option for quantitative measurement is Bayesian structural break analyses. An advantage of this approach is that it can be applied across all asset classes (I2). Nevertheless, the advantages and disadvantages of individual measurement methods regarding crypto asset risk management are still uncertain (I3).

Strategy: This dimension involves developing and planning strategies and measures to manage, minimize, or avoid assessed risks. These strategies must address legal and compliance issues, as well as organizational resource sharing. Overall, it is crucial to consider the FSP's objectives and align the risk strategy with the corporate strategy.

REQ4: When considering risk management for crypto assets, it is advisable to thoroughly examine the applicable **regulatory compliance** [38]. Compared to traditional finance assets, there is still regulatory uncertainty [17]. Nevertheless, the experts agree that regulation gives FSP security and can foster risk mitigation (I1–5). "*We need some kind of an alignment in global regulators. This alignment will provide more certainty in the space asset tracing and recovery asset tracing*" (I1). Crypto asset service providers that perform critical functions should be licensed and authorized [3, 17]. This includes companies that provide transfer, exchange, settlement, and custody services [3]. New regulations, such as 'Markets in Crypto-Assets' (MiCAR), control the market more strictly (I1, I2). Organizations' requirements for crypto assets could be more extensive (I3). Regulatory risks can also vary by country, and it is a challenge presently that we need to align regulations globally (I1, I5). BCBS 239 is a standard that governs threat reporting by financial institutions. It requires FSP to limit Group 2 crypto assets to less than 1 percent of their Tier 1 capital for risk management purposes. The decision to enter into such transactions (I2, I4) must be entirely consistent with the FSP's risk appetite and strategic objectives, as determined and approved by the bank's board of directors (I2). In addition, financial institutions' stress testing analyses must include crypto transactions [6].

REQ5: Unclear and inconsistent **governance** structures and processes can pose risks to investors, financial institutions, and the broader financial system. Governance encompasses various factors, including transparent decision-making processes, efficient risk management practices, and robust internal controls [6, 7]. By prioritizing governance as a requirement for risk management, organizations can better manage the unique hazards of crypto assets and build trust with stakeholders (I3, I5). Consensus-oriented governance models in crypto assets allow stakeholders to develop assets, enabling innovative risk management and achieving political goals. However, these models also pose challenges in determining responsibility for damages. The decentralized nature of decision-making makes it difficult to determine who is accountable for any harm that may arise [14].

REQ6: To assess newly emerging threats promptly, it is necessary to **continuously monitor** the crypto asset market and its interconnectedness with the broader financial system (I2, I4). The implementation of regulations such as the EU proposal MiCAR is required to **mitigate already identified risks**. Due to the rapid pace of developments in the crypto market and the potential for influential players to accelerate adoption, continuous monitoring is necessary to identify critical exposures should they arise [64]. Monitoring crypto assets' use on any crypto market presents a significant challenge. While conducting a comprehensive analysis of direct and indirect exposures is difficult, it is still possible to gain valuable insights (I3, I5). Official statistics are already helpful in shedding light on aggregated indirect exposures of the main economic sectors to crypto assets [25]. For instance, the European Securities and Markets Authority has published a risk monitoring framework for the crypto asset market, which covers stablecoins, crypto asset service providers, and decentralized financial services [15].

REQ7: By fostering a culture of **continuous learning for organizations**, FSP can ensure that their staff is up-to-date with the trends, threats, and best practices in the industry [19]. This culture can help organizations stay informed on the latest developments in the crypto asset market and adjust their risk management strategies accordingly (I3, I5). Organizational learning is essential for risk management in crypto assets, as the market is rapidly evolving, and new threats and opportunities are constantly emerging [63, 65]. By promoting ongoing education, organizations can build a more knowledgeable and skilled workforce, which can help them better manage risks and stay ahead of the curve in the rapidly evolving crypto ecosystem [39]. Organizations can provide training and development opportunities for their staff (I1–5). Additionally, organizations can encourage their staff to stay informed by reading publications (I1, I3) and attending events (I1, I3, I5).

Control: Implementing specific control measures and procedures involves ongoing monitoring and adjustment of risk management measures to ensure effectiveness and keep threat exposure within acceptable limits. Effective risk control necessitates a continuous assessment of the risk landscape and the effectiveness of the implemented controls, as well as inter- and intra-organizational resource sharing.

REQ8: FSP should have a **clear and robust risk management framework** appropriate to the threats of their crypto asset exposures and services (I2, I5). Given the anonymity and limited regulatory oversight of crypto assets, banks should fully **integrate** their risk management framework for cryptos into their overall risk management processes (I5), including those related to anti-money laundering and countering the financing of terrorism and sanctions evasion and increased fraud monitoring [6, 53]. One way to manage these risks is to integrate frameworks into existing processes [32]. FSP should assess whether they adequately incorporate the features of these mostly new and untested markets into their risk frameworks. In the longer term, methodologies and calibrations will likely need to be adjusted [4].

REQ9: The highly volatile and decentralized nature of crypto assets makes them particularly risky [41, 48]. Therefore, a lack of **diversification** can lead to significant losses. "*It is essential to differentiate between the banking perspective, which involves holding cryptos on its books with the intention of selling them to customers, and the investment perspective*" (I5). Most crypto assets must provide diversification benefits to investors. Smart Contracts, Proof of Work coins, Proof of Stake coins, and Masternodes are the best out-of-sample diversifiers. They consistently outperform the benchmark portfolio [31]. The diversification benefits of crypto assets must be less beneficial for risk-averse investors (I1, I3, I5). During uncertain economic environments, crypto assets offer similar diversification benefits to traditional assets [42]. There is a need to consider not only the number of different assets but also their specific characteristics (I1–5). A diversified portfolio could include assets with varying market capitalization, trading volume, and risk profiles [55]. Banks must adhere to strict credit risk standards when valuing crypto assets and cannot exploit diversification benefits. "*Holding Bitcoin and Ether will not allow me as a bank to claim any diversification benefits from a credit risk perspective. Unless the investment is hedged, the bank has to hold one euro in capital reserves for every euro it invests in ether. Similarly, for every euro invested in Bitcoin, the bank is required to hold a corresponding capital reserve for every euro invested. This is an additional burden on the bank*" (I2).

REQ10: A **cross-functional approach** enables looking at risks from different perspectives, thereby conducting a more comprehensive assessment. Through the collaboration of experts, potential risks can be identified early and managed appropriately (I1–5). Crypto assets risks are of particular concern due to their high volatility, lack of regulation, and cybersecurity concerns [2]. In addition, a cross-functional approach can help increase transparency and accountability in risk management of crypto assets (I3, I5). Organizations that adopt an interdisciplinary approach can better demonstrate that they have taken appropriate measures to minimize potential risks [40].

5 Evaluation

We evaluate our requirements mixed-methods [8] by a quantitative survey and qualitative insights from expert interviews. First, we proceeded with the survey, measuring the degree of agreement for each requirement, including keywords and descriptions, with a 7-point Likert scale. We interviewed 200 portfolio managers and financial advisors at asset and wealth management firms. Fig. 5 shows an average agreement of 87.3% on all requirements. We recognize the highest values for the risk

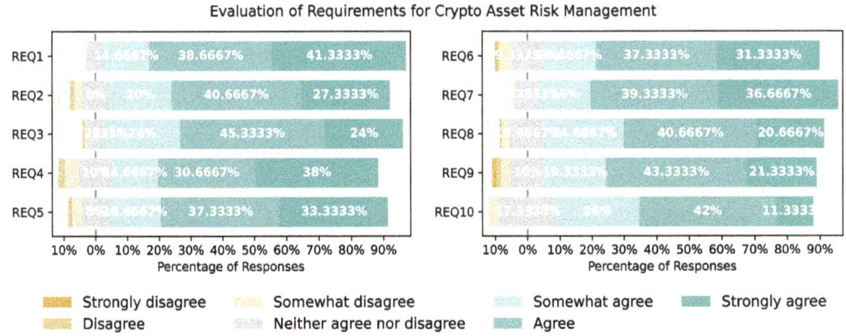

Fig. 5 Quantitative evaluation of the requirements with a survey (n=200)

analysis (REQ1), the quantitative risk methods (REQ3), and organizational learning (REQ7). On the contrary, the participants perceive the minimum agreement for the cross-functional approach (REQ10) and diversification (REQ9).

In addition, we conducted semi-structured interviews with nine highly qualified experts from academia and practice who specialize in risk management, crypto finance, or organizational adaptation. We presented the elaborated dimensions and requirements. Regarding understandability, the experts mention a high degree (IE1, IE4, IE9) as the requirement, including the high-level abstraction in Fig. 4, and the descriptions and explanations (IE2) support each other. The experts really like the focus of the requirements, as it combines risk assessment and mitigation with organizational aspects of learning and integration (IE1, IE3, IE6). The scope of the requirements is rated quite well. Some experts might add ethical perspectives, fairness, or other aspects (IE1, IE2, IE5, IE8, IE9). In addition, the experts appreciate the aspects of governance and integration of frameworks, organizational learning, and cross-functional approach, as these points are most lacking in reality (IE1, IE2, IE6). Finally, the requirements could enrich the common understanding of crypto assets as well as the awareness of crypto assets and specific risk management across the organization. The requirements highlight components for implementing their risk management processes and structures (IE6, IE9). Summarizing the results of the twofold evaluation, the study participants and the experts from the interviews underline the importance of combining qualitative and quantitative risk assessment. As a discrepancy, the experts emphasized inter- and cross-organizational integration (REQ8, REQ10) and governance.

6 Discussion

By developing requirements for establishing and improving risk management of crypto assets for FSP, we aim to boost their stability, ensuring they remain unshaken in turbulent markets. Risk factors and their management in crypto assets are complex and require a multidisciplinary approach. FSP must, therefore, not only navigate the intricate regulatory landscape but also develop robust internal systems to monitor and manage risks.

Both traditional financial assets and crypto assets are subject to a range of risk factors. However, there are notable differences between the two. Crypto assets, for instance, often display higher volatility and a paucity of historical data for risk assessment [27, 64]. This complicates the application of quantitative models based on data and necessitates a more comprehensive approach that entails the incorporation of qualitative factors [33], (I1–5). Qualitative methods and expert judgment are particularly important in regulatory uncertainty, which presents a significant challenge in developing appropriate risk management strategies. Large banks have begun to employ scenario analysis for the risk management of crypto assets in a manner similar to that observed for traditional financial assets (I4). Clear and coherent regulation is crucial for enhancing risk management [15, 17]. Coupled with diversification strategies, the implementation of clear and consistent regulatory frameworks can mitigate risks in the crypto asset market. However, the high correlation among these assets, particularly Payment Tokens, limits diversification's efficacy. Compared to Payment Tokens, managing risks associated with so-called Utility Tokens is focused on understanding and evaluating the adoption and usage of the underlying protocol, as the value of these tokens is less influenced by market speculation (I3).

Although technological challenges can be scary, they are solvable with further research and development. However, legal and regulatory risks are more complex. The regulatory landscape is trying to keep up with the pace of digital innovation within the crypto market but requires harmonized global efforts [51]. Frameworks such as the MiCA, GDPR, or AML regulation provide decision-making platforms, but the complexity of compliance requires continued efforts by FSP (I1). Market risks from extreme volatility and changes in sentiment emphasize the need for modern financial instruments and infrastructures. Overall, monitoring the crypto asset space and taking appropriate measures to manage the risks and capitalize on the opportunities is crucial.

7 Conclusion

Summary. This research paper examined the requirements for crypto asset risk management for financial service providers. In particular, it focused on elements of strategy, assessment, and control, which provide a comprehensive and organizational approach that extends beyond the mere implementation of legal requirements. We used a literature review and interviews with experts in assessing and managing crypto risks as a knowledge base. For evaluation, 200 participants, focusing on portfolio managers and financial advisors, completed our questionnaire and rated the requirements. Additionally, we conducted nine interviews with experts from academia and practice to obtain more profound qualitative feedback for refinement. In total, we collected ten requirements.

Limitations and Further Research. Our approach's rigid structure and implementation were both advantages and limitations. Using a structured literature review and semi-structured interviews to gain knowledge encountered obstacles such as conceptualizing the proper search string, selected databases, or the experts' and study participants' quantity and profile. Further insights can be gathered by integrating focus groups or empirical surveys. Including different FSP types and sizes as well as different crypto assets offered, promising research can be initiated based on our results. Furthermore, adopting emerging technologies, such as artificial intelligence, has immense potential to enhance risk management by facilitating improved decision-making. Nevertheless, further research needs to address data privacy, cybersecurity, and quality control challenges.

Implications. We contribute to the knowledge base of blockchain governance, security management in banking, and DeFi risk management. Our requirements should form the foundation for creating organization-specific, robust risk management frameworks that consider the correlation between different crypto assets, the impact of market volatility, and regulatory changes. Our results contribute to the IS research field and address the financial sector. For practical implications, FSP can adapt our requirements by creating new or modifying their existing risk management frameworks based on their type of FSP service offer or size. Comprehensive risk management does not depend solely on the further development of regulations. With our requirements, we deliver many aspects that FSP must proactively address to compete in the crypto asset ecosystem in the long term.

Acknowledgements This work has been developed in the project InKryBa and is partly funded by the DZ-Bank-Stiftung under grant number FRFMM-788/2022. The authors are responsible for the content of this publication.

References

1. Apostolaki, M., Zohar, A., & Vanbever, L. (2017). Hijacking bitcoin: Routing attacks on cryptocurrencies. In *2017 IEEE symposium on security and privacy (SP), IEEE* (pp. 375–392).
2. Arner, D. W., Zetzsche, D. A., Buckley, R. P., & Barberis, J. N. (2019). The identity challenge in finance: From analogue identity to digitized identification to digital kyc utilities. *European Business Organization Law Review, 20*, 55–80.
3. Bains, P., Ismail, A., Melo, F., & Sugimoto, N. (2022). *Regulating the crypto ecosystem: The case of stablecoins and arrangements*, International Monetary Fund.
4. Bank of England. (2023). *Prudential regulation authority annual report 2022–23, Technical report*. Accessed on March 1, 2024.
5. Barbereau, T., Sedlmeir, J., Smethurst, R., Fridgen, G., & Rieger, A. (2022). Tokenization and regulatory compliance for art and collectibles markets: From regulators' demands for transparency to investors' demands for privacy. In *Blockchains and the token economy: Theory and practice* (pp. 213–236). Springer.
6. Basel Committee on Banking Supervision. (2022). *Prudential treatment of cryptoasset exposures*. https://www.bis.org/bcbs/publ/d545.pdf
7. Brown, I., Steen, A., & Foreman, J. (2009). Risk management in corporate governance: A review and proposal. *Corporate Governance: An International Review, 17*(5), 546–558.

8. Bryman, A. (2006). Integrating quantitative and qualitative research: How is it done? *Qualitative Research, 6*(1), 97–113.
9. Chalmers, D., Fisch, C., Matthews, R., Quinn, W., & Recker, J. (2022). Beyond the bubble: Will nfts and digital proof of ownership empower creative industry entrepreneurs? *Journal of Business Venturing Insights, 17*, e00309.
10. Chen, Y., & Bellavitis, C. (2020). Blockchain disruption and decentralized finance: The rise of decentralized business models. *Journal of Business Venturing Insights, 13*, e00151.
11. Chimienti, M. T., Kochanska, U., & Pinna, A. (2019). Understanding the crypto-asset phenomenon, its risks and measurement issues. *Economic Bulletin Articles, 5.*
12. Chornous, G., & Ursulenko, G. (2013). Risk management in banks: New approaches to risk assessment and information support. *Ekonomika, 92*(1), 120–132.
13. Conti, M., Kumar, E. S., Lal, C., & Ruj, S. (2018). A survey on security and privacy issues of bitcoin *IEEE Communications Surveys Tutorials, 20*, 3416–3452.
14. Elliott, D. J., & De Lima, L. (2018). Crypto-assets: Their future and regulation. *Oliver Wyman*, 1–14.
15. European Securities and Markets Authority. (2022). *Crypto-assets and financial stability*. https://www.esma.europa.eu/sites/default/files/library/esma50-165-2251_crypto_assets_and_financial_stability.pdf. Accessed on March 15, 2023.
16. European Union. (2018). *Regulation (EU) 2018/843 of the European Parliament and of the Council of 30 May 2018*. https://eur-lex.europa.eu/legal-content/EN/TXT/?uri=CELEX%3A32018L0843. Accessed on March 15, 2023.
17. Ferreira, A., & Sandner, P. (2021). Eu search for regulatory answers to crypto assets and their place in the financial markets' infrastructure. *Computer Law and Security Review, 43*, 105632.
18. Financial Action Task Force. (2019). *Guidance for a risk-based approach to virtual assets and virtual asset service providers*. https://www.fatf-gafi.org/publications/fatfrecommendations/documents/guidance-rba-virtual-assets.html
19. Gephart, M. A., Marsick, V. J., Van Buren, M. E., Spiro, M. S., & Senge, P. (1996). Learning organizations come alive. *Training & Development, 50*(12), 34–46.
20. Gramlich, V., Guggenberger, T., Principato, M., Schellinger, B., & Urbach, N. (2023). A multivocal literature review of decentralized finance: Current knowledge and future research avenues. *Electronic Markets, 33.*
21. Hacibedel, B., & Perez Saiz, H. (2023). *Assessing macrofinancial risks from crypto assets*. International Monetary Fund.
22. Hartwich, E., Ollig, P., Fridgen, G., & Rieger, A. (2023). Probably something: A multi-layer taxonomy of non-fungible tokens. *Internet Research, 34*(1), 216–238.
23. Hopkin, P. (2018). *Fundamentals of risk management: Understanding, evaluating and implementing effective risk management*, Kogan Page Publishers.
24. Hsieh, S.-F., & Brennan, G. (2022). Issues, risks, and challenges for auditing crypto asset transactions. *International Journal of Accounting Information Systems, 46*, 100569.
25. International Monetary Fund. (2023). 11th statistics forum: Session iv—Urszula Kocha'nska. https://www.imf.org/-/media/Files/News/Seminars/2023/11th-stats-forum/session-iv-urszula-kochanska.ashx. Accessed on March 2, 2024.
26. International Organization of Securities Commissions. (2023). *Report on financial technologies (Fintech), innovation, regulation and sustainable growth*, Technical report, IOSCO. Accessed on March 1, 2024.
27. Jeegers, T. (2023). Cryptoasset taxonomies. In *Understanding crypto fundamentals: Value investing in cryptoassets and management of underlying risks* (pp. 121–137). Springer.
28. Jorion, P. (1996). Risk2: Measuring the risk in value at risk. *Financial nalysts Journal, 52*(6), 47–56.
29. Jorion, P. et al. (2007). *Financial risk manager handbook* (Vol. 406). John Wiley & Sons.
30. Kaiser, T. (2023). *Praxis des non-financial risk managements im Finanzsektor*. Springer.
31. Kajtazi, A., & Moro, A. (2019). The role of bitcoin in well diversified portfolios: A comparative global study. *International Review of Financial Analysis, 61*, 143–157.

32. KPMG (2022). *Cryptoassets: A risk management perspective.* https://kpmg.com/xx/en/home/insights/2022/04/cryptoasset-risk.html. Accessed on March 8, 2024.
33. Leo, M., Sharma, S., & Maddulety, K. (2019). Machine learning in banking risk management: A literature review. *Risks, 7*(1), 29.
34. Litterscheidt, R., & Streich, D. J. (2020). Financial education and digital asset management: What's in the black box? *Journal of Behavioral and Experimental Economics, 87*, 101573.
35. Ma, C., Colon, L., Dera, J., Rashidi, B., & Garg, V. (2021). Caraf: Crypto agility risk assessment framework. *Journal of Cybersecurity, 7*(1), tyab013.
36. Maia, G., & dos Santos, J. V. (2021). *Mica and defi ('proposal for a regulation on market in crypto-assets' and 'decentralised finance').* SSRN Electronic Journal.
37. Mayring, P. (2020). *Qualitative Forschungsdesigns* (pp. 3–17). Springer Fachmedien Wiesbaden.
38. Mikhaylov, A. (2023). Understanding the risks associated with wallets, depository services, trading, lending, and borrowing in the crypto space. *Journal of Infrastructure, Policy and Development, 7*(3).
39. Mishra, R., Singh, R. K., Kumar, S., Mangla, S. K., & Kumar, V. (2023). Critical success factors of blockchain technology adoption for sustainable and resilient operations in the banking industry during an uncertain business environment. *Electronic Commerce Research, 1.*
40. Mizrak, F. (2023). Integrating cybersecurity risk management into strategic management: A comprehensive literature review. *Research Journal of Business and Management, 10*(3), 98–108.
41. Piñeiro-Chousa, J., Ángeles López-Cabarcos, M., Sevic, A., & González-López, I. (2022). A preliminary assessment of the performance of defi cryptocurrencies in relation to other financial assets, volatility, and user-generated content. *Technological Forecasting and Social Change, 181.*
42. Platanakis, E., Sutcliffe, C., & Urquhart, A. (2018). Optimal vs naïve diversification in cryptocurrencies. *Economics Letters, 171*, 93–96.
43. Pytel, N., Zeiß, C., & Winkelmann, A. (2023). Enabling utxo-based backwards and forwards traceabilty. *ECIS 2023 Research Papers, 319*, 5–11. https://aisel.aisnet.org/ecis2023_rp/319
44. Qin, K., Zhou, L., Afonin, Y., Lazzaretti, L., & Gervais, A. (2021). *Cefi vs. defi—comparing centralized to decentralized finance.* arXiv:2106.08157v2.
45. Qu, S. Q., & Dumay, J. (2011). The qualitative research interview. *Qualitative Research in Accounting Management, 8*, 238–264.
46. Rehman, M. H., Salah, K., Damiani, E., & Svetinovic, D. (2020). Trust in blockchain cryptocurrency ecosystem. *IEEE Transactions on Engineering Management, 67*, 1196–1212.
47. Schär, F. (2021). ecentralized finance: On blockchain-and smart contract-based financial markets. *FRB of St. Louis Review.*
48. Schär, F. (2021). Decentralized finance: On blockchain- and smart contract-based financial markets. *Fed. Reserve Bank St. Louis Rev., 103.*
49. Schwiderowski, J., Pedersen, A. B., & Beck, R. (2023). Crypto tokens and token systems. *Information Systems Frontiers.*
50. Stulz, R. M. (2008). Rethinking risk management. In *Corporate risk management* (pp. 87–120). Columbia University Press.
51. Teng, H. W., Härdle, W. K., Osterrieder, J., Baals, L. J., Papavassiliou, V. G., Bolesta, K., ... & Orhun, E. (2023). Mitigating digital asset risks. Available at SSRN: https://ssrn.com/abstract=4594467 or https://doi.org/10.2139/ssrn.4594467 or https://papers.ssrn.com/sol3/papers.cfm?abstract_id=4594467
52. Thakor, A. V. (2020). Fintech and banking: What do we know? *Journal of Financial Intermediation, 41*, 100833.
53. The Bank for International Settlements. (2019). *Statement on crypto-assets.* https://www.bis.org/publ/othp14.htm
54. Tomitza, C., Schaschek, M., Straub, L., & Winkelmann, A. (2023). What is the minimum to trust ai?—a requirement analysis for (generative) ai-based texts. *Wirtschaftsinformatik 2023 Proceedings.*

55. Trimborn, S., Li, M., & Härdle, W. K. (2020). Investing with cryptocurrencies—a liquidity constrained investment approach. *Journal of Financial Econometrics, 18*(2), 280–306.
56. U.S. Securities and Exchange Commission. (2019). *Framework for "Investment contract" analysis of digital assets*. https://www.sec.gov/corpfin/framework-investment-contract-analysis-digital-assets. Accessed on March 15, 2023.
57. Valeonti, F., Bikakis, A., Terras, M., Speed, C., Hudson-Smith, A., & Chalkias, K. (2021). Crypto collectibles, museum funding and openglam: Challenges, opportunities and the potential of non-fungible tokens (nfts). *Applied Sciences, 11*, 9931. https://www.mdpi.com/2076-3417/11/21/9931
58. Verlande, L., Rudel, S., & Lechner, U. (2023). Requirements for a federated learning system to strengthen it security in human resource management. *Wirtschaftsinformatik 2023 Proceedings*.
59. vom Brocke, J., Simons, A., Niehaves, B., Riemer, K., Plattfaut, R., & Cleven, A. (2009). Reconstructing the giant: On the importance of rigour in documenting the literature search process. *17th European Conference on Information Systems* **o. A.**, 1–12.
60. Voskobojnikov, A., Wiese, O., Koushki, M. M., Roth, V., & Beznosov, K. K. (2021). The u in crypto stands for usable: An empirical study of user experience with mobile cryptocurrency wallets. In *Proceedings of the 2021 CHI conference on human factors in computing systems* (pp. 1–14). ACM. https://doi.org/10.1145/3411764.3445407
61. Whitaker, A., & Kräussl, R. (2020). Fractional equity, blockchain, and the future of creative work. *Management Science, 66*, 4594–4611.
62. Wurgler, J. (2000). Financial markets and the allocation of capital. *Journal of Financial Economics, 58*, 187–214.
63. Zeiß, C., Straub, L., Hahn, V., Lang, K., Schaschek, M., Tomitza, C., & Winkelmann, A. (2024). *Designing for banking resilience: A DeFi E-Learning solution* (Vol. 14621, pp. 325–338). Springer.
64. Zeiss, C., Straub, L., Schaschek, M., & Winkelmann, A. (2024). The obscure world of digital assets—design principles for user-centered platforms. In *ECIS 2024 proceedings* (Vol. 4, pp. 1–16). https://aisel.aisnet.org/ecis2024/track16_fintech/track16_fintech/4
65. Zetzsche, D. A., Arner, D. W., & Buckley, R. P. (2020). Decentralized finance. *Journal of Financial Regulation, 6*, 172–203.

Evaluation of Outlier Detection Methods for Anomaly Detection in Journal Entries: A Use Case Analysis

Tobias Schreier, Nicolai Gnoss, Marina Tropmann-Frick, and Martin Schultz

Abstract Detecting anomalous journal entries in a company's general ledger is essential for external auditors. An increasing trend employs outlier detection (OD) methods, especially machine learning methods, for anomaly detection in journal entry data. Recent research often lacks comparative analysis of OD methods. Thus, this study provides a comparative analysis of OD methods for journal entry anomaly detection using real-world accounting data. Additionally, in the context of domain-specific data preprocessing, we give special consideration to the amount, due to its importance for auditors. This yields three different dataset variants. We conduct our analysis based on three example accounts manually labeled by external auditors. Autoencoders, clustering-based local outlier factor (CBLOF), and histogram-based outlier score (HBOS) consistently outperform other methods across different accounts and dataset variants. With the provided results, this research enhances the understanding and applicability of OD methods for journal entry anomaly detection.

1 Introduction

Many companies are required by law to have their financial statements audited annually by external auditors. This annual audit aims to assure prospective stakeholders that the entity's published financial information complies with applicable accounting standards and is free from misstatements due to fraud or errors. Nowadays, companies try to standardize and automate their business processes as much as possible, relying mainly on information systems. For example, enterprise resource planning (ERP) systems process many business transactions on a daily basis, the financial impact of which is recorded as journal entries in the financial accounts. Consequently, this leads to an increasing amount of electronically available data that is relevant for auditing.

T. Schreier (✉) · N. Gnoss · M. Tropmann-Frick · M. Schultz
Hamburg University of Applied Sciences, Hamburg, Germany
e-mail: tobias.schreier@haw-hamburg.de

C. M. Flath et al. (eds.), *Digital Innovation and Organizational Transformation*, Lecture Notes in Information Systems and Organisation 83,
https://doi.org/10.1007/978-3-032-08483-5_22

The International Standard on Auditing (ISA) 240 deals with the auditor's responsibilities relating to fraud in an audit of financial statements [14]. One way to identify misstatements in financial statements, whether caused by fraud or error, is the analysis of accounting data at a detailed level, namely at journal entry level. With computer-assisted audit techniques (CAATs; [5], auditors can examine the entirety of journal entries, which is referred to as *journal entry testing*. Although required by auditing standards, there are no generally accepted rules or indicators that should be used to detect anomalous journal entries. In most cases, static rules are applied, which only check a few attributes of a journal entry at a time (e.g., postings with a high amount, postings close to fiscal year-end, or users with few postings), resulting in a high false positive rate. To cope with this problem and the large amount of data, the application of machine learning (ML) methods has been discussed in auditing research recently [15, 17]. Several research studies have shown that for anomaly detection tasks in auditing, ML methods can indeed achieve valuable results [27–29].

Against this background, this paper explores which outlier detection methods are suitable for detecting anomalous journal entries. We select multiple outlier detection (OD) methods from different algorithm types, apply them to a real-world accounting dataset, and compare their performance. We split the dataset into individual financial accounts to consider that accounts are the main structuring element of a company's financial statements. In addition, we incorporate domain knowledge in the preparation of the dataset by adding several computed attributes that mimic audit-relevant aspects of journal entries and explore different methods for handling the amount of a journal entry.

The remainder of the paper is structured as follows: Section 2 covers related research regarding anomaly detection in the context of external auditing. In Sect. 3, we describe the data preprocessing and the selected OD methods. Section 4 presents the results of our analysis. In Sect. 5, the principal findings, our main contributions, the limitations of our study, and future research are discussed. Finally, we conclude in Sect. 6 with a summary of our research.

2 Related Work

In recent decades, it has often been noted that the field of auditing has lagged behind technological progress due to the delaying effect of a large number of regulations and auditing standards [15]. However, various research studies have shown that the use of ML can have a huge impact on auditing and change it significantly [17, 31]. A major obstacle in identifying suspicious journal entries is the absence of labels. To overcome this problem, unsupervised learning methods like autoencoders can be used [22]. Reference [29] proved that anomaly detection using an autoencoder is also possible on smaller datasets by training the autoencoder not on all journal entries of a complete fiscal year but only on those of individual financial accounts. Reference [33] developed a prototype web application that uses a variational autoencoder and a long short-term memory architecture for detecting unusual journal entries. Reference [21] conducted a systemic review of existing studies which apply unsupervised anomaly detection in an auditing context. Reference [26] proposed a self-supervised learning framework to learn task invariant accounting data representations. Reference [4] applied seven supervised ML techniques, such as isolation forest and autoencoders, on a real-world general ledger dataset. Recently, [10] proposed the concept of artificial intelligence co-piloted auditing, which emphasizes the collaborative potential of auditors and foundation models such as LaMDA and GPT-4 in the audit domain. Using a developed chain-of-thought prompting strategy, the models were instructed to accomplish complex tasks such as journal entry testing.

The state of the art shows that several methods have been presented for anomaly detection in the context of financial auditing. However, the methods are only compared to a few other OD methods or to no other methods at all. Thus, this paper provides a comparison of different OD methods for journal entry anomaly detection. Due to the importance of the amount to auditors, our analysis is combined with the domain-specific preprocessing of the amount.

3 Feature Engineering and Outlier Detection Method Selection

3.1 Dataset Description

The dataset used in this study was sourced from the SAP ERP system of a food production and trading company and is the same dataset as in [29]. It comprises all journal entries recorded over the course of one fiscal year. The dataset consists of 72,917 journal entries with 302,365 line items, each of which is characterized by 29 features. In total, the dataset contains journal entries for 321 individual accounts. Since we conduct our analysis on a per account basis and line items from the same account are each associated with exactly one journal entry, we refer to line items as journal entries in the following. Three of the accounts were manually labeled by external auditors, as detailed in [29]. Thereby, the journal entries for the accounts *revenue domestic*, *revenue foreign*, and *expenses* were labeled as anomalous or not. We chose these accounts carefully in consultation with external auditors because we expect that they follow a standardized accounting system and are mainly handled through automated processes. Additionally, it is important to note that the revenue cycle is a critical area of focus in audits as it is classified as a high-risk area under auditing standards. With this selection of accounts, we also want to investigate how the OD methods perform with financial accounts of different sizes. Consequently, our sample comprises one large account and two relatively small accounts. The *revenue domestic* account contains 6,643, the *revenue foreign* account 651, and the *expenses* account 778 journal entries. Of these journal entries, 242 (3.64%), 21 (3.23%), and 27 (3.47%) were labeled as anomalous.

3.2 Data Preprocessing

Several preprocessing steps are undertaken to prepare the data for our analysis. In the context of domain-specific data preparation, first, four additional features are computed based on other features from the dataset (*DatesEqual*, *OneDateOutsideAccountingYear*, *PostingCloseToFiscalYearEnd*, and *CreationDateDayOfWeek*, see Table 1). The addition of these features is motivated by insights gathered from discussions with external auditors. In order to take into account the structure of the journal entries, sorted lists of all account numbers and names on the debit and credit side of a journal entry are created and added as additional features. The same approach is applied to the creditor and debtor numbers, names, and countries of origin. Note that the creditor and debtor numbers are combined in one feature *CredDebNumberList*. Together with the twelve additional features, each journal entry consists of 41 features.

All features are categorical except *AmountLocalCurrency*, which is numerical. Features with the same value across all accounts and entries are removed. Also, features with the same value on one or two accounts are dropped for the respective accounts but kept for the remaining accounts. Furthermore, features with duplicate meaning, features where each value is unique, and features that contribute to the additional computed features are removed. This decreases the number of features to 18 for the *revenue domestic*, 17 for the *revenue foreign*, and 15 for the *expenses* account. Table 1 shows the resulting set of features. The categorical features are one-hot encoded. We choose one-hot encoding because it is the state-of-the-art method for encoding categorical features. However, we acknowledge that there are other alternative category encoding methods like category embedding [11] that could be explored by future work. After one-hot encoding, the number of features is 358 for the *revenue domestic*, 125 for the *revenue foreign*, and 60 for the *expenses* account.

For the numerical feature *AmountLocalCurrency*, three different approaches are investigated, as the amount of a journal entry is of great importance for auditors, as many concepts (e.g. materiality thresholds) and risk assessments are based on the amount.

1. **Standardized Amount**: The amount is standardized using standard scaling.
2. **Binned Amount**: First, the amount is transformed by subtracting the mean and dividing by three times the standard deviation. To divide by three times the standard deviation is a heuristic decision and a value derived from statistics. After the transformation, the amount is replaced by a binary feature that indicates whether the amount is greater than or equal to 1 (1) or less than 1 (0). Thus, the binary feature indicates whether the amount is greater than three times the standard deviation.
3. **Separated Amount**: First, the amount is transformed as described before. Then, the amount is removed from the dataset, and the OD methods are applied to the dataset without the amount. After obtaining the labels from the OD methods, the labels are adjusted using the transformed amount. If the transformed amount is

Table 1 Features of the accounting dataset. Features marked with an asterisk (*) are added as additional domain-specific features. Crosses (x) indicate whether features are present in the data for the *revenue domestic* (RD), *revenue foreign* (RF), and *expenses* (E) account

Feature Name	*Feature Description*	*RD*	*RF*	*E*
DocNo	Unique identifier for journal entry	x	x	x
DocType	Type of journal entry (e.g. invoice)	x	x	x
PostingKey	Controls the posting of journal entry	x	x	x
DebitCreditIndicator	Debit/ credit indicator (D/C)	x	x	x
AmountLocalCurrency	Absolute amount	x	x	x
TaxCode	Tax code (e.g. input tax, sales tax)	x		
UserId	Unique identifier of the user	x	x	x
TCode	Function used to create journal entry	x	x	x
ReversalDocNoTrueFalse	Indicator for journal entry reversal	x	x	
DocOrigin	Origin (ERP module) of journal entry			x
DatesEqual*	Indicator for *PostingDate*, *DocDate*, *CreationDate* being equal	x	x	x
OneDateOutsideAccountingYear*	Indicator for one of the dates lying outside the fiscal year under review	x	x	
PostingCloseToFiscalYearEnd*	Indicator for the *PostingDate* being close to fiscal year end	x	x	x
CreationDateDayOfWeek*	Day of week of the *CreationDate*	x	x	x
DebitAccountNoList*	Sorted list of debit account numbers	x	x	x
CreditAccountNoList*	Sorted list of credit account numbers	x	x	x
CredDebNumberList*	Sorted list of creditor/ debtor numbers	x	x	x
DebtorNameList*	Sorted list of debtor names	x	x	x
DebCredCountryList*	Sorted list of creditor/ debtor countries	x	x	
		18	17	15

greater than or equal to 1, the label is set to 1 (outlier). The label is left unchanged if the transformed amount is less than 1. This approach is adopted from [29].

The OD methods are applied to each of the three dataset variants and the three accounts, and the results are compared in the evaluation.

3.3 Selected Outlier Detection Methods

With our selection of outlier detection (OD) methods, we aim to cover all popular OD algorithm types and include widely used OD methods. In total, we compare fifteen OD methods, spanning the algorithm types density-based, probabilistic, linear models, proximity-based, outlier ensembles, and neural networks. The selected OD methods are shown in Table 2. The *Python Outlier Detection* (PyOD) [32] library is utilized for most methods, while for DBSCAN, the implementation in the *scikit-learn* [23] library is used. The custom autoencoder is adopted from [29] and implemented using *Keras* [7] and *Tensorflow* [1].

DBSCAN and the PyOD methods, except the autoencoders, are optimized using repeated grid search. Thereby, the area under the receiver operating characteristic curve (ROC AUC) is used for scoring. The grid search is conducted on the revenue domestic account with the standardized amount. For the autoencoders (AE, VAE, and CAE), the configuration (architecture and hyperparameters) presented in [29] is used, which provides a significant performance boost over PyODs' default configuration.

For the PyOD methods and the CAE, the threshold, which decides whether an entry is classified as an outlier, is set to 0.1, meaning that the 10% of entries with the highest anomaly score are classified as anomalies. For DBSCAN, setting a custom threshold is not possible, as DBSCAN does not return anomaly scores but directly returns the cluster labels where -1 indicates outliers. The choice of the 10% threshold for PyOD methods and the CAE is based on discussions with external auditors, prioritizing recall over precision. This decision aims to minimize the risk of potentially anomalous journal entries being overlooked and is thus in line with the risk-oriented view in auditing. This threshold is preferred over thresholds determined based on each account's actual percentage of outliers. These thresholds could be calculated since we know the actual percentage of outliers for each of the three analyzed accounts from the labeling by the external auditors. The thresholds representing the actual

Table 2 Selected outlier detection methods

Abbreviation	*Method*	*Type*	*Reference*
DBSCAN	Density-Based Spatial Clustering of Applications with Noise	Density-based	[8]
ECOD	Empirical-Cumulative-distribution-based Outlier Detection	Probabilistic	[19]
PCA	Principal Component Analysis	Linear Models	[30]
MCD	Minimum Covariance Determinant	Linear Models	[12]
OCSVM	One-Class Support Vector Machine	Linear Models	[25]
LOF	Local Outlier Factor	Proximity-based	[6]
CBLOF	Clustering-Based Local Outlier Factor	Proximity-based	[13]
HBOS	Histogram-Based Outlier Score	Proximity-based	[9]
KNN	K Nearest Neighbors	Proximity-based	[3]
SOD	Subspace Outlier Detection	Proximity-based	[18]
IForest	Isolation Forest	Outlier Ensembles	[20]
LODA	Lightweight On-line Detector of Anomalies	Outlier Ensembles	[24]
AE	AutoEncoder	Neural Networks	[2]
CAE	Custom AutoEncoder	Neural Networks	[29]
VAE	Variational AutoEncoder	Neural Networks	[16]

percentage of outliers in the data would be 0.04 for the *revenue domestic* and 0.03 for the *revenue foreign* and *expenses* account.

4 Results

In our study, we analyze the performance of various OD methods. The methods are evaluated using labels manually created by external auditors. As performance metric, we use the ROC AUC score. Each method is executed ten times to account for randomness, and the results are averaged. Standard deviations are calculated to assess variability.

We split our analysis into three sections. Section 4.1 analyzes the methods' performance on the three dataset variants. The goal is to determine which preprocessing approach for the amount results in the highest performance. In Sect. 4.2, we compare the methods' performance on the three different financial accounts. We aim to investigate whether the methods perform differently on larger and smaller journal entry populations. Finally, in Sect. 4.3, we evaluate the methods' overall performance across all dataset variants and accounts. Additionally, we address the methods runtimes.

4.1 Performance on Different Dataset Variants

Figure 1 displays the ROC AUC scores for each dataset variant, averaged over the three accounts. For the binned and separated amount variants, deviations from the standardized amount are shown if they exceed 0.01. With the standardized amount, the top-performing methods are KNN, AE, CAE, and VAE. For the binned amount, CAE, VAE, CBLOF, HBOS, IForest, and AE perform best. For the separated amount, CAE, ECOD, HBOS, and AE are the leading methods. Conversely, LODA, MCD, and SOD consistently show the poorest performance across all dataset variants.

Binning the amount yields a slight performance improvement for some methods, such as IForest (+0.04), HBOS (+0.03), and CAE (+0.02), but significantly degrades performance for others, like MCD (−0.11), DBSCAN (−0.09), and OCSVM (−0.09). Overall, binning reduces average performance from 0.84 to 0.82. Thus, whether the OD methods should be trained with the binned amount instead of the standardized amount depends on the individual OD method employed. Separating the amount maintains an overall average performance of 0.84. While some methods benefit from separating the amount, such as LODA (+0.1), ECOD (+0.03), PCA (+0.03), HBOS (+0.03), and IForest (+0.03), others experience performance declines, including DBSCAN (−0.05), OCSVM (−0.05), LOF (−0.04), and KNN (−0.04). Thus, as with binning the amount, whether the amount should be separated depends on the utilized OD method.

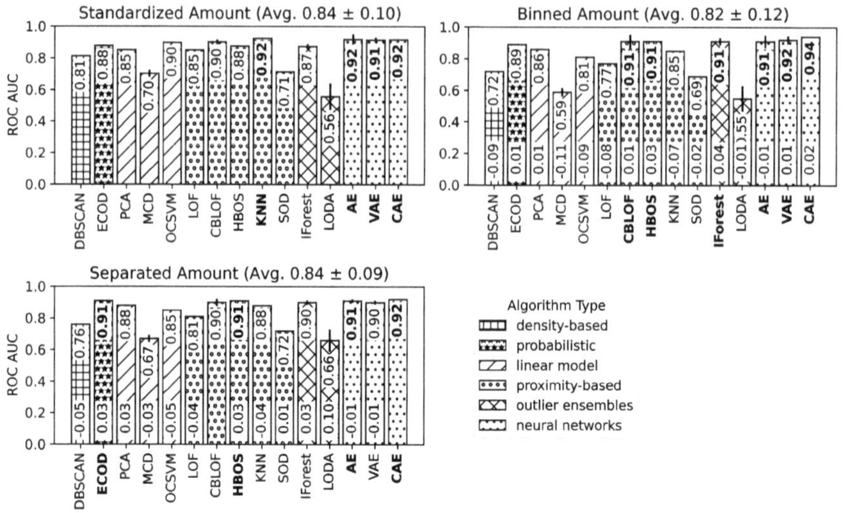

Fig. 1 ROC AUC scores per dataset variant (averaged across the three accounts). Best-performing methods are in **bold**. Error bars show standard deviation over ten iterations

Overall, we do not recommend binning or separating the amount but instead training the OD methods with the standardized amount. While for some methods binning or separating the amount can increase performance, overall performance does not change when separating the amount and even decreases when binning the amount. Thus, we recommend to use the standardized amount.

4.2 Performance on Different Financial Accounts

Figure 2 illustrates the ROC AUC scores for each financial account, averaged over the three dataset variants. Deviations from the *revenue domestic* account are shown for the *revenue foreign* and *expenses* accounts when they exceed 0.01.

Most methods perform better on the smaller *revenue foreign* and *expenses* accounts than on the larger *revenue domestic* account. Notably, LOF shows significantly better performance on smaller accounts (*revenue foreign*: +0.22; *expenses*: +0.26), while MCD performs much worse on smaller accounts (*revenue foreign*: −0.27; *expenses*: −0.25). The average performance increases from 0.81 on the *revenue domestic* account to 0.82 on the *revenue foreign* account and 0.85 on the *expenses* account. For the *revenue domestic* account, the best-performing methods are OCSVM, AE, CAE, and HBOS, while LODA, LOF, and SOD are the worst. On the *revenue foreign* account, CAE, VAE, CBLOF, and AE perform best, with MCD and LODA performing worst. For the *expenses* account, many methods, including ECOD, PCA, KNN, CBLOF, HBOS, IForest, VAE, and CAE, perform well, while MCD, LODA, and SOD perform poorly.

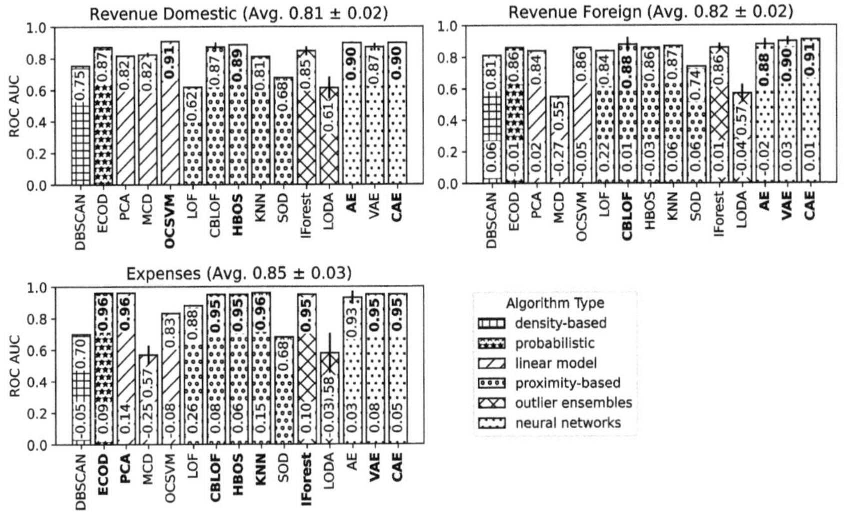

Fig. 2 ROC AUC scores per account (averaged across the three dataset variants). Best-performing methods are in **bold**. Error bars show standard deviation over ten iterations

In summary, for larger accounts, we recommend OCSVM or autoencoders, while for smaller accounts we recommend autoencoders, HBOS, or CBLOF.

4.3 Overall Performance and Runtime

Figure 3 presents the overall ROC AUC scores, averaged across all dataset variants and accounts. The top-performing methods overall are CAE, VAE, AE, CBLOF, and HBOS, while LODA, MCD, and SOD are the worst. Significant variability is noted for LODA, CBLOF, and AE across iterations.

The experiments are conducted on a system with 128 GB DDR4 RAM, an Intel Core i9-10980XE, and an NVIDIA TITAN RTX with 24 GB VRAM. Figure 4 shows method runtimes for each account, averaged across dataset variants. Runtimes include training and prediction times. On the *revenue domestic* account, the fastest methods are PCA, LODA, HBOS, and CBLOF, while on the *revenue foreign* and *expenses* accounts, PCA, HBOS, and OCSVM are fastest. MCD, KNN, and LOF are slowest on *revenue domestic*, MCD and CAE on *revenue foreign*, and the autoencoders on *expenses*.

In conclusion, for larger datasets, OCSVM or autoencoders are recommended, with CBLOF or HBOS being suitable if runtime is a concern. For smaller datasets, autoencoders, CBLOF, or HBOS are recommended, with CBLOF and HBOS being the faster methods.

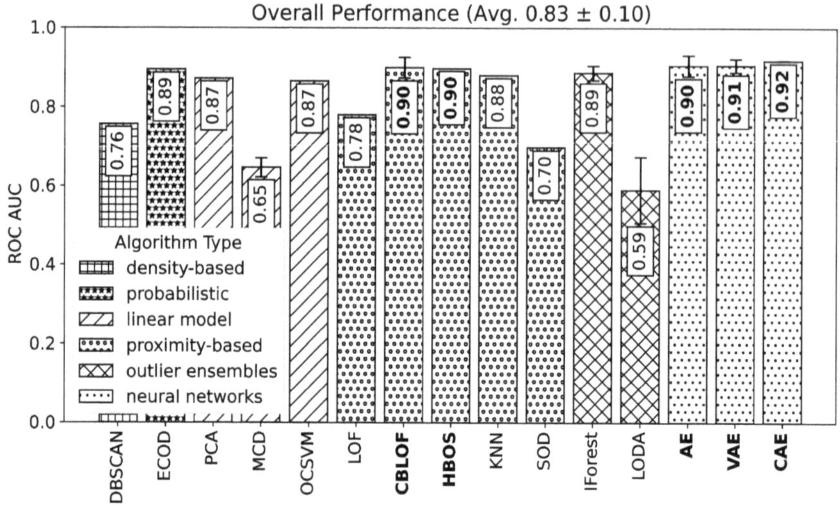

Fig. 3 ROC AUC scores averaged across all dataset variants and accounts. Best-performing methods are in **bold**. Error bars show standard deviation over ten iterations

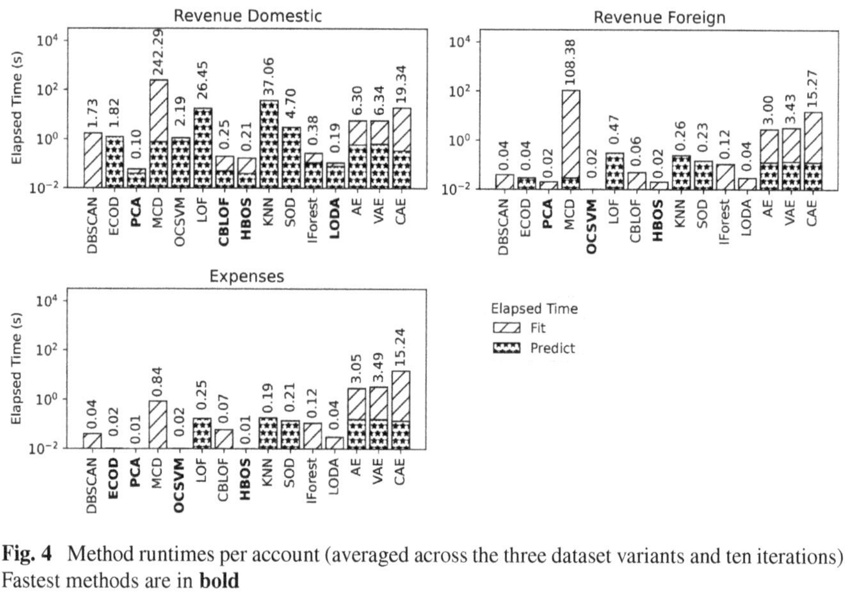

Fig. 4 Method runtimes per account (averaged across the three dataset variants and ten iterations). Fastest methods are in **bold**

5 Discussion

5.1 Principal Findings

Regarding the influence of domain-specific data preprocessing, standardizing the amount emerges as the best preprocessing approach. Binning the amount, while beneficial for some methods, generally leads to a slight decrease in average performance from 0.84 to 0.82. Separating the amount maintains an overall stable performance, with some methods benefiting, while others experience performance declines. Since standardizing the amount is the simpler preprocessing method and yields similar performance as separating the amount, the amount should be standardized.

In terms of performance on different financial accounts, the results vary based on the size of the accounts. A notable trend is that the smaller *revenue foreign* and *expenses* accounts yield better performance from most OD methods compared to the larger *revenue domestic* account. Overall, the methods CAE, VAE, AE, CBLOF, and HBOS are consistently among the top performers across all dataset variants and financial accounts. Significant variability in performance is observed for LODA, CBLOF, and AE, indicating that while these methods can be highly effective, their performance may be inconsistent.

Based on these findings, we recommend using the standardized amount for training OD methods. For larger datasets, OCSVM or autoencoders are recommended, with HBOS or CBLOF as suitable alternatives if runtime is a concern. For smaller datasets, autoencoders, CBLOF or HBOS are preferred, with CBLOF or HBOS being advisable if runtime is important.

5.2 Contributions

Our study offers valuable insights into the performance of OD methods for anomaly detection in journal entry data. By providing a comparative analysis of selected OD methods using a real-world accounting dataset, we address a gap in existing research, which often lacks such detailed evaluations. Our focus on the domain-specific preprocessing of the amount, a critical aspect for auditors, adds an understanding of how different preprocessing techniques impact the performance of various OD methods.

We select a diverse range of OD methods that encompass various algorithm types. One of the key contributions of our study is the practical guidance it offers on preprocessing the amount. Our results indicate that standardizing the amount is the best and simplest approach. We also highlight the mixed effects of binning and separating the amount, emphasizing that while these techniques can benefit certain methods, they may also degrade the performance of others.

Furthermore, our analysis reveals how different OD methods perform across financial accounts of varying sizes. For larger accounts, OCSVM and autoencoders are recommended, while for smaller accounts we recommend autoencoders, CBLOF, and HBOS. In addition to performance considerations, our study also addresses the practical aspect of method runtime. We identify HBOS and CBLOF as suitable alternatives when runtime is a concern, providing actionable insights for auditors who must balance accuracy with efficiency in their anomaly detection tasks.

Overall, our research enhances the understanding and applicability of OD methods for journal entry anomaly detection, offering both theoretical contributions and practical recommendations that can benefit the field of auditing.

5.3 Limitations

Our comparison is limited to a selected set of OD methods. Although we considered a comprehensive array of OD methods from various algorithm types, it is possible that other methods not included in our study might achieve better results. Additionally, our analysis is based on data from one fiscal year and one company, which may limit the generalizability of our results. The dataset may not encompass the variety and complexity present in other industries or companies. This context-specific nature of our dataset means that our findings might not be directly applicable to different settings without further validation.

Moreover, our analysis focused on three specific accounts due to the availability of labeled data. While these accounts were carefully selected in consultation with external auditors to represent different sizes and types of accounts, they may not fully capture the diversity of the entire dataset. Other accounts, possibly with different characteristics and anomaly patterns, might yield different results. Lastly, the reliance on manually labeled data introduces a dependency on the accuracy and consistency of the labeling process. The labels provided by external auditors, although thorough, are subject to human judgment and may contain biases or errors. This inherent subjectivity in the labeling process could affect the evaluation of the OD methods' performance.

In summary, while our study provides valuable insights into the performance of various OD methods for journal entry anomaly detection, these limitations suggest that further research is needed to validate and extend our findings across different methods, datasets, and contexts.

5.4 Future Research

To address these limitations, future research could expand the array of OD methods included in the analysis. Additionally, extending the analysis to multiple fiscal years or different companies would provide a broader perspective and improve the generalizability of the findings. By examining data from various time periods and diverse organizational contexts, researchers can better understand the variability and consistency of OD methods' performance. Finally, collaborating with external auditors to generate labels for additional accounts is another promising avenue for future research. A more comprehensive set of labeled data would enable a deeper evaluation of OD methods across a wider range of financial accounts.

In conclusion, future research should aim to broaden the scope of OD methods evaluated, extend the temporal and organizational range of the datasets analyzed, and collaborate with auditors for more comprehensive labeling. These efforts will contribute to a more robust and applicable understanding of anomaly detection in journal entry data, ultimately enhancing the effectiveness of automated auditing processes.

6 Conclusion

In this paper, we conducted an analysis of various OD methods to identify anomalous journal entries in financial data. Our study addressed a gap in the literature by providing a comparative evaluation of multiple OD methods using a real-world accounting dataset. We investigated the impact of different preprocessing techniques for the amount, a crucial aspect in the context of auditing, and assessed the performance of the methods across financial accounts of varying sizes.

Our findings demonstrate that standardizing the amount is the best and simplest method for preprocessing the amount. While binning and separating the amount can benefit certain methods, these techniques generally result in mixed performance, thereby making standardization the better approach. We also observed that the performance of OD methods varies significantly with the size of the financial accounts. Larger accounts benefit from methods like OCSVM and autoencoders, whereas smaller accounts perform well with autoencoders, CBLOF, and HBOS.

Overall, our study highlights CAE, VAE, AE, CBLOF, and HBOS as consistently high-performing methods across the different dataset variants and accounts. LODA, MCD, and SOD demonstrated poor performance. Additionally, we provided practical guidance on method selection based on performance and runtime, recommending methods like HBOS and CBLOF for scenarios where runtime efficiency is critical. Despite the valuable insights, our study has limitations, including the focus on a single company's dataset and the reliance on manually labeled data for specific accounts. These limitations suggest the need for further research to validate our findings across diverse datasets and contexts. Future work should also explore additional OD methods.

In conclusion, our research provides a detailed evaluation of OD methods for journal entry anomaly detection, offering both theoretical contributions and practical recommendations. By addressing the specific needs of auditors and highlighting the performance and efficiency of various methods, we aim to enhance the effectiveness of automated auditing processes and contribute to the broader field of financial anomaly detection.

References

1. Abadi, M., Barham, P., Chen, J., Chen, Z., Davis, A., Dean, J., Devin, M., Ghemawat, S., Irving, G., Isard, M., Kudlur, M., Levenberg, J., Monga, R., Moore, S., Murray, D. G., Steiner, B., Tucker, P., Vasudevan, V.,… & Warden, P. (2016). TensorFlow: A system for large-scale machine learning. In *Proceedings of the 12th USENIX Conference on Operating Systems Design and Implementation, OSDI'16* (pp. 265–283). USENIX Association.
2. Aggarwal, C. (2017). *Outlier analysis* (2 ed.) Springer Cham. https://doi.org/10.1007/978-3-319-47578-3
3. Angiulli, F., & Pizzuti, C. (2002). Fast outlier detection in high dimensional spaces. In T. Elomaa, H. Mannila, H. Toivonen (Eds.), *Principles of data mining and knowledge discovery* (pp. 15–27). Springer Berlin Heidelberg. https://doi.org/10.1007/3-540-45681-3_2
4. Bakumenko, A., & Elragal, A. (2022). Detecting anomalies in financial data using machine learning algorithms. *Systems, 10*(5), 130. https://doi.org/10.3390/systems10050130
5. Braun, R. L., & Davis, H. E. (2003). Computer-assisted audit tools and techniques: analysis and perspectives. *Managerial Auditing J, 18*(9), 725–731. https://doi.org/10.1108/02686900310500488
6. Breunig, M. M., Kriegel, H. P., Ng, R. T., & Sander, J. (2000). LOF: Identifying density-based local outliers. *SIGMOD Rec, 29*(2), 93–104. https://doi.org/10.1145/335191.335388
7. Chollet, F., & et al. (2015). Keras. https://github.com/fchollet/keras
8. Ester, M., Kriegel, H.P., Sander, J., & Xu, X.(1996). A Density-Based algorithm for discovering clusters in large spatial databases with noise. In *Proceedings of the Second International Conference on Knowledge Discovery and Data Mining, KDD'96* (pp. 226–231). AAAI Press. https://doi.org/10.5555/3001460.3001507
9. Goldstein, M., & Dengel, A. (2012). Histogram-Based Outlier Score (HBOS): A fast unsupervised anomaly detection algorithm. In *KI-2012: Poster and Demo Track*.
10. Gu, H., Schreyer, M., Moffitt, K., & Vasarhelyi, M. (2023). Artificial intelligence co-piloted auditing. *SSRN Electron J*. https://doi.org/10.2139/ssrn.4444763
11. Guo, C., & Berkhahn, F. (2016). Entity embeddings of categorical variables.
12. Hardin, J., & Rocke, D. (2004). Outlier detection in the multiple cluster setting using the minimum covariance determinant estimator. *Computational Statistics & Data Analysis, 44*(4), 625–638. https://doi.org/10.1016/S0167-9473(02)00280-3
13. He, Z., Xu, X., & Deng, S. (2003). Discovering cluster-based local outliers. *Pattern Recogn Lett, 24*(9), 1641–1650. https://doi.org/10.1016/S0167-8655(03)00003-5
14. IAASB: ISA 240. (2024). The auditor's responsibilities relating to fraud in an audit of financial statements. https://www.iaasb.org/publications/proposed-international-standard-auditing-240-revised-auditor-s-responsibilities-relating-fraud-audit
15. Issa, H., Sun, T., & Vasarhelyi, M. (2017). Research ideas for artificial intelligence in auditing: The formalization of audit and workforce supplementation. *Journal of Emerging Technologies in Accounting, 13*(2), 1–20. https://doi.org/10.2308/jeta-10511
16. Kingma, D., & Welling, M. (2022). Auto-Encoding variational bayes.
17. Kokina, J., & Davenport, T. (2017). The emergence of artificial intelligence: How automation is changing auditing. *Journal of Emerging Technologies in Accounting, 14*(1), 115–122. https://doi.org/10.2308/jeta-51730
18. Kriegel, H.P., Kröger, P., Schubert, E., & Zimek, A. (2009). Outlier detection in Axis-Parallel subspaces of high dimensional data. In T. Theeramunkong, B. Kijsirikul, N. Cercone & T. B. Ho (Eds.), *Advances in knowledge discovery and data mining* (Vol. 5476, pp. 831–838). Springer Berlin Heidelberg. https://doi.org/10.1007/978-3-642-01307-2_86
19. Li, Z., Zhao, Y., Hu, X., Botta, N., Ionescu, C., & Chen, G. (2023). ECOD: Unsupervised outlier detection using empirical cumulative distribution functions. *IEEE Transactions on Knowledge and Data Engineering, 35*(12), 12181–12193. https://doi.org/10.1109/TKDE.2022.3159580
20. Liu, F., Ting, K., & Zhou, Z. H. (2008). Isolation forest. In *2008 Eighth IEEE International Conference on Data Mining* (pp. 413–422). https://doi.org/10.1109/ICDM.2008.17

21. Nonnenmacher, J., & Gómez, J. (2021). Unsupervised anomaly detection for internal auditing: Literature review and research agenda. *The International Journal of Digital Accounting Research*, 1–22. https://doi.org/10.4192/1577-8517-v21_1
22. Nonnenmacher, J., Kruse, F., Schumann, G., & Gómez, J. M. (2021). Using autoencoders for data-driven analysis in internal auditing. In Proceedings of the 54th Hawaii International Conference on System Sciences. https://doi.org/10.24251/HICSS.2021.697
23. Pedregosa, F., Varoquaux, G., Gramfort, A., Michel, V., Thirion, B., Grisel, O. , Blondel, M., Prettenhofer, P., Weiss, R., Dubourg, V., Vanderplas, J., Passos, A., Cournapeau, D., Brucher, M., Perrot, M., & Duchesnay, E. (2011). Scikit-learn: Machine Learning in Python. *The Journal of Machine Learning Research, 12*(85), 2825–2830.
24. Pevný, T. (2016). Loda: Lightweight on-line detector of anomalies. *Mach Learn, 102*(2), 275–304. https://doi.org/10.1007/s10994-015-5521-0
25. Schölkopf, B., Platt, J., Shawe-Taylor, J., Smola, A., & Williamson, R. (2001). Estimating the support of a high-dimensional distribution. *Neural Computation, 13*(7), 1443–1471. https://doi.org/10.1162/089976601750264965
26. Schreyer, M., Sattarov, T., & Borth, D. (2021). Multi-view contrastive self-supervised learning of accounting data representations for downstream audit tasks. In *Proceedings of the Second ACM International Conference on AI in Finance, ICAIF '21*. Association for Computing Machinery. https://doi.org/10.1145/3490354.3494373
27. Schreyer, M., Sattarov, T., Borth, D., Dengel, A., & Reimer, B. (2017). Detection of anomalies in large scale accounting data using deep autoencoder networks. CoRR.
28. Schreyer, M., Sattarov, T., Schulze, C., Reimer, B., & Borth, D. (2019). Detection of accounting anomalies in the latent space using adversarial autoencoder neural networks. CoRR.
29. Schultz, M., & Tropmann-Frick, M. (2020). Autoencoder neural networks versus external auditors: Detecting unusual journal entries in financial statement audits. In *Proceedings of the 53rd Hawaii International Conference on System Sciences* (pp. 5421–5430). https://doi.org/10.24251/HICSS.2020.666
30. Shyu, M.L., Chen, S.C., Sarinnapakorn, K., & Chang, L. (2006). Principal component-based anomaly detection scheme. In T. Young Lin, S. Ohsuga, C.J. Liau & X. Hu (Eds.), *Foundations and novel approaches in data mining, studies in computational intelligence* (pp. 311–329). Springer Berlin Heidelberg. https://doi.org/10.1007/11539827_18
31. Sun, T., & Vasarhelyi, M. (2017). Deep learning and the future of auditing: How an evolving technology could transform analysis and improve judgment. *The CPA Journal, 87*(6), 24–29.
32. Zhao, Y., Nasrullah, Z., & Li, Z. (2019). PyOD: A python toolbox for scalable outlier detection. *Journal of Machine Learning Research, 20*(96), 1–7.
33. Zupan, M., Budimir, V., & Letinic, S. (2021). Journal entry anomaly detection model. *Intelligent Systems in Accounting, Finance and Management, 27*(4), 197–209. https://doi.org/10.1002/isaf.1485

When to Use Smart Contracts Instead of Traditional Contracts—A Conceptual Analysis

Anna Hupe

Abstract Smart contracts are code-based representations of business logic that encapsulate predefined rules that they verify and execute autonomously. As self-executing agreements, these contracts running on a blockchain facilitate interactions be-tween untrusted parties, eliminating the need for intermediaries. They speed pro-cesses, increase transparency, and facilitate data exchange across national and or-ganizational boundaries, providing a competitive advantage. However, there are significant costs associated with implementing smart contracts. In our study, we conduct a comparative analysis of these costs and compared them to traditional contracts. Using a combination of literature review and expert interviews, we dissect the cost structures of both approaches at an abstract level. We then construct a matrix to systematically compare traditional contracts with smart contracts. This framework allows us to model the conditions that favor the use of smart contracts over traditional ones, and to identify instances where each approach has a distinct advantage.

1 Introduction

Please Since Szabo [26] defined smart contracts already back in the mid-1990s as a "*computer protocol that digitally facilitates, verifies, and enforces the contract's performance*", the term should be widely known and applied by organizations. Eggers et al. [10] see smart contracts as the "*next revolutionary innovation toward extensive automation*". However, to date, smart contracts are rarely implemented by organizations. This is despite the fact that they offer several solutions, such as automating processes, reducing transaction costs, eliminating sources of error, and increasing trust between contracting parties. Smart contracts can be implemented wherever business logic can be defined as a clear if-then relationship. Current automation technologies such as enterprise resource planning systems, workflow management

A. Hupe (✉)
University of Kassel, Kassel, Germany
e-mail: anna.hupe@uni-kassel.de

C. M. Flath et al. (eds.), *Digital Innovation and Organizational Transformation*, Lecture Notes in Information Systems and Organisation 83,
https://doi.org/10.1007/978-3-032-08483-5_23

systems, and robotic process automation differ from smart contracts in one important way: the location of their storage. Smart contracts are stored on a blockchain, its content is stored in a decentralized manner. After they are programmed and stored on a blockchain, they serve three functions. They (1) store rules, (2) verify rules, and (3) self-execute them [14]. Although there has been some research on smart contracts [12–15, 18], no one has yet looked at how they compare to traditional contracts. However, comparing traditional contracts to smart contracts is an important first step in facilitating their implementation. It provides the basis for making informed decisions for or against a smart contract. With our study, we provide a basis for organizations and individuals to classify whether and in which cases a traditional contract should be used and when the use of a smart contract is appropriate. The following research question forms the basis of our study:

RQ "*In what cases and under what conditions are smart contracts more appropriate than traditional contractual arrangements*?"

To answer the research question, we compare the costs of creating and executing a traditional contract with the costs of creating and executing a smart contract. In doing so, we focus on the most prominent blockchain on which smart contracts run: Ethereum. This paper is structured as follows: first, we explain the concept of smart contracts and use cases where smart contracts are already implemented. Second, we present other use cases that are particularly suitable for the application of smart contracts. In the third part, the methodological part, we explain the procedure of our literature review, the expert interviews and the framework on which our analysis is based. In the fourth part, we examine the cost structures of conventional and smart contract arrangements. We use the matrix developed in part 3 as the basis for this analysis. The underlying assumption is that smart contracts are perfectly programmed and free from corrupting influences. We then summarize and discuss our results (part 5) and present a conclusion and the contribution of our research to theory and practice (part 6).

2 Background

2.1 Smart Contracts

According to the first existing definition, given by Szabo [26], "*a smart contract is a set of promises, specified in digital form, including protocols within which the parties perform on these promises*". Richard et al. [21] state that smart contracts "*enforce autonomous verification in any transaction in the network under some pre-defined conditions*". Thus, smart contracts are promises in digital form, with accompanying protocols that fulfill those promises. Programs that execute a protocol under certain circumstances and are stored on a blockchain can be categorized as a smart contract [34]. Smart contracts map business logic and execute agreements and transactions, even complex ones, between blockchain participants automatically and without intermediaries [34]. They are computer protocols that map, verify, or provide technical support for the execution of contracts [27]. A smart contract is a program code written to be deployed, verified, and executed on a blockchain platform [25]. It is immutable, decentralized, open source, self-executing, accurate, and fast. Therefore, the smart contract technology is an attractive decentralized application that enables computations on top of a blockchain [31]. In order to run and execute a smart contract, it is necessary to have a money exchange via cryptocurrency to incentivize validators to solve cryptocraphic puzzles. Therefore, in the following analysis, we assume that the appropriate and necessary wallet is set up and available. Since the analyzed case focuses on the Ethereum blockchain, the gas fees are paid in Ether [16]. The fee for the operation of smart contracts is called "*gas fee*" [16]. The exact cost of the gas fee depends on supply and demand, similar to the price of electricity. When all this is set up, smart contracts allow users to create self-executing algorithms with immutable rules on blockchain systems [21]. The computer protocols can manage large sums of money, execute asset transactions, and govern the transfer of digital rights between multiple parties [18]. There is a consensus in the scientific community that the application domain for smart contracts is much broader than the currently widely known use cases in the financial sector [8, 12, 31]. Wherever business logic can be described as an if-then relationship by exchanging events and value, smart contracts (and their sub smart contracts) can be implemented [12]. The principle of "*code is law*" applies [31]. The three main tasks that smart contracts are overtaking are (1) storage of rules, (2) verification of rules, and (3) self-execution of the terms of an agreement between untrusted parties [19], [14]. Storage on the blockchain ensures that a smart contract is immutable and that transactions initiated by the contract are autonomously and truthfully executed. A smart contract is subsequently unalterable, making it all the more important for the parties involved to agree on all contract contents and contingencies.

2.2 *Common Use Cases for Smart Contracts*

As mentioned earlier, smart contracts have great applications when intermediaries need to be trusted and when contracting parties agree on a contractual object that can be described by simple or nested if-then relationships [12]. By using smart contracts, processes can be managed with greater speed, efficiency, and accuracy. Trust and transparency can be created because there is no central third party involved and the encrypted records of transactions are shared with network participants [14]. This eliminates the question of whether information has been altered for personal gain. Because of the blockchain approach, smart contracts create great security and enable savings by eliminating intermediaries and the associated time delays and fees. In the financial sector, smart contracts are used to make international trade faster and more efficient [32]. Standardized rules agreed upon by the parties involved enable an ecosystem of trust. Banks as trusted parties become redundant and credit checks can be automated with smart contracts [32]. Furthermore, smart contracts facilitate data exchange and thus serve as a driver for industrial business models [6]. In the case of Walmart's pilot project, smart contracts enable automatic penalties for late deliveries [15]. The food companies Nestlé, Dole, Unilever, and Tyson Foods are part of the pilot project. By tracking deliveries, transfers are made automatically as soon as the goods are delivered. These smart contracts are processed via a private blockchain on Hyperledger Fabric. If deliveries do not happen within the agreed timeframe specified in the smart contract, a penalty payment is due [15]. According to Walmart, the pilot project has resulted in significant savings due to a reduction in transaction costs [15]. The exact amount of savings generated by the implementation of smart contracts has not yet been disclosed. In addition to their use in supply chains, smart contracts also have great potential applications in the public sector. They can be used to automate the transfer of ownership of real estate and the associated land registry entries [24]. This saves the parties involved expensive notary fees and time-consuming procedures. The smart contract would then formulate in a way that the land registry entry changes automatically [24]. This could be, for example, the receipt of the transfer of the real estate price from the buyer to the seller. Once the smart contract detects such a transfer ("*if function*"), the land registry entry is changed ("*then function*").

Estonia recently launched an "*e-residency*" program based on smart contracts that allows anyone in the world to apply for a "*transnational digital identity and authentication to access secure services, as well as to digitally encrypt, verify, and sign documents*" [28]. Further applications in the public sector currently tested are registration of property titles (prototyped inter alia in Sweden, Georgia, Honduras and Ghana), tax administration and electronic invoice insurance (initiated in China), digital identity (initiated in Italy), managing identification of state residents (planned in the United States), transfer of ownership (planned in the United States) and online votes (tested inter alia in Denmark, France and The Netherlands) [28]. According to the World Bank, close to 2% of the Global Gross Domestic Product ends up in the hands of corrupt government agents [28]. As implementing smart contracts in the public sector creates transparency, the World Bank identifies them as a key technology to overcome corruption [28]. Once the required infrastructure for the relevant use case is in place, there are significantly more applications for smart contracts. For example, self-driving taxis can independently bill users for their services [17]. In that case, the smart contract is programmed in a way that it opens the door if the car as soon as a solvent passenger is interested in a ride. The location of the car is tracked by an oracle as soon as the passenger is getting into the car. The oracle records the trip and then feds this information into the smart contract. The computer protocol calculates the amount to be paid, which is automatically debited from the deposited account when the passenger completes the trip and leaves the vehicle. Following the same principle, it is possible to automate the process of renting vacation homes, bicycles, etc. In the manufacturing industry, smart contracts enable networked machines to automatically request services. For example, repair slots are automatically booked when the machine needs to be repaired or serviced [3]. Smart contracts also provide use cases for facilitating and automatizing administration within organizations. In human resources, for example, smart contracts can be used to automatically manage bonuses and expense reimbursements. Besides, they can verify the originality of certificates and skills which assists the process of (intraorganizational) staffing.

3 Methodology

In order to compare traditional and smart contracts and their associated costs in a structured manner, we created a framework to guide our analysis. Specifically, we developed a matrix that allows us to capture and compare the factors relevant to setting up and operating both traditional and smart contracts and their associated costs. In the first column, we distinguish the number of contracting parties. We distinguish between cases where (1) two parties (1:1) or (2) more than two parties (1) are involved in the contract. For the contract duration in the second column, we analyze (1) non-recurring/one-time use contracts and (2) longer contract durations (see Fig. 1). For the different contract durations, we then distinguish the costs associated with the contract; we differentiate between one-time and recurring costs. The resulting matrix allows us to evaluate which type of contract is most appropriate in each case, focusing on the predictable costs incurred over the lifetime of the contract. In our model, we assume that the subject matter of the contract is fulfilled. Costs that may be incurred as a result of non-compliance are not included in the analysis to ensure comparability of cases.

As a basis for our analysis, we conducted a systematic literature review following vom Brocke et al. [30] and using Cooper's related taxonomy (vom [30]. We defined existing research on smart contracts and directly related concepts and technologies (phases 1 and 2) to provide a framework for our literature analysis. In addition to information systems databases AIS eLibrary and Information Systems Research Journals, we selected the computer science databases ACM Digital Library and IEEE

Contractual Relationship	**Contract Period: Non-recurring**		**Contract Period: Recurring**	
	One Time costs*	**Recurring costs***	**One Time costs***	**Recurring costs***
1:1 contracting parties				
1:n contracting parties				
* Costs for contract creation, contract verification, and execution of contract, *assuming contract compliance*				

Fig. 1 Analysis framework for comparing contract related costs

(phase 3). By selecting highly ranked databases and including papers published in them, we ensure the quality of the papers included and thus the validity of our analysis. As suggested by Cooper in his taxonomy, it is also necessary to define keywords that form the basis of the literature analysis (vom [30]. Our search strings ("smart contracts" AND "transaction costs") and ("smart contracts" AND "gas fee") and ("transaction costs" AND "business contract") yielded a total of 1,886 potentially relevant documents as of February 10, 2024, with a starting year of 2008, as 2008 is considered the beginning of blockchain technology with the publication of the white paper around bitcoin. After reviewing the titles and abstracts, we divided the papers into the categories "highly relevant" and "relevant", where the title and abstract indicated that the paper detailed transaction costs for smart or conventional contracts. If neither the title nor the abstract indicated that the paper detailed transaction costs in conventional or smart contracts, the paper was considered "not relevant". This process resulted in 100 highly relevant and relevant papers. After reading the articles in their entirety, we were able to index 17 papers that we included in the analysis based on their content on transaction costs in smart contracts or conventional contract design (phases 3 and 4). Based on these highly relevant articles, we developed theoretical overview matrices of the cost structures of traditional and smart contracts (phase 5), which we present in the following sections of the paper. To validate and challenge our findings, we conducted a qualitative study. We interviewed twelve smart contract practitioners (Table 1). Six of them are currently deploying smart contracts in their organizations, three are programming smart contracts, and three are lawyers who review smart contracts before they are translated into code.

In these semi-structured interviews, which lasted between 30 and 60 min, we presented our findings from the literature review and the matrix (Fig. 1). We then asked for their feedback and suggestions for changes. After transcribing the recorded interviews, we coded them using MAXQDA. We included all aspects and feedback of the analysis framework that were mentioned by three or more of the experts during the interviews. We included them in our model when three or more experts recommended the same changes. An overview of the methodological approach is shown in Fig. 2.

Table 1 Overview of interview partners

Interviewee	Reason for including expert in data collection process
1–6	Smart contract users in banking, insurance and retail sectors
7, 8, 9	Smart contract developers with $\geq$ 3 years of experience
10, 11, 12	Legal professionals with $\geq$ 10 years of experience and an additional smart contract qualification for $\geq$ 3 years

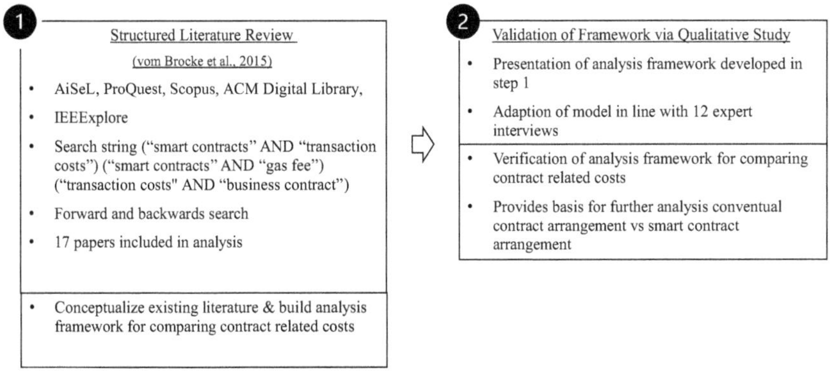

Fig. 2 Analysis framework for comparing contract related costs

4 Analysis

4.1 Conventional Contract Agreement

Following the analytical framework derived above (Fig. 1), we will first analyze the costs incurred in the case of *two contractors* (1:1) and a *single contract term.* We will then compare these costs to the case where *more than two contractors* (1:n) are involved. After analyzing the two one-time contract cases, we will consider the case of *recurring* contracts. Again, we start with the case where *two parties* are involved and then compare it to the case where *more than two parties* are part of the contract.

Many contracts are concluded by *two parties.* This applies for the majority of B2B supply contracts as well as for rental, employment, and sales contracts. In all cases, it is important that the subject matter and terms of the contract, as well as any related contingencies, are clarified and stated. The more complex the subject matter of the contract, the more likely it is that the parties will involve legal counsel in drafting the contract, also in the case of a *non-recurring contract* agreement. This ensures that the contract is legally binding and free of errors. The total one-time cost of agreeing on the content of the contract (including legal experts) comes at a cost; the more complex it is and the longer it takes to agree on its content, the more expensive the one-time cost of drafting it. Since in the first scenario the contract is *non-recurring*, there are no recurring costs.

In case *more than two parties* (1:n) are involved in the contract, the effort required to draft the contract is greater than in a two-party setting. This is because the interests of several parties must be coordinated when drafting the contract. Also, the effort to define the subject matter of the contract is obviously more complex than the process when only two parties are concerned. The more contractors involved and the more complex its content, the higher the coordination costs. Thus, the one-time costs in the 1:n setting are greater than those in the 1:1 setting. Since the duration of the contract is limited to a single event, no recurring costs arise. In case of a *recurring contract* between *two parties* (1:1), the one-time costs are just as high as in the case of a non-recurring contract (see above). This is because in both cases, all contingencies must be addressed. In the case of a recurring contract, recurring costs are incurred because both parties must verify compliance with the agreed-upon subject matter. Depending on the application, this can also be done by third parties (service providers). The total recurring cost is therefore the sum of the verification costs of both parties.

In case *more than two parties* (1:n) are involved in a *recurring* contract, the one-time costs are just as high as in the case of a 1:n non-recurring contract. This is because in both cases, all possible contingencies must be addressed. The overall recurring costs (verification costs) in a 1:n setting are higher than in a 1:1 setting. Similar to the 1:1 setting, the verification costs comprise all expenses for checking the compliance of contractual objects, possibly completed by service providers. The more complex the contract setting (contracting parties and contract complexity) the higher the verification costs since the compliance with the contract must be checked by all contractors individually.

4.2 Smart Contract Arrangement

After having structured the costs of conventional contract creation (see Fig. 3), we will now do the same for smart contracts (see Fig. 4). In the first case, where a contract is *non-recurring* and concluded between *two contracting parties*, the onetime costs are higher than those for traditional contract creation. This is because additional costs are incurred because not only do all parties need to agree on the subject matter of the contract and clarify contingencies, but the agreement also needs to be translated into a smart contract and programmed accordingly. The process leading up to the actual programming of the smart contract is also more expensive than creating a traditional contract agreement. This is because lawyers with special training in smart contract law are needed to validate its content. Lawyers without this training are not permitted to review the content of a contract that is to be translated into a smart contract and declare it legally binding ("*Many legal professionals have not yet fully grasped what smart contracts are or how they function.*", expert 10). Lawyers with the additional training to declare a smart contract legally binding are rare these days, so they have high hourly rate ("*Many do not see the potential and therefore do not perceive the necessity to undergo the appropriate further education.*", expert 11). If the programmer has questions about the content of the contract during the coding process, both parties to the contract and the aforementioned legal experts will need to come to the table to resolve the ambiguity. The experts in our qualitative study agree that the cost of creating a smart contract is three to ten times higher than the cost of creating a traditional contract. Even though the contract is set up for a one-time event, there are still recurring costs. This is because the smart contract is responsible for verifying and enforcing its terms. It increases the cost of verification. These costs come from the price of gas and the amount of gas used.

Contractual Relationship	**Contract Period: Non-recurring**		**Contract Period: Recurring**	
	One Time costs*	**Recurring costs***	**One Time costs***	**Recurring costs***
1:1 contracting parties	- Agreement and review of contract contents by **A and B** - Legal verification by **legal advisor** - Cost for verifying the occurrence of contractual objects by A and B (if necessary, by service providers) Costs < one-time costs for 1:n contracting parties for conventual contracts	No recurring costs as contractual object is nonrecurring	- Agreement and review of contract contents by **A and B** - Legal verification by **legal advisor** - Cost for verifying the occurrence of contractual objects by A and B (if necessary, by service providers) Costs = one-time costs for 1:1 contracting parties for conventual contracts	- Costs for verifying the occurrence and compliance of contractual objects by **contracting parties A and B** (if necessary, by service providers) - Overall verification costs = x * 2 Costs < recurring costs for 1:n contracting parties for conventual contracts
1:n contracting parties	- Agreement and review of contract content by **contracting parties (n)** - Legal verification by **legal advisor** - Costs for verifying the occurrence and compliance of contractual objects by **contracting parties (n)** (if necessary, by service providers) Costs > one-time costs for 1:1 contracting parties for conventual contracts	No recurring costs as contractual object is nonrecurring	- Agreement and review of contract contents by **contracting parties (n)** - Legal verification by **legal advisor(s)** Costs = one-time costs for 1:n contracting parties for conventual contracts	- Costs for verifying the occurrence and compliance of contractual objects by **contracting parties (n)** (if necessary, by service providers) - Overall verification costs = x * n Costs > recurring costs for 1:1 contracting parties for conventual contracts
* Costs for contract creation, contract verification, and execution of contract, *assuming contract compliance*				

Fig. 3 Overview of costs in a conventional contract arrangement

Contractual Relationship	Contract Period: Non-recurring		Contract Period: Recurring	
	One Time costs*	**Recurring costs***	**One Time costs***	**Recurring costs***
1:1 contracting parties	- Agreement and review of contract contents by **A and B** - Legal verification by **special legal advisor(s)** - The contract's content is programmed as a smart contract by an **external party** and stored on Ethereum. Costs < one-time costs for 1:n contracting parties for smart contracts > one-time costs for 1:1 contracting parties for conventional contracts	- Costs for verifying the occurrence and compliance of contractual objects by **smart contract** - Overall verification costs = total gas used * gas price (gas price is fluctuating) Costs < recurring costs for 1:n contracting parties for smart contracts	- Agreement and review of contract contents by **A and B** - Legal verification by **special legal advisor** - The contract's content is programmed as a smart contract by an **external party** and stored on Ethereum. Costs = one-time costs for 1:1 contracting parties for smart contracts	- Costs for verifying the occurrence and compliance of contractual objects by **smart contract** - Overall verification costs = total gas used * gas price (gas price is fluctuating) Costs < recurring costs for 1:n contracting parties for conventual contracts
1:n contracting parties	- Agreement and review of contract content **by contracting parties (n)** - Legal verification by **special legal advisor(s)** - The contract's content is programmed as a smart contract by an **external party** and stored on Ethereum. Costs > one-time costs for 1:1 contracting parties for smart contracts	- Costs for verifying the occurrence and compliance of contractual objects by **smart contract** - Overall verification costs = total gas used * gas price (gas price is fluctuating) Costs > one-time costs for 1:1 contracting parties for smart contracts	- Agreement and review of contract contents by **contracting parties (n)** - Legal verification by **special legal advisor(s)** - The contract's content is programmed as a smart contract by an **external party** and stored on Ethereum. Costs = one-time costs for 1:n contracting parties for smart contracts	- Costs for verifying the occurrence and compliance of contractual objects by **smart contract** - Overall verification costs = total gas used * gas price (gas price is fluctuating) Costs < recurring costs for 1:n contracting parties for conventual contracts

* Costs for contract creation, contract verification, and execution of contract, *assuming contract compliance*

Fig. 4 Overview of costs in a smart contract arrangement

If *more than two* (1:n) contracting parties enter a smart contract for a *one-time* contractual relationship, the one-time costs for agreeing on the content of the contract are greater than in the 1:1 case. Because more parties with different interests are involved.

in agreeing on the subject matter of the contract, the associated setup costs are higher than when creating a smart contract. Since the contract terms are more complicated than in the 1:1 contract constellation, the cost of translating and programming a smart contract based on the agreement(s) is also higher. Since the contract is agreed for a longer period of time, the smart contract continuously monitors the occurrence of the deposited conditions. For the continuous monitoring of the smart contract, a gas fee is permanently incurred (recurring costs). These costs are higher compared to 1:1 contractual relationship because the associated smart contract is more complex in 1:n contractual relationships.

In case a contract is *recurring* and concluded between *two contracting parties*, the onetime costs are equal to the onetime costs that arise when two parties are entering a smart contract that is non-recurring. This is because all contingencies and cases need to be agreed, whether the contracts are recurring or non-recurring. Similar to the previous cases, lawyers with special training in smart contract validation are required. The recurring costs in a 1:1 recurring smart contract setting are higher than in a one-time smart contract setting, because gas fees are due throughout the term of the contract.

In the last scenario in which a contract is *recurring* and concluded between *more than two contracting parties* (1:n), the onetime costs for setting up a smart contract are equal to the costs that arise when a 1:n contract is set up for a non-recurring period. Due to the recurring contract period, the recurring costs of a 1:n smart contract relationship are higher than in case of a 1:n non-recurring smart contract relationship (see Fig. 3).

5 Analysis

The analysis shows that the total one-time cost of setting up smart contracts is much higher than the cost of setting up conventional contracts (experts 1 - 12). This is because in addition to the cost of agreeing the terms of the contract, there are legal fees and programming costs to translate the content of the contract into smart contracts. The total recurring cost of smart contracts depends on the complexity and duration of the contract. In the case of a 1:n contractual relationship, the recurring cost of smart contracts to automatically verify and execute contract elements is less than the sum of the costs incurred when all parties manually verify and execute contracts. Depending on the complexity of the contract between two contracting parties, the recurring costs are lower in a traditional contracting environment. This is because if the contract is entered into once, the one-time review of the contract terms is low and easily verifiable. However, if the contract terms between two contractors are highly complex, for example, involving various external databases, it may be more advantageous to implement smart contracts. In general, our analysis has shown that the more complex a contract (determined by the contract objects and the parties involved), the higher the one-time costs. In these cases, the use of smart contracts is preferable. Despite the high setup costs, smart contracts offer the advantage that checking and executing rules is less expensive than doing it manually. The less complex the contracts are, and only from a cost perspective, the traditional contract can still be used. However, if security is the primary concern and transaction costs are secondary, smart contracts should be used. This is also in line with the original idea and goal of all blockchain applications: the primary decision for blockchain and smart contract solutions should not be based on cost aspects, but on security aspects.

6 Conclusion and Contribution to Theory and Practice

Although there have been studies on the cost structure of smart contracts, such as the composition of gas fees [29] and energy consumption to run smart contracts [33], we are the first to directly compare the costs associated with setting up traditional and smart contracts. This comparison provides the basis for further research around the computing protocols analyzed. Based on our findings, use cases such as Walmart can be quantitatively analyzed once the relative savings generated by using smart contracts are published. The matrix we developed provides a starting point for analyzing other key factors that influence a decision for or against smart contracts. Kannengiesser et al. [13] identify technical challenges associated with smart contracts. They provide initial solutions to the identified challenges. Based on this, our matrix offers another important step to sensitize organizations for the use of smart contracts. In addition, we create a first relevant tool for practitioners and academics to determine whether to choose conventional or smart contracts. In addition to the existing 10-step decision path for blockchain applications [20], we introduce a criteria catalog through our morphological box. This catalog aims to determine when it is appropriate to use a smart contract, and when a conventional contract should be preferred.

Overall, the paper provides a basis for evaluating the use of smart contracts in terms of effectiveness. For practitioners, our results help them to better assess when the use of smart contracts in their organization is worthwhile or not. We provide them with concrete evaluation dimensions. We also contribute to theory, as our work is the first to provide a basis for evaluating smart contracts in terms of effectiveness. So far, and since smart contracts are a rather new phenomenon, there has been quite a lot of research on this topic [1–5, 7, 8, 9, 11–14, 22, 23, 25–29, 31]. The various application scenarios of smart contracts have been extensively analyzed and presented in the literature. It is common for new digital innovations to be surrounded by extensive research, and smart contracts are no exception. However, there is a lack of evaluation regarding the cost structures of smart contracts compared to conventional contracts. Our research addresses this gap by comparing the costs associated with deploying smart contracts versus traditional contracts. In doing so, we provide a foundation for further research to evaluate smart contracts across different aspects and on blockchains other than Ethereum, such as Hyperledger Fabric. These aspects may include employee adoption, organizational knowledge required for successful implementation, and exploration of additional applications and use cases for smart contracts.

Literaturverzeichnis

1. Albizri, A., & Appelbaum, D. (2021). Trust but verify: The oracle paradox of blockchain smart contracts. *Journal of Information Systems, 35*(2), 1–16. https://doi.org/10.2308/ISYS-19-024
2. Bai, X., Cheng, Z., Duan, Z., & Hu, K. (2018). Formal modeling and verification of smart contracts. In *Proceedings of the 2018 7th International Conference on Software and Computer Applications. ICSCA 2018: 2018 7th International Conference on Software and Computer Applications. Kuantan Malaysia, 08 02 2018 10 02 2018*. ACM (pp. 322–326).
3. Balcerzak, A. P., Nica, E., Rogalska, E., Poliak, M., Klieštik, T., & Sabie, O. M. (2022). Blockchain technology and smart contracts in decentralized governance systems. *Administrative Sciences, 12*(3), 96. https://doi.org/10.3390/admsci12030096
4. Carvalho, A., & Karimi, M. (2021). Aligning the interests of newsvendors and forecasters through blockchain-based smart contracts and proper scoring rules. *Decision Support Systems, 151*, 113626. https://doi.org/10.1016/j.dss.2021.113626
5. Chen, T., Li, Z., Zhou, H., Chen, J., Luo, X., Li, X., & Zhang, X. (2018). Towards saving money in using smart contracts. In *Andrea Zisman und Sven Apel (Hg.): Proceedings of the 40th International Conference on Software Engineering: New Ideas and Emerging Results. ICSE '18: 40th International Conference on Software Engineering*. Gothenburg Sweden, 27 05 2018 03 06 2018. ACM (pp. 81–84).
6. Chong, A. Y. L., Lim, E. T., Hua, X., Zheng, S., & Tan, C. W. (2019). Business on chain: A comparative case study of five blockchain-inspired business models. *Journal of the Association for Information Systems*, 1308–1337. https://doi.org/10.17705/1jais.00568
7. Christidis, K., & Devetsikiotis, M. (2016). Blockchains and smart contracts for the internet of things. *IEEE Access, 4*, 2292–2303. https://doi.org/10.1109/ACCESS.2016.2566339
8. Cuccuru, P. (2017). Beyond bitcoin: An early overview on smart contracts. *International Journal of Law and Information Technology, 25*(3), 179–195. https://doi.org/10.1093/ijlit/eax003
9. Egelund-Müller, B., Elsman, M., Henglein, F., & Ross, O. (2017). Automated execution of financial contracts on blockchains. *Business & Information Systems Engineering, 59*(6), 457–467. https://doi.org/10.1007/s12599-017-0507-z
10. Eggers, J., Hein, A., Weking, J., Böhm, M., & Krcmar, H. (2021). Process automation on the blockchain: An exploratory case study on smart contracts. In *Tung Bui (Hg.): Proceedings of the 54th Hawaii International Conference on System Sciences. Hawaii International Conference on System Sciences: Hawaii International Conference on System Sciences (Proceedings of the Annual Hawaii International Conference on System Sciences).*
11. Halaburda, H. (2020). Understanding smart contracts as a new option in transaction cost economics. S.l.: SSRN.
12. Huang, Y., Zhang, P., & Jin, Z. (2021). Improving business operation efficiency by using smart contract. In *2021 2nd Asia Service Sciences and Software Engineering Conference. ASSE '21: 2021 2nd Asia Service Sciences and Software Engineering Conference*. Macau Macao, 24 02 2021 26 02 2021. ACM (pp. 34–40).
13. Kannengiesser, N., Lins, S., Sander, C., Winter, K., Frey, H., & Sunyaev, A. (2022). Challenges and common solutions in smart contract development. *IIEEE Trans. Software Eng, 48*(11), 4291–4318. https://doi.org/10.1109/TSE.2021.3116808

14. Khan, S. N., Loukil, F., Ghedira-Guegan, C., Benkhelifa, E., & Bani-Hani, A. (2021). Blockchain smart contracts: Applications, challenges, and future trends. *Peer-to-peer networking and applications, 14*(5), 2901–2925. https://doi.org/10.1007/s12083-021-01127-0
15. Lacity, M. C., & Van Hoek, R. (2021). How Walmart Canada used blockchain technology to reimagine freight invoice processing. *MIS Quarterly Executive*, 219–233. https://doi.org/10.17705/2msqe.00050
16. Li, C. (2021). Gas estimation and optimization for smart contracts on ethereum. In 2021 36th IEEE/ACM International Conference on Automated Software Engineering (ASE). 2021 36th IEEE/ACM International Conference on Automated Software Engineering (ASE). Melbourne, Australia, 15.11.2021 - 19.11.2021: IEEE (1082–1086).
17. Li, M., Chen, Y., Lal, C., Conti, M., Martinelli, F., & Alazab, M. (2023). Nereus: Anonymous and secure ride-hailing service based on private smart contracts. *IEEE Transactions on Dependable and Secure Computing, 20*(4), 2849–2866. https://doi.org/10.1109/TDSC.2022.3192367
18. Liu, H. (2020). A novel supply chain model based on smart contract. In *Proceedings of the 2020 2nd International Electronics Communication Conference. IECC 2020: 2020 2nd International Electronics Communication Conference.* Singapore Singapore, 08 07 2020 10 07 2020. ACM (pp. 115–120).
19. Mohanta, B. K., Panda, S. S., & Jena, D. (2018). An overview of smart contract and use cases in blockchain technology. In *2018 9th International Conference on Computing, Communication and Networking Technologies (ICCCNT). 2018 9th International Conference on Computing, Communication and Networking Technologies (ICCCNT).* Bangalore, 10.07.2018 - 12.07.2018: IEEE (pp. 1–4).
20. Pedersen, A. B., Risius, M., & Beck, R. (2019). A ten-step decision path to determine when to use blockchain technologies. *MIS quarterly executive, 18*(2), 99–115. https://doi.org/10.17705/2msqe.00010
21. Richard, R., Prabowo, H., Trisetyarso, A., & Soewito, B. (2020). Smart contract development model and the future of blockchain technology. In *2020 the 3rd International Conference on Blockchain Technology and Applications. ICBTA 2020: 2020 the 3rd International Conference on Blockchain Technology and Applications.* Xi'an China, 14 12 2020 16 12 2020. ACM (pp. 34–39).
22. Shahab, S., & Allam, Z. (2020). Reducing transaction costs of tradable permit schemes using blockchain smart contracts. *Growth and Change, 51*(1), 302–308. https://doi.org/10.1111/grow.12342
23. Shailak, J. (2020). Smart contracts: Building blocks for digital transformation. Unpublished.
24. Shinde, D., Padekar, S., Raut, S., Wasay, A., & Sambhare, S. S. (2019). Land registry using blockchain—A survey of existing systems and proposing a feasible solution. In *2019 5th International Conference on Computing, Communication, Control And Automation (ICCUBEA). 2019 5th International Conference On Computing, Communication, Control And Automation (ICCUBEA).* Pune, India, 19.09.2019—21.09.2019. IEEE (pp. 1–6).
25. Simić, S., Marković, M., & Gostojić, S. (2021). Smart contract and blockchain based contract management system. In *7th Conference on the Engineering of Computer Based Systems. ECBS 2021: 7th Conference on the Engineering of Computer Based Systems.* Novi Sad Serbia, 26 05 2021 27 05 2021. ACM (pp. 1–8).
26. Szabo, N. (1996). Smart contracts: Building blocks for digital markets. *EXTROPY: The Journal of Transhumanist Thought, 18*(2).
27. Taherdoost, H. (2023). Smart contracts in blockchain technology: A critical review. *Information, 14*(2), 117. https://doi.org/10.3390/info14020117
28. Triana Casallas, J. A., Cueva-Lovelle, J. M., Rodríguez, M., & José, I. (2020). Smart contracts with blockchain in the public sector. *International Journal of Interactive Multimedia and Artificial Intelligence, 6*(3), 63. https://doi.org/10.9781/ijimai.2020.07.005
29. Vatiero, M. (2018). Smart contracts and transaction costs. *SSRN Journal*. https://doi.org/10.2139/ssrn.3259958

30. vom Brocke, J., Simons, A., Riemer, K., Niehaves, B., Plattfaut, R., Cleven, A. (2015). Standing on the shoulders of giants: Challenges and recommendations of literature search in information systems research. *Communications of the Association for Information Systems, 37*. https://doi.org/10.17705/1CAIS.03709s
31. Wan, Z., Xia, X., Lo, D., Chen, J., Luo, X., & Yang, X. (2021). Smart contract security: A practitioners' perspective. In *2021 IEEE/ACM 43rd International Conference on Software Engineering (ICSE). 2021 IEEE/ACM 43rd International Conference on Software Engineering (ICSE)*. Madrid, ES, 22.05.2021—30.05.2021: IEEE (pp. 1410–1422).
32. Wang, X., & Xu, F. (2022). The value of smart contract in trade finance. *Manufacturing & Service Operations Management, 25*(6), 2056–2073. Artikel msom.2022.1126. https://doi.org/10.1287/msom.2022.1126
33. Zhang, R., & Chan, W. K. V. (2020). Evaluation of energy consumption in block-chains with proof of work and proof of stake. *Journal of Physics: Conference Series, 1584*(1), 12023. https://doi.org/10.1088/1742-6596/1584/1/012023
34. Zheng, Z., Xie, S., Dai, H. N., Chen, W., Chen, X., Weng, J., & Imran, M. (2020). An overview on smart contracts: Challenges, advances and platforms. *Future Generation Computer Systems, 105*, 475–491. https://doi.org/10.1016/j.future.2019.12.019

Digital Industry and Retailing

Development and Future Research Directions of AI-Based Anomaly Detection in Smart Manufacturing: A Bibliometric Analysis

Maximilian Nebel, Philip Stahmann, and Christian Janiesch

Abstract Manufacturing companies face a vast increase of data. Connected sensors turn physically isolated objects into nodes in data communication networks. This development enables but also forces companies to harness their data to gain a competitive edge. In this regard, anomaly detection enables seamless processes, so that production failures can be avoided. Artificial intelligence (AI) and especially machine learning and deep learning constitute instruments to leverage statistical complexity necessary to identify anomalies in these vast amounts of data. AI-based anomaly detection has therefore been subject to an intensive academic discourse in Information Systems. This short paper provides preliminary results from a bibliometric analysis highlighting the development over time of scientific contributions in this field. Our findings show that the academic discourse has gained momentum but is still premature. Additionally, we find that a technical perspective on the topic prevails in literature.

1 Introduction

As is the case with numerous other sectors, the manufacturing industry is subject to considerable competitive pressure driven by the relentless pursuit of optimization. This is especially pertinent in the manufacturing sector, given that the potential for improvement is consistently being tapped into through the use of technologies such as anomaly detection to minimize flaws in the production. Therefore, there is increased pressure to optimize manufacturing processes to save costs and offer

M. Nebel (✉) · P. Stahmann · C. Janiesch
TU Dortmund University, Dortmund, Germany
e-mail: maximilian.nebel@tu-dortmund.de

P. Stahmann
e-mail: philip.stahmann@tu-dortmund.de

C. Janiesch
e-mail: christian.janiesch@tu-dortmund.de

C. M. Flath et al. (eds.), *Digital Innovation and Organizational Transformation*, Lecture Notes in Information Systems and Organisation 83,
https://doi.org/10.1007/978-3-032-08483-5_24

products at lower prices. Artificial Intelligence (AI)-based anomaly detection has been identified as a driver for manufacturing process optimization [1].

Anomaly detection targets the identification of unexpected events [2]. In manufacturing, the aim is to alert decision-makers regarding about the occurrence of anomalies such as unexpected machinery wear or production defects to entail initiate remediate corrective actions [3]. The capability to leverage complex statistical models using machine learning supports the inference of information from data [4].

Despite the importance of AI-based anomaly detection in manufacturing, related literature is scattered into isolated publications. Aggregating literature that characterizes the development of the topic in science is scarce. However, publications in adjacent fields in Information Systems (IS) show that an aggregated understanding of scientific pathways of topics opens potentials for further development in academia and practice for example, [5–7]. On this basis, we formulate the following research question (RQ):

RQ *How has research on AI-based anomaly detection in manufacturing developed over time?*

To answer the RQ, we conducted a bibliometric study based on 161 publications. More specifically, we analyzed types of outlets, citations, and keywords over the past six years. This short paper includes preliminary answers to the RQ. Further bibliometric analyses that build on an extended literature database to address the RQ in greater detail are still ongoing.

2 Research Methodology

To find answers to both research questions, we structured our research into the three phases of data acquisition, data preparation, and data analysis [8]. Data acquisition marks the *first phase*, the focus was on ensuring that required information is included in the data. Due to their vast diffusion in IS, we adhered to the guidelines established by vom Brocke et al. [9]. We first defined the scope on what we look for in the gathered search results. Until now, in our search we did not focus on the results or methods presented in the publications, rather than on the meta data, such as citations or keywords. In this short paper, we searched the databases IEEE Xplore, Scopus, Web of Science, EBSCOhost and AISEL as these cover a broad variety of high-quality outlets on relevant topic.

Our search term consists of three connected blocks of terms and their abbreviations. Each block represents one of the three core topics that define the AI-based anomaly detection in manufacturing domain. The first block contains terms regarding AI. The second one focuses on anomalies. Lastly, the third block refers to manufacturing terminology. The final search term is the following: (AI-based OR "Artificial Intelligence-based" OR ML-based OR "machine learning-based" OR DL-based OR "deep learning-based") AND (anomaly OR outlier OR error) AND ("Industrie 4.0"

OR "industry 4.0" OR "intelligent manufacturing" OR "smart factory" OR "smart manufacturing" OR "IIoT" OR "industrial Internet of things").

In total, we found 717 publications. After deduplication and filtering of the titles, 161 sources remain. The oldest results are from 2016 with one Outlier in 2006. Independent of this, we identified the most cited authors in Google Scholar.

Subsequently, the *second phase* focuses on data preparation for data analysis in the third phase. The gathered data from the literature databases was structurally heterogeneous. To enable analysis, we aligned the data formats. The meta data includes the corresponding databases, authors, titles, publication years, countries of the authors institutions, keywords, and whether the publication is from a journal or proceeding.

The design of data and data formats is based on other bibliometric analyses in the IS domain for example [10–12]. Besides structural homogenization, data preparation also included semantic alignment of keywords. For example, "industrial Internet of things (IIoT)" was reduced to "industrial Internet of things". We hereby aimed to do as little alterations as necessary.

Phase three covers data analysis. Rather than a static, predefined procedure, we used an explorative, iterative approach as intermediate results may open avenues for further research. To determine the most cited publications according to Google Scholar, we used a Python script provided by Wittmann [13].

3 Theoretical Background

Anomaly detection is a method of identifying patterns in data that deviate from the norm [2]. This approach is employed in manufacturing, because the time-series sensor data can be analyzed by computers to identify faults during production [14]. AI has the potential to be a significant factor in this process. By employing sophisticated statistical machine learning techniques, AI can discern the attributes of patterns and indications of anomalies. The advantage of AI is that it enables the use of a variety of statistical methods, each of which may be suited best to different types of data [15].

Classification algorithms delineate data into normal and anomalous classes for example [16]. It is a supervised technique, which requires a training phase before algorithm deployment. As an unsupervised technique, clustering algorithms constitute a more explorative approach, where data are assigned to homogeneous clusters for example, [17]. Data points that are not assigned to expected clusters are considered anomalous. Furthermore, predictive analysis enables forecasting future states in production processes [18].

Companies can take advantage of this by selecting the most appropriate machine learning methods for their needs. Machine learning can be used to predict known anomalies at an early stage, enabling intervention even before critical failures occur for preventive actions ensuring seamless processes and to minimize downtimes [19]. With the decision making behavior of AI, it has the potential to expand the automation of manufacturing processes [20, 21]. For instance, an AI detects an anomaly and triggers the corresponding reaction automatically.

4 Preliminary Results and Contributions

In the following, preliminary analysis results are structured into citation analysis, outlet analysis, and keyword analysis.

Citation analysis. First, we identified the most cited publications to understand which publications constitute the most relevant basis for further scholars. To get a reliable picture, we also considered the average citations per year. These support an evaluation whether a publication constitutes a lasting foundation for future research. Figure 1 displays the most cited publications in AI-based anomaly detection in smart manufacturing. Noteworthy, the top four most cited publications in total are also the most cited publications on average over the last years. The oldest publication is from 2016 [22], the others are from 2020 [23, 24], 2021 [25, 26] or 2022 [27].

Outlet analysis. To further identify the development of the field of the academic discourse over the last years we investigated the distribution of outlet types over time. whether a publication distributed as part of a journal or conference. Figure 2 shows the absolute number of publications in conference proceedings and journals.

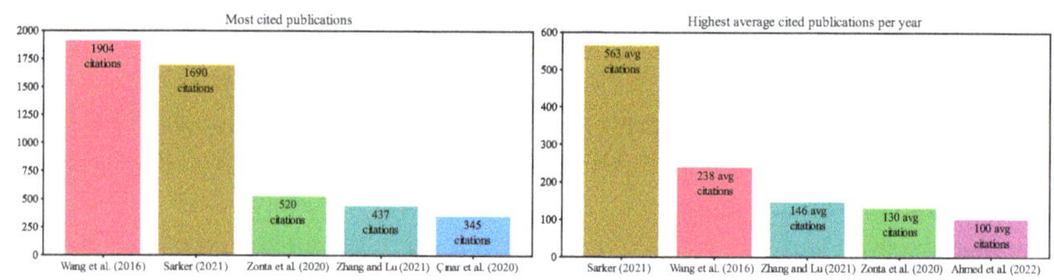

Fig. 1 Most cited publications

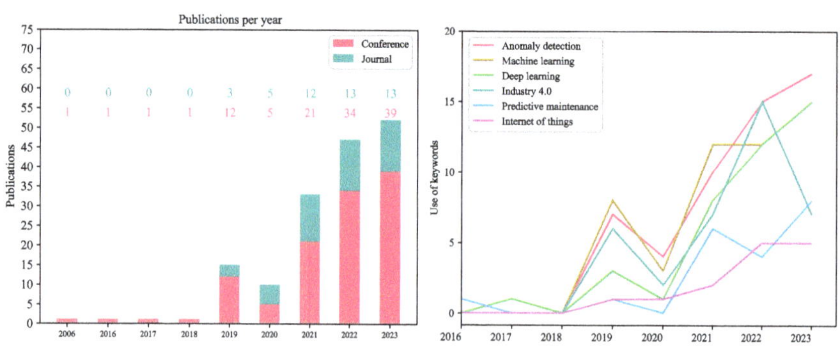

Fig. 2 Annual published articles (left) and top six most used keywords (right)

Beginning from 2019, the number of publications increases with an average rate of 162% per year (185% in conference proceedings and 154% in journal publications). It is worth noting that the proportion of journal publications is gradually increasing in comparison to conference proceedings, with 25% of the publications in 2023 appearing in journals.

Keyword analysis. The analysis of keywords aims to provide an understanding of the most relevant topics in AI-based anomaly detection in manufacturing and how they developed over time. Figure 2 shows on the right side the development of the six most frequently used keywords as chosen by the authors of the identified publications.

The most prominent keywords are "anomaly detection", "machine learning", and "deep learning". "Machine learning" dominated until 2022 and has then been overtaken by "deep learning". Deep learning is usually used for more complex problem-solving that may be due to data variety in manufacturing [28]. Four out of the six most frequently used keywords relate to manufacturing as application domain. Out of these "predictive maintenance" constitute the majority in 2023. (Industrial) "Internet of things" and "industry 4.0" derive from national initiatives towards the digitization of manufacturing. The industrial Internet of things is the US American term, whereas industry 4.0 has its roots in Germany.

Preliminary practical and theoretical contributions. Our research aims for a contribution to both practice and academia. Academics can use the results as starting points for future research and by newcomers to the field to gain an overview and familiarize themselves with the various aspects of the field. Additionally, our work supports researchers in identifying relevant topics and keywords for their own literature search in their work and thus creates an incentive to explore AI-based anomaly detection in manufacturing. The results of our research offer practitioners benefits as well. They can use the findings to more accurately assess past developments and identify potential issues caused by outdated technologies. The insights into future trends enable companies to anticipate changes and capitalize on them.

5 Conclusion, Limitations, and Outlook

In our preliminary study, we conducted a bibliometric analysis following Donthu et al. [8] to observe the development and future directions of AI-based anomaly detection. In particular, for this research-in-progress paper, we focused on the timely developments regarding the citations and keywords used in the data.

To answer our RQ: The findings suggest that the field is transitioning from a young and fast changing area towards a more mature research field. This is seen in the development of the conference to journal ratio towards journals from 2021 and onwards. We also showed the most cited works, that are journal articles that predominantly describe a state of the art or fundamentals relevant to the field.

With the keyword analysis, we find indications of a development towards more sophisticated statistical models for anomaly detection as deep learning characterizes by more complex model building than machine learning. The prominence of "Internet of things" and "industry 4.0" indicates that AI-based anomaly detection has a significant share in digitization initiatives from the perspective of the academic discourse. Furthermore, we find that the academic discourse seems to be considered through a methodological or technical lens, as "machine learning" and "deep learning" occur more frequently than terms relating to the digitization of manufacturing. An academic discourse guided by methodological considerations indicates a focus on problem-solving, that is ensuring seamless manufacturing processes with provided data.

Despite rigorous adherence to scientific guidelines of vom Brocke et al. [9], the literature search process has some limitations. Choices on databases, search strings, and parameters have a significant influence on results of bibliometric analyses. Additionally, the selection of publications as well as database depends on subjective content interpretation. There is no guarantee that we did not miss publications that would have been relevant to investigating the research questions. Furthermore, keywords used in bibliometric analyses to reflect content of publications and literature streams [5, 12] are only proxies that address essential aspects of content, but can never fully depict the complexity of contributions.

In order to obtain a broader representation of the field, we plan to expand our research by not only increasing the number of publications as a database for bibliometric analysis, but also by expanding our methodological toolbox. We will add publications found for example in the databases ACM or Springer Link. The choice of databases is due to their broad and complementary coverage of various outlets that engage with the topics of applied computer science, AI, and smart manufacturing.

In our further research, we will detail the presented analyses based on the broader literature coverage. In terms of citations, and keyword use, we plan to conduct network analysis to identify (covert) groupings by topic and geographic distributions to further investigate local clusters and focal points. We will not only look at the quantity of publications over the years, but also on the geographical diffusion of different key aspects in the domain over certain time spans. For example, we plan on investigating whether the network shows signs of saturation in regard to expansion and networking. Additionally, this can be used by practioners to identify global trends, such as on-demand machine learning as part of artificial intelligence as a service solutions e.g., [29]. Regarding outlets, we will extend the perspective on outlet types towards analyzing which conferences and journals engage with which topics over time. This may foster an understanding of the development today and reveal future research avenues [12]. Broader keyword analyses including their topic-wise relations will support the identification clusters suitable to project future research directions [8]. The expected contribution of our full research yields at a characterization of the development of research on AI-based anomaly detection in manufacturing (RQ). In addition, we want to expand with complementary RQs to include further perspectives and also identify future research directions.

Acknowledgements This research and development project is funded by the German Federal Ministry of Research, Technology and Space (BMFTR) within the „Zukunft der Wertschöpfung—Forschung zu Produktion, Dienstleistung und Arbeit" (Funding No. 02K23A070) and managed by Projektträger Karlsruhe (PTKA). The authors are responsible for the contents of this publication.

References

1. Peres, R. S., Dionisio Rocha, A., Leitao, P., & Barata, J. (2018). IDARTS—Towards intelligent data analysis and real-time supervision for industry 4.0. *Computers in Industry, 101*, 138–146. https://doi.org/10.1016/j.compind.2018.07.004
2. Chandola, V., Banerjee, A., & Kumar, V. (2009). Anomaly detection. *ACM Computing Surveys, 41*, 1–58. https://doi.org/10.1145/1541880.1541882
3. Huang, H., Yang, L., Wang, Y., Xu, X., & Lu, Y. (2021). Digital twin-driven online anomaly detection for an automation system based on edge intelligence. *Journal of Manufacturing Systems, 59*, 138–150. https://doi.org/10.1016/j.jmsy.2021.02.010
4. Janiesch, C., Zschech, P., & Heinrich, K. (2021). Machine learning and deep learning. *Electron Markets, 31*, 685–695. https://doi.org/10.1007/s12525-021-00475-2
5. Schöbel, S., Saqr, M., & Janson, A. (2021). Two decades of game concepts in digital learning environments—A bibliometric study and research agenda. *Computers & Education, 173*, Article 104296. https://doi.org/10.1016/j.compedu.2021.104296
6. Wanner, J., Wissuchek, C., Welsch, G., & Janiesch, C. (2023). A taxonomy and archetypes of business analytics in smart manufacturing. *SIGMIS Database, 54*, 11–45. https://doi.org/10.1145/3583581.3583584
7. Zschech, P., Bernien, J., Heinrich, K. (2019). *Towards a taxonomic benchmarking framework for predictive maintenance: The case of NASA's turbofan degradation.* In ICIS 2019 Proceedings.
8. Donthu, N., Kumar, S., Mukherjee, D., Pandey, N., & Lim, W. M. (2021). How to conduct a bibliometric analysis: An overview and guidelines. *Journal of Business Research, 133*, 285–296. https://doi.org/10.1016/j.jbusres.2021.04.070
9. vom Brocke, J., Simons, A., Niehaves, B., Riemer, K., Plattfaut, R., & Cleven, A. (2009). Reconstructing the giant: On the importance of rigour in documenting the literature search process. In *ECIS 2009 Proceedings.*
10. Honey, K., Robb, A., & Rohde, F. (2022). *Are we contributing? The who, when, where, & what of the Blockchain research landscape.* In ICIS 2022 Proceedings.
11. Smacchia, M., & Za, S. (2022). *Artificial intelligence in organisation and managerial studies: A computational literature review.* In ICIS 2022 Proceedings.
12. Schöbel, S., Schmitt, A., Benner, D., Saqr, M., Janson, A., Leimeister, J. M. (2023). Charting the evolution and future of conversational agents: A research agenda along five waves and new frontiers. *Information Systems Frontiers, 26*(2), 729–754. https://doi.org/10.1007/s10796-023-10375-9
13. Wittmann, F. M. (2017). Optimization applied to residential non-intrusive load monitoring.
14. Stahmann, P., Rieger, B. (2021). *Requirements Identification for Real-Time Anomaly Detection in Industrie 4.0 Machine Groups: A Structured Literature Review.* In Proceedings of the 54th Hawaii International Conference on System Sciences (HICSS). https://doi.org/10.24251/hicss.2021.696
15. Russell, S., Norvig, P. (2021). *Artificial intelligence. A modern approach.* Pearson Education Limited.
16. Saci, A., Al-Dweik, A., & Shami, A. (2021). Autocorrelation integrated gaussian based anomaly detection using sensory data in industrial manufacturing. *IEEE Sensors J., 21*, 9231–9241. https://doi.org/10.1109/JSEN.2021.3053039

17. Mucchielli, P., Bhowmik, B., Ghosh, B., & Pakrashi, V. (2021). Real-time accurate detection of wind turbine downtime—An Irish perspective. *Renewable Energy, 179*, 1969–1989. https://doi.org/10.1016/j.renene.2021.07.139
18. Stefani, K., & Zschech, P. (2018). *Constituent elements for prescriptive analytics systems.* In ECIS 2018 Proceedings.
19. Corallo, A., Crespino, A., Dibiccari, C., Lazoi, M., & Lezzi, M. (2018). Processing big data in streaming for fault prediction: An industrial application. In *2018 14th International Conference on Signal-Image Technology & Internet-Based Systems (SITIS)*. IEEE (pp. 730–736). https://doi.org/10.1109/SITIS.2018.00117
20. Arinez, J.F., Chang, Q., Gao, R.X., Xu, C., & Zhang, J. (2020). Artificial intelligence in advanced manufacturing: Current status and future outlook. *Journal of Manufacturing Science and Engineering, 142 (11)*, 110804. https://doi.org/10.1115/1.4047855
21. Yang, T., Yi, X., Lu, S., Johansson, K. H., & Chai, T. (2021). Intelligent manufacturing for the process industry driven by industrial artificial intelligence. *Engineering, 7*, 1224–1230. https://doi.org/10.1016/j.eng.2021.04.023
22. Wang, S., Wan, J., Li, D., & Zhang, C. (2016). Implementing smart factory of industrie 4.0: An outlook. *International Journal of Distributed Sensor Networks, 12*, 3159805. https://doi.org/10.1155/2016/3159805
23. Zonta, T., Da Costa, C. A., Da Rosa Righi, R., Lima, M. J. de, Da Trindade, E. S., & Li, G. P. (2020). Predictive maintenance in the industry 4.0: A systematic literature review. *Computers & Industrial Engineering, 150*, 106889. https://doi.org/10.1016/j.cie.2020.106889
24. Çınar, Z.M., Abdussalam Nuhu, A., Zeeshan, Q., Korhan, O., Asmael, M., & Safaei, B. (2020). Machine learning in predictive maintenance towards sustainable smart manufacturing in industry 4.0. *Sustainability, 12*, 8211. https://doi.org/10.3390/su12198211
25. Sarker, I. H. (2021). Machine learning: Algorithms, real-world applications and research directions. *SN computer science, 2*, 160. https://doi.org/10.1007/s42979-021-00592-x
26. Zhang, C., & Lu, Y. (2021). Study on artificial intelligence: The state of the art and future prospects. *Journal of Industrial Information Integration, 23*, Article 100224. https://doi.org/10.1016/j.jii.2021.100224
27. Ahmed, I., Jeon, G., & Piccialli, F. (2022). From artificial intelligence to explainable artificial intelligence in industry 4.0: A survey on what, how, and where. *IEEE transactions on industrial informatics, 18*(8), 5031–5042. https://doi.org/10.1109/TII.2022.3146552
28. Wang, J., Ma, Y., Zhang, L., Gao, R. X., & Wu, D. (2018). Deep learning for smart manufacturing: Methods and applications. *Journal of Manufacturing Systems, 48*, 144–156. https://doi.org/10.1016/j.jmsy.2018.01.003
29. Lins, S., Pandl, K. D., Teigeler, H., Thiebes, S., Bayer, C., & Sunyaev, A. (2021). Artificial intelligence as a service. *Business & Information Systems Engineering, 63*, 441–456. https://doi.org/10.1007/s12599-021-00708-w

Monte Carlo Simulation to Analyse the Impact of Uncertain Telemetry Data on the Calculation of CO_2e Emissions for Trailer Traffic

Justus Leskow, Steffen Greiser, Laura Gregorc, and Stelios Damalas

Abstract This paper analyses the impact of a map-matching algorithm on the uncertainties of GPS coordinates in the calculation of carbon dioxide emissions for trailer transport based on telemetry data. Using trailer type, load, journey and route parameters, the Transport Carbon Footprint can be calculated based on DIN EN ISO 14083 and using the *GLEC* Framework. A Monte Carlo simulation was used to analyse the effects of GPS coordinate uncertainties on the *Graphhopper* map matching algorithm. Based on this, the effects of route deviations on the calculation of the Transport Carbon Footprint were analysed. The results of this investigation indicate that the use of a map matching algorithm leads to a relative deviation of less than 0.02% in the calculation of the carbon footprint of transport due to GPS uncertainties.

1 Introduction

Anthropogenic climate change, driven by the increased concentration of greenhouse gases such as carbon dioxide (CO_2), methane (CH_4), and nitrous oxide (N_2O) in the atmosphere, represents one of the greatest threats to humanity to date. The enhanced greenhouse effect, resulting from these elevated levels of greenhouse gases, leads to a net warming of the Earth's surface. This process is quantified in terms of carbon dioxide equivalents (CO_2e), which standardize the impact of various gases based on their global warming potential [1–4]. Scientific evidence indicates that the continuous warming of our planet contributes to severe environmental disruptions. These disruptions include increased frequency and severity of crop failures, natural disasters like hurricanes and wildfires, and widespread water shortages. Such effects of anthropogenic climate change not only threaten ecosystems but also have the potential to

J. Leskow (✉) · S. Greiser · L. Gregorc
Hochschule Osnabrück, Faculty of Management and Technology, Lingen, Germany
e-mail: Justus.Leskow@hs-osnabrueck.de

S. Damalas
Virtual Vehicle Research GmbH, Contextual Information Systems & Operational Insights (CISO), Graz, Austria

C. M. Flath et al. (eds.), *Digital Innovation and Organizational Transformation*, Lecture Notes in Information Systems and Organisation 83,
https://doi.org/10.1007/978-3-032-08483-5_25

exacerbate international conflicts over resources [5, 6]. To mitigate these dire consequences, significant reductions in CO_2e emissions are imperative. The transportation sector, accountable for 20.68% of global greenhouse gas emissions in 2022, presents a critical area for intervention [7]. Within this sector, road transport alone is responsible for 73% of the emissions, highlighting its potential for optimization [8]. Long-term emission reductions in the transport sector can be achieved through the adoption of more efficient fuels, advancements in vehicle technology, and modal shifts towards sustainable transport options [9]. Efficient transport management, which includes strategic route planning and traffic congestion avoidance, is essential for environmental protection. This requires the systematic collection, analysis, and utilization of data [10]. A key strategy to enhance transport efficiency and reduce CO_2e emissions involves the use of telemetry data. The Global Positioning System (GPS) enables the collection of positioning data from mobile phones and vehicles, complemented by anonymized Call Detail Records (CDR) from mobile phone providers [11]. By analysing this data, it is possible to calculate the CO_2e emissions associated with specific travel routes, thereby enabling targeted interventions to reduce the carbon footprint of transportation. Furthermore, this data-driven approach can lead to the development of new business models. Companies can leverage these insights to offer innovative services such as eco-friendly route planning, real-time traffic management, and personalized carbon footprint tracking for consumers and businesses alike, creating economic opportunities while contributing to environmental sustainability.

2 Problem Statement and Scientific Question

Several companies have already recognized the potential of these business models. For calculating Corporate Carbon Footprints (CCF), the DIN EN ISO 14064 [12] standard is widely used. Solutions like *ClimatePartner* and *Carbon Trust* offer services based on this standard. *EcoTransIT World* and initiatives such as the *Sustainable Freight Buyers Alliance* provide an alternative calculation focus: the Transport Carbon Footprint (TCF). For calculating TCFs, the earlier DIN EN 16258 [13] standard has been superseded by the more advanced DIN EN ISO 14083 [14]. This extension provides the normative basis for calculating the TCF for entire transport chains and has influenced frameworks such as the Global Logistics Emissions Council (GLEC) Framework [15]. GLEC represents a voluntary and independent partnership of companies, green freight programs and industry associations, supported by researchers and experts, led by the Smart Freight Centre, which provides comprehensive guidelines for calculating logistics emissions [16]. However, these methods require values for the distances travelled. The direct input of actual telemetry data from transport operations cannot therefore be used directly to calculate CO_2e emissions in scenarios. The GLEC framework offers three possible ways of calculating distances: Shortest Feasible Distance (SFD) as the shortest practical route between two places, Great Circle Distance (GCD) as direct distance and Actual Distance (AD) as distance generally based on odometer readings from transport management systems that need corrections with Distance Adjustment Factors (DAF). For this DAF, a value of 1.05 is specified in the GLEC framework in the event of possible uncertainties in the data, so that the distances and thus the emissions are not too low. It is now questionable whether the actual distances, which can be calculated using telemetry data and a map matching algorithm, would also be uncertain to such an extent. The paper aims to assess the impact of utilizing telemetry data and the *GraphHopper* map matching algorithm on the uncertainty in calculating travelled distances and thus CO_2-equivalent (CO_2e) emissions for trailer traffic, comparing these method with the conventional approach specified in the GLEC framework. For this a Monte Carlo Simulation is used.

3 Methods and Techniques

The DIN EN ISO 14083 is an international standard by the International Organization for Standardization (ISO) that focuses on the quantification and reporting of greenhouse gas (GHG) emissions and energy consumption in the transportation sector. It provides methodologies for calculating the environmental impacts of various transport services, including road, rail, water, and air. The standard defines system boundaries, requiring the inclusion of all relevant energy consumption and emissions from the extraction of energy resources to their end use [17]. Key requirements include the use of joules for energy consumption and grams of CO_2-equivalent (CO_2e) or multiples thereof for GHG emissions. The standard mandates accounting for emissions from onboard electronics, propulsion energy, ancillary services, and both loaded and empty trips, as well as the full life cycle emissions of fuels and electricity [14]. Building on DIN EN ISO 14083, the GLEC Framework provides practical guidelines for logistics and transport companies. It translates the ISO standard into actionable steps for measuring and reporting emissions, promoting consistency and reliability [15]. The ISO 14083 and the GLEC Framework provide comprehensive methodologies for calculating emissions across entire transport chains [18]. However, this paper focuses specifically on a single transport process, referred to as a Transport Chain Element (TCE). By narrowing the scope to a TCE, we aim to provide a detailed analysis of the emissions associated with this particular segment of the transport chain, contributing to a more precise understanding of its environmental impact. Even for a single TCE, the full emissions are calculated as Well-to-Wheel (WTW) emissions to comply with the GHG Protocol [19]. WTW emissions encompass both Tank-to-Wheel (TTW) and Well-to-Tank (WTT) emissions. WTT emissions include greenhouse gas emissions generated during the extraction, production, and transportation of fuel to the point where it is ready for use. TTW emissions, on the other hand, cover the greenhouse gas emissions produced during the actual use of the fuel in a vehicle or machinery, typically from the combustion process in the engine [15]. This approach ensures a comprehensive assessment of the environmental impact of each TCE, aligning with global standards for emissions reporting and sustainability assessments in the transportation sector. The derivation of the transport carbon footprint based on the GLEC Framework can be divided into three steps. Firstly, the transport activity is calculated from the distance travelled and the payload of the TCE according to Formula 1. [1]

$$T_{\mathrm{TCE}} = m_{\mathrm{TCE}} \cdot d_{\mathrm{TCE}} \quad (1)$$

$$G_w = T_{\mathrm{TCE}} \cdot g_w \cdot DAF \quad (2)$$

In the second step, the emission factors are determined as a function of the utilisation. The respective values are provided by the GLEC Framework in Table 18 [15]. The third step describes the calculation of the WTW GHG emissions from the two previously derived values and a DAF based on Formula 2. [2] When using actual distances, the GLEC Framework recommends a DAF because actual distances, typically calculated using odometers, may result in lower amounts. However, as the distances in this paper are calculated using post-processing and a map-matching tool, this factor will have the value 1 for the further calculations.

The general methodology for calculating the transport carbon footprint is illustrated in Fig. 1. Since the distance travelled is directly incorporated into the calculation of the transport activity and, thus, indirectly influences CO_2e emissions and the TCF, it raises the question of how accurate the determination of the distances travelled is and, consequently, how accurate the calculated emissions are. Due to uncertainties in the raw GPS coordinates, as shown in Figs. 2 and 3, routing tools without map-matching functions can have considerable deviations in the determination of the distances travelled, as uncertainties can be interpreted as possible reversals of direction. As a result, the distances in some segments can deviate many times over from the actual routes travelled. These uncertainties can usually be compensated by using map matching algorithms. Table 1 provides an example of how large the differences are due to different calculation methods. The values of different methods for calculating the distances travelled for five real routes are presented. Graphhopper uses a map-matching algorithm, that snaps the coordinates to the street in direction of the next coordinate, while the geodetic model calculates a linear distance between coordinates. The telemetry unit of the trailer also transmits the odometer distances, which, according to the GLEC framework, would represent the actual distances that would have to be corrected by the DAF. Nevertheless, it remains questionable how significant the deviations will be even after the coordinates have been corrected. The effects of the map-matching tool are therefore being investigated further. The average uncertainty of GPS coordinates is specified by the US Department of Defence as ≤ 3.8 m in 2020 [20]. Schön and Kutterer also provide the same results [21]. Based on this uncertainty, it is assumed that the GPS coordinates gathered from telemetry

---

[1] T_{TCE} = Transport Activity of TCE (tkm), m_{TCE} = Payload of TCE (t), d_{TCE} = Transport Distance of TCE (km).

[2] G_w = WTW-Greenhousegas-Emission ($kg\ CO_2e$), T_{TCE} = Transport Activity of TCE, g_w = WTW-Emission-Factor ($\frac{kg\ CO_2e}{tkm}$), DAF = Distance Adjustment Factor.

data are normally distributed. Initially, the mean geographical latitude and longitude values ($\overline{\phi}$ and $\overline{\lambda}$) of the route are calculated. Based on this, the departure a of the Earth is determined using the following formula:

$$a = \frac{\Delta\lambda}{360^\circ} \cdot 2 \cdot \pi \cdot R \cdot \cos(\phi) \tag{3}$$

Here, $\Delta\lambda$ represents the difference in geographical longitudes in degrees, R denotes the Earth's radius in meters, and ϕ is the geographical latitude of the route in degrees. The GPS uncertainty $\sigma_{\text{GPS},0}$ of the Standard Positioning Service in meters corresponding to the uncertainty σ_{GPS} in degrees latitude/longitude is computed as follows:

$$\sigma_{\text{GPS}} = \frac{\sigma_{\text{GPS},0}}{\sqrt{a(\phi)^2 + m^2}} \tag{4}$$

where $a(\phi)$ is the departure at the geographical latitude and m is the associated meridian arc length. The latitude/longitude coordinates of the telemetry data are then altered n times using the calculated inaccuracies, assuming a normal distribution. This is achieved by adding normally distributed noise to the original coordinates:

$$\phi_i' = \phi_i + \mathcal{N}(0, \sigma_{\text{GPS}}) \tag{5}$$

$$\lambda_i' = \lambda_i + \mathcal{N}(0, \sigma_{\text{GPS}}) \tag{6}$$

Here, ϕ_i and λ_i represent the original latitude and longitude coordinates, while ϕ_i' and λ_i' denote the perturbed coordinates for the i-th simulation. Simulations are then carried out with these randomly modified GPS coordinates to determine the accuracy of the map-matching algorithm. If the simulation is executed n times, a statistical distribution of the total distance (TD) is obtained. A histogram of the total distances can be created in the same way. From this histogram, the standard deviation of the total distance is estimated. This enables further calculations for estimating the sample size n required for assessing the uncertainty of the total distance and thus indirectly for assessing the uncertainty of CO_2e emissions. For each of the n simulated trajectories, the traveled distance is determined using the Graphhopper map-matching algorithm. This algorithm matches the perturbed coordinates to a map to calculate the actual traveled distance. The expected distance E[d_{orig}] is the distance calculated via map-matching for the original telemetry data coordinates. It can be described as follows:

$$E[d_{\text{orig}}] = \text{MapMatching}(\phi_i, \lambda_i) \tag{7}$$

where ϕ and λ are the original latitude and longitude coordinates. The standard deviation of the distances of the n simulated trajectories is then computed. The standard deviation is calculated as follows:

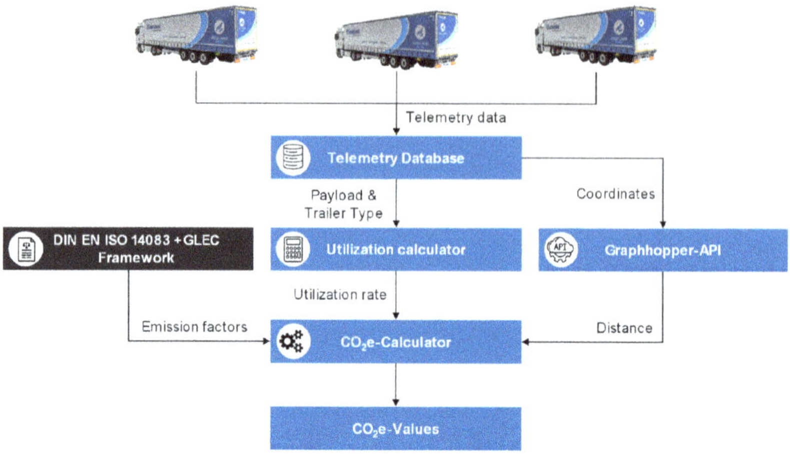

Fig. 1 Approach for the CO_2e Calculator

$$\sigma_{\mathrm{TD}} = \sqrt{\frac{1}{n-1}\sum_{i=1}^{n}(d_i - \overline{d})^2} \tag{8}$$

where d_i is the traveled distance for the i-th simulation and $\overline{d}$ is the mean distance of all simulations. The confidence interval for the traveled distances is determined as follows:

$$\left[\overline{d} - z_{\alpha/2} \cdot \frac{\sigma_{\mathrm{TD}}}{\sqrt{n}}; \overline{d} + z_{\alpha/2} \cdot \frac{\sigma_{\mathrm{TD}}}{\sqrt{n}}\right] \tag{9}$$

where σ_{TD} is the standard deviation of the travelled distances, n is the number of simulations, and $z_{\alpha/2}$ is the critical value of the standard normal distribution for the confidence interval.

4 Application and Results

The first step in calculating the uncertainties of the TCF is to take the GPS uncertainties into account. While the distance between two arcs of latitude is almost stable, the distance between two arcs of longitude differs significantly depending on the geographical latitude value ϕ due to the departure of the earth. Therefore, the GPS uncertainty of the coordinates is calculated based on the departure a as a function of the mean value of the latitude $\overline{\phi}$ and the associated meridian arc length m according to formulae 3 + 4. The uncertainty $\sigma_{\mathrm{GPS},0}$ with the value of 3.8 m is used for this [20, 21]. The coordinates assumed to be true from the telemetry data are then modified

Fig. 2 GPS Uncertainties - GPS-Jitter

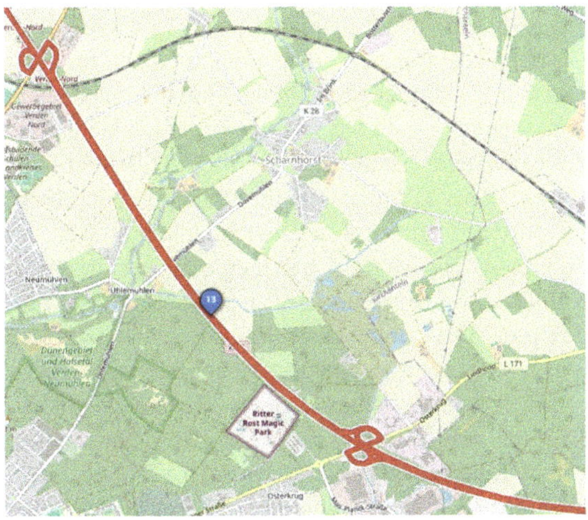

Fig. 3 GPS Uncertainties - ORS-Routing with GPS-Jitter and segment looping

Table 1 Calculated distances by method in m

Route	Graphhopper	Geodesic	Telemetry (Odometer)	Open Route Service (ORS) API
1	251500	244734	247000	368409
2	274602	262825	270000	301965
3	264168	246682	259000	269270
4	302496	268238	290000	306631
5	340851	328009	335000	356252

according to formulae 5 + 6 with a normally distributed uncertainty of 3.8 m. An example of this procedure is shown in Table 2. The original coordinates describe an exemplary route from Würzburg in the direction of Frankfurt am Main. These coordinates have now been altered with a normally distributed standard deviation of 3.8 m. The geodetic distance between the original coordinates and the altered coordinates is additionally shown. Despite the actual proximity of a few metres, the calculation of the distance travelled based on the altered coordinates using the Open Route Service (ORS) API would result in a distance of around 103.4 km instead of the actual 87.4 km, as some coordinates are too close to the lanes leading in the opposite direction and are thus interpreted by the ORS API as a change of direction, as seen in Fig. 3. The calculation of the distance using the Graphhopper API results in a distance of 87.5 km despite the altered coordinates. This underlines the necessity of a map-matching algorithm when calculating distances from uncertain GPS coordinates. Since the GPS uncertainties can be compensated for with the map-matching algorithm, it still remains questionable how strongly the GPS uncertainties affect the calculation of the total distance. A Monte Carlo simulation is therefore carried out. Using the calculated standard deviations for longitude and latitude, GPS coordinates based on real telemetry data are altered and the distances travelled by n coordinate variants are simulated using the GraphHopper map-matching API. The calculation time increases with the sample size n, but leads to a reduction in the uncertainty of the calculated distances of the Monte Carlo simulation [22]. The aim is to find a compromise. In this paper, the standard deviation of the total distance σ_{TD} is used for different values of the sample size n (10, 25, 50, 75, 100, 150, 200, 300, 400, 500, 600). The Monte Carlo method is performed ten times for each sample size n, resulting in a distribution of the deviation σ_{TD}. Figure 4 shows the corresponding box plot. The sample size was chosen at n = 400, as the box and the whiskers no longer vary as much with larger sample sizes n. By determining the required number of simulations, 5 routes of trucks can now be taken from the telemetry data, which are simulated 400 times each. The respective simulation results are shown in Table 3, where Total Distance is the expected value of the original coordinates according to Formula 7. In Table 4 the mean values of the total distances and their 95% confidence intervals of the five routes are shown. The results have been calculated by applying formulae 8 + 9. Due to the lowest standard deviation for route 3 and the highest standard deviation for route 4, it seems appropriate to take a closer look at the distribution of the total distances. The cumulative probability distributions and their lower (red) and upper (green) threshold values of the 95% confidence intervals are therefore shown in Figs. 5 and 6. It is noticeable that route 3 with the lowest standard deviation has an almost ideal normal distribution. Route 4, on the other hand, shows a large plateau in the cumulative probability distribution around the actual mean value. This can be explained by threshold values, to which distanced coordinates are matched to certain points, in GraphHopper's map-matching algorithm. This also explains the conspicuously wide limits of the confidence interval. Even if route 4 has the greatest deviation in relation to the total length, the inaccuracy of approximately 6 cm per kilometer travelled is to be regarded as very small. The question is to what extent uncertainties in GPS coordinates impact the precision of the calculated CO_2e emissions. Therefore, the distributions of the standard deviations of the CO_2e emissions of the routes are analysed based on formulae 1–2. In Table 5 the corresponding CO_2e emissions of the routes are presented. The results of the CO_2e calculations are given as WTW emission values in accordance with the GHG Protocol and therefore include all emissions caused by the production of the fuel and during its combustion. Table 6 contains the average WTW emissions and the 95% confidence intervals of the simulated routes. Route 3 still has the smallest and route 4 the largest standard deviation for the CO_2e values. The shape of the cumulative distributions of the routes, shown in Figs. 7 and 8, also indicates that the emissions behave exactly like the distances of the routes. This seems plausible, as the other values from formulae 1 + 2 remain constant. Since route 4 varies the most in terms of both route length and CO_2e emissions, the following can be derived from this example: The probability that the map matching algorithm calculates the total distance of a random 300 km route with an accuracy of 37.18 m is therefore 95%. This would be equivalent to a relative deviation of 0.014%. With regards to the uncertainties in the calculation of emissions, for a random route that is 300 km long, the probability, that the calculation would have a deviation of less than 56.2 g, is 95%. This would correspond to a relative deviation of 0.0123%. The utilization of a map-matching tool incorporating telemetry data enables precise determination of distances traveled, thereby facilitating accurate calculations of CO_2e emissions within the transport sector. This approach is particularly significant when considering the methods recommended by the GLEC Framework for determining distances in road transport, specifically the SFD method or distance measurements using odometry and a DAF. The importance of actual movement data becomes evident: rather than relying on static start and end points, the distances actually traveled are employed to compute the transport carbon footprint. This methodology allows for the inclusion of unforeseen events, such as detours or traffic congestion, in the calculations, which would otherwise be lost in other calculation methods. The integration of a map-matching tool with telemetry data therefore represents an opportunity to improve more accurate modelling and thus a possible future reduction in greenhouse gas emissions.

Table 2 Example of altered coordinates

Waypoint	Original Coordinates		Altered Coordinates		Geodetic
	Longitude	Latitude	Longitude	Latitude	Distance (m)
1	9.907651	49.754719	9.907689368009276	49.75475736800928	5.98
2	9.638704	49.762104	9.638692174665875	49.762092174665874	1.84
3	9.511619	49.839225	9.511595222056805	49.83920122205681	3.71
4	9.350629	49.932655	9.350574725787768	49.932600725787765	8.46
5	9.140104	49.994733	9.14003231571496	49.99466131571496	11.18
6	8.939787	50.029489	8.93974104069887	50.029443040698865	7.17

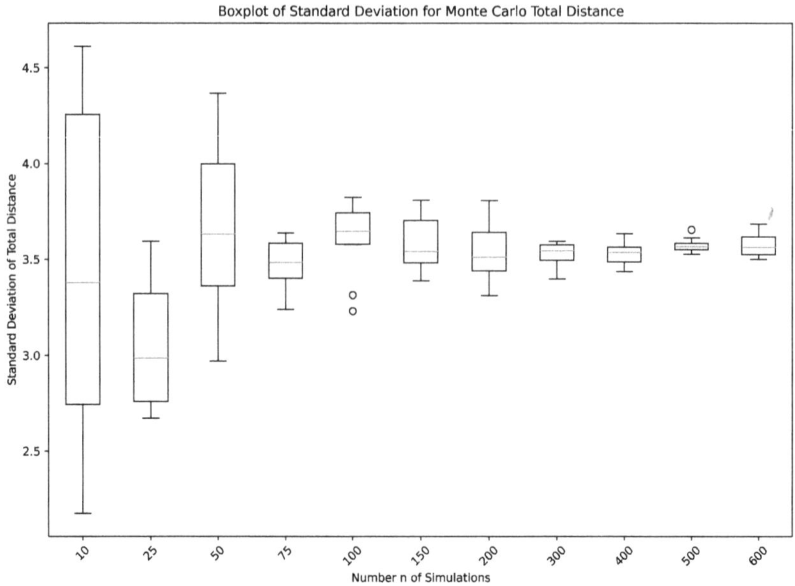

Fig. 4 Determination of the simulation size n of the Monte-Carlo Simulation

Table 3 Standard Deviation of the simulated Routes

Route	Total Distance (m)	Standard Deviation	Standard Deviation per km
1	251500	11.44	0.0455
2	274602	6.56	0.0239
3	264168	1.17	0.0044
4	302496	18.59	0.0614
5	340851	3.41	0.0100

Table 4 95% Confidence Interval Total Distances

Route	Mean Value (m)	95% Confidence Interval (m)
1	251501	(251478, 251523)
2	274600	(274588, 274613)
3	264168	(264166, 264170)
4	302509	(302472, 302545)
5	340851	(340845, 340858)

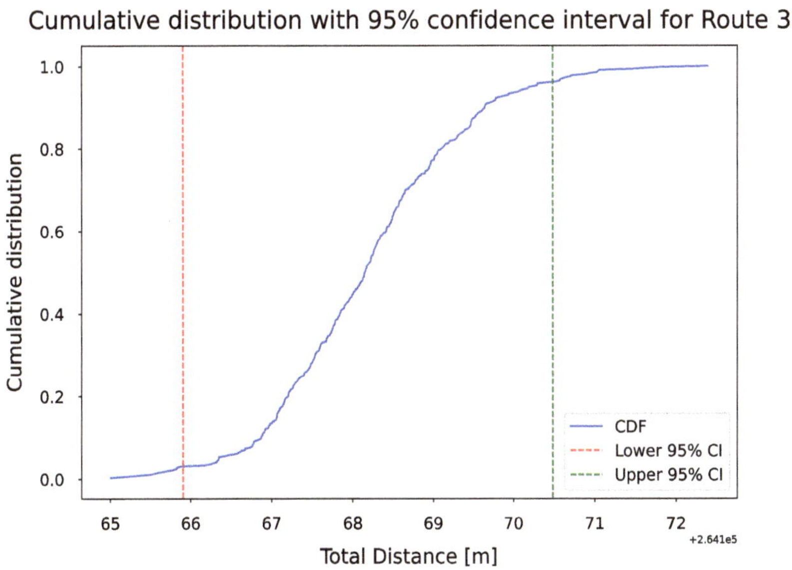

Fig. 5 Cumulative Distribution of the Total Distances of Route 3

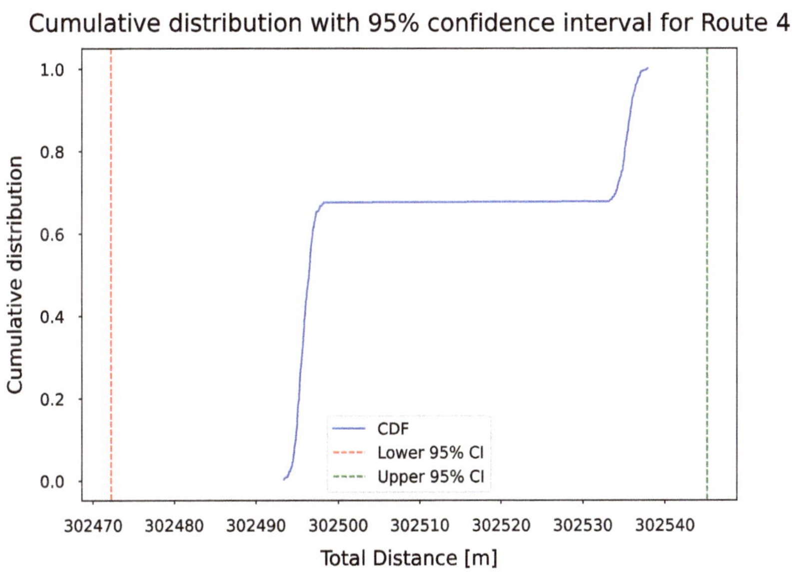

Fig. 6 Cumulative Distribution of the Total Distances of Route 4

Table 5 Standard Deviation of the WTW GHG Route Emission

Route	Total Emission (kg CO_2e)	Standard Deviation	Standard Deviation per km
1	298.283	0.0136	5.3965e-05
2	322.836	0.0077	2.8106e-05
3	311.697	0.0014	5.2167e-06
4	456.436	0.0281	9.2743e-05
5	494.716	0.0049	1.4521e-05

Table 6 95% Confidence Interval of WTW GHG Route Emission

Route	Mean Value of the Total Emission (kg CO_2e)	95% Confidence Interval (kg CO_2e)
1	298.284	(298.258, 298.311)
2	322.834	(322.819, 322.85)
3	311.697	(311.695, 311.7)
4	456.455	(456.4, 456.51)
5	494.717	(494.707, 494.726)

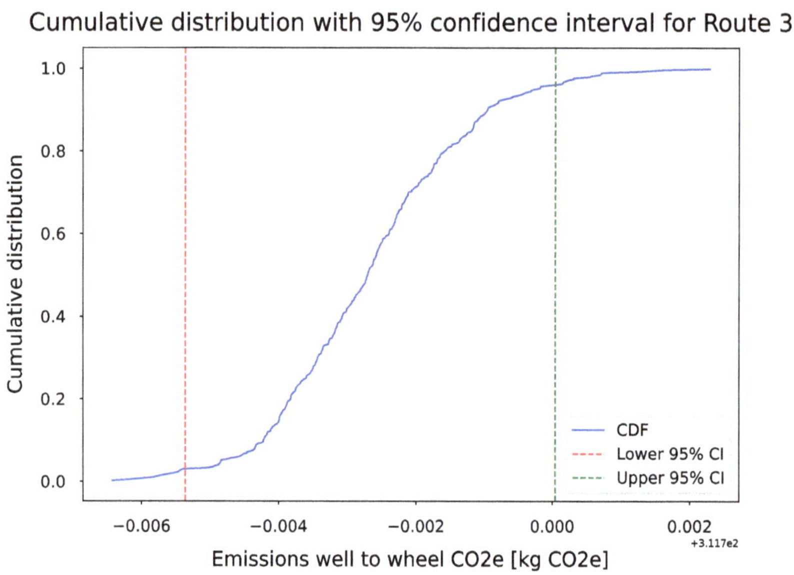

Fig. 7 Cumulative Distribution of the WTW GHG Emission for Route 3

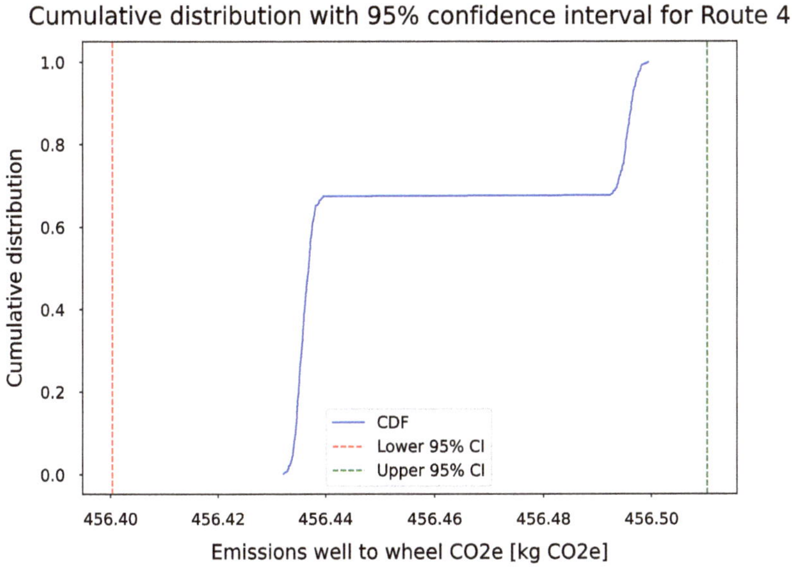

Fig. 8 Cumulative Distribution of the WTW GHG Emission for Route 4

5 Summary and Outlook

This paper analyses the impact of a map-matching algorithm on the uncertainty of GPS coordinates in the calculation of travelled distances and thus carbon dioxide emissions for trailer traffic. The method is based on DIN EN ISO 14083 and the GLEC Framework for the calculation of CO_2e emissions. A Monte Carlo simulation is used to analyse the effects of GPS uncertainties on the total route distance and CO_2e emissions. The results indicate that the use of the map-matching algorithm leads to an accurate calculation of the length of the distance travelled and thus to an accurate calculation of the transport carbon footprint. Moreover, this method enables the inclusion of unforeseen events such as detours or traffic congestion in the calculations, which would otherwise be lost in other calculation methods recommended by the GLEC Framework. Moreover, this method offers a novel approach to enhancing distance determination within the GLEC Framework. Furthermore, it enables the real-time calculation of CO_2e emissions. In the future, the model could be enhanced to achieve more precise emission factor calculations by incorporating not only varying payloads, but also route elevation profiles, velocity profiles or differing tire pressures, which are often available in the telemetry data. This spatial and temporal transparency in CO_2e emissions could serve as an intriguing starting point for optimizing transport processes. Since the CO_2e emissions of transport processes are directly influenced by fuel consumption and therefore also incur direct costs for the company, the integration of map-matching with telemetry data offers a viable means to improve accurate modeling and potentially reduce future greenhouse gas emissions and company costs.

Acknowledgements The authors would like to thank Fahrzeugwerk Bernard KRONE GmbH & Co. KG and Kemena GmbH for providing the telemetry data in compliance with data protection. Under the consortium leadership of the Krone Group, Spelle, with partners from industry and science, the three-year EDNA project (funding code: 01MD22001C; funding programme: "EDGE Data Economy"), funded by the German Federal Ministry of Economics and Climate Protection (BMWK), is researching the potential of digital technologies for more sustainable production in the transport and logistics sector (www.edna-projekt.de).

The project was funded by the program "Digitale Technologien" of the Austrian Federal Ministry for Climate Action, Environment, Energy, Mobility, Innovation and Technology (BMK). The publication was partially funded within the COMET K2 Competence Centers for Excellent Technologies from the Austrian Federal Ministry for Climate Action, Environment, Energy, Mobility, Innovation and Technology (BMK), the Austrian Federal Ministry for Labour and Economy (BMAW), the Province of Styria (Dept. 12) and the Styrian Business Promotion Agency (SFG). The Austrian Research Promotion Agency (FFG) has been authorised for the programme management.

References

1. NOAA Climate.gov: Global temperature anomalies - graphing tool (2023). https://www.climate.gov/maps-data/dataset/global-temperature-anomalies-graphing-tool
2. Ramanathan, V., & Feng, Y. (2009). Air pollution, greenhouse gases and climate change: Global and regional perspectives. *Atmospheric Environment, 43*(1), 37–50. DOI https://doi.org/10.1016/j.atmosenv.2008.09.063. https://www.sciencedirect.com/science/article/pii/S1352231008008583
3. Saunois, M., Stavert, A. R., Poulter, B., Bousquet, P., Canadell, J. G., Jackson, R. B., Raymond, P. A., Dlugokencky, E. J., Houweling, S., Patra, P. K., Ciais, P., Arora, V. K., Bastviken, D., Bergamaschi, P., Blake, D. R., Brailsford, G., Bruhwiler, L., Carlson, K. M., Carrol, M., … Zhuang, Q. (2020). The global methane budget 2000–2017. *Earth System Science Data, 12*(3), 1561–1623. https://doi.org/10.5194/essd-12-1561-2020
4. Tian, H., Xu, R., Canadell, J. G., Thompson, R. L., Winiwarter, W., Suntharalingam, P., Davidson, E. A., Ciais, P., Jackson, R. B., Janssens-Maenhout, G., Prather, M. J., Regnier, P., Pan, N., Pan, S., Peters, G. P., Shi, H., Tubiello, F. N., Zaehle, S., Zhou, F., … Yao, Y. (2020). A comprehensive quantification of global nitrous oxide sources and sinks. *Nature, 586*(7828), 248–256. https://doi.org/10.1038/s41586-020-2780-0
5. Malhi, G. S., Kaur, M., & Kaushik, P. (2021). Impact of climate change on agriculture and its mitigation strategies: A review. *Sustainability, 13*(3), 1318. https://doi.org/10.3390/su13031318
6. von Uexkull, N., & Buhaug, H. (2021). Security implications of climate change: A decade of scientific progress. *Journal of Peace Research, 58*(1), 3–17. https://doi.org/10.1177/0022343320984210

7. Statista: Co2-ausstoß weltweit nach sektoren — statista (2024). https://de.statista.com/statistik/daten/studie/167957/umfrage/verteilung-der-co-emissionen-weltweit-nach-bereich/
8. Lamb, W. F., Wiedmann, T., Pongratz, J., Andrew, R., Crippa, M., Olivier, J. G. J., Wiedenhofer, D., Mattioli, G., Khourdajie, A. A., House, J., Pachauri, S., Figueroa, M., Saheb, Y., Slade, R., Hubacek, K., Sun, L., Ribeiro, S. K., Khennas, S., de La Rue Can, S., … Minx, J. (2021). A review of trends and drivers of greenhouse gas emissions by sector from 1990 to 2018. *Environmental Research Letters, 16*(7), 073005. https://doi.org/10.1088/1748-9326/abee4e
9. Blok, K., Afanador, A., van der Hoorn, I., Berg, T., Edelenbosch, O. Y., & van Vuuren, D. P. (2020). Assessment of sectoral greenhouse gas emission reduction potentials for 2030. *Energies, 13*(4), 943. https://doi.org/10.3390/en13040943
10. Ravi, S., & Mamdikar, M. R. (2022). A review on its (intelligent transportation systems) technology. In *2022 International Conference on Applied Artificial Intelligence and Computing (ICAAIC)* (pp. 155–159). IEEE. https://doi.org/10.1109/ICAAIC53929.2022.9792638
11. Markovic, N., Sekula, P., Vander Laan, Z., Andrienko, G., & Andrienko, N. (2019). Applications of trajectory data from the perspective of a road transportation agency: Literature review and maryland case study. *IEEE Transactions on Intelligent Transportation Systems, 20*(5), 1858–1869. https://doi.org/10.1109/TITS.2018.2843298
12. Deutsches Institut für Normung e. V.: Din en iso 14064-3:2020-05, treibhausgase_- teil_3: Spezifikation mit anleitung zur validierung und verifizierung von erklärungen über treibhausgase (iso_14064-3:2019); deutsche und englische fassung en_iso_14064-3:2019 (2020). https://doi.org/10.31030/3023312
13. Deutsches Institut für Normung e. V.: DIN EN 16258:2013-03, Methode zur Berechnung und Deklaration des Energieverbrauchs und der Treibhausgasemissionen bei Transportdienstleistungen (Güter- und Personenverkehr); Deutsche Fassung EN_16258:2012, vol. 03.220.01. Beuth Verlag GmbH, Berlin (2013). https://doi.org/10.31030/1894795
14. Deutsches Institut für Normung e. V.: Din en iso 14083:2024-06, treibhausgase_- quantifizierung und berichterstattung über treibhausgasemissionen von transportvorgängen (iso_14083:2023); deutsche fassung en_iso_14083:2023 (2024). https://doi.org/10.31030/3532135
15. Global Logistics Emissions Council: Global logistics emissions council framework v3.1 (2024). https://smart-freight-centre-media.s3.amazonaws.com/documents/GLEC_FRAMEWORK_v3_UPDATED_04_12_24.pdf
16. Ehrler, V. C., Seidel, S., Lischke, A., Davydenko, I., Dobers, K., Lewis, A., Val, S., & Luzzini, D. (2018). *Standardization of transport chain emission calculation – status quo and what is needed next*. https://doi.org/10.5281/ZENODO.1487520
17. Dehdari, P., Wlcek, H., & Furmans, K. (2023). An updated literature review of CO2e calculation in road freight transportation. *Multimodal Transportation, 2*(2), 100068. https://doi.org/10.1016/j.multra.2022.100068. https://www.sciencedirect.com/science/article/pii/S2772586322000685
18. Fancello, G., Vitiello, D. M., & Serra, P. (2023). Evaluating the environmental sustainability of an intermodal freight logistic chain using the GLEC framework. In O. Gervasi, B. Murgante, A. M. A. C. Rocha, C. Garau, F. Scorza, Y. Karaca, & C. M. Torre (Eds.), *Computational science and its applications—ICCSA 2023 workshops, Lecture notes in computer science* (pp. 563–576). Springer Nature Switzerland and Imprint Springer. https://doi.org/10.1007/978-3-031-37123-3_39
19. World Resources Institute: Greenhouse gas protocol corporate value chain (scope 3) accounting and reporting standard (2011).
20. United States Department of Defense: Global positioning system (GPS) standard positioning service (SPS) performance standard - 5th edition (2020, April). https://www.gps.gov/technical/ps/2020-SPS-performance-standard.pdf
21. Schön, S., & Kutterer, H. (2005). Realistic uncertainty measures for GPS observations. In F. Sansò (Ed.), *A window on the future of geodesy, International Association of Geodesy Symposia* (Vol. 128, pp. 54–59). Springer. https://doi.org/10.1007/3-540-27432-4_10
22. Harrison, R. L. (2010). Introduction to monte carlo simulation. *AIP conference proceedings, 1204*, 17–21. https://doi.org/10.1063/1.3295638

Overcoming Lemon Markets with Business Reputation Ecosystem—A Multi-Agent Simulation on Monetary Ratings

Ulvi Ibrahimli, Simon Hemmrich, Simon Zauke, and Axel Winkelmann

Abstract Business reputation ecosystems are a widely untapped research field. In these ecosystems, agents can selectively exchange (monetary) ratings to inform about the experienced quality in a market. We build a model for conducting a multi-agent simulation that can be used to simulate and evaluate business reputation ecosystems as a new system class. We explore the factual occurring voluntary payment to create positive (pay) or negative ratings (no pay), selling ratings selectively to alleviate information asymmetry, and the workings of counter-ratings to prevent buyers' dishonest ratings. Thereby, we analyze, among others, agent profitability, the occurrence of dishonest ratings, and reputation bias and sensitivity. The results provide simulation-based empirical evidence that the concept of monetary reputation systems provides necessary incentives for participation, and high-quality sellers and honest buyers benefit from such a system. The results indicate that counter-ratings prompt buyers to rate sellers honestly, albeit incurring the monetary cost for positive ratings.

1 Introduction

Information asymmetry between buyers and sellers can lead to a downward spiral of the provided quality in business-to-business (B2B) markets [1, 2]. Reputation systems can reduce or even reverse this dynamic [3, 4]. As information systems (IS), they collect, aggregate, and disseminate information about a product [5]. In the business-to-consumer (B2C) context, they demonstrated practical usefulness in

U. Ibrahimli (✉) · A. Winkelmann
Julius-Maximilians-Universität Würzburg, Würzburg, Germany
e-mail: ulvi.ibrahimli@uni-wuerzburg.de

A. Winkelmann
e-mail: axel.winkelmann@uni-wuerzburg.de

S. Hemmrich · S. Zauke
Universität Paderborn, Paderborn, Germany
e-mail: simon.hemmrich@uni-paderborn.de

C. M. Flath et al. (eds.), *Digital Innovation and Organizational Transformation*, Lecture Notes in Information Systems and Organisation 83,
https://doi.org/10.1007/978-3-032-08483-5_26

the form of review systems [6] or recommender systems [7] for marketplaces like Amazon or eBay. Despite their significant benefits and daily use for product search, reputation systems poorly exist in B2B settings [6, 8–10]. Several design weaknesses contribute to the underutilization of these system classes in B2B markets [11, 12]. These include inter alia low incentives to submit ratings [13], the prevalence of distorted or reciprocal ratings, and the system's vulnerability to fake or unfair ratings [14, 15]. Furthermore, businesses fear revealing capable suppliers to competitors and are challenged to compare products and services as well as to align conflicting stakeholder interests. Often, there is deliberate non-transparency regarding price and quality from the sellers' side [16]. Nevertheless, the research indicates that low product quality, delayed transactions, or volatile supplier performance are detrimental to forming trust, a critical factor in data exchange in B2B setups [17, 18]. Consequently, we argue that such instances of intercompany misconduct necessitate establishing robust reputation systems in a B2B context. Reputation systems are viewed as essential technologies that digital ecosystems rely on to build or restore trust and foster corporate collaborations between agents [8].

Designing business reputation ecosystems as a new system class [11] is an upcoming advance to address the previously mentioned weaknesses [19]. In this new system class, companies—denoted as agents—collect and distribute ratings, which they can selectively communicate to one another. Two novel ideas proposed by Hemmrich [20] are particularly relevant to this paper. (1) Sellers offer product discounts, expecting buyers to compensate by paying the full price. Buyers can freely and selectively choose to grant this compensation through positive ratings, effectively costing them the discounted amount.[1] On the other hand, sellers perform counter-ratings to penalize the exploitative rating of such buyers (e.g., when they do not pay the pre-agreed money), which becomes only visible (upon threshold) if the buyer consistently fails to pay the offered discount. Payments linked to ratings establish a direct quantifiable connection between a rating and a business transaction, incorporating a reputation mechanism that quantifies trust between agents [20]. (2) Buyers own their ratings and decide to whom (typically other buyers) they sell the rating information for profit. This incentive offers an alternative to hitherto seller-induced incentive schemes with potentially biased ratings [13]. Systems in which agents can validate stored quality information based on these ratings are generally superior to those that test only for honesty [17, 21]. The ability to select ratings individually also appears essential for a business reputation ecosystem to function effectively [11, 22].

We employ Agent-Based Modeling and Simulation (ABMS) to study and evaluate the effects of the proposed system class [23]. A simulation is a particularly suitable means of investigating novel designs not implemented in the real world and assessing IS-induced phenomena (e.g., selection behavior of agents of trustworthy sellers) before practically instantiating an artifact [24]. Moreover, agent-based simulation enables configuring heterogeneous agents with self-learning adaptive strategic behavior. This capability closely mirrors the chain of complex interactions that take

[1] In this paper, the term "buyers" refers to purchasing companies in the B2B context. To avoid potential confusion, we will refer to buyers in B2C transactions as "consumers" where necessary.

place within such information systems. The engineering of environment variables allows for evaluating the effectiveness of such IS in real B2B settings [25]. The IS scholarship also reflects on its epistemic status—that is, mechanism-based methods are viewed as credible approaches for studying novel socio-technical IS phenomena and making epistemic inferences [23]. Therefore, simulation furnishes strong scientific rigor [23, 26]. No simulation study has examined this kind of system class with monetary ratings or counter-ratings. To gain prima facie empirical evidence of whether such a system functions, we formulate the following research question (RQ):

RQ: How do the incentives offered by monetary reputation ecosystems contribute to reducing information asymmetry between agents?

The paper continues by describing the theoretical background comprising information asymmetry, reputation systems, and ABMS. The subsequent section deals with agent-based model setup and parameters, followed by outcome analysis, evaluation, and discussion before concluding the study.

2 Research Background

2.1 Information Asymmetry

Akerlof's seminal work on 'The Market for Lemons' explores the impact of information asymmetry, exemplified in car markets. Sellers know more about product quality than buyers, leading to buyer uncertainty and reduced willingness to pay high prices. High quality going unrecognized disincentivizes sellers from offering higher quality, leading to a downward spiral of quality dominated by low-quality "lemons" [1]. This effect of information asymmetry is also seen in most B2B transactions [2], where sellers cannot prove quality upfront. One form of ex-ante quality signaling is through reputation [27–29], which can contribute to mitigating this problem (Fig. 1) [30]. Reputation affects the perceived quality and facilitates sales transactions [31, 32]. Adverse selection and moral hazard can be addressed through pre- or post-contractual measures [33], while trusting buyers contribute to a company's reputation and instill trust in uncertain sellers [34].

Reputation systems help signal good quality, thereby reducing information asymmetry and building trust [4, 32]. Positive ratings from a positive reputation lower perceived risk for buyers, thus making them more willing to engage in transactions previously deemed too risky [29, 35]. The reliance on reputation increases the willingness to transact with sellers, fostering economic stability and growth [36, 37]. High-quality sellers aim to build a positive reputation for higher profits, while low-quality sellers try to avoid or manipulate ratings to appear more favorable [38, 39]. Reputation systems, rooted in real-tested product quality, combat information asymmetry effectively [21]. While reputation may not perfectly reflect quality [29], ratings

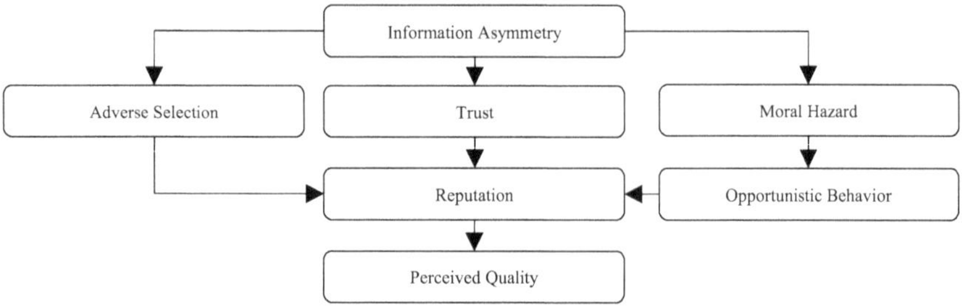

Fig. 1 Lemon market theory: nomological network for antecedents of perceived quality [30]

from peer buyers in a reputation system serve as the best approximation [35, 40]. Trustworthy identities, such as known companies, contribute to the credibility of their ratings [22, 41], promoting efficient and trustworthy markets [42].

2.2 *Reputation Systems in B2B Context*

A business reputation system involves a seller offering a buyer a rating opportunity, with the payment as a rating being optional and indicative of the seller's delivered quality. Other buyers can observe monetary ratings received by a seller and request this information based on the trustworthiness of the identity. Unlike B2C applications, where the identity of the rating agent (consumer) is less relevant, in business ratings, the identity significantly influences the trustworthiness of the given rating [22, 34]. Ratings from renowned companies are deemed more trustworthy, given the perceived reluctance to risk their public reputation for a forged rating [43, 44], particularly when stored immutably [20]. A counter-rating mechanism in the form of a star rating initially restricts the visibility of negative ratings, becoming apparent only after a threshold of excessive negative ratings across all sellers is reached [20]. Moreover, the buyer has the discretion to confirm or refuse to pass on the requested rating, weighing the benefits (receiving compensation and potentially other ratings) against potential detriments (disclosing relevant information to competitors). Buyers selectively submit information about a seller's product quality, and other buyers can learn which identity of buying agents appears trustworthy, building a simulated self-learning adaptive system [45] (Fig. 2).

Yet such reputation systems are yet to evolve in the future [11, 47]. Notably, B2B transactions between companies present unique challenges compared to B2C contexts, such as differences in purchase intention, decision-making, complexity, information asymmetries, payment processes, product characteristics, usage, supplier relationships, logistics [17, 48, 49], and rising information opacity [50]. Hence, business reputation systems face greater challenges than B2C systems in incentivizing rating agents, as submitting ratings involves resource commitment and time [46]. Consequently, the justification for rating efforts should align with a tangible

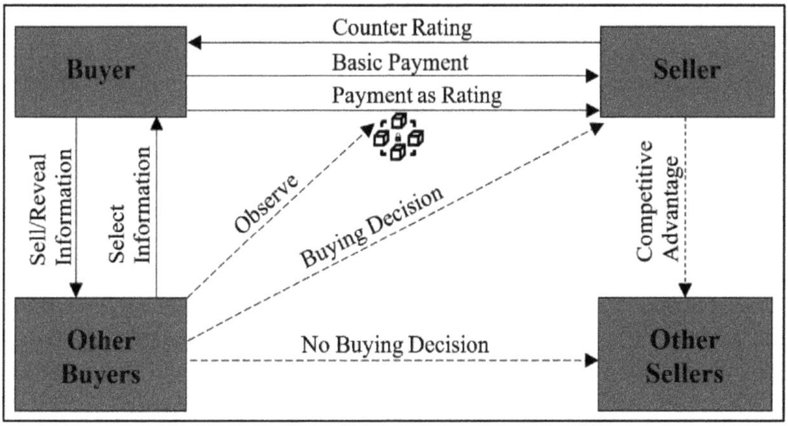

Fig. 2 Mechanisms of the business reputation system [46]

business benefit (notably monetary incentives [51]). Additional challenges include the rater's experience or expertise in rating products [8] and concerns about competitive disadvantages, potentially leading to hesitancy in sharing information [16]. Competitive situations may also influence rating submission, as companies might be reluctant to enhance the reputation of good suppliers, fearing the loss of a strategic advantage [13]. However, this concern is less pronounced in low- or non-competitive environments. *Selective* forwarding of information, where the original buyer verifies the authenticity of a rating, is considered a viable solution [11].

The context of B2B entails specific agent interactions. The following incentives should hold to show that our model works and can achieve solid simulation results. Companies evaluate costs and benefits and must reproduce three incentives in the system design for agents [11]: (1) Sellers with a high reputation command a price premium in the long term, expecting higher profits than non-participation,(2) Buyers can profit by selling rating information, allowing their revenue to exceed rating payments; (3) Buyers minimize losses by avoiding sellers that fail quality expectations.

3 Research Method

3.1 Agent-Based Modeling and Simulation

Agent-based models are a particularly good fit for examining new properties of systems with simulations [52]. ABMS method helps understand complex patterns that emerge in markets due to the presence of many individual agents [25]. ABMS is well suited since many agents can conduct parallel interactions, such as selling and buying rating information, to maximize profit, thereby simulating a platform network.

It is a system design tool to investigate economic effects in dynamic markets with information asymmetries and to develop new theoretical insights [53, 54]. In the agent-based approach, properties of a system occur from individual, autonomous agents and their interactions in a shared environment [55].

Agents are discrete and identifiable individuals with assigned characteristics and rules that determine their behavior and decisions in a defined environment. They interact with their environment, including other agents, restricted to predefined rules. Agents recognize the characteristics of other agents, act autonomously in a goal-oriented manner, and compare the outcomes of their behavior with their goals. This way, they can store what they learned and adapt to experiences [56]. Agents can have different capability levels: individual *if–then* execution (e.g., drive and stop), dynamic autonomous according to their state (e.g., refuel), interactivity with the environment (e.g., tow another car), adaptivity and learning based on experience (e.g., foresighted driving) [55].

3.2 Application and Evaluation Framework

We apply ABMS as a research method to empirically test how the described incentives contribute to reducing information asymmetry in monetary reputation ecosystems. For the research setup of simulation in IS research, our approach is based on the guidance of Beese et al. [23] and Rand and Rust [25]. We first derive a conceptual model that serves as a foundation for the simulation. Based on this, we generate model parameters to run simulation scenarios with variations in agent numbers, the occurrence of dishonest ratings, the extent of price adjustments, the regulation of trading with ratings, and mechanisms for calculating the reputation of sellers.

The ABMS software NetLogo was chosen based on criteria like free availability, widespread use in research, moderate development effort, graphical display of simulation results with export options in textual data format, and portability.

In the application phase, we show that the model helps create the intended incentives (described in 2.2) necessary for the simulation and, thus, the ecosystem to function. In the evaluation phase, we assess to what extent the monetary reputation ecosystems reduce information asymmetries in a B2B market scenario. For this purpose, one can evaluate the model in terms of *utility* (main purpose), *fitness* (future permanence), and *usefulness* (practical use) [57]. We evaluate the model's *utility* to develop an understanding of the dynamics of information asymmetries in B2B markets using the metrics of Schlosser et al. [58]. The *fitness* of the model will be assessed as the reputation ecosystem evolves and new requirements emerge [57], so this metric is skipped at this stage. To evaluate the model's *usefulness*, we study the behavior of the agents, e.g., to generate honest ratings for blacklisting sellers, and whether they achieve benefits within this system. Our model undergoes summative evaluation after the application phase. We avoid earlier formative evaluation due to the deterministic programming of the ABMS as a discrete system [59]. The chosen evaluation strategy allows for simulating different market scenarios with moderate time expenditure within this artificial evaluation [26].

4 Agent-Based Model for Simulation

4.1 Agent Properties and Model Parameters

The agent-based model represents a decentralized market with seller and buyer agents, each representing a company. Sellers, $S = \{s_1, s_2, ..., s_n\}$, offer homogeneous products of varying quality, cost and price. Quality is modeled with a normal distribution ($\mu = 50$, $\sigma = 30$). Quality, combined with a normally distributed random factor, co-determines production costs per product. Sellers set prices 20 percent above their costs, allowing for price adjustments. Buyers, $B = \{b_1, b_2, ..., b_m\}$, have properties like quality expectation quality exp_b N(50,30),, budget per purchase, price-reputation sensitivity, probability of unfair rating behavior, and star rating. The price-reputation sensitivity coefficient influences the purchase decision, a uniformly distributed random number (0,1), which prevents bias with sufficiently generated agents. Values below (or above) 0.5 indicate a preference for price (or reputation). Opportunistic rating behavior in the model occurs when b_j (any buyer) withholds the rating payment despite the s_j (any seller) meeting or exceeding the b_j's expectations. The likelihood of such behavior is a normally distributed random number ($\mu = 0$) with a (later) specified standard deviation (*sd-malicious-behavior* [0.00,1.00]). Buyers possess a star-$rating_b$ [0.0,5.0] to regulate such behavior, which is the arithmetic mean of all received ratings.

In buyer–seller interactions within the ABM, the negotiated rating payment (rpay $amount_b^s$) and basic payment (price reduced by rpay $amount_b^s$) vary for each pair (b, s) upon negotiation. b_j computes the selection probability of s_j based on budget and price sensitivity (excluding blacklisted sellers where $quality_s$<quality exp_b), price compared to min_s × price sensitivity $coef_b$. Other buyers can acquire reputation information from buyers through purchases or trading rating information. If b_j possesses reputation information about s_j, the selection probability involves adding the price comparison metric to the product of locally calculated reputation for s_j and b_j's reputation sensitivity (price compared to min_s × price sensitivity $coef_b$) + rep_s × reputation sensitivity $coef_b$. The rating payment amount is modeled with a continuously equally distributed random number ranging from 5 to 20 percent of S's price. The transaction's non-performance-dependent component (basic payment, *bpay*) is derived by subtracting the generated rating amount from the s_j's price. In addition, each buyer agent holds distinct properties: transaction $history_b$, own reputation $information_b$, bought reputation $information_b$, and all reputation $information_b$.

Model parameters facilitate the simulation of various scenarios. Four parameters affect sellers' pricing behavior post-monetary transactions. If the share of received performance (rating) payments surpasses a certain threshold, there is a price increase. Conversely, if the share falls below a threshold, prices decrease. Six model parameters regulate the trade with ratings. The *premium-for-sale-of-reputation information* [-1.00,1.00] determines the premium or discount for buyer agents' selling ratings. The model prevents an excessive number of ratings from being sold via a single provider (*nr-max-purchasable-repinfo-per-seller* [1,100]) and sets an upper limit for buyers from whom rating information can be purchased (*nr-max-buyers-to-buy-repinfo-from* [0,50]). Buyers can purchase a limited number of additional ratings (*base-nr-purchasable-reputation-information* [0,20]) beyond their offer to buy. The *threshold-purchase-amount* [1,100] determines the minimum basic payment amount a buyer must pay so that trading with rating information becomes possible, and *reputation-information-to-buy* determines the criteria (newest, oldest, or all ratings) for purchasing rating information from another buyer.

To perform an artificial simulation scenario, we establish a set of base model parameters such that the subsequent variations of individual parameters can be ex-post evaluated against the base model. Some examples include: *sd-malicious-buyer-behaviour* = 0.10; *threshold-buyer-star-rating* = 3.0; *premium-for-sale-of-reputation-information* = 0.20; *good-seller-share-of-rpays-received* = 0.80; *price-premium-after-good-seller-performance* = 0.05; *bad-seller-share-of-rpays-received* = 0.40.

4.2 *Model for Simulation*

Setup. The agent behavior is simulated in ten procedures, executed consecutively in a unit of time (*tick*) (Fig. 4). Here, the simulation generates seller and buyer agents with corresponding properties. Before the first tick run, no b_j has any reputation information about s_j.

Matching. If no tick has yet elapsed, the first procedure is choosing a seller. In the first tick, each buyer *b* chooses a random *s* and creates a link to *s*. From the second tick onwards, each buyer initially creates a set of sellers within their budget and builds a link to each seller. Subsequently, a selection probability$_b$ a is calculated for each link. Only the link with the highest selection probability$_b$ remains. In the next process, sellers delete the links to buyers who have a star-rating$_b$<*threshold-buyer-star-rating* to prevent a possible systematic dishonest rating.

Payment Process. The remaining sellers and buyers calculate the amount of the rating payment in *negotiate-rpay*. This is followed by payment of the basic amount, *bpay*. Before *rating-process*, buyers inspect the quality of the product and decide whether they rate it negatively or positively (paying rpay). Based on the result, buyers make or do not make the rating payment and store this information in their transaction history. In another step, buyers can blacklist sellers. Based on rating payments received, sellers adjust their prices. Finally, the data on seller reputation are saved, and all links between sellers and buyers are deleted.

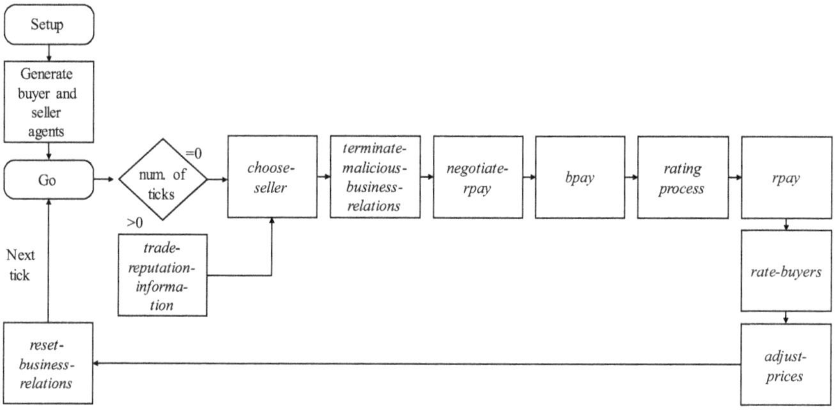

Fig. 3 Model of simulating payment as ratings between agents

Trading with Ratings. *trade-reputation-information* is only executed if at least one tick has already been passed. Here, each buyer collects ratings that are within their budget from a set of *S*. This set contains sellers who performed at least one sale, are not on the buyer's blacklist, and for whom these b_j have bought at most as many ratings as technically possible. When a tick starts, b_j randomly selects a seller s_j from this set. Subsequently, each b_j has a maximum set of other buyers b_j for this seller s_j, defined by the model parameter *nr-max-buyers-to-buy-repinfo-from*, who have already interacted with this s_j and had a transaction via *threshold-purchase-amount*. If a buyer does not find suitable other buyers, their set stays empty. Each b_j in this set sells, depending on *reputation-information-to-buy*, the oldest, newest, or all available ratings of the desired seller from own reputation information_b to the other rating b_j. Each buyer stores the purchased ratings and calculates a reputation value for each potential seller and stores this individually in all-reputation information_b (Fig. 3).

5 Simulation Outcome

5.1 Application

Following the setup phase, seller (N = 30) and buyer agents (N = 50) are created with their properties in the time unit ticks = 0. We observe heterogeneity among sellers in terms of quality, cost, and price and among buyers regarding quality expectations and budgets. The scenario is initially simulated over 50 ticks to gauge the results of seller behavior.

The sellers' profit is calculated from the rating and basic payments received minus the cost per unit multiplied by the number of sales. Due to a few outliers, we study median profit instead of average. The analysis shows that sellers with above-average

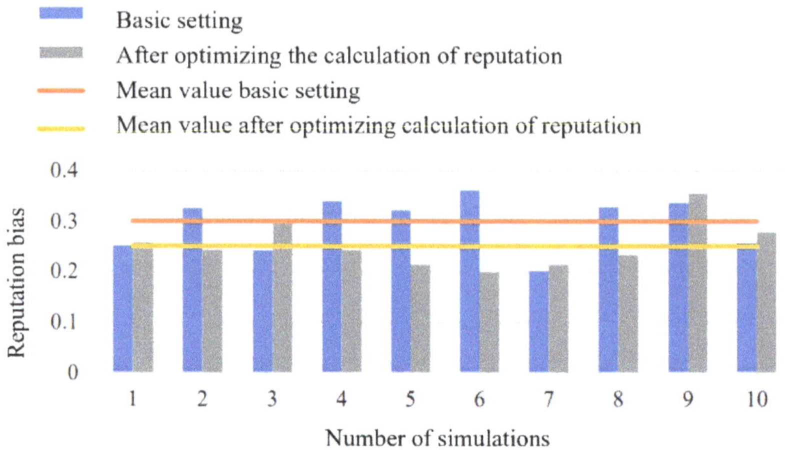

Fig. 4 ABMS reputation bias comparison with basic model setup

product quality run at a loss after 50 ticks, albeit a smaller loss than low-quality sellers. To assess the long-run effects, we extend the simulation by an additional 150 ticks. We find that high-quality sellers eventually become profitable, whereas low-quality sellers suffer even greater losses. This finding highlights that consistently offering high-quality products pays off in the long run within a money-based reputation mechanism.

Looking at buyers, the difference between made rating payments and revenue from the sale of ratings is relevant as a profit metric. After 50 ticks, this difference averages positive and increases as buyers interact with more sellers. Buyers made the rating payments 80 percent of the time. The cluster analysis reveals that buyers with the highest probability of dishonest rating surprisingly achieve high profits initially, yet this effect diminishes in the long term. Also, reputation-sensitive buyers tend to be more profitable than price-sensitive buyers. These findings emphasize that buyer profitability is positively shaped by the interplay of distinct features of the reputation system.

Thus, we observe that the model works as intended. The first incentive (1) is validated as high-quality sellers achieve higher profits when the reputation system is switched on, and low-quality sellers benefit when switched off. The second incentive (2) also occurs, as buyer profits are positive on average and median. To test the third incentive (3), we measure each rating trade as to how much each buyer spends on buying rating information about sellers that do not meet their quality expectations and compute how high the losses would have been if they had bought from those sellers. After 200 ticks, for all buyers, the sum of potential losses incurred when choosing a bad seller exceeds the cost of buying the respective ratings. Thus, (3) incentive is also observed.

5.2 Evaluation

Evaluating the *utility* of choosing a capable seller, the reputation bias is computed as suggested in [58] with small modifications. The bias measures how much the average reputation of each seller deviates from the reputation it should receive. The mean reputation bias is computed based on the base setting of the model parameters. The average mean reputation bias achieved in ten simulations is 0.30 (Fig. 4). To observe the influence of variations of relevant model parameters on reputation bias according to One-Factor-At-a-Time (OFAT) sensitivity modeling, six parameters are selected that govern the trade with ratings and reputation building: *nr-max-purchasable-repinfo-per-seller* ([10,100] with an interval of 10), *nr-max-buyers-to-buy-repinfo-from* ([1,45] with an interval of 5), *base-nr-purchasable-reputation-information* ([1,20] with an interval of 1), *threshold-purchase-amount* ([10,100] with an interval of 10), *reputation-information-to-buy* and *rep-computation-method* (all methods, see Sect. 4.1). Subsequently, for each parameter we perform ten simulations (100 Ticks each), holding other parameters constant at the base model setup. We later set variables at values that individually generated the lowest average reputation bias and performed ten more simulation rounds. The optimized parameter setting indeed leads to overall reduced reputation bias (Fig. 4).

To evaluate the *usefulness*, we study the effect of buyers' dishonest rating behavior through reputation bias and buyers' mean profit with a bias-optimized model parameter setting. The results show that reputation bias and buyers' mean profit increase with the probability of dishonest ratings. Buyers who often rate dishonestly have lower expenses for making rating payments than those who never or rarely rate dishonestly. However, a poor star rating discourages sellers from transacting with those buyers. Nonetheless, dishonest buyers can still profit from selling rating information. To address this, we adjusted the model parameter so that buyers do not purchase ratings from other buyers whose star ratings fall below $\text{threshold-buyer-star-rating}_b$. We observe that although the buyers with the lowest probability of dishonest rating receive the highest profit, those with the highest probability still manage to generate high profits.

6 Discussion and Implications

The study provides simulation-based empirical evidence that the concept of money-based reputation systems in B2B markets can effectively incentivize participation. The results of this study have several implications for the research. We find that, albeit with short-term losses, sellers who consistently offer high-quality products benefit from participating in such a system in the long run. The fact that buyers typically make the rating payments in most cases implies that, in the long run, they are likely to find a seller that matches their quality expectations in such systems. This, coupled with the finding that fair rating buyers receive the highest profit from trading the rating information, indicates an overall reduced information asymmetry regarding the seller quality compared to the lemon market at the "cold start". The system incentivizes buyers to rate honestly, and honest buyers benefit the most from the monetary reputation system. However, dishonest raters also make significant profits. One likely explanation is that dishonest buyers often avoid paying rating payments, positively impacting their net profit. The adjusted star rating emerged as a suitable instrument to alleviate this problem as the model with a star rating shows lower reputation bias than the one without such an instrument. Yet future research needs to design a more robust counter-mechanism, as buyers may rate dishonestly not only for financial but also for strategic purposes [60].

On the other side, our study presents practical implications. The model developed can serve as a prototypical testing framework on, for example, digital B2B marketplaces for capital goods or E-Commerce platforms. Our model can be used to inform platform design and policies aimed at optimizing platform-based matchmaking and promoting trust in B2B transactions. Understanding the buyer–seller dynamics through the lens of reputation systems can help platforms design algorithms that highlight reputable sellers and allow buyer profits, thereby fostering a trustworthy digital marketplace. Nonetheless, certain caveats are to be considered. The fact that buyer profit increases as they interact with more sellers (Sect. 5.1) suggests a buyer's tendency to switch sellers frequently to sell more rating information. Thus, it is advised that practitioners design a countermeasure to address potential intercompany malpractices. Also, the dishonesty remains undetected when untruthful rating information is not sold to other buyers on such platforms. A remedy could be encouraging purchasing and comparing multiple ratings [20].

Altogether, our work contributes to scholarly discourse within IS research by studying how B2B agents are incentivized to participate in money-based reputation systems. It sheds light on how the monetary nature of such ecosystems reduces information asymmetry. Through the lens of multi-agent simulation, our research offers a more nuanced empirical understanding of monetary reputation ecosystems in the B2B arena.

7 Conclusion

This study explores the design, functionality, and impact of monetary transaction-based reputation systems on information asymmetry to be used in B2B markets.

The study demonstrates the model's functionality by simulating a comprehensive market scenario and provides an initial evaluation of the concept of the business reputation ecosystem. It shows that it provides the necessary incentives for participation. Also, the information asymmetry is reduced since buyers, in the long run, are likely to find a seller that matches their quality expectations, and fair-rating buyers receive the highest profit from trading with ratings. Yet introducing a risky advance here in the form of monetary ratings is necessary to help digitize trust, as it entails a risk for sellers of receiving poor ratings and, consequently, less payment

[20]. Our study reveals that the counter-rating instrument helped minimize dishonest rating behavior. However, the continued profitability of dishonest buyers indicates a need for future research to address this market failure comprehensively. The simulation model presented can unlock the potential of business reputation ecosystems. It sets the stage for further research on developing more robust reputation systems with dynamic agent parameters and exploring real-world applications of monetary reputation systems.

Our study comes with certain limitations. Given the choice of the ABMS as a research method, abstraction decisions were necessary. The abstractions include infinite supplier budgets and do not model the possibility of suppliers charging prices below production costs. Also, a more robust financial penalty mechanism is necessary for strategic dishonest ratings as it distorts such a system [60]. For the results to be extrapolated to real-world situations, it must be verified whether the chosen abstraction leads to deviating agent behavior compared to real test subjects. In addition, future research still needs to address issues such as dynamic parallel adjustment of the model parameters and handling positive dishonest ratings.

References

1. Akerlof, G. A. (1970). The market for “Lemons”: Quality uncertainty and the market mechanism. *The Quarterly Journal of Economics, 84*(3), 488–500.
2. Banerjee, A., Ries, J. M., & Wiertz, C. (2020). The impact of social media signals on supplier selection: Insights from two experiments. *International Journal of Operations & Production Management, 40*(5), 531–552.
3. Rice, S. C. (2012). Reputation and uncertainty in online markets: An experimental study. *Information Systems Research, 23*(2), 436–452.
4. Thierer, A., Koopman, C., Hobson, A., & Kuiper, C. (2016). How the internet, the sharing economy, and reputational feedback mechanisms solve the lemons problem. *University of Miami Law Review, 70*(3), 830–878.
5. Resnick, P., Kuwabara, K., Zeckhauser, R., & Friedman, E. (2000). Reputation systems. *Communications of the ACM, 43*(12), 45–48.
6. Gutt, D., Neumann, J., Zimmermann, S., Kundisch, D., & Chen, J. (2019). Design of review systems—A strategic instrument to shape online reviewing behavior and economic outcomes. *The Journal of Strategic Information Systems, 28*(2), 104–117.
7. Jannach, D., & Jugovac, M. (2019). Measuring the business value of recommender systems. *ACM Transactions on Management Information Systems, 10*(4), 1–23.
8. Dikow, H., Hasan, O., Kosch, H., Brunie, L., & Sornin, R. (2015). Improving the accuracy of business-to-business (B2B) reputation systems through rater expertise prediction. *Computing, 97*(1), 29–49.
9. Mai, E. S., & Liao, Y. (2021). The interplay of word-of-mouth and customer value on B2B sales performance in a digital platform: An expectancy value theory perspective. *Journal of Business & Industrial Marketing, 37*(7), 1389–1401.
10. Poniatowski, M., Neumann, J., & Kundisch, D. (2019). Reviewing the Vendor or the product-analyzing vendor versus product representation in B2B review systems. In *25th Americas conference on information systems, Cancun* (pp. 1–5).
11. Hemmrich, S., Bobolz, J., Beverungen, D. & Blömer, J. (2023). Designing business reputation ecosystems—A method for issuing and trading monetary ratings on a blockchain, In *Proceedings of the 31st European conference on information systems (ECIS), Kristiansand.*

12. Seutter, J., Kutzner, K., Stadtländer, M., Kundisch, D., & Knackstedt, R. (2023). "Sorry, too much information"—Designing online review systems that support information search and processing. *Electronic Markets, 33*(1), 47.
13. Neumann, J., & Gutt, D. (2019). Money makes the reviewer go round–ambivalent effects of online review elicitation in B2B markets. In *25th Americas conference on information systems (AMCIS), cancun* (pp. 1–10).
14. Ansari, S., & Gupta, S. (2021). Review manipulation: Literature review, and future research agenda. *Pacific Asia Journal of the Association for Information Systems, 13*(4), 97–121.
15. Mayzlin, D., Dover, Y., & Chevalier, J. (2014). Promotional reviews: An empirical investigation of online review manipulation. *American Economic Review, 104*(8), 2421–2455.
16. Zhu, K. (2002). Information transparency in electronic marketplaces: Why data transparency may hinder the adoption of B2B exchanges. *Electronic Markets, 12*(2), 92–99.
17. McKnight, D. H., Lankton, N. K., Nicolaou, A., & Price, J. (2017). Distinguishing the effects of B2B information quality, system quality, and service outcome quality on trust and distrust. *The Journal of Strategic Information Systems, 26*(2), 118–141.
18. Mehta, S. C., & Durvasula, S. (1998). Relationships between SERVQUAL dimensions and organizational performance in the case of a business-to-business service. *Journal of Business & Industrial Marketing, 13*(1), 40–53.
19. Hevner, A. R., March, S. T., Park, J., & Ram, S. (2008). Design science in information systems research. *Management Information Systems Quarterly, 28*(1), 6.
20. Hemmrich, S. (2023). Business reputation systems based on Blockchain technology—A risky advance. In *Proceedings of the 31st European conference on information systems (ECIS), Kristiansand.*
21. Kennes, J., & Schiff, A. (2007). Simple reputation systems. *Scandinavian Journal of Economics, 109*(1), 71–91.
22. Marti, S., & Garcia-Molina, H. (2003). Identity Crisis: Anonymity vs Reputation in P2P Systems. *'Proceedings Third International Conference on Peer-to-Peer Computing, P2P '03* (pp. 134–141). IEEE.
23. Beese, J., Haki, M. K., Aier, S., & Winter, R. (2019). Simulation-based research in information systems: Epistemic implications and a review of the status quo. *Business & Information Systems Engineering, 61*(4), 503–521.
24. Sonnenberg, C., & vom Brocke, J. (2012), Evaluations in the science of the artificial–reconsidering the build-evaluate pattern in design science research. In *International conference on design science research in information systems (DESRIST 2012).* Design Science Research in Information Systems. Advances in Theory and Practice, Las Vegas. Berlin (pp. 381–397). Springer.
25. Rand, W., & Rust, R. T. (2011). Agent-based modeling in marketing: Guidelines for rigor. *International Journal of Research in Marketing, 28*(3), 181–193.
26. Venable, J., Pries-Heje, J., & Baskerville, R. (2016). A framework for evaluation in design science research. *European Journal of Information Systems, 25*(1), 77–89.
27. Li, L., Tadelis, S., & Zhou, X. (2020). Buying reputation as a signal of quality: Evidence from an online marketplace. *The RAND Journal of Economics, 51*(4), 965–988.
28. Mui, L., Mohtashemi, M., & Halberstadt, A. (2002). Notions of reputation in multi-agents systems. In *Proceedings of the first international joint conference on autonomous agents and multiagent systems Part 1 (AAMAS), Bologna* (pp. 280–287).
29. Shapiro, C. (1982). Consumer information, product quality, and seller reputation. *The Bell Journal of Economics, 13*(1), 20–35.
30. Devos, J., Van Landeghem, H., & Deschoolmeester, D. (2012). The theory of the lemon markets in IS research. In Y. K. Dwivedi, M. R. Wade & S. L. Schneberger (Eds.), *Information systems theory: Explaining and predicting our digital society* (pp. 213–230). Springer Science & Business Media.
31. Ba, S., & Pavlou, P. A. (2002). Evidence of the effect of trust building technology in electronic markets. Price premiums and buyer behavior. *MIS Quarterly, 26*(3), 243–268.

32. Saeedi, M. (2019). Reputation and adverse selection: Theory and evidence from eBay. *The RAND Journal of Economics, 50*(4), 822–853.
33. Mavlanova, T., Benbunan-Fich, R., & Koufaris, M. (2012). Signaling theory and information asymmetry in online commerce. *Information & Management, 49*(5), 240–247.
34. Jøsang, A., Ismail, R., & Boyd, C. (2007). A survey of trust and reputation systems for online service provision. *Decision Support Systems, 43*(2), 618–644.
35. Moreno, A., & Terwiesch, C. (2014). Doing business with strangers. Reputation in online service marketplaces. *Information Systems Research, 25*(4), 865–886.
36. Biong, H. (2013). Choice of subcontractor in markets with asymmetric information: Reputation and price effects. *Journal of Business & Industrial Marketing, 28*(1), 60–71.
37. Ghose, A., & Ipeirotis, P. G. (2010). Estimating the helpfulness and economic impact of product reviews: Mining text and reviewer characteristics. *IEEE Transactions on Knowledge and Data Engineering, 23*(10), 1498–1512.
38. Salminen, J., Kandpal, C., Kamel, A. M., Jung, S., & Jansen, B. J. (2022). Creating and detecting fake reviews of online products. *Journal of Retailing and Consumer Services, 64*, 1–15.
39. Shapiro, C. (1983). Premiums for high quality products as returns to reputations. *The Quarterly Journal of Economics, 98*(4), 659–679.
40. Shapiro, S. P. (1987). The social control of impersonal trust. *American Journal of Sociology, 93*(3), 623–658.
41. Whetten, D. A. (1997). Part II: Where do reputations come from?: Theory development and the study of corporate reputation. *Corporate reputation review, 1*, 25–34.
42. Kreps, D. M., & Wilson, R. (1982). Reputation and imperfect information. *Journal of Economic Theory, 27*(2), 253–279.
43. Keh, H. T., & Xie, Y. (2009). Corporate reputation and customer behavioral intentions: The roles of trust, identification and commitment. *Industrial Marketing Management, 38*(7), 732–742.
44. van der Merwe, A. W., & Puth, G. (2014). Towards a conceptual model of the relationship between corporate trust and corporate reputation. *Corporate reputation review, 17*, 138–156.
45. Sabzian, H., Shafia, M. A., Bonyadi, N. A., Jandaghi, G., & Sheikh Mohammad, J. (2018). A review of agent-based modeling (ABM) concepts and some of its main applications in management science. *Iranian Journal of Management Studies, 11*(4), 659–692.
46. Hemmrich, S., Schäfer, J., Hansmeier, P., & Beverungen, D. (2024). The value of reputation systems in business contexts—A qualitative study taking the view of buyers. In *Proceedings of the 57th Hawaii international conference on system sciences, Hawaii international conference on system sciences, Hawaiian village.*
47. Narang, S., Byali, M., Dayama, P., Pandit, V., & Narahari, Y. (2019). Design of trusted B2B market platforms using permissioned blockchains and game theory. *IEEE international conference on blockchain and cryptocurrency (ICBC)* (pp. 385–393). IEEE.
48. Chen, S., He, Q., & Xiao, H. (2022). A study on cross-border e-commerce partner selection in B2B mode. *Electronic Commerce Research, 22*(2), 1–21.
49. Choy, K. L., Lee, W. B., & Lo, V. (2003). Design of a case based intelligent supplier relationship management system—The integration of supplier rating system and product coding system. *Expert Systems with Applications, 25*(1), 87–100.
50. Zhou, Z. Z., & Zhu, K. X. (2010). The effects of information transparency on suppliers, manufacturers, and consumers in online markets. *Marketing Science, 29*(6), 1125–1137.
51. Miller, N., Resnick, P., & Zeckhauser, R. (2005). Eliciting informative feedback: The peer-prediction method. *Management Science, 51*(9), 1359–1373.
52. Wall, F. (2016). Agent-based modeling in managerial science: An illustrative survey and study. *Review of Managerial Science 10*(1), 135–193. https://doi.org/10.1007/s11846-014-0139-3
53. Dong, J. Q. (2022). Using simulation in information systems research. *Journal of the Association for Information Systems, 23*(2), 408–417.
54. Poggio, T., Lo, A. W., LeBaron, B., & Chan, Nicholas T. (2001). *Agent-based models of financial markets: A comparison with experimental markets* (MIT Sloan School of Management Sloan Working Paper 4195-01) (eBusiness@MIT Working Paper 124).

55. Macal, C. M. (2016). Everything you need to know about agent-based modelling and simulation. *Journal of Simulation, 10*, 144–156.
56. Macal, C. M., & North, M. J. (2009), Agent-based Modeling and Simulation. In *Proceedings of the 2009 Winter Simulation Conference (WSC), Austin* (pp. 86–98). IEEE.
57. Gill, T. G., & Hevner, A. R. (2013). A fitness-utility model for design science research. *ACM Transactions on Management Information Systems, 4*(2), 1–24.
58. Schlosser, A., Voss, M., & Bruckner, L. (2004). Comparing and evaluating metrics for reputation systems by simulation. In *Proceedings of the IEEE workshop on reputation in agent societies. Citeseer*.
59. Shannon, R. E. (1998). Introduction to the art and science of simulation. In *1998 winter simulation conference*. Proceedings (cat. no. 98ch36274) (Vol. 1, pp. 7–14). IEEE.
60. Panagopoulos, A. D., Koutrouli, E., & Tsalgatidou, A. (2017). Modeling and evaluating a robust feedback-based reputation system for e-commerce platforms. *ACM Transactions on the Web (TWEB), 11*(3), 1–55.

GPSR Compliance
The European Union's (EU) General Product Safety Regulation (GPSR) is a set of rules that requires consumer products to be safe and our obligations to ensure this.

If you have any concerns about our products, you can contact us on

ProductSafety@springernature.com

In case Publisher is established outside the EU, the EU authorized representative is:

Springer Nature Customer Service Center GmbH
Europaplatz 3
69115 Heidelberg, Germany

www.ingramcontent.com/pod-product-compliance
Ingram Content Group UK Ltd.
Pitfield, Milton Keynes, MK11 3LW, UK
UKHW021639180926
475650UK00001B/34
* 9 7 8 3 0 3 2 0 8 4 8 2 8 *